14

Franciscan Institute Publications

PHILOSOPHY SERIES NO. 12
Edited by Allan B. Wolter, O. F. M.

PHILOTHEUS BOEHNER, O. F. M., Ph. D.

Collected Articles on Ockham

Edited by

ELIGIUS M. BUYTAERT, O. F. M.
S. T. D., D. Litt. et Hist. Orient., L. G.

Published by
THE FRANCISCAN INSTITUTE
ST. BONAVENTURE, N. Y.

and

E. NAUWELAERTS   F. SCHÖNINGH
LOUVAIN, BELGIUM   PADERBORN, GERMANY
1958

I. FRANCISCAN INSTITUTE PUBLICATIONS

Philosophy Series

1. *The Tractatus de successivis Attributed to William Ockham*, edit. Ph. Boehner, 1944. $ 2.00.

2. *The Tractatus de Praedestinatione et de praescientia Dei et de futuris contingentibus of William Ockham*, edit. Ph. Boehner, 1945. $ 2.00.

3. *The Transcendentals and Their Function in the Metaphysics of Duns Scotus*, by Allan B. Wolter, 1946. $ 2.00.

4. *Intuitive Cognition. A Key to the Significance of the Later Scholastics*, by Sebastian Day, 1947. $ 2.00.

5. *The De primo principio of John Duns Scotus. A Revised Text and a Translation*, by Evan Roche, 1949. Exhausted. New Edition with Commentary by Allan B. Wolter in preparation.

6. *The Psychology of Love According to Saint Bonaventure*, by Robert P. Prentice, Second edition. 1957 $ 3.50.

7. *Evidence and Its Function According to John Duns Scotus*, by Peter C. Vier, 1951. $ 2.00.

8. *The Psychology of Habit According to William Ockham*, by Oswald Fuchs, 1952. Exhausted.

9. *The Concept of Univocity Regarding the Predication of God and Creature According to William Ockham*, by Matthew C. Menges, 1952. $ 2.50.

10. *Theory of Demonstration According to William Ockham*, by Damascene Webering, 1953. $ 2.50.

11. *The Category of the Aesthetic in the Philosophy of Saint Bonaventure*, by Emma Jane Marie Spargo, 1953. $ 2.50.

12. *Philotheus Boehner. Collected Articles on Ockham*, edit. Eligius M. Buytaert. 1958.

13. *Motion, Time and Place According to William Ockham*, by Herman Shapiro. 1957. $ 3.85.

History Series

1. *Three Saints' Lives by Nicholas Bozon*, edit. M. Amelia Klenke, 1947. $ 2.00.

2. *Seven More Poems by Nicholas Bozon*, edit. M. Amelia Klenke, 1951. $ 2.00.

Philotheus Boehner
COLLECTED ARTICLES ON OCKHAM

𝔉ranciscan 𝕴nstitute 𝕻ublications

PHILOSOPHY SERIES NO. 12
Edited by Allan B. Wolter, O. F. M.

PHILOTHEUS BOEHNER, O. F. M., Ph. D.

COLLECTED ARTICLES ON OCKHAM

Edited by

ELIGIUS M. BUYTAERT, O. F. M.
S. T. D., D. Litt. et Hist. Orient., L. G.

Published by

THE FRANCISCAN INSTITUTE
ST. BONAVENTURE, N. Y.

and

E. NAUWELAERTS
LOUVAIN, BELGIUM

F. SCHÖNINGH
PADERBORN, GERMANY

1958

PHILOTHEO BOEHNER, O. F. M.
PIAE MEMORIAE
BIOLOGIAE DOCTORI
LECTORI GENERALI
PRIMO DIRECTORI INSTITUTI FRANCISCANI
INCEPTORI PROROGANS
MAGISTRO DISCIPULUS
AMICO AMICUS
D. D. Editor

Cum permissu Superiorum

TABLE OF CONTENTS

INTRODUCTION

After the death of Father Philotheus Boehner (May 22, 1955), a number of his friends started thinking about publishing in book-form all his articles on Ockham. Late in 1955 two powerful voices were added to the chorus of admirers. Fr. Pacificus Borgmann, O.F.M. (Warendorf) and Professor Heinrich Scholz (Münster) let it be known to the Editor that such a project would meet with their whole-hearted support. The idea was not only to build a spiritual monument to Father Philotheus with the very stones he himself had moulded, but also to prevent Father's exceptional knowledge of Ockham from being, partly at least, lost in not always easily accessible publications.

It was not the intention to reprint in one volume whatever had been done by Father Boehner in the line of Ockham research[a]. We could not very well reproduce in one book the following volumes: Guillelmi Ockham *Quaestio prima principalis Prologi in Primum Sententiarum*, Paderborn, 1939; *The Tractatus de successivis Attributed to William Ockham*, St. Bonaventure, 1944; *The Tractatus de praedestinatione et de praescientia Dei et de futuris contingentibus of William Ockham*, St. Bonaventure, 1945; William Ockham, *Summa Logicae*, vol. I—II, St. Bonaventure, 1951 and 1954. Likewise excluded was Father's edition of the *Centiloquium* [FrancStud 1 (1941) n. 1 58—72, n. 2 35—54, n. 3 62—70; 2 (1942) 49—60, 146—157, 251—301]. A critical edition of this work will be found among the "Dubia et Spuria" of the projected *Opera omnia philosophica et theologica* of Ockham. The articles *Ein Gedicht auf die Logik Ockhams* [FranzStud 26 (1939) 78—85] and *Scotus' Teachings according to Ockham* [FrancStud 6 (1946) 100—107 and 362—375] deal with

---

[a] Cfr E. M. Buytaert, *Bibliography of Fr. Philotheus Boehner, O. F. M.*, Franc. Stud. 15 (1955) 321—329. No. 11 of the *Bibliography* (The Life, Writings, and Teachings of William Ockham) has been published under the title: Ockham. Philosophical Writings. A selection edited and translated by Ph. Boehner, O. F. M., [Edinburgh], 1957.

border problems and were not incorporated. And it would have been completely out of line to reproduce here what Father Boehner has written on Ockham in *Christliche Philosophie von ihren Anfängen bis Nikolaus von Cues* (with E. Gilson; 3d edit. Paderborn, 1954), and in *Medieval Logic: An Outline of Its Development from 1250 to c. 1400* (Manchester and Chicago, 1952). Both books are sufficiently accessible to anyone interested.

To insure that the present volume be of value even to those students who would have the good fortune of having all the originals on hand, we did not simply reprint the articles. Nor did we follow the chronological order of their appearance. We tried to enhance the value of the articles by adding notes and cross-references. And we ordered them topologically in this fashion:

I. General Studies.

    1. *Der Stand der Ockham-Forschung,* FranzStud 34 (1952) 12—31.

    2. *Ockham's Philosophy in the Light of Recent Research,* Proceedings of the Tenth International Congress of Philosophy (Amsterdam, August 11—18, 1948), Amsterdam, 1949, 1113—1116.

II. Critical Studies (authenticity, chronology, codicography).

    1) In General.

        3. *Manuscrits des oeuvres non-polémiques d'Ockham,* La France Franciscaine 22 (1939) 171—175.

        4. *On a Recent Study of Ockham,* FrancStud 10 (1950) 191—196.

    2) In Particular.

        5. *A First Redaction of the Expositio Aurea of Ockham,* FrancStud 8 (1948) 69—76.

        6. *The Hypothetical First Redaction of Ockham's Expositio Aurea,* FrancStud 14 (1954) 374—386.

        7. *Zur Echtheit der Summa Logicae Ockhams,* FranzStud 26 (1939) 190—193.

4) Theodicy-Theology

5) Politics.

These twenty-four articles were reprinted without changes, if one does not count the correction of obvious typographical errors and occasional *lapsus calami*[b]. The additions of the Editor are easily recognizable. They are printed either in square brackets[c] — in the text as well as in the original footnotes — or in notes exclusively indicated by letters. Omitted from some articles are text editions, as is made clear in the preceding list.

We are very grateful to the Editors of the periodicals and books in which the articles originally have been published for permitting us to re-edit the studies in the present volume. Specifically we thank the Editors of Franziskanische Studien, The New Scholasticism, Proceedings of the American Catholic Philosophical Association, Review of Metaphysics, Review of Politics, and Traditio.

---

[b] Father Boehner himself insisted that an editor should correct such occasional slips of his author; cfr *infra* 132.

[c] The author used square brackets on very rare occasions only.

1. DER STAND DER OCKHAM-FORSCHUNG[a]

Ockhams Philosophie und Theologie haben in den letzten Jahr-
zehnten die Aufmerksamkeit der Forscher mehr auf sich gelenkt als
in den Jahren vor 1926. Man kann mit gutem Grund sagen, daß vor
dem Erscheinen der gründlichen Studie Hochstetters zur Erkenntnislehre Ockhams[1] Ernstzunehmendes zur Philosophie Ockhams kaum
veröffentlicht worden ist. Hochstetter und dann Vignaux[2] gebührt
das Verdienst, die erste Bresche in den Wall von zum Teil unglaub-
lichen Vorurteilen geschlagen zu haben, die ein historisch getreues
Verständnis der Gedankenwelt Ockhams verhinderten. Verzögert
haben eine bessere Beurteilung sicher die Arbeiten von Ehrle und
Michalski,[3] so wertvoll sie auch in anderer Hinsicht sein mögen. Auf
jeden Fall wurde einer sachlichen Erforschung erst durch Hochstetter
und Vignaux der Weg gewiesen, auf dem dann andere, und hier vor
allem Baudry in Paris und Moody in New York, vorwärtsgegangen sind.

Im folgenden sollen nun die Ergebnisse dieser Forscher und unsere eigenen in knapper Form dargestellt werden. Wir lassen bewußt
das politische Schrifttum[b] außer acht.

[1] Erich Hochstetter, Studien zur Metaphysik und Erkenntnislehre
Wilhelms von Ockham, Berlin 1927.

[2] Paul Vignaux im Dictionnaire de théologie catholique, Artikel:
Nominalisme, und (mit E. Amann) Artikel: Occam, t. XI. Paris 1931,
col. 717—784: 876—889.

[3] Vgl. besonders F. Ehrle, Der Sentenzenkommentar Peters von
Candia, des Pisanerpapstes Alexanders V. (Beihefte zu den Franziska-
nischen Studien, H. 9), Münster 1925. — Wir verzichten auf eine ausführliche Angabe der verschiedenen Beiträge von Michalski, die in den Handbüchern der Geschichte der Scholastik (De Wulf und Überweg-Geyer)
oder in den Bibliographien, vor allem Guelluy's (siehe Anm. 28) oder von
Valens Heynck in: FranzStud 32 (1950) 164—183 eingesehen werden kann.

[a] Erst herausgegeben in: FranzStud 34 (1952) 12—31. Vgl. unten
S. 23—38, Ockham's Philosophy in the Light of Recent Research.

[b] Vgl. unten, S. 442 ff.

I. OCKHAMS LEBEN

Bislang sind wir nur in einigen aber wichtigen Einzelheiten über die grundlegende Studie Hofers[4] hinausgekommen. Unser englischer Mitbruder Konrad Walmesley[5] entdeckte eine äußerst wichtige Urkunde, nach der ein Wilhelm Ockham im Jahre 1306 die Subdiakonatsweihe erhalten hat. Da wir mit gutem Grund annehmen dürfen, daß es sich hier um den Venerabilis Inceptor handelt, haben wir endlich ein gesichertes Datum vor 1324, dem Jahre, in welchem Ockham nach Avignon zitiert worden ist. Da das alte Recht ein Alter von 20 Jahren für den Empfang der Subdiakonatsweihe vorschrieb, muß Ockham um 1286 oder noch früher geboren sein, also nicht, wie Hofer annahm, "nur wenige Jahre vor 1300."[6] Diese Vordatierung des Geburtsjahres von Ockham ist wichtig für die Beurteilung der Frage, ob Ockham Duns Scotus gekannt hat oder nicht. Hofer glaubte diese Frage verneinen zu müssen. Das geht nicht mehr an. Es ist sogar wahrscheinlich, daß Ockham den Doctor Subtilis persönlich gekannt hat; ob er aber sein Schüler gewesen ist, bleibt eine offene Frage.

Für das Todesjahr Ockhams wird nach der letzten Studie von Rudolf Höhn O.F.M.[7] am Jahr 1349 (9. April) festzuhalten sein.

Die folgenden Daten sind also wohlgesichert:

ca. 1285 Geburt Ockhams
ca. 1306 Subdiakonatsweihe
ca. 1324 Vorladung nach Avignon
ca. 1328 Flucht aus Avignon
ca. 1329 Ankunft in München
ca. 1349 (9. April) Tod Ockhams

Ockhams Grab war in der Franziskanerkirche in München, und zwar im Chor. Für weitere Einzelheiten verweisen wir auf die schon

---

[4] J. Hofer, Biographische Studien über Wilhelm von Ockham O. F. M. in: ArchFrancHist 6 (1913) 209—233; 439—465; 654—669.

[5] Vgl. Die Bemerkung in: Guillelmi de Ockham Opera Politica [I], accuravit J. G. Sikes, Manchester 1940, p. 288.

[6] 1. c. 232.

[7] Rudolf Höhn O. F. M., Wilhelm Ockham in München, in: FranzStud 32 (1950) 142 ff.

erwähnte Studie Höhns, auf unsere biographische Skizze in der Edition des Tractatus de Successivis[8] und auf die kürzlich erschienene weitausholende Zusammenfassung und Weiterführung bei Baudry.[9]

II. OCKHAMS NICHTPOLITISCHE WERKE

Eine kritische Sichtung der Ockham zugeschriebenen Werke wurde von Ehrle und Michalski angebahnt und vor allem von Hochstetter, Baudry und dem Verfasser weitergeführt. Im folgenden werden wir gelegentlich auch noch nicht veröffentlichte Ergebnisse miteinfließen lassen. Die Frage der Datierung der Werke Ockhams stößt auf größere Schwierigkeiten. Hier müssen wir uns im wesentlichen mit einer relativen Datierung begnügen, die aber gerade für den an der inneren Entwicklung Ockhams interessierten Forscher ausreicht. Um eine Klärung dieser Frage haben sich vor allem Baudry[10] und der Verfasser bemüht. Iserlohs weitausholende Studie ist leider zu wenig sachlich, daß heißt zu wenig von einer Kenntnis der Handschriften und einer auf Texten beruhenden Begründung bestimmt und kann darum hier nicht ernstlich in Betracht gezogen werden.[11]

Es ist sicher, daß Ockhams Sentenzenkommentar bereits im Jahre 1323 vorlag; es ist auch sicher, daß die Summa Logicae vor 1328 geschrieben worden ist und daß die Quodlibeta sicher vor 1333 existierten. Innerhalb dieses Rahmens ist es nun möglich, eine relative

---

[8] The Tractatus de Successivis Attributed to William Ockham. Edited with a Study on the Life and Works of Ockham (Franciscan Institute Publications, [Philosophy Series] No. 1), The Franciscan Institute, St. Bonaventure N. Y. 1944 [1—15].

[9] Léon Baudry, Guillaume d'Occam. Sa vie, ses oeuvres, ses idées sociales et politiques. Tome I: L'homme et les oeuvres. (Etudes de Philosophie Médiévale), Paris 1950 [17—249].

[10] Es würde zu weit führen, alle Beiträge Baudrys hier aufzuzählen; wir verweisen auf die Bibliographien und vor allem auf das in Anm. 9 genannte Werk, das Baudrys Forschungen zusammenfaßt und weiterführt.

[11] E. Iserloh, Um die Echtheit des "Centiloquium". Ein Beitrag zur Wertung Ockhams und zur Chronologie seiner Werke, in: Greg 30 (1949) 78 ff.; 309 ff. [Beurteilt in: On a Recent Study of Ockhan, unten 33 ff.].

Datierung der übrigen Schriften vorzunehmen, die wir mit einer Besprechung dieser Werke verbinden wollen.

1. Reportatio Ockham

Dieses Werk, das so in den Handschriften zitiert wird, umfaßt das zweite, dritte und vierte Buch der Sentenzen, oder vielmehr es stellt eine mehr oder weniger lose Sammlung von Quästionen über die drei letzten Sentenzenbücher dar. Zu Anfang des zweiten und am Ende des vierten Buches wird in den Handschriften häufig eine Distinktioneneinteilung angeführt.

Wir müssen aber hervorheben, daß nicht alle Quästionen, die sich in der einzigen Edition dieses Werkes (Lyon 1495) finden, zur Reportatio gehören. Leider ist diese Edition sehr unzuverlässig. Nicht nur gehören verschiedene Quästionen nicht zur Reportatio, wenigstens nicht zu ihrem ursprünglichen Bestand, sondern auch der Text und die Reihenfolge der Quästionen bedürfen einer gründlichen Revision. Auch zeigen die Handschriften kein eindeutiges Bild. Nach einer eingehenden vergleichenden Studie von elf Handschriften und der Edition können wir behaupten, daß die Lyoner Ausgabe als Grundstock die gesamte Reportatio Ockham enthält und dazu noch mit Quästionen Ockhams angereichert ist, die zum Teil sicher einer späteren Periode angehören. Am besten stimmt das vierte Buch der Edition mit der handschriftlichen Überlieferung überein. Problematisch sind nur die Dubitationes additae, die sich nur in vier der Lyoner Ausgabe überhaupt nahestehenden Handschriften nachweisen ließen, und ein längerer Abschnitt am Ende der 13. Quaestio, der sich nur in den vier Handschriften, aber nicht in der Lyoner Ausgabe findet; er beginnt: *Ad septimum dico, istud non est supra formatum* ... Das zweite und dritte Buch weisen dagegen größere Verschiedenheiten auf, die sich heute auf Grund einer größeren Zahl von Handschriften deutlicher aufweisen lassen als es uns früher[12] möglich war. Von Buch II gehören zweifellos zum Grundstock der Reportation: qq. 1, 2, 4—7, 9—16 (17, 18 wird von der Mehrzahl der Handschriften im dritten Buche geführt), 19, 20 (aber nicht U: Ad quintum dubium, das sich nur in zwei Handschriften nachweisen ließ), 21—24 (26 findet sich fast in allen Handschriften im dritten Buche). Von Buch III gehören zweifellos zum Grundstock der Reportatio: qq. 1—4, 6—11.

Der Rest der Quästionen, der nicht zum Grundstock der Reportatio gehört, scheint dagegen eine gewisse Einheit zu bilden. Es sind die qq. II, 3, 8, 25; III, 5, 12—15 und die Dubitationes additae am Schluß des vierten

---

[12] The Notitia Intuitiva of Non-existents according to William Ockham. With a Critical Study on the Text of Ockham's Reportatio and a Revised Edition of Rep. II, Q. 14—15, in: Traditio 1 (1943) 242 f. [unten 293 f.]

Buches. Von diesen ist II, 8: *Utrum mundus potuit fuisse ab aeterno per potentiam divinam* in sieben Handschriften und wenigstens in einer anderen in der Tabula angegeben. In dieser Quästio wird die Reportatio Ockham (Sic!) zitiert, und zwar in J, wo die Editio und nur diese liest: . . . *patet in Reportatione nostra;* in ähnlicher Weise in N, wo sogar nach den Handschriften die Ordinatio Ockham zitiert wird. Daraus folgt, daß diese Quaestio nicht zur Reportatio gehört. Die Authentizität braucht aber nicht bezweifelt zu werden, da sich Ähnliches in dem Traktat über die Prädestination findet.[13] Eine späte Handschrift, Paris, Nationalbibliothek 16398, hat allerdings von derselben Hand als Marginalnote zu dieser und der quaestio II, 3 die Bemerkung gefügt: *Hic ponuntur aliquae quaestiones extravagantes quae non sunt, videtur mihi, de mente huius doctoris* (fol. 161 b). Die Quaestio II, 3 scheint eine quaestio disputata zu sein; auf jeden Fall erscheint in ihr der Hinweis auf einen „opponens" (in B). Diese scheint mit den Additiones (am Schluß des vierten Buches) und mit den qq. III, 12—15, die miteinander durch Hinweis verbunden sind und in denen auch wiederholt ein Opponens oder Adversarius auftritt, eine straffere Einheit zu bilden. Ich habe vorgeschlagen,[14] diese Gruppe von Quaestionen als Q u a e s t i o n e s d i s p u t a t a e zusammenzufassen. Auf keinen Fall gehören diese zur Reportatio und werden darum in der geplanten Ausgabe mit einigen anderen Quaestionen gesondert behandelt werden. Quaestio II, 25 nimmt dagegen eine gewisse Sonderstellung ein; sie ist in fünf Handschriften bezeugt; dem Inhalt nach zu urteilen (nur die Fictum-Theorie wird vorausgesetzt) gehört sie zur Periode der Reportatio; ihre Form deutet darauf hin, daß sie ein größeres Fragment ist. Zwei Handschriften bringen sie im dritten Buche. — Im dritten Buche ist die q. 5: *Utrum praeter Spiritum Sanctum tripliciter datum sit necesse ponere caritatem* nur von zwei Handschriften bezeugt, ebenfalls qq. 14 und 15, während 13 von drei Handschriften bezeugt ist. Q. 12: *De connexione virtutum* ist dagegen sehr gut bezeugt, in fünf Handschriften der Reportatio, in einer Handschrift der Quodlibeta (Vat. Chigi B. VII. 93) und als Einzelquaestio in einer anderen Handschrift der Vaticana (lat. 380).

Innere Kriterien zwingen uns, die Reportatio als das älteste der uns überkommenen Werke Ockhams anzusprechen. Die Behandlung der notitia intuitiva und abstractiva weist auf ein frühes Stadium hin; vor allem aber beweist die unbeirrte Annahme der Fictum-Theorie und die eindeutige Ablehnung jeder Theorie, die aus dem Begriff eine psychische Realität macht, daß die Reportatio zeitlich vor allen anderen auf uns gekommenen Schriften

---

[13] Vgl. The Tractatus de Praedestinatione . . . of William Ockham Edited by Philotheus Boehner O. F. M. (Franciscan Institute Publications [Philosophy Series] N. 2), St. Bonaventure, N. Y. 1943, p. XI.

[14] Vgl. The Notitia Intuitiva, in Traditio 1 (1943) 243 [und unten 298].

Ockhams anzusetzen ist. Baudrys Versuch, die Kommentare zu philosophischen Schriften vor den Sentenzenkommentaren zu datieren, ist sicher
verfehlt.[15]

Als Entstehungszeit der Reportatio kann etwa 1318 oder sogar ein
etwas früherer Zeitpunkt angenommen werden. Die Reportatio des ersten
Buches ging offenbar der uns erhaltenen Reportatio voraus, wie die Hin-
weise auf das erste Buch in der Reportatio beweisen.

2. Ordinatio Ockham

Dieses umfangreiche Werk, das nur das erste Buch des Sentenzen-
kommentares enthält und bei weiten länger ist als die drei letzten Bücher
zusammengenommen, muß als die Hauptquelle für die Philosophie und
Theologie Ockhams angesehen werden. Sie ist in etwa zwanzig (zum Teil
unvollständigen) Handschriften und in zwei Drucken (Straßburg 1483 und
Lyon 1495) erhalten. Ihre Entstehungszeit ist sicher vor 1323 und wahrscheinlich um 1318 anzusetzen. Bei der Ausarbeitung kam Ockham Aureoli's
Sentenzenkommentar (Ordinatio) zur Kenntnis, der sicher in Reinschrift
im Jahre 1317 vorlag. Auf Grund der Handschriften können wir wenigstens
zwei wenig verschiedene Redaktionen unterscheiden, wobei wir jene
Redaktion, die Michalski auf Grund von einigen Marginalnoten annehmen
zu müssen glaubte, nicht als eigentliche Redaktion, sondern als Korrektur
betrachten, die während der Ausarbeitung selbst vorgenommen wurde.
Die von uns angenommene zweite Redaktion wurde sehr wahrscheinlich
veranlaßt, als Ockham mit Aureolis Sentenzenkommentar bekannt wurde.
Als Ockham in dist. 27, q. 3 sich mit Aureoli auseinandersetzen mußte und
bei ihm auf eine Theorie stieß, die seiner bis dahin verfochtenen Theorie
über die Begriffe ähnlich war, wurde er auf bedenkliche Folgen aufmerksam.
Bislang hatte er, wie die erste Redaktion seines Werkes zeigt (nur erhalten
in Florenz Bibl. Naz. A. 3. 801 und als Abbreviation in Vatic. Borgh. 68),
die Ansicht vertreten, den Begriffen komme nur ein gedankliches (esse
objectivum oder fictum) Sein zu. Es ist eigenartig und sicher bezeichnend,
daß die Florenz-Handschrift an der genannten Stelle in dist. 27, q. 3 einfach
abbricht und erst mit der dist. 30 wieder beginnt. Alle anderen Handschriften
haben aber den vollständigen Text und dazu überall, wo Ockham früher nur
die Fictum-Theorie vertrat, Zusätze etwa von der Form: *vel secundum aliam*

---

[15] Vgl. Baudry, Guillaume d'Occam; vor allem Appendice IV (260 ff.),
wo Baudry unsere Argumente zu entkräften sucht. Wir glauben in unserer
Antwort, die in den Franciscan Studies (1951) erscheinen wird, diese Frage
endgültig entschieden zu haben [vgl. Franciscan Studies 11, Commemorative Volume (1951) 305 ff.; und unten 96 ff.]. Ockham war zuerst Theologe
und hat sich dann der Erklärung philosophischer Schriften zugewandt.
Wie es scheint, war dies das Normale für die Scholastiker aus den Orden.

opinionem quam etiam reputo probabilem . . . Diese andere Opinio ist jene, die dem Begriff eine psychische Realität zuspricht. Es ist sicher eine gute Stütze dieser Annahme, daß vielleicht die beste Handschrift, Troyes 718, diese Zusätze häufig in Marginalnoten hat. Unsere beiden Editionen [1483, 1495] enthalten nur die zweite Redaktion.

3. Die Erklärung zu logischen Schriften

Diese sind die Expositio super Porphyrium, Expositio super librum Praedicamentorum, Expositio super duos libros Perihermenias und Expositio super duos libros Elenchorum. Es steht fest, daß diese Erklärungen in der angegebenen Reihenfolge entstanden sind. Da Ockham schon in der Expositio super Porphyrium die Fictum-Theorie nur mehr als probabel oder sogar als weniger probabel als die andere vorträgt, sind wir gezwungen anzunehmen, daß er diese Kommentare nach der Reportatio und nach der ersten Redaktion der Ordinatio verfaßt hat, und zwar schon sehr bald, etwa kurz nach 1318.

Markus von Benevent hat die drei erstgenannten Erklärungen unter dem Namen Expositio aurea im Jahre 1496 herausgegeben. Der Name ließ sich bis jetzt handschriftlich nicht nachweisen. Leider taucht gelegentlich noch die Bemerkung auf, Markus von Benevent habe diese drei Werke überarbeitet (wie Prantl ohne jeden Beweis zuerst behauptet hat). Ein Vergleich mit den Handschriften zeigt, daß von einer Überarbeitung keine Rede sein kann: leider hat Markus keine besonders gute Vorlage für seinen Text benützt; seine Edition sollte nur unter Zuziehung von guten Handschriften benützt werden. Die bislang noch nicht edierte Expositio super duos libros Elenchorum ist in sieben Handschriften bekannt, die anderen in zehn. Von einer ersten Redaktion, die Anneliese Maier in einer Handschrift der Vaticana vermutete, kann nicht die Rede sein; es handelt sich dort nur um eine Abbreviation oder besser noch um Auszüge (Notabilia).[16]

4. Expositio super libros Physicorum

Von diesem recht umfangreichen Kommentar zur Aristotelischen Physik sind etwa zehn Handschriften bekannt, von denen aber einige nur die ersten Bücher und keine das achte Buch vollständig enthält. Das Werk

---

[16] Vgl. unsere Antwort auf A. Maier (Ein neues Ockham-Manuskript. Die Originalform der Expositio aurea?, in: Gregorianum 28 [1947] 101—133) in Franciscan Studies 8 (1948) 69—76: A first Redaction of the Expositio aurea of Ockham [und unten 42 ff.; vgl. auch A. Maier, Zu einigen Problemen der Ockhamforschung, in: ArchFrancHist 46 (1953) 191—192, und Ph. Boehner, The Hypothetical First Redaction of Ockham's Expositio aurea, in FrancStud 14 (1954) 374—386, hier wiederholt 50--65].

ist also unvollendet geblieben. Diese Tatsache rückt wohl die Abfassungszeit dieses Werkes näher an das Jahr der Zitierung Ockhams nach Avignon.
Auf jeden Fall ist das Werk, wie die Zitate beweisen, nach den Erklärungen
der logischen Schriften entstanden. Eingehende Diskurse reihen diese bis
jetzt noch unedierte Schrift unter die wichtigsten Quellen für Ockhams
Lehre. Mit Ausnahme des Prologs, der in zwei Redaktionen erhalten ist,
scheint dieses Werk keine besonderen textkritischen Probleme zu bieten.

5. Summa Logicae

Dieses vielleicht bedeutendste, sicher aber meist gelesene und benutzte
Werk Ockhams — etwa 50 Handschriften sind bekannt und die von Markus
von Benevent besorgte Edition wurde häufig bis zum 17. Jahrhundert
aufgelegt — stellt die erste umfassende systematische Darstellung der
mittelalterlichen Logik dar. Prantls in der Ockham-Literatur leider häufig
wiederholte textkritische Bemerkungen zu der alten Ausgabe sind völlig
aus der Luft gegriffen (Prantl hat keine einzige Handschrift geprüft). In
unserer provisorischen etwa dreißig Handschriften berücksichtigenden
Ausgabe, deren erster Teil soeben erschienen ist,[17] haben wir nochmals
die Unhaltbarkeit der Behauptungen Prantls nachgewiesen. An Hand der
Handschriften, von denen etwa zehn noch vor Ockhams Tode geschrieben
sind, ließ sich dartun, daß die alte Ausgabe im wesentlichen die älteste
Tradition widerspiegelt. Mit Ausnahme des Kapitels über die Relation:
Et quod haec non sit opinio Aristotelis (51 unserer Edition [S. 147—156]
und 53 der alten Edition) können alle Kapitel als gesichert bezeichnet
werden. Dieses kritische Kapitel findet sich in achtzehn Handschriften,
darunter der ältesten uns bekannt gewordenen (von 1339); trotzdem scheint
es nach unserer Meinung nicht direkt von Ockham selbst herzurühren,
obwohl der Inhalt ganz ockhamistisch ist. Ockham hat offenbar in seinem
Original Verbesserungen und Zusätze angebracht, die sich gewöhnlich durch
eine gewisse Unsicherheit in den Handschriften verraten, da die Schreiber
nicht immer wußten, wo die Zusätze dem Text eingefügt werden sollten.
Zwei größere Zusätze verdienen unsere Beachtung. Die Kapitel 13—16
(des dritten Teiles des dritten Hauptteiles der alten Ausgabe): *Quia circa
modalium propositionum aequipollentias et repugnantias . . .* finden sich in
allen Handschriften mit Ausnahme von drei, die sicher nicht zu den ältesten
zu rechnen sind, aber sie sind an verschiedenen Stellen eingefügt worden.
Ein ähnliches Bild zeigt der Tractatus de obligationibus, der nur von drei
späteren Handschriften ausgelassen wird, dafür aber von zwei Handschriften

---

[17] William O c k h a m, Summa Logicae. Pars Prima. Edited by Philo-
theus B o e h n e r O. F. M. (Franciscan Institute Publications. Text Series
No. 2), St. Bonaventure, N. Y. 1951 [und 1957; inzwischen auch Pars
Secunda et Tertiae prima, ebd. 1954].

zweimal an verschiedenen Stellen gebracht wird. Für weitere Einzelheiten darf wohl auf die Einleitung zur neuen Edition hingewiesen werden [S. V—XII].

Es ist nicht leicht, die Abfassungszeit dieses reifen Werkes Ockhams festzulegen. Der Venerabilis Inceptor hat offenbar längere Zeit daran gearbeitet. Ein Hinweis in der Handschrift O 67 der Amploniana in Erfurt berechtigt uns als Terminus ante quem 1328 anzunehmen; die Erwähnung des Magister abstractionum, also des Franciscus de Mayronis, der im Jahre 1323 die Magisterwürde erhielt, berechtigt uns als Terminus post quem 1323 anzunehmen. Der Geleitbrief (nach der ältesten Handschrift an Wilhelm von Ambersberg gerichtet [vgl. edit. Böhner 7]) deutet darauf hin, daß die Summa Logicae wohl in Avignon vollendet wurde.

6. Quodlibeta VII

Zur handschriftlichen Überlieferung dieses wichtigen Werkes Ockhams vergleiche unsern Aufsatz „Zu Ockhams Beweis der Existenz Gottes" in: Franziskanische Studien 32 (1950) 54 f. (auch infra 403 f.) Die Echtheit der Quodlibeta steht außer Zweifel, und zwar für alle sieben. Das ergibt sich aus der äußeren und inneren Kritik. Es sind mehr als zehn Handschriften bekannt und mehrere unabhängige alte Ausgaben. Von diesen scheint der Straßburger Druck von 1491 am meisten gebraucht und am wenigsten zuverlässig zu sein. Die Anordnung der Quästionen weist sowohl in den Drucken wie in den Handschriften einige Verschiedenheiten auf. Die q. IV, 6: De connexione virtutum des Straßburger Druckes fehlt in andern Ausgaben und ist nur in einer Handschrift der Quodlibeta bezeugt (vgl. oben unter 1); sie paßt auch nicht in den Stil der Quodlibeta. Q. VII, 14: *Utrum tres personae sint unus Deus numero . . .* fehlt in den meisten Handschriften und ist nur von zweien bezeugt.

Über die Abfassungszeit der Quodlibeta wissen wir sicher, daß sie vor 1333 und nach der Expositio super 8 libros Physicorum entstanden sind. Ob sie in Oxford oder vielleicht eher in Avignon oder sogar in München verfaßt worden sind, wissen wir nicht. Baudry[18] neigt mehr zu Oxford und möchte darum die Quodlibeta vor 1324 datieren. Es bleibt die Möglichkeit offen, daß sie in einem Studienhaus des Ordens gehalten wurden. Die Quodlibeta tragen ganz das Gepräge des Unvollendeten und Skizzenhaften an sich. Es könnte sein, daß sie Reportationen sind.

7. Quaestiones super libros Physicorum

Diese Sammlung von 151 durchweg kurzen Quaestionen gehört wegen ihres Stiles und vor allem auch wegen der häufigen Zitierung der Quodlibeta in die zeitliche Nähe der Quodlibeta. Sie sind noch mehr als die

---

[18] Baudry, Occam 76.

2*

Quodlibeta skizzenhaft und unvollständig durchgeführt. Leider sind uns nur zwei vollständige und voneinander abhängige Handschriften bekannt nebst einem größeren Fragment.

8. Summulae in libros Physicorum

Wie wir aus gelegentlichen Bemerkungen Ockhams in seinen Kommentaren zu philosophischen Werken wissen, hatte er die Absicht, alle Werke des Aristoteles zu erklären. Dabei muß ihm auch vorgeschwebt haben, den Lehrgehalt dieser Werke in systematischer Form getrennt darzustellen. Er hat dies für die Logik getan. Für die Physik hat er wenigstens einen Anfang gemacht, der uns in Form eines größeren Bruchstückes des geplanten Werkes erhalten ist. Es geht auch unter dem Namen Summulae physicales oder Philosophia naturalis. Die drei letzten Kapitel der Drucke finden sich als Tractatus de Loco im Tractatus de Successivis [edit. Böhner 69—96]; sie sind wörtlich der Expositio super libros Physicorum entnommen. Das Werk ist in etwa zehn Handschriften erhalten und in mehreren alten Drucken. Für weitere Einzelheiten verweisen wir vor allem auf Baudry[19], der das Werk zeitlich noch vor die Summa Logicae anzusetzen scheint; wir ziehen es vor, es nach der logischen Summe anzusetzen, weil es nicht vollendet wurde.

9. Tractatus de Corpore Christi
oder Primus Tractatus de Quantitate

Dieser Traktat, dessen Incipit lautet: Sicut dicit quaedam glossa... und in der Handschrift Angelica (1017) die Überschrift trägt: Quaestio de quantitate, ist jetzt in fünf Handschriften bekannt. Baudry hatte schon früher darauf hingewiesen, daß dieser Traktat eine selbständige Schrift ist und nur durch die Herausgeber der alten Drucke mit dem folgenden Werk: De Sacramento Altaris verbunden und als Teil dieses Werkes behandelt worden ist. Leider ist ihnen darin Birch in seiner Edition ([Burlington] Iowa 1930), die recht mangelhaft ist, gefolgt. Für die Abfassungszeit dieses Werkes fehlen klare Anhaltspunkte; wir nehmen an, daß sie nach dem Sentenzenkommentar und den Kommentaren zu den philosophischen Schriften entstanden ist, vielleicht sogar bedeutend später, wie der Ton verschiedener Stellen nahelegt; man vergleiche z. B. den gereizten, an spätere Schriften erinnernden Ton auf S. 112, 116, 126 der Edition von Birch.

10. Tractatus de Sacramento Altaris oder
Secundus Tractatus de Quantitate

Dieses Werk ist uns in sieben Handschriften bekannt; es ist nach Juli 1323 geschrieben, da der Doctor communis schon Sanctus genannt wird.

---

[19] Baudry, Occam 52 ff.

Alles scheint aber darauf hinzudeuten, daß es noch in Oxford verfaßt ist, vor allem der Hinweis, daß in strittigen Fragen die Autorität des Papstes anzurufen sei (ed. Birch S. 442). Für weitere Einzelheiten verweisen wir auf Baudrys eingehende Diskussion, der aber leider sehr wenig über den Tractatus de Corpore Christi zu sagen hat.[20]

11. Tractatus de Praedestinatione et de Praescientia Dei et de Futuris Contingentibus

Diese in etwa zehn (zum Teil unvollständigen) Handschriften bekannte Schrift wurde zuerst von Markus von Benevent in der Expositio Aurea herausgegeben und später von mir.[21] Über die Abfassungszeit wissen wir wenig; doch liegt es sehr nahe, sie nach dem Sentenzenkommentar anzusetzen.

12. Compendium Logicae oder Tractatus Logicae minor

Bis vor kurzem habe ich an der Echtheit dieses Werkes gezweifelt. Nach eingehendem Studium dieser (und der folgenden) Schrift habe ich mich persönlich von der Echtheit überzeugt. Das Werk ist uns, soweit wir feststellen konnten, nur in der Handschrift Assisi 690 erhalten. Ludger Meier O. F. M. hat aber eine andere, leider am Ende des Krieges vernichtete Handschrift dieses Werkes in der Bibliothek des Minoritenklosters zu Würzburg entdeckt, die im Jahre 1346 geschrieben ist und Ockham ausdrücklich als Autor nennt, also noch drei Jahre vor seinem Tode.[21a] Das Incipit lautet: *Logica cum dicatur a logos . . .* Das Explicit: *. . . sit vera vel concedenda. Explicit minor tractatus novae logicae Guilelmi Occam.* Die Schrift ist keine Abbreviatio der Summa Logicae oder der gleich zu erwähnenden Logik und gibt in gedrängtester Kürze, aber durchaus selbständiger Form den Inhalt der Logik Ockhams. Die Abfassungszeit dieser Logik muß wohl nach 1330 anzusetzen sein, fällt also in die Münchener Periode.[22]

13. Elementarium Logicae oder Tractatus Logicae medius

Diese Schrift wurde von P. Apollinaris van Leeuwen O. F. M. in der Handschrift der Münchener Staatsbibliothek 1060 (4379) entdeckt und von ihm als ein echtes Werk Ockhams bezeichnet. Heute, nach eingehender Prüfung dieses Werkes, möchten wir unsere Bedenken gegen seine Echtheit

---

[20] B a u d r y , Occam 88 ff.

[21] Vgl. Anm. 13.

[21a] L. M e i e r O. F. M., Aufzeichnungen aus vernichteten Handschriften des Würzburger Minoritenklosters, in ArchFranchHist 44 (1951) 194. 202 f.

[22] Philotheus B o e h n e r , Three Sums of Logic attributed to William Ockham, in: FrancStud 11 (1951) 173 ff. [auch unten 70 ff.].

[The Tractatus de successivis Attributed to William Ockham, Franciscan
Institute Publications, Philosophy Series 1, St. Bonaventure, N. Y. 1944,
19 *]* fallen lassen. Die bislang einzig bekannte Handschrift ist datiert; sie
wurde im Jahre 1348, also einem Jahre vor den Tode Ockhams, in Deutschland geschrieben. Inhaltliche Bedenken können kaum erhoben werden.[23]
Alles deutet darauf hin, daß diese selbständige Logik, die im Ganzen kürzer
ist als die Summa Logicae, aber den Traktat über die Trugschlüsse aus-
führlicher bringt, in München entstanden ist.

14. Verschiedene Quästionen

In der Baseler Handschrift F. II. 24 finden sich einige Quästionen,
die Ockham zugeschrieben werden. Wahrscheinlich ist nur eine De Relatione authentisch: sie ist inzwischen von Gaudenz Mohan O. F. M. ediert
worden.[24] Die noch von Baudry erwähnte Quaestio de quantitate in
se,[25] die in einer Münchener Handschrift bekannt ist, ist nur ein kleines
Fragment der Summa Logicae. Adam Wodham's Hinweis „*Ockham . . .
in utroque tractatu de quantitate*" kann sich nur auf die beiden oben er-
wähnten Traktate über die Quantität beziehen (nr. 9 u. 10).

Vielleicht lassen sich alle jene Quästionen, die sicher nicht zu einem der
bereits genannten Werke gehören, unter dem Sammelnamen Quaestiones
disputatae vereinigen. Weitere Forschungen sind aber notwendig, um
dies zu rechtfertigen.

Es scheint nunmehr angebracht, einige Schriften zu besprechen, deren
Echtheit durchaus nicht erwiesen ist und die wir als unecht bezeichnen
möchten.

Der Tractatus de Successivis ist in mehreren Handschriften bekannt und wird gewöhnlich Ockham zugeschrieben. Ich habe in meiner
Edition nachgewiesen, daß dieses Werk vollständig, mit Ausnahme einiger
überleitender Sätze, der Expositio super libros Physicorum wörtlich entnommen ist. Da wir nicht annehmen, daß Ockham selbst diese Kompilation
gemacht hat — obwohl das natürlich möglich ist —, betrachten wir dieses
Werk als unecht, wenn auch fast jeder Satz von Ockham stammt.[26]

Das Centiloquium, das gerade in neuerer Zeit häufig zitiert wird,
und zwar gewöhnlich, um Ockhams gefährliche Lehren nachzuweisen,

---

[23] Philotheus B o e h n e r, Does Ockham know of material Implication?
in: FrancStud 11 Commemorative Volume (1951) 203 ff. [auch unten 320 ff.].
[24] FrancStud 11 Commemorative Volume (1951) 273—303.
[25] B a u d r y, Occam 285.
[26] Vgl. Anm. 8. Vgl. dazu Iserloh's unbegründete Bemerkungen in
seinem Aufsatz: Um die Echtheit des "Centiloquium". Ein Beitrag zur
Wertung Ockhams und zur Chronologie seiner Werke, in: Greg. 30 (1949)
78 ff.; 309 ff. [auch Anm. 11].

halte ich für unecht. Später, und unabhängig von uns, hat Baudry auch die Echtheit in Frage gezogen.[27] Gründliche Ockhamkenner wie Hochstetter und Vignaux teilen diese Bedenken. Die ersten beiden Handschriften des bis 1938 handschriftlich unbekannten Werkes wurden von mir gefunden, später hat Dom Bascour eine Handschrift des 15. Jahrhunderts in Spanien (Burgo de Osma, Kathedrale, *ms.* 61, jetzt *ms.* 202, fol. 84r—115r) entdeckt.[28]

Ein Defensorium logicae Ockham ist in einer Vatikanischen Handschrift (Angelica [1017]) enthalten. Diese sehr interessante Schrift, die nur die Lehre von den Termen behandelt, scheint auf einen Schüler Ockhams zurückzugehen.

Wie sich aus dieser Diskussion der nichtpolitischen Werke Ockhams ergibt, sind noch manche Probleme zu lösen, obwohl nicht verkannt werden darf, daß sich das Bild in den letzten zehn Jahren wesentlich geklärt hat.

III. DIE LEHRE OCKHAMS

Es ist nicht leicht, in einem kurzen Überblick den augenblicklichen Stand der Forschung bezüglich der Lehre Ockhams darzulegen. Dies kann nur in einer schematischen Form geschehen, wobei auf die wichtigste Literatur hingewiesen werden soll.

Sehr wenig ist bislang auf dem Gebiete der Theologie Ockhams gearbeitet worden. Guelluy's[29] Untersuchung über das Verhältnis von Philosophie und Theologie beschäftigt sich mehr mit Grenzfragen und läßt den Inhalt der Theologie ziemlich unberücksichtigt. Obwohl die Arbeit teilweise einen Mangel an Verständnis der mittelalterlichen Logik im allgemeinen und der positiven Leistung Ockhams auf diesem Gebiete einschließlich seines realistischen Konzeptualismus im besonderen verrät, muß sie doch als ein erster und grundsätzlich gelungener Versuch angesehen werden, Ockhams Stellungnahme zum Problem Glaube und Wissen, Philosophie und Theologie zu klären. Das Ergebnis ist, daß Ockham im wesentlichen

---

[27] Vgl. Baudry, Occam 270 f. und 286.

[28] Vgl. meine Antwort auf Iserloh's Artikel (Anm. 26): On a recent Study of Ockham, in: FrancStud 10 (1950) 191 ff. [und unten 33 ff.].

[29] Robert Guelluy, Philosophie et Théologie chez Guillaume d'Ockham (Universitas Catholica Lovaniensis. Dissertationes ... Series II — Tomus 39), Louvain 1947.

die Tradition fortsetzt, also weder Fideist noch Rationalist noch
Skeptiker ist; daß aber bei ihm eine deutliche Akzentverschiebung
zu den rein logischen Problemen in diesem Fragenkomplex zutage
tritt zugleich mit einem stärkeren Gefühl für die teilweise aber weit-
reichende Unzulänglichkeit der Aristotelischen Philosophie, die dem
christlichen Kontingenzgedanken nicht gerecht wird. Guelluy's Ergebnis läßt sich vielleicht schärfer und auf jeden Fall gerechter in
der folgenden klassischen Zusammenfassung Vignaux's ausdrücken:

> Même si, comme nous le croyons, on peut discerner dans une telle
> doctrine la part de notions et de raisons proprement philosophiques, l'univ-
> ers de ce nominalisme est l'univers d'un théologien que la Révélation a
> introduit au point de vue divin: il n'a pas du réel une autre appréhension
> que l'incroyant, mais, croyant, il en affirme des prédicats spécifiquement
> théologiques; en les pensant soumises à une *potentia absoluta*, il juge des
> choses comme Dieu les voit.[30]

Als einzige größere und rein theologische Arbeit ist nur die Untersuchung über die Eucharistielehre Ockhams von Gabriel Buescher[31]
erschienen. Daraus geht hervor, daß Ockham im wesentlichen daran
interessiert ist, wie seine Theorie über die Quantität auf die Trans-
substantiation und die Gegenwart Christi im Allerheiligsten Sakra-
ment des Altares angewandt werden kann. Bekanntlich nimmt Ockham an, daß die Quantität nichts bedeutet, was nicht entweder
Substanz oder Qualität ist; ein eigenes Sein der Quantität gibt es
nicht. Grund dieser Behauptung ist die Aristotelische Lehre, daß
kein Akzidens Substrat für ein anderes Akzidens sein kann; wäre
aber die Quantität "susceptibilis contrariorum", so hätte sie eine
wesentliche Eigenschaft der Substanz. Im Rahmen dieser Lehre
sucht Ockham durchaus im orthodoxen Sinne das Geheimnis der
Eucharistie zu erklären, und zwar vom Standpunkt des absolut
Möglichen aus. Der Einfluß von Skotus ist unverkennbar.

---

[30] P. Vignaux, Nominalisme au XIVe Siècle. Les Conférences Albert-
le-Grand. Inst. d'Etudes Médiévales, Montréal 1948, p. 96.

[31] G. Buescher, The Eucharistic Teaching of William Ockham
(Franciscan Institute Publications. Theology Series No. 1), St. Bonaventure,
N. Y. 1950.

Hinzuweisen wäre hier noch auf einen Aufsatz von Eligius B u y t -
a e r t O.F.M.[32] über Ockham's Stellung zur Frage der Unbefleckten
Empfängnis der Muttergottes. Er kommt zu dem Ergebnis, daß
Ockham in der Dogmengeschichte beachtet zu werden verdient, und
zwar nicht nur wegen seiner wesentlich geistigen Definition der Erb-
sünde, sondern auch darum, weil er die Möglichkeit der Unbefleckten
Empfängnis zugibt.

Im übrigen ist Ockhams Theologie noch recht unerforscht. Bemerkungen in der Literatur und vor allem den Handbüchern über
die Theologie des Venerabilis Inceptor sollten mit größter Vorsicht
angenommen werden. Es ist sicher, daß Lutterell in seiner Anklage-
schrift gegen Ockham die Lehre seines Gegners mißdeutet hat. Darum
ist es zu bedauern, daß H o f f m a n n[33] nicht einmal die Möglichkeit
berücksichtigt, daß Lutterell nicht zuverlässig ist, vielmehr von der
unbewiesenen Voraussetzung ausgeht, daß Lutterell ein objektiver
Gewährsmann sei und aus reiner Liebe zur Reinerhaltung des Glaubens gehandelt habe. Ein Mann ist nicht schon darum glaubwürdig,
weil er Ockham anklagt und auf Gefahren hinweist, die erst noch
bewiesen werden müssen; ein Mann ist sicher wenig glaubwürdig,
wenn feststeht, daß er ein persönliches Interesse daran hatte, Ockham
zu verdächtigen. Hoffmann gibt selbst dafür die notwendigen Unter-
lagen. Lutterell mußte ja die peinliche Erfahrung machen, als Kanzler der Universität [Oxford] seines Gegners und auf Verlangen der
Professoren seines Amtes enthoben zu werden. Noch größere Bedenken müßte Hoffmann gehabt haben, als er feststellen mußte,
daß Lutterells eigene Rechtgläubigkeit durchaus nicht außer Zweifel
stand und wahrscheinlich auch angezweifelt wurde. Denn in der
Frage der Visio beatifica teilte er die später zurückgenommene Ansicht seines Freundes, des Papstes Johann XXII. Zöge man all dieses

---

[32] Eligius B u y t a e r t O. F. M., The Immaculate Conception in the
Writings of Ockham, in FrancStud 10 (1950) 149 ff.

[33] F. H o f f m a n n, Die erste Kritik des Ockhamismus durch den Ox-
forder Kanzler Johannes Lutterell (Breslauer Studien zur historischen
Theologie, Neue Reihe Bd. IX), Breslau 1941. Leider sind, soweit in Erfahrung gebracht werden konnte, die angekündigten Texte, die allein Wert
haben, bis jetzt nicht veröffentlicht worden.

in Betracht, so könnte man vielleicht zu einer verständlicheren Erklärung der bislang unerklärten Tatsache kommen, daß Ockham
trotz des Gutachtens der Theologen-Kommission, das Pelzer und
Koch veröffentlicht haben, nie verurteilt worden ist. Es ist doch
sonderbar, daß ein Johann XXII. das wirksamste Mittel einer Ver-
urteilung theologischer Ansichten Ockhams nicht angewandt hat
und es lediglich mit Drohungen bewenden ließ. Wir müssen lernen,
Ockham und die mit seiner Persönlichkeit und Lehre verbundenen
Probleme unvoreingenommen zu prüfen, und das bedeutet, zunächst
einmal Ockham nicht in dem berühmten oder vielmehr berüchtigten
historischen Zusammenhang zu sehen, der häufig nur ein konstruiertes
Rahmenwerk ist, in das Tatsachen gepreßt werden.

So dürfen wir behaupten, daß es bis jetzt nicht bewiesen ist, daß
Ockhams Theologie für den ebenfalls noch zu beweisenden Niedergang der scholastischen Theologie des 14. und 15. Jahrhunderts verantwortlich zu machen ist; daß es aber vor allem noch nicht bewiesen
ist, daß Ockhams Theologie Luthers dogmatische Verirrungen vor-
bereitet habe. Was den zweiten Punkt betrifft, so haben Denifle und
Grisar — beide sind im wesentlichen eins, da Grisar Denifle aus-
giebig benützt — sich eigentlich vergeblich bemüht, eine Brücke
zwischen Ockham und Luther zu schlagen. Vignaux hat bereits
Warnungstafeln aufgerichtet. In seinem Geiste und in deutlichem
Gegensatz zu Lortz und anderen kommt R. Weijenborg O.F.M.[34]
in seiner Studie über die Charitaslehre Luthers zu dem Ergebnis, daß
die Ockhamistische Lehre, die Luther durch Biel kannte, für Luthers
Theologie nicht entscheidend war. Diese sehr gründliche und empfeh-
lenswerte Untersuchung kommt zu dem Ergebnis:

La théologie de Luther nous paraît avoir pris son point de départ dans
les conceptions personelles qu'il a nourries depuis 1509, notamment dans
celle qui affirme qu'on doit toujours suivre les inspirations de la charité.
De la sorte, elle a altéré l'ockhamisme authentique dont nous avons
esquissé les lignes générales suivant la doctrine gabriéliste de la charité
infuse . . .

---

[34] R. Weijenborg O. F. M., La Charité dans la Première Théologie
de Luther (1509—1515), in: Revue d'histoire ecclésiastique 45 (1950)
617—669.

Zu einem noch mehr überraschenden Ergebnis kam Vignaux,[35] der eine Einzelstudie der 57. und der 97. These Luthers gewidmet hat, die einen radikalen Gegensatz zwischen Luther und Ockham erkennen lassen, der leider von Denifle nicht im rechten Licht gesehen worden ist. Studien wie diese sind sehr zu begrüßen, um aus dem Halbdunkel vager Analogien und der Verwechselungen von Ursache und Anlaß ins helle Licht der Geschichte zu kommen, die, soll sie nüchtern bleiben, zunächst einmal feststellen muß, wie es nun eigentlich wirklich gewesen ist. Ehe wir Synthesen machen und große Zusammenhänge aufweisen können, muß zuvor noch viel Kleinarbeit geleistet werden, die bekanntlich viel schwieriger ist als Geschichtskonstruktion im Hegelschen Sinne.

In diesem Zusammenhang sei auf eine irreführende und lange kritiklos hingenommene Bemerkung im Chartularium Universitatis Parisiensis hingewiesen [*Chartularium* II 505—507]. Es handelt sich dort um einen Erlaß der Artistenfakultät gegen Irrtümer und Verirrungen, die gewissen "Occanici" zugeschrieben werden. Da Ockham genannt wird, hat man geglaubt, seine Lehren seien mit diesem Erlaß gemeint. Michalski hatte bereits Schwierigkeiten, diesen Erlaß, der unter Buridan, also einem unter Ockhams Einfluß stehenden Scholastiker, herausgekommen ist, mit Buridans Ehrlichkeit in Einklang zu bringen. Es gelang ihm mit dem naheliegenden Hinweis, daß Buridan in diesen Punkten Ockham nicht folge. Tatsächlich ist, wie ich nachweisen konnte,[36] Ockham geradesowenig wie Buridan von diesem Erlaß betroffen; im Gegenteil, dieser Erlaß ist durchaus im Sinne Ockhams gehalten. Unabhängig von mir sind Moody und Hochstetter zu demselben Ergebnis gelangt.[37]

In der Logik hat Ockham vor allem dahingearbeitet, sie von aller Metaphysik zu säubern und sie rein formal aufzubauen. Moo-

---

[35] P. Vignaux, Sur Luther et Ockham, in: FranzStud 32 (1950) 21—30.

[36] Philotheus Boehner O. F. M., Supposition and the Notion of Truth, in: FrancStud 6 (1946) 275 ff. [unten 248 ff.].

[37] Vgl. Ernest A. Moody, Ockham, Buridan and Nicholas of Autrecourt, in: FrancStud 7 (1947) 123 ff.

dy's Darstellung der Logik Ockhams[38] zeigt vor allem, wie Ockham die platonischen Elemente unerbittlich ausmerzt. Die Formalisierung der Logik wird durch eine weitgehende Anwendung der Suppositionstheorie und der Consequentiae erreicht. Zur Grundlage aller Formen des Schließens, einschließlich der Syllogistik, ist tatsächlich, wenn auch noch nicht äußerlich kenntlich, die Konsequenzenlehre gemacht. Die grundlegenden Theoreme der modernen Aussagenlogik sind Ockham bekannt.[39] Er ist, soweit wir bis jetzt wissen, der erste, der die sogenannten De Morganschen Regeln (De Morgan, Mathematiker um die Mitte des 19. Jahrhunderts) klar formuliert, und zwar als Regeln der Aussagenlogik und nicht, wie De Morgan, der Klassenlogik. Die Suppositionstheorie wird mit Hilfe der Consequentiae entwickelt. Ockham ist wohl der erste gewesen, der die stark in Verwirrung geratene Modalitätenlogik in der Ersten Analytik entwirrt und in einer klassischen Form entwickelt hat. Dessen war er sich auch bewußt, wie er, etwas temperamentvoll, im Elementarium hervorhebt, wo wir die bezeichnenden Sätze lesen:

"Et unde provenerit, quod doctrina de syllogismis huiusmodi (i. e. modalibus) ibi (i. e. in libro Priorum) ita confuse est tradita, an videlicet ex defectu transferentis vel alia causa, ignoro. Qui tamen non vult merito bestiae comparari, propter verba ista et quaecumque alia scripta in libris, qui dicuntur esse Aristotelis vel cuiuscumque alterius infidelis et in multis errantis, suum ingenium in obsequium ignorantis quam plurima non captivet, sed sermonibus quibuscumque huiusmodi rationem praeferat evidentem: et si rationis non est capax, se de huiusmodi perdendo tempus suum nullatenus intromittat" (München, Staatsbibl. 1060, fol. 155 rb. s.).

Ockham hat streng an der Allgemeingültigkeit der Logik festgehalten und bereits eine Idee von einer dreiwertigen Logik gehabt, die er aber ablehnt.[40]

---

[38] Ernest A. Moody, The Logic of William of Ockham, London 1935.

[39] Vgl. J. Salamucha, Die Aussagenlogik bei Wilhelm Ockham (aus dem Polnischen übersetzt von Johannes Bendiek O. F. M.), in: Franz Stud 32 (1950) 97 ff.

[40] Vgl. The Medieval Crisis of Logic and the Author of the Centiloquium attributed to Ockham, in FrancStud 4 (1944) 151 ff. [und unten 351 ff.]. Für die Idee der dreiwertigen Logik vgl. unsere Ausführungen zur Ausgabe des Traktates De Praedestinatione (siehe Anm. 13).

In der Erkenntnistheorie ist Ockham naiver Realist in bezug auf die Sinneserkenntnis (im Gegensatz zu Aureoli). Er hat einen unerschütterlichen Glauben auch an die Objektivität der Verstandeserkenntnis, und zwar wegen des Kausalnexus unserer unmittelbaren Begriffe mit der Wirklichkeit. Solche Allgemeinbegriffe, die ihr Entstehen seinem naturhaften und rein kausalbedingten Prozeß verdanken, geben die objektive Wirklichkeit in geistiger Form wieder. Das Erkennen schreitet vom Einzelnen, das in der Notitia intuitiva intellektuell und direkt erfaßt wird, über die intellektuelle abstraktive Erkenntnis desselben Einzeldinges zu abstrakten Allgemeinbegriffen vor. Ockham lehnt stillschweigend die Aristotelische, in fast endlosen Variationen vertretene Abstraktionstheorie ab, und vor allem ihre Begleiterscheinungen von Species intelligibilis und Intellectus agens und possibilis. Er kennt nur eine psychologische Abstraktion.

Ockhams Lehre, daß es durch die absolute Macht Gottes möglich sei, eine intuitive Erkenntnis von nichtexistierenden (aber möglichen) Dingen oder Tatsachen zu haben, ist in skeptischem Sinne ausgelegt worden. Diese Ansicht beruht auf einer irrigen Deutung der Texte, wie wir nachgewiesen haben.[41] Nach Ockham ist gerade die intuitive Erkenntnis jene, die uns berechtigt, mit absoluter Evidenz über kontingente Tatsachen zu urteilen, daß sie existieren, wenn sie existieren, und daß sie nicht existieren, wenn sie auch tatsächlich nicht existieren. Der noch gelegentlich in der Ockhamliteratur auftauchende Dämon Descartes', der uns täuschen könnte, hat keinen Platz in der Evidenzlehre Ockhams, sondern höchstens in der Lehre von der Gewißheit, die ein subjektiver Zustand ist. Wo Evidenz gegeben ist, ist ein Irrtum unmöglich. Ockham hat an keiner Stelle anders gelehrt.

Ockham hat gleichfalls die Möglichkeit einer spekulativen Erkenntnis rückhaltlos anerkannt, falls sie mit Allgemeinbegriffen operiert und nicht mit Singulärbegriffen im strengen Sinne. Eine Singulär-Erkenntnis, also jene, die sich nur auf ein Ding bezieht und in der nur ein Individuum erkannt ist (singularis simplex et

---

[41] Vgl. The notitia intuitiva, in: Traditio 1 (1943) 242 f. [und unten 296 f.].

propria), kann nie zur Einzel-Erkenntnis eines anderen Dinges führen. Die Erkenntnis von einer einzelnen Wirkung garantiert die Erkenntnis der bisher nicht wahrgenommenen einzelnen Ursache; ein solcher Übergang ist nur möglich, wie ja auch die Erfahrung vollauf bestätigt, wo Allgemeinbegriffe im Spiel sind. Leider ist diese Lehre ebenfalls arg mißverstanden worden.[42]

Die erkenntnistheoretische Stellung Ockhams kann als r e a - l i s t i s c h e r   K o n z e p t u a l i s m u s bezeichnet werden.[43] Der Venerabilis Inceptor lehnt jegliche Form von Allgemeinheit in den Dingen ab. Er ist überzeugt, daß auch in der abgeschwächten Form einer Natura communis die Lehre vom Universale in re mit einer untragbaren Hypothese über die Struktur des Einzeldinges belastet ist. Die Individualität eines Dinges bedarf keiner Erklärung, sondern nur die Tatsache, daß wir Allgemeinbegriffe haben.

In der M e t a p h y s i k bleibt Ockham seinen erkenntnistheoretischen Prinzipien treu. Trotz aller gegenteiligen blindgläubig wiederholten Behauptungen, er habe oder könne keine Metaphysik haben, hat er eine wenigstens in den Grundrissen ausgeführte Metaphysik, wenn sie auch bedeutend einfacher ist als die von Duns Scotus. Ockham hat offenbar nicht die Zeit gefunden, eine ausführliche Metaphysik zu entwickeln, obwohl er, wie wir gelegentlichen Bemerkungen entnehmen können, eine Erklärung der Aristotelischen Metaphysik im Sinne hatte, die uns sicher weitere Aufschlüsse über seine eigene Metaphysik gegeben hätte.

Die Hauptsorge verlegt Ockham auf eine sorgfältige Gegenstandsanalyse. Der Begriff muß am Gegenstand und nicht umgekehrt gemessen werden. Gerade in der Projizierung von Begriffen in die Wirklichkeit sieht er einen der Hauptfehler der Scotisten. Das gilt vor allem auch von den Distinktionen. Darum nimmt er im Bereich des geschöpflichen Seins nur eine Real-Distinktion an; die Formal-Distinktion läßt er nur in der Trinität gelten. Dagegen gehört die Distinctio rationis nur der Begrifflichen Welt an. Aus dem Bestreben,

---

[42] Vgl. Ockham's Theory of Signification, in FrancStud 6 (1946) 143 ff. [und unten 201 ff.].

[43] Vgl. Philotheus B o e h n e r O. F. M., The Realistic Conceptualism of William Ockham, in: Traditio 4 (1946) 307 ff. [und unten 156 ff.].

die Begriffe am Gegenstand zu messen, reduziert er die Kategorien auf zwei, Substanz und Qualität. Über die Reduzierung der Relation auf diese beiden letzten Seinsunterschiede hat uns G. Martin eine recht interessante Studie[44] geschenkt, in der trotz der zu stark hervortretenden Tendenz, Ockham mit den Augen Kants zu sehen, doch klar herausgearbeitet wird, wie Ockham eine bereits früher einsetzende Entwicklung zu Ende führt und zu echten Transzendentalbegriffen vorstößt.

In ähnlicher Weise hat Ockham auch die Lehre von der Univokation des „Seins" weitergeführt und geklärt. „Sein" wird in univokem Sinne von Gott und den Geschöpfen ausgesagt, und zwar in einer Univokation, die dem unendlichen Abstand im Sein zwischen Gott und Geschöpf Rechnung trägt. Es scheint, daß Ockham eine Art Strukturgleichheit des Begriffes mit inhaltlicher Verschiedenheit vorschwebt. Solche strukturgleiche Begriffe schlagen die Brücke von den Geschöpfen zu Gott.[45]

Da Gott sich der unmittelbaren Erfahrung unseres Verstandes entzieht, kann er nicht intuitiv, sondern nur durch Allgemeinbegriffe erkannt werden. Ockham hat die Bedingungen einer solchen Erkenntnis in kritischer Auseinandersetzung mit Scotus genau geprüft. Gottes Existenz läßt sich in strengem Sinne beweisen. Nach Ockham leidet der Beweis von Scotus — dessen Grundgedanken er annimmt — darunter, daß Scotus mit der Wirkursächlichkeit im Sinne der Produktion von Sein arbeitet. In der Produktionsordnung läßt sich nach Ockham ein Regressus in infinitum nicht ausschließen; dieser läßt sich aber wohl ausschließen, wenn man statt der produktiven die konservative Ursächlichkeit zugrunde legt. Darum kann Gott als der höchste Erhalter der Welt erschlossen werden.[46] Im übrigen bedarf die natürliche Gotteslehre Ockhams noch weiterer Untersuchun-

---

[44] Wilhelm von Ockham. Untersuchungen zur Ontologie der Ordnungen, Berlin 1949.

[45] Vgl. Matthew Menges O. F. M., The Concept of Univocity Regarding the Predication of God and Creature according to William Ockham (Franciscan Institute Publications, Philosophy Series No. 9), St. Bonaventure N. Y. 1952.

[46] Vgl. unsern Aufsatz: Zu Ockhams Beweis der Existenz Gottes, in FrancStud 32 (1950) 50 ff. [unten 399 ff.].

gen, die aber die feinen Unterschiede in der Terminologie vor allem auch
der Probatio, Persuasio und Demonstratio berücksichtigen müßten.
    Wir können es nicht unterlassen, auf eine interessante Studie
hinzuweisen, die all jenen besonders empfohlen sei, die in den land-
läufigen Handbüchern der Philosophie und Theologie die einzige
Quelle ihrer Kenntnis der Philosophie und Theologie Ockhams haben.
P. Allan W o l t e r hat die Frage ausgewählt: Sind nach Ockham
unmögliche Dinge unmöglich, weil Gott sie nicht machen kann, oder
kann Gott sie nicht machen, weil sie unmöglich sind. Er weist nach,
daß diese Frage für Ockham eine sinnlose Frage ist und daß der
Venerabilis Inceptor das Problem der inneren Möglichkeit der Dinge
im wesentlichen wie der hl. Thomas gelöst hat. Die Absurditäten,
die man Ockham zugeschrieben hat, zum Beispiel, daß Gott „ein
vernünftiges und unvernünftiges Wesen, ein totes und lebendiges
zur selben Zeit hervorbringen könne" (Bittle), existieren lediglich
in der lebhaften Einbildungskraft dieser Neuscholastiker.[47]
    Ockhams P h y s i k bedarf noch weiterer und eingehenderer Unter-
suchungen, die viel mehr die bis jetzt noch nicht editierten Quaestiones
super libros Physicorum und die Expositio super libros Physicorum
heranziehen müßten. Es ist sicher, daß Ockham nicht der Aristotelischen Bewegungslehre folgt. Was er geleistet hat, ist, wie Moody[48]
mit Recht hervorgehoben hat, die Klärung der Grundfragen der
Bewegung vom Standpunkt des Philosophen und Logikers und nicht
so sehr vom Standpunkt des Mathematikers und Empirikers. Seine
Hauptleistung war, daß er das berühmte Axiom: "Omne quod
movetur ab alio movetur" (zu übersetzen: Alles, was in Bewegung
ist, wird von einem anderen bewegt) so interpretierte, daß es auch
eine Bewegung gibt, wenn ein Körper nicht von etwas anderem bewegt wird. Damit hat er dem Trägheitsprinzip und der modernen
Definition der Kraft als philosophische Möglichkeiten den Weg bereitet.
    Die P s y c h o l o g i e und E t h i k Ockhams sind wohl noch am
wenigsten untersucht. Vor allem und gerade wegen der Studie von

---

[47] Allan W o l t e r O. F. M., Ockham and the Textbooks: On the Origin
of Possibility, in FranzStud 32 (1950) 70 ff.
    [48] Vgl. Ernest A. M o o d y, Galileo and Avempace, in: The History of
Ideas 12 (1951) 163—193 und 375—422; bes. S. 399.

Anita G a r v e n s,[49] die durchaus unzulänglich ist, warten wir noch
auf eine gründliche und unvoreingenommene Untersuchung der
Ethik Ockhams. Leider ist auch auf diesem Gebiete zuviel den voneinander abschreibenden Lehrbüchern geglaubt worden.
Wir möchten schließen mit einer Bemerkung, die nicht bitter gedacht ist, wenn sie auch bitter lauten mag. Wie ist es möglich, daß
in einer ernstzunehmenden Zeitschrift ein durchaus ernstzunehmen-
der Mann an die Absurdität glauben kann, Ockham habe den Satz
vertreten: Credo quia absurdum?[50] Nicht einmal Tertullian, dem
man diesen Unsinn gern zuschiebt, hat diese Absurdität aufgebracht.
Was ist uns mit Unwahrheiten gedient? Ehe wir große Konstruktio-
nen entwerfen dürfen, muß wenigstens für das 14. und 15. Jahrhundert noch viel Kleinarbeit geschehen. Wir müssen erst wissen,
wie es gewesen ist, um dann zu erklären, wie es so sein konnte, soweit
dies im rein menschlichen Raum überhaupt möglich ist. Ferner
möchten wir, in der Hoffnung nicht mißverstanden zu werden, um
etwas Nachsicht bitten für die Beurteilung eines Zeitalters, das doch ein
notwendiges Bindeglied in der katholischen Tradition bleibt. Ist die Re-
formation auf jeden Fall auch dadurch charakterisiert,daßsie ganze Jahr-
hunderte einfach als Dekadenz verwarf, so möchten wir gerade die echt
katholische Haltung darin finden, daß die ganze Tradition bejaht wird.

2. OCKHAM'S PHILOSOPHY IN THE LIGHT OF RECENT RESEARCH[a]

A truer picture of Ockham as a Philosopher is slowly beginning
to emerge from a maze of prejudices and uncritically repeated opinions
about his life, works and doctrine.

---

[49] Anita G a r v e n s, Die Grundlagen der Ethik Wilhelms von Ockham,
in FranzStud 21 (1934) 243—273, 360—408. [Für die Psychologie Ockhams,
siehe Oswald F u c h s O. F. M., The Psychology of Habit According to William Ockham (Franciscan Institute Publications, Philosophy Series No. 8),
St. Bonaventure, N. Y. 1952].

[50] R. S c h w a r z, Das Problem der christlichen Philosophie, in PhJb 60
(1950) 222.

[a] First published in: Proceedings of the Tenth International Congress
of Philosophy (Amsterdam, August 11—18, 1948), edit. E. W. Beth,

Concerning his life. Since Hofer's basic biographical sketch two important facts have been discovered. First, Fr. Conrad Walmesley, O.F.M. found a document stating that a William Ockham was ordained a subdeacon in 1306; the second discovery is the Incipit of an extract from Burley, De puritate artis Logicae in Amploniana 0 67, where it is stated that the Summa of Ockham was written before 1329. Both dates with their implications force us to suppose that Ockham was born before 1290, probably around 1285. Hence Ockham was about 25 years old when Scotus died. It is probable that Ockham personally knew Scotus.

Concerning his works. The difficult problem which is important for every scholastic—viz. which works are authentic and to what extent the available texts are faithful, has been studied by Baudry, Bascour, Boehner, Maier. Here are the results (excluding the political works):

1. Works which are without any reasonable doubt authentic.

I. Ordinatio, that is, the commentary on the first book of the Sentences. There is clear evidence for at least two redactions. Of the first redaction we know one complete ms., one abbreviation, and one ms. which shows the additions of the second redaction usually on the margin.

II. Reportatio, that is questions on the second, third and fourth books of the Sentences. Many questions, however, which are printed in the edition of Lyons 1495, do not belong to the Commentary and are partly of doubtful authenticity, they are: lib. II, q. 3, q. 8, q. 20 (beginning with U), q. 25; lib. III, q. 5, q. 12, qq. 13—15, and the Additiones [read: Dubitationes] additae at the end of this edition.

III. Expositio super librum Porphyrii, super librum Praedicamentorum, super libros Perihermenias (these three expositions, also called Expositio aurea, were edited by Marcus de Benevento 1496), super libros Elenchorum. Maier has recently suggested that there is a second redaction of the Expositio aurea; her reasons, however, are without any foundation.

H. J. Pos and J. H. A. Hollak, II (Amsterdam 1949) 1113—1116. Cfr. supra 1—33, where usually more details have been given.

IV. Expositio super libros Physicorum (the work seems to be incomplete, since no ms. is known which has the 8th book completed).

V. Summa Logicae. Salamucha and Boehner have proved that Prantl's doubts as regards this work are without any foundation.

VI. Tractatus de Sacramento Altaris. Baudry has shown that this tract is really composed of two; one we can call De corpore Christi, the other De Sacramento Altaris. They are usually separated in the mss.

VII. Tractatus de Praedestinatione.

VIII. Summulae in libros Physicorum (a fragment).

IX. Quodlibeta VII. Quodl. IV. q. 6 of the Strassburg edition does not belong to the Quodlibeta.

X. Quaestiones super libros Physicorum. Only three mss. are known; it is closely related to the Quodlibeta.

2. Works which are most probably non-authentic.

I. De principiis Theologiae.

II. De successivis, which is a compilation from the Expositio super libros Physicorum.

III. Centiloquium theologicum.

Since the majority of these works are accessible in older editions (a few in modern editions), we have to ask whether their text is faithful.

None of the earlier editions has a faithful text; the same is true for the edition of De Sacramento Altaris published by Birch.

The Incunabula editions of the Ordinatio have a fair text; they follow a deteriorated tradition of the second redaction.

The Reportatio is in a bad condition and its use without manuscripts may lead to serious errors.

The editions of the Summa Logicae have in general a fair text, though serious errors have been discovered by Salamucha.

The old edition of the Expositio aurea presents a bad text, so that it should not be used without the help of mss.

The editions of the Quodlibeta present a fair text only.

3*

A critical edition of the non-political works of Ockham is being prepared by the Franciscan Institute, St. Bonaventure, N. Y., U. S. A., in cooperation with the Abbey of Mont César, Louvain, Belgium,[b] and with several other scholars. For the time being no study of Ockham's doctrine should omit to consult the manuscript tradition also.

Concerning the doctrine. Various tendencies have impeded a correct understanding of Ockham's teaching in Philosophy. Many scholars have been intent upon finding in Ockham one or even the main cause of the breakdown of Scholasticism. Since the reason for this breakdown is now rarely attributed to Scotus' Philosophy, the burden of responsibility is laid more heavily on Ockham. Michalski's Studies, important as they are for the literary history of the 14th century, seem to suffer under this prejudice. However, many of his misinterpretations have been corrected by more recent investigations. Unfortunately these corrections are slow in reaching the textbooks. As witness of this slowness, see the third volume of De Wulf, Histoire de la Philosophie médiévale (1947), which is in need of a complete revision in regard to its representation of Ockham's doctrine, since Ockham would not recognize it as his own.

1. In Logic (cfr. Salamucha, Bochenski, Moody, Boehner and Guelluy), Ockham carries on the scholastic tradition, combining the genuine Aristotelian Logic with that of Petrus Hispanus and leading it to a high degree of perfection. This Logic is essentially formal; a clear concept of material implication is found, many theorems of the propositional and functional calculus of modern Logic are already known in their verbal form, and even a faint idea of a three-valued Logic is encountered. The concept of truth is being redefined with the help of a refined logic. A new arrangement of the system of Logic is prepared.

---

[b] At the end of 1951 Dom Bascour, of Mont-César, notified Fr. Philotheus that his numerous occupations did not allow him any longer to contribute to the critical edition in preparation. The edition is now entirely in the hands of the Franciscan Institute. Cfr. *infra* p. 75—76 and 112.

2. In Epistemology and Metaphysics (cfr. Vignaux, Weinberg, Boehner, Day, Guelluy), Ockham's supposed scepticism, agnosticism, fideism, empiricism, etc., have disappeared in the light of original text-analysis. Ockham lays the foundation and origin of true knowledge in intuitive cognition of singular facts; this guarantees the truth of evident judgements, about states of things. Intuitive cognition never leads into error, even if there is an intuitive cognition of something that does not exist. Ockham thus is the continuator of the Augustinian doctrine of the infallibility of judgments regarding immediately given facts. Hence Ockham's foundation for every cognition lies in experience. Ockham's abstract knowledge and all scientific knowledge is by means of universal concepts which, formed on immediate cognition, are only universalized by predication. Hence his theory is realistic, insofar as the concepts are representing reality, it is conceptualistic insofar as the universal concepts are entities in the mind whilst there is no universality whatsoever outside the mind, except by voluntary intuition. Ockham's ideas about the relation between faith and reason are in the line of tradition, he only emphasizes the insufficiency of reason as regards certain — not all — matters of faith, by applying and pushing his logic to its last consequences. Ockham is not an agnostic, since he admits a proof of the existence of God and certain attributes—though he does not admit a strict demonstration for the unicity, liberty or the omnipotence of God. For these latter, however, he admits moral certitude.

3. As regards Ockham's political ideas (cfr. Boehner, Hamman[c]), it becomes more and more apparent that Ockham's place amongst the curialist and laicist parties in the struggle between the Pope and the Emperor takes a moderate and traditional position; he teaches a clear distinction between temporal and spiritual power and requests a peaceful cooperation between both. It is worthwhile to quote here a statement of Ockham's which is full of significance at our present time "Therefore he is not truly zealous for the common good, who does

---

[c] Cfr. *infra*, 442 ff. — Adalbert Hamman, O. F. M., La doctrine de l'Eglise et de l'Etat chez Occam — Etude sur le "Breviloquium" (Etudes de science religieuse 1) Paris 1942.

not desire and work, as much as he can in his station, that the whole world be subject to one monarch." This is Ockham's expression of a union of all people and nations of this globe under one government.

There is need for further studies on Ockham's Metaphysics and Ethics which are partly already in preparation.

For a complete Bibliography cfr. Robert Guelluy, Philosophie et Théologie chez Guillaume d'Ockham, Louvain-Paris, 1947 [Léon Baudry, o. c. 273—306, and Valens Heynck, O.F.M., Ockham-Literatur 1919—1949, in FranzStud 32 (1950) 164—183].

3. MANUSCRITS DES OEUVRES NON-POLEMIQUES D'OCCAM[a]

Cette liste a été composée avec l'aide bienveillante de M. l'abbé Baudry (Paris), des RR. PP. Dom Bascour (Mont-César), V. Doucet (Quaracchi), Fr.-M. Henquinet (Quaracchi), W. Lampen (Nimègue). La Liste reste ouverte.

I. — Expositio aurea super artem veterem.

Incipit: *Cum (quoniam) omne operans quod in suis operibus et actibus potest errare aliquo indiget directivo . . .*

(Incipit liber Elenchorum: *Circa librum Elenchorum primo videndum est . . .*)

Bruges.	499 (olim 59) (cum Elench.).	s. XIV.
Firenze.	Bibl. Naz. G. 3. 803 (sine Elench.).	s. XIV.
Firenze.	Bibl. Naz. B. 4. (cum Elench.).	1331.
Firenze.	Bibl. Laurenz. Leop. Gadd. 153 (sine Elench.).	s. XV.
Oxford.	Bodl. Misc. 558 (cum Elench.).	s. XIV.
Paris.	Bibl. Nat. 6431 (incompl. sine Elench.).	s. XIV.
Paris.	Bibl. Nat. 14721 (cum Elench.).	s. XIV.
Vaticana.	Palat. lat. 998 (sine Elench.).	s. XIV.
Los Angeles.	University 6 (sine Perih. et Elench.).	s. XIV.

II. — Summa totius logicae.

Incipit (primus prol.): *Quam veritatis sectatoribus afferat . . .*

Incipit (secund. prol.): *Dudum me frater et amice carissime tuis litteris studebas inducere . . .*

Incipit: *Omnes logicae tractatores intendunt astruere quod argumenta...*

---

[a] First published in La France Franciscaine 22 (1939) 171—175. — Cfr. L. Baudry o. c. 273—287.

Assisi.	187 (secunda pars).	s. XIV.
Assisi.	647 (tertia pars tert. part.).	s. XIV.
Assisi.	666 (quarta pars tert. part.).	s. XIV.
Assisi.	670.	
Avignon.	1086.	1343.
Basel.	F. II. 25.	1342.
Bologna.	Univ. 137 (103).	
Bruges.	497.	s. XIV.
Bruges.	498.	1340.
Cambrai.	942 (841).	s. XIV.
Cambridge.	Gonv. and Caius 464/571.	1341.
Cambridge.	Peterhouse 102 (1. 0. 7.).	s. XIV.
Cesena.	Malatestiana Plut. X. sin. 6.	s. XIV.
Cracau.	Bibl. Jag. 719 DD II 38.	1352.
Erfurt.	Amplon. O 67.	1339.
Erfurt.	Amplon. Q 259.	1340.
Erfurt.	Amplon. Q 257.	in. s. XIV.
Erfurt.	Amplon. F. 301.	1348.
Fabriano.	Bibl. com. 24.	s. XV.
Firenze.	Bibl. Naz. E. 5. 802.	s. XIV.
Firenze.	Bibl. Naz. S. Marco. I. II. 5.	s. XIV.-XV.
Firenze.	Bibl. Laur. Plut. XII. sin. cod. 4.	s. XIV.
Firenze.	Bibl. Laur. Plut. XII. sin. cod. 2.	s. XIV.
Laon.	431.	s. XIV.
London.	Brit. M. Arundel, 367.	s. XIV.
München.	Staatsbibl. 23 530.	s. XV.
Napoli.	Bibl. Naz. VIII. G. 98.	s. XIV.
Napoli.	Bibl. Naz. VIII. E. 62.	s. XIV.
Padova.	Univ. 1913.	
Padova.	Univ. 2092.	
Padova.	Univ. 1123.	
Padova.	Anton. XII. N. 544.	
Padova.	Anton. XXII. N. 537.	
Paris.	Bibl. Nat. 6430.	1399.
Paris.	Bibl. Nat. 6431.	s. XIV.
Paris.	Bibl. Nat. 6432.	s. XIV.
Paris.	Bibl. Nat. 3521.	s. XIV.
Reims.	888.	s. XIV.
Vaticana.	Lat. 674.	s. XIV.
Vaticana.	Lat. 947.	s. XIV.
Vaticana.	Lat. 948.	s. XIV.
Vaticana.	Lat. 949.	s. XIV.
Vaticana.	Lat. 950.	s. XV.

Vaticana.	Lat. 951.	s. XV.
Vaticana.	Lat. 952.	1369.
Vaticana.	Lat. 953.	s. XIV.
Vaticana.	Borgh. 151.	
Vaticana.	Chigi E. IV. 99.	
Vaticana.	Chigi E. VII. 220.	
Vaticana.	Chigi E. VII. 221.	
Vaticana.	Ottoboni 2071.	s. XIV.
Venezia.	S. Marco. Cod. 250 a. 243. I. 170 (L. VI.	1366.
	CCXCII).	
Venezia.	Seminario. F. III. 12.	

III. — Compendium logicae (Dubium).

| Assisi. | 690. | s. XV. |

Incipit: *Logica cum dicatur* . . .
(Explicit minor tractatus nove Loyce fratris Guillelmi Ocham)

| München. | Staatsbibliothek, 1060 (4379). | s. XIV. |

IV. — Summulae in libros Physicorum.

Incipit: *Studiosissime saepiusque rogatus a litteratis quam plurimis* . . .

Bruges.	496.	s. XIV.
Cracau.	Bibl. Jag. 736.	s. XIV.
Paris.	Bibl. Nat. 15880.	s. XIV.
Paris.	Arsen. 830.	
Reims.	888.	s. XIV.
Rodez.	56.	s. XV.
Vaticana.	Palat. lat. 1202.	s. XV.

V. — Expositio super Physicam.

Incipit: *(Nos) philosophos plurimos sapientiae titulo decoratos* . . .
Sive: *Valde reprehensibilis videtur qui in sua perfectione* . . .

Assisi.	294.	s. XIV.
Berlin.	Staatsbibl. 974.	s. XIV.
Bruges.	557.	init. s. XIV.
Chambéry.	23.	s. XIV.
Napoli.	Bibl. Naz. VIII. E. 26.	s. XIV.
Oxford.	Merton Coll. 293.	s. XIV.
Stettin.	Bibl. d. Marienstiftgymn. Camp. 13.	s. XV.
Vaticana.	Lat. 3062.	s. XIV.

VI. — Quaestiones in Physicam.

Incipit: *Circa materiam de conceptu quaero primo: utrum conceptus sit*
aliquod fictum . . .
Sive: *Quaeritur utrum possit probari quod artificialia aliquid addunt* . . .

Paris.	Bibl. Nat. 17841.	s. XV.
Upsala.	Univ. Bibl. cod. C. 665.	s. XIV.
Vaticana.	Lat. 956.	s. XIV.
Wien.	Bibl. Palat. 5460 (Univ. 911).	s. XV.
Wien.	Dominik. 153.	

VII. — **Quodlibeta VII.**

Incipit: *Utrum possit probari per rationem naturalem quod tantum est unus Deus . . .*

Basel.	F. II. 24 (Quodl. I et II).	s. XIV.
Bruxelles	Bibl. roy. 4771.	s. XV.
Giessen.	733.	s. XV.
München.	Staatsbibl. 8943.	s. XV.
Paris.	Bibl. Nat. 16398.	s. XV.
Paris.	Bibl. Nat. 17841 (Quodl. I—IV. 1).	s. XV.
Paris.	Bibl. Maz. (Quodl. I—II. 15).	s. XIV.
Vaticana.	Lat. 3075.	1333.
Vaticana.	Lat. 956.	s. XIV.
Vaticana.	Chigi B. VI. 93.	s. XIV.
Wien.	Dominik. 153 (Quodl. I—IV).	s. XV.

VIII. — **Commentarius in IV. libros Sententiarum.**

Incipit 1. lib.: *Circa prologum quaero primo: Utrum sit possibile intellectum viatoris habere notitiam evidentem de veritatibus theologiae . . .*

Incipit 2. lib.: *Circa secundum Sententiarum quaeritur: utrum creatio actio qua deus dicitur formaliter creans differat ex natura rei a creatore . . .*

Incipit 3. lib.: *Circa tertium librum primo quaeritur: utrum solus filius univit sibi naturam humanam in unitatem suppositi . . .*

Incipit 4. lib.: *Utrum sacramenta novae legis sint causae effectivae gratiae.*

Assisi.	199 (Quaest. extr. ex Comment. in Sent.).	s. XIV.
Basel.	A. VI. 22. (Sent. I d. 1. q. 1—4.).	s. XIV.
Bruxelles.	Bibl. roy. 1284 (1. Sent.).	1471.
Bruxelles.	Bibl. roy. 3512 (2—4 Sent.).	s. XIV.
Cambridge.	Gonv. a. Caius 101/53 (1. Sent.).	s. XIV.
Cambridge.	Gonv. a. Caius 325/525 (1. Sent.).	s. XIV.
Cambridge.	Gonv. a. Caius 285/678 (qq. in prol. 1—4).	s. XIV.
Erfurt.	Amploniana. Q. 109 (Abbrev.).	s. XIV.
Firenze.	Bibl. Naz. F. 6. 800 (1. Sent.).	s. XIV.
Firenze.	Bibl. Naz. A. 3. 801 (1—4 Sent.).	s. XIV.
Göttingen.	Theol. 118 (1—4 Sent.).	

Milano.	Ambr. C. 281 inf. (2—4 Sent.).	
München.	Universitätsbibl. 52 (1—4. Sent.).	s. XIV.
München.	Staatsbibl. 8943 (2—4 Sent.).	s. XV.
Oxford.	Merton Coll. 100 (1—4. Sent.).	s. XIV.
Oxford.	Merton Coll. 106 (1. Sent.).	s. XIV.
Oxford.	Balliol Coll. 299 (1—4. Sent.).	s. XIV.
Padova.	Bibl. Anton. X. 184.	s. XV.
Padova.	Bibl. Univ. 927.	s. XV.
Paris.	Bibl. Nat. 15561 (Tabula et consp. qq.).	s. XIV.
Paris.	Bibl. Nat. 15904 (1—2. Sent. incompl.).	s. XIV.
Paris.	Bibl. Nat. 16398 (3—4. Sent.).	s. XV.
Paris.	Bibl. Maz. 894 (1. Sent.).	s. XIV.
Paris.	Bibl. Maz. 893 (2—4. Sent.).	s. XIV.
Paris.	Bibl. Maz. 962 (1. Sent. incompl. d. 30, q. 3).	s. XIV-XV.
Troyes.	718 (1. Sent.).	s. XIV.
Vaticana.	Borgh. 68 (Abbrev. 1. Sent.).	s. XIV.
Vaticana.	Ottob. 2088 (1. Sent.).	s. XIV.
Venezia.	Bibl. S. Antonii.	

IX. — **Tractatus de successivis.** (Invenitur etiam in Summulis Physic.).

Incipit: *Quia communis opinio est quod motus tempus et locus* . . .

Basel.	Univ. F. II.	s. XIV.
Bruges.	500 (Inc.: Videndum est de loco quem Philoso- phus 4⁰ Phis. def . . .).	s. XIV.
Erfurt.	Amplon. O. 76.	s. XIV.
Paris.	Bibl. Nat. 16130.	s. XIV.

X. — **Tractatus de praedestinatione et de futuris contingentibus.**

Incipit:*Circa materiam de praedestinatione et scientia est advertendum...*

Basel.	Univ. F. II. 24.	s. XIV.
Bruges.	469.	s. XIV.
Erfurt.	Amplon. F. 345 (sine sec. parte).	c. 1360.
Paris.	Bibl. Nat. 14579.	s. XV.
Paris.	Bibl. Nat. 14580.	s. XIV.
Paris.	Bibl. Nat. 14715.	s. XIV.
Paris.	Bibl. Nat. 14909 (sine sec. parte).	s. XV.
Paris.	Bibl. Nat. 16130 (sine sec. parte).	s. XIV
Vaticana.	Ottob. 179.	s. XIV.

XI. — **Tractatus de sacramento altaris.**

Incipit: *Circa conversionem panis* . ..
Sive: *Stupenda super munera* . . .
Sive: *Sicut dicit quaedam glossa* . . .

Basel.	F. II. 24.	s. XIV.
Giessen.	733.	s. XV.
Oxford.	Balliol Coll. 299.	s. XIV.
Oxford.	Merton Coll. 137.	s. XIV.
Paris.	Bibl. Nat. 15888.	s. XIV.
Rouen.	561.	s. XV.
Troyes.	718.	s. XIV.
Vaticana.	Ottob. 179.	s. XIV.
Wien.	Dominik. 153.	s. XIV.

XII — Fragmenta et dubia.

1) *Quaestio de relatione.*
Incipit: *Alia de relatione vane referentur . . .*

| Basel. | F. II. 24. | s. XIV. |

2) *Quaestio: Utrum essentia divina et relatio distinguantur ex natura rei . . .*

| Basel. | F. II. 24. | s. XIV. |

3) *Propositio, an sit concedanda: essentia divina est quaternitas . . .*

| Basel. | A. VII. 13. | s. XIV. |

4) *Centiloquium theologicum (*sive *De principiis theologiae)*[b].
Incipit: *Anima nobis innata eo potius naturaliter appetit . . .*
Sive: *Humana nobilis natura eo potius naturaliter nititur . . .*

| Erfurt. | Ampl. Q. 104 (fragmentum). | s. XIV. |
| Vaticana. | Palat. 378. | s. XV. |

4. ON A RECENT STUDY OF OCKHAM[a]

Father Iserloh's rather long article: "Um die Echtheit des Centi-loquium. Ein Beitrag zur Wertung Ockhams und zur Chronologie seiner Werke," in *Gregorianum* XXX (1949) 78—103, 309—346, is a plea for the authenticity of the *Centiloquium* attributed to Ockham. In the first part, the author tries to find a place for the *Centiloquium* in the chronological order of Ockham's works; in the second part, he examines and rejects all the reasons we have advanced against the authenticity of the *Centiloquium*. The main purpose of Father Iserloh's article is to give support to those who think that Ockham was responsible for the breakdown of scholasticism (cfr. p. 346). His

---

[b] The *Centiloquium* and the *Tractatus* are different works.

[a] *Franciscan Studies* 10 (1950) 191—196.

criticism, on the other hand, is directed mostly against certain opinions of the present writer.

After a careful study of Iserloh's criticism, we are convinced that, apart from a few minor details, our position on the non-authenticity of the *Centiloquium*, remains secure. We leave it, therefore, to serious and competent students of the history of medieval philosophy to judge. There is no point in a repetition of our arguments; repeating a statement does not add to its truth.

However, there is a serious reason for us to protest [against] Father Iserloh's criticism, and we wish to make this protest as strong as possible. Iserloh has misinterpreted one of our statements in such an unfortunate manner that it makes us appear to be insulting others. He has imputed to us the opinion that the greater part of the old and new literature on Ockham is worthless almost without exception to one who would properly evaluate Ockham's teachings. He writes:

> Er ist sich klar darüber, daß er mit seiner Ansicht fast allein dasteht, aber er fühlt sich berechtigt, über den größten Teil der alten und neuen Literatur „als fast ausnahmslos wertlos zur Beurteilung der Lehre Ockhams" hinwegzugehen (p. 81).

We deny emphatically that we have ever expressed this sweeping judgment, either explicitly or by implication. We deeply regret that Iserloh has distorted our intention and has made a phrase we have used to mean something it does not mean in its context. This he has done by the well-known method of cutting off a few of our words and placing them into an entirely different context. To show the reader that Iserloh has used this regrettable method, we here submit our complete text, italicizing the few words Iserloh chose to quote:

> Auch der Neuscholastik ist es bis heute nicht gelungen, den „omnium nominalium monarcha" in seiner wahren Bedeutung zu würdigen. Wenig erhebende Beweise dafür sind Aufsätze aus neuerer Zeit, die mit vorgefaßten Meinungen ohne die auch bei wissenschaftlichen Arbeiten notwendige Haltung des Verstehenwollens seine Lehre ideengeschichtlich untersucht haben. Sie sind *fast ausnahmslos als wertlos zur Beurteilung der Lehre Ockhams* zu bezeichnen. Dagegen wirken Arbeiten, wie die von Hochstetter, Baudry, Vignaux, Moody und A. van Leeuwen, O. F. M., nicht nur wegen ihrer Zuverlässigkeit, sondern vor allem wegen ihrer unpartei-

ischen Einstellung erfrischend (,,Ein Gedicht auf die Logik Ockhams", in *Franzisk. Studien* 26 (1939) 78).

It is clear that we are not speaking about most of the old and recent literature concerning Ockham, but only about certain articles. These particular articles which were written with preconceived opinions we *do* aver are almost without exception worthless for one who would properly evaluate Ockham's teachings. We have explicitly excluded the books and articles of the scholars mentioned by us. We are at a loss to understand such a misrepresentation. It gives no credit to the method used by Iserloh, who is responsible for still further misrepresentations, but these we shall abstain from discussing.

In general Iserloh seems to rely on vague feelings and intuitions rather than on solid, albeit tedious, research into the manuscript tradition. Iserloh's embarassingly lighthearted manner of doing away with solidly established conclusions of others is shown in his treatment of the *Tractatus De Principiis Theologiae* — edited by Baudry who on good evidence refuses to consider it Ockham's work — and the *Tractatus De Successivis*. Iserloh, in face of scholarly opinion, denies that these works are compilations and persists in attributing them to Ockham. We believe that neither Baudry nor we are in need of defense. We have spent months of wearisome research in manuscript-reproductions difficult to read; and we have, following a suggestion of Baudry, finally succeeded in finding every line of the *Tractatus De Successivis* — except the opening lines and a few connecting phrases — in the *Expositio super libros Physicorum* of Ockham. In our edition of the *Tractatus De Successivis* we have carefully marked what is not in the *Expositio;* we also indicated the variants of two of the mss. of the *Expositio;* we have noted where the compiler continues, etc. According to the rules of a stringent historical method we were entitled to call this tract a compilation. For if a work composed of parts literally found in another work is not a compilation, what is? As to the authenticity of the tract, we stated that since practically every line is found in an authentic work of Ockham, the Medieval scribes or the compiler were right in ascribing this compilation to Ockham; yet we doubted that the compilation was made by Ockham himself. But, Iserloh does away with all this simply by writing: "Die Annahme einer Kompilation halte ich nicht für notwendig und sehe keinen Grund, Ockham "De Successivis" abzusprechen" (p. 85). This, we confess, is irritating. The fact that four manuscripts (the only ones known to us — when we published our edition and the only ones still known to Iserloh though in the meantime we have discovered a few others) ascribe this *Tractatus* to Ockham is really no proof of its authenticity in the modern sense. If Iserloh is to be consistent, he must deny the character of compilation and affirm the authenticity in the modern sense of all the abbreviations and the *notabilia* encountered frequently in Medieval manuscripts and usually ascribed to their author. In fact, Iserloh will experience little difficulty in doing so, since even the fact that in such works for instance in the *Tractatus Theologiae* almost every paragraph starts with the word "Ponit" (viz. Ockham) does not prove anything. He would say: Ockham is only hiding himself behind another person. That is an easy explanation; too easy, we believe.

Concerning the chronology of the works of Ockham, Iserloh's contribution is practically nil, though he does not fail to give the impression that he has established a chronological order (for instance: he says ,,Unter Berücksichtigung aller angegebenen Gesichtspunkte möchte ich folgende Reihenfolge der Werke Ockhams aufstellen", p. 94). Following the suggestions of others, mostly of Baudry who deserves much credit in these matters, we have relied mostly on the cross-references found in Ockham's works, and employing this good historical method, with the necessary precautions, we have established a relative chronological order of the more important philosophical and theological writings. This, we are happy to say, has been taken over by Iserloh without quibble. The main problems concern the absolute date of the *Quodlibeta* and the *Quaestiones super libros Physicorum* — both works are closely connected — and the *Summa Logicae*. Baudry had shown that the *Quaestiones* had been written before the *Quodlibeta*, and there can be no doubt that this opinion is correct. Was the *Summa Logicae* written before these works or after? We have no convincing proof on either side.

Iserloh, apparently following his intuition and relying mostly on his judgment of the different tenor of these works, believes that the

Quodlibeta and the *Quaestiones* were written in Oxford, the *Summa Logicae* in Avignon. For the former assumption he advances the reason that the *Quodlibeta* and the *Quaestiones* are more radical hence Ockham could not yet have been in trouble; and since the *Quodlibeta* were definitely written before 1333, the only reasonable date appears to him to be before 1323, while Ockham was still at Oxford. What makes us reluctant to accept this hypothesis is first, the almost complete lack of references in this to other works; second, the clear and unflinching adherence to the *intellectio*-theory on the nature of universals and the rejection of the *fictum*-theory. In all the other works there is still a trace of hesitation, even in the *Summa Logicae;* not, however in the *Quodlibeta* and the *Quaestiones.* On the other hand, we are sure that the *Quodlibeta* were written after the *Commentary on the Sentences* and all the commentaries on philosophical works, since the *Commentary on the Sentences* and the *Expositio super libros Physicorum* are quoted. That means that Ockham composed or rather sketched the two works after the greater part of his non-political writings was finished.

In favor of placing the *Summa Logicae* after 1323 and therefore probably at Avignon, there is at least one strong argument which escaped Iserloh. According to Iserloh's intuition the *Summa Logicae* gives signs of caution and carefulness on the part of Ockham; there-fore, Iserloh concludes, Ockham must have been in trouble while writing the *Summa Logicae.* The only text that serves as basis for this construction is the following:

> Ideo est alia opinio de quantitate, quae mihi videtur esse de mente Aristotelis, sive sit haeretica sive catholica, quam volo nunc recitare, quamvis nolim eam asserere. Et ideo quando illam opinionem posui et scripsi super philosophiam, non scripsi eam tamquam meam, sed tamquam Aristotelis, quam exposui, ut mihi videtur; et eodem modo nunc sine asser-tione recitabo eam . . . *Summa Logicae* pars I, cap. 44 (edit. Ph. Boehner, p. 125 lin. 134—139) (edit. [antiqua] cap. 46).

Before going on we cannot forbear to correct a minor detail which, we admit, is a mere trifle; but Iserloh has brought pedantic scrutiny upon himself by the rather pretentious attitude which pervades his article. In the above quoted text, reproduced by Iserloh, he has

written *Physicam* instead of *philosophiam* and he adds in parenthesis:
„Böhner liest mit der Edition Bologna 1498 Philosophiam." This is
quite incorrect. We do not have the edition of Bologna; we
rather read in the oldest manuscripts. However, Iserloh adduces
for his reading „Physica" three manuscripts of the Vatican library.
We checked them: Vat. lat. 947 has ph'ia 3, 948 has: ph'iam; Ottoboni 2071 phy[aa]. We have also checked 949 which has: ph'iam,
950 phiam, 951 phyām, and in all these cases, the best analysis of
these abbreviations is *philosophiam;* only Vat. lat. 952 has *Physicam.*
This confirms us in our belief that Iserloh has not had much experience with manuscripts.

However, we are more interested in the text itself which is at the
basis of Iserloh's intuition, and from which he gathers that Ockham
was in trouble when he wrote these lines. What little this proves is
shown by the fact that Ockham employed similar expressions at a time
when he was supposed not to have been in trouble. We read in his
Expositio super librum Perihermenias, ad: Quoniam autem ... the
following:

> ... quamvis aliquo modo possit concedi secundum theologos. Sed de
> hoc non est curandum modo, quia in illo libro et in aliis libris Philosophi
> non intendo aliquid asserere quod sit falsum, sed tantum intendo explanare
> intentionem Aristotelis, sive fuerit vera sive falsa.

Hence, we do not believe that such expressions can help us much
in dating Ockham's works.

There is still another indication that the *Summa Logicae* might
have been written after 1323; we should like to call attention to it
for the first time. In *Summa Logicae* III, 1, cap. 4 [Edit. Ph. Boehner,
p. 334, lin. 40—41] Ockham writes: *Et ideo errat Magister Abstractionum assignando in praedictis syllogismis fallaciam accidentis* ...
Now, the *Magister Abstractionum* is Francis Mayron. He became
Master in 1323 and, as it seems, was called *Magister Abstractionum*
because of his great interest in the formalities and their abstract
wordings. This would bring the date of the *Summa Logicae* definitely
up to the time of Avignon. Of course, we should not forget that
Ockham probably had been working on the *Summa* for quite a while,
as is indicated by his dedicatory letter [Edit. Ph. Boehner, p. 7].

In any case, we consider such evidence much more valuable in dating a work than vague guesses based on the general tenor of the work.

It is interesting to note that the error of Francis Mayron which is rejected by Ockham is favored by the author of the *Centiloquium* (cfr. *Centiloquium* Concl. 80C [edit. Ph. Boehner, *Franciscan Studies*, vol. 3, 1942, p. 290]). And this brings us to another of the reasons which has induced us to answer Iserloh's article. There are more indications against the authenticity of the *Centiloquium* than we have given so far. One point very striking, and in our opinion, very strong is the following:

The unknown author of the *Centiloquium* mentions in at least two places certain opinions of the "moderni". In both cases the *moderni* are followers of Ockham or even Ockham himself. Anyone who has studied Ockham, not just in a cursory way, but thoroughly, knows that in Ockham's language the *moderni* are definitely people different from himself. Years ago Moody called attention to this in his excellent study on the Logic of Ockham. He writes:

> . . . if Ockham had actually been inspired by a desire for novelty and by a spirit of rebellion against tradition, it is strange that he did not keep up with the progressive movements of his own times, and number himself among the *moderni*. It is strange that he constantly criticized them and stated his own preference for the opinions of the *antiqui*, on the ground that they (the *antiqui*) stayed closer to the authentic thought of Aristotle (*The Logic of William of Ockham*, London: Sheed and Ward 1935, p. 7).

Moody also informs us in a footnote that he has noted at least fifteen references to the *moderni* in Ockham's logical writings, and that the theories of those *moderni* are usually those of fourteenth century Scotists as Francis Mayron and others and of realists as Walter Burleigh, Aegidius Romanus etc. (cfr. footnote on p. 7). Our own experience with the works of Ockham can but confirm the statement of Moody.

It is a strange fact that the unknown author of the *Centiloquium* refers twice at least to theories of the *moderni*, and that in both cases these *moderni* are Ockham and his followers, and, what is even more strange, these *moderni* are supposed to be quite numerous.

4 Boehner, Articles on Ockham

We read, for instance in Concl. 39D (our edition [*Franciscan Studies*, vol. 3, 1942] p. 254):

Sed quia ista opinio non communiter tenetur, ideo ponebatur conclusio secundum secundam[b] opinionem quae reliquis communior reputatur, praecipue a modernis.

This second opinion which is regarded as more common, especially by the *moderni* is the opinion of Ockham. Could Ockham, who scorns the *moderni*, write that? We are safe in stating that psychologically speaking it was impossible for Ockham to write these lines. The remark of the unknown author also proves that Ockham's theory was already widespread and that there had already come into being a kind of school. This school, or rather this group of scholastics, knew that they belonged to the *Via moderna*. To our unknown author and to them the term '*moderni*' had become a sign of progress and in any case, had a meaning different from that which it has in the works of Ockham. From this we can conclude that the time of the composition of the *Centiloquium* is the latter part of the fourteenth century.

Again, we read in Concl. 73A (our edition [*loc. cit.*] p. 286):

Si vero relatio accipiatur pro re, quae non est signum vel terminus, sicut quasi omnes theologi tenent, tunc adhuc per fidem oportet tenere plures relationes in divinis existere, utpote paternitatem realem . . ., ad quas relationes reales ponendas, iudicio ecclesiae semper salvo, nulla videtur ratio cogens: quia sicut in creaturis a maiori multitudine modernorum ponitur relationem nihil aliud esse quam terminum relative significantem, sic etiam in divinis, fide semper salva, poni potest probabiliter.

We do not intend to discuss the doctrinal content of this text. Our main point of interest here is that a "multitude of moderns" is mentioned who adhere to the theory of Ockham concerning relation or even to a theory which goes beyond the position of Ockham. Since these *moderni* are Ockhamists in a broad sense and since there is already a multitude of them, we must suppose that the date of composition is in any case much later than 1323—1324 as suggested by Iserloh. And, from what we have heard before, it would be psycho-

---

[b] The word *secundam* is omitted in the first edition of the article, but is found in the edition of the *Centiloquium*, and requested by the context.

logically impossible for Ockham to write these lines and to refer to his own followers as *moderni*. Fortunately, in this case we have a text from the *Summa Logicae* — supposedly written after the *Centiloquium* according to Iserloh's construction — where in regard to the same problem Ockham mentions the *moderni*, but here in accord with Ockham's own usage, the *moderni* referred to are not his own followers. In the *Summa Logicae* I, cap. 53 of the edition (in the mss. 51 [and edit. Ph. Boehner p. 152, lin. 183—198]) we read[e]:

> Quae vero assueta sunt dici de relationibus, multa (im)propria, nonnulla falsa et fabulosa esse constat, sicut latissime patet perscrutanti volumina edita de his a modernis, licet aliqua eorum habeant verum intellectum, ut quod pater paternitate est pater et filius filiatione est filius et similis similitudine est similis et his similia, in quibus locutionibus non oportet fingere rem aliquam . . .

According to this text (the chapter in which it is contained is found in the oldest manuscript known to us and in two others written before 1344 and altogether in eighteen of all the thirty mss. we have checked) the *moderni* are the realists and not of the flock of Ockham. According to the unknown author of the *Centiloquium* and in regard to the same problem the *moderni* are precisely those of Ockham's flock.

There are still other places where the unknown author of the *Centiloquium* uses unockhamistic language or, where he defends theories rejected by Ockham. We may come back to these in a later publication. For the time being we would like to mention at least that, since the time of our edition of the *Centiloquium*, our friend Dom Hildebrand Bascour, O.S.B., has discovered another manuscript of the *Centiloquium* in Spain [Burgo de Osma, Cathedral *ms. 61*, presently *ms. 202*][d]; it seems to be of the late fifteenth century and has for title: *Centiloquium Magistri Okan*. It has no proper *Explicit;* the table of contents ascribes it to Gerson. In order to facilitate the finding of other manuscripts we shall communicate here the *Incipits* of the *Centiloquium* known to us:

---

[e] The word order of the full edition does not always correspond to this quote.

[d] Cf. *Franciscan Studies* 13 (1953) 2—3, pp. 40—41.

4*

Humana nobilis natura eo potius naturaliter cognoscere . . .
Quia natura nobilis potius naturaliter nititur cognoscitur . . .
Anima nobis innata eo potius naturaliter appetit cognoscere . . .

Since we have only fifteenth century attributions of the *Centiloquium* to Ockham, and since there are serious objections to crediting the authenticity of this tract, the work cannot be attributed to Ockham. If Iserloh wishes to find in Ockham the reason for the breakdown of scholasticism, he must prove it by a much more thorough study of work authentically his, and above all, he must show himself better acquainted with Medieval Logic. In the meantime, those who are criticized by him have a right to demand that he represent their thought correctly, and not in a distorted manner.

5. A FIRST REDACTION OF THE EXPOSITIO AUREA OF OCKHAM

A Critical Comment on Anneliese Maier, *Ein neues Ockham-Manuskript* (Die Originalform der Expositio Aurea?)[a]

Ockham wrote several works on Logic.[b] One is the *Summa Logicae*, or *Summa Totius Logicae*, sometimes simply called the *Logica* of Ockham. This is the most widely known and distributed work of the Venerabilis Inceptor and is still extant in about fifty manuscripts.[c] The other logical works form a group by themselves. They are Expositions or Commentaries to various logical writings. We

---

[a] First published in *FrancStud* 8 (1948) 69—76. Cfr. the next article in the present volume where one can find the more recent literature on the problem. The art. of A. Maier discussed in the present article was published in *Greg* 28 (1947) 101—133.

[b] Cfr *infra*, 70—96.

[c] In addition, see A. Maier, *Handschriftliches zu Wilhelm Ockham und Walter Burley* in *A. F. H.* 48 (1955) 226—227; T. Barth, O. F. M., *Die Summa Logicae des Wilhelm Ockham und der Traktat de puritate artis Logicae des Walter Burleigh in zwei Handschriften der Kommunalbibliothek von Treviso* in *FranzStud* 37 (1955) 411—413. These new discoveries bring the number of mss. of the *Summa Logicae* to about sixty (cfr. the list of mss. in Boehner's edit. of the *Summa* I vi—viii).

know four of them, and they are most probably the only ones of this kind composed by Ockham. They are: *Expositio super librum Porphyrii, Expositio super librum Praedicamentorum, Expositio super duos libros Perihermenias, Expositio super duos libros Elenchorum.* Of these expositions we know eleven manuscripts; one contains only the *Expositio super duos libros Elenchorum,* five do not contain this work; the rest contain all the mentioned Expositions. If we disregard two editions of longer parts from the *Expositio super duos libros Perihermenias* made by the author,[1] we can say that there exists only one edition of the three first Expositions on logical writings, viz., the Incunabula edition of 1496 arranged by Marcus di Benevento of the Celestine branch of the Benedictine Order. The *Expositio super libros Elenchorum* has never been printed.

The fact that Marc of Benevent edited only the three first expositions under the title: *Expositio super totam artem veterem,* also known as the *Expositio Aurea,* should not mislead us to believe that Ockham intended these three works to be one work. We failed to find any evidence for this in the manuscripts. On the contrary, the fourth commentary is added to the others in the same manner in the manuscripts as the preceding ones. Fr. Marc of Benevent did not edit the *Expositio super duos libros Elenchorum* either because he did not know of it or he did not have at his disposal a manuscript which contained it, or because he intended only to publish Ockham's commentary on the "Ars Vetus". The latter reason was most probably decisive for the lack of the fourth exposition in the manuscripts, at least for three of them, it would seem. However, the opinion, which still exists in textbooks and other publications, that Ockham wrote the *Expositio aurea super artem veterem* and also as a separate work an *Expositio super libros Elenchorum,* is without foundation. For this reason, the Ockham-Commission in charge of the edition of all the non-political works of Ockham will treat all these expositions

---

[1] The *Tractatus De Praedestinatione* ... of William Ockham, Franciscan Institute Publications No. 2, *The Franciscan Institute,* 1945, pp. 104—113. *The Realistic Conceptualism* of William Ockham in *Traditio* IV, 1946, pp. 320—335.

as one group and each exposition individually. At present, Professor Ernest A. Moody is working on the *Expositio super Porphyrium.*[d]

Anneliese Maier has recently published a study on the *Expositio Aurea of Ockham* in which she suggests that a certain manuscript discovered by her in the Vatican library probably represents an earlier redaction of this work.[2]

A careful study of this article has convinced us that the reasons advanced by the author, who has chosen the 14th century and mainly its scientific culture as her special field of research, are partly without any weight and partly in contradiction with well-established facts. Since the article was published in the well-known review of the Jesuit Fathers in Rome and since the author, too, has gained the confidence of students of medieval philosophy, it is to be feared that her suggestions may be taken over even as a probability by those who have no immediate access to the sources. Hence we are forced to the thankless task of criticism. We wish to assure the author that in this criticism her suggestions have been taken into serious consideration.

It was Prantl who first cast some doubts on the authenticity of the *Expositio Aurea*, or rather of the printed text of the *Expositio Aurea* which he exclusively used whilst writing his History of Logic in the Occident.[e] It is known that his reasons lacked a serious foundation as we shall see later. Anneliese Maier approaches the problem of authenticity from a different angle. She has discovered in the Cod. Borgh. 151 (which, by the way, is known to the Ockham-Commission) an anonymous tract on logic. This tract is divided into three parts which bear the respective titles: Notabilia Porphyrii, Notabilia Praedicamentorum, Notabilia libri Perihermenias. The old Catalogue refers to the entire manuscript as Scriptum Guillelmi Auquam super logicalia (p. 103). A closer study led the author to the discovery that this work is a kind of redaction of the Expositio Aurea; it is only shorter than the work known in the edition of Marco di Benevento.

---

[2] *Ein neues Ockham-Manuskript* (Die Originalform der Expositio aurea?).

[d] In press as the first volume of our edition of *Opera omnia philosophica et theologica* of Ockham.

[e] Cfr *infra*, 65—70.

All text divisions and most explanations are lacking. Furthermore, no Notabilia are given from the second part of Porphyry's Isagoge and of the second book of Perihermenias which, both as the author maintains (p. 103), contain only text-analyses (die in der Expositio nur derartige Textanalysen enthalten), but no comments of Ockham, which are usually introduced by expression as: *Notandum, Sciendum, Intelligendum*. However, the number of such *Notabilia* discovered in the work by the author, is much less than in the *Expositio Aurea* as we know it. Furthermore, the author of these *Notabilia* several times remarks that he has omitted less important things (p. 103 s.). In general, however, there is a far reaching agreement between the text of the *Notabilia* and that of the *Expositio Aurea;* usually the *Notabilia* correspond to the comments of Ockham, but sometimes also to the text-analysis (p. 104) which, however, are also given as *Notabilia* (p. 103). According to Anneliese Maier, only two rather long *Notabilia* do not have a corresponding text in the *Expositio.* In order to show the correspondence, she presents in parallel columns the *Notabilia* of the first chapter of Porphyry and the corresponding parts of the *Expositio.* The agreement between both is striking; it leaves no doubt that the one is dependent on the other. Of the rest, she gives only the beginning of each chapter (of Porphyry and of the *Praedicamenta*), the beginning of a few *Notabilia* of the first book of *Perihermenias* and finally the two entire *Notabilia* which according to her are lacking in the *Expositio.*

There is no doubt that the author has proven that the *Notabilia* and the *Expositio* are Redactions of the same work (p. 131). We also readily agree with the author that we are not dealing with two different *Reportationes* of the same lectures (p. 131). We finally agree that one of the two possibilities has to be chosen, either the *Notabilia* are an *Abbreviatio* of the *Expositio* or they are an early redaction of the *Expositio* and the *Expositio* is an enlarged edition of the *Notabilia*. She is convinced that the latter possibility has more probability in favor of it than the former. These are her reasons:

1. The *Expositio Aurea* has been considered to be worked over; and hence, even before the *Notabilia* were known, it was suspected that there was an earlier redaction (p. 131).

2. In the *Notabilia* such peculiarities are lacking as have caused doubts as regards the full authenticity of the *Expositio:* viz., the long, mostly pedantic and clumsy text divisions and text explanations and the tiresome repetitions in the comments, and above all the unequal stylistic presentation (p. 132).

3. The most decisive reason, however, is that two long *Notabilia* have no corresponding text in the *Expositio* (p. 131).

Unfortunately, these reasons do not prove the point that the author is making. For they are either irrelevant or incorrect. This we shall presently show.

To 1.: It is a fact that some scholars have considered the *Expositio Aurea* to be contaminated by additions. It is difficult to say how many were of this opinion. It is especially difficult to say how many are still of this opinion after Abbagnano has shown that the basis for Prantl's statement to that effect is without any foundation. Since Prantl's erroneous opinion and its repercussions still seem to have some weight for Anneliese Maier, we are forced to expose it again. In *Die Geschichte der Logik im Abendlande,* v. 3, p. 329, note 739, Prantl writes:

> Jedoch am Schluß des Buches (of the printed text, because Prantl used no manuscript for Ockham) lesen wir: Et sic est finis tum expositionum super totam artem veterem secundum mentem venerabilis inceptoris Guilielmi de Occham . . . und es ist hieraus nach der üblichen Bedeutung der Worte "ad mentem" zu schließen, daß das Ganze nicht aus erster Hand von Occham herrührt . . . sondern allenfalls auf nachgeschriebenen Heften beruht;[3] auch wird ja in jenen Teilen des Commentars, welche nicht dem Albert de Saxonia angehören, öfters der "venerabilis inceptor," oder der "venerabilis expositor Occham" selbst genannt (z. B. Praedicam. c. 3 zweimal), und bei der arbor Porphyriana (Praedicab., de specie) lesen wir die ergötzlichen zwei Distichen: Sum litis genitrix, solis sed nota peritis, Per me quam plures erubuere viri; Sed decus et splendor nitidissimus Occham Ingenio claram me facit esse suo.

Already in 1939 (*Franziskanische Studien,* 26 (1939), 193 we have called attention to the effective and definitive refutation of the thesis of Prantl made by N. Abbagnano (*Guglielmo di Ockham,* Lan-

---

[3] We have checked all the manuscripts and can only say that "ad mentem Ockham" is in none of them.

ciano, 1931). We repeat it here even at the risk of appearing to be repetitious:

Abbagnano weist auf S. 28—29 nach, daß Markus von Benevent in seiner Ausgabe manches hinzugefügt hat, aber seine Zusätze immer sorgfältig durch F. M. kenntlich macht. Markus macht selbst darauf aufmerksam. Es heißt fol. 7: "Notandum est hic quod interdum tam in quaestionibus Alberti parvi quam in expositione textus quaedam inter has duas literas, scilicet F. M., intercepta reperiuntur: quae dicta solum fratri Marco operis correctori sunt ascribenda." Hätte Prantl diese Zeilen in dem ihm vorliegenden Texte gelesen, so hätte er sich seine Anmerkung 739 ... sparen können.

There is, indeed, no reason why this doubt or suspicion of Prantl which has no foundation in the manuscript tradition but only in a superficial reading of the edition[4] should even be taken seriously. Anneliese Maier is ready to admit that (p. 101). However, she seems to entertain suspicion on the authenticity of the *Expositio Aurea*, and in order to mitigate Prantl's error she points to the fact that sometimes Frater Marcus left out "F.M." when he made an addition. That is true in one instance at least. Where the others are we do not know. But this instance is so obviously an addition and is set off so clearly from the other text of the *Expositio Aurea* that it will not help Prantl very much. The addition is the *arbor Porphyriana*. On top of it is the first distich found in Prantl's footnote, and at the bottom the other which contains the name of Ockham. Perhaps Frater Marcus was so enraptured by his poetry that he forgot to add his initials; or, it may be that the transscriptores or the printer forgot this notation. It is beautiful to find excuse for a person; an error, however, must not be excused, but eliminated. Only scholars who did not make a special study of the *Expositio Aurea* have followed Prantl blindly, the few who consulted the manuscripts have thought quite differently. In fact, there is no sign of serious interpolations or

---

[4] The printer has even explained how it happened that the notes went into the text though Marc of Benevent had them added on the margin of the corrected copy: *quod ita evenit, quod cum in marginibus utriusque exemplari quaedam annotata essent cum F. M. litteris hinc inde, quae transscriptores putantes ea esse de utriusque exemplaris integritate, intus apposuerunt . . .*

additions, when we compare the old edition with the manuscripts; there are, however, omissions on the part of the edition, the text of which is in a rather bad condition.

To 2.: We are unable to offer any serious discussion of this rather vague reason. *De gustibus non est disputandum.* Others are inclined to find Ockham's *Expositio* clear and even interesting.

To 3.: The main reason of the author can be easily eliminated. The two long *Notabilia* have in fact a corresponding text in the *Expositio Aurea,* and not only in the manuscripts but also in the edition. The author has simply overlooked them. It was easy for us to recognize them, since we have published them in the appendix of our study on Ockham's De Praedestinatione. It may suffice to give in parallel columns only the beginning and the end of both.

Notabilia ed. Anneliese Maier, Greg. XXVIII, 1 (1947) p. 130	*Expositio super 1*ᵐ *L. Perihermenias* *ed.* Philotheus Boehner, O.F.M. The *Tractatus de Praedestinatione* . . . 1945, p. 109 s.

Item nota quod ista propositio: "omne quod est, quando est, necesse est esse" de virtute sermonis est simpliciter falsa, et hoc quia ista non potest esse de virtute sermonis nisi temporalis vel de temporali subiecto. Et si sit . . .	Sciendum est quod ista propositio: Omne quod est quando est necesse est esse, de virtute sermonis est simpliciter falsa, et hoc quia ista non potest esse de virtute sermonis nisi temporalis vel de temporali subiecto. Si sit . . .
. . . Et ita non est de ista: "Omne quod est, necesse est esse," non enim sequitur: "tunc⁵ est, igitur *a* est," sit *a* aliquid quod est, sicut sequitur: "hoc tunc est, igitur *a* est," si *a* sit in hoc tempore.	. . . Et ita non est de ista: Omne quod est necesse est esse; non enim sequitur: Tempus est,⁶ igitur A est, si A sit aliquid quod est, sicut sequitur: Hoc tempus est, igitur A est, si A sit in hoc tempore.

p. 130	p. 106 s.
Item nota quod in propositionibus singularibus de futuro, in qui-	Sciendum est hic, quod in propositionibus singularibus de futuro,

---

⁵ The reading "tunc" in the *Notabilia* seems to be an error (of the scribe ?).

⁶ The reading "tempus" in the *Expositio* is certain in all mss. and also in the edition.

bus subiicitur praecise pronomen demonstrativum vel nomen simplex proprium . . .

in quibus subiicitur praecise pronomen demonstrativum vel nomen simplex proprium . . .

. . . igitur haec est possibilis: hoc est nigrum; sed non sequitur; album potest esse nigrum, igitur haec est possibilis: album est nigrum, et sic de aliis.

. . . igitur haec est possibilis: Hoc est album, et tamen non sequitur: Nigrum potest esse album, igitur haec est possibilis: Nigrum est album, et sic de aliis.

Thus breaks down the entire basis on which the suggestion was built that these *Notabilia* are an early form of the *Expositio*. They are not an original redaction; they are just *Notabilia*, noteworthy excerpts or extracts, made from another work which the writer of these *Notabilia* had before him. If we read his closing note without any prejudice, but taking it at its face value, it proves that he had a work before him in which already *Notabilia*, viz., the *Notabilia* which he transcribed, were existing. For he says:

Tanta igitur notata sint de propositionibus de futuro in materia contingenti; et in hoc terminantur notabilia primi libri, quae alicuius sunt ponderis, quia notabilia puerilia multa omisi propter brevitatem (p. 131).

In order to omit some *Notabilia puerilia*, it is necessary that they are already given; at least we should not assume the role of the famous medieval "protervus" and take refuge in the certainly not obvious sense, that *possible Notabilia* are omitted.

For the sake of historical truth we would like to add a few minor corrections which do not concern primarily the thesis of Anneliese Maier.

On p. 102 she states that the *Expositio Aurea* in the Mss. is called mostly *Summa in artem veterem*. We have no evidence for this.

On p. 103, note 9, the author maintains that the majority of Mss. containing the *Expositio Aurea* does not contain the *Expositio super duos libros Elenchorum*. This is not correct, as far as we know at present. There is an equal number of Mss. which contain them and do not contain them, viz. 5.

On p. 132, footnote 30, the author refers to another manuscript which contains Ockham's commentary to the first book of the Sentences. It was of interest to us to learn from the author that this manuscript was written by the same scribe who wrote the *Notabilia*. Cod. Borgh. 68 is indeed an *Abbreviatio* (up to dist. 30) as we were finally assured by Msgr. Pelzer and Fr. Julius Reinhold, O.F.M., who were so kind as to give every modern means at their disposal in order to decipher the partly erased *Explicit*. However, before this final work, we were inclined to see in this Codex a *reportatio* of Ockham's first book on the Sentences. We were convinced that it could not be an *Abbreviatio* of the text tradition which is represented by most of the Mss. and also by the editions of this work. A more protracted study of the text convinced us that it is an *Abbreviatio*, made of the first redaction of Ockham's commentary on the Sentences. Thus it happened that Anneliese Maier had texts of an "original form" of one of Ockham's works in her hands, but nevertheless rightly concluded that it was an *Abbreviatio*. The manuscript tradition of medieval works can be sometimes extremely complicated.

6. THE HYPOTHETICAL FIRST REDACTION OF OCKHAM'S EXPOSITIO AUREA[a]

In 1947, Anneliese Maier, noted for her scholarship in the field of scholastic philosophy and especially of scholastic physics, published an article[1] in which she called attention to an already known manuscript of the Vatican Library, Borgh. 151. Besides the *Summa Logicae* and the second tract on *De Sacramento Altaris* of Ockham, this codex also contains *Notabilia Porphyrii*, *Notabilia libri Praedicamentorum*, and *Notabilia libri Perihermenias*. A preliminary study convinced Dr. Maier that the *Notabilia* are either an abbreviation

---

[1] [*Ein neues Ockham-Manuskript (die Originalform der Expositio aurea?)*, in *Gregorianum* 28 (1947) 101—133; cfr also]: *Zu einigen Problemen der Ockhamforschung* in *A. F. H.* 46 (1953) 161—194, cf. especially 191—192; however, the ms. Miss Maier is referring to is rather 151 (not 150); cf. her catalogue *Codices Burghesiani* (Rome 1952) 197—198.

[a] First published in *FrancStud* 14 (1954) 374—386. Reply of A. Maier to this article in *Handschriftliches zu Wilhelm Ockham und Walter Burley* in *A. F. H.* 48 (1955) 227—232.

or a first redaction of the *Expositio aurea* of Ockham. She also advanced a few reasons in favor of the possibility that the *Notabilia* are an original work of Ockham. These reasons were linked up with the idea that the *Expositio aurea* might be the work of an editor other than Ockham. In my reply[2] to Dr. Maier's article, I "energetically" rejected the opinion, repeatedly refuted by others as well as by myself, that the *Expositio aurea* as represented by the edition of 1496 is not substantially the work of Ockham. Again I called attention to the fact that Prantl's statement to the contrary was due to a superficial reading of the old edition, the only text, by the way, that he consulted. The "hypothesis" (*Annahme, Vermutung*, etc., Dr. Maier called it) that the *Notabilia* are the first redaction and an original work of Ockham, I did not take too seriously, since the only concrete evidence that Dr. Maier produced in support of it — the lack of two rather long passages of the *Notabilia* in the *Expositio aurea* — was easy to eliminate, since the lack was obviously due to an oversight on the part of the author. On the other hand, the differences between the texts of the *Notabilia* and the *Expositio aurea*, which Dr. Maier showed by publishing extensive parts of both in parallel columns, were not pronounced enough, in my opinion, to eliminate the probability that the *Notabilia*, as their name indicates, are noteworthy extracts, or a kind of *abbreviatio* made by a compiler from the *Expositio aurea*. Hence I believed that this chapter on the textual criticism of Ockham's works could be considered closed. This belief, however, proved too optimistic. Very soon after the publication of my article, Anneliese Maier answered in a long footnote in the Gregorianum.[3] My insistence that *"notabilia"* in medieval manuscripts usually means excerpts of noteworthy texts from longer works, did not convince her. In my article I remarked that if anyone says he leaves out or omits *"notabilia"* — as the author of the *Notabilia* repeatedly does — then he must have something (that is, *"notabilia"*) to omit, for it is hardly believable that *"possible notabilia"* were left

---

[2] *Franciscan Studies* VIII (1948) pp. 69 ff. [*supra*, 42—50].

[3] Cf. *Literarhistorische Notizen über Aureoli, Durandus, und den Cancellarius' nach der Handschrift Ripoll* 77bis *in Barcelona*, in *Gregorianum* XXIX (1948), p. 250.

out. To this remark I received the surprising answer that the author
of the *Notabilia* left out only possible *notabilia*. This, according to
Dr. Maier, is proved by the following passage found toward the end
of the *Notabilia Perihermenias:*

> Alia notabilia quae possent notari circa oppositionem propositionum
> obmitto ad praesens, quia non sunt nisi puerilia et occurrunt prima facie
> inspicienti textum.

Dr. Maier continues: "Hier ist doch ohne Zweifel an mögliche
notabilia gedacht."

I am afraid that I shall be blamed for deflecting the discussion
into logical subtleties. A remark rather jokingly made was taken
seriously. Hence for me the penalty of having to refute it. This,
however, is not too difficult. For to say that in the text quoted
above there is "without any doubt" the thought of "possible notabilia" is hardly sound logic. There are no doubts but very good
reasons to believe positively that in the text quoted there is no
question at all of "possible notabilia". The *possent* of the text obviously does not refer to *notabilia* but to *notari*. And *notari* is the
typical activity of a scribe or a compiler. The compiler of the *Notabilia*, therefore, merely said that other *notabilia*, that is, other noteworthy passages, could be noted, that is, could be copied. It is most
likely that he said this with *"notabilia"* before him. In fact, it is quite
possible that he had a manuscript before him — I know of at least
one — where the *notabilia* were clearly and neatly marked on the
margins as *Primum notabile, Secundum notabile*, etc. That he copied
such *notabilia* becomes even more probable when we consider that
he qualifies some of them as childish *(puerilia)*. How could he call
"possible notabilia" childish? Now, if Ockham were the author of
the *Notabilia*, then we would have to imagine the strange situation
of Ockham's first considering certain possible ideas or glosses (the
"possible notabilia" of Anneliese Maier) as childish and not worth
writing down, but later, when revising this text of his, inserting the
childish *notabilia*. For at every place where the *Notabilia* mention
the omission of *notabilia puerilia*, there are *notabilia* in the *Expositio
aurea*. Is it not more natural and more in line with sound psychology
to say that some man other than Ockham and probably one not too

well disposed toward him — the manuscript originally belonged to the Pontifical library at Avignon — had these *notabilia* in a manuscript of the *Expositio aurea* before him, but did not consider them worth copying, since he thought them too childish?

Indeed, the usual sense of *notabilia*, when found in medieval manuscripts, designates excerpts of noteworthy passages from larger works. Such *Notabilia* collections were quite often made by a student or by an abbreviator. Our libraries contain many of them. Even Annaliese Maier has dealt with such *Notabilia*, which she unhesitatingly proves to be excerpts or abbreviations, viz., the *Notabilia Cancellarii*. Charles Balić writes of them:

"Il faut bien remarquer, tout d'abord, que notre document n'est qu'un abrégé, une sorte de compte rendu sommaire, que le reportateur a fait pour son usage. Il l'indique déjà clairement en l'intitulant "*Notabilia*": de ce qui s'est passé, il a relevé ce qui lui a paru "notabile".[4] This statement is made more precise by Anneliese Maier when she shows that these *Notabilia* are notes made by or for the "Cancellarius" taken from other works. In this case, therefore, she takes *Notabilia* in the commonly accepted medieval sense and not in the unique sense she postulated for the *Notabilia* of Borgh. 151.[5] With just reason, then, it can be asked why the *Notabilia* of Borgh. 151 should be given Dr. Maier's highly unusual meaning. In her replies to me — even in the last one —[6] she always shifts to me the burden

---

[4] Cf. *Les Commentaires de* Jean Duns Scot *sur les quatres livres des Sentences* (*Biblioth. de la Rev. d'Hist. Eccl., Fasc.* I, Louvain, 1927), p. 187.

[5] Cf. *art. cit.*, p. 246: „Diese Vermutung stimmt auch zu dem, was Glorieux für den anschließenden Teil der Notabilia festgestellt hat: es handelt sich hier um Aufzeichnungen nach einer Quaestio des Thomas von Wylton, bei der der „Kanzler" interveniert hat. Glorieux vermutet, daß die Notizen der Worcester Handschrift für Thomas hergestellt worden sind; aber es ist natürlich ebenso gut möglich — und wie uns scheint, wahrscheinlicher —, daß sie für den Kanzler abgeschrieben wurden und dann gleichfalls ein Stück seines persönlichen Materials bildeten, das dann später in Bausch und Bogen als "Notabilia Cancellarii" bezeichnet worden ist.

[6] „Zu einigen Problemen der Ockhamforschung", *Arch. Franc. Hist.* XLVI (1953). . . . Boehner . . . hat die Notabilia ohne weiteres als spätere Abbreviation erklärt, ohne wirkliche Beweise für diese Behauptung anführen zu können . . ." p. 32, footnote.

of proving that the *Notabilia* of Borgh. 151 are not excerpts. This is rather strange, to say the least. What reason is there for me to prove that *Notabilia* are *Notibilia* in the ordinary sense, as we know them, for instance, for works of Scotus, Ockham, and Burleigh? Since Dr. Maier is pleading for a most uncommon sense of the term *"notabilia"* as the title of an independent work, the burden of proving her opinion or suspicion or hypothesis lies with her.

With good reason and in all justice to the requirements of sound scholarship, I could rest the case here — and confidently wait for more objections to appear in footnotes, Nevertheless I shall try to advance a few reasons why the *Notabilia* must be considered *Notabilia*, that is, why they must be regarded as being exactly what their title says they are, and not an original work of Ockham. First, there is the fact that the *Expositio aurea* is a running commentary on the classical text of logic, the *Ars Vetus*. The *Notabilia* exactly follow the division of the text that occurs in the *Expositio aurea*. Hence it appears fairly obvious that the *Notabilia* must go back to a commentary on or an exposition of some text, or other, and not vice versa. If, however, the *Notabilia* are an exposition, and if they are not *Reportationes* — as Anneliese Maier has correctly conceded — then it is quite remarkable that they should be only *"notabilia"*, that is, only notations concerning ideas that came to the mind of the author after the explanation of the text. Equally remarkable is the fact that there is no real exposition of any text, nor is there any division of texts.[7] But textual divisions were necessarily required and textual exposition was precisely the aim of such works. The complete lack of textual divisions and textual expositions are in my opinion, the best proof that the *Notabilia* are not an original work but are simply that which their name indicates — "notabilia".

---

[7] When Dr. Maier mentions, „die langen, meist sehr pedantischen und schwerfälligen Texteinteilungen und -erklärungen . . ." (Cf. *art. cit.*, p. 132), I am at a loss to understand this. The text division of Saint Thomas in his commentaries to Aristotelian writings are as „pedantisch und schwerfällig" (if not even more) as those of Ockham. This is the style of the *expositiones* or running commentaries.

Furthermore, at the time of Ockham many *Abbreviationes* were being made at Avignon. Anneliese Maier informs us that the MS. Borghese 151 is mentioned in a list of books of the Pontifical library at Avignon under the date 1396.[8] In the same volume of Gregorianum in which Dr. Maier published her first article concerning this question, Z. Alszeghy, S.J., mentioned that John XXII introduced at the Papal Court a new office, that of *Abbreviator originalium*. Since the manuscript of the *Notabilia* which we are discussing comes from Avignon, it is quite possible, if not most probable, that it goes back to an *Abbreviator* belonging to the Papal Court in Avignon. For, as Dr. Maier has pointed out, the scribe who wrote Borgh. 151 also wrote the first part of Borgh. 68, which is an *abbreviatio* of Ockham's *Ordinatio*. It seems very likely that the scribe and the abbreviator were one and the same person. In any case, it is certain that the Notabilia originated in a milieu that was interested in *abbreviationes* and had them made and copied.

I may mention here a fact that would seem to place the manuscript in the first half of the Fourteenth Century, for it represents an excellent textual tradition. When the abbreviator introduces a new *notabile*, usually by the stereotyped formula: *Item notandum*, adding a few words that place the *notabile* in the context of the *Expositio aurea*, he then gives a text which rates among the best of the manuscripts of the *Expositio*. A comparison of many parallel texts proved that the Notabilia of Borgh. 151 is most closely related to the oldest dated manuscript, that of Firenze B. Nat. B. 4. 1618, written in 1331, and that it has remarkably few single variants. Other and especially later manuscripts have many more deviations from the text that will be adopted by the critical edition. Now, if the *Notabilia* were a first redaction or a first draft of Ockham's exposition of the *Ars Vetus*, we could justly expect more variants in the *Notabilia* than we actually find. In fact, the text of the *Expositio aurea* could stand an improvement. There is, for instance, the long discussion at the beginning of the *Expositio libri Perihermenias* on the nature of the universal. The complete text, which I have

---

[8] Cf. *art. cit.*

published in *Traditio*,[9] is also in the *Notabilia*. Now in this lengthy text there is an arrangement that is by no means well-ordered. First Ockham deals with four kinds of theories about the nature of the universal in the mind — the *habitus*, the *species*, the *intellectio*, and the *fictum* theories, Ockham writes:

> Igitur propter istas rationes magis debet poni, quod tales passiones animae, de quibus loquitur hic Philosophus, sunt qualitates mentis, quam quod sint talia idola sive ficta.

And then he starts again:

> Dico igitur, quod Philosophus passiones animae vocat illa, ex quibus componitur propositio in mente vel syllogismus vel componi potest. Sed quid sit, potest esse triplex opinio in genere.

Following this, Ockham enumerates three theories concerning the nature of the universal. But this time the first is the *res*-theory, that is, that the universal is a real universal thing and the concept is the conception of a universal thing. This is briefly refuted. After the refutation follows the unqualified *qualitas*-theory (*habitus-species-intellectio*-theories). Finally the *fictum*-theory is discussed, and objections raised against it before in the first presentation of it are answered.

It can hardly be denied that this arrangement is somewhat disorderly; in fact it is definitely confused and confusing. The only explanation I can offer for this is that the first part of the discussion was added later. But this need not concern us here. The point I wish to make is this, that the same poor arrangement is in both the *Notabilia* and in the *Expositio aurea*. If the *Expositio aurea* were a second redaction, we would surely find a better and more logical arrangement of the matter under discussion, and the needless repetitions omitted. Ockham did exactly this later, in the *Quaestiones super libros Physicorum*. It would seem that the obvious explanation for lack of good order in the *Expositio* is that it is the original redaction of Ockham, and since the *Notabilia* has the same confused arrangement, it seems equally obvious that it was copied from the *Expositio*.

---

[9] *The Realistic Conceptualism of William Ockham*, in *Traditio*, IV (1946), pp. 320—335.

This explanation is further strengthened by an interesting passage in the discussion of the second opinion of the second part of the *Expositio*. I shall present here in parallel columns corresponding passages taken from the *Notabilia*, from Manuscript A (the oldest one known) and from our critical edition.

Notabilia	Ms. A	Final Text
Alia est opinio quam reputo probabilem, quod passiones animae sunt quaedam qualitates mentis existentes subiective in mente ita vere et ita realiter sicut albedo existit in pariete vel frigus in aqua. Et pro ista opinione videtur esse Commentator 7ᵐᵒ Metaphysicae commento [follows a blank of about two words]. Ubi videtur dicere quod universalia sunt qualitates mentis et non sunt de substantia...	Sed alia potest esse opinio quam reputo probabilem, quod passiones animae sunt quaedam qualitates subiective in mente ita vere et ita realiter sicut albedo existit in pariete vel frigus in aqua. Et ista opinio videtur esse Commentatoris 7⁰ Metaphysicae* [two and a quarter of a line free]. Et ita secundum Commentatorem universalia sunt qualitates mentis et non sunt de substantia ...	Alia potest esse opinio quam reputo probabilem, quod passiones animae sunt quaedam qualitates mentis existentes subiective in mente ita vere et ita realiter sicut albedo existit in pariete vel frigus in aqua. Et pro ista opinione videtur esse Commentator 7⁰ Metaphysicae [commento 23⁰ ubi dicit: Sanitas dicitur duobus modis etc.] Ita secundum Commentatorem universalia sunt qualitas mentis et non sunt de substantia ...

* *Here the marginal note:* Hic solum deficit auctoritas Commentatoris.

This passage suggests that when Ockham wrote the *Expositio aurea* he left space for the quotation from Averroes in order to supply it later — a procedure which is encountered in other works of his — but he never added it. The later sribes tried to cover the lacuna. The *Notabilia* has a faint trace of this lacuna; the space has been partially filled — only about two words are omitted. But the filling of this lacuna in the *Notabilia* is quite individual, different from the known manuscripts. This would indicate that the compiler of the *Notabilia* did not have a text where the lacuna was intelligibly filled. Hence he supplied the lack by writing: *Ubi videtur dicere quod.*

All the differences between the final text of the *Expositio* and the *Notabilia* are of a similar nature. They can be easily explained as the changes that an abbreviator would naturally consider necessary to provide a smoothly reading text; they never introduce new ideas. This is true even of the Prologue to which Anneliese Maier has recently shifted the burden of carrying the main evidence for her hypothesis. I freely admit that the differences here are more pronounced than in other parts of the *Notabilia;* however, I cannot convince myself that they are of such a nature as to corroborate Dr. Maier's claim that they are two different redactions by the same author. The differences are within the boundaries of *Notabilia* characteristics. Although Dr. Maier has published both Prologues in parallel columns, for the benefit of the reader, I shall publish them again, but completely, using the final text of the critical edition and also a better text of the *Notabilia.* For the former text I owe thanks to Professor Ernest Moody, editor of the *Expositio super Porphyrium;* for the latter text, to Fr. Julius Reinhold, of the Scotus Commission in Rome, who has checked my transcription from photostats against the original manuscript. The reader may judge for himself whether the differences between these two Prologues are sufficient for considering the *Notabilia* an original work of Ockham. I am not able to convince myself that Dr. Maier's hypothesis is in the least tenable. Therefore the forthcoming critical edition of the *Expositio aurea*, the first volume of which is already going through the press, will not consider the *Notabilia* to be a first redaction but only a collection of excerpts from Ockham's work.

Notabilia	Expositio aurea
	Quoniam omne operans, quod in suis operationibus et actibus potest errare, aliquo indiget directivo, et intellectus humanus in acquirendo scientiam et suam perfectionem ab ignotis ad nota discurrit necessario, circa quod directivum errare potest

Quia propter errorem in logica *multi antiquorum in errores varios* inciderunt ut testantur *Philosophus* et Commentator eius *primo Physicorum,* ad memoriam logicalium promptius habendam sunt quaedam notabilia memoriter retinenda.

Primo igitur nota *quod logica non est unus habitus numero nec unum individuum sicut Sortes vel Plato vel ista albedo vel illa nigredo; sed est una collectio multorum habituum quibus syllogismus in communi et partes suae tam subiectivae quam integrales et passiones, in alia parte cognoscitur syllogismus demonstrativus et suae passiones, et in alia parte cognoscitur (rep. cognoscitur) propositio et suae passiones et sic de aliis.* Et similiter *in alia parte logicae cognoscitur propositio enuntians hanc passionem de syllogismo in communi et in alia parte* propositio *enuntians aliam passionem de eodem syllogismo in communi, ita quod secundum quod praedicata vel subiecta propositionum notarum in logica variantur, secundum hoc partes logicae variantur, quae tamen*

multipliciter, necessario fuit aliquam artem inveniri, per quam evidenter cognosceret veros discursus a falsis, ut tandem posset certitudinaliter inter verum et falsum discernere. Haec autem ars est logica, propter cuius ignorantiam testante Philosopho primo Physicorum, multi antiqui in errores varios devenerunt.

Circa autem istam artem sunt aliqua generalia primo praemittenda; secundo est ad expositionem diversorum librorum logicae accedendum, Circa primum, primo videndum est de istius scientiae entitate et quidditate, secundo de ipsius subiecto, tertio de ipsius utilitate, quarto de ipsius ad alias scientias differentia essentiali, quinto cui parti philosophiae supponatur.

Circa primum breviter dicendum est quod logica non est unus habitus numero, nec unum individuum sicut Sortes et Plato, vel iste asinus vel iste bos vel ista albedo vel ista nigredo, sed est una collectio multorum habituum quibus syllogismus in communi, et partes suae tam subiectivae quam integrales, et passiones earum, cognoscuntur; ita quod una parte logicae cognoscitur syllogismus et suae passiones, et alia parte cognoscitur syllogismus demonstrativus et suae passiones, alia parte cognoscitur propositio et suae passiones, et sic de aliis. Et non tantum hoc, immo alia parte cognoscitur propositio enuntians hanc passionem de syllogismo in communi, et alia parte enuntians aliam passionem de eodem syllogismo in communi ita quod secundum quod subiecta

60 — *Ph. Boehner: Collected Articles*

omnes partes unam logicam constituunt, non quidem tamquam unam
rem numero sed ad modum quo
multi homines faciunt unum populum et diversae civitates faciunt
unum regnum.

Et pro isto potest adduci talis
ratio: *Quando*cumque *aliqua sic se
habent quod aliquid stat cum uno
illorum et non stat cum alio, illa
non sunt eiusdem rationis; sed cum
scientia qua scitur una conclusio
libri Posteriorum*, puta A, *stat error
circa* aliam conclusionem eiusdem
libri, puta B, et *cum scientia qua scitur*
B *non stat error circa* B, *igitur* scientia qua scitur A *et* scientia qua scitur
B *non sunt eiusdem rationis*. Et
ultra per *Philosophum* 7⁰ *Metaphysicae ex* illis quae *sunt alterius*
et alterius *rationis* numquam *fit
per se unum numero, nisi unum sit
actus et aliud potentia: igitur ex
talibus notitiis non fit una scientia
numero*.

Item nota *quod* scientiae logicae
*sicut et cuiuslibet alterius scientiae
sunt tantum duae causae essentiales*

vel praedicata propositionum notarum in logica variantur, secundum
hoc partes logicae variantur; quae
tamen omnes partes unam logicam
constituunt, non quidem tamquam
unam rem numero, sed ad modum
quo multi homines unam populum
faciunt et civitates diversae unum
regnum, et sic de aliis diversis; de
quibus dicimus quod aliquando ex
multis eiusdem rationis aliquod
unum constituitur, et aliquando ex
multis diversarum rationum constituitur aliquod unum.

Pro praedicta conclusione ad
praesens sufficit ratio ista, quia
quando aliqua sic se habent quod
aliquid stat cum uno illorum et non
stat cum alio, ista non sunt eiusdem
rationis. Sed accipio scientiam qua
scitur una conclusio libri Posteriorum et scientiam qua scitur
alia conclusio eiusdem libri, et
sit una A et alia B; tunc cum scientia qua scitur A stat error circa
B, sed cum scientia qua scitur B
non stat error circa B, ergo A et B
non sunt eiusdem rationis. Ex hoc
arguo ultra; quandocumque aliqua
sunt alterius rationis, ex eis non
fit per se unum numero nisi unum
sit actus et aliud potentia, secundum Philosophum 7⁰ Metaphysicae;
sed nulla scientia componitur ex
talibus, quia secundum Philosophum ibidem nullum accidens componitur ex partibus talibus sed
tantum ex partibus eiusdem rationis; igitur ex talibus notitiis non fit
una scientia numero.

Secundo videndum est de istius
scientiae causis essentialibus. Circa
quod sciendum quod istius scien-

proprie loquendo de causa, scilicet efficiens et finalis. Cuius ratio est quia scientia est quaedam *res simplex non composita ex partibus alterius et alterius rationis, et nulla* talis *res potest habere plures quam duas causas proprie loquendo, scilicet* efficientem et finalem. Cuius probatio est, *quia omnis causa vel est intrinseca* rei et sic *materia vel forma, vel extrinseca* et sic *efficiens vel finis.* Sed nulla res simplex quae est simplex *per carentiam compositionis ex partibus alterius rationis habet materiam et formam tamquam causas intrinsecas, quia si haberet, componeretur ex eis sicut ex partibus alterius rationis, igitur nulla* scientia *potest* proprie loquendo *habere plures quam duas causas* [not readable] et finalem.

Et quod dicitur communiter quod [not readable] *scilicet materialis, formalis* etc. *non est verum proprie loquendo de causa, quomodo loquitur Philosophus 2⁰* [not readable] *et 5⁰ Metaphysicae* capitulo de causa. *Sed* illud dictum vulgare solum habet veritatem *extendendo nomen causae et improprie loquendo.* Unde *illud quod vocatur causa materialis magis deberet vocari subiectum scientiae vel praedicatum vel obiectum quam causa. Et sic accipiunt* homines *si bene intelligant causam materialem pro obiecto, quod tamen si sit causa nisi in genere causae efficientis vel forte finalis.*

tiae, sicut et cuiuslibet scientiae, tantum sunt duae causae essentiales, proprie loquendo de causa; cuius ratio est quia nulla res simplex, non composita ex partibus alterius et alterius rationis, potest habere nisi duas causas, scilicet efficientem et finalem; sed quaelibet scientia est simplex per carentiam compositionis ex partibus alterius rationis; ergo nulla scientia habet plures quam duas causas. Maior est manifesta, quia omnis causa rei vel est causa intrinseca et tunc est pars rei sicut est materia et forma, vel est causa extrinseca sicut efficiens et finis; sed nulla res simplex per carentiam compositionis ex partibus alterius rationis habet materiam et formam tamquam causas intrinsecas, quia si haberet componeretur ex eis sicut ex partibus alterius rationis; igitur nulla res simplex potest habere plures quam duas causas.

Et ideo quod dicitur communiter, quod cuiuslibet scientiae sunt quatuor causae, scilicet materialis, formalis, efficiens et finalis, non est verum proprie loquendo de causa, quomodo loquitur Philosophus 2⁰ Physicorum et 5⁰ Metaphysicae, sed extendendo nomen causae, et improprie loquendo de causa. Et ideo illud quod vocatur causa materialis magis deberet vocari subiectum scientiae vel praedicatum vel obiectum, quam causa; et sic accipiunt, si bene intelligant, causam materialem pro obiecto; quod tamen, si sit causa, non potest esse causa nisi in genere causae efficientis vel forte finalis.

Item nota, *quod causa efficiens logicae usitatae fuit Aristoteles; unde ipse fuit primus traditor istarum collectionum vel librorum* logicae modo quo nos *utimur. Tamen de causa efficiente logicae tuae vel meae dicendum est proportionaliter sicut de causa efficiente* aliorum habituum *intellectualium, quod ad librum De Anima pertinet magis.*

Item nota, quod *causa finalis logicae, accipiendo logicam pro collectione habituum vel pro habitu est actus cognoscendi, ex quo* actu vel quibus actibus *talis habitus generatur. Et finis illorum actuum qui est finis mediatus habitus, est ille, propter quem eliciuntur. Sed de hoc pertinet tractare ad scientiam naturalem.*

Item nota, quod *scientiae* logicae *multae sunt utilitates, quarum una est facilitas discernendi inter verum et falsum. Nam ista scientia perfecte habita faciliter iudicat quid verum et quid falsum, et hoc quantum ad illa quae per propositiones per se notas possunt sciri. Cum enim in talibus non oporteat nisi ordinate procedere a propositionibus per se notis ad ultima quae sequuntur ex eis et talem processum et discursum docet logica, sequitur quod per eam in talibus faciliter verum invenitur et eadem ratione faciliter verum a falso discernitur.*

Alia utilitas *est promptitudo respondendi. Nam per istam artem docetur quid est proposito repugnans, quid consequens, quid antecedens.*

Viso igitur, quod scientia non habet nisi duas causas, sciendum quod causa efficiens logicae usitatae vocatur Aristoteles, quia ipse primus eam tradidit et fuit primus traditor istarum collectionum vel librorum, quibus utimur; tamen de causa efficiente logicae tuae vel meae est dicendum proportionaliter, sicut de causa efficiente aliorum habituum intellectualium; quod ad librum De anima pertinet magis. Causa finalis logicae, accipiendo logicam pro habitu vel collectione habituum, est actus cognoscendi ex quo talis habitus generatur. Finis autem istorum actuum, qui est finis mediatus habitus vel habituum, est ille propter quem eliciuntur; de hoc tamen pertinet tractare ad scientiam naturalem.

Tertio videndum est de istius scientiae utilitate. Circa quod sciendum quod istius scientiae sunt multae utilitates, inter quas una est facilitas discernendi inter verum et falsum. Nam ista scientia perfecte habita, faciliter iudicatur quid verum et quid falsum, et hoc quantum ad illa quae per propositiones per se notas possunt sciri. Cum enim in talibus non oporteat nisi ordinate procedere a propositionibus per se notis ad ultima quae consequuntur ex eis, et talem discursum et processum docet logica, sequitur quod per eam faciliter in talibus verum invenitur, et eadem ratione faciliter verum a falso dicernitur.

Secunda facilitas est promptitudo respondendi. Nam per istam artem docetur quid est proposito repugnans, quid consequens, quid anteccdens; quibus notis faciliter repugnans negatur, consequens conceditur, et ad antecedens secundum sui qualitatem, sicut ad impertinens, respondetur.

Per istam etiam artem solutio omnium argumentorum peccantium in forma docetur, nec est possibile in quacumque scientia ex veris inferre falsum, quin per regulas certas in ista scientia traditas talis defectus faciliter deprehendatur, et sine arte logicae et usu illius impossibile est hoc facere. Et *ideo* logicam *ignorantes multas demonstrationes sophismata reputant, et econverso multa sophismata tamquam demonstrationes acceptant.*

Per istam etiam artem solutio omnium argumentorum peccantium in forma docetur, nec est possibile in quacumque scientia ex veris sophistice inferre falsum, quin per regulas certas in ista scientia traditas talis defectus faciliter deprehendatur, et sine ista arte vel usu ipsius est hoc impossibile; et ideo istam scientiam ignorantes multas demonstrationes sophismata reputant, et econservo multa sophismata tamquam demonstrationes acceptant, nescientes inter syllogismum sophisticum et demonstrativum distinguere.

Tertia *utilitas* huius scientiae — et est consequens ad primam — *est facilitas percipiendi virtutem sermonis et proprium modum loquendi, quid,* scilicet, *ab auctoribus dicitur proprie* et *de virtute sermonis* et quid improprie et *secundum usitatum modum loquendi.* Unde multa dicta auctorum intelligenda sunt non de virtute vocum sed secundum usitatum modum loquendi auctorum et ad intentionem dicentis, et illud percipere est valde *necessarium omni studenti in dictis auctorum, quia qui omnia* verba *auctorum de virtute sermonis et proprie accipiunt, incidunt in multos errores* ex hoc *et* in *difficultates inexplicabiles.*

Item nota, *quod ista scientia seipsa distinguiter ab omni alia,*

Alia utilitatis logicae est facilitas virtutem sermonis et proprium modum loquendi percipiendi. Nam per istam artem faciliter scitur, quid ab auctoribus de virtute sermonis profertur, quid non de virtute sermonis sed secundum usitatum modum loquendi vel secundum intentionem dicentis; quid dicitur proprie, quid metaphorice; quod est maxime necessarium omnibus studentibus in dictis aliorum, quia qui semper omnia dicta auctorum de virtute sermonis et proprie accipiunt, incidunt in multos errores et inexplicabiles difficultates.

Quarto videndum est de istius scientiae ab aliis differentia et di-

quia de aliis est ista scientia et scientiae aliae. Nam ista scientia tradit primam(?) *scientiam sive notitiam conceptuum vel intentionum per animam fabricatarum.* Et *hinc est quod ista scientia dicitur rationalis. Istae autem scientiae dicuntur reales non quin ista scientia* sicut et ceterae *sit vera res et vera qualitas perficiens intellectum sicut aliae scientiae, sed quia determinat de his, quae sine ratione esse non possunt, sed aliae scientiae de rebus existentibus extra animam.*

Item nota, quod logica dici potest scientia practica, quia ut *dicit Avicenna in I° Metaphysicae suae, distinctio est inter scientias practicas et speculativas, quia practicae sunt de operibus nostris, sed speculativae non sunt de operibus nostris.* Cum igitur logica *tractet de syllogismis, propositionibus* argumentis, discursibus et huiusmodi, *quae non possunt fieri a nobis, sequitur quod est de operibus nostris non de exterioribus nisi forte secundario, sed de interioribus, quae vera sunt opera nostra,*

stinctione. Circa quod sciendum quod ista scientia seipsa distinguitur ab omni alia, quia de aliis est ista scientia et de aliis aliae scientiae. Nam ista scientia, saltem principaliter, tradit notitiam conceptuum vel intentionum per animam fabricatarum, non extra se, quomodo fabricantur res artificiales, sed intra se. Verumtamen qualia sunt ista fabricata, scilicet conceptus et intentiones, cuiusmodi sunt syllogismi, propositiones, termini et huiusmodi an scilicet sint realiter et subiective in anima existentes, an aliquo alio modo, non ad logicam sed ad metaphysicam pertinet; et ideo hic est pertranseundum. Et hinc est quod ista scientia dicitur rationalis, ceterae autem scientiae demonstrativae dicuntur scientiae reales; non quin ista scientia sit vera res et vera qualitas perficiens intellectum, sicut aliae scientiae, sed quia determinat de his quae sine ratione esse non possunt, aliae autem scientiae de rebus existentibus extra animam determinant.

Ultimo videndum est, cui parti philosophiae supponatur logica, an scilicet ista scientia sit notitia practica vel speculativa. Et dicendum est, quod sicut dicit Avicenna in principio suae Metaphysicae, quod distinctio est inter practicas et speculativas scientias, quia scientiae practicae sunt de operibus nostris, scientiae autem speculativae non sunt de operibus nostris. Ex quo patet quod logica practica est dicenda, quia cum scientia logicae tractet de syllogismis, pro-

et per consequens logica erit scientia *practica non speculativa.*

positionibus et huiusmodi, quae non nisi a nobis fieri possunt, sequitur quod est de operibus nostris; non quidem exterioribus nisi forte secundario, sed de interioribus quae vere opera nostra sunt; et per consequens ista scientia est practica et non speculativa. Cum sit necessarium Grisasori...

Item nota quod liber Porphyrii *non habet unum subiectum tantum sicut nec aliquis alius liber traditus...*

Iste liber est primus secundum ordinem doctrinae inter omnes libros logicae, cuius notitia non est una secundum numerum, sed est collectio multarum notitiarum; nec etiam habet unum subiectum sicut nec aliquis liber traditus...

7. ZUR ECHTHEIT DER SUMMA LOGICAE OCKHAMS[a]

Die Summa Logicae, das verbreitetste Werk Wilhelm Ockhams, soll demnächst in einer kritischen Ausgabe vom Institute of Medieval Studies zu Toronto (Kanada) der wissenschaftlichen Welt zugänglich gemacht werden. Die Vorbereitungen sind soweit gediehen, daß in absehbarer Zeit dieses Meisterwerk mittelalterlicher Logik dem Druck übergeben werden kann.[1]

---

[1] [Das Vorhaben des Institute of Medieval Studies zu Toronto ist um 1942 dem Franciscan Institute überlassen worden, und P. Boehner hat die Summa Logicae, Pars Prima (St. Bonaventure, N. Y. 1951) und Pars Secunda et Tertiae prima (ebd. 1954) herausgegeben.] Wir werden in nächster Zeit weitere Schriften Ockhams der Öffentlichkeit zugänglich machen: Die ersten Quästionen des Prologs zum Sentenzenkommentar sind schon im Druck und werden im Verlag Schöningh, Paderborn, erscheinen [nur die Quaestio prima principalis Prologi erschien, Paderborn, 1939]. Ferner sind in Vorbereitung der Traktat De successivis [vgl. edit. Boehner, St. Bonaventure, 1944] und De praedestinatione [vgl. edit. Boehner, St. Bonaventure, 1945]. L. Baudry (Paris) bereitet die Editio der Expositio aurea, der Quodlibeta und der Quaestiones in Physicam vor.

---

[a] Erst erschienen in: FranzStud 26 (1939) 190—193.

Über die Echtheit bestimmter Teile dieser in mehreren älteren Drucken vorliegenden Schrift und die Brauchbarkeit der uns bislang zugänglichen Textgestalt hat Prantl sich ein Urteil erlaubt, das seine wissenschaftliche Zuverlässigkeit wieder einmal in Frage stellt. In seiner Geschichte der Logik im Abendlande heißt es: „Aber wenn der aufmerksame Leser alsbald entdecken muß, daß dieser Text unmöglich in seiner Totalität so aus Occams Händen hervorgegangen sein kann, so geben nur die genannten jüngeren Drucke (in den Dedicationen und am Schlusse) den Aufschluß, daß wir eine Überarbeitung der echten Summa Occams vor uns haben, welche gegen Ende des 15. Jahrhunderts in Oberitalien veranstaltet wurde, als dortselbst sich eine förmliche Schule des occamistischen „Nominalismus" etablierte. Man druckte ja damals in solchen Dingen nur dasjenige, was man brauchte und wie man es brauchte, d. h. häufig ohne mit diplomatischer Treue ein älteres Original als solches reproduzieren zu wollen . . . Kurz, es zeigt sich (s. z. B. die Kehrseite des Titelblattes und den Schluß, d. h. f. 81 v. B., der Ausgabe v. 1522), daß der Cölestiner Marcus de Benevento, "inter eos, quos nominales vocent, minimus", das Werk Occams, welcher als Inceptor sacrae scholae invictissimorum Nominalium galt, neu redigierte . . . Von diesem Marcus von Benevent rührt nun nicht bloß jener Prolog her ("Quam magnos veritatis" etc.), welcher in allen Ausgaben vorangestellt wird, sondern auch sämtliche Titelüberschriften der einzelnen Kapitel und außerdem mannigfache Erweiterungen des Lehrstoffes, welche sich bald deutlicher bald undeutlicher als spätere Zusätze verraten. Wenn wir z. B. I, 10, f. 5 r. B lesen: "Nunc de alia divisione nominum, quibus scholastici frequenter utuntur, est dicendum", so kann dies unmöglich Occam selbst geschrieben haben; oder wenn

---

P. Apollinaris van Leeuwen hat eine Editio des Compendium Logicae angekündigt [aufgegeben] und Dom Bascour von der Abtei Mont César in Belgien die des ersten Buches des Sentenzenkommentars [1951 hat Dom Bascour sein Vorhaben dem Franciscan Institute überlassen]. Eine Liste der bis jetzt bekannten Handschriften der nicht kirchenpolitischen Werke Ockhams wird voraussichtlich in diesem Jahre in der Zeitschrift La France Franciscaine erscheinen [vgl. Manuscrits des oeuvres non-polémiques d'Ockham, in: La France Franciscaine 22 (1939) 171—175, und oben 28 ff.].

III, 3, 38, f. 70 v. A. gesagt wird "Ideo ad istius summae completionem, quae de omni modo arguendi generalem tradit notitiam, sunt aliqua perscrutanda et primo disserendum est de obligationibus", so bedarf es nach solchem Geständnis keines weiteren Beweises, daß die dort eingereihten Obligationes und Insolubilia eine spätere Interpolation sind. Aber wenn ich somit in der Darstellung der Summa totius logicae mit möglichster Vorsicht verfahren und vorerst kritisch das Spätere ausscheiden soll, so bleibt, wie die Dinge einmal liegen, zur Beantwortung der Frage, ob etwas noch von Occam selbst herrühren könne oder nicht, häufig nur das Kriterium des subjektiven Gefühls übrig; und wenn auch der Leser hoffentlich zu mir das Vertrauen hegt, daß ich mich in diese ganze Literatur hinreichend hineingelebt habe, um mein Gefühl möglichst zu schärfen, so möge doch bei mangelnden äußeren Zeugnissen hiermit meine Irrtumfähigkeit ausdrücklich vorbehalten sein. Entzogen soll dem Leser darum nichts werden, sondern was ich für unecht halte, wird eben später in Abschn. XX bei den übrigen Interpolationen eine Darstellung finden." (C. Prantl, Geschichte der Logik im Abendlande, 3. Bd., Leipzig 1867 [Graz 1955], S. 329, Anm. 740.)

Was Prantl so temperamentvoll und selbstsicher behauptet, hält einer kritischen Nachprüfung nicht stand [siehe auch William Ockham, Summa Logicae Pars Prima, edit. Ph. Boehner, St. Bonaventure, N. Y., 1951, S. VIII ff.]. Es sind mehr als 40 Handschriften der Summa Logicae bekannt,[b] davon die zwei ältesten in Deutschland (Erfurt, Amploniana [Q 259 und O 67]). Leider hat es der berühmte Gelehrte versäumt, auch nur eine Handschrift zu Rate zu ziehen.

Bei unsern Vorbereitungsarbeiten für die kritische Ausgabe mußten wir dem Urteil des Historikers der Logik im Abendlande auf jeden Fall Rechnung tragen und so haben wir alle von Prantl als unecht erklärten Stellen in den ältesten Handschriften nachgeprüft. Es zeigte sich, daß alles, was Prantl nach seinem Gefühl als unecht erklärte, sich bereits um 1340 handschriftlich nachweisen läßt.

Es ist wahr, der Prolog des großen Ockhamschülers Adam Wodham findet sich nicht in allen Handschriften, wohl aber schon in

---

[b] Jetzt etwa 60; siehe oben S. 42, Note c.

den beiden Mss Amploniana O 67 (aus dem Jahre 1339) und Basel F II 25 (aus dem Jahre 1342). Sein Verfasser ist also auf keinen Fall jener Marcus von Benevent, der den Druck der Summa Logicae besorgte. Von wem die Titelüberschriften stammen, läßt sich bis heute nicht entscheiden, aber auch sie kann Marcus sehr wohl den Handschriften entnommen haben. Die Handschriften zeigen darin eine große Mannigfaltigkeit [vgl. edit. Boehner, S. IX].

Wichtiger, oder besser gefährlicher ist die Unechtheitserklärung des Tractatus de obligationibus, den Prantl sogar einem "Pseudooccam" zuschreibt. Dieser Pseudooccam existiert nur in Prantls Geschichte der Logik. Jedenfalls findet sich jener Traktat in allen älteren Handschriften. Für seine Unechtheitserklärung bucht Prantl mit "Genugtuung", daß Thurot (In: Revue crit. d'hist. et littér. 1876. Nro 13. p. 195 u. 198) diesen Passus in einer Pariser Handschrift nicht hat finden können. Möglicherweise hat Thurot Ms Bibl. Nat. 6431 im Auge, wo ich tatsächlich unsern Traktat nicht entdecken konnte. Jedenfalls findet er sich in allen älteren Handschriften. Doch ist zu beachten, daß er nicht immer an der gleichen Stelle angetroffen wird. Es steht also fest, daß unser Traktat schon ein Jahrzehnt vor dem Tode Ockhams in den Handschriften war. Da Prantl auch hier nur sein Gefühl sprechen läßt, wird man sich der Fides codicum beugen müssen [vgl. *Summa*, edit. Boehner, S. IX].

Für die weiteren Unechtheitserklärungen Prantls beschränken wir uns darauf, die von ihm gemachten Zitate in einer Konkordanz mit dem Ms Amploniana Q 259 zusammenzustellen. Prantl zitiert nach der Ausgabe: Venetiis 1522.

Prantl	Amplon. Q 259
I, 10, f. 5rB (Prantl 3. Bd. Anm. 740)	f. 8v
II, 36, f. 35vA („ 3. „ „ 961)	f. 63ra
II, 37, f. 35vB („ 3. „ „ 962)	f. 63rb
II, 64, f. 49rB („ 3. „ „ 999)	f. 85va
II, 68, f. 49vA („ 3. „ „ 1005)	f. 86va
III, 38, f. 70vA („ 4. „ „ 162)	f. 100ra

(Dasselbe gilt für die Anmerkungen 163—172 = Pseudooccam!)

Demnach hält keine der Unechtheitserklärungen Prantls der historischen Wahrheit stand.

Leider haben Prantls Gefühlsurteile nachgewirkt. Kardinal Ehrle (Der Sentenzenkommentar Peters von Candia ... FS Beiheft 9, 1925, 99) schreibt wesentlich vorsichtiger schon als Prantl: "Der Text ist im Druck von dem bekannten Nominalistenhaupt Markus von Benevent humanistisch etwas überarbeitet", und beruft sich in der Fußnote auf Prantl. Doch weiß er bereits, daß der I. Prolog (Quam magnos veritatis ...) nicht von Markus, sondern von Ahdam Wodham stammt. Die dann folgende Edition des Prologs, die von Pelster stammt, gibt allerdings noch keinen einwandfreien Text.

Diese Vorsicht des großen Forscher-Kardinals hat Nicola Abbagnano (Guglielmo di Ockham, Lanciano, 1931, 30—31) wieder fallen lassen und schreibt die Irrtümer Prantls noch einmal ab. Er schließt: Indubbiamente queste espressioni come altre che si potrebbero rilevare in qualche altro punto della logica provano, se non altro, qualche aggiunta posteriore e qualche interpolazione fatta alla logica dalla scuola occamistica.

E. Moody (The Logic of William of Ockham, London, Sheed and Ward 1935), der uns die beste Darlegung der Logik Ockhams mit reichhaltiger Textauswahl geschenkt hat, verweist auf Prantl und kennt auch das wesentlich vorsichtigere Urteil Ehrles, ohne sich weiter zur Echtheitsfrage zu äußern.

So mögen diese Ausführungen wenigstens den einen Nutzen haben, daß eine andere Legende Prantls aus der Welt geschafft ist.

Wir können es nicht unterlassen, bei dieser Gelegenheit noch auf einen anderen Irrtum Prantls hinzuweisen, den bereits N. Abbagnano korrigiert. Prantl bezweifelt auch die Echtheit der Expositio aurea, mit deren Neuherausgabe sich L. Baudry in Paris beschäftigt. Abbagnano weist auf S. 28—29 nach, daß Markus von Benevent in seiner Ausgabe manches hinzugefügt hat, aber seine Zusätze immer sorgfältig durch F M kenntlich macht. Markus macht selbst darauf aufmerksam. Es heißt fol. 7: "Notandum est hic quod interdum tam in quaestionibus Alberti parvi quam in expositione textus, quaedam, inter has duas litteras, scilicet F. M., intercepta reperiuntur: quae

dicta solum fratri Marco operis correctori sunt adscribenda." Hätte
Prantl diese Zeilen in dem ihm vorliegenden Texte gelesen, so hätte
er sich seine Anmerkung 739 (3. Bd. S. 329) sparen können.

8. THREE SUMS OF LOGIC ATTRIBUTED TO WILLIAM OCKHAM[a]

To disentangle and to clarify the text-tradition of the writings
of the scholastics certainly constitutes one of the most necessary
and at the same time most tedious tasks in the historical research
of medieval thought. In order to understand the thought of a man
one has to know what he really wrote and the sequence in which
he composed his works. Critically edited or at least trustworthy
texts are absolutely indispensable. Where there are none extant in
editions, the student must take the road of manuscript research. Yet,
even more basic is the solution of the preliminary problem concerning
the authenticity of the works which are themselves attributed to an
author. In this regard the literary bequest of William Ockham still
posits doubts in spite of the much research that has been done in
recent years. It is true that a general agreement has been reached
amongst scholars as regards the authenticity of the main works of
the Venerabilis Inceptor.[1] In fact, it seems that all outstanding
scholars in the field of Ockhamistic studies, such as Hochstetter,
Vignaux and Baudry agree with the present writer on the authenticity
of all the non-political works enumerated by him in his study published in 1944.[2] They even agree with him in qualifying as doubtful
or certainly non-authentic a few other works, viz., the *Centiloquium*,
the *Tractatus de principiis Theologiae*, the *Tractatus de Successivis*
and a certain tract on logic. However, this agreement is not adduced
here as a proof; it can have weight only in as much as the authorities

---

[1] Cf. the excellent comprehensive study of Léon Baudry, *Guillaume
d'Occam. Sa vie, ses oeuvres, ses idées sociales et politiques*, in *Etudes de
Philosophie Médiévale*, t. XXXIX (Paris: Vrin, 1949), I, 273—294.

[2] Cf. Philotheus Boehner, O. F. M., *The Tractatus de Successivis attributed to William Ockham*, in *Franciscan Institute Publications*, No. 1 (St. Bonaventure, N. Y., 1944), pp. 16—23.

---

[a] First published in FrancStud 11 (1951) 173—193.

behind it have substantiated their opinion. This restriction, obvious though it may appear, will be proved necessary by this investigation. For, although the present writer is convinced that it is extremely hard to restore to Ockham's authorship the *Centiloquium*, the *Tractatus de Principiis Theologiae* and the *Tractatus de Successivis*, most likely it will be necessary to count "the certain tract on logic", and also another one, among the genuine works of Ockham, for it is particularly this work which has not been subjected to a thorough study, whilst the other three have not only been studied but also edited.

Among the many logical writings which are expressly attributed to Ockham by scribes of the 14th century also several systematical works on logic are found. For want of a better name, let us call them "Logical Summae". These are to be distinguished from another literary type concerning logic, viz., from explanations of classical logical texts. Ockham has written such explanations or *Expositiones* of at least four logical works, namely of the *Isagoge* of Porphyry, of Aristotle's *Categories*, *Perihermenias* and *Sophistical Refutations* *(Expositio super Porphyrium, super Praedicamenta, super duos libros Perihermenias, super duos libros Elenchorum)*. These expositions are running commentaries on the text and usually add sometimes quite long discourses introduced by *Notandum* or *Sciendum* or some such similar expressions. It is obvious that in these commentaries Ockham follows the thought of his author and merely writes down the inspirations he gets from him.

In the *Summae*, on the other hand, we have before us independent systematical works. Here, the science of logic as understood by the scholastics, is brought into a systematic order and composed according to the idea of the author himself. Hence a *Summa* of logic represents in the Middle Ages what we would call a handbook or textbook of logic. There are many such logical *summae* written by medieval logicians and known to us; they are by no means as monotonous as our neo-scholastic works on logic.

Ockham has composed at least one such *summa* of logic the authenticity of which is firmly established beyond any doubt. It is his famous *Summa logicae* or, as it is sometimes called, *Summa totius logicae*. Widely distributed in the Middle Ages it was printed many

times before the 17th century. Yet, we find that in older and sometimes even in recent literature other systematical works on logic are
attributed to Ockham. Most, or indeed practically all, of these attributions are, however, so vague that it seems useless to discuss them
here. This holds especially for Wadding and Sbaralea in the *Scriptores
Ordinis Minorum.* One gets the strong impression that they quote
the same work, viz., the *Summa Logicae,* under different titles. In
order to bring some light into the prevailing confusion we have to
follow the only safe method, viz., that of manuscript research.

It was Apollinaris van Leeuwen, O.F.M., who in a letter called our
attention some time ago to another systematic work of Ockham on
logic which he discovered in a manuscript of the Staatsbibliothek
in Munich. He realized that it was a work different from the *Summa
logicae.* In 1938 when collecting information on manuscripts attributed
to Ockham we were informed by our friend Victorin Doucet of the
existence in Assisi of a manuscript containing a logic of Ockham.
Finally, we were able to locate still another systematical work on
logic bearing the name of Ockham in the Vatican library with the
title *Defensorium logicae Ockham.*[b] Thus in a short time three distinct
and definitely located works on logic and connected with the name
of Ockham had come to our knowledge. This was still before 1939.
Unfortunately the war made it impossible to obtain microfilms of
these works. Finally this year we were able to secure them, and thus
we are now in a position to form a substantiated opinion concerning
their authenticity.

Here, however, we shall not enter into a discussion of the work
known as *Defensorium logicae Ockham,* first, because it does not seem
to have any claim to authenticity, since, as the title suggests, it is
a defense of Ockham's logic, which could hardly be attributed to
Ockham himself; secondly, because an edition of this work is being
prepared by Gaudens Mohan, O.F.M. who will resume in a more
thorough manner the problem of authenticity. The present study,
therefore, will be confined only to three systematical works on logic
all of which are expressly attributed to Ockham; they are the *Summa
logicae (S1),* the *Logica* of Munich *(S2)* and the *Logica* of Assisi *(S3).*

---

[b] Angelica 1017 (R. 6. 32), f. 21r—36r.

1. SUMMA LOGICAE. TRACTATUS LOGICAE MAIOR *(S1)*

There are about 50 known manuscripts of the *Summa Logicae* of Ockham. It is probable that more are still hidden in smaller libraries. In order to identify this work in the manuscripts at least three *Incipits* are required. Some manuscripts start with the introductory preface written probably by Adam Wodham, a disciple of Ockham: *Quam magnos veritatis sectatoribus afferat fructus sermocinalis scientia* ... Others start with the dedicatory letter of Ockham: *Dudum me frater et amice carissime tuis litteris* ... Again, several manuscripts start with the logic itself: *Omnes logicae tractatores intendunt astruere* ... The explicits in various manuscripts also vary, mostly, however, due to a transposition of the tract on *Obligationes* (to the end), and for other reasons. More important for an exact identification of this work will be a survey of its content which shall be made in presenting its division.

The *Summa* is divided into three main parts, and the third again in several parts. Following the edition of 1508 (Venice) we have the following division and subdivisions which to a certain extent follow the order of the logical writings of Porphyry and Aristotle.

I. On terms. 1. On terms in general. 2. On the predicables. 3. On the predicaments. 4. On supposition.

II. On propositions.

III. On Syllogisms. 1. On syllogism in general. 2. On the demonstrative syllogism. 3. On the topical arguments (syllogisms and consequences). 4. On the *obligationes* and the insolvable. 5. On the fallacies.

The *Summa logicae* which we shall call from now on *S1* treats its subject matter in a rather comprehensive manner. It has very little on the hypothetical syllogism, perhaps because it aims at a systematization of the Aristotelian logic in a broad sense. Of course it is not strictly confined to Aristotelian logic in the proper sense, but rather to that trend of logic which was mainly developed in the 13th century, which as it seems has little interest in hypothetical syllogisms.

6*

There has never been advanced a serious reason against the authenticity of this work or of the parts of it. Prantl's[3] pretentious assertions about the inauthenticity of certain parts (On Hypothetical Propositions, On Obligations, and On the Insolvable and minor additions, corrections and changes) which even in this year 1950 have still found an echo, and his creation of a Pseudo-Ockham are based only on vague intuitions and feelings; Prantl has not made the slightest effort to study the manuscript tradition of the works of Ockham but consulted only old printed editions. We do not want to again repeat our reasons against this pure invention. However, since Prantl and those who have uncritically followed him, did not examine the manuscripts of this work, it escaped them that there are a few parts of *S1* which need a critical evaluation. Whilst the *Tractatus de Obligationibus* is found in all of the manuscripts written certainly between 1339—1348 (at least six manuscripts), the Chapter on relation (Cap. 53 of the editions) is missing in 12 of the 30 manuscripts we studied. Hence this major part, that is an entire chapter, posits a serious problem. However, since the *Tractatus de Obligationibus* and *De insolubili*, and chapters 13 ff. (III, III of the editions: *Quia circa modalium propositionum aequipollentias et repugnantias…*) are inserted at different pages in some manuscripts, and even in some of the oldest ones, there is a strong suspicion that they have been added after the first draft of *S1* was finished. But there is no evidence whatsoever that these parts were not added by the author himself.

As we have proved elsewhere and as it is now generally accepted even by Baudry,[4] *S1* must have been composed before 1329. We are inclined to believe that it was *completed* in Avignon, probably between 1324 and 1327. Our opinion is based on the fact that the work is prefaced by a letter to Adam Wodham who was in England, and secondly because Francis of Mayronis is called *Magister abstractionum;* but this Franciscan scholastic became Master in 1324. However, it is sufficient for us to know for sure that *S1* was written before 1329.

---

[3] Cf. C. Prantl, *Geschichte der Logik im Abendlande*, III (Leipzig, 1867), 399, n. 740, and IV (1870), 41 ff.

[4] Op. cit., p. 77 ff.

Before we go on to a discussion of other tracts on logic, let us exclude from our study another type of work which must not be confused with the following tracts. As is well known, there are many abbreviations or compilations made from lengthy works of scholastics. They have the title *Abbreviatio*, or *Notabilia*, or *Conclusiones*. We know of at least one such work of *S1* preserved in *Vat. lat.* 674. It contains *Conclusiones* of the first part of *S1* and an abbreviation of the Tract on Fallacies of *S1*. The literal repetition of the text of *S1* clearly proves that this is the work of a compiler different from Ockham.

2. THE ELEMENTARIUM OCKHAM OR TRACTATUS LOGICAE MEDIUS *(S2)*

As we mentioned before it was Apollinaris van Leeuwen who first maintained that a work contained in *Clm* 1060 is a work due to the pen of Ockham, that it is different from *S1*, and an important work. At the time when Fr. Apollinaris made this statement we were rather sceptical about his assertion, and we remained sceptical until recently. In 1944 we still wrote: "We doubt its authenticity." [cfr. *The Tractatus de successivis* (St. Bonaventure, 1944) p. 19]. However, we must confess that our doubt was not based on any acquaintance either with the manuscript or with its content. Our doubt was only one of these vague feelings which should not be allowed to determine a position in historical research. After several futile attempts, finally last year we were able to secure a microfilm of this manuscript through the kind help of Palmaz Rucker, O.F.M. On the basis of the document itself we are now in a condition to form a substantiated opinion.

First let us give a few details of this manuscript. *Clm (München, Staatsbibliothek) 1060* is written in a difficult current hand and contains several works on logic. Some of these are enumerated on fol. *136*vb, and there fortunately the date of completion is added. The scribe tells us:

In isto volumine continentur haec subscripta videlicet conclusiones...(?)
Item logica Burle cum declarationibus quarumdam propositionum com-

munium cum regulis libri Priorum. Item logica Okkam cum expositione communium et regulis libri Posteriorum. Haec collecta sunt per fratrem Fridericum (?) de Nordlingham (?) prout studente in Constantia anno d. MCCCXLVIII in cathedra Petri Apostoli.

We are here interested only in the "logica Okkam". On top of folio *135*r (recent numbering) we find the superscription: *Incipit logica Magistri Gwilhelmi Okkam Ordinis Fratrum Minorum tractatus medius.* In order to help further discovery of possibly existing manuscripts and, in order to give an idea of the content, we will now communicate the entire introduction and the first lines of the work:

Occupationibus, quas interrumpere mihi durum est, paucas per vices lucubras morulus interponens ad utilitatem parvulorum cupientium primo discere logicae elementa, quibus lacte simplicis sapidaeque doctrinae opus est (non) solido cibus sententiarum subtilium, praesens duxi opusculum componendum, quod poterit elementarium appellari, ut tenella ingenia, nondum vaniloquiis fabulosis ac ridiculosis imbuta figmentis, planis ac lucidis nec non et utilibus nutriantur gratius rudimentis, quibus delectati adhaereant, quinimmo nauseant(!) super insipides et obscuris atque phantasticis nec non vix opinabilibus non intelligibilibus doctrinis. Aestimo autem, quod si in his studuerint diligenter ac lecta et intellecta memoriae custodierint in thesauris, parvo tempore poterint adipisci, quod quam multi studentes mali in annis plurimis attingere nequiverunt, et ad intelligenda altiora et difficiliora non solum sed etiam in aliis scientiis non mediocriter adiuvabit. Quod autem in hoc opere minus vere, obscure, confuse, superflue, diminute vel nugatorie aut aliter minus recte dictum reperierit, hoc respuat, corrigat et informet et meae imperitiae vel discretioni mentis, quam his attente applicare non valui, deputans propter hoc utilia non dimittat.

Hic sunt octo libri distincti per capitula, quorum Primus tractat de terminis, de quibus etiam tractatur in libro Porphyrii et Praedicamentorum Aristotelis.

Secundus liber de propositionibus, de quibus etiam tractatur in libro Perihermenias.

Tertius de suppositionibus, de quibus alibi in libris Aristotelis non tractatur.

Quartus de syllogismis, de quibus tractatur in libro Priorum.

Quintus de locis, de quibus tractatur in libro Topicorum.

Septimus de demonstratione, et de hac tractatur in libro Posteriorum

Octavus de fallaciis, de quibus tractatur in libro Elenchorum.

Et si quis aliquid vitiosi vel non correcti in scriptura istius compendii reperit, non studio scribentis imputetur, sed velocitati etc.

Explicit prologus

(Incipit tractatus) Finis logicae principalis est scire discernere in omni materia sophisticum argumentum a vero. Est autem argumentum unius propositionis ex pluribus vel una propositione illatio. Est autem argumentum triplex, scilicet vocale, mentale et scriptum. Argumentum vocale est, quod de ore profertur ac audiri potest. Scriptum est quod in libro scribitur vel re corporali scribitur et legi ac videri potest. Mentale quod solummodo mente concipitur et nullius idiomatis vel linguae existit et corporaliter nec audiri nec videri potest . . .

In order to identify possible manuscripts of this work, we shall also add a longer passage of the end:

. . . Haec de logica saepe rogatus a pluribus compendiose perscripsi, ne opus prolixius parvulos nimium oneraret, ut et ista, quae omisi cum maiore aviditate quaerantur; pro quibus ab illis, qui doctrinam suis phantasticis et vix opinabilibus assertionibus obvitiantes (obnubilantes?) non per rationem sed per personam odio, amore privato, timore, invidia, malitia et superbia stimulati nituntur destruere, detractationes et persecutiones expecto. Sed ego eorum conatus contemno malignos et veritatis amore eorum stultitias (stultissimas!), cum opportunitatem habuero et maiora non impedierint, propalabo, benevolem, si defeci, desiderans correctorem. Erit enim mihi gratissimum, si cognovero quempiam verius, rationabilius, clarius, aptius et plenius vel quomodolibet utilius notitiam tradere praedictorum vel aliorum scibilium quorumcumque.

Deo gratias. Deo gratias. Explicit logica Magistri Wilhelmi Okkam Ordinis Fratrum Minorum. Explicit medius tractatus logicae Magistri Gwilhelmi Okkam.

Hence the work is called *Elementarium* by the author himself. And the scribe calls it twice *Tractatus Medius logicae Okkam*. The work is ascribed four times to William Ockham, in the title and in the *Explicit* (2x) and again in the passage quoted above which also gives the date 1348. This, certainly, is a rare documentation. There can be no doubt, as far as the external evidence is concerned, that the work is authentic. Since Ockham died most probably in 1349, the attribution by the scribe is contemporary with Ockham. And this attribution gains in weight if we also consider the fact that the scribe lived in South Germany (Constance), hence not too far from Munich, where Ockham lived.

Unfortunately, up to the present, we know only of this one manuscript of the *Elementarium*, and hence we have practically only one witness, a very good one at that, as to its authenticity. Nevertheless, until exterior evidence can be arrayed against the authenticity, we are forced to accept the testimony of the scribe, unless there are reasons based on the content of this work which prove that it is morally impossible that Ockham could be the author of *Elementarium*. Though we have not yet advanced our study to such a point that we can be absolutely sure, nevertheless, while transcribing this work, we had the strong impression that the teaching in this work is generally in very good agreement with that of certainly authentic works of Ockham. We have to take into account, however, that this (and the following *S3*) leaves out theological discussions. In this *S2* is quite different from *S1* which purposely takes into consideration theological problems, especially in its examples. However, this can hardly be an objection against the authenticity of *S2*. For *S2* addresses itself only to beginners, and it means it. Whilst *S1* expressly states: *Tractatum hunc duxi scribendum, nonumquam regulas per exempla tam philosophica quam theologica declarando* (Dedicatory letter).

Some other points creating certain difficulties, can be reasonably explained, as we shall try to show partly here and partly in our edition which we are preparing. For the time being let us repeat that we have not found any disagreement between *S1* and *S2*, which in our opinion excludes the authenticity of *S2*.

It is also obvious that in an elementary tract we can hardly expect references to other works of the author himself. We know that Ockham likes to quote his own works. But there are also exceptions. For instance the *Quodlibeta* have only a few such references, and the *Quaestiones super libros Physicorum* quote only the *Quodlibeta*. Nevertheless, we discovered four references of the author to his "logica". And here a certain surprise is in store for us. Let us, however, first indicate these references, and then partly discuss them here, partly in the following chapter.

The first reference is embedded in a quite personal text which we believe worthwhile publishing here *in toto* (fol. *163*va):

Alius locus ponitur locus ab auctoritate, et ille locus debilis est, nisi arguatur ab auctoritate illius qui fallere et falli non potest. Et ideo non sequitur: Aristoteles dicit hoc, ergo hoc est verum, quia ipse decipi potuit. Nec sequitur: Astrologus dicit hoc, ergo ita est, quia quilibet astrologus decipere et decipi potest. Propter quod non est necesse credere cuilibet qui putatur expertus in arte vel scientia sua, quia in multis artibus et scientiis nullus potest esse perfectus, sed quilibet errare potest, sicut (*ms.* sic cum) quia multi putantur experti esse qui non sunt, sed vel omnino sunt opinantes et ignari vel solummodo habent memoriam sententiarum vel illorum quae audierunt (et) viderunt de eis, certum et clarum iudicium non habentes. Multi enim vigent memoria, quae bestiis et hominibus, viris et mulieribus, pueris et adultis, stultis et sapientibus est communis, et tamen in iudicio omnino deficiunt, vel habent iudicium valde debile. Vidi enim aliquos pueros et mulieres ac etiam naturaliter stultos quibusdam viris intelligentibus et profundi iudicii in potentia memoriae praevalere. Verumtamen expertis et qui etiam experti communiter reputantur ista est reverentia exhibenda ut dicta eorum non spernantur nec reprobentur nec negentur, antequam constiterit quod sunt dissona veritati, sed suspensa teneatur sententia sive sint dicta antiquorum vel modernorum ut nec propter novitatem vilipendantur nec propter veritatem (! reverentiam ?) teneantur, sed veritas in omnibus extollatur, quia sive antiqui sive moderni, sive amici sive inimici fuerint assertores, sanctum est praehonorare veritatem.

Haec de locis ad praesens sufficiant. Multa autem quae dimittuntur in logica, quam dudum edidi, et in Topicis Aristotelis et Boethii, qui voluerit, poterit invenire. Nec tamen omnia quae dici possent, reperiet, quia nec omnia ab aliquo sunt inventa, sed novae regulae evidentissimae possunt a studiosis excellentem (!) habentibus iudicium rationis quotidie inveniri.

A second reference is found fol. 177rb:

Ad cuius evidentiam, ut aliquo modo apertius et exquisitius et completius quantum ad aliquid dicatur, quam dixi in logica, est sciendum . . .

Fol. *182*vb we read:

. . . sicut dixi in logica tractando de isto modo fallaciae accidentis . . .

Fol. *184*va:

. . . licet sit fallacia consequentis penes primum modum, et sic debet intelligi quod dictum est de hoc in logica . . .

The first reference can be connected with *S1* which indeed has much more about the topical rules than *S2*. It is furthermore noteworthy that the reference is to a logic which has been edited "dudum". We cannot help but attach some significance to this word, "dudum"

since it calls to our mind the first word of the dedicatory letter of
S1: Dudum me frater . . ., but also because the word implies that the
logic referred to, has been written a long time ago. We do not know
any systematical work on logic written in the spirit and the terminology of Ockham which has been composed, let us say, before 1340.
Burleigh is definitely out of question, and so is Richard Campsale,[5]
for both wrote against Ockham. Buridan's Logic can hardly be meant
for his *Summulae* are to a large extent only a revision of Petrus
Hispanus' *Summulae logicales.* Furthermore, as far as our acquaintance
with Buridan goes, he avoids the expression "De virtute sermonis"
which however is used in *S2.* However, we must not forget that
very little is known about this period in general and of its logic
in particular. We can only maintain that to the best of our knowledge this mentioning of a logic can be referred to the *Summa
Logicae* of Ockham, and in this sense we consider it a confirmation
of the authenticity of *S2.*

Although the reference just discussed can be traced to *S1,* it was
not possible to trace the other references to *S1.* This result was
disappointing and first appeared to us a serious objection against the
authenticity of *S2.* Nevertheless, we hope to be able to give a quite
satisfactory solution of this problem, but we will have to do that in
the following chapter.

However, before we go on we would like to call the attention of
the reader to other texts found in *S2* which in our opinion point to
Ockham as author.

On fol. *172*vb we read:

Sicut ad habendum sensum improprium istius orationis: Italia est
rebellis imperatori . . .

Without maintaining that this is an unquestionable indication
of Ockham's authorship, we, nevertheless, believe that this expression
is easier understood when we assume that the author lived in Munich
after the emperor's retreat, forced by the rebellious Italians.

---

[5] Victorin Doucet, O. F. M., "L'oeuvre scholastique de Richard de
Connington, O. F. M.," in *Arch. Franc. Hist.* 29 [1936] 420; here the author
mentions a *ms.* of the logic of Campsale, viz. *Bologna Univ.* 2635.

On fol. *172*vb we read the truly Ockhamist sentences:

Ex his potest advertere studiosus, quod fingentes nomina vel voces ad modum nominum abstractorum de nominibus propriis, pronominibus, adverbiis, coniunctionibus, praepositionibus, interiectionibus ac etiam de verbis, nominibus, participiis, ubi non possunt aperte assignare res distinctas, de quibus constat quod sunt distinctae, cuiusmodi sunt talia, quae putantur nomina, quae in nullo auctore reperiuntur: haeceitas vel haectitas, Sorteitas, Martemeitas, quandalitas, ubeitas, enimitas, velitas, sieitas, aditas, anitas, abeitas, quamobreitas, usquequoeitas, albedineitas, animeitas, lectoreitas (? or: lecteitas?), de scientia facili scientiam difficillimam reddiderunt et difficultates inextricabiles, ubi nulla est vel parvissima, induxerunt. Et ideo ad ratiocinationes eorum, in quibus tales voces accipiuntur, vel respondendum est, quod proferunt voces non significativas, vel dicendum est, quod orationibus utuntur impropriis, quarum sensus, quem prima facie sonat, est negandus quem intendunt taliter arguentes. Et aliquando poterit eius dari sensus verus improprius. Sicut si accipiatur ista: Haec haeceitas aliquo modo distinguitur ex natura rei a subiecto, potest habere sensum improprium verum, istum scilicet vel alium, non ad propositum loquentium: Hoc pronomen "haec" non tantum est demonstrativum substantiae sed etiam partium suarum et aliarum rerum. Melius tamen esset omnino deridendo tales non intelligentes, quae loquuntur, dicere quod voces non significativas accipiunt. Quamvis enim aliquando liceat ex necessitate vel aliqua utilitate vocabula fingere, non tamen licet vocabula (fingere) ad decipiendum simplices per involutiones vocum et ad insinuandum res aliquas quae non sunt nec esse possunt, et ad inducendum difficultates, ubi nulla deberet esse vel parva; quemadmodum ex improprio et figurativo modo loquendi antiquorum propter ignorantiam posteriorum multorum nescientium antiquos fuisse figurative locutos et improprie, difficultates innumerabiles et nocivae quam plurimae sunt inductae. Ita enim ab antiquo adolevit (ms. abolevit) modus loquendi improprius, ut vix a quoquam valeat evitari. Quod scio mihi saepius accidisse scienter vel etiam et brevitatis causa vel conformando me modo loquendi communi etiam improprie locutus (sum; *ms.* proprie), propter quod forte aliqui in quibusdam dictis meis vel mihi contradictionem imponent, quae per distinctionem solvi debet, vel ab intentione mea penitus discordabunt.

Anyone who is acquainted with Ockham's writings will remember that he has met with similar invectives of Ockham against the creations of new terms by the Scotists and that he gives practically the same example of this verbalism. In addition, the tone of this passage reveals an old man who looks back at a long career of writing.

3. THE TRACTATUS MINOR LOGICAE OCKHAM *(S3)*

The failure to locate the rest of the above mentioned references in *S1 forced* us to look elsewhere. It was obvious that we should look for them in another *Summa* of Logic which is likewise attributed to Ockham, viz., that which is preserved in *ms. 690* of Assisi. Through the kind help of Victorin Doucet we obtained a microfilm of this work and thus are now in a condition to make a comparative study. The manuscript is written in a half current hand of the 14th century. The *Incipit* reads:

> Logica cum dicatur a logos, quod est sermo et ideo merito latine sermo-cinalis et rationalis scientia appellatur. Ipsa enim docet et tradit regulas quibus omnes ratiocinationes in omni scientia et arte, mentales, vocales et scriptae, debent, ut non sint sophisticae, regulari. Quamobrem non irrationabiliter scientia scientiarum et ars artium nuncupatur, quia in omni arte et scientia docet discernere sophisticum argumentum a vero, et ideo nulla scientia potest perfecte et artificiose sine ipsa tradi et haberi, quia nullus sine ipsa regulante potest per artem ex veritate nota racio-cinando ignotam accipere veritatem, licet interdum nonulli a casu et abs-que certitudine evidenti per notas ad alias ignotas perveniant veritates. Propter quod istius artis ignorantia decipiuntur in multis ita ut multi in errores vix inopinabiles prolabuntur quia argumenta sophistica et apparen-tia pro veris accipiuntur.
>
> Sic argumentum est triplex, scilicet mentale quod componitur ex cogitationibus mentis, vocale quod componitur ex vocibus ab ore prolatis et scriptum . . .

The division of this work follows exactly the same pattern as *S2*, but it omits a discussion of the demonstrative syllogism. For the rest this tract is considerably shorter than *S2*.

The explicit reads:

> . . . Est autem ista fallacia extra dictionem quia potest quis solummodo mentaliter respondendo huiusmodi responsiones formare et decipi putando quod una alia propositio affirmativa vel negativa formata ex eisdem sit vera vel concedenda.
>
> Explicit minor tractatus novae logicae fratris Gwilhelmi Ockham.

Again, we have an explicit attribution of a systematic work on logic to Ockham, hence we shall call it *S3*. It must be our rule to believe such a medieval explicit attribution unless we have grave reasons to doubt it. Let us therefore assume the authenticity of this tract *S3*, at least for the time being.

What strikes us first is the fact that it is called *logica nova*. Two meanings can be attached to this expression, 1. that it follows the new logic, viz., the logic introduced by the Summulists like Peter of Spain etc., or 2. that it is another logic of the same author. This second meaning is certainly preferable, since a comparison with the logic of the Summulists shows that they start with a tract on propositions; at least Peter of Spain, William of Shyreswood and Buridan have this arrangement in their *Summulae*. The division of *S2* and *S3* follows Ockhams *Summa Logicae (S1)* except for the place of the supposition (and of induction which *S1* has at the end, and in the tract on topical consequences; the tract on Obligations is had only in *S1*).

What is more striking is the fact that *S3* is called *tractatus minor.* Hence there must be a *tractatus maior.* This *tractatus maior* cannot be *S2*, since it is expressly called the *tractatus medius;* there remains the only possibility that it is *S1*, if, of course, the attributions to Ockham are correct. In this assumption it follows furthermore that the chronological order of these *Summae* must be: *S1—S3—S2* since *S2* is called *tractatus medius*, which logically presupposes the two extremes of which it is the middle. In order to verify our deduction, we have now to go back to our quotations. There are no quotations of any work of the author in *S3*.

Our first quotation (of fol. *163*vb of *S2*) cannot refer to *S3* but only to *S1* which has a very extensive treatment of topical rules. This part of *S1* fills about 130 typewritten pages whilst it occupies in *S2* 32, in *S3* only 7.

It is, however different with the tract on the fallacies. In *S2* it has 112 typewritten pages, (the whole has 308, hence a third), in *S3* it has 28 typewritten pages, of 68, hence more than a third. In *S1* it has (in the printed edition) 12 folios of 107, that is a little more than one tenth. In order to compare the length of the tract on fallacies with that of the others we can say, that *S1* has approximately 80, *S2* more than 112, *S3* 28 typewritten pages. It is evident that the interest of the author has shifted towards the tract on fallacies.

The rest of the quotations could not be verified in *S1*, but we believe that they can be verified in *S3*. In order to make this evident and also to show a possible dependence of *S1*, *S2*, *S3*, we will present the texts in parallel columns:

S1 (fol. *99ra*)
P. III, IV, c. 8

Post haec dicendum est de compositione et divisione coniunctim. Et primo sciendum, quod tunc est aliqua oratio multiplex secundum compositionem et divisionem, quando aliqua oratio prolata vel scripta propter solam diversam punctuationem dictionum potest habere diversos sensus. Sicut ista oratio sic prolata: Quidquid vivit semper est, si punctuaretur sic: Quidquid vivit semper, est, habet unum sensum; si autem punctuetur sic: Quidquid vivit, semper est, habet alium sensum, ita quod causa apparentiae istius fallaciae est identitas earundem dictionum in oratione composita et divisa. Causa non existentiae est diversitas punctuationis.

Istius autem fallaciae sunt duo modi principales. Primus est

S2 (f. *177b*)
1. 8. c.

Sequitur de fallacia compositionis et divisionis, quae est deceptio proveniens ex hoc quod alicuius unius orationis dictiones possunt componi vel dividi ab invicem, sicut ista est distinguenda: Quidquid vivit semper est. Potest enim haec dictio 'semper' componi cum hac dictione vivit vel dividi ab ea. Non autem differunt istae fallaciae per hoc quod quando oratio in sensu composito est falsa, est fallacia compositionis et quando in sensu diviso est falsa est fallacia divisionis, quia eadem propositio potest esse primo falsa in sensu composito et non in sensu diviso, sed postea potest esse in sensu diviso et non composito. Sic ista: Omnis homo currens velociter addiscit, poterit esse vera, si velociter componatur cum hac dictione currens,

S3 (f. *240r*)

Tertia fallacia in dictione vocatur compositio et quarta divisio. *Circa quod non est curiose disputandum, an sit una fallacia vel plures, aut quis vocandus sit sensus compositionis et quis divisionis; hoc enim parum vel nihil prodest ad alias scientias intelligendas.* Est autem fallacia compositionis et divisionis deceptio proveniens ex hoc quod partes orationis eiusdem possunt diversimode componi vel dividi ab invicem. Unde causa apparentiae est identitas orationis. Causa non existentiae est diversitas sensuum, propter quod dictiones eiusdem orationis aliter et aliter possunt componi et dividi ab invicem.

Sunt autem duo modi principales.

Primus est, quando retento eodem ordine dictionum (secundum

quando tota oratio sive composita sive divisa remanet in utroque sensu categorica vel hypothetica. Secundus modus est, quando sensus compositus est propositio categorica et sensus divisionis est propositio hypothetica. Et secundum hoc posset poni distinctio inter compositionem et divisionem, ut illae orationes dicantur multiplices secundum compositionem, quando uterque sensus est propositio categorica vel uterque est propositio hypothetica.

Illae autem dicuntur multiplices secundum divisionem, quando unus sensus est propositio categorica et reliquus est propositio hypothetica. *Utrum tamen isto modo sit accipienda distinctio istarum fallaciarum, non multum curo, quia hoc scire non reputo multum utile specialibus scientiis, quamvis notitia distinguendi tales orationes magnam habet utilitatem.*

Iuxta primum modum sunt tales orationes multiplices . . .
There follow only discussions of examples of

et falsa, si dividatur ab ea, puta si aliquis currat velociter et nullus homo addiscat, et postea poterit accidere econverso, puta si nullus currit velociter et tamen aliquis currens addiscat velociter. Fallacia autem non putatur propter solam mutationem rei vocibus eodem modo dispositis, ergo tali modo non distinguitur fallacia compositionis et fallacia divisionis, sed eadem propositio potest primo esse falsa in sensu composito et non in sensu diviso, et postea poterit esse falsa in utroque sensu. Et ita in eodem argumento sophistico esset primo fallacia compositionis et postea non esset fallacia compositionis.

Ideo aliter potest dici, quod quandoque aliquo modo eadem est fallacia compositionis et divisionis et aliquando aliquo modo possunt distingui.

Ad cuius evidentiam, ut aliquo modo apertius et exquisitius et completius quantum ad aliquid dicatur quam dixi in logica est sciendum, quod com-

eundem ordinem dictio cum!) patenter in tardis et rudibus possunt esse diversi sensus propter hoc, quod aliqua dictio potest componi vel dividi ab alia, quod apparet ex sola punctuatione diversa. Sic distinguendae sunt tales: Quidquid vivit semper est. Haec dictio 'semper' potest componi cum hoc verbo vivit, et est vera vel potest dividi ab eo, et tunc est falsa.

Secundus modus est, quando eadem dictio non habet patenter plures sensus retento eodem dictionis ordine, sed in explicatione sensuum est aperta et patens diversitas sensuum propter hoc, quod aliqua vel termini diversimode componuntur vel dividuntur ab invicem, sicut patet hic: Quinque sunt duo et tria. Nam unus sensus est iste: Quinque sunt duo et quinque sunt tria, ubi iste terminus 'quinque' componitur ibi in diversis propositionibus cum illis duobus terminis 'duo' et 'tria'. Alius sensus est: Quinque sunt duo et tria con-

this fallacy, mostly taken from theology.

positionis et divisionis possunt assignari duo modi principales. Unus est, quando ex sola diversa punctuatione tam in loquendo quam in scribendo faciliter, clare et aperte possunt de eadem oratione haberi diversi sensus, ita ut rudes valeant discerne unum ab alio, sicut patet de ista: Omnis homo currens velociter movetur,quae potest punctuari sic: Omnis homo currens *velociter movetur,* et sic: Omnis homo *currens* velociter... Et sic numquam vel raro fallacia compositionis distinguitur a fallacia divisionis ex hoc quod eadem dictio potest componi cum una vel cum alia, sicut in exemplo praedicto patet, quia non potest ratio assignari, quare magis iste sensus, in quo haec dictio 'velociter' componitur cum hac dictione 'currens', quam ille in quo componitur cum hac dictione 'movetur'. Si autem aliqua est alia ratio, nec ex sola punctuatione diversa faciliter et clare pateant diversi sensus in quorum uno eadem dic-

iunctim, quinque sunt aliqua quae comprehendunt duo et tria.

Dicitur autem quod iste modus compositionis coincidit cum primo modo amphibologiae quantum ad orationes in quibus ponuntur dictiones inter terminos facientes propositiones hypotheticas. Etiam dicitur quod penes secundum modum distinguendae sunt propositiones in quibus ponitur dictum propositionis cum dictione faciente propositionem modalem. Sensus compositionis exprimitur per propositionem in qua modus praedicatur de propositione de inesse. Sicut sensus istius compositionis: Omnem hominem esse animal est scitum a te, exprimitur per istam: Omnis homo est animal est scita a te. Sensus divisionis explicatur per propositiones, in quibus modus est determinatio compositionis vel in ipsis ponitur verbum modale; sicut praedictae propositionis intellectus: Omnem hominem esse animal est necessarium, explicatur per istam:

tio componitur cum alia dictione et in alio sensu non componitur cum alia sed permaneat per se, tunc potest sensus compositus distingui a sensu diviso, quia ille sensus est compositus, in quo dictio componitur cum alia dictione, et ille est divisus, in quo eadem dictio cum nulla alia immediata sibi componitur.

Omnis homo necessario est animal.

Et[b] sic etiam in praedicto exemplo potest distingui sensus compositus a sensu diviso, non ex eo quod haec dictio 'velociter' potest componi cum hac dictione 'currens' vel cum hac dictione 'movetur', sed ex hoc quod haec dictio 'movetur' potest componi cum hac dictione 'velociter' vel dividi ab ea, quia tunc nulla alia copulatur immediate. Et isto modo aliquis idem sensus est compositus et divisus; si aliter, erit compositus et non divisus. Compositum enim et divisum in illa significatione, in qua accipiuntur, quando attribuuntur fallaciae compositionis et divisionis non sunt opposita, licet connotent diversa, sed possunt competere eidem.

Secundus modus principalis compositionis et divisionis est, quando non ex sola punctuatione retenti omnino eisdem dictionibus nulla alia addita potest faciliter rudibus clare et aperte patere diversitas sensuum, sed quando in clara et aperta expressione sensuum interdum aliquibus dictionibus additis vel aliqua eadem aut aliquibus eisdem replicata vel repetita eadem dictio componitur cum una vel pluribus, vel in uno sensu non in alio. Sicut ista: Quinque sunt duo et tria, vel non habet vel non patet rudibus habere diversos sensus ex hoc quod istae dictiones retento eodem ordine nulla addita vel subtracta possunt diversimode punctuari, sed in expressione sensuum talis clara patet diversa compositio eiusdem dictionis cum alia vel aliis; nam unus sensus est . . . *Here follows a discussion of this proposition and also of modal propositions* . . .

Porro, quamvis praedicto modo possit fallacia compositionis distingui a fallacia divisionis et utriusque possint assignari duo modi principales, quorum sensus dividitur in duos, ut unus dicatur, quando oratio composita est categorica, et divisa hypothetica, alius quando utraque est categorica, sicut in propositionibus in quibus ponitur dictum propositionis cum modo,

---

[b] What follows, in *S2* only.

tamen, sicut tactum est prius, de hoc minimum est disputandum et contenden-
dum; est magis curiosum quam utile pro aliis scientiis, sicut et curiosum est
nimis investigare, an propositiones, quae secundo modo distinguuntur, scilicet
modales sint distinguendae secundum compositionem et divisionem vel am-
phibologiam, et si secundum utramque, an magis proprie secundum amphibo-
logiam vel secundum compositionem et divisionem. Sufficit enim scire pro
aliis scientiis, ad quas notitia fallaciarum sicut et aliorum logicalium ordina-
tur, quod tales orationes possunt habere tales diversos sensus.

If we compare these texts, we find many relations between *S1*,
S2 and *S3*. In each text we find the admonition that it is not of much
value to distinguish the fallacy of composition from that of division.
None of the early or contemporary logicians have this as far as we
were able to check. The almost identical wording of this warning is
quite remarkable.

Furthermore each *Summa* distinguishes only two principal modes,
which is also quite characteristic, and each *Summa* puts special
emphasis on the difference in the punctuation, even the mentioning
of which we could not discover in any other logic of the time; hence
it also seems to be Ockhamistic. Finally, it appears to us that *S2*
and *S3* are more closely related than *S1* and *S2*. *S1* makes the distinction between the two principal modes of these fallacies under
the general idea that the punctuation is the cause of the fallacy, the
first mode being when the proposition is either categorical or hypothetical, the second when they are mixed or can be either categorical or hypothetical. *S3*, however, maintains that only the first mode
is due to a difference in the punctuation, the second principal mode
refers more to the fact that the composition or division must be
made apparent by an explanation. This division is in fact further
explained and clarified by *S2*. But it is in regard to this explanation
that the author refers to his *logica*. Hence we are to conclude that
he does not refer to *S1* but to *S3*.

There appears then a definite development from *S1* over *S3* to
S2 to a more definite and clearer distinction of the two modes of the
fallacy of composition and division. In order to show this development
even better, we shall add now a text from the still unedited *Expositio*
super libros Elenchorum, which shows the same peculiarities common
to all the texts mentioned above (admonition not to bother too much

about a distinction, and secondly the emphasis on punctuation). This text is definitely earlier than *S1*. We read *(ms. Oxford Bodl. 558)*:

Ad: Secundum compositionem autem huiusmodi . . . Circa totam istam partem est primo notandum, quod quandocumque retentis eisdem dictionibus et eodem ordine dictionum propter solam diversam punctuationem causatur diversitas sensus recte intelligentibus, et tunc est ibi multiplicitas secundum compositionem et divisionem et aliter non. Et ideo quando aliqua talis oratio scribitur vel profertur et una dictio non plus ex modo proferendi vel scribendi conjungatur cum una dictione quam cum alia, tunc est multiplicitas nec habetur expresse in quo sensu scribitur vel profertur. Unde si sic scribatur ista oratio: Quicumque vivit semper est, non habetur . . .

Secundo notandum, quod diversi sunt modi distinguendi compositionem et divisionem . . .

Aliter potest dici, quod tunc est fallacia compositionis, quando in utroque sensu propositio est categorica vel utraque hypothetica; et tunc est fallacia in divisione, quando in uno sensu est propositio categorica et in alio hypothetica. Et hoc videtur innuere littera Aristotelis, quia sic est in exemplis positis ab Aristotele. Et tunc illa littera: Ergo posui te . . . debet legi sic ut in ea exemplificet quomodo composita et divisa non semper idem significant vel quod ibi ponit paralogismos compositionis.

Sed ista difficultas non est multum utilis et magis est ad placitum hominis dicere quod voluerit et accipere vocabula sicut placuerit quam ex re ipsa, ideo de ipsa transeundum est. Hic tamen intelligendum est, quod ubicumque est fallacia compositionis, est ibi aliquo modo fallacia divisionis et econverso. *Quae autem oratio debeat vocari composita et quae divisa, non est multum curandum.*

There can be no doubt that the *Expositio* is more closely related to *S1*, but it also clearly shows relation to *S2* and *S3*. Some of the same characteristic peculiarities occur in all the four texts. We can hardly believe that this can be explained by chance.

The quotation of fol. *182*vb concerns the *fallacia accidentis*. Here again we will compare the pertinent texts of the three *Summae*.

S1 (fol. *104*ra)	*S2* (fol. *182*vb)	*S3* (fol. *242*r)
Secundus modus principalis fallaciae accidentis est, quando aliqua coniunguntur	Secundus modus principalis fallaciae accidentis, sicut dictum est prius, est quando	Secundus modus, quando ex hoc quod duo extrema coniunguntur separatim ter-

7*

per praedicationem cum tertio non variato in diversis propositionibus et in conclusione coniunguntur illa eadem cum illo tertio non variato. Sicut sic arguendo: Iste canis est tuus et iste canis est pater, ergo est tuus pater.

Verumtamen non semper quando sic arguitur est fallacia accidentis. Hic enim nulla est fallacia accidentis: Iste homo est albus, iste homo est animal, ergo iste homo est animal album. Et ideo ad cognoscendum quando in tali modo arguendi est fallacia accidentis et quando non, videndum est an ex propositione in qua ista duo praedicantur coniunctim de aliquo contingat inferre praedicationem unius de altero, et an talis oratio sit propria. Et si sic, non est ibi fallacia accidentis. Ut hic: Sortes est rationalis, Sortes est animal, ergo Sortes est animal rationale.

Si autem talis oratio sit impropria, tunc non valet, sicut non sequitur: Sortes est homo, Sortes est animal, ergo

ex hoc quod duo extrema in praemissis coniunguntur per praedicationem affirmativam vel negativam cum tertio termino non variato *sophistice concluditur,* quod ista duo extrema subintellecta vere affirmative vel negative praedicantur de eodem tertio termino non variato, quam est sciendum, quod in tali modo, arguendi (quod) utraque praemissa est mere de inesse et mere de praesenti et mere categorica, aut non. Si sic aut utraque propositio est singularis, aut non. Si utraque est singularis, numquam est proprie fallacia accidentis, sed poterit esse aliqua alia large saltem accipiendo aliam fallaciam, et hoc quia vel conclusio non sequitur ex praemissis propter improprietatem locutionis, quae apparebit in conclusione et poterit ibi assignari fallacia figurae dictionis sic arguendo; Sortes est animal, Sortes est homo, ergo Sortes est homo animal; vel aliter accipitur aliquis terminus in aliqua praemissa et in conclusione *et poterit*

tio *sophistice concluditur,* quod coniunctim praedicantur affirmative vel negative de eodem tertio non variato. Propriissime autem iste modus accidentis est, quando propositiones sunt mere de inesse et mere de praesenti et pure affirmativae vel negativae et nulla determinatio vel modus ponitur in eis, et propositiones omnes sunt congruae, si terminus sumptus sit terminus discretus; sed tunc poterit esse fallacia aequivocationis vel figurae dictionis. *Hic enim proprie est fallacia aequivocationis: Iste canis est eius, iste canis est pater, ergo est pater eius, et non est propria fallacia accidentis, quia aliter accipitur haec dictio "eius" in praemissa et in conclusione.* Haec autem: Iste est albus, iste est animal, ergo iste est animal album, magis proprie est fallacia figurae dictionis quam accidentis. Sed quando terminus sumptus est discretus, tunc potest esse fallacia accidentis, si propositiones aliquae sunt de praeterito vel

Sortes est homo animal. Nec sequitur: Sortes est lapis, Sortes est homo, ergo Sortes est homo lapis. Similiter si ex tali praedicatione propria non contingat inferre praedicationem unius illorum coniunctorum de reliquo est ibi fallacia accidentis. Et ideo quia non sequitur: Iste canis est pater tuus, ergo est tunc, ista consequentia non valet: Iste canis est tuus, et est pater, ergo est pater tuus, sed fallacia accidentis. Similiter non sequitur: Iste est monachus albus, ergo est albus; ideo hic est fallacia accidentis: Iste est albus, iste est monachus, ergo iste est albus monachus. Et ita de consimilibus.

Verumtamen sciendum est, quod semper in tali argumento est fallacia figurae dictionis. Et ita semper in tali modo arguendi concurrunt fallacia figurae dictionis; tamen quando quis credit, quod sequitur conclusio propter hoc quod illa coniungebantur eidem termino in praemissis decipitur per fallaciam accidentis. Si

ibi assignari fallacia aequivocationis saltem large, non strictissime sumendo fallaciam aequivocationis, quando scilicet est fallacia aequivocationis propter hoc, quod aliqua propositio est distinguenda penes aliquem modum fallaciae aequivocationis, sicut dixi in logica tractando de isto modo fallaciae accidentis. Large autem accipiendo fallaciam accidentis vel similitudine potest dici in tali modo arguendi esse fallacia accidentis, propter quod sic arguendo: Iste canis est tuus, iste canis est pater, ergo iste canis est pater tuus, non est proprie fallacia accidentis, sed magis fallacia aequivocationis, licet non strictissime: in quo modo arguendi potest etiam assignari fallacia figurae dictionis. Si vero in tali modo arguendi (in) aliqua praemissarum sit terminus communis poterit ibi esse proprie fallacia accidentis. Unde haec est proprie, quamvis non propriissime, fallacia accidentis: Animal est album, animal est homo, ergo animal est homo albus.

de futuro vel de (modo *lacuna*) sicut in talibus: Sortes fuit puer, Sortes fuit sapiens, ergo Sortes fuit sapiens puer, Sortes est senex, Sortes erit robustus, ergo erit robustus senex, Sortes dubitatur decrepitus esse, Sortes dubitatur esse sansus, ergo Sortes dubitatur esse decrepitus sanus.

Quando autem terminus tertius est terminus communis etiam in propositionibus mere de praesenti et de inesse, fallacia nonumquam fit accidentis, sic arguendo: Aliquod animal est corvus, aliquod album est animal, ergo aliquod animal est corvus albus. Quando autem in tali modo arguendi est fallacia accidentis et quando non, semper vel frequenter potest sciri per hanc regulam: quando ex huiusmodi praemissis in quibus praedicatur aliqua divisim, si determinatio potest syllogistice inferre unum istorum de reliquo tunc potest illa determinatio inferri coniunctim, nisi aequivocatio vel incongruitas locutionis impediat, et ideo hic non est fallacia acci-

autem credat huiusmodi conclusionem sequi propter similitudinem illarum dictionum ad alias dictiones in quibus scit tenere talem modum arguendi, decipitur per fallaciam figurae dictionis. Et in illo casu potest assignari aliqua multiplicitas in fallacia figurae dictionis propter hoc quod unus terminus aliter accipitur in propositione una et in alia, quia tamen nulla oratio una est multiplex, ideo ibi non est aequivocatio nec amphibologia nec compositio nec divisio nec accentus. Unde sciendum est quod si semper quaelibet dictio in tali modo arguendi uniformiter accipiatur non committeretur aliqua fallacia dictarum, immo si servaretur forma syllogistica non ponendo medium terminum in conclusione non esset ibi fallacia accidentis. Sicut hic non est fallacia: Iste canis est tuus, iste canis est pater, igitur aliquis pater est tuus. Similiter nec hic: Iste est albus, iste est monachus, ergo aliquis monachus est albus. *Sed in tali modo*

Si autem propositiones sint de praeterito vel de futuro vel de modo, poterit esse fallacia accidentis sive tertius terminus sit communis sive discretus seu singularis. Unde hic est fallacia accidentis: Sortes fuit albus, Sortes fuit puer, ergo Sortes fuit puer albus, quia si Sortes fuit albus in senectute non in iuventute, praemissae sunt verae et conclusio falsa. Hic etiam est fallacia accidentis: Sortes fuit infans, Sortes fuit infans sapiens. *(there follow discussions of similar fallacies.)*

Responsio autem generalis ad omnia talia sophismata debet esse ista: Aliqua interdum possunt praedicari divisim de aliquibus non variato (termino), quamvis (enim) non praedicentur coniunctim de eo. Sed praeter istam generalem responsionem oportet assignare regulas speciales, quare in diversis casibus non sit necesse... *there follow two rules and long discussions about similar fallacies.*

dentis: Omne animal est corvus, aliquod animal est album, ergo aliquod animal est albus corvus, quia ex praemissis infertur discursus iste: Aliquod album est corvus, quae infertur ex praemissis secundum discursum. Quando autem ex praemissis huiusmodi infertur, ubi praedicatur unum ⬛ istorum dictorum de reliquo, scitur quae de syllogismis tradi debent. Et ita potest cognosci iste modus fallaciae accidentis.

arguendi aliqua dictio accipitur diversimode in diversis propositionibus. Unde in ista: Iste canis est tuus, li tuus significat possessionem; in ista autem: Iste canis est tuus pater, li tuus non significat possessionem sed significat patrem istius hominis; propter quod aliter accipitur in una propositione quam in alia; nulla tamen oratio est multiplex.

The same relation as in the preceding texts prevails in the present texts. It is apparent that *S2* is closer related to *S3* than to *S1*. It also seems clear that the reference in *S2* to the *logica* can be verified only in *S3*, because *S3* assumes that there is in a certain case a *fallacia aequivocationis*, and *S2* has to mitigate that statement which appears too strong to the author. For the rest we abstain from a detailed discussion, since we have adduced the texts only as documentary proofs so that the reader can form his own mind.

It is furthermore interesting that the treatment of the *Fallacia accidentis* in the *Expositio super libros Elenchorum* seems to represent the earliest stage. In order to prove it, we shall add a few excerpts from this earlier work.

Expos. sup. 1. Elench.

Dicto aliqualiter de duobus primis modis fallaciae accidentis quamvis multa in particulari sint omissa . . . dicendum est aliquod de tertio modo, qui est quando ex hoc quod aliqua coniunguntur cum aliquo tertio non variato infertur illa coniungi simul respectu eiusdem tertii non variati. Et penes istum modum peccant tres ultimi paralogismi positi hic a Philosopho. Et distinguitur iste modus a primis duobus, quia in primis accipitur aliquis terminus in praemissis qui non accipitur in conclusione, in isto autem modo quilibet terminus qui accipitur in praemissis accipitur in conclusione, sicut patet in isto paralogismo: Iste canis est pater, iste canis est tuus, igitur iste canis est tuus pater. Et ideo in isto modo non est proprie medium, quia medium non ingreditur conclusionem, et ideo iste modus non est ex variatione medii, quia non habet proprie medium. Tamen quia illud quod est loco medii scilicet ponitur in utraque praemissa in nullo variatur sicut patet intuenti, quia nec secundum se nec secundum suum significatum nec secundum suppositionem nec quocumque modo aliter quam in optimo syllogismo.

... Hic tamen intelligendum quod numquam hoc contingit nisi quando alterum illorum aliter significat quando accipitur divisim et quando accipitur coniunctim, sicut hic: *Iste canis est tuus significat possessionem; quando dicitur sic: Iste canis est tuus, ly tuus non significat possessionem sed aliud.* Sed tunc videretur quod numquam talis modus esset fallacia extra dictionem, sed semper in dictione, quia ad dictionem pertinet significare. Dicendum, quod in isto modo semper coincidunt fallacia accidentis et alia (aliqua?) in dictione; sed propter aliud dicitur fallacia accidentis et fallacia in dictione. Dicitur enim fallacia accidentis propter hoc quod ex hoc quod aliqua sunt unum cum tertio per praedicationem divisam non convenit inferre illa esse unum cum eodem tertio non variato per praedicationem coniunctam; et ex hoc scitur quod ex propositione in qua praedicatur coniunctim de tertio non convenit inferre unum praedicari de tertio, sed est ibi fallacia figurae dictionis propter variationem dictionis in una propositione et in alia ... fol. *131*rb s.

The quotation of fol. *183*rb concerns the *fallacia consequentis.* First we shall present the pertinent texts.

S 1 (fol. *104*rb) III, IV, c. 12	S 2 (fol. *184*rb)	S 3 (fol. *243*r)
Unde sciendum quod quandoque committitur fallacia consequentis arguendo enthymematice et quandoque arguendo ex pluribus propositionibus. Si autem est ex pluribus propositionibus, ad hoc quod sit consequens requiritur quod consequens inferat quamlibet propositionem positam in antecedente et non econverso. Et si arguatur in futura,	Secundus modus principalis istius secundi modi principalis est, quando illa consequentia quae est consequens et non antecedens, sit in aliquo argumento sophistico antecedens, et illa quae vere est antecedens et non consequens sit consequens, id est quando sequitur econtra et non sic. Ista enim propositio: Omnis homo currit, vere est	Secundus modus est, quando illa propositio quae vere est consequens vel per aliquam conditionalem expresse. Secundus modus est, quando illa propositio quae vere est consequens vel per aliquam conditionalem expresse denotatur esse consequens, ponitur loco antecedentis sic: Omnis homo currit, ergo omne animal currit;

semper simul cum hoc erit fallacia accidentis.

consequens et non antecedens ad istam: Omne animal currit, et ista: Omne animal currit, vere est antecedens et consequens. Et ideo, si ista: Omne animal currit, fiat consequens in alia consequentia vel argumento, et ista: Omnis homo currit fiat antecedens, committitur fallacia consequentis penes illum modum. Propter hoc distinguitur iste secundus modus a primo modo istius secundi principalis, quia in priori modo potest committi fallacia consequentis, quamvis nulla propositio accepta sit consequens ad aliam, sicut hic: Si homo est albus, asinus est albus; nullus homo est albus, ergo nullus asinus est albus.

Potest autem adhuc iste modus subdividi quia aut antecedens est una propositio aut plures.

nam sequitur econverso et non sic; idem enim quod est vere consequens, ponitur loco antecedentis. Si domus est, paries est, nulla domus est, ergo nulla paries est. Nam per istam conditionalem: Si domus est, denotatur, quod ista: Nulla domus est, est consequens respectu alterius: Nulla paries est, per istam regulam: Si aliqua conditionalis est bona, oppositum consequentis est antecedens ad oppositum antecedentis. Et ideo quia ista: Nulla domus est, ponitur in antecedente, in praedictis sophisticis, committitur fallacia consequentis, quia in consequentia, qua una propositio infertur ab una consequentia, ponitur loco alterius. Et ideo non sequitur sic, sed econverso . . .

Si[c] plures (sequitur) ad hoc quod sit fallacia consequentis penes istum modum non sufficit, quia conclusio inferat unam tantum praemissarum et non econtra, sed oportet quod inferat utramque praemissarum et non econverso. Et propter hoc non semper est fallacia consequentis penes hunc modum arguendi etiam ex omnibus universalibus affirmativis in secunda figura, sed semper fit fallacia consequentis penes primum modum. Et sic debet intelligi quod dictum est de hoc in logica. Si autem antecedens sit una propositio et non plures, responsio generalis debet esse ista: sequitur econverso et non sic . . .

[c] What follows, in *S2* only.

CONCLUSION

Our study has shown that there are definite ties between the three *Summae*. They at least insinuate that they may be written by the same author, though, of course, they are no proofs of this fact.

There remains the question, whether there are serious contradictions between the three *Summae*. When we first met with the author's explanation of material consequence in *S2* we were almost convinced that at least this doctrine was in disharmony with that in *S1*. After we have given some thought and study to this point we came to the conclusion that there is no real contradiction on this point between *S1, S2* and *S3*, but that they are in agreement. The less clear statement in *S2* and *S3* is probably due to the more elementary and shorter treatment of logic in these latter works. Though we had prepared texts to prove it, we prefer to deal with them in connection with another study that we have prepared on the problem of material implication in Ockham's logic. There we hope to clarify some confusions which stem from the lack of a clear distinction between material and formal consequence and material and formal implication.

Hence, since there is no objection from the part of inner criticism and since exterior evidence is unequivocally in favor of the authorship of Ockham, we are forced to add to the list of Ockham's genuine works two more tracts on Logic: The *Elementarium* or *Tractatus logicae medius* and the *Tractatus logicae minor*.

9. THE RELATIVE DATE OF OCKHAM'S COMMENTARY ON THE SENTENCES*

A study on Ockham coming from the pen of L. Baudry always carries the weight of authority. The present volume is intended as a comprehensive study of Ockham's life and works. A second volume,

---

* Léon Baudry, *Guillaume d'Occam. Sa vie, ses ouvres, ses idées sociales et politiques. Tome I. L'homme et les oeuvres.* ("Etudes de Philosophie Médiévale," Directeur: Etienne Gilson, de l'Académie Française, t. XXXIX) (Paris: Vrin, 1950), 316 pp. [This book review was first published by Fr. Philotheus in FrancStud 11, Commemorative Volume (1951) 305—316.]

yet to be published, will be devoted to the social and political ideas of Ockham. Combining the biographical and bibliographical data at the expense of a clear systematical exposition, Baudry follows Ockham's life step by step, first setting the historical background and milieu in which Ockham lived and the circumstances under which he wrote his works. Then this great pioneer in Ockham research weaves into the biographical account, a discussion of the works of the *Venerabilis Inceptor.* Thus the work falls naturally into three main chapters: Ockham at Oxford (the philosopher and theologian), Ockham at Avignon (the ally of Michael of Cesena), Ockham at Munich (in the service of Louis the Bavarian).

Baudry's account of the life and the works of Ockham understandably contains some *lacunae*, as well as many interesting hypotheses and constructions. Occasionally his explanations, in the opinion of this reviewer, are too ingenious. But even Baudry's errors are usually of such a nature as to provoke a serious re-examination of the data in question, for he seldom advances a theory without some basis in the manuscript tradition with which he shows a rare familiarity. Though the present reviewer does not always agree with this excellent scholar, he has, nevertheless, learned much from him and before starting a discussion of these differences, he would like to make it clear that Baudry's theories are a far cry from that type of fiction with which Ockham literature still abounds.

It will be impossible to do justice to all of Baudry's arguments in this review. Since we hope to take up the question of the text tradition of the works of Ockham on purely philosophical and theological problems in a comprehensive study that will appear in the *Franciscan Studies*, here only a few points will be mentioned, *viz.*, mainly those on which Baudry explicitly disagrees with the present reviewer.

In the list of authentic works of Ockham, Baudry (p. 285) still enumerates under no. XIV, *De quantitate in se. (Munich 276)*. Through our friend Hochstetter, we have received photostats of this manuscript which prove that these two chapters are the same as chapters 44 and 45 of the edition of the *Summa Logicae* part I. Hence it is not a special work of Ockham. Fragments of parts of the *Summa*

Logicae (and for that matter of other works of Ockham) quite frequently appear in manuscripts. Adam Wodham, in consequence, is
not referring to this fragment, when he writes: *"Ockham in libro* 4⁰
sententiarum et in utroque tractatu de quantitate," but he has in mind
the two tracts on the Holy Eucharist.

Under *Ouvrages douteux*, no. v, Baudry lists the *Compendium
logicae (Munich 1060)*, which he suggests, at least, is to be found
also in *Assisi 690*. We have made a thorough study of these two
manuscripts. *Munich 1060* contains an *Elementarium logicae* or a
Tractatus medius; Assisi 690 contains a *Tractatus minor logicae*.
Both are distinct, but related; both are ascribed to Ockham (the
Munich *ms.* is written 1348). We were unable to discover any serious
reason against the authenticity of these two tracts. Hence, we have
to abide by the explicit testimony of the manuscripts. My former
statement that Ockham's purely philosophical and theological writings had been composed before his arrival in Munich, probably needs
a revision, since it is not only possible, but probable, that these two
tracts were composed in Munich.

The main differences between Baudry and the present reviewer
concerning the works of Ockham is the chronological order of the
non-political works. Unfortunately, Baudry had completed his work
and submitted it to the press before he had an opportunity to take
into account the results of our research. He found them important
enough, however, to dicuss them in an appendix, and it is natural
that he tries to defend his main thesis.

Baudry first questions our *proof* for the earlier date of the *Summa
Logicae*. This is rather surprising, since he had abandoned already in
this volume his former opinion that it was written around 1340.
Already before the war, we called attention to the fact that we know
several manuscripts of Ockham written before 1340; furthermore,
that *ms. Erfurt (Amploniana) 0 67* bears a note of a scribe stating
that Burleigh wrote his *De puritate artis logicae*, after the *Summa
Logicae* and that Frater Johannes Nicolai made an abbreviation of
this work of Burleigh when he studied in Paris in 1329. Of course,
this date of an abbreviation of a work that was written after the
Summa Logicae, pushes the terminus *ante quem* of the composition

back to at least 1329, or very probably before 1327. Baudry questions the correctness of the date 1329 as found in the manuscript, since Schum in his description has added a question mark after 1329. Why Schum has done that, we do not know. There is absolutely no correction, nor any erasure, visible, in the manuscript, and the date is very clearly written. Baudry's doubt is, therefore, as far as the document is concerned, entirely unfounded. In this connection Baudry writes incorrectly: *"Comment, écrivant dix ans plus tôt, Jean Nicolas pouvait-il la (date) connaître?"* It was the scribe, and not Joannes Nicolai (!), who wrote in 1339 that Johannes Nicolai made his abbreviation in 1329. How he knew that is quite a futile question to ask, since the scribe is the only one who knew it and he is dead. Let us adhere to the *fides codicum* until we have a serious reason against it.

A more serious point is raised by Baudry concerning the relative chronology of the non-political writings. Against my assertion that Ockham first lectured on the *Sentences*, then started to convert his *Reportatio* of the first book into an *Ordinatio* (which was probably never finished), and that after his start he began to comment on philosophical writings in the following order (with which Baudry agrees) *Expositio super Porphyrium, super Praedicamenta, super Perihermenias, super libros Elenchorum, super libros Physicorum.* According to Baudry all these works have preceded the *Commentary on the Sentences.* In our opinion the reverse is true, or at least it is true that Ockham had lectured on the *Sentences* and had started his *Ordinatio* (the first redaction of the first book on the *Sentences*) and while he was preparing this he started commenting on the philosophical works. If this hypothesis is correct, it follows that the oldest writing of Ockham is the *Reportatio* (certainly the 2nd-4th books are preserved in this state).

In favor of this relative chronology we have advanced two main reasons. The first is based on a development of a certain doctrine from one opposite to the other. As is well known, Ockham has advanced two theories concerning the nature of universals. The one is called the *"Fictum*-theory". According to this a concept or a universal does not have real being, and therefore is not an accident of the soul as its subject, but has only the being of an object of thought, an "esse objectivum", a purely ideal existence. This is called, following St. Augustine (and Abaelard), *"fictum"* (not fiction!). The other theory is called *"Intellectio*-theory", according to which the concept or the universal is a real accident of the soul, identical with the act of understanding *(intellectio)* and hence it exists in the soul as subject, it has an *"esse subiectivum"*.

We take for granted, as commonly agreed upon, that Ockham finally adopted the *"Intellectio*-theory" exclusively. This is proved by the fact that the *"Fictum*-theory" is unequivocally rejected in the *Quodlibeta* and the *Quaestiones super libros Physicorum*, and the *"Intellectio*-theory" professed in the *Summa Logicae* which mentions this as the only probable opinion (the *"Fictum*-theory" is never taken into account). As far as these theories are concerned, the final outcome therefore is clear. It is further agreed that Ockham considers both theories as probable in the Commentaries to philosophical works preceding the three works mentioned before. Hence it is only logical to conclude that Ockham in these works had not yet made up his mind. But, we can still go further. If there is a work in which Ockham does not consider these two theories as probable and not only does not accept the *"Intellectio*-theory", but strongly embraces the *"Fictum*-theory" and rejects the other, then we must concede that such a work belongs to the first period of Ockham's philosophical and theological activity, and that such a work must have been composed prior to those in which he considers both theories at least probable.

Unfortunately Baudry has not made a thorough study of the development of Ockham's theories concerning the nature of universals. It has escaped his attention that Ockham firmly defends the *"Fictum*-theory" in the *Reportatio* (Book 2—4 of the *Sentences*) and that he expressly rejects the *"Intellectio*-theory" or any theory which regards the universal as a quality. The only natural explanation of this fact is that Ockham wrote the *Reportatio* before the other works where he considers the *"Intellectio*-theory" successively as probable, more probable, and finally as the only acceptable view. It has also escaped the attention of Baudry that in the first redaction of the *Ordinatio*, at least up to distinction 18, Ockham knows the *"Fictum*-theory" and develops his doctrine and explanation solely on the basis of this theory. In the second redaction the *"Intellectio* theory" is taken into account and is clearly discernible as an addition to explanations given on the basis of the *"Fictum*-theory". In the Commentaries on philosophical works, both theories are presented, but already a definite preference is given to the *"Intellectio*-theory". As evidence for this view, we may consider the following texts. We read in:

> *Report.* II, q. N: ... absolutum et respectivum dicunt duos conceptus communes Deo et creaturis, qui nec habent esse in Deo nec in creaturis subiective, sed tantum obiective.
> *Report.* II, q. 11 C and E: Quarto dico, quod mensura aliquando immo ut saepius est imperfectior mensurato. Hoc probatur, quia aut mensura habet esse obiective in anima aut extra. Si primo modo, tunc est imperfectior, quia sic est tantum ens rationis, quod est imperfectius ente reali.
> *Report.* II, 12 F: ... et ista unitas est tantum quidam conceptus in anima habens tantum esse obiective et nullo modo subiective ...
> *L.c.* L: Tertio modo dicitur tempus motus imaginatus sive conceptus qui tantum habet esse obiective in anima et nullo modo subiective.

Instructive is *Rep.* II, qq. 14—15, especially MM, where we read:

> Alia autem est abstractio, per quam producit universale sive conceptum rei universalem in esse obiectivo, sicut alias dictum est.

The question arises, of course, where did Ockham speak about this abstraction? He does it definitely in another question of the same book that *follows* questions 14—15, *viz.*, in II, 25 (especially O). He may, however, allude to dist. 2, q. 8 of the first book. But in any case, it can refer only to a passage where the *"Fictum*-theory" was exclusively presented. That is the case in II, q. 25, and that was the case in the first redaction of I, d. 2, q. 8. It is surprising, that Ockham so consistently forgets any other theory but the *"Fictum*-theory" in the *Reportatio*, whilst he is so careful to listen to both theories in the second redaction of the *Ordinatio* and in the Commentaries on philosophical works.

In *Report.* IV, q. 11 E we read:

> Tertio modo accipitur quidditas pro definitione composita ex diversis conceptibus generis et differentiae, et illa quidditas non est idem realiter cum eo cuius est quidditas, quia illa habet solum esse obiectivum in anima et nullo modo subiectivum.

In the light of this it is rather surprising to be informed by Baudry (p. 266, footnote 2):

Le Père Boehner (The *Tractatus de Successivis* ... p. 17), nous dit que dans les trois derniers livres *(the Reportatio!)* Guillaume se refère toujours à la théorie du fictum et qu'il la tient "pour assurée". La première de ces affirmations est juste. Pour s'en convaincre, il suffit de se reporter aux passages suivants: lib. II, q. 1L, M, q. 15 SS, q. 24 O. Mais rien dans ces passages ne permet d'affirmer qu'il tient cette théorie "pour assurée". L'ayant signalée comme probable dans le premier livre, il n'avait pas besoin de revenir sur ce point.

First, let us emphasize the fact that Baudry agrees with us that the *"Intellectio-*theory" is never mentioned in the *Reportatio*. Even if only this much were true, knowing what we do of Ockham's habits, we could not dispose of the fact that the *"Intellectio-*theory" is not mentioned, in such easy fashion as does Baudry.

If it is maintained that the Commentaries to philosophical works have preceded the *Commentary on the Sentences,* and that the *Reportatio* or even the first redaction of the first book on the Sentences admits both theories, then psychologically speaking, it is highly improbable that the constant mention of the two theories in the second redaction of the first book and the philosophical commentaries is suddenly followed by the consistent omission of any mention of the *"Intellectio-*theory" in the *Reportatio*, book II—IV. However, we do not even need to appeal to Ockham's usual habits at all. It is only necessary to read the texts, not only those we quoted above, but also the texts to which Baudry refers. It then will be plainly evident, that Baudry has failed to read these texts carefully. In the first two texts referred to, Ockham says that universals have *only (tantum, solum)* an objective being or ideal existence. Now, "tantum" and "solum" are exclusive terms. Hence, we can only conclude that at this time Ockham rejected all the other theories on the nature of the universals and defended the *"Fictum-*theory" only. But, even if this is considered too much of an interpretation—though Ockham, great logician that he was, would unconditionally accept it—let us look at the other reference adduced by Baudry (II, q. 15 SS). We read:

Ideo dico, quod actio intellectus est realis, quia terminatur ad cognitionem realem intuitivam vel abstractivam modo praedicto. Et quando dicit, quod intellectus agens facit universale in actu, verum est, quia facit quoddam fictum et producit quemdam conceptum in esse obiectivo, qui terminat eius actum, qui tantum habet esse obiective *et nullo modo subiective.*

Here, and in at least three of the texts quoted by us, Ockham definitely and unequivocally states that the universals have no "subjective existence" whatsoever. In other words he rejects any theory which makes of the universals any kind of real being. Hence, Baudry's statement that nothing in these passages allows us to affirm that Ockham takes this *"Fictum-theory"* for granted is contradicted by the texts. Our former statement (quoted by Baudry) was still too mild. We should have said that Ockham not only took the *"Fictum-theory"* for granted but that he rejected any theory according to which the universals or concepts have real being, hence also the *"Intellectio-theory"* (provided he even knew of it at this time). But, whether he had an idea of the *"Intellectio-theory"*, or not, is irrelevant here.

When we now turn to the *Ordinatio*, we arrive at a surprising confirmation of our assumption. It has been known for a long time that there are several redactions of this *Ordinatio*. They are proved by marginal notes discovered by Michalski and found in several manuscripts. We succeeded in showing that there must be still another redaction even after that which is mentioned in the marginal notes. We found one complete text *(Firenze F A 3—801)* and one abbreviation *(Vat. Borg. 68)* which omit many parts of the *Ordinatio* existing in our editions; these texts are manifestly additions. Some manuscripts, and one of the best ones, very often have them on the margin. The striking feature of those additions, in so far as they concern our present problem, is this: they usually follow those passages where Ockham had explained a certain doctrine on the basis of the *"Fictum-theory"*.

Already in the first question of the Prologue we have such a case. In Prol. q. 1, Z we read:

Sciendum tamen, quod notitia abstractiva potest accipi dupliciter. Uno modo, quia est respectu alicuius abstracti a multis singularibus; et sic cognitio abstractiva non est aliud quam cognitio alicuius universalis abstrahibilis a multis, de quo dicetur postea.

8 Boehner, Articles on Ockham

And now follows the addition:

Et si universale sit vera qualitas existens subiective in anima, sicut potest teneri probabiliter . . .

Clearer still is the addition in Prol. q. II, Y:

Totum quod dicitur de praedicatione rei in divinis debet intelligi secundum illam opinionem, quae ponit, quod intellectio non est subiectum nec praedicatum propositionis sed obiectum intellectionis, quam opinionem reputo probabilem. Secundum autem aliam opinionem, quam etiam reputo probabilem, scilicet quod omne subiectum propositionis in mente est intellectio vel aliqua qualitas inhaerens menti, debet dici, quod propositio illa, quam format intellectus de deitate distincte, non componitur ex re sed ex intellectione . . .

It is evident that Ockham first explained his theory about predication concerning divine attributes exclusively according to the *"Fictum-*theory", but later, in a second or a third redaction, for some reason or other he had lost complete confidence in the *"Fictum-*theory", and as the probability of the *"Intellectio-*theory" took shape, he felt compelled to make this addition. This is the only obvious and sound explanation which does not do violence to the facts.

A similar case is found in Prol. q. 3 principalis (sive 7 in ordine) under S. Again such an addition is made after Ockham had explained an idea according to the *"Fictum-*theory". Then he adds a possible explanation on the basis of the *"Intellectio-*theory". We read:

Et istud dicendum, si teneatur, quod conceptus non est intellectio vel cognitio, sed aliquid fictum per actum intelligendi habens tale esse obiectivum quale habet res in esse subiectivo. Secundum autem opinionem quae ponit, quod conceptus praedicabilis de re, non pro se sed pro re, est ipsa intellectio et quod universalia omnia sunt quaedam intellectiones inhaerentes menti, videtur esse dicendum . . .

Again in Prol. q. 5 principalis (sive 9 in ordine) under R we have the addition:

Et hoc secundum opinionem, quae ponit, quod universalia non habent nisi esse obiectivum.

Under U we read:

Secundum opinionem, quae ponit, quod conceptus seu intentio praedicabilis de re pro re est ipsa intellectio, potest dici . . .

Under Y we have the addition:

Vel est actus intelligendi.

Again under AA a long text has been added:

Si autem teneatur opinio, quae ponit, quod praedicabilia sunt intellectiones animae, quae sunt realiter ipsae cognitiones intellectus . . .

The famous *quaestio* of the second distinction in which Ockham deals with the problem of the nature of universals *ex professo* fits perfectly into this picture. We have edited this question and we have nothing to add, except to state that Ockham gave clear preference to the *"Fictum*-theory" when he first composed this question. In the later additions and corrections, recognizable by the fact that they are found in marginal notes and omitted by the first redaction, Ockham changed his opinion so that the *"Fictum*-theory" and the *"Intellectio*-theory" appear to be equally probable. (Cf. our edition in *The New Scholasticism*, XVI [1942] 224—240.)

Now, it is partly this attitude, (*viz.*, that both theories are held to be equally probable) and partly a clear preference for the *"Intellectio*-theory" that we find in the commentaries to the philosophical writings beginning with the *Commentary on Porphyry* to the *Physics*.

Already in the *Expositio super Porphyrium* we read (ad: Sit autem unoquoque . . .):

Tertio notandum, quod aliquid esse in aliquo genere . . . quia species et genera non sunt verae substantiae nec significantur per substantias, immo secundum opinionem, quae ponit quod intentio in anima sive conceptus sunt in anima subiective eo modo quo albedo est in pariete . . . species vere sunt qualitates.

The *"Fictum*-theory" is not even mentioned, though the *"Intellectio*-theory" is not defended. The same is the case in ad: Descendentibus vero . . . (tertio notandum). The same (without mentioning the *"Fictum*-theory") in *Expos. super Praedicamenta*, cap. 9 ad: Secundarum vero substantiarum . . . In *op. cit.* Cap. 12, ad: Ad aliquid vero talia . . . the *"Intellectio*-theory" is not even qualified as an opinion but taken for granted. The same assertion without any qualification in *op. cit* cap. 18 ad: Videtur autem praeter . . .

8*

The famous treatment of our problem in the Prologue to *Perihermenias* we have already edited and needs no further discussion. We have shown (*Traditio*. IV [1946] 315 ff.) that in this text Ockham is already uncertain in mind and no longer gives the *"Fictum* theory"* clear preference. That the *"Intellectio-*theory" occupies the first place appears already in *Periherm.* cap. 5 De oppositis ad: Quoniam autem sunt.... There an explanation is given first according to the *"Intellectio-*theory" and then according to the*" Fictum-*theory".

Let us go now a step further to the *Expositio super libros Elenchorum* in lib. II ad: In illis qui deducunt ... We find again that both opinions are mentioned, but now first the *"Intellectio-*theory" and then the *"Fictum-*theory". Here is the text:

> Et si dicatur quod alterum contradictoriorum est non ens quia utrumque vel est ens reale vel ens rationis. Unde secundum illam opinionem quae ponit quod intentiones animae seu conceptus sunt quaedam qualitates subiective existentes in anima, utrumque contradictoriorum est vere ens secundum aliam opinionem quae ponit quod intentiones seu conceptus reale; animae non habent alicubi nisi esse obiectivum neutrum contradictoriorum est ens reale sed utrumque est ens rationis.

The same situation is encountered in the *Expositio super libros Physicorum.* Here we read in I, ad: Quod autem dividitur ...:

> Dicendum est quod si teneatur opinio quae ponit quod intentio animae est qualitas inhaerens animae. ... Secundum autem illam viam, quae ponit quod universalia non habent esse subiectivum sed tantum esse fictum ...

In the *Summa Logicae,* Ockham presents only the *"Intellectio* theory"* as probable and does not take into account the *"Fictum* theory".* However, he does not defend it either. It is in the *Quodlibeta* and in the *Quaestiones super libros Physicorum* that Ockham squarely rejects the *"Fictum-*theory" and admits only the *"Intellectio-*theory". There is no necessity to adduce any texts to this effect since on this point we are in complete agreement.

Thus we have proved that in the *Reportatio* (books II—IV) of the *Commentary on the Sentences* Ockham defends the*"Fictum-*theory" and flatly rejects the *"Intellectio-*theory". In the second redaction of the *Ordinatio,* or at least in the *Redactio* which has come down to us in most of the manuscripts, the *"Intellectio-*theory" is usually added as another probability. In the Commentaries to logical and physical writings both theories are considered to be more or less on equal grounds, though it is safe to say that the "*Intellectio*-theory" is definitely preferred, since it now always appears in the first place, and sometimes even without mentioning the other. In the *Summa Logicae* only the "*Intellectio*-theory" is mentioned as the probable one, and in the *Quaestiones super libros Physicorum* and the *Quodlibeta* this theory is the only one which is defended whilst the "*Fictum* theory" is definitely rejected. It is hardly just to call this picture of the development a mere theory or an opinion; to our mind it is historically certain.

However, we did not state that we believe the *Summa Logicae* preceded the *Quodlibeta* and the *Quaestiones*. This problem needs a much more thorough investigation.

Our second reason for stating that the *Commentary of the Sentences* has preceded the Commentaries on philosophical writings is based on at least one explicit quotation. We agree with Baudry that vague references, for instance, *sicut alibi dixi*, etc., do not prove much. But before we offer our main quotation let us call attention to the fact that in the *Expositio super Praedicamenta*, cap. *De Relatione*, the following text occurs: "Multa alia possent adduci sicut alibi adduxi ad demonstrandum quod est de intentione Philosophi, quod relatio non est alia res distincta ab omni re absoluta." According to Baudry the only work which preceded this is Ockham's tract on *De indivisibilibus* (and this appears to us to be doubtful; perhaps it is identical with the first part of *De Sacramento Altaris*) and the *Expositio super Porphyrium*. Of course, Ockham does not deal with this problem in the *Expositio super Porphyrium*. But he has a special question on this in the *Ordinatio*, dist. 30, q. 3, where he definitely says "multa" about our problem. The title of the quaestio is: "Utrum de intentione Philosophi fuit ponere quemcumque respectum a parte rei distinctum ab omnibus absolutis et ab omni absoluto." This question is very long.

A decisive quotation, however, is found in *Expositio super libros Elenchorum*. Baudry knew of it. Unfortunately the limited number of manuscripts at his disposal has lead him astray. For at this particular place the only manuscript to which he had access, *viz.*, *ms. Paris, Bibl. Nat. 14731*, is faulty. It reads, fol. 119vb: "Et sic frequenter loquuntur de nominibus connotativis tam super philosophiam quam super sententias." We disagree with Baudry when he says that this text as it reads here makes much sense, certainly not in the context which must have been known to Baudry. The far better reading is certainly that of all the other manuscripts we have checked and which contain this part *(Firenze, Bibl Naz. B. 4*, written in 1331, *Oxford, Bodl. 558, Assisi, 670)*. All of these read:

> Et quia frequenter locutus sum de nominibus connotativis tam super philosophiam quam super sententias, et non est sufficienter dictum de distinctione, ideo ad sciendum . . .

Then follows a long discourse on this distinction. This text is found in at least three manuscripts, all written in the 14th century, one in 1331. Baudry tries to show the improbability of this reading guaranteed by at least three manuscripts; he writes (p. 263):

> Remarquons d'abord que, lu de la sorte (as it is in the three manuscripts), ce texte s'harmonise mal avec l'hypothèse émise par le Père Boehner. Dans cette hypothèse, en effet, Guillaume n'avait rien publié avant de commenter les *Sentences;* dans cette hypothèse encore l'Expositio a fait immédiatement suite à cet ouvrage. Comment Guillaume pouvait-t-il renvoyer à des oeuvres philosophiques, alors que de telles oeuvres n'existaient pas encore?

Baudry knows the manuscript tradition of Ockham's works. He knows as well as we do that there is no work in the manuscripts called *Expositio aurea;* there are only commentaries to Porphyry, to the *Categories*, to *Perihermenias*, and then to *De Sophisticis Elenchis*. Hence Ockham was able to refer to at least three philosophical works. But Ockham does not even say that he is referring to philosophical works, not even that he had published anything; he says only that he has *spoken* about these terms frequently when dealing with or rather lecturing *(super!)* on philosophical works and on the *Sentences*. We believe that we can definitely dismiss this tortuous interpretation.

However, his second objection is of a more serious nature. For a few columns further Ockham definitely refers to the *Commentary on the Sentences* in the future tense. Ockham writes there: "Ista responsio super Metaphysicam et super librum sententiarum diffusius ostendetur." It is to be noted that this reference still occurs in the same discourse as the former dealing with connotative terms. Whilst the former refers to them more in general, the latter refers to a treatment of connotative terms in connection with a special problem, *viz.*, with the *accidentia copulativa et non-copulativa*. This problem Ockham promises to take up more *in extenso* when he comes to an explanation of Aristotle's *Metaphysics* and in the *Commentary on the Sentences.* It is obvious that this will be done in the fourth book of the *Commentary on the Sentences* when dealing with the problem of the accidents in the Holy Eucharist. There was not yet (and never was) a published work on it, but only a *Reportatio*. The meaning of this reference can, therefore, be only that Ockham intends to discuss this problem at length when he will be working on the *Ordinatio* of the fourth book of the *Sentences*. In view of everything that has been said before, we do not believe that any other explanation is even probable. We agree with Baudry that it can hardly be assumed that Ockham was so absent-minded that in the same lecture he stated that he had lectured *(locutus sum)* on the *Sentences*, and that he still intended to lecture on the *Sentences*. However, understood in the sense in which we have explained it, the second does not mean "when we shall lecture", but only that it will be shown *(ostendetur)* in the *Ordinatio* of the *Commentary on the Sentences.*

From all that has been said, we believe that we are entitled to state that Ockham first lectured on the *Sentences*, and only then started with his exposition of philosophical texts. From this it follows that a study of the development of Ockham's thought must not start with the *Expositio aurea* and the other philosophical works, but with the *Reportatio* and the *Ordinatio*'s first redaction.

All the other problems of the chronological order of the non-political writings of Ockham we consider of minor importance. Baudry gives reasons that Ockham first wrote the *Summa Logicae*, then the *Quodlibeta*, and after them the *Quaestiones super libros Physicorum*. He believes that it was written between 1320—1324 (p. 80). We are inclined to hold that the *Summa Logicae* was *completed* probably in Avignon and after 1324, but before 1327, since Francis of Mayronis who became Magister in 1324 is called *Magister Abstractionum*. In any case we agree with Baudry that the *Summa Logicae* was written after the Commentaries.

We are happy to find that Baudry agrees with us in considering the authenticity of the *Centiloquium* as doubtful.

Let us conclude by congratulating this excellent scholar for having accomplished a work on Ockham which no one who attempts any serious research in the philosophy, the theology, or the political doctrine of the *Venerabilis Inceptor* may ignore.

10. THE TEXT TRADITION OF OCKHAM'S ORDINATIO[a]

A. Textual Discussion

There can be no doubt that William Ockham must be ranked amongst the most important Scholastics. His doctrine and his influence may be judged in a negative sense, but his philosophical and theological personality cannot be excluded from even the smallest textbook of the History of Scholasticism which pretends to give at least a general view of Christian thought in the Middle Ages. Every historian, interested in the Philosophy and Theology of the 14th century, is forced to start with or go back to the Venerabilis Inceptor. The necessity, however, of studying the works of Ockham meets with an enormous difficulty. It is not only the more developed scientific culture expressed in a complicated technical language which a modern reader has to master, but it is especially the difficulty of having a text which can be safely used as a sufficiently reliable basis for our research-work. Although we have printed texts of a great deal

---

[a] First published in The New Scholasticism 16 (1942) 203—241; we omitted, however 222—241 (text edition with immediate introduction). A study on the text tradition of the *Reportatio* may be found in the art. *The notitia intuitiva, infra* p. 268—300.

of Ockham's writings,[1] nevertheless, they are neither easy to reach nor in such condition that they present in every case the true teachings of Ockham. In spite of many attempts in recent years to prepare critical editions, practically nothing has been achieved. Even the De Sacramento Altaris, the only modern edition of the non-polemical work of Ockham,[b] does not satisfy the demands of a critical edition, and certainly, did not solve the problem whether this treatise is one work or is composed of two different tracts later united to one work. The older printed editions of the other non-polemical works consequently will remain, for the time being, the basis of our research work.

Our purpose, therefore, in the present study is to ascertain the reliability of the printed text of one work of Ockham viz. the first book of the Commentary on the Sentences. We believe this task a very urgent one, because the first book of the Commentary on the Sentences is the most important theological work of the Venerabilis Inceptor. Its dimensions surpass more than twice those of the three other books taken together, and it discusses the problems with a thoroughness which makes it the most reliable source for Ockham's true ideas. Therefore it must be the basis of any study of the theological and even the philosophical teachings of Ockham. Consequently, the reliability of the printed text of the first book is the most important problem concerning the non-polemical works of Ockham. We will discuss this problem in our present study, and in doing so, we intend to justify a preliminary edition of the first questions of the prologue, of which the first fasciculus was published last year.[2]

---

[1] Of Ockham's non-polemical and authentic works are not printed: Expositio super librum Elenchorum; Expositio super libros Physicorum; Quaestiones in libros Physicorum. The statement in our textbooks and in other publications on Ockham that the Quaestiones in libros Physicorum are printed (even in several editions!) seems to be an error, because no copy has ever been dicovered.

[b] The De Sacramento Altaris of William of Ockham Edited by T. Bruce Birch, Burlington, Iowa, 1930.

[2] Textuum Guilelmi Ockham fasciculus I[us]: Quaestio prima principalis Prologi in primum librum Sententiarum ad fidem codicum restituta a P. Philotheo Boehner, O. F. M., Paderborn, Schöningh [1939]. I made this

The Incunabula-edition of the Commentary on the Sentences of Lyons (1495)[3] has suggested at least the false opinion that all the four books were one work. In reality they have to be distinguished as two different works, the first book being the "Ordinatio Ockham", the three other books being the "Reportatio Ockham".[4]

What is the difference between an Ordinatio and a Reportatio? A Reportatio generally speaking, is a copy of lectures taken by a pupil at school and often worked over later by him or by the teacher: In the latter case it is an authorized Reportatio. An Ordinatio on the contrary, is a text composed for publication by the author himself. Of course, the basis for this Ordinatio are almost always the lectures, but they are worked over, enriched and hence bear less traces of the spoken language. Let us add the explanation of another term which we shall also use viz. Abbreviatio. An Abbreviatio is the text of an Ordinatio or Reportatio shortened by somebody who wanted only the essential parts of the original texts. After these explanations we can proceed to our main problem.

A remark of Michalski, probably taken too literally, but in any case exaggerated, may have, and in fact, has had dangerous consequences for the appreciation of the texts found in the Incunabula-edition. The famous Polish scholar writes: "En ce qui concerne le premier livre, les éditions imprimées ne diffèrent en rien du texte des manuscrits."[5] What does this extraordinarily optimistic expression "en rien" mean? I think we wrong this scholar, who is to be commend-

---

edition in agreement with Dom H. Bascour, O. S. B., of Louvain, who is preparing a critical edition of the first book. I myself am preparing the other three books. [The four books will be edited by E. M. Buytaert.]

[3] The Strassburg-edition of 1486 contains only the first book. As the differences between this and the other edition are only very slight, we shall mean in our discussion by Incunabula-edition always the Lyons-edition.

[4] This was definitely proved by K. Michalski: Le criticisme et le scepticisme dans la Philosophie du XIVe siècle, in: Bull. intern. de l'Acad. Pol.... Classe d'Hist. et de Phil. I. Partie 1925, Cracovie, Impr. de l'Un. 1926, p. 43—45.

[5] Les courants critiques et sceptiques dans la philosophie du XIVe siècle, ... Cracovie 1927, p. 8. Michalski studied the following manuscripts of our list: 1, 3, 4, 8, 10, 11, 12, 13.

ed for his investigations of the fourtheenth century, if we understand his words as meaning that the Incunabula-edition is already a critical editions. We should rather take his words as meaning that there are no important variants between the manuscripts he examined and the edition of 1495, that is, in any case, no longer omissions and additions. Our investigations of the manuscripts examined by Michalski lead us to a less optimistic opinion.

I. The manuscripts examined.

We examined seventeen manuscripts and the two Incunabula-editions, partly in their originals, partly in photostats or microfilms. In the following we shall give a short description of the manuscripts, adding to certain manuscripts sigla and to all a general indication of their value which, of course, will be proved by our discussion later. Furthermore, we will indicate which manuscripts were only partly examined.

1)   Bruxelles, Bibl. Royale 1284 (written 1471 in a poor current hand on paper). Fol. 407: Expliciunt questiones super primo sentenciarum de ordinacione fratris Guillelmi Ockham de Ordine fratrum minorum, scripte et complete Lovanii pro venerabili viro domno et magistro Johanne Grymberch sacre pagine baccalario formato per manus Johannis Pistoris de Herenthals. Anno domini 1471, die quidem martis XXIII septembre.

       After a study of the first question we excluded the text of this manuscript completely, because it is the worst of all.

2) C   Cambridge, Gonville and Caius 285/678 (written in the 14th century in a neat half-current hand on vellum). The manuscript contains only a fragment of the prologue and ends abruptly fol.168v: ... qualis non est theologia respectu credibilium non est evidens ..., that is to say, in the tertia quaestio principalis prologi.

       The text is not too bad.

3) C_1 Cambridge, Gonville and Caius 101/53 (written in the 15th century on vellum in "a small and terrifically contracted hand" — I find this remark of the Catalogue exaggerated) fol. 192: Explicit scriptum Wilhelmi de Hockam super primum sentenciarum.

       We studied only the prologue.

       The Text of this manuscript is not bad and in any case better than C and even better than C_2.

4) C_2 Cambridge, Gonville and Caius 325/525 (written in the late 14th century in a neat and not too contracted current hand on vellum) fol. 183: Explicit scriptum Willelmi de Ocham supra primum sentenciarum.

      We studied only the prologue.

      The text is fair and seems to rank between C and C_1.

5) F   Firenze, Bibl. Naz. A. 3. 801 (written probably in the first half of the 14th century in several very contracted and bad hands on vellum) fol. 132: Explicit scriptum venerabilis doctoris (cancelled by points: doctoris and inceptoris written above) Guilelmi de occham. super primum sentenciarum.

      This manuscript ranks among the best ones and presents the first "redaction".

6 F_1 Firenze, Bibl. Naz. F. 800 (written in the late 14th century in a contracted half-current hand on vellum) fol. 171: Explicit scriptum Wilhelmi de hocham super primum sentenciarum.

      The text is not too good and has some additions not yet found in other manuscripts which certainly are non-authentic.

7) M   München, Staatsbibliothek 52 (written at the end of the 14th century in a neat half-current hand on vellum) fol. 198v: Explicit scriptum Willide Hockam super primum sentenciarum. Deo gracias. The manuscript was discovered bay Fr. Ludger Meier (Cfr. Die Erforschung der Franziskanerscholastik, in: Franz. Studien 18 [1931] 138).

      The text is just fair, but is very interesting because it often unites different traditions and gains in importance by its marginal notes.

8) Ma Paris, Bibl. Mazarine 894 (written in the 14th century in a neatly arranged gothic hand on vellum) fol. 198r: Hic expliciunt questiones super primum librum sentenciarum de ordinacione fratris Guillelmi de Ockam de ordine minorum Oxonie.

      The text seems to be good and is important because it constitutes a different family from FTOb. Most of its marginal notes seem to be non-authentic.

9)   Paris Bibl. Mazarine 962 (written in the early 15th century in a contracted half-current hand on vellum). This manuscript was discovered a few years ago by Glorieux. The first initial is cut out. The text which ends at the d. 30, q. 3: ... possuerunt tales respectus esse res reales ... seems to be good.

      I studied only the first question and had the impression that it is closely related to Ma, but has not the marginal notes of Ma.

10) O Oxford, Merton College 100 (written in the 14th century in a neat but every contracted gothic hand on vellum; the two last pages seem to be rewritten by another hand, likewise the tabula). Explicit hic liber primus ... (the following is erased).
The text is not bad.

11) O₁ Oxford, Merton College 106 (written in the late 14th century in a terrifically contracted and poor hand on vellum).
We studied only the prologue, which revealed a relation to Ob with a deteriorated text.

12) Ob Oxford, Balliol College 299 (written before 1368 according to the catalogue in a very bad and contracted current hand). Explicit scriptum fratris Gilli(?) de Hocham super primum sentenciarum.
The Text ranks among the best, though many homoioteleuta are found.

13) Paris, Bibl. Nat 15 904 (written in the 14th century in a terrifically poor and contracted half-current hand). Explicit primus liber sentenciarum secundum Occham. et sic patent questiones primi libri sentenciarum. amen.
After having received photostats of this manuscript a detailed study of the first questions of the prologue forced me to exclude this text completely. It is one of the worst.

14) Paris, Bibl. Nat. 15 561 (written in a very bad hand of the late 14th century on vellum and paper). Contains on fol. 246 r—249 v schemes and a list of the questions.

15) Troyes 718 (written in the early 14th century in a terrifically contracted half-current hand on vellum). Explicit scriptum fratris Wilelmi a Hocham super primum.
This manuscript ranks with the best ones and often surpasses even F.

16) V Vaticana, Ottob. 2088 (written in the 14th century in a poor half-current hand on vellum).
We studied only the questions of the prologue.
The text is only fair; it is difficult to place it definitely in a certain family.

17) Vaticana, Borgh. 68 (written in the 14th century in a neat half-current hand on vellum).
We studied only the questions of the prologue.
The text is an Abbreviatio but otherwise good.

18) E Editio Lugdunesis (Lyons 1495).

19) Editio Argentina (Strassburg 1486).
Both the editions have a fair text.

Besides these manuscripts there are some others which we did not study; they are:

Assisi, Bibl Com. 199. According to a letter from Fr. Athanasius Ledoux, it is written on paper and vellum in the 14th century and contains the following parts:
  fol. 1—5a: 2 quaestiones prologi (Ockham);
  fol. 6r—86v: quaestiones Petri de Candia;
  fol. 87r—179: quaestiones secundum Ockham.
Basel, Stadtbibliothek A. VI. 22. According to Hochstetter, Studien zur Metaphysik und Erkenntnislehre Wilhelms von Ockham, Berlin 1927, p. 2 this manuscript written in a good hand of the 14th century on paper contains only I. Sent. d. 1, q. 1—4.
Erfurt, Amploniana Q 109. According to Hochstetter l. c., this is an Abbreviatio, and many questions are missing.

Of the manuscript: Padova Bibl. Anton. X. 184 of the 15th century I have no further knowledge; the same is true of the manuscript: Göttingen Theol. 118 of the 14th century. Fr. Ephrem Longpré informed me that the two manuscripts at Giessen seem to be the "Collectorium" of Gabriel Biel (DCCXXXI B. G. XV and DCCCIV B. G. XV).

II. Discussion of the value of the manuscripts in general.

In order to form a general opinion on the value of the different manuscripts and editions, we studied chiefly the first nine questions of the prologue in detail, and extended our research to other parts only for a few more important manuscripts, as is indicated in the list and will become evident from our discussion. For a general evaluation we used three criteria: a long quotation of Scotus in the first question, some critical marginal notes and the agreement or disagreement of the variants.

An excellent criterion for judging the value of manuscripts can be, under certain conditions, a quotation. These conditions are: The author must intend to quote exactly, the quoted text must be known, and finally the quoted text must not be a "locus communis", for instance, it must not be a quotation taken from Aristotle, St. Augustine or other commonly quoted authors. The three conditions are fully realized in one long quotation found in the first question of the prologue. Here (LL), Ockham criticizing some Scotists refers them to their master and quotes a long passage of Scotus (Ox. IV, d. 45, q. 3. n. 17; ed. Vivès t. 20, p. 349). Ockham writes: "Ne autem ista opinio quantum ad notitiam intuitivam sensibilium et aliquorum mere intelligibilium tamquam nova contemnatur, adduco verba Doctoris Subtilis libro 4⁰ distinctione 45ᵃ quaestione 3ᵃ duas praedictas conclusiones expresse ponentis ... dicit sic de verbo ad verbum." Here we find an excellent occasion to compare the text of our manuscripts with the text of Scotus, because we are sure that Ockham not only intends to quote the essential content of that passage of Scotus, but he will carefully and exactly repeat the true words of the Doctor Subtilis.[c] Therefore, two conditions are fulfilled. What about the third condition? In order to procure a sufficiently good text of Scotus, I compared the quotation with the following five manuscripts Assisi Bibl. Com. 137, Erfurt, Amplon. 2⁰ 130, Paris, Bibl. Nat. 3114 and 15854, Worcester Cath. F. 60.

After having secured the text of Scotus, we compared the various manuscripts of Ockham with the common text of the Scotus-manuscript. If we count only the important variants (the transpositions and other unimportant variants as illum, istum, ergo, igitur do not change our result), we can arrange the manuscripts in the following list:

F 3 variants;
ObT 4 variants;
O_1MaM 8—10 variants;
C_1OC_2F 11—15 variants;
CV about 20 variants;
E more than 30 variants.

We do not conclude that this list already gives the exact value of the different manuscripts in general or of every part; the place of the Incunabula-edition is certainly too low. But in any case we found a primary well-founded indication that the best manuscripts probably are FObT.

---

[c] Cfr. the next article in the present volume, 127 ff.

Another excellent criterion for judging the value of the text of manuscripts are critical marginal notes. By critical marginal notes we mean remarks made by the scribe on the margin indicating the condition of the original which he copied. In our case all these critical marginal notes refer to Ockham's original. They appear to be noticed first by Michalski who discovered them in the Oxford and Cambridge manuscripts. We succeeded in finding them in other manuscripts as well. At present we will take into consideration only a certain group found in the Quaestio secunda principalis of the prologue. Other marginal notes and their importance will be discussed later.

The critical marginal notes are the following:

1) Istud scripsit continue cum alio, sed postea cancellavit: Similiter omnis conceptus, sicut habeat alias declarari . . .[6]
Found in FTOb (C$_1$ in the text; Ma has the original composition of Ockham in the text and the corrected text of Ockham in a marginal note without a critical remark).

2) Ante correctionem pro illo: adhuc etc., fuit sic: aut ergo subiectum primum est species . . .
Found only in M.

3) Consequenter scripsit sic nec cancellavit, licet forte cancellare intendit: Quarta conclusio est, quod passiones tales negativae non possunt probari — post scripsit in additionibus, sed totum cancellavit: Quarta conclusio est ista, quod passiones negativae . . .
Found in FTObOO$_1$M (CC$_1$C$_2$V in the text).

4) Hic scripsit primo et post cancellavit illud quod hic sequitur; et tunc illud quod est hic primum, fuit secundum, et secundum tertium, et tertium quartum: Dico primo quod aliqua habet pro medio . . .
Found in FTObM (CC$_1$ in the text).

5) Littera habet secundum quid (instead of propter quid).
That error of Ockham is marked by FM as a marginal note; by OC$_2$ in the text. Ma has secundum quid in the text without any remark.

These marginal notes are obviously made by one and the same scribe; consequently, all the manuscripts which have these marginal notes belong to one family. Therefore, Ma represents another family. Within the family with the critical marginal notes, one group is

---

[6] The entire text of these notes with their variants will be published in our edition, fasc. 2[us]; here we communicate only the remarks of the scribe and the beginning of Ockham's text.

more faithful to the original tradition, viz. FTOb and somehow C_1M. That leads us again to almost the same conclusion that certainly the three first mentioned manuscripts contain a good text.

This conclusion is definitely confirmed, if we take into account the last criterion: the agreement or disagreement of the different manuscripts with the common text of the majority of manuscripts. In my list of variants FTOb have less single variants (i. e. in disagreement with the common text of the majority) than any other text. In this comparison Ma gains in value, and so does the Incunabula-edition, M loses, but neither Ma nor E reaches the value of FTOb. Among these three manuscripts T has sometimes a better text than F and less homoioteleuta; Ob is less valuable than FT because of its many homoioteleuta.

Therefore our general conclusion from this more mechanical procedure is, that FTOb represent the best text-tradition, and these, with the overwhelming majority of all the manuscripts known, belong to one family. This family goes back to one manuscript which was carefully made from the original of Ockham.

But our general conclusion meets some difficulties which arise from a further detailed study of the manuscripts FTObMMa. The clarification of these difficulties will give a more precise evaluation of the mentioned manuscripts.

III. Discussion of single marginal notes and of lacunae in F.

There are certain short critical marginal notes in F which are found, as far as I could verify it, only in F. These marginal notes refer to the lacunae in the original of Ockham or, and that seems to be more probable, in the first official copy made under the supervision of Ockham. The scribe of F or, more probably, the scribe of its original copied very carefully the original of Ockham or the first official copy even as regards its size. Therefore, sometimes it leaves a part of a column blank. If there is nothing left out, the scribe may remark on the margin: hic nihil deficit. Sometimes that remark is not found, and we have a right to conclude that the scribe did not know what the free space in his original meant. But, there are other instances where we are informed of the meaning of the lacunae. In the Dist. 2, q. 4 D (2. col.) we read in the text of F after an explanation of the opinion of Scotus: "quere alias vias in Johanne libro secundo et in metaphysica." Here, a marginal note says: "hic dimisit spacium pro aliis viis." The entire text which is here omitted in F is found in the Incunabula-edition, but also in all the other manuscripts including Ma. Therefore, this part was added later. We have the immediate proof for this in T. This manuscript brings the entire passage partly in the text (first it starts like F: quere, but this word is cancelled), partly on the margin and partly transposed to a wrong place. This proves to one who is acquainted with manuscripts that the addition was in the original of T on the margin. But in which original? In the first original of FTOb etc. or in the original of Ockham? We think it was in both, because Ma has this addition also in the text. This seems to suggest that the addition was made by Ockham himself at a later date and implies at once that Ockham went over his work at least twice.[7] The other possibility of course remains, that somebody else added the text of Scotus in the original of Ockham and in the first official copy. But this is extremely improbable, because Ockham brought his original with him to Avignon, and there he made additions which are not found in any manuscript. That seems to prove that his original did not have any influence on the text tradition after Avignon. Before Avignon (1324—1328) he most probably kept his own original with him at all times.

Unfortunately, other instances do not so clearly fit into the scheme of the first one just discussed, though I believe that they, in the light of later discussions, are no real objection. In the text of F d. 2. q. 6 (9[a] ed. B) we read: quere in Scoto d. 3. et 8 primi libri. A marginal note says: Hic dimisit spacium pro residuo. The "residuum" is found in TOb etc. and in the Incunabula-edition where it covers about two columns; Ma, however, reads (without a marginal

---

[7] The second time at Avignon, which is proved by the testimony of the Commission in charge of his cause. Cfr. J. Koch, „Neue Aktenstücke zu dem gegen Wilhelm Ockham in Avignon geführten Prozeß", in: Rech. de Théol. Anc. et Méd., VII (1935), 195—197. These additions, however, are neither very numerous nor long.

note) like F and omits the text of Scotus. Here, we have to conclude — if my theory is right — that the text was either never in the original of Ockham or was added after the scribe of Ma or its original copied the original of Ockham, or the copyist left it out. This last alternative is very improbable. The same is true of a marginal note in d. 3. q. 5 B.

To this same category belong two lacunae in F. In d. 2 q. 7 (10ª ed. F) after the words: quia necesse esse nihil includit quod non dicit necesse esse vel ratio essendi (exposition of the proof of the existence of God after Scotus) half a column of our edition and TOb-family is left out. F has a lacuna; Ma leaves the text out without a lacuna.

There is another lacuna which is more interesting, because it is able to throw some light on the relation between Ockham and Aureoli. In d. 5. q. 3. (L) at the end of the "dubium tertium", a lacuna is found in F without a critical marginal note (another marginal note in F. says: "op. pe. au.," i. e. opinio Petri Aureoli). Here, more than one column is left out by F and Ma, but in addition to it, the last passage of the text in these two manuscripts differs from all the others. T has the last part of the omitted column again in a marginal note. This shows that the exposition of the opinion of Aureoli was later added and even changed, but not the criticism, which proves that Ockham already knew Aureoli when he wrote the first "redaction" of his Ordinatio; therefore the opinion of some scholars, who think that Ockham's critique on Aureoli implies a second redaction is not well founded, neither in the text-tradition nor by their own reasoning.

Michalski writes:

Am Schluß sei unser Augenmerk noch auf eine Besonderheit im Kommentar Wilhelm Ockhams hingelenkt. Bei Bekämpfung der Ansichten des Petrus Aureoli über die Universalien behauptet der Venerabilis Inceptor, daß er nicht nur diese Frage, sondern das ganze erste Buch seines Kommentars zum Lombarden schon bearbeitet hatte, bevor er das Werk seines französischen Konfraters gelesen habe (Sent. I. d. 27, q. 3). Trotzdem finden wir schon im Prolog seines Kommentars eine ziemlich breit angelegte Polemik gegen die Anschauungen Petrus Aureoli's die Frage betreffend, ob der Theologe wegen seiner öfteren Spekulation über Glaubensgeheimnisse neben der Tugend des Glaubens noch einen anderen Habitus in seiner Seele gewinnen könne. Wenn nun Ockham in der dist. 27 behauptet, daß er das

dort besprochene Problem der Universalien vor Kenntnisnahme des Aure-
olschen Kommentars vollständig bearbeitet hat, so müssen wir schließen,
daß er in den ursprünglichen Text seiner Lectura noch verschiedene Er-
gänzungen hinein getragen hat, da er die Anschauungen Petrus Aureoli's
bereits am Anfang seines Kommentars fast wörtlich angibt, um sie nachher
zu bekämpfen. Es ist also zwischen der ersten Lectio und der letzten Be-
arbeitung eines jeden Buches zu unterscheiden.[8]

This proof is not valid though the conclusion is obviously true,
if taken in the sense, that between the Lectura Prima and the Ordinatio there is a difference. And nobody will doubt it. The real and
serious problem only is, whether we have to admit different "Re-
dactiones" of the Ordinatio itself. Michalski seems to imply it. And
here, too, the conclusion seems to be true, but his proof is not valid.
Michalski did not read carefully enough the text which he used as
basis for his proof; therefore he gave a misleading interpretation of
it. Ockham writes:

> Ista opinio quantum ad conclusionem, pro qua rationes priores sunt
> adductae, videtur mihi falsa. Quia tamen pauca vidi de dictis illius Doctoris
> (i. e. Petri Aureoli) — si enim omnes vices, quibus respexi dicta sua, simul
> congregarentur, non complerent spatium unius diei naturalis — ideo contra
> opinantem istum nolo multum arguere; possem enim leviter ex ignorantia
> dictorum suorum magis contra verba quam contra mentem suam arguere.
> Possent autem contra istam conclusionem adduci aliqua argumenta, quae

---

[8] Michalski, „Die vielfachen Redaktionen einiger Kommentare zu
Petrus Lombardus," in: Miscellanea Ehrle, 1 (1924) 260. We chose this
more cautious text of Michalski and not another in: "Le criticisme et le
scepticisme dans la Philosophie du XIVe siècle." in: Bulletin . . . Cracovie,
1926, p. 43—45. Here, he writes: "Ockham a dû probablement remanier la
rédaction primitive du premier livre sur Lombard, puisqu'il dit lui-même
(Sent. I. d. 27, q. 3) qu'il avait déjà refait presque en entier le premier
livre, avant d'avoir pris connaissance du commentaire d'Auriol, ce qui ne
nous empêche pas de trouver des citations de cet auteur déjà dans le prologue et dans les premiers passages du livre I (Sent. I, d. 1. q. 3). Elle
suffisent par conséquent à prouver, que le premier livre a été remanié par
l'auteur lui-même, de sorte que la forme sous laquelle nous connaissons
l'édition imprimée, ne correspond ni à la rédaction primitive, ni à un
reportatum tiré des leçons." Amann (in Dictionnaire de Théol. Cath. t. 11,
col. 873) apparently refers to this text of Michalski when he writes: "Pour
le commentaire des Sentences, Michalski a montré que le text du premier
livre est une ordinatio, revue par l'auteur."

feci dist. 26ª huius libri de esse cognito. Quam materiam tractavi et fere omnes alias de primo libro, antequam vidi opinionem hic recitatam...(H)...ex quibus responsionibus forte apparebunt aliqua contra mentem dicentis, non tamen sum certus, quia non vidi eum in aliis de illa materia (J). I. d. 27,q. 3.

A careful reader of this quotation will find that Michalski read too much into the text. Ockham does not say that he did not read the work of Aureoli before he completed all the other parts of the first book. On the contrary, he expressly says that he did read some parts of Aureoli's work, and consequently he was able to use them. He further states that as regards the problem under consideration (de illa materia!) he did not see or read other passages in Aureoli which referred to it; finally, he makes the very important statement, that he finished already the dist. 26 (he writes his words in the dist. 27) and almost all the other distinctions (we can take materia et fere omnes alias in this sense), before he became aware of this particular opinion of Aureoli which is refuted by him.

If we bear this careful interpretation in mind, one lacuna in F may be of great importance and probably capable of an explanation. In F, the d. 27 q. 3 only a very small part of the beginning is found: ending with: Si dicatur . . . secundum realem emanationem vel generationem . . . The rest to dist. 29 q. u. inclusive, is left out, a quarter of a column being blank in F without a marginal note. This is the part in which we find the above quoted text of Ockham. I would suggest the following explanation: When Ockham wrote this part, he had already finished all the other parts of the Ordinatio. In other words d. 27, q. 3—d. 29, q, u. are the last questions completed by Ockham, but they were still unfinished or not yet written at all when the official copy was made. In any case, I do not see another more probable explanation of this strange fact. It is, of course, possible that the scribe did not finish his copy, but I must ask, why just here and why just in that part of which Ockham says that he wrote last did the scribe make this peculiar omission? If somebody would suggest that the "Petia" system could explain this lacuna, I have to object, that I have no indication for it, at least not in this part.

Therefore, we agree with Michalski on his statement that Ockham went over his work at least twice, but for entirely different reasons.

IV. Discussion of omissions in F and their significance.

In the light of our theory of a "second redaction" of the first book, we are able to explain other facts, especially omissions in F. These omissions in F (and they occur very often in Ma, too, which was studied by Michalski) are by no means simple homoioteleuta, and cannot be explained by an error of the scribe; neither are they a sign of an Abbreviatio. How, for instance, will we explain why in the first question of the prologue (X, p. 20 ss of our edition) the words: "vel importata per extrema" in their different variations are constantly omitted? The easiest explanation is that they were later added on the margin. That could explain why T, too, at least once has this omission. These are additions of Ockham, because they are found in Ma. But even if they were not found in Ma, I would not hesitate to attribute them to Ockham, because they are guaranteed by T.

Our theory is confirmed by the following omission in F. In Quaestio 2ª prologi we read: Praedicta opinio de unitate . . . (at the end of P). T transposes the text, and Ob has the text here and on the margin, a fact which definitely proves that the passage was a marginal note in the original of T and Ob. Another text (I. c. Q): ista non competunt Deo, is omitted by FMaObV; T transposes it, O$_1$ has it on the margin.

Another instance is more striking. In the Quaestio 3ª (prima incidentalis 2^{ae} principalis M) the text: "Tamen sciendum . . . pro ipsis concretis" is omitted in FMaV; all the other manuscripts like the edition have this text, but T and M have here the marginal note: "Additio". This probably means that the passage was found in a separate copybook of Ockham, because we know that he wrote: in additionibus (see footnote 7).

These instances could be multiplied. We often find texts, sometimes longer ones, sometimes only a few words which are omitted (sometimes by Ma and by V, too) which can be found either in the text or quite frequently in marginal notes of other manuscripts. These additions, taken together, would constitute a considerable part, probably more than 50 pages. These "additions" prove a second "redaction" made by Ockham; but the critique on Aureoli does not prove anything of this kind. A more careful study of these additions will probably reveal that we can distinguish additions of different periods and consequently that Ockham went over his works several times. But this will be the task of a future critical edition.

Though I am not of the opinion that these additions will essentially change the result of a study on Ockham based on the first book of the printed text, nevertheless, they are useful indications for a development in Ockham's doctrine. One instance may illustrate it. Hochstetter (l. c., p. 177), in discussing the problem of a "scientia realis" according to Ockham, is of the opinion that the praedicatio rei de re was first admitted by Ockham and later discarded. The texts which he uses, are not in F; therefore they are later additions and consequently are not in favor of his theory.[9] Other omissions are in favor of another theory of Hochstetter, viz. of texts which refer to the opinion that the concept is something "subiective existens in anima". Ockham, giving a solution to a problem answers first, according to the opinion that the concept is "obiective" existing in the soul, and second, according to the other opinion ("vel secundum aliam opinionem . . ."). The second answer is left out by F except d. 18, q. 1, J; d. 27, q. 2, CC; d. 35, q. 4, E. The omission of the "secunda opinio" is especially important in Quaestio prol. 2ª principalis Y, because T has it on the margin. This fact certainly is in favor of a development of Ockham's doctrine which was suggested by Hochstetter (see our edition of qu. 8 (J. 2).

V. Single critical notes in the text of M.

Although the manuscript Munich 52 is comparatively late, nevertheless, it will be of some importance for a future critical edition. The scribe of M or of its original was an intelligent man and copied not only one text but studied different manuscripts and tried to make some sort of a critical edition, though with little success. Therefore we find sometimes the remark in the text: "alia littera habet sic." Some instances may give an idea of this peculiarity of M. In the second question of the prologue, after having transcribed the

---

[9] The words: "si res possit praedicari" (q. 2ª principal. Y. prol.) were not in the text used by the Magistri at Avignon; cfr. Koch, art. cit., p. 197, 33).

text of the family of FTOb, the scribe adds: "alia littera habet sic: primo videtur falsum . . ." This comparatively long addition is found as text in Ma. Another time we read after an "et": "vel secundum aliam litteram: nisi etiam." These additions often are the text of Ma, but there are many exceptions. Nevertheless, they increase the value of M, although its text is not always good and often worse than E.

VI. The marginal notes of Ma.

Baudry made a careful study of the three last books of the Commentary of the Sentences of Ockham in the manuscript Paris, Mazarine 893.[10] He discovered some remarkable differences between that manuscript and the Incunabula-edition, although in other respects the Mazarine-text approaches the Edition more than any other manuscript known to me. This manuscript, I believe, was written by the same scribe who wrote Ma. Such a relation may be important for a reciprocal appreciation of both manuscripts.

The manuscript Mazarine 893 has the "Additiones" which are found at the end of the Incunabula-edition, and as far as I know, only in this Manuscript. Ma has likewise many additions, but on the margin, and especially on his first pages. The problem arises whether they are authentic or not. After a detailed study of these marginal notes which are sometimes very long, I came to the conclusion that they are non-authentic. I do not think anyone will admit that the following remark could be written by Ockham himself: Hoc quod hic dicit . . . contradicit huic quod dicit in logica sua . . . (a later hand added: non est verum . . .). From this and similar instances of additions which always are written in the same neat gothic hand, we are allowed to conclude that all the other marginal notes which are not supported by any other manuscript, are additions made by some intelligent readers, and they were copied by the scribe of Ma. This of course, presupposes that Ma was transcribed from a copy of Ockham's original, because it seems impossible for many reasons to believe that these instances against Ockham could be written by Ockham himself or somebody else on his original. Nevertheless, the

---

[10] Sur trois manuscrits Occamistes, in: Archives d'Hist. Doctr. et Litt. du M. A., Paris, Vrin, 1936, p. 157—162.

value of Ma remains as the main representative of a family different from the FTOb-family.

There are, of course, many other points which deserve discussing. But I hope that we succeeded in proving or making probable our theory regarding the value of the different manuscripts of the first book of Ockham's Commentary on the Sentences, viz.: there are to be distinguished at least two families, and within the family of FTOb we can call F an earlier state of the Ordinatio than TOb. The Incunabula-edition has not the value which Michalski's statement about it could have given it. In another sense, however, it is true that, for the time being, the Incunabula-edition of the first book is a fairly safe basis for our research-work, if one tries to study the doctrine of the Venerabilis Inceptor as a whole or if one does not forget to base his results on more than one passage.

New discoveries concerning the doctrine of Ockham can hardly be expected from a future critical edition of this first book. Such an edition, however, will have another effect, viz. a revision of the exposition of Ockham's doctrine in our textbooks and of many articles written by incompetent students. If one is not able to grasp the meaning of Ockham's conceptualism and his criticism (not scepticism — this disease certainly is in Holkot) and his serious endeavour to find a new solution for Christian philosophy in a new situation, a solution which satisfied him and others, and even Saints, he may take our advice and leave the Venerabilis Inceptor alone.

B. Edition of Quaestio 8^a Dist. 2^{ae} of Ockham's Ordinatio

[We omit here this edition, and its immediate introduction; cfr. The New Scholasticism 16 (1942) 222—241.]

11. THE CRITICAL VALUE OF THE QUOTATIONS OF SCOTUS' WORKS FOUND IN OCKHAM'S WRITINGS[a]

Comment to: *La valeur critique des citations des oeuvres de Jean Duns Scot*, by Charles Balic, O.F.M., in *Mélanges Auguste Pelzer*, Louvain, 1941, pp. 531—556.

[a] First published in FrancStud 8 (1948) 192—201.

Father Balic, the well-known prefect of the Scotus Commission in Rome, has devoted a special study to the problem of the critical value of quotations of works of Scotus encountered in the writings of other scholastics. The discussion centers mainly on three questions: 1. whether such quotations can serve as a secure basis in order to establish the original text of Scotus, 2. whether they help to fix the date of certain writings of Scotus, 3. whether they may be of assistance in solving the problem of the authenticity of certain works attributed to Scotus. Father Balic has confined his study exclusively to those scholastics who seem to be more significative in this regard. They are: Hervaeus Natalis, Thomas of Sutton, Robert of Cowton, William of Nottingham, John of Reading, William Ockham,[1] William of Alnwick and John Rodington. His main interest is focussed on Scotus' *Ordinatio* and the various *Reportationes* of the Doctor Subtilis, the other writings of Scotus being treated only incidentally.

The general conclusion as regards the first problem is stated as follows:

> Les citations de l'*Ordinatio* de Duns Scot ne nous aident donc point à en connaître et à en fixer le texte original: exception faite cependant pour certaines affirmations où on dit, par exemple, qu'il a changé d'opinion, qu'il a changé tel ou tel mot... (p. 553).

We understand the author to mean by this that quotations are of no help whatsoever in re-establishing the original text, unless they indicate changes made by Scotus himself.

Concerning the second and third problem, the author is more optimistic. He summarizes his position in the following statement:

> Cependant, si les citations ne peuvent en général nous guider dans l'établissement du texte original, elles peuvent être très précieuses pour le critique ayant en vue l'authenticité des textes scolastiques, leur autorité, leur succession chronologique, etc. (p. 555).

The author points especially to Scotus' *Reportatio examinata*, the *Lectura* of Oxford, *De Primo Rerum Principio*, *De Theorematibus*, *Additiones Magnae*, to show the importance of such quotations.

---

[1] We prefer to call Ockham "William Ockham" and not "William *of* Ockham", since many of the oldest manuscripts do so, as likewise Pope John XXII in official documents.

Since all of them are attributed to *Joannes Scotus*, already by authors of the first half of the 14th century, their authenticity is thus confirmed and hence they will find a place in the critical edition now being prepared.

In this connection it will be of special interest to our readers to learn that Balic places the authenticity of *De Primo Rerum Principio* and *De Theorematibus* on the same level as the *Summa Theologica* of Alexander of Hales. That means the two works are authentic in this sense, that Scotus had the will to produce these works; that he has had the idea of them and has conceived their plan and indicated the material to be used (qui a voulu l'oeuvre, en a eu l'idée, en a conçu le plan et indiqué la matière p. 556). For the rest, it is immaterial whether the style is different and the whole execution of the work not completely in line with the manner of the "author" himself. If this be so, then we may legitimately ask whether Balic wishes to admit that such a work of an "author" may even contradict his certainly and absolutely genuine works. Since he cites the case of the *Summa Halensis*, it appears he is willing to go even this far. For he also gives the prudent advice which we ourselves wish to emphasize:

Tâchons de ne pas confondre *Ordinatio* et *Reportationes,* de distinguer dans un texte écrit la part vraiment sienne de celle qui revient aux collaborateurs et fut rédigée par eux sous sa direction ou selon son programme (p. 556).

We gather from this: A student of Scotus who uses the "less authentic" works as *De Primo Rerum Principio* and *De Theorematibus* will not be safe from criticism, if he cannot substantiate his findings in these writings with the "authentically authentic" works of Scotus. This is tantamount practically excluding *De Primo Rerum Principio* and *De Theorematibus* from serious studies on *Scotus'* doctrine, at least in the sense, that they cannot be used as primary sources. Or to put it in another way, the debate about the authenticity of these works as such is futile; the only fit subject of dispute would be the meaning of the particular doctrines expounded in these works.

Ockham is awarded special consideration by Balic, because he claims to quote Scotus literally (p.540). We shall confine the remainder of our comments to Fr. Balic's treatment of Ockham.

Several times we have pointed at the importance of the *Venerabilis Inceptor* as a secondary source of clarifying the original text of Scotus.[b] Unfortunately, it seems that the war conditions prevented the author from reading our publications, though one was published in Europe in 1939. Had Fr. Balic known of them, we are sure he would have been more cautious in his criticism, particularly since we had already published a critical revision of the very text Fr. Balic quotes as an instance of Ockham's inaccurate citation of Scotus.[c]

Ockham does not always pretend to quote faithfully according to modern standards, that is, literally. Yet, we have found, that he is usually quite faithful and makes little or no changes. Of course, he leaves out texts which are not to the point, and adds words to link up texts. But, there is one instance where Ockham has not only quoted Scotus, as he usually does, but states expressly that he will quote him literally, or, as he puts it, *de verbo ad verbum*. It was this lengthy quotation (in our edition, Paderborn, Schöningh, 1939, p. 32—34), which we used to evaluate the various manuscripts of the *Ordinatio* of Ockham [cf. note c] by confronting it with the better manuscripts of the *Ordinatio* of Scotus. It so happened, that Balic has made the same comparison of a certain common text of Scotus established on the basis of a few good manuscripts (we both used the Scotus mss. of Erfurt, Assisi, and Worcester; in addition we each used a few different ones). Whilst Balic compared the common text of Scotus with the Incunabula-edition of Ockham and *one* manuscript of Ockham (Vatic. Ottoboni 2088), we compared the common text of Scotus with 12 mss. of Ockham's *Ordinatio*. To anyone acquainted with the manuscript tradition of scholastic works, this will explain the difference in our results. The meager result of Balic's comparison is this: If we place the common text of Scotus alongside the text of the Incunabula-edition of Ockham, more than thirty variants appear. (We had made the same discovery). If we compare it with the Ockham ms. of the Vatican Library, the "number of divergences is sensibly diminished" (p. 450). Our result was, of

---

[b] E. g. in FrancStud 6 (1946) 100—101. Cf. especially *supra*, p. 110 ff.

[c] Guillelmi Ockham *Quaestio prima principalis Prologi in Primum Librum Sententiarum* (Paderborn 1939) 32—34.

course, more graded. We found that there is one group of Ockham manuscripts, and to it belongs the Vatican ms., which shows about twenty variants. Another group, which shows a somewhat intermediary position, has about ten variants. A third group, which represents the best texts, has at most *five variants of any importance.* Now, to show not more than five variants in such a long text is not a bad recommendation at all for Ockham's faithfulness in quoting Scotus *de verbo ad verbum.* It remains true, of course, that Ockham quoted that manuscript of Scotus' *Ordinatio,* which was available at Oxford. But we dare say that it was not too bad a one, for it must have been a manuscript of the very early 14th century, and certainly was written before 1315. To substantiate our statements, we shall edit at the end of this article Ockham's text as it will appear in the critical edition at present in preparation.[d] To this we shall add the variants of the Assisi ms., which is the only one at our present disposal, as our former notes are lost.

By these remarks we do not, of course, intend to imply that a large number of critically established texts of Scotus may be gleaned from a critical edition of Ockham's *Ordinatio.* Balic rightly defends the need of basing a critical edition on the *Fides Codicum.* However, we know from our own experience that sometimes very important texts cannot be re-established merely on the basis of the manuscripts. The editor who slavishly follows manuscripts alone is trusting a purely mechanical device, and will invariably perpetuate mistakes. If, for instance, an equal number of good manuscripts yield different, or even contradictory texts, we must have recourse to criteria other than the manuscripts themselves contain. Among such criteria are literal quotations by later writers, especially, if they lived close to the time of the author. For there is a great chance, or at least a better chance, that such writers understood the original thought of the text quoted better than we do. We mention this, not because we believe that the editors of Duns Scotus are not aware of it, but because we are under the impression that their emphasis on the *Fides Codicum*

---

[d] The Editor of the present volume will edit, God willing, the *Ordinatio* of Ockham. He does not claim that his text will entirely correspond to the one published here.

could be misunderstood. The manuscripts or the *Fides Codicum* must have the first word, but not always the last word. Otherwise, we would have to go so far as to re-establish the original text of the author with all its *lapsus calami* and *lapsus linguae*, or even of the errors caused by the scribe's failure to catch the dictation of the author. We have noticed such *lapsus linguae* or *calami* in the *Ordinatio* of Ockham. More than once certain manuscripts will add the remark: *Littera habet sic*, and then follows an erroneously written word, which was previously corrected. To illustrate: In speaking of the *demonstratio propter quid*, Ockham had at one place in his original copy, the words "secundum quid". Some manuscripts have here: *Secundum quid*, which is wrong, others have: *propter quid*, which is obviously right, but was not in Ockham's own copy. A third group has: *propter quid*, but adds either in the text or on the margin: *littera habet: secundum quid*. Should we put this error *"secundum quid"* in the final critical edition? I think common sense and charity would not allow it. Such a change, however, should be noted in a footnote.

Again, we do not think that the editors of the Scotus-works think differently. But in order to fret out some of these errors, quotations can be of considerable help.

This leads us to consider another reason [given] by Balic against the faithfulness of the quotations found in Ockham. According to Balic, an early Scotist, John of Rodington, has blamed Ockham for being inexat in his quotation of Scotus.[2] Admitting that John's remark carries some weight, we must take this testimony *cum grano salis*. In order to evaluate it properly, we went through the tedious work of checking everything that we possibly could. Refuting an allegation from Scotus made by Ockham, John states:

> Ad illud — sic ait — 'in substantiis non est abstractio nisi a suppositis propriae naturae', dico quod libri correcti habent sic: 'in substantiis non est communiter abstractio, etc.'

Unfortunately, Balic has given references neither to Scotus nor to Ockham. We finally succeeded in locating the texts in Scotus and

---

[2] Cfr. p. 540 [of Mélanges Auguste Pelzer], and De critica textuali Scholasticorum scriptis accomodata, in *Antonianum* 20 (1945) 277.

Ockham, and are convinced that John of Rodington refers to this passage in Ockham:

Praeterae, quod dicit (viz. Scotus) quod in substantiis non est abstractio nisi a suppositis propriae naturae . . . (Ordinatio, d. 5, q. 1, G).

However, this is not the text, where Ockham quotes Scotus in the strict sense, since Ockham merely summarizes here the literal quotation of Scotus which he has cited at the outset of his discussion. In D (of the Lyon edition) on the same question we read the fuller quotation:

Maior declaratur: In substantiis est tantum una abstractio, scilicet quidditatis a supposito propriae naturae, quia substantiae non sunt natae concernere aliquid alterius naturae . . .

The Codex Assisiensis of the Oxoniense of Scotus reads here as follows:

Huius syllogismi maiorem declaro sic: In substantiis (here follows a long passage, with the sign on the margin: Sco. extra, and which corresponds to the *additio* in the Garcia-edition, p. 506) tantum est abstractio a supposito propriae naturae communiter, quia non sunt natae concernere aliquid alterius naturae . . .

Now, the first redaction of the Ordinatio of Ockham, preserved in the ms. Firenze Bibl. Naz. A. 3. 801, reads as follows:

Maior declaratur: In substantiis est tantum una abstractio, scilicet communiter, a supposito propriae naturae, qui . . . etc. as in the edition.

It is true, the "communiter" in the Firenze ms. is written so that with some good will "quidditatis" can be read also, and that may explain, why the other manuscripts of Ockham have the reading "quidditatis". However, it is also possible that because of the close resemblance of the "q" and "con" and the endings "tis" and "ter" there may be a confusion already in the manuscripts of Scotus. In any case, the addition which according to John of Rodington was in the "corrected" text of Scotus, is or has its equivalent in the text of Ockham.

Let us now draw the conclusion from this discussion: John of Rodington did not quote Ockham correctly, *sicut patet intuenti*. Instead of quoting Ockham's quotation of Scotus, he quotes a short reference to that quotation. Furthermore, we can maintain with a high degree of probability that Ockham quoted the "corrected" text of Scotus, which John seems to deny, and that Ockham understood it even as an addition, as the expression "scilicet" indicates. Therefore, the criticism of John of Rodington, if he really intended his remark as a criticism, which we doubt, loses its weight. And consequently, Balic's argument likewise. As Balic rightly emphasizes, however, it remains correct to say that Ockham's quotations are only a witness of the manuscript which he used.

We have found it necessary to eliminate the unwarranted suspicion cast by Balic on the trustworthiness of Ockham's citations of Scotus, not merely because we regard it as unfounded, but principally to justify our publication of some of these quotations in recent issues of *Franciscan Studies* (*Scotus' Teachings According to Ockham*, Franc Stud 6 [1946] 100—107, 362—375; note, however, the mis-print on p. 102 in the reference to the Ordinatio of Ockham: read "d. 2, q. 9 in ordine" instead of "d. 2, q. 3 in ordine"). For we had previously asserted that Ockham is in the main very reliable when he quotes Scotus [*ibid.* 100], and we feel it our duty to substantiate our contention in view of the statements of Father Balic to the contrary. Not that we would dream of maintaining that the texts we have so far published should be considered as critically established texts of Scotus. But we do insist that these quotations of Ockham represent a very early text tradition.[e]

In view of Father Balic's critical remarks which first appeared in the *Antonianum* [cf. note 2], we were hesitant about continuing our publication of such quotations. Now that he has revealed the

---

[e] On this occasion the Editor of the present volume wants to express his regret that the Scotus Commission did not check the quotations of Aureoli. Aureoli's *Scriptum* or *Ordinatio* was certainly finished in 1316, and a manuscript of this work from 1316—1317 is still in existence. This manuscript, and the redaction of the work contained in it, are much closer to Scotus, at least chronologically, than the Assisi manuscript of the new Scotus Edition. We noticed already one important difference between Aureoli and the Assisi manuscript: in the first question of the First Distinction Aureoli quotes at length texts which, according to the Assisi manuscript, were deleted by Scotus; cfr. our edit. vol. I 342—345, with references to the new edition of Scotus on p. 345.

reasons for his misgivings, we see that they are not valid and are convinced all the more of the usefulness of publishing Ockham's citations of Scotus.

In this connection we add the text referred to previously where Ockham claims to quote Scotus literally. Our text is established critically on the basis of all the manuscripts (16) of the *Ordinatio* of Ockham that are known to us [1948]. It is the text of the critical edition being prepared at the Franciscan Institute, with the cooperation of various scholars, especially of Dom Bascour, O.S.B. [cf. *supra*, p. 26], the first volume of which we hope will soon appear in print. In order that the reader may be able to compare this text with the text of Scotus, we shall add the variants of the Assisi manuscript [Commun. 137] of Scotus' *Ordinatio*, omitting only the very unimportant ones, such as transpositions, or *iste* for *ille*, *ergo* for *igitur*, or vice versa.

APPENDIX

Ockham, Ordinatio Q. 1 Prologi, KK-LL

Ne autem ista opinio quantum ad notitiam intuitivam sensibilium te aliquorum mere intelligibilium tanquam nova contemnatur, adduco verba Doctoris Subtilis libro quarto, distinctione 45ᵃ, quaestione 3ᵃ duas praedictas conclusiones expresse ponentis, videlicet quod intellectus noster intuitive cognoscit sensibilia et quod intuitive cognoscit aliqua mere intelligibilia. Unde concedens quod pars intellectiva habet actum recordandi proprie dictum, et per consequens quod intuitive cognoscit actum cuius postea recordatur tanquam obiecti proximi, dicit sic de verbo ad verbum.

"Dico igitur ad istum articulum, quod in intellectiva est memoria et actus recordandi proprie dictus. Supposito enim quod intellectus non tantum cognoscat universalia, quod quidem verum est de intellectione abstractiva, de qua loquitur Philosophus, quia sola illa est scientifica, sed etiam intuitive cognoscit illa quae sensus cognoscit, quia perfectior et superior cognoscitiva in eodem cognoscit illud quod inferior, et etiam quod cognoscat sensationes — et utrumque probatur per hoc quod cognoscit propositiones contingenter veras et ex eis syllogizat; formare autem[1] propositiones et syllogizare proprium est intellectui; illarum autem veritas est de obiectis ut intuitive cognitis, sub ratione scilicet existentiae suae[2], sub qua cognoscuntur a sensu — sequitur quod in intellectu possunt inveniri

---

[1] *om.* A.   [2] *om.* A.

omnes conditiones prius dictae pertinentes ad recordari. Potest enim percipere tempus et habere actum post tempus et sic de caeteris. Et potest breviter recordari cuiuscumque obiecti, cuius potest ipsa[3] memoria sensitiva recordari, quia potest illum actum qui est proximum obiectum intuitive cognoscere quando est et ita recordari postquam fuit. Potest etiam recordari multorum proximorum obiectorum, quorum non potest sensitiva recordari, utpote[4] intellectionis praeteritae et volitionis. Quod enim talium recordetur homo, probatur: quia alia non posset poenitere de malis volitionibus nec etiam praeteritam intellectionem ut praeteritam conferre ad futuram, nec per consequens ex eo quod ista speculatus est ordinare se ad speculandum alia sequentia ex istis. Et breviter destruimur[5] multipliciter[6], si intellectionum et volitionum non recordamur. Illarum autem non potest aliquis sensus recordari, quia non cadunt sub obiecto alicuius sensus. Ergo ista recordatio est propria intellectui et hoc ratione obiecti proximi. Est et[7] alia propria non solum ratione obiecti proximi sed remoti, ut est[8] recordatio quae tendit in necessarium ut necessarium ut in obiectum remotum, cuiusmodi est recordatio habens pro obiecto remoto triangulum habere tres. Nam obiectum proximum recordationis, scilicet actus tendens in tale obiectum non potest esse nisi actus partis intellectivae. Sic igitur patet, quod aliqua recordatio est propria intellectui ex ratione utriusque obiecti[9], scilicet tam proximi quam remoti. Aliqua etiam in ratione obiecti proximi est ita propria quod non posset competere sensui. Aliqua autem[10] ex ratione obiecti proximi competit intellectui, tamen potest competere sensui, utpote si intellectus intuitive intellexit me videre album, et postea intellectus intelligit vel recordatur me vidisse album. Hic quidem[11] obiectum proximum et remotum posset esse obiectum recordationis intellectivae et est, quandocumque collatio fit ex tali recordatione per discursum ad aliud syllogistice concludendum. Alicuius tamen sensitivae, utpote supremae, sensatio praeterita non potest esse obiectum proximum nisi tantum recordationis intellectivae, ut tactum est in articulo praecedenti. Nulla tamen recordatio pertinet ad intellectum inquantum praecise abstractive intelligens".

12. A RECENT PRESENTATION OF OCKHAM'S PHILOSOPHY[a]

De Wulf's *Histoire de la Philosophie Médiévale* belongs to the standard histories of medieval philosophy. More personal than Geyer's work, *Die Patristische und Scholastische Zeit*, it runs the risk of being

[3] *om.* A.   [4] omnis *add.* A   [5] destruuntur A
[6] *om.* A.   [7] etiam A   [8] ut est]utpote A.
[9] actus *add.* A   [10] *om.* A.   [11] et *add.* A.

[a] First published in FrancStud 9 (1949) 443—456.

more subjective as well. Whilst Geyer carefully collects the results of the latest studies in the particular fields, De Wulf apparently aims at a more rounded picture of the philosophers under consideration. In such a synthesis, however, there is a greater danger of being led by preconceived ideas or the consistency of an imaginary system and in consequence arriving at a subjective interpretation. We still believe that history should first ascertain facts, and it should attempt to reconstruct a "system", if there is any, only after a thorough acquaintance with the sources. We also believe that history should be absolutely impartial. We do not deny that history has also the task of judging; but its judgment must be guided by something more important and more objective than the personal convictions of the historian. And above all, the historian should with due regard to human frailty always be ready to understand the thought of a philosopher in the better and more intelligible sense, whenever his statements permit it. Scotus promulgated this golden rule of interpretating texts and judging about them when he said: *Ex dictis eorum volo rationabiliorem intellectum accipere quem possum* (*Ox.* I, d. 8, q. 5, n. 8). We are convinced and intend to prove that such sound rules of historical research have not been observed in De Wulf's treatment of the philosophy of Ockham.

We were reluctant at first to make an issue of this, especially since the man whose work we are to criticize, is justly regarded a pioneer in the field of the history of medieval philosophy. We were even more hesitant of censuring his work on learning of the death of this great historian. But can we strictly adhere to the rule of charity, *De mortuis nil nisi bene*, if a dead man's work still lives and perpetuates what are clearly errors and misunderstandings manifest to those who went through the tedious labor of checking his work against the historical facts? We believe, we can adhere to the rule, if we separate the person from his work, and avoid setting one personal conviction against the other. With this understanding, we shall in spite of our original hesitation undertake, at the request of several friends, an objective criticism of De Wulf's presentation of Ockham's philosophy. And while we shall have to point out almost incredible errors, still it is only these errors we wish to expose, not the man, whom we admire

10*

and to whom we are indebted. For that reason we shall not refer to De Wulf in the following pages, but only to the *Histoire*. Our criterion will be the evidence of the texts.

Ockham's philosophy is treated on pp. 27—51 of the third volume of the *Histoire de la Philosophie Médiévale*, published in 1947. We shall read one paragraph after another, indicating each by its number in the *Histoire* and then shall offer our comment.

Nr. 377 deals with the life of Ockham and his works. This part, as is acknowledged, was rewritten partly by making use of our own research. There is one sentence, however, which in the face of the sources is hardly admissable.

Quand Louis de Bavière voulut légitimer le marriage adulterin de son fils, contrairement aux lois de l'Eglise, Guillaume défendit l'omnipotence de l'Etat en matière politique (p. 29).

It will be very difficult or rather impossible to prove this sweeping statement on the basis of Ockham's text itself in the work that he has written about this matrimonial cause. We shall refer to it in the edition of H. S. Offler (*Guillelmi de Ockham, Opera Politica*, Manchester 1940). Ockham discusses this individual case under the assumption that the marriage under question is not valid (cfr. p. 281, 24—27) — an assumption which was later confirmed by the Church in 1349. He further maintains that the emperor has no jurisdiction as to the purely spiritual and sacramental character of a marriage case.

In specie autem de sacramento matrimonii ... dicitur quod ad imperatorem inquantum solummodo imperator, eo quod pluries existit infidelis, causa matrimonialis quantum ad illa quae specialiter ultra legem naturae et ius gentium et leges civiles sunt in scripturis sacris prohibita vel praecepta, minime spectant (p. 282—283, n. 30—2); cfr. almost the same words a little further, p. 283, 9—13).

Matrimonial cases amongst infidels have to be decided by the Emperor as successor of the old Roman emperors. For the rest, Ockham seems to admit that the Emperor has the right to interfere, though Ockham is not fully decided in his answers, since he is constantly giving alternatives. In any case, Ockham declares that the marriage under question can be declared to be annulled by the emperor, since it is proven that no true marriage exists. The emperor can do this either because he has this power as successor of the Roman emperors, or because he has the right to use *epikeia* (p. 282, 1), owing to urgent necessity and the impossibility of recourse to the Pope.

This is all that remains of the alleged omnipotence of the state according to Ockham.

In the same number on p. 30 we read: "Dans la seconde partie de sa carrière, Guillaume mène campagne contre le Pape, dont il conteste les droits temporels et la suprématie politique." It is true that Ockham has denied the political supremacy of the Pope, which, after all, is correct teaching. However, Ockham has never denied the temporal rights of the Pope, on the contrary, he believes that a Pope, by the fact that he is instituted the Supreme Pontiff, is free and subject to no secular jurisdiction (cfr. *Dialogus*, pars III, tract. I, lib. 1, c. 17; and *Octo quaestiones . . .*, q. 3, c. 3; ed. Sikes, p. 105).

Nr. 378. We read: "Duns Scot est son principale adversaire . . ." (p. 30). The statement that Scotus was the main adversary for Ockham can be correctly or incorrectly construed. It is true that none of the great scholastics has been more criticized by Ockham than Scotus. One has but to read the Venerable Inceptor's writings in order to find overwhelming evidence for it, so much, indeed, that a fruitful study of Ockham requires constant use of Scotus's works as well. However, if the statement means that Ockham is always in opposition to Scotus, it is definitely exaggerated. Ockham admires Scotus and he has learned much from him, in spite of his differences. We could say that Ockham has developed his own philosophy and theology in constant critical discussion with Scotus. He has performed a true "crisis", a discrimination, discarding many Scotistic doctrines, but also retaining an equal if not a greater number of them.

In this connection we would like to expose the peculiar manner in which the *Histoire* distorts quotations from Ockham's works. We read on p. 32:

Réalisme outré . . ., réalisme modéré . . . et surtout formalisme des scotistes . . . sont tour à tour déclarés absurdes, remplis de contradictions, impensables: *falsa, absurda, irrationalis* (*Logica*, I, c. 16).

Here we have an express reference to the sixteenth chapter of the first part of Ockham's *Summa Logicae*. In this chapter Ockham only rejects the formal distinction of Scotus in regard to the problem of universals. The only text which substantiates one third of the alleged quotation is this: "Sed haec opinio videtur esse irrationabilis." We suspect that the rest was taken from Ockham's criticism in the *Ordinatio*, but, to be sure, not of Scotus, but of the others, for in d. 2, q. 6 where Ockham criticizes Scotus by naming him neither the term "absurd", nor "irrational" occurs. In fact, it does not even occur in the chapter of the *Summa Logicae* quoted by the *Histoire;* for the *fides codicum* testifies that instead of *irrationalis* or rather *irrationabilis* Ockham wrote: *omnino improbabilis*.

In Nr. 379. On pp. 31—32 we are informed about the terrible individualism and pluralism of the Venerable Inceptor. We read:

Individualisme et pluralisme renforcés: telle est la thèse fondamentale et elle est énoncée à satiété. Tout être est individuel par tout ce qu'il est. Etant d'une pièce, farouchement isolé, et réellement distinct de tout autre, il ne contient rien qui soit semblable ou commun entre lui et quelque autre individu. L'universel n'existe donc à aucun titre dans la nature.

The last sentence is unquestionably true for Ockham, and that is about all. However, it is definitely not true that, according to Ockham, an individual does not contain anything that is similar or common with another individual. Unfortunately the wording of the *Histoire* is equivocal. We can hardly believe that "common" means here something which is identically the same in two individuals. For such a universality has been denied by everyone of the classical scholastics. "Common" can also hardly mean, something which is not individual in a concrete existing being; for it is just this commonness which is resented by Thomists in the solution of Scotus' formal distinction between the common nature and the individual difference. The Thomists, too, defend the thesis that everything in an individual is individual, even if they prefer to say, individualized. But that which is individualized is individual. Hence "common" can mean only "similar". Therefore, the assertion of the *Histoire* will only apply to Ockham, if and only if, he denied similarity between the individuals. Only then could we speak of an isolationism. Unfortunately the facts, that is the texts of Ockham, clearly affirm what the *Histoire* denies. How else, could Ockham write (*Reportatio* III, p. 9, Q):

... uno modo accipitur [univocum] pro conceptu communi aliquibus habentibus perfectam similitudinem in omnibus essentialibus sine omni dissimilitudine, ita quod hoc sit verum tam in substantialibus quam in accidentalibus, sic quod in forma accidentali non est reperire quod est dissimile cuilibet formae in alia forma accidentali ... Et sic accipiendo univocum, conceptus solus speciei specialissimae est univocus, qua in individuis eiusdem speciei non est reperire aliquid alterius rationis in uno et alio.

It is true, as the *Histoire* maintains, that in Ockham's system there is no place for an Aristotelian or Thomistic abstraction; the reason, however, is not this isolationism, but the denial of any principle of individuation which is according to Ockham "vide de sens", as the *Histoire* correctly states.

Passing over a few lines of equally dubitable correctness, we read:

Il n'est de distinction possible que la distinction réelle, car la distinction de raison (virtuelle) et la distinction formelle sont des vains artifices n'ayant pas plus de valeur que le réalisme thomiste ou scotiste dont elles font fonction.

We wonder why Ockham can say just the opposite (*Quodl.* I, q.):
... *quia omnis distinctio vel est formalis vel realis vel rationis.* And furthermore, if this statement of the *Histoire* were correct, it is hard to understand, why Ockham, even in one of his latest works, can speak of a formal distinction and explain it in the sense of Scotus' formal non-identity? In the *Summa Logicae*, part II, c. 2, Ockham says:

Non est aliud dicere, quod essentia et tres Personae distinguuntur formaliter secundum unum intellectum, nisi quod essentia est tres personae et persona non est tres personae ...

In fact, Ockham has always admitted the formal distinction in its negative wording (and probably more scotistic meaning), but only in God, not in creatures.

After a few lines of fairly correct statements we are stopped short by a quite inaccurate exposition of Ockham's doctrine on the categories. We read (p. 33):

...les accidents "absolus" ne sont pas distincts de la substance, et se reduisent à des *concepts* répondant à des aspects de cette substance.

In other words — another confirming text will be given a little later — according to the *Histoire* Ockham maintains that the only things *(res)* in this world are substances or the parts of substances, viz. matter and form; all accidents are reduced to concepts. We have not the slightest idea, on which text in Ockham's collected works this statement is, or possibly could be, based. It is true that, according to Ockham's clearly favored and often defended theory, quantity is not an entity distinct from substance or quality; quantity is only a mode of being of material substances or corporeal qualities, for it is their mode of having parts outside parts. However, and this was apparently overlooked by the *Histoire*, a material substance can exist without the mode of having parts outside parts, as the body of Christ does in the Holy Eucharist; hence to say: "Dès lors, comme pour Descartes, l'étendue se confond avec l'essence du corps," is incorrect. For actual extension has nothing to do with the "essence" of a body or material substance, since it can be absent, as in the case of the body of Christ existing in non-quantitative manner in the Holy Eucharist. But still for another reason the identification of extension with the essence of bodies is incorrect, since corporeal qualities are quantitative in the same manner that bodies are.

But what about quality? According to the sweeping statement mentioned before, the absolute accidents, hence also the qualities, are not real entities distinct from their substance. This the *Histoire* even expressly maintains: "A leur tour les qualités corporelles se confondent avec la substance" (p. 33). In other words, according to the *Histoire*, Ockham teaches that corporeal qualities are the same as substance and they are only different aspects of substance in the same manner as quantity is. This is expressly stated as regards all the four species of qualities distinguished by the scholastics: "Aucun des quatre types de qualités reconnues par les scolastiques (à la suite d'Aristote) ne trouve grâce devant le franciscain" (p. 33). If only Ockham's most explicit words, time and again reiterated, would have found grace before the *Histoire*. However, in this case, we can even quote the *Histoire* against itself. A few lines further the *Summa Logicae* is quoted to the effect that relation is not a distinct entity from substance and quality — which is correct; but we are surprised to read here: *Praeter res absolutas, scilicet substantias et qualitates, nulla res est imaginabilis (Sum. totius log.*, 1ᵃ p., c. 49) (p. 34). Thus the *Histoire* quotes a text against its own statement. There is no text to be found in Ockham's works where he has ever denied that certain qualities, though not all, are distinct entities *(res)* and are not identical in any way with substance. For further evidence we shall quote the following text from the same work quoted by the *Histoire* (c. 49).

> Sunt autem quaedam in genere qualitatis, quae important res distinctas a substantia, ita quod illa res non est substantia, sicut sunt albedo et nigredo, color, scientia, lux et huiusmodi. Quaedam autem sunt, quae alias res a praedictis qualitatibus et substantia non important, cuiusmodi sunt figura, curvitas, rectitudo, densitas, raritas et huiusmodi.

This text also proves the futility of the restriction quoted, strangely enough — from a *non authentic* work.

> Ont seules une réalité propre autre que la substance les qualités qui sont affranchies de liens avec l'étendue, à savoir les actes conscients: visio, intellectio, dilectio et omnes actus anime cognitivi et appetitivi sunt qualitates reales in anima. *Tractatus de principiis theologiae*, p. 120.

What is most amazing is, that at the bottom of the same page this exclusive statement of the *Histoire* is falsified even by the *Tractatus*. For there we read: *Ideo gravitas, levitas, color, sapor et huiusmodi ... sunt res inherentes* (p. 120s).

Nr. 380 deals with Ockham's Psychology. This part again, is a strange mixture of truth and fiction. We noticed with satisfaction that the explanation of Ockham's doctrine on intuitive and abstractive cognition (pp. 34s) is fairly correct. Certain serious misunderstandings of the intuitive cognition of non-existents do not reappear in the *Histoire*. The only critical observation we wish to make here is that we have not found any evidence in the texts of Ockham to show that he limits abstractive cognition to intellective cognition alone. On the contrary in *Ordinatio* (prol. q. 1, TT) Ockham equates *phantasia* with *notitia abstractiva*.

Likewise the short account of Ockham's theory of signification is fairly correct, except for two probably minor misunderstandings. First, the *Histoire* maintains that Ōckham's term for the function of signification is *notare;* we have no evidence for that. On the same page (36) *connotare* and "consignifier" seem to be brought into a similar relation. In Ockham's language it would be more appropriate to call the significative function of the syncategoremata like "Every", "and" etc. co-signification, because such terms signify only in connection with categorematic terms. The categorematic terms are to be subdistinguished into absolute and connotative terms. Connotative terms have signification and no co-signification since they signify an object or usually individuals. "White" is for instance a connotative term, since it directly signifies an individual that has whiteness. "Whiteness", however, is an absolute term and not a connotative term, and so is "intellection" according to Ockham, which, however the *Histoire* unfortunately uses as an example of connotative term. We hope that it is only a misprint, since it should be "intellectus". In fact, according to Ockham "intellectus" is a connotative term which signifies directly the soul and indirectly an intellection.

If after these misunderstandings we continue to read the *Histoire*, we find ourselves in a swamp of confusion and ignorance of Ockham's technical language. We read (p. 36):

> Or, tandis que les termes du language et de l'écriture ont avec le réel signifié un rapport de signification conventionelle (suppositio materialis), le terme qui désigne un individu (suppositio personalis) et le terme abstrait (suppositio simplex) sont liés de façon naturelle aux objects pensés.

Let us try somehow to disentangle this confusion of *suppositio*, *impositio* and *intentio*. We have given a complete explanation of these terms and connected theories in the *Franciscan Studies* (VI, 1946, 143 ss, 261 ss)[b] and hence will only explain what the terms mean. A term has personal supposition when it is used in a proposition —this applies to simple and material supposition as well — and signifies its object; it does not matter, whether the term is a concept or an intention of the mind, or a spoken or a written word. When we

---

[b] Cfr. *infra* p. 201 ss, 232 ss.

use the term "word" as predicate in a proposition it signifies every word and has personal supposition. The spoken or written word "man" was instituted at will *(ad placitum)* to signify individual men; when it is used in this significative function, it has personal supposition. Furthermore, the term "man" is instituted by human beings in order to signify real objects which are not words or concepts, in a word, which are not signs; for that reason the word "man" is called a name of first imposition. On the other hand, the term "word" is instituted to signify words, like "man", "noun" etc., hence it signifies objects which are signs instituted at will. The term "word" is a sign of a sign, and for this reason is a word of second imposition. Ockham also distinguished first and second intention, only making now the distinction between intentions of the mind and intentions of the mind which signify intentions, which in turn signify objects outside the mind. Every concept and every spoken and written word, when used in its original signification, which is natural in the case of concepts and arbitrary in the case of words, has personal supposition. When not used in its significative function it may represent either the intention as such or the material word, be it spoken or written. In the first case the term has simple supposition regardless of whether it is a first or second intention that is represented. When the term represents the material spoken or written word whether it be of first or second imposition, it has material supposition. It is somewhat ironical to find the *Histoire* attributing to Ockham the very idea of simple supposition that he so often rejected namely that in simple supposition the term supposits for its abstract signified object, for instance that "man" supposits for "humanity" or "white" for "whiteness". Ockham writes:

Ex quo sequitur quod falsum est quod aliqui ignorantes dicunt, quod concretum a parte praedicati supponit pro forma, videlicet quod in illa: *Sortes est albus,* ly "albus" supponit pro albedine. *Summa Logicae,* p. I, c. 63 [ed. Boehner, 176].

A similar confusion of various theories is found on the following pages (p. 37—39). They deal with the nature and the value of universals. The *Histoire* asks: "Les signes sont-ils en rapport avec les êtres qu'ils signifient et quel est ce rapport?" A distinction is required, we are told. The acts of sensation or of intellective intuitive cognition bring us in direct contact with the real, with the experienced. Abstractive cognition, on the contrary, is but a fiction and applies only to thought objects. However, the most explicit texts of Ockham militate against such a distinction. For instance:

> Idem totaliter et sub eadem, ratione a parte obiecti est obiectum intuitivae et abstractivae notitiae . . . *Ordinatio,* prol. q. 1, CC.

It is not difficult to indicate the cause of this misunderstanding. The *Histoire* fails to do what Hochstetter has masterly done, namely to distinguish between two theories of Ockham in regard to the nature of concepts. According to the first theory which was later completely abandoned, the concept or universal is a *fictum,* that is a mental picture which exists only as thought object or has an "esse objectivum", since it is not a reality or a thing, but only a thought, or more exactly, the object of a thought. The term "ideal" being would probably apply to this "esse objectivum", since it is constituted by an act of thinking. Unfortunately the *Histoire,* inattentive to Ockham's terminology, calls this *fictum* a *figmentum.* Ockham, when dealing with this theory, has never called the concept, for instance of man or of cause, a *figmentum,* but always a *fictum.* For a *figmentum,* as Ockham explains in the same context, is something which is an impossibility as "chimaera", a *hircocervus* (stag-goat) etc. A *figmentum,* is of course the result of a *fictio,* and thus can be called a *fictum;* but not every *fictum* is a *figmentum.* Since a *fictum* is the product of mental picturing of something that is real or can be real, it has not the connotation of "unreal" as the modern word "fiction" has. *Figmentum,* however, has this connotation. For that reason, Ockham can maintain, that *fictum* and *fictio* (as the act of producing a *fictum*) are related to reality, that is, that a *fictum* is a concept which is similar to things in their subjective, that is, their real, being. Now let Ockham speak for himself.

> . . . universale non est aliquid reale habens esse subiectivum nec in anima nec extra animam, sed tantum habet esse obiectivum in anima, et est quoddam fictum habens esse tale in esse obiectivo, quale habet res extra in esse subiectivo. Et hoc per istum modum, quod intellectus videns aliquam rem extra animam fingit consimilem rem in mente, ita quod si

haberet virtutem productivam, sicut habet virtutem fictivam, talem rem in esse subiectivo numero distinctam a priori produceret extra ... Illud fictum in mente ex visione alicuius rei extra esset unum exemplar. Ita enim, sicut domus ficta, si fingens haberet virtutem productivam realem, est exemplar ipsi artifici, ita illud fictum esset exemplar respectu sic fingentis ... *Ordinatio* d. 2, q. 8, E.

This certainly exposes as untenable the following lines (p. 37) of the *Histoire*.

... il (l'universel) n'est qu'une fiction forgée dans l'âme de toutes pièces: abstractio quae non est nisi fictio quaedam. Pures étiquettes mentales qui servent à cataloguer les individus réels dans les cadres génériques et spécifiques, les notions abstraits n'attaignent pas ces individus que par la surface et le dehors, et non par le dedans.

All this is being said on the basis of that theory which Ockham held when he lectured on the *Sentences*, but which was gradually abandoned when he worked on his *Ordinatio*. When he wrote his *Summa Logicae* and the *Quodlibeta* he definitely rejected it as false. However, of this important development in Ockham's teaching, the *Histoire* makes no mention. The second and truly Ockhamistic theory about the nature of concepts, namely that a concept or universal is the act of knowing itself, and therefore a quality of the mind and a real entity in the soul, because as such it is more similar to the object known, is only mentioned by the *Histoire* at the end of this treatment without attaching much importance to it. Hence the exposition of Ockham's theory is deficient in two respects: First, too much emphasis is put on the theory which Ockham abandoned at an early stage of his career, and secondly, this theory itself is misrepresented.

This misrepresentation is revealed in the following passage.

Toutes attaches avec l'extramental étant brisées, les universaux deviennent un matériel logique que les sciences conbinent. Tout se passe *comme si* les vues de l'esprit s'adaptaient aux individus réels, mais elles ne les atteignent pas ...

There is no text in Ockham's works which substantiates these lines, and, of course, no quotations are given. However, we would like to ask, what does "atteindre" really mean? As far as we are able to make out, it can only mean that our concepts, according to Ockham, do not "reach" the individuals, because they do not represent them. If this is meant, it is contradicted by Ockham everywhere where he deals with this topic. For, as we have seen before, he insists in the character of similarity between concepts and individual natures. For that reason, we believe that Ockham's "Nominalism" or rather Conceptualism is closer, if not much the same, as the theory of Abaelard, which the *Histoire* denies, and precisely for this reason very far from the conceptualism of Kant with whom the *Histoire* associates Ockham. The interested reader may get more information and also textual evidences from our article "The realistic conceptualism of Ockham", in *Traditio* Vol. IV (1946), *infra*, 156—174.

Setting aside all the other partially true and partially false statements of the *Histoire*, let us select only the following incorrect statement:

> La notion *abstraite* d'être perd son charactère univoque (Scot) ou analogique (Thomas) (p. 38).

No reference to any work of Ockham is given. In fact, no reference could be given, because Ockham defends the univocity of the term "being", following Scotus and dissenting in an extremely mild manner from St. Thomas, for he admits univocity and also analogy in a certain sense. Let the texts speak for themselves.

> Pro univocatione [entis] nescio nisi tantum unam rationem, in cuius virtute omnes aliae rationes tenent, et est ista: Omnes concedunt quod aliquam notitiam incomplexam habemus de Deo pro statu isto, et etiam de substantia creata materiali et immateriali . . . Igitur oportet necessario ponere, quod intelligendo Deum pro statu isto cognoscam eum in conceptu communi sibi et aliis . . .
>
> In virtute rationis praedictae tenet ratio prima Joannis [id est Scoti!] de conceptu dubio et certo, aliter non . . . *Report.* III, q. 9.

In the same question Ockham also explains in which sense one can speak of analogy.

The scanty remarks expressing convictions more than accurate facts and the few lines of Ockham's speculative psychology shall be passed over here.

Nr. 381. The presentation of the *Theodicy* of Ockham suffers under all the shortcomings pointed out in our previous discussions.

Only here they have the cummulative effect of making Ockham's serious and important theodicy simply a caricature. We have written a detailed critical review of this part which will appear early next year in *Franziskanische Studien* (Münster).^c Hence we shall single out only a few of the extremely surprising statements of the *Histoire*.

We should not be surprised, of course, to read on p. 41 that our notions in regard to God and especially the notion of causality are of no help.

> ... la notion de cause est un *figmentum* de l'esprit. Le principe de causalité ne peut établir avec rigueur l'existence de Dieu, car il est difficile, sinon impossible de démontrer que les causes ne peuvent s'enchaîner à l'infini et sans point d'arrêt. Quia difficile est vel impossibile probare contra philosophos quod est processus in infinitum in causis eiusdem rationis (*I Sent.*, d. II, q. 5).

We charitably suppose that the author of the *Histoire* has never seen the context of his quotation. First, because the quotation is wrong, it is to be found in I, d. 2, q. 10, Q. Secondly, because it has quite the opposite meaning in its context. For we read:

> Dico ergo quantum ad primum articulum, quod ratio probans primitatem efficientis est sufficiens, et est ratio omnium philosophorum. Videtur tamen, quod evidentius posset probari primitas efficientis per conservationem rei a sua causa quam per productionem, secundum quod dicit rem accipere esse immediate post non esse. (And now follows the text quoted by the *Histoire*). Cuius ratio est, quia difficile est vel impossibile probare contra philosophos quod non est processus in infinitum in causis eiusdem rationis.

As the reader can ascertain for himself, Ockham expressly states that the primacy of a first efficient cause can be proved and even demonstrated — the latter is clearly maintained by Ockham in one of his latest works, the *Quaestiones super libros Physicorum*. However, the worst of all is this: the words quoted by the *Histoire* do not even prove the point which it intends to make. In fact, an extraordinary blunder has been committed. Which scholastic has ever maintained that a process *ad infinitum* is impossible in the order of *causae eiusdem rationis*? *Eiusdem rationis* is dropped in the French text. St. Bona-

---

^c Cf. *infra*, 399—420.

venture and a few others, yes; but not St. Thomas nor Duns Scotus
nor most of the other scholastics. How else could St. Thomas
maintain that in the case of the generation of one man from another
a process *ad infinitum* is possible? For he says:

> Unde non est impossibile quod homo generetur ab homine in infinitum.
> Esset autem impossibile, si generatio huius hominis dependeret ab hoc
> homine, et a corpore elementari, et a sole, et sic in infinitum. *Summa Theol.*
> I, 47, 2, ad 7um.

Unfortunately the immediately following lines of the *Histoire*
are of the same type:

> Que si, pour éviter une régression à l'infini dans la série des causes, on
> s'arrête à un premier efficient, celui-ci prime sans doute tous les autres êtres;
> mais pourquoi serait-il le plus parfait possible? Conclusion: l'existence de
> Dieu est objet de foi et non de démonstration. Non potest sciri evidenter
> quod Deus est *(Quodl.* I, 1).

Here again, we are forced to show that the text of Ockham was
not understood and that a maimed text is used to prove something
that Ockham has denied. The *Histoire* uses the expression "primer"
which means "to surpass" and "to be the first". There would be no
harm in using this expression in the latter sense, viz. to be the first,
if the *Histoire* had abstained from adding that it is the first in regard
to all other things. By this addition the *Histoire* makes a supposition
which Ockham denies; for, if this first efficient cause surpasses all
other beings, it follows according to Ockham, that it can be but one
and is also the most perfect being that is possible. But it is exactly
this notion of God, viz. that God surpasses all other beings, which
according to Ockham cannot be the result of any demonstration
possible to us. In order to give the reader a clear picture of the really
distorted presentation of Ockham's teaching in the *Histoire*, we have
to go into closer discussion of the text quoted from the *Quodlibeta*.

In *Quodlibetum* I, 1 the question is asked: Whether it can be proved
by natural reason that there is but one God. In answering this question
Ockham gives two definitions of the term "God". One meaning is:
Deus est aliquid nobilius et melius omni alio a se. It is obvious and also
later emphasized by Ockham, that that which is more noble and

better than anything else, surpasses all other beings. A second meaning of the term "God" is this: *Deus est illud quo nihil est melius et perfectius*. This definition expresses that God is first only in the sense that He is not surpassed by anything else, but not in the sense that He surpasses everything else. After this Ockham gives an answer to the question according to the two different descriptions of God. First, he answers according to the first description of God. In order to enable the reader to judge for himself how inadequate the quotation in the *Histoire* is we shall quote the entire answer of Ockham and italicize the text selected by the *Histoire;* we also add in parenthesis a few words which are in most of the manuscripts but not in the edition used by the *Histoire:*

Dico quod accipiendo Deum secundum primam descriptionem non potest demonstrative probari, quod tantum est unus Deus. *Cuius ratio est, quia non potest evidenter sciri, quod Deus est* (sic accipiendo Deum); ergo non potest evidenter sciri, quod est tantum unus Deus, sic accipiendo Deum.

It is or rather should be obvious that Ockham's denial of a demonstrative proof of God's existence refers only to the first description of God. Ockham's indication that he is speaking of God in the first meaning occurs twice in the edition used by the *Histoire* and even three times in the original form of the *Quodlibeta*, and thus it shows, how anxious Ockham was not to be misunderstood.

Unfortunately, it did not help him. Nor did his express and absolutely unequivocal affirmation that God's existence can be demonstrated, if "God" is taken in the meaning of the second description. And, strangely enough (from the viewpoint of the *Histoire*) the reason Ockham gives is that otherwise there would be a process *ad infinitum*. Let the text speak for himself:

Sciendum tamen, quod potest demonstrari Deum esse accipiendo Deum secundo modo prius dicto, quia aliter esset processus in infinitum nisi esset aliquid in entibus, quo non est aliquid prius et perfectius...

We abstain from commenting on the rest of this Number, since it would lead us too far and would mostly be a matter of favorable or unfavorable interpretation.

No. 382. Here the *Histoire* deals with Ockham's Ethics and Logic. Ockham's Ethics is still little explored and probably less understood.

This is reflected in the scanty remarks of the *Histoire* which are at least exaggerated. However, let us discuss a few of them. On p. 42 we read:

> Il n'y a ni bien ni mal en soi, la différence entre l'un et l'autre reposant sur un décret de Dieu qui eût pu renverser l'ordre existant.
>
> Dieu est un autocrate qui pourrait, sans tenir compte de ce qu'il y a de rationnel ou non dans ses volontés, provoquer chez l'homme des actes d'amour aussi bien que des actes de haine (II *Sent.* q. 19).

According to Ockham at least one act is bad in itself, so that it can never be good, viz. to disobey God; and there is one act that is absolutely good, so that it can never be bad, viz. to obey or to love God. For the latter part of our statement we quote the following text.

> Nam iste actus [quo Deus diligitur super omnia et propter se] est sic virtuosus, quod non potest esse viciosus, nec potest iste actus causari a voluntate creata nisi sit virtuosus: Tum quia quilibet pro loco et tempore obligatur ad diligendum Deum super omnia, et per consequens, iste actus non potest esse viciosus; tum quia iste actus est primus omnium actuum bonorum. *Quodl.* III, 13.

In other words, Ockham admits one absolute norm of Ethics, viz. the obligation to obey God, Ockham has never maintained that anyone, not even God, can dispense from this obligation. However, to obey God means to love God. But here, a difficulty arises. Does Ockham not maintain that it is possible that God can command that a creature hates Him? According to the evidence of the texts, it cannot be doubted that Ockham admitted this. However, in order to understand this correctly we must not overlook that "potest" in Ockham's language has two meanings. In one meaning it has the sense of consistency or rather lack of contradiction; this is subdistinguished into a possibility based on the lack of logical contradiction or contradiction with a necessary truth, and a possibility based on the lack of contradiction with contingent facts. From this logical possibility we have to distinguish psychological possibility or capability. When Ockham maintains that God can command hatred of Him it is only in the first sense; never in the second. By this he means that such a command is not selfcontradictory on logical grounds. How does he prove that? It is based on the theological truth that God is the primary cause of every effect. Now, a creature can command to hate God, this act of commanding the hatred of God is caused by God as first cause and by the creature as second cause. Hence it cannot include a contradiction — on purely logical grounds — that God can command hatred of Himself.

Up to now, we have dealt with the logical possibility as such. Let us now assume that God would command that a created will hates Him. There, according to Ockham, would be a genuine perplexity or ethical antinomy. In such a case, the created will simply could not act. For if it obeys, and consequently hates God, it would love God. Let us listen to Ockham himself, who presents this case in a slightly milder form.

Si dicatur, quod Deus potest praecipere, quod pro aliquo tempore non diligatur Ipse, quia potest praecipere quod intellectus sit intentus circa studium et voluntas similiter, ut nihil possit illo tempore de Deo cogitare . . .

Respondeo: Si Deus posset hoc praecipere, sicut videtur quod potest sine contradictione, dico tunc, quod voluntas non potest pro tunc talem actum elicere, quia ex hoc ipso quod talem actum eliceret, Deum diligeret super omnia, et per consequens impleret praeceptum divinum, quia hoc est diligere Deum super omnia, diligere quidquid Deus vult diligi. Et ex hoc ipso quod sic diligeret, non faceret praeceptum divinum per casum et per consequens sic diligendo Deum diligeret et non diligeret. *Quodl.* III, 13.

To qualify Ockham's position as ethical positivism is perhaps more a matter of words. For the Venerabilis Inceptor knows one invariable norm of Ethics, viz. the obligation to obey the will of God or to love God. For the rest, ethical norms are commanded by the will of God and have to be obeyed in virtue of the general and absolute ethical norm. Thus Ockham does not base his ethics on some anonymous and impersonal law pervading nature, or on something to which God Himself is subject, for instance on "ethical values" of which the *Histoire* speaks. Ockham bases his ethics on one Personal principle, on God who is most powerful, most good and most wise and most just. Hence it is absolutely incorrect to say that ethical laws depend on the subjective viewpoint of those who consider and judge them, as we read in the *Histoire:*

11*

Puisque les valeurs morales ne sont pas des absolus, elles varient suivant le point de vue subjectif de qui les considère et les juge.

No text reference is given, since there is no text in Ockham which substantiates this statement.

The following short remarks on the Logic of Ockham are rather vague. The *Histoire* does not explain what Ockham, and almost all the scholastics meant by "demonstration", namely something that modern scholastics no longer strive for. To some extent, we think they are right. In Aristotelian Axiomatics a demonstration is a necessary conclusion obtained by a syllogistic process from necessary and evident premisses. It was not Ockham's fault that such high and almost impossible requirements were demanded of a demonstration, since it was Aristotle who, under the influence of Mathematics, wrote the *Posterior Analytics*. But Ockham was not such a fool to believe, that:

Tout ce qui n'est pas démontrable est relégué dans la sphère des conclusions probables (p. 42).

For, Ockham not only knew of *propositiones per se notae* and immediate formal consequences, but also of absolutely evident contingent propositions based on experience. In all these cases absolute certitude is given and no fear of deception. But even a "probable" syllogism or a dialectical proof which often is a *persuasio*, as the *Histoire* rightly mentions, may give the highest degree of certitude. Ockham says concerning the "probabile" in the *Summa Logicae*, part III, I, c. 1 [Ed. Boehner, 328]:

Sequitur etiam aliud, quod non omnis syllogismus topicus facit semper praecise dubitationem et formidinem, sed etiam frequenter facit primam fidem sine omni dubitatione, quia ita aliquando adhaeremus probabilibus sicut evidenter notis.

What is said about science on page forty-three is of such a nature that we hardly believe that Ockham would recognize this as his own doctrine:

Tout se ramène à une technique (comme dans la logique mathématique moderne) et celle-ci ne peut conduire à un enrichissement du savoir, car le sujet et le prédicat des propositions analytiques sont identiques.

It is definitely not the case that analytical propositions enter a science — at least as long as it is not logic.

The famous razor of Ockham must, of course, also appear in the *Histoire*. There is nothing wrong about this, for the principle was known to Aristotle and every philosopher is bound to use it. For philosophy is a science, and a science has to prove what it affirms. However, it is not quite historical to impute the wording: *Pluralitas non est ponenda sine necessitate ponendi*, to Ockham. These exact words are found in the non-authentic *Tractatus de principiis Theologiae* (ed. Baudry p. 125). Ockham has several forms for it. The most common one is: *Pluralitas non est ponenda sine necessitate.* We also find the form: *Frustra fit per plura, quod potest fieri per pauciora.* The most explicit form is this: *Nihil debet poni sine ratione assignata nisi sit per se notum vel per experientiam scitum vel per auctoritatem scripturae probatum (Ordin.* d. 30, q. 1 E).

In No. 383 the *Histoire* deals with Ockham's physics. Here we find the expression: "La qualité étant réduite à la quantité.. " Before we read that quality was reduced to substance. As our texts have shown both statements are in disagreement with Ockham's most explicit words. Only certain qualities are not distinct from substance whilst quantity is not distinct from substance or quality.

No. 384 deals with the relation between Philosophy and Theology. We certainly can abstain from a detailed discussion of this part, since a masterly Dissertation has been published about this by Guelluy. Let us simply confront two quotations.

The *Histoire* reads (p. 45):

D'une part la sphère des vérités chrétiennes est inaccessible à la raison et réservée à la foi; d'autre part, la théologie doit renoncer à établir ses affirmations par la voie du raisonnement. Articuli fidei non sunt principia demonstrationis, nec sunt probabiles, quia omnibus vel pluribus vel sapientibus apparent falsi (*Summa t. log.* III, 1 — to be more correct: III, I, 1). C'est la condamnation de la théologie spéculative et toute collaboration avec la philosophie est impossible.

After only mentioning here that to render "demonstrationis" with "du raisonnement" only emphasizes the fact that the meaning of demonstration is unknown to the *Histoire*, we quote now Guelluy's *Philosophie et Théologie chez Guillaume d'Ockham* (Louvain 1947, p. 364):

Notons, d'autre part, qu'Ockham refuse de séparer le domaine de la théologie de celui de la métaphysique . . .
Le Venerabilis Inceptor ne semble, dans aucun des textes que nous avons étudiés, se donner pour but d'opposer la foi et la raison ou de soustraire le domaine de la révélation à toute investigation intellectuelle . . .

To this statement of a scholar who has studied this problem *ex professo* in the text of Ockham himself, we add a passage from one of the latest works of Ockham:

Contra: Nisi eadem veritas posset probari in scientia naturali et Theologia, Philosophia non iuvaret ad Theologiam. *Quodl.* V, 1.

The following reflexions are therefore without any foundation in the texts of Ockham.

Much criticism could be applied to the following number on the political doctrines of Ockham. Most of it is fiction as can be gathered from the article of Morrall in this number of the *Franciscan Studies*.[d]

We have led the patient reader through a veritable forest of misunderstandings wildly grown up, not so much because of the fault of one man, but because of careless and sloppy treatment of a scholastic who *per fas et nefas* must serve as the explanation of the decadence of scholasticism. All this only proves that we need serious studies on the Theology and Philosophy of Ockham in order to find out what he really thought and wrote. Only after that we have the right to judge, to condemn or to praise.

13. THE REALISTIC CONCEPTUALISM OF WILLIAM OCKHAM[a]

Students of medieval scholasticism are accustomed to apply the name 'conceptualism' to Ockham's doctrine concerning the nature and scope of universals. This seems to be an apt designation, provided that its meaning is not burdened with idealistic connotations. Unfortunately, quite a number of neo-scholastics qualify conceptualism as a doctrine which severs the bond between thought and reality,

[d] Vol 9 (1949) 335—369.
[a] First published in: Traditio 4 (1946) 307—335; we omitted, however, the text edition and its introductory remarks, 319—335.

and is therefore essentially idealistic. Small wonder, then, that such a conceptualism imputed to William Ockham falls an easy prey to their violent, and to a large extent justified, attack against idealism in general. However, as far as Ockham's conceptualism is concerned, their victory in this regard is an illusion, for the simple reason that his alleged idealistic conceptualism does not exist. Hence it appears to us that Ockham's genuine conceptualism enjoys, for the time being, a relative security from neo-scholastic criticism.

It is the aim of the following paper to prove that Ockham's doctrine as regards universals is a realistic conceptualism. As additional evidence, a revised edition of a comparatively inaccessible text will be offered.[b]

I. UNIVERSALS AND REALITY ACCORDING TO WILLIAM OCKHAM

Father Bittle's *Epistemology* (with the title: *Reality and the Mind*) is outstanding for the sober position it adopts amongst conflicting neo-scholastic theories, as well as for its clarity of expression. According to this distinguished author, the main point in conceptualism

'is the contention that the content of our universal ideas is *not realized* in any form whatever in the individual sense-objects; there is no foundation in the things themselves which would justify the intellect in forming universal ideas. Our universal ideas are thus purely subjective products of the mind without a correlative in nature; in other words, there is nothing in the individuals in nature which is genuinely represented by these universal ideas. This, of course, gives to the universals only a strictly intra-mental significance; as "universals" they have no objective value.'[1]

In this illuminating passage the connection between conceptualism and idealism is made as explicit as could be desired. And when Fr. Bittle, a few lines later, says that at least Ockham's doctrine was really conceptualism, we are left in no doubt that he thinks the

---

[b] Cfr. note a.

[1] C. N. Bittle, O. M. Cap., *Reality and the Mind, Epistemology* (New York 1938) 237. Cfr. also J. Gredt, O. S. B., *Elementa philosophia Aristotelico-Thomistica* (7th ed. Freiburg i. Br. 1937) I, 94: 'Conceptualistae (veteres Stoici, Conceptualistae saeculi XIV et XV: Guilelmus Ockham..., tandem Kant ... et Kantiani) admittunt quidem conceptus universales, quos tamen merum mentis figmentum esse docent, cui nihil in rerum natura respondeat.'

ockhamistic conceptualism to be of the idealistic type. For this unambiguous statement Fr. Bittle has apparently relied on the customary treatment of Ockham's doctrine in our textbooks which, as it happens, have been led astray by certain medievalists. We have no intention of blaming him for this. However, we consider it our duty to rectify an injury — not in order to save Ockham or to exculpate him (for the guilt of Ockham has still to be proved), but to serve truth, a task which, in our opinion, is included in the virtue of religion.

Let us first state that Ockham, far from being an idealist, has not even a place in his system for the critical aporia from which idealism has started its subjective journey; for the problem, whether and how we can know anything of reality by conceptual knowledge, does not even enter Ockham's system, since in his system the immediacy of cognition and the firm causal nexus between object and thought does not admit of any separation between thought and reality. Hence he is remarkably innocent of *the* 'philosophical sin' committed, according to certain neo-scholastics, by many of their brethren who have suffered under the critical aporia and who have, in the spirit of St. Thomas, refuted idealism by granting, and not by simply denying, the critical aporia. We, for our part, side with the latter, amongst whom are very eminent names. Hence we do not consider the lack of this aporia in Ockham as something to be praised.

On the other hand, there can be no doubt that Ockham radically denied the existence of any universality in singular things.[2] The *universale in re*, even as common nature, or in any other form which entails any real existence of the universal in individuals, is eliminated by him on metaphysical grounds.[3] However, we are unable to see

---

[2] Cfr. in the text edited below [i. e. in Traditio], N and Y.

[3] Cfr. Ockham's extensive criticism of any kind of such a realism in Ordinatio (I Sent. d. 2, qq. 4—7; especially q. 7 S: "Ideo aliter dico ad quaestionem, quod nulla res extra animam nec per se nec per aliquod additum reale vel rationis, nec qualitercumque consideretur vel intelligatur, est universalis; ita quod tanta est impossibilitas, quod aliqua res extra animam sit quocumque modo universalis, nisi forte per institutionem voluntariam, quomodo ista vox: Homo, quae est vox singularis, est universalis, quanta impossibilitas est, quod homo per quamcumque considerationem vel secundum quodcumque esse sit asinus" (Revised text).

how idealism follows from such a denial of a *universale in re*, since such a careful distinction between thought and reality is not equivalent to a divorce of thought from reality. The 'idealistic Ockham' is a historical monstrosity. If idealism is characterized at least by the denial of a correspondence of our thought with reality, and so that our thought is not determined by reality but at most occasioned by reality, then Ockham is remarkably free from any idealistic tendencies.

Of course, we cannot expect from him an *ex professo* refutation of idealism, since idealism was unknown to him. But he has implicitly denied the thesis of idealism by affirming the following theses:

FIRST THESIS: *The content of our concepts is the conception or grasping of reality.*

According to Ockham, the starting point of all our knowledge is intuitive cognition. Intuitive knowledge — naturally speaking — is the immediate intellectual grasp of an existing and present thing. The object which is sensibly known is likewise known immediately by the intellect. This intellectual knowledge of a singular is the *notitia intuitiva intellectiva*, which is a proper, simple and incomplex cognition of a singular fact. This knowledge or this intellection is caused by two partial causes —: the object which is known or rather makes itself known, and the intellect which knows or becomes 'knowing-the-object'. The object is the active cause, which as *causa univoca* produces an effect similar to itself.[4]

Besides this intellective intuitive cognition, an abstractive cognition of the same singular object is caused, either immediately by the object itself, or mediately by the object and immediately by the first intuitive cognition. This abstractive knowledge remains as habitual knowledge in the intellect.[5]

Again, besides these two cognitions, which concern only singular facts, the intellect forms another cognition, based on the former, which is not proper to one singular fact, but which is common to an indefinite number of singular facts of the same kind, since it does not concern this individual more than that individual. This abstractive cognition is universal cognition, also called common or confused

---

[4] *Reportatio* II, q. 15 EE; ed. Traditio 1 (1943) 263.
[5] Cfr. *ibid.* G—M; ed. cit. 250—253.

cognition. Thus the common intellection of the universal concept 'man' does not concern Sortes more than Plato or any other real or possible man, since it concerns all men equally, being so common or generalized or universalized that it does not regard their individual differences.[6]

The transition from simple and proper knowledge of singulars to simple and common knowledge of universals is in any case a natural one and does not involve a special activity of the intellect.[7] However, Ockham does not give detailed information about this psychological process of forming universals by 'abstraction'.[8]

---

[6] Cfr. the text edited below, E. Note that "confused cognition" has a technical meaning, since it refers to universal concepts, which are 'common' and capable of 'confused' supposition. The universals are not confused cognitions in the modern sense of the word. Cfr. the unedited *Expositio super libros Physicorum*, lib. I, ad textum 4: "Et ideo, cum universalia sint simplicia, sicut alias ostendi, proprie non cognoscuntur confuse, et ita proprie non sunt confusa . . ."

[7] Cfr. *Ordinatio* d. 2, q. 7 CC: "Ad septimum dico, quod natura occulte operatur in universalibus, non quod producat ipsa universalia extra animam tamquam aliqua realia, sed quia producendo cognitionem suam in anima quasi occulte saltem mediate (vel immediate [addition of the second redaction]) producit illa universalia illo modo, quo nata sunt produci. Et ideo omnis communitas isto modo est naturalis et a singularitate procedit; nec oportet illud, quod isto modo fit a natura, esse extra animam, sed potest esse in anima" (Revised text).

[8] Ockham has given more indications of this transition on the basis of the *fictum*-theory in *Reportatio* II, qu. 25 O (this question is missing in some manuscripts, but seems to be authentic): "ad aliud dico, quod universalia et intentiones secundae causantur naturaliter sine omni activitate intellectus et voluntatis a notitiis incomplexis terminorum per istam viam: Quia primo cognosco aliqua singularia in particulari intuitive vel abstractive; et hoc causatur ab obiecto vel habitu derelicto ex primo actu; et habita notitia statim ad eius praesentiam, si non sit impedimentum, sequitur naturaliter alius actu distinctus a primo terminatus ad aliquid tale esse obiectivum, quale prius vidit in esse subiectivo; et ille actus secundus producit universalia et intentiones secundas et non praesupponit eas. Exemplum: Aliquis videns albedinem intuitive vel duas albedines abstrahit ab eis albedinem in communi ut est species, et non est aliud nisi illae duae notitiae incomplexae terminatae ad albedinem in singulari, sive intuitivae sive abstractivae, causantur naturaliter, sicut ignis calorem, unam tertiam notitiam distinctam ab illis, quae producit talem albedinem in esse obiec-

At any rate, it can be safely affirmed that, according to Ockham, universal conceptual knowledge, which is based ultimately on intuitive knowledge, or on a knowledge which is at least as immediate as intuitive knowledge, by a natural and therefore necessary process, is conception of reality.[9]

SECOND THESIS: *The content of our thought is in the relation of similitude with reality.*

The similarity or similitude, or the correspondence between thought or universal intellection and reality follows immediately from the causal relation in which thought stands with reality. We have already quoted a text in which the object is called a univocal cause as regards cognition: this means that the object causes an effect similar to it. The similarity between concept and reality is very often affirmed by the *Venerabilis Inceptor*, so that it is superfluous to quote texts in direct support of this statement. We prefer to present texts in indirect support of it. In anticipation of certain

---

tivo, qualis prius fuit visa in esse subiectivo, sine omni activitate intellectus vel voluntatis, quia talia naturaliter causantur." As to the *intellectio*-theory cfr. the text edited below, E. This same text is found with significant variants in *Quaestiones super libros Physicorum* (unedited) q. 7 where we read: "Respondeo, iste est modus ponendi: Intellectus apprehendens intuitive (intentionem?) rem singularem elicit unam cognitionem intuitivam in se, quae est tantum cognitio illius rei singularis . . ." For a more detailed explanation of this process *ad mentem Ockham*, see in Gabriel Biel, *Collectorium* I, d. 3, q. 5 B (Tübingen 1501).

[9] The immediacy of intuitive and abstractive cognition with the exclusion of any "medium" between the cognition and its object is strongly emphasized by Ockham in *Ordinatio* d. 27, q. 3. J. Here he affirms such an immediacy as probable also for the universal abstractive cognition (that is, for a concept). It seems that he affirmed it as certain in his later period. This should dispose of all objections raised against Ockham's theory of cognition which are based on the causal relation between object and cognition. For the cognition of the object is immediately caused; but the cognition is not the effect *from* which or *by* which a cognition of the object is obtained. There are not two or even three cognitions necessary in order to know the object; there is only one cognition, viz. immediate cognition of reality. For this reason Ockham could not place on the same level the natural signs which are concepts and the natural signs found in nature or instituted by man. Cfr. note 16.

critics who understand the similarity between concept and thing too crudely as a physical mirroring of reality in the mind, and in consequence ridicule such a similitude, Ockham is clear-sighted enough to stress the limits of this similarity. For, as far as sensible reality is concerned, its similitude in the mind is of another type of being, namely, of intellectual or spiritual being.[10] For this reason, Ockham prefers to make himself clear on this point by using terms which refer directly to the peculiar intellectual grasp of reality. In his *Summa logicae* he describes this relation, in the particular case of universal concepts of substances (*species, genus,* etc.), by saying: 'The universal concept expresses or explains, declares, imports and signifies the substances of things, or the essence of things — i. e., their nature, which is their substance.'[11]

It is therefore Ockham's genuine teaching that universal concepts are in the relation of similarity with reality, that there is a correspondence between them and a representation of the one by the other.

---

[10] This is certainly the case according to the *intellectio*-theory as regards concepts. According to the *fictum*-theory the dissimilitude between concept and reality is even greater. Nevertheless Ockham affirms the similitude between concept and reality, also, and even more — for obvious reasons — on the basis of the *fictum*-theory. Cfr. my edition of Ordinatio d. 2, q. 8 E: "The Text Tradition of Ockham's Ordinatio," *The New Scholasticism* 16 (1942) 227. Cfr. also in the text edited below, L. As to the dissimilarity between a universal concept and reality Ockham says, expressing at the same time also the similarity, in *Ordinatio* d. 2, q. 8 J (ed. cit. 234): "Ad secundum dico, quod talia ficta non sunt realiter similia, sed magis dissimilantur et distant quam accidentia, tamen sunt talia in esse obiectivo, qualia sunt alia in esse subiectivo . . ." *Realiter similia* here means something which is similar in the manner of a real being. However, *ficta* are no real beings. Consequently the *intellectio*-theory, according to which universals are real beings (that is real accidents of the mind), grants more similarity between concept and reality, as is expressly stated by Ockham. Cfr. M in the text edited below.

[11] *Summa logicae* 1, 17: "Sed magis proprie loquendo debet concedi, quod universale exprimit vel explicat essentiam substantiae, hoc est naturam quae est substantia . . . Unde omnes auctoritates quae sonant, universalia esse de essentia substantiarum vel esse in substantiis vel esse partes ipsarum, debent sic intelligi, quod auctoritates non aliud intendunt, nisi quod talia universalia declarant, exprimunt, explicant, important et significant substantias rerum."

In order to make as explicit as possible the true nature of Ockham's conceptualism, it may suffice to paraphrase Fr. Bittle's definition of conceptualism, so that it can apply to Ockham: The content of our universal ideas is realized in individual sense-objects, if they concern such objects and not psychic objects; there is a foundation in the things themselves which does justify the intellect in forming universal ideas. Our universal ideas are by no means purely subjective products of the mind without a correlative in nature; in other words, there is something in nature, namely the individual essence or nature, not something or some nature different from the individuals, which is genuinely represented by these universal ideas. This, of course, gives to the universals a strictly extra-mental significance; as 'universals' they have objective value. However, only the content, not the universality (i. e., predicability of many), corresponds to reality; and finally, only the content grasped by the intellect, not the peculiar status of universals as psychic realities, corresponds to reality (if the universal concerns sensible facts). The character of universality and spirituality applies only to universal concepts and by no means to extra-mental sense-objects.

Since conceptualism is characterized by the affirmation of universals in the mind and by the denial of any universality outside the mind, Ockham's theory is conceptualism. Since, however, realism can be characterized by the affirmation of a correspondence or similarity between concepts and reality, or by the intentionality of concepts as regards reality — a correspondence which is either denied or at least not affirmed by idealism —, Ockham's conceptualism has to be qualified as realistic conceptualism, and not as idealistic conceptualism. Its connection with idealistic conceptualism seems to be not justified and, hence, unjust.

II. HOCHSTETTER'S AFTER-THOUGHT

What we have stated above is in general affirmed by Hochstetter,[12] who gives additional documentary evidence. However, his interpretation of some of these texts is biased by the distinguished author's

---

[12] E. Hochstetter, *Studien zur Metaphysik und Erkenntnislehre Wilhelms von Ockham* (Berlin-Leipzig 1927).

urge to find traces of idealism in Ockham's doctrine. Still, he has to confess that Ockham apparently never felt himself to be involved in the critical aporia concerning the similarity between thing and concept,[13] though Ockham has seen this difficulty, according to Hochstetter, in the *species*-theory.[14] And, indeed, Ockham's doctrine on intuitive knowledge leaves no room for the critical doubt. However, Hochstetter thinks that this absence of the critical doubt in Ockham is only apparent. In a seemingly thorough manner he tries to convince his readers that Ockham has made some limitations as regards the similarity between thought and reality. In one instance he even discovers that Ockham goes so far as to state that in an act of cognition the object is no more given than is Caesar (whom we have never seen) through his image.[15]

This inaccurate interpretation will be rectified on another occasion. Here it may suffice to state that without any doubt a universal is a natural sign of reality and that, as such, it does not represent one individual more than another, and that in this it is like the statue of the unknown Caesar or Hercules which to me represents all unknown men equally, neither one more than the other. But here the analogy ends. For the natural sign which is a universal is gained from intuitive knowledge. Hence, at least one object corresponding to such a universal (which is simple knowledge and not composed) is, or was, known. The other objects or individuals of the same class are not known individually by this common knowledge — i. e., not by a proper and not-common concept —, but only by a common concept, for the simple reason that they are not known individually

---

[13] *Op. cit.* 103: "Sieht man Ockham grob-realistisch immer wieder die similitudo von Ding und Begriff hervorheben, so hat man zunächst den Eindruck, daß er sich ihr gegenüber niemals in der bekannten kritischen "Verlegenheit wegen der Art, wie ich a priori hiervon etwas wissen könne' (Kant, Kr. d. r. Vern. Vorrede S. SVII) befunden hat."

[14] *Op. cit.* 44; cfr. here the reference to Reportatio II, q. 15 S, T.

[15] *Op. cit.* 104: "Einmal geht er, wie wir oben sahen (S. 48), schließlich so weit zu sagen, daß bei einem Erkenntnisakt (der ja für ihn gleichfalls stets similitudo rei ist; here Hochstetter adds a note referring the reader to *Sent.* I, d. 27, q. 3. X; *Sent.* II, q. 15 EE), das Objekt uns nicht mehr gegeben sei als Caesar (den wir nie sahen) durch sein Bild."

— i. e., by intuitive knowledge. Since, as regards the natural signs which concepts, we have a special case of semantics, Ockham (and this was certainly overlooked by Hochstetter and, as far as I know, by others as well), in his characterization of signs which are terms or concepts, drops the requirement or qualification that they lead only to recordative knowledge.[16] That is to say, the *sign*-relation between concept and object is not the same as between an effect and a cause, since the concept as effect is the very cognition, and not the cognition of a cognition which calls to mind a former cognition. We consider this distinction (which, by the way, is obvious) as pivotal in Ockham's semantics and theory of knowledge.

Unfortunately, idealistic prejudices have pushed Hochstetter to a rather desperate interpretation of a text found in the *Quodlibeta*. Here the distinguished author is convinced that the separation between thought and reality is most clearly and definitely expressed by Ockham. We shall first present the text:

Ad istam quaestionem dico, quod repraesentare multipliciter accipitur:

Uno modo accipitur pro illo, quo aliquid cognoscitur, et sic repraesentans est cognitio et repraesentare est esse illud, quo aliquid cognoscitur, sicut cognitione aliquid cognoscitur.

Secundo modo repraesentare est cognoscere aliquid, quo cognito aliquid aliud cognoscitur, sicut imago repraesentat illud, cuius est imago, per actum recordandi.

Tertio modo accipitur repraesentare pro aliquo causante cognitionem, sicut objectum (vel intellectus) causat cognitionem (*Quodl.* IV, q. 3).

Of this very innocent text Hochstetter gives the following interpretation:

In den Quodlibeta (IV, 2. 3) stellt er bei dem Versuch einer Gliederung der Repraesentantia neben der Repräsentation durch Objekte (bei der er vielleicht an willkürliche objektive Zeichen, wie z. B. den "circulus",

---

[16] *Summa logicae* I, 1: "Propter tamen protervos est sciendum, quod signum accipitur dupliciter: Uno modo pro omni illo quod apprehensum aliquid aliud in cognitionem facit venire, quamvis non faciat mentem venire in primam cognitionem (that is, only in secundam vel recordativam) eius, sicut alibi est ostensum, sed in actualem post habitualem eius ... Aliter accipitur signum pro illo quod aliquid facit in cognitionem venire et natum est pro illo supponere vel addi in propositione ..." I shall deal with Ockham's semantics in a forthcoming article in Francican Studies; [cf. *infra*, 201 ff.]

der den Weinausschank in der Taverne ankündigt (Logik I, cap. 1), oder natürliche Zeichen, wie z. B. den Rauch, der das Feuer zu erkennen gibt, denkt), die repräsentative Funktion der cognitio ausdrücklich der Repräsentation durch ein Abbild, die eine Erinnerung an das früher wahrgenommene Repraesentatum erfordere, gegenüber. Die auf andere Fragen abzielende Untersuchung selbst zieht die hierin unausweichliche erkenntnistheoretische Konsequenz nicht; daß demzufolge die cognitio oder intellectio zwar eine Repräsentation, aber nicht die eines Objektes durch ein anderes ihm naturaliter zugeordnetes und auch nicht mehr eine similitudo objecti ist (*op. cit.* 105).

I am at a loss to understand this. Hochstetter intends to give the gist of the above-quoted text. He suggests (if I understand him correctly) that Ockham, by the second mode of representation, has in mind representation by arbitrary signs, and by the third mode of representation understands representation by objective signs — i. e., by natural signs (smoke, a sign of fire). These two kinds of representation are distinguished from the representation of cognition. If this is the case, Hochstetter concludes, then cognition is neither an arbitrary sign nor a natural sign of that which is representated by it.[17] Hence the representation of a cognition is that of an unknown X— i. e., of an unknown cause.

The best answer to Hochstetter is a correct interpretation of this text which, according to Hochstetter himself, is basic. Ockham says that the term *repraesentare* can be understood in a threefold manner. He does not say that the three meanings of *repraesentare* are exclusive. Then he goes on to distinguish the three meanings:

1. In the first sense, 'to represent' is applied (i. e., is predicated) to that by which something is known. Hence we can use this word

---

[17] That this is Hochstetter's intention is confirmed by the words immediately following (*Op. cit.* 105): "Die Übereinstimmung mit dem Grundgedanken des Bildgleichnisses in der Kritik der Speziestheorie (s. o. S. 44) ist unverkennbar. Ebenso ist die Erweiterung des Repräsentationsbegriffs. Dort fußt der Einwand ausschließlich auf dem Gedanken der Abbildrepräsentation, an anderen Stellen ruht die repräsentative Zuordnung auf der Kausalrelation." And now it comes: "Hier ist die cognitio ausdrücklich aus beiden Gruppen herausgenommen und als eine Sonderart hingestellt, die sowohl von der genannten Kritik nicht mehr getroffen wird, wie auch unabhängig vom Kausalproblem ist. Über das 'Wie' und die Möglichkeit dieser Repräsentation schweigt Ockham."

in the following proposition: *Cognitio est repraesentans;* and this again means that by a cognition something is known. Where in this text does Ockham say that the object of this cognition is not the cause of the cognition or that the cognition is not similar to the object?

2. In the second sense, 'to represent' means a special kind of cognition, namely, the cognition of something by something else which is a sign of it, either an arbitrary or a natural sign. Such a case of representation is given, for instance, when an image represents something else; for it recalls to my mind recordative knowledge of what is representated by it. The representation by a cognition or intellection of objects as such is different from the representation by which a man, through his image, is recalled to my mind. These two cases have to be distinguished, as they were always distinguished by Ockham from the earliest days of his literary activity; for his criticism of the species theory is based on this distinction.

3. In the third sense, 'to represent' is applied to that which causes a cognition. As we know, according to Ockham the cognition is caused by the object and by the intellect; as causes of cognition, or because they make something to be represented, both object and intellect can be said to represent, or it can be said that through them something is present to the mind. This too is in perfect agreement with Ockham's teachings from his earliest scholastic days.

I am afraid that Hochstetter has here offered a gratuitous construction. Certain prejudices have led him to read something into a text because he wished to find it in that text, but he did not faithfully follow the text of Ockham himself. The 'basic' text of Hochstetter not only does not contradict our denial of idealism, or even of idealistic traces in Ockham, but rather it confirms our denial.[18]

---

[18] It is not without satisfaction that we draw the attention of medievalists to the outstanding study on scholastic semantics by John A. Oesterle: "Another Approach to the Problem of Meaning," *The Thomist* 7 (1944) 233—63, which briefly discusses the notion of *repraesentare* according to the Thomistic tradition in John of St. Thomas, on page 241 f. We read on page 242: "Repraesentare — which concerns everything by which something is made present to the knowing power — embraces three of the causes, the objective, formal and instrumental." These three causes are found in the three meanings assigned by Ockham to the term *repraesentare*.

III. THE HISTORICAL VALUE OF THE EDITED TEXT

As regards the nature of universals, Ockham's teachings have undergone a development which, in its very general outlines, was accurately seen by Hochstetter. However, the distinguished author had only a limited knowledge of the chronological sequence of Ockham's works, since only a few manuscripts, and those mostly of minor value, were at his disposal. Nevertheless the sequence which he considered most probable seems to be fairly correct, namely: The *Commentary on the Sentences, De sacramento altaris, Quodlibeta, Summa logicae,* and the *Expositio aurea* somewhere before the *Summa logicae* — though I still have difficulty in correctly locating the *De sacramento altaris,* or rather the treatises on *De sacramento altaris,* since the edition of this work really consists of two quite different tracts, probably composed at different times.

Our own research, based on a more detailed study of manuscripts and on the many *supra* and *infra*-references found in Ockham's writings, has led to the following conclusions: Ockham started his career as a writer by lecturing on the *Sentences.* Of these lectures or *Reportata* only the *Quaestiones super 2um, 3um et 4um librum* are known and published in the Lyons edition of 1495. They are quoted in the middle ages as the *Reportatio Ockham* and represent his first work (they are either his own notes or notes taken by his pupils). The *Reportatio* or lecture notes on the first book of the *Sentences* was then transformed by Ockham into an *Ordinatio* destined for publication. Of this original *Ordinatio* only one manuscript is known to me (Firenze, Bibl. Naz. A. 3. 801). After he had almost finished the *Ordinatio,* Ockham began commenting on philosophical writings: first on Porphyry's *Isagoge,* then on the *Categories,* then on *Periher-menias,* then on the *Elenchi,* then on the *Physics,* as can be definitely established on the basis of cross-references which I have collected. Since there are various *infra*-references to almost all the other works of Aristotle, we can be sure that Ockham intended to comment on them also, but either these commentaries are lost or more probably, Ockham did not find time to compose them. Ockham's *Quodlibeta* and the *Quaestiones super libros Physicorum* (which has many ref-

erences back to the *Quodlibeta*) belong to a later period. The latest
work seems to be the *Summa logicae* or, perhaps, the *Summulae in
libros Physicorum* (of which we know only a small fragment). The
Summa logicae was written before 1329, according to an old manuscript.

The text edited here, together with another published in *The
New Scholasticism*,[19] namely *Ordinatio* d. 2, q. 8, gives us a clue for
a further precisation of Ockham's literary activity. In the *Ordinatio*-
text a long addition is found which was in Ockham's first redaction
(since the Florence MS does not have it and since the Troyes MS,
which is the best, has it as a marginal note). Before we go any further,
a few words have to be said about Ockham's theory concerning the
nature of universals.

Ockham admitted only two theories, which at various times
satisfied him. The one can be called the *fictum*-theory, according to
which universals have no subjective reality (i. e., no *esse subjectivum*
or the being of real accidents in a subject) but have only an *esse
objectivum* (as objects of thought); as objects of thought they are
ficta or *figmenta* or idola of the mind, not in the sense that they are
pure constructions, but in the sense that they are produced by the
mind as thought-objects in correspondence with reality. As such
they have universality, but have no categorical being, since they
are neither accidents nor substance (cf. the text below, L and W).
The other theory can be called the *intellectio*-theory, according to
which universals do have an *esse subjectivum*, since they are real
accidents of the mind, namely, the intellection or cognition itself
(cf. text E *et seq.* and O).

In the text edited below, both theories are offered as possible
solutions of the problem regarding the nature of universals, though
the *intellectio*-theory is already preferred. Let us now examine the
other writings of Ockham in reference to these theories.

1. The *Reportatio* of Ockham (books 2—4 of the Commentary on
the *Sentences*) admits only the *fictum*-theory and hardly mentions
the *intellectio*-theory.

2. The *Ordinatio* of Ockham (the first book of his Commentary
on the *Sentences*) also, in its first redaction, shows hardly any traces

---

[19] Cfr. note 10, above.

12*

of the *intellectio*-theory and always speaks in terms of the *fictum*-theory.

3. The Commentaries on Porphyry and on the *Categories* of Aristotle show clear signs of the *intellectio*-theory, which they already prefer, though usually only conditionally.

4. The *Commentary on Perihermenias*, of which the decisive text is here edited, explains both theories for the first time *in extenso*, giving, however, preference to the *intellectio*-theory (cf. text E).

5. To this period of Ockham's literary activity — i. e., when he was working on, or had just finished, the *Commentary on Perihermenias* — we have to assign the second redaction of the *Ordinatio*, which is represented by the Lyons edition. For in an addition to this second redaction we have a reference to his *Commentary on Perihermenias* (d. 2, q. 8 T[Q]). Now, this addition is nothing but a reinforcement of the *intellectio*-theory, which formerly was amongst the four opinions dismissed by the author (cf. *ibid.* B). But it is still weak and in the form: 'Cui non placet ista opinio de talibus fictis in esse objectivo . . .' (*ibid.* T [Q]). Nevertheless, by revising the entire text of the *Ordinatio*, Ockham now added, almost wherever an occasion presented itself, a reference to the *intellectio*-theory, usually with the words: 'vel secundum aliam opinionem.'

6. In his later works, in the *Quodlibeta*, the *Quaestiones super libros Physicorum* and the *Summa logicae*, only the *intellectio*-theory is mentioned and the *fictum*-theory is rejected or not even mentioned at all.

If we bear in mind the fact that the text edited here belongs to the transitional stage in Ockham's development regarding the nature of universals, we may be able to explain some of its peculiarities. The most striking trait is the repeated treatment of various opinions. The first treatment enumerates four possible opinions; the second treatment lists three possible opinions. Only one opinion of the second treatment (namely, the *fictum*-theory) is found in the first treatment *(opinio* IV*a)*; the first opinion of the second treatment has no equivalent in the first treatment; the second opinion of the second treatment, however, has an equivalent in the first three opinions of the first treatment — i. e., instead of the as yet unspecified *qualitas*-theory of the second treatment, three opinions are offered in the first treatment, all of which consider the universal as a quality of the mind, namely, the *habitus-*, *species-*, and *intellectio*-theories. However, before drawing any conclusion from these relations, let us first glance at the opinions enumerated in *Ordinatio* d. 2, q. 8. In the first redaction it presents four theories as improbable: the *intellectio*-theory, the *species*-theory, the *habitus*-theory, and the convention-theory;[20] and it presents one theory as probable, namely, the *fictum*-theory. The second redaction adds a reinforcement of the *intellectio*-theory, which now appears at least as probable as the *fictum*-theory.

Let us furthermore enumerate the opinions discussed in one of the latest writings of Ockham, the *Quaestiones super libros Physicorum* (not yet edited). Here, five opinions are expressed in the very titles of the questions. These opinions will be identified by adding in parentheses the names given to the various opinions above:

1. 'Utrum conceptus sit aliquid fictum habens tantum esse objectivum in anima' (*fictum*-theory); this is rejected.

2. 'Utrum conceptus sit res extra concepta' (the realistic theory, corresponding to *Opinio* Ia *in genere;* cf. text N); this, of course is rejected.

3. 'Utrum conceptus sit qualitas mentis' *(Opinio* IIa *in genere);* this theory is admitted, but Ockham does not yet specify the nature of this quality.

4. 'Utrum conceptus sit qualitas, quae est species vel habitus' *(Opinio* IIa*);* this *species*-theory is also rejected.

5. 'Utrum conceptus sit qualitas terminans actum intelligendi' *(Opinio* Ia*);* this *habitus*-theory is likewise rejected.

6. 'Utrum conceptus communis sit intellectio generalis' *(Opinio* IIIa*);* this *intellectio*-theory is adopted and, in the following question, applied to singular concepts as well.

---

[20] As to the meaning of these terms, see the text edited below; for the convention-theory, cfr. *Ordinatio* d. 2, q. 8 E; "Quarta posset esse opinio, quod nihil est universale ex natura sua, sed tantum ex institutione, illo modo quo vox est universalis, quia nulla res habet ex natura sua supponere pro alia re, nec vere praedicari de alia re sicut nec vox, sed tantum ex institutione voluntaria. Et ideo sicut voces sunt universales per institutionem et praedicabiles de rebus, ita omnia universalia."

Let us now compare the various opinions offered by Ockham. In the following scheme the certain and, as to the two treatments in our text, probable chronological succession of these opinions will be indicated by their location, reading from left to right. We indicate by an asterisk those opinions which at that time were admitted as at least equally probable. We also present these opinions in the order given by Ockham, since their place is significant.

ORDINATIO Ia Redactio	ORDINATIO IIa Redactio	PERIHERMENIAS 2nd Treatment	PERIHERMENIAS 1st Treatment	Qq. S. L. Physic.
Intellectio-th. Species-th.		Realistic-th. Qualitas-th.* (not specified	Habitus-th. Species-th.	Fictum-th. Realistic-th.
Habitus-th.		Fictum-th.*	Intellectio-th.*	Qualitas-th. (not specified)
Convention-th. Fictum-th.*			Fictum-th.*	Species-th.
				Habitus-th.
	Reinforcement of Intellectio-theory*			Intellectio-th.*

Now we are in a position to offer at least a probable opinion regarding the relation between the two treatments in *Perihermenias*. It seems to be more natural to presuppose that Ockham, when he was shaken in his belief in the *fictum*-theory and had become more inclined towards the *qualitas*-theory, did not yet have a clear idea as to the nature of this quality. But he soon realized that, in accordance with his whole system and with the principle of economy, the *intellectio*-theory could best satisfy him. Hence we presume that he first developed the three opinions in the second treatment *(Opiniones in genere)*, but after a very short time (as it seems) added a more detailed treatment. This addition starts (inB) right after the enumeration of three (!) opinions. He says here:

Qualis autem sit ista passio animae, an scilicet sit aliqua res extra animam, vel aliquid realiter existens in anima, vel aliquid ens fictum existens tantum in anima objective . . .

This is indeed discussed, and in the same order, in the *second* treatment. However, immediately after the announcement of the *three* opinions Ockham turns to a discussion of four opinions, of which, only one corresponds to those announced just before; and, of those announced before, the first is not treated at all, and the second is treated in three sub-divisions. This strange fact seems to suggest that Ockham first proceeded to a discussion of the three opinions *in genere*, but later inserted the first treatment in which he specified the quality which is a concept and identified it with the intellection.

If we consider the first treatment as an addition, another odd fact can be easily explained. In X we find answers to objections against the *fictum*-theory. But the objections are not in the second treatment of the three opinions *in genere*, but in the first treatment of the four opinions. This fact is very significant. Apparently Ockham took the objections against the *fictum*-theory out of the second treatment (chronologically the first!) and added them to the first treatment. Since the value of the *fictum*-theory was very much diminished for him, he left these objections there without an answer. But the answers remained in the second treatment. Finally, our hypothesis also explains why the quotation from Averroes (O) was omitted by Ockham from the first treatment, since he already had it in the second treatment (S).

However, Ockham himself must have realized the puzzling condition of his discussions on the nature of universals in *Perihermenias*. He certainly felt the need of rearranging the whole in a more systematic manner. Thus we can explain why the seven first questions of the *Quaestiones super libros Physicorum* again present the whole of the discussions, reshaped in a thoroughly systematic way. Most of the text in these *Quaestiones* is found literally in the text of *Perihermenias*, so that the former was called by Hochstetter[21] only a compilation from *Perihermenias*. However, I am firmly convinced

---

[21] *Op. cit.* 4: "Zum mindesten die ersten Quästionen über das Problem des Begriffes scheinen erst von späterer Hand zusammengestellt zu sein." L. Baudry ("Sur Trois Manuscrits Occamistes," *Archives d'histoire doctrinale et littéraire du Moyen Age* 11 [1936] 148) remarks: "Ces questions sont certainement de Guillaume d'Occam."

that this 'compilation' was at least made by Ockham himself in order
to bring the somewhat confusing exposition in *Perihermenias* into
a logical order. For I know compilations from Ockham's works which
were made by others; but the 'compilation' of the *Quaestiones super
libros Physicorum* is that of a master who made significant changes.
In fact, it is a new redaction of the discussions on this problem,
composed after Ockham had reached his maturity.

A detailed discussion of the various opinions, even beyond the
text published here, may be found in Hochstetter's study. One point
is absolutely certain — Ockham finally held only the *intellectio*-theory.

IV. REMARKS ON THE FOLLOWING EDITION

[Cfr. Traditio IV (1946) 319—335; both the Remarks and the
text are omitted by us.]

14. OCKHAM'S THEORY OF TRUTH[a]

The AIM of the following investigation is to show that the
concept of truth during the entire classical period of scholasticism
was connected with the theory of signification and supposition and
that this trend reached its complete development in Ockham's
teachings by a consistent and resolute application of the theory of
supposition. The *Venerabilis Inceptor* was not the first scholastic
theologian to adopt the theory of supposition from the medieval
logicians. We already recognize traces of this theory in theological
writings, not only as early as in the *Summa Theologica* of Alexander
of Hales,[1] but in the writings of Alexander's immediate predecessors
as well;[2] we find many references to the theory of supposition in
St. Bonaventure's work, as the index added to the first four volumes
of the Quaracchi edition clearly indicates. St. Thomas likewise

---

[1] Cf., e. g., *S. Theol.*, 1, n. 365, p. 541: *suppositio personalis*. [In the
present article "Alexander of Hales" always means the "Summa fratris
Alexandri"].

[2] In *S. Theol.*, 1, n. 364, I-II; p. 540, Alexander uses ideas of Prae-
positinus connected with supposition.

---

[a] First published in: FrancStud 5 (1945) 138—161.

makes use of the theory of supposition[3] and still more does Duns Scotus. However, the most extensive use of this truly medieval and genuine scholastic theory was made by Ockham in his theology and philosophy; in his writings it is present everywhere and applied with unsurpassed rigor, especially when he attempts to elucidate the concept of truth of statements, i. e., the concept of logical truth. It appears to us that, by this consistent reinterpretation of the concept of logical truth with the help of the theory of supposition, Ockham has presented a theory of truth which is truly scholastic, since basically it is what is nowadays called the theory of correspondence.

Hence we do not intend, nor do we wish, to propound radically new ideas contained in the writings of the *Venerabilis Inceptor;* we only intend to present Ockham's theory of truth as a most convenient means for a clearer understanding of the scholastic concept of truth. At the same time we hope that the theory of supposition, which is one of the greatest achievements of scholastic Logic, will again play that decisive rôle in neo-scholasticism which was assigned to it by the scholastics.

Our immediate task however, and in fact our main task will be to offer a historical presentation of this theory of truth. Hence we are obliged to regard the teachings of Ockham in a historical light, and, therefore, we shall deal first with the concept of truth developed or explained by some prominent scholastics of the thirteenth century and we will show that, insofar as they use the theory of signification and supposition, they lead to Ockham's theory. The second part of our study will deal with Ockham's own theory of signification. The third and final part will examine Ockham's application of the theory of signification and supposition to the analysis of logical truth.

HISTORICAL NOTES ON THE CONCEPT OF TRUTH IN SCHOLASTICISM

This historical sketch is not a complete history of the scholastic concept of truth. Such a history can not be presented within the limits of this survey nor is it necessary in order to attain the main

---

[3] E. g., in *S. Theol.*, I, 39, 3—6.

purpose of this study. In particular, the writer regrets that he was not able, for practical reasons, to include the prominent figure of Albertus Magnus in this sketch. For, insofar as medieval logic is concerned, Albertus Magnus is certainly of the utmost historical importance. Nevertheless it seems to be sufficient to select a few prominent Franciscan scholastics and St. Thomas in order to show that there has been a certain unity in the interpretation of the concept of logical truth by means of the theory of signification and supposition. Needless to say, since we are only interested in this particular aspect of their theory, we pass over the rest of their theory without denying thereby the existence of further clarifications and their importance.

If we consult neo-scholastic textbooks in regard to the concept and explanation of truth, we find but few which do not place special emphasis on the commonly called scholastic or Aristotelian or even Thomistic definition of truth: "Veritas est adaequatio rei et intellectus" (in this form or in one of its many variants). Almost every seminarian has to know it by heart and every teacher has to endure the affliction of explaining this definition to his pupils. For its fame certainly equals its obscurity. This statement may be shocking, at first sight, to some neo-scholastics. However, it is not altogether novel or radical. We are so fortunate as to be able to corroborate it by quotations from at least two authorities, one from the ranks of genuine late Thomism and another from the ranks of neo-scholastic Scotism. Cajetanus, the famous interpreter of St. Thomas, says: "Ex his autem patet quartum, quod obscuritatem magnam in hac materia ponit, scilicet quod veritas est conformitas intellectus et rei."[4] And Father Zacharias Van de Woestyne, O.F.M., remarks that the classical or traditional definition of truth, quoted by St. Bonaventure and St. Thomas, has to be interpreted by his own previous explanations, and since it has much obscurity, as Cajetanus states with many others, it is better to put it aside.[5] If this is so,

---

[4] *S. Theol.*, 1, 16, 2; comment. VII; ed. Leonina, p. 209.

[5] ... quia tamen ut cum multis declarat Caietanus (In S. Theol., 1, q. 16, a. 2) obscuritatem magnam facit, melius est eam seponere (*Cursus Philosophicus*, I [Mechliniae, 1921], 113, note 2). Does the author think of

then it is the more surprising that neo-scholastics cling to it so tenaciously.

However, we are told that it is famous, classical, Aristotelian, and even Thomistic. Let us, therefore, make clear at the beginning, that this definition was not formulated by St. Thomas, as he himself acknowledges; nor was it invented by Aristotle, who has left us many an obscure formula but not this one. According to Dr. G. Phelan: "For centuries it was believed and repeated that Isaac the Jew, Honain ben Ishak, an historian of Bagdad, who died in 876 A. D., was the author of the famous definition of truth . . ., but recent investigation has failed to reveal it in the writings of the Jewish compiler."[6] This substantially correct statement of Dr. Phelan needs a few clarifications, and as a Franciscan I feel it my duty to offer them. It is true that St. Thomas ascribes this definition to Isaac Israeli and that he believed it to be the definition given by the Jewish philosopher. But if "centuries of belief" means that scholastics of, let us say at least, the thirteenth and fourtheenth centuries commonly ascribed this definition to Isaac, the statement is hardly correct. For, we look in vain for any mention of Isaac as the author of this formula in Alexander of Hales, in Albertus Magnus, in St. Bonaventure, in Richard a Mediavilla, not to mention Scotus and Ockham who do not have this definition at all; and one is naturally led to wonder whether, besides St. Thomas, any scholastic (at least outside the Thomistic tradition, which can hardly be identified with the scholastic tradition in general) attributes this formula to Isaac. This much is certain: the main scholastic Franciscan tradition either

---

Cardinal Mercier also? The latter remarks with caution: "La définition traditionnelle: *Veritas est adaequatio rei et intellectus*, est donc irréprochable, mais il faut bien l'entendre" (*Critériologie générale, Cours de Philosophie*, IV [Louvain-Paris, 1923], 32). Cf. with this statement: "In my opinion the best definition of truth is the traditional scholastic definition, provided we understand and interpret it correctly, for it may be easily misunderstood and misinterpreted" (Ch. R. Baschalo. "The Nature, Source and Object of Truth", in *The New Scholasticism*, XII (1938), 232).

[6] "Verum sequitur esse rerum," *Medieval Studies* (published for the Institute of Medieval Studies by Sheed and Ward, New York, 1939), 1, 12.

attributes this formula only to a "quidam philosophus" or does not make use of it at all.

A second point needs clarification. Dr. Phelan speaks of "recent investigation" which "has failed to reveal it in the writings of the Jewish compiler", and substantiates his statement by a reference to an article written by Fr. T. J. Muckle.[7] Sincerely acknowledging the value of the brief study of Fr. T. J. Muckle, we must claim the credit for having discovered the absence of this definition in Isaac Israeli for the editors of the works of St. Bonaventure. Fr. Muckle himself acknowledges this by his reference to the investigation already made by the editors of Quaracchi. The latter tell us[8] that they have looked in vain for the famous definition, which was ascribed by St. Thomas to Isaac Israeli, in Aristotle and in Isaac Israeli's *De Definitionibus* — i. e., the wording of the formula, not the sense of it: "Si verba tantum spectas, definitio veritatis a S. Doctore hic proposita neque in uno neque in altero occurrit, sed si ad sententiam intendis, illa definitio habetur apud utrumque."

They then inform us that they have examined a manuscript of Munich which contains Isaac's work *De Definitionibus*, and that they have found a definition of truth different from the classical one. As evidence of this, they publish the entire definition of truth as given by Isaac.[9] Not satisfied, however, with this negative result,

---

[7] "Isaac Israeli's Definition of Truth," *Archives d'histoire doctrinale et littéraire du Moyen Age*, Paris, Vrin, VIII 1933, 1—8.

[8] *St. Bonaventurae Opera Omnia*, Quaracchi, 1, 707, note 5.

[9] Fr. Muckle's investigation goes farther insofar as he has examined other manuscripts also, with the same negative result. Cf. also J. T. Muckle, "Isaac Israeli *Liber de Definicionibus*," in *Archives d'histoire doctr. et litt. du M. A.*, (Paris Vrin, XI [1938]), where on pp. 307, 322, 323, 332 and 338, Isaac's definitions of truth are found. His starting point was apparently the erroneous remark in Ueberweg-Geyer, Die Patristische und Scholastische Philosophie, (11. Auflage, Berlin, 1938), p. 334; "Bonaventura (1 Sent. d. 40 a. 2, q. 1), Heinrich von Gent (M. de Wulf, *Hist. de la philos. scol. dans les Pays-Bas* usw. Louvain-Paris 1895, 166), Thomas von Aquin (*De verit.* 1 a. 1; *S. theol.* 1, q. 16 a. 2 ad 2) entnehmen die bekannte scholastische Wahrheits-definition; veritas est adaequatio rei et intellectus dem "Buch der Definitio-

they searched for a possible other source for the classical formula, and they tentatively point to Averroes and Avicenna. And, in fact, the definition given by Averroes certainly comes very close to the wording of the famous definition. For in his work, *Destructio Destructionum*, Averroes says: "Veritas namque, ut declaratum est in sua declaratione (definitione), est aequare rem ad intellectum scilicet quod reperiatur in anima, sicut est extra animam."[10]

It is strange that this remarkable investigation of the editors is so much overlooked, despite the fact that the editors always, at every occurrence of the famous formula, refer back to their discussion in the first volume, and the editors of Alexander of Hales[11] again referred to it and again printed the text of Averroes.

There is, therefore, much evidence, as the editors of St. Bonaventure have pointed out, that the famous, classical Aristotelian and even Thomistic definition goes back to Arabian sources. Hence neither its obscurity nor its origin recommend it for use in our textbooks.

---

nen Isaaks." Fr. Muckle, justly criticizing Geyer's statement, briefly mentions the important investigation of the editors of the works of St. Bonaventure; "He [Geyer] makes a reference to St. Bonaventure's Commentary on the First Book of Sentences (d. 40, a. 2, q. 1) where the definition is found. It is not there attributed to Isaac by St. Bonaventure and the footnote referred to below is repeated distinctly saying it does not occur in Isaac."

[10] Quoted by the editors according to the edition of Venice, 1495. Closely approaching the famous definition, though not as much as the preceding, is that of Avicenna, quoted by the editors from his *Metaphysics*, c. 9: "Veritas autem ... intelligitur dispositio dictionis vel intellectus, qui signat dispositionem in re exteriori, cum est ei aequalis." D. H. Pouillon, "Le premier traité des propriétés transcendantales. *La Summa de bono* du Chancelier Philippe," in *Revue Néoscolastique de Philosophie*, XLII (1939), 59, referring to the editors of Alexander of Hales and P. Minges, who are both more in favor of an Averroistic origin, decides rather, for historical reasons, in favor of an Avicennian origin of this formula. Cf. Parthenius Minges, O. F. M., "Philosophiegeschichtliche Bemerkungen über Philip von Grève," in Philosophisches Jahrbuch der Görresgesellschaft XXVII (1914), 21—32.

[11] *S. Theol*, t. I, p. 142, note 2.

1. ALEXANDER OF HALES

As far as we know at present, the famous definition of truth makes its first appearance in scholasticism with William of Auxerre, who according to Grabmann, died between 1231 and 1237, and with Philip the Chancellor (sometimes confused with Philip Greve) who died 1236 and wrote his *Summa de Bono* about 1230.[12] This work has deeply influenced Alexander's Summa and through it the early Franciscan school. It was from the *Summa de Bono* that Alexander most probably took the classical definition of truth when he wrote: "Item ponitur alia (definitio) a quodam philosopho: Veritas est adaequatio rei et intellectus, sicut generaliter adaequatio signi et significati."[13]

It is worthwhile to discuss this definition a little more in detail. For, what is striking is this, that the "famous" definition is linked up at once with the idea of signification as developed by St. Anselm, who in turn was undoubtedly under Aristotelian influence when he connected the idea of signification with the idea of truth, in his *Dialogus de Veritate*. We need but read the first chapters of Aristotle's *Perihermenias* and Anselm's work in order to convince ourselves of such an influence.[14] In Alexander's, or rather Philip the Chancellor's,

---

[12] Cf. M. Grabmann, *Geschichte der katholischen Theologie seit dem Ausgang der Väterzeit* (Herder Freiburg, 1933), p. 58—59. According to D. H. Pouillon (loc. cit., p. 59), William of Auxerre twice has the definition: "adaequatio intellectus ad rem" (*Summa aurea*, L. I. c. 10, p. 5, and L. I. Fr. 14, q. 3).

[13] *S. Theol.*, I, n. 89 IV; t. 1, p. 142. In the footnote to this definition the editors refer to the findings of the editors of St. Bonaventure, which we have already mentioned, and then quote Philip Grève (that is, Philip the Chancellor), who has literally the same definition as Alexander.

[14] ... Compare for instance St. Anselm, *Dialogus de Veritate*, c. 13 (or 14); PL, t. 158, c. 484C: "Cum enim significatur esse, quod est, aut non esse, quod non est, recta significatio est et constat esse rectitudinem, sine qua significatio recta nequit esse. Si vero significetur esse, quod non est, aut non esse, quod est, aut si nihil omnino significetur, nulla erit rectitudo significationis, quae nonnisi in significatione est...," with Aristotle, *Categories* (in the translation of Boethius, lib. I, PL, 64, c. 195D): "Nam quo res est vel non est, eo etiam oratio vera aut falsa esse dicitur..." The *Perihermenias* supplied Anselm with the idea and the terms of signification, probably through Boethius, where text and commentary give ample evi-

formulation of the classical definition, therefore, we see an attempt to interpret the obscure "classical" definition by means of Aristotelian terms through the influence of St. Anselm. And that is certainly a strange and unexpected fact.

As we are informed by the definition, the *adaequatio rei et intellectus* is only a special case of the relation of *signum* and *signatum*. Hence "intellect" has to be understood as "signifying intellect", and "thing" has to be understood as "signified thing". Thus we obtain the first clarification of this definition: Truth is the conformity *(adaequatio)* of the intellect, which is a sign, with the thing which is signified by this sign. Or, and more in Anselmian terms: Truth is the correctness or rightness *(rectitudo)* of the relation between a sign and that which is signified by this sign, i. e., in our case, between the intellect and the thing.

We must, however, leave open the question, whether Alexander means by "intellect" or "understanding" the concept and the mental proposition or the sensible sign and sensible proposition, since he does not distinguish between mental propositions and oral propositions, or at least he does not do so as clearly as one might desire. He does, however, distinguish the truth of simple comprehensions given by tradition to the truth of comprehension, whilst the classical one is referred to the truth of *signum* et *signatum*, that is to propositions.[15]

It seems certain that Alexander always links up the truth of signification at least with the truth of oral propositions, as was done by St. Anselm himself.[16] He also knows, of course, the Anselmian

dence of it. Anselm's own contribution seems to be the emphasis laid on the relation of conformity between *signum* and *signatum*, the correctness of which or the *rectitudo* of which is truth.

[15] "Nam quaedam [definitiones] datae sunt de veritate comprehensionis, ut illae Soliloquiorum, quae coincidunt in idem: Verum est, quod ita, ut est, videtur, et alia: Verum est, quod ita est, ut cognitori videtur, si velit possitque cognoscere. — Quaedam de vero signi sive significationis, ut illa: Veritas est adaequatio signi etc. vel intellectus etc." (*S. Theol.*, I, n. 89; t. 1, p. 143a).

[16] Cf. the relevant references to St. Anselm in *S. Theol.*, I, n. 89, ad 3; p. 143 b; and n. 94; p. 151.

distinction between the truth of cogitation, the truth of signification, and the truth of things, since he expressly refers to it.[17] But "cogitation" can hardly be interpreted in the sense of concept or mental proposition, but rather as imagination, i. e., as mental construction or even fiction, according to its etymology: *co-agitatio*.[18] On the other hand, *significatio* does not apply to the word as mere sound, but to a word insofar as it conveys meaning, which of course is given or perceived only by the intellect. This may account for the lack of a distinction between the signification of the word and the signification of that which is in the mind and the relation between both.

We must not, however, overlook another very important distinction which was made already by St. Anselm and which was taken over by many scholastics, since it brings us as close to the theory of supposition as is possible here. For, with St. Anselm, Alexander distinguishes between a signification which is made or applied by actually signifying the signified, and the signification which is assigned to a proposition as such and which is given to it or assigned to it regardless of its actual use and application to a concrete fact. For instance, the proposition *Dies est* has received *(accepit significare)* or has been assigned the signification that it is day, whether it is day or not; that is, it simply signifies by itself because of this

---

[17] "Sicut distinguit Anselmus, quod est veritas rei et veritas cogitationis et significationis, sic falsitas multipliciter: falsitas rei, ut homo pictus est homo falsus; et falsitas cogitationis, ut montes aurei falsi montes; et falsitas enuntiationis vel significationis, ut hominem esse asinum est falsum. Dicendum ergo, quod falsitas rei est in rebus, falsitas cogitationis est in anima — prout dicitur in Psalmo: Anima mea impleta est illusionibus — falsitas enuntiationis in voce prout est signum" (*S. Theol.* n. 96, Resp.; p. 154).

[18] Wilpert, in his article quoted in note 30, points out the importance of the right understanding of the term *cogitare*. He writes (p. 73, note 1): "Wenn z. B. Suarez, Joh. a Sancto Thoma und andere die Ausdrucksweise des hl. Thomas mißdeuten, so liegt der Grund dafür zum größten Teil in einer Wandlung der Begriffe. Wir dürfen das thomistische cognoscere häufig geradezu mit Bewußtseinhaben von, denken übersetzen. Dagegen bezeichnet cogitare bei Thomas noch durchwegs das discursive Denken entsprechend seiner ursprünglichen Bedeutung co-agitare. Nicht mehr so bei Suarez. Vg. Descartes: Mens semper cogitat (hat Bewußtsein)."

assignment that it is day. Such a signification is, of course, by definition always correct, since the proposition retains this signification as
long as it is assigned to it, and consequently is not affected by the state
of thing or by reality. But when signification is made, i. e., when
such a proposition with this definite signification is applied to a
concrete situation or state of thing (in our case, when it is used in
order to express that it is now actually day), then the proposition
either actually signifies the fact or it does not; if it does, it is right
as to its signification and consequently the proposition is true; if
it does not, then it is not right as to its actual or made signification,
and consequently it is false.[19]

The distinction between assigned and made signification ultimately comes down to the distinction between signification as such
and the actual use of signification in a proposition about facts, i. e.,
supposition. That signification as such and supposition is here referred to the whole proposition rather than to the terms makes no
essential difference. What is important for us, is that such a distinction is made between signification as such and the application of
this signification in or as a proposition, and that truth or falsity is
only given in applied signification, whilst the assigned signification
is not susceptible of falsity. The Anselmian term for the correctness
of such a signification, or the *rectitudo* as truth of a proposition in
applied signification, means, therefore, that the "supposition" of
this proposition (or its terms) is right, and only if that is given, is
the proposition true; if not, the proposition is false. Alexander

---

[19] "Alia est rectitudo et veritas enuntiationis, quia significat ad quod
significandum est facta; alia quia significat quod accepit significare. Facta
est enim ad significandum rem esse dum est, et non esse dum non est;
accepit autem significare rem esse indifferenter, dum est et dum non est.
Verbi gratia, sive dies sit sive non sit, haec oratio "dies est" accepit significare diem esse. Primo modo veritas dicta est mutabilis et separabilis in
contingentibus; secundo modo, inseparabilis. Primo modo est susceptiva
veri et falsi; veritas in hac enim vita non attenditur secundum id, quod
accepit enuntiatio, sed secundum id, ad quod est; secundo modo non, quia
attenditur id, quod accepit. Unde Anselmus dicit quod primam veritatem
habet accidentaliter, secundam naturaliter" (*S. Theol.*, I, n. 89, ad 3;
p. 143). For the whole quotation, cf. Anselmus, *Dialogus de Veritate*, c. 2;
PL, t. 158, c. 470 B s.

merely substitutes the term *adaequatio* for *rectitudo:* "Est enim veritas signi, secundum quod dicimus orationem veram esse, cum ostendit rem esse sicuti est; et secundum hoc veritas est adaequatio signi ad id cuius est signum."[20]

We may conclude, therefore, that in the writings of Alexander of Hales, through St. Anselm and ultimately through Aristotle, we find a definition of logical truth in terms of signification and of the equivalent of supposition.

2. ST. BONAVENTURE

As is to be expected, the Seraphic Doctor in general follows the line of thought of his master, Alexander. He takes over the "classical" definition of truth understood and interpreted with Anselmian terms. On the other hand, he brings more to the fore the Aristotelian background of the interpretation in Anselmian terms. These various historical relations are made more apparent when St. Bonaventure states that truth concerning a *complexum* (the Aristotelian term for a proposition) is the truth of signification, and that this truth is given when the sign signifies the thing as it is, and furthermore, that this conformity of sign and thing signified is the *adaequatio* intended by the classical definition:

> Verum enim dictum de complexo respicit compositionem, sicut dicit Philosophus, quia veritas et falsitas circa compositionem consistit; et ideo dicit veritatem signi. Signum autem est verum, quando significat, rem se habere, sicut se habet; tunc enim dicitur adaequari . . .[21]

There is no doubt that this statement is couched in the terminology of Anselm as well as Aristotle and perhaps that of Aristotle more so than of St. Anselm. This becomes even more obvious in the answer to the third objection of the same question, where the Seraphic Doctor quotes Aristotle's notification of truth in the *Categories* (in the chapter on substance) but falls immediately in line with St. Anselm, so that the editors here refer to St. Anselm alone:

---

[20] *S. Theol.,* n. 93, ad 1—2; p. 150 b. St. Anselm's famous and more general definition: "Veritas est rectitudo sola mente perceptibilis," is quoted by Alexander in n. 89, VIII; p. 142.

[21] I *Sent.,* d. 46, a. u., q. 4, t. 1, p. 828.

Unde Philosophus non dixit: "Ab eo, quod res *est* tantum," sed: "*est* vel *non est*." Et est sensus: ad eo quod res *est*, est oratio vera, quae significat ipsam *esse*, et ab eo quod *non* est, est falsa, quae significat *esse;* e contrario intelligendum in re, quae *non est*.[22]

We may gather from all this that, according to the Seraphic Doctor, the truth of a proposition is given, if the affirmative proposition signifies a thing that is, and the negative proposition signifies a thing that is not (certain qualifications will be added later). If the opposite cases are given, we have falsity of proposition. Saint Bonaventure, therefore, like Alexander of Hales, understands the classical definition of truth to be a case of the signification of propositions; and, like his master, he explains it with Aristotelian and Anselmian ideas.[23]

However, we look in vain in St. Bonaventure's works for a clear and expressly stated distinction between a mental and an oral or written proposition. On the other hand, the Seraphic Doctor follows his master in making St. Anselm's distinction between signification which is assigned to a proposition and the signification which is made or applied. In other words, he too has an equivalent of supposition. Instead of assigned and applied signification he adopts the Anselmian terms of essential (or natural) and accidental signification (which are also used by Alexander). Thus in every proposition *(enuntiatio)* we have an essential truth which is due to the fact that the signs used are instituted to signify certain objects, and this instituted signification of a proposition is always given, whether the proposition is true or false. Hence the proposition, considered only in its meaning of signification, without its application to a concrete

---

[22] *Loc. cit.* ad 3 m. p. 829, Justly the editors refer here to St. Anselm only, since they have given the reference to Aristotle already in note 4, p. 828; here in note 2 they refer both to Aristotle's *Perihermenias* and to St. Anselm's *Dialogus de Veritate!*

[23] St. Bonaventure quotes the Anselmian definition: "Veritas est rectitudo sola mente perceptibilis," in II *Sent.*, prol., t. 2, p. 4a in connection with the classical definition; he links up the classical definition with the Anselmian idea of *signum* and *significatum*, in II S., d. 37, a. 2, q. 3, ad opp. 2, t. 2 p. 875. He links up the classical definition with the Aristotelian notification of truth in I *Sent.*, d. 40, a. 2, q. 1, ad 1—3, t. 1, p. 707, and elsewhere.

fact, is always true and never false (let us add, as long as a certain signification is assigned to the terms). From this essential and always given truth, we have to distinguish the accidental truth, which, as the term indicates, is not given with the proposition as such, but which is given only if the signification of the proposition is applied to a fact and squares with the fact or the actual thing which is represented or expressed by the proposition. If thus the actual state of affairs is represented by the proposition, we have the adequation or conformity between sign and signified; if not, we have falsity.[24]

It is clear then, that according to the Seraphic Doctor, we have to look for truth in the relation of signification; more exactly, we learn that truth is a property, a condition, of the relation between the *signum* and the *significatum* in and through a proposition, the *significatum* being anything which can be signified in this way. Hence the basis for the truth of a proposition is not only being, but non-being as well, not only position, but also privation and defect.[25]

---

[24] "In omni enuntiatione duplex est veritas: una essentialis, et haec est veritas, qua propositio repraesentat illud, ad quod repraesentandum instituta est; et haec numquam privatur ab enuntiatione; omnis enim enuntiatio significat illud, ad quod instituta est, sive sit vera, sive falsa. Alia vero est veritas accidentalis, quae attenditur in propositione in hoc, quod repraesentat rem, secundum quod est — tunc enim dicitur adaequari signum signato; et veritas enuntiationis non est aliud quam quaedam adaequatio — et haec veritas privatur per falsitatem. Tunc enim est propositio vel enuntiatio falsa, quando signum non repraesentat rem, sicut est, vel res non est, sicut repraesentatur per signum. Et hoc est, quod dicit Philosophus: Ab eo, quod res est, vel non est, dicitur oratio vera; hoc est dicere, ab eo, quod res est, sicut repraesentatur, dicitur oratio vera; ab eo quod res non est, sicut repraesentatur, dicitur oratio falsa. Sicut igitur iniustitia est privatio rectitudinis, sic falsitas est defectus adaequationis . . ." (II *Sent.*, d. 37, a. 2. q. 3, t. 2, p. 874).

[25] "Ideo cum quaeritur, super quid fundetur veritas enuntiationis; non oportet, quod ex parte rei respondeat aliqua veritas. Sicut enim verum ens contingit vere significari ipsum esse, sic etiam de illo, quod nullo modo est, contingit vere significare, quod ipsum non est. Sicut enim significatio dicit relationem, quae non requirit significatum esse in actu; sic etiam veritas signi, quae quidem dicit conditionem illius relationis, non exigit fundari super aliquam rem actualiter existentem . . ." (II *Sent.* d. 37, a. 2, q. 3, ad 4m, t. 2, p. 875).

This is very important and it is worthwhile to emphasize it, since one could be misled by the formula which is sometimes quoted: *Verum sequitur esse rerum*, to believe that truth is always *directly* based on being. For we are convinced that the extension of this formula to propositions of non-existence leads necessarily to the theory of signification. The Seraphic Doctor does not deny that being is the ultimate basis of the truth of propositions, but he denies very clearly that it is always the direct basis of truth. This will become evident from an interesting addition to I *Sent.*, d. 46, a. u., q. 4 ad 3m, where the problem discussed is: What is the basis of the truth in a true proposition?

Some people, according to the Seraphic Doctor, distinguish three kinds of true propositions and to each type they assign a different basis of their truth: In an affirmative or positive proposition, for instance in the proposition: *Caesar est homo*, the basis of truth is the reality itself, namely, the being which is Caesar. In a privative proposition, for instance in the proposition: *Caesar est homo mortuus*, the basis of truth is reality only in a certain sense *(secundum quid)*, since a privation (the term *mortuus*) connotes something, that is a being, which is deprived. In a negative proposition, however, for instance in the proposition: *Caesar non est*, the basis of truth is nothing. However, at least the last basis assigned does not satisfy the Seraphic Doctor, for he objects: when we say: "this proposition is true," the predicate "true", which here qualifies the proposition, predicates some condition of being, and consequently must be based on something which is a being.[26]

Others maintain that the basis of truth in such statements is the principles of reality — in the case of Caesar, matter and form. However, such a basis cannot account for the truth of propositions of non-existence. For let us assume that Caesar be completely destroyed as to both matter and form; nevertheless, the proposition: *Caesar fuit*, or *Caesar non est*, remains true.

---

[26] "Sed tamen illud non videtur sufficere, quia, cum dicitur: haec oratio est vera, verum praedicat aliquam conditionem entis: ergo necesse est super aliquid fundari, quod sit" (I *Sent*, d. 46, a. u. qu. 4, ad 3m, t. 1, p. 829).

Others, finally, maintain that the basis of truth of such propositions is the understanding subject. This opinion, however, is refuted at once by the Seraphic Doctor by the brief but very remarkable statement that even if no one actually understands the proposition: *Caesar fuit,* and if it were written on a wall, it nevertheless would be true.[27] Hence there can be no doubt that the Seraphic Doctor does not confuse the truth of a statement with the cognition of the truth of a statement and that he, like Ockham, puts special emphasis on the fact that a proposition as such is true or false, i. e., in objective verification regardless of subjective verification.

In his positive answer to our problem, the Seraphic Doctor once more falls back on St. Anselm's theory of signification. The truth of a proposition is the truth of a sign, as we have explained before. But this truth is not an absolute quality or property of a proposition, but only a relative property, given in the relation of the sign to that which is signified. That means: if the relation of signification is correct, the proposition is true; if it is not correct, the proposition is false. Now it does not belong to the essence or definition of signification that that which is signified is a being or something in reality; it is only required that it be something that can be known, a *cognoscibile.* Consequently signification and even true signification does not imply the reality or being of that which is signified. On the other hand, since everything which the intellect grasps or understands is either grasped or understood as being or grasped or imagined in comparison with being or as related to being, it follows that every signification or the truth of signifying speech is either directly *(simpliciter)* based on being or indirectly, in relation *(in ordine)* to being. The first instance is given in the true statement: *Petrus est,* provided, of course that Peter exists. The second instance is given in the statement: *Petrus fuit,* or *Petrus erit* — here we have a relation to the present time —, or even in the true statement: *Caesar non est,* since this proposition is equivalent to: *aliquod est ens, quod non est Caesar.* The same is also assumed for the statement: *Chimaera non est hirco-*

---

[27] "Sed adhuc illud non videtur sufficiens: quia esto quod nullus intelligat actu, adhuc oratio ista est vera, scripta in pariete: Caesar fuit" *(loc. cit.).*

cervus.[28] Unfortunately, the Seraphic Doctor does not point out and declare the relation to being in the last statement. We assume that he means that that which is signified by the term *chimaera* is not the same as that which is signified by the term *hircocervus*. But where in this case is the relation to being, if we do not form new propositions? Or does he mean: the concept of the one is not the same as the concept of the other? The relation to being is of course easily seen in the former instance: *Caesar non est*, since the Seraphic Doctor resolves it, reminding us of a similar resolution of existential propositions made by modern logic: There is something, and this something is not Caesar.

This may suffice, since our intention was only to show that St. Bonaventure's theory of truth is an outstanding example of the theory of correspondence interpreted in terms of signification and an equivalent of supposition. Summarizing, we may say that truth is the conformity between the signifying proposition and that which it signifies. Falsity, consequently, is the difformity of the signifying proposition with that which it signifies.[29]

3. ST. THOMAS

It is only "with fear and trembling" that I deal here with St. Thomas' theory of truth in relation to signification. For I know well that there is no unanimous interpretation of the texts of St. Thomas

---

[28] Ideo dicendum, quod cum veritas orationis sit veritas signi, et veritas signi non dicat qualitatem absolutam — sicut nec necessitas consequentiae— sed respectivam, sicut signum; cum omne, quod contingit significare contingit vere significare, et etiam falso: sicut ad rationem significandi non oportet rem esse entem, sed cognoscibilem, sic nec ad rationem verae significationis. Et quoniam omne, quod intellectus capit, vel est ens, vel capit sive imaginatur per comparationem ad ens; ideo omnis significatio et veritas orationis significantis vel fundatur simpliciter super ens, ut si dicatur: Petrus est, vel in ordine ad ens. Unde propositio de praeterito fundatur super ordinem eius ad praesens; similiter propositio de futuro, sicut propositio negativa, ut si dicatur: Caesar non est; aliquod enim ens est, quod non est Caesar, et sic de aliis; similiter si dicatur; chimaera non est hirco cervus" *(loc. cit.)*.

[29] Cf. II *Sent.*, d. 37, a. 2, q. 3, ad opp. 2: "Item veritas est adaequatio rei et intellectus, et falsitas est inadaequatio rei et intellectus, per oppositum . . ." In his answer St. Bonaventure links up these definitions with the theory of signification.

even amongst the Thomists. And furthermore, it may appear almost ridiculous to go into a discussion of the definition of truth according to the Common Doctor, because any textbook of Thomistic philosophy, of which there is no scarcity, should suffice to enlighten us with the clarity of St. Thomas' philosophy itself. I thought so, too. But I was disappointed. In fact, they appeared rather confusing to me. I then hoped for light from those Thomists who have devoted special studies to the theory of truth according to their great master, and there is certainly no scarcity of such historical articles either.[30]

---

[30] We have examined the following articles:

Baumgartner, Matth., "Zum thomistischen Wahrheitsbegriff," *Festgabe für Clemens Bäumker* (*Supplement-Band, Beiträge zur Geschichte der Mittelalterlichen Philosophie*, herausg. von Cl. Bäumker) (Münster, 1913), pp. 241—260. There is no mention of any connection between the theory of truth and the theory of signification.

Roland-Gosselin, M. D., "Sur la théorie thomiste de la vérité" *Revue des Sciences Philosophiques et Théologiques*, X, (1921). The result is likewise negative; the author, however, is more interested in the epistemological problem.

The same, "La théorie thomiste de l'erreur," *Mélanges thomistes, Bibl. Thom.*, III (1923), 253-274. The same result.

Wilpert, P., "Das Urteil als Träger der Wahrheit nach Thomas von Aquin," *Philosophisches Jahrbuch der Görresgesellschaft*, XLVI (1933). This remarkable study, too, does not mention the aforesaid connection.

Kremer, R., C. SS. R., "La synthèse thomiste de la vérité," *Revue Néoscolastique de Philosophie*, XXXV (1933), 317—338. The result is essentially negative, though a few lines on p. 327 repeat what St. Thomas says in S. Theol., I, 16, 2 (cf. note 35); this is used by the author for a friendly and just criticism of Mercier, in footnote 4.

Keeler, L. W., "St. Thomas' Doctrine Regarding Error," in *The New Scholasticism*, 1933, p. 26—57. Does not mention the theory of signification, though there is a reference to the text in our footnote 35 (p. 40, note 47).

Phelan, G., "Verum sequitur esse" (see note 6), likewise does not mention it and is more interested in the metaphysical background of the classical formula.

Muller-Thym, B., "The To be which signifies the truth of propositions," *Proceedings of the American Catholic Philosophical Association*, XVI (1940), 230—254. See the following note.

Ryan, J. K., "The problem of Truth" *Essays in Thomism*, edited by R. E. Brennan, O. P. (Sheed and Ward, 1942), pp. 65—79. Here too, the

Again, I was sadly disappointed, and hardly found what I was looking for. Most of them, as also the textbooks, try to make the classical formula of truth more savory, interpreting it with speculations, some of which are difficult for me to accept. Almost all of them, however, observe a strange silence concerning the theory of signification and supposition in relation to the Thomistic theory of truth.[31]

On the other hand, it cannot be denied that St. Thomas also has something to say about signification in relation to truth, and in my opinion, much better things than Thomists usually discover in the texts of their master. Hence, once more, I had to turn or return to the texts of St. Thomas himself, and even more so, because I was warned by a Thomist, who happens to be an expert in modern logic, that one of the best elucidations concerning the truth of propositions given by St. Thomas no longer plays a rôle in the textbooks.[32]

In order to do justice to those who have dealt with the Thomistic theory of truth, let us first state that we do not maintain that they misinterpreted St. Thomas; we only say that they have not said enough and certainly not that which, in our opinion, is most lucid in St. Thomas. Secondly we wish to state that many of them (Wilpert at least is an exception) have not carefully followed the development of St. Thomas himself. No one can reasonably deny that there is

---

result is essentially negative, though two lines on p. 66 repeat in free translation what is said in note 35 by St. Thomas.

I was not able to consult Romeyer, B., "La théorie de Saint Thomas sur la vérité. Esquisse d'une synthèse" *Ann. Phil.*, III. 2 (1925).

It may be well to repeat that I have not made a universal statement about the lack of the connection between the theory of signification and the theory of truth in modern Thomistic literature.

[31] B. Muller-Thym, *op. cit.*, is at least somehow an exception, since he uses freely the term "signify" and devotes even a few lines (pp. 248—249) to the signification of subject and predicate in true proposition.

[32] Bochenski, I. M., O. P., "Notes historiques sur les propositions modales," *Revue des Sciences Philosophiques et Théologiques*, XXVI (1937), 674, note 3: "*Summ. Theol.*, I, q. 13, a. 12. Cette théorie thomiste si remarquable ne figure plus dans les manuels."

evidence of a development in St. Thomas' ideas, but, as in the case of Aristotle, this fact is much overlooked, especially in regard to the works following the Commentary on the Sentences. Dismissing here for our study the Commentary on the Sentences, we can consider the following sequence of the works of St. Thomas relevant to our problem as safely established:

Quaestiones de veritate: 1256—1259.
Summa contra gentiles: completed 1264.
Summa theologica: since 1266.
In libros Perihermenias: since 1269.

Now, it seems that the theory of signification is not linked up with the theory of truth in the first two works, but it is definitely connected with it in the two last works. In consequence, there can be expected a difference — not a contradiction — of interpretation of the Thomistic theory of truth according as the principal source is the former of the latter works. In this study we shall follow St. Thomas exclusively in the latter writings, in accordance with our purpose.

We must concede to Dr. Phelan that the definition of truth, expressly attributed to Isaac Israeli by the Common Doctor, plays an important rôle in St. Thomas' latter writings as it does in his former works. But it is likewise true that in the *Summa Theologica* St. Thomas uses the terms significare and signum in order to explain what is meant by this obscure definition. After one has read Thomistic explanations of truth burdened with heavy metaphysical specula- tions, it is a relief to find St. Thomas himself saying that the truth of an affirmative proposition is a case of signification. For such an affirmative proposition is then true, if subject and predicate signify somehow the same, insofar as the thing or the reality is concerned, but something different, insofar as the meaning of the terms is concerned: "Ad cuius evidentiam sciendum est, quod in qualibet propositione affirmativa vera, oportet quod praedicatum et subiec- tum significent idem secundum rem aliquo modo, et diversum secundum rationem." And he explains what he means, using as example the proposition *Homo est albus.* The meaning of *homo* and the meaning of *albus* differ, but both refer to the same concrete *suppositum.*[33]

When, therefore, St. Thomas a little later (in 16, 2) defines truth as the conformity between intellect and thing: "Et propter hoc per conformitatem intellectus et rei veritas definitur," we have to understand this formula in the sense previously explained. Hence the *intellectus* is the entire proposition, with its various relations of signification of subject and predicate and the copula, the thing is the reality or the being about which the proposition is made. Hence, if the plurality of subject and predicate, both usually (the statement of identity would be an irrelevant exception) conveying different meanings, signify the same thing or *suppositum*, they stand for the same thing in this proposition; this identity of the thing for which subject and predicate stand is signified by the composition of the two terms in the proposition, which composition is signified by the copula *est:* "Huic vero diversitati, quae est secundum rationem, respondet pluralitas praedicati et subiecti; identitatem vero rei significat intellectus per ipsam compositionem" (*loc. cit.*, 13, 12).

At any rate, the conformity or correspondence (the *adaequatio*) of a proposition (the *compositio*) with the actual state of affairs or with the thing, is truth. To know this conformity means to know truth. Both the conformity and the knowledge of this conformity are different.[34] To know truth only reveals this already established conformity to the mind, but does not create it. On the other hand,

---

[33] "Manifestum est enim, quod homo et albus sunt idem subiecto et differunt ratione; alia enim est ratio hominis, et alia ratio albi. Et similiter cum dico: Homo est animal; illud enim ipsum quod est homo vere animal est; in eodem enim supposito est et natura sensibilis, a qua dicitur animal, et rationalis, a qua dicitur homo. Unde et hic etiam praedicatum et subiectum sunt idem supposito, sed diversa ratione" (*S. Theol.*, I, 13, 12).

[34] Wilpert, in his article quoted in note 30, shows clearly the difference between the *verum* as object and as content of an act of judgement or of the *enuntiatio* and he decides against Johannes a Sto Thoma in favor of Caietanus, that the *verum* as content is the subject of truth: "Es ist das Hindenken eines Sachverhalts auf einem Gegenstand rein als solches, das die für die Wahrheit charakteristische Beziehung und Vergleichung schafft, und es ist das Urteil als Denken eines Sachverhalts als eines gegenständlichen, das den primären Träger der Wahrheit bildet" (p. 72).

the knowability (this term being taken in its broadest sense) is essential to the relation which establishes truth of composition or the logical truth. Hence, only where there is a conformity knowable by the intellect can we speak of logical truth. In the act of simple apprehension, either of the senses or of the intellect, there is only the act of knowing the object and no composition of known objects, and consequently no knowing or knowability of a conformity. Hence such an act of simple apprehension does not reveal or manifest or make known the relation in which it stands to the known object. But only if the intellect applies one form which is signified by the predicate, to a thing signified by the subject (affirmative proposition) or removes the one from the other (negative proposition) do we have composition or division and with this either truth or falsity.[35]

Here again the act of composition or forming an affirmative or negative proposition is linked up with signification. For, it is expressly stated that predicate and subject signify the same thing, though under a different aspect.

We will stop here, since it is sufficient for us to have shown that St. Thomas in his *Summa Theologica*, i. e., in his later period, certainly links up his theory of truth with his theory of signification. A comparison with his Commentary on Perihermenias can only confirm this. But we shall abstain from such a discussion, since it does not reveal essentially new ideas concerning our problem. We shall add only two remarks. St. Thomas' theory of signification is not generally accepted by the scholastics; for, whilst the Angelic Doctor, certainly in agreement with tradition since Boethius, emphasizes indirect signification of words, meaning that the word signifies the concept and through the concept the thing, Scotus and Ockham decide in favor of direct signification of the thing by the word with which a certain meaning is connected. This problem will be taken up later.

---

[35] "Sed quando iudicat rem ita se habere sicut est forma quam de re apprehendit, tunc primo cognoscit et dicit verum. Et hoc facit componendo et dividendo; nam in omni propositione aliquam formam significatam per praedicatum, vel applicat alicui rei significatae per subiectum, vel removet ab ea. Et ideo bene invenitur quod sensus est verus de aliqua re, vel intellectus cognoscendo quod quid est; sed non quod cognoscat aut dicat verum" (*S. Theol.*, I, 16, 2).

On the other hand, it is remarkable that St. Thomas makes evident the distinction between words or spoken signs and the mental terms or concepts. He prefers to call the former signs in the strict sense, whilst he reserves for the latter the term *similitudo*.[36] This however, appears to us to be a matter of terminology rather than of serious disagreement with other scholastics, since those who call the concepts signs, also emphasize the fact that mental signs are natural similitudes of reality.

4. DUNS SCOTUS

The *Doctor Subtilis* does not, as far as we were able to ascertain, use the famous definition of truth, though there are unmistakable allusions to it. Furthermore, he does not deal with our problem *ex professo* in his theological works and his remarks on the notion of truth are scarce. However, we are fortunate in having at our disposal at least one question concerning our problem, namely, in his *Quaestiones in libros Metaphysicorum*. Since we have some doubts,

---

[36] Cf. for instance: "Comparantur autem ad intellectum voces quidem sicut signa, res autem sicut ea quorum intellectus sunt similitudines . . ." (*Lectura* III *in Periher.*, n. 7, ed. Leon., p. 16). Cf. also n. 9, p. 17: "Quod quidem iudicium, si consonet rebus, erit verum, puta cum intellectus iudicat rem esse quod est, vel non esse quod non est; falsum autem quando dissonat a re, puta cum iudicat non esse quod est, vel esse quod non est. Unde patet quod veritas et falsitas sicut in cognoscente et dicente non est nisi circa compositionem et divisionem. Et hoc modo Philosophus loquitur hic. Et quia voces sunt signa intellectuum, erit vox vera quae significat verum intellectum, falsa autem, quae significat falsum intellectum . . ."

Cf. also the following text in which St. Thomas explains why he does not call the concepts or the *passiones animae* or the *intellectus* "signa", though they signify things: "Ubi attendendum est quod litteras dixit esse notas, id est signa vocum et voces passionum animae similiter; passiones autem animae dicit esse similitudines rerum: et hoc ideo, quia res non cognoscitur ab anima nisi per aliquam sui similitudinem existentem vel in sensu vel in intellectu. Litterae autem ita sunt signa vocum, et voces passionum, quod non attenditur ibi aliqua ratio similitudinis, sed sola ratio institutionis, sicut et in multis signis; ut tuba est signum belli. In passionibus autem animae oportet attendi rationem similitudinis ad exprimendas res, quae naturaliter eas *designat*, non ex institutione" (*op. cit.*, lect. II, n. 9, ed. Leon., p. 14).

though no definite proof, as to the authenticity of the *Quaestiones in libros Perihermenias* (at least of the *Opus secundum*), we prefer to disregard the latter for our study, and to base it on Quaestio 3ª libri VI^i of his Commentary on the Metaphysics of Aristotle, though a preliminary study has convinced us that there is substantial agreement between the latter and the former work.

The *Doctor Subtilis* clearly distinguishes ontological and logical truth, and in the sphere of logical truth or the truth of the intellect he makes the customary distinction between the truth of simple apprehension and of composition and division or of propositions.[37] In regard to the latter he distinguishes again, as St. Thomas did, between the truth of a proposition as such and the truth of a proposition as comprehended by the intellect.[38] We are here concerned only with the former. In his first approach to the question the *Doctor Subtilis* says that the truth of a proposition considered in itself is exactly the conformity of the sign, which is the proposition, with the thing, or the object that is signified: "Sed verum in signo dicit significatum esse id, quod manifestatur per signum, et in hoc signum manifestare illud, quod est, et ita conformitatem signi ad signatum."[39]

However, the *Doctor Subtilis* is well aware of the ambiguity of this preliminary formula or definition of truth, since it applies to the sign-relation of simple concepts as well as to the sign-relation of complex concepts or propositions. Without going into details, we can say that according to Scotus the difference between these two relations is this, that the meaning (the *signatum*) of the simple concept has no other existence than to be the object of this conceptual act, i. e., it is as it is conceived, and hence no difformity can enter this sign-relation. On the other hand, the sign-relation of a complex

---

[37] Loc. cit., n. 6, ed. Vivès, t. V, p. 338 *et seq.*

[38] The latter is apprehended in a reflexive act; cf. loc. cit., n. 7, p. 339. Scotus here mentions again the *propositiones neutrae*, which however have nothing to do with a third "truth-value" besides truth and falsity by the intellect. I have dealt with this problem in the second volume of *Franciscan Institute Publications: William Ockham, Tractatus de praedestinatione...*, edited with a study on the medieval problem of a three valued logic, which is at present in the hands of the printer; [St. Bonaventure, 1945, p. 58—88].

[39] Loc cit., n. 8, p. 34ob.

concept (i. e., here, of a proposition) *presupposes* the sign-relation of the simple concept; in other words, the sign-relation of the simple concept naturally precedes the sign-relation of the proposition and thus is the basis for the agreement or disagreement, for conformity or difformity of the sign which is the proposition with the signs which are the simple concepts. The objects or the meanings of the simple concepts thus measure the proposition and account for its truth or falsity. Because they are in virtual agreement or disagreement before they are formed into a proposition, they measure the actual agreement or disagreement of a proposition when it is actually formed.[40]

Hence truth considered in itself and not considered as object of the intellect is the conformity of a complex concept or a proposition with the relation virtually given by the extremes or the simple concepts. If the proposition is in conformity with the *significatum* (meaning) of its elements, the proposition is true; if it is in difformity, it is false. This is stated so generally that it comprises all the possible relations, given in any true or false proposition.[41]

There still remains the task of specifying a little more the relation of conformity or difformity which is given in true propositions. In a proposition we have the comparison of two terms. If the comparison of the one simple concept with the other concerns the same thing, we have an affirmative proposition; if it concerns a different thing,

---

[40] "Propter illud notandum est, quod obiectum simplex, quod est signatum conceptus simplicis, nullum esse habet aliud, quam in conceptu, secundum quod esse debet mensurare illum conceptum; obiecta conceptus complexi, quae sunt extrema, aliud esse habent, quam ut sunt in conceptu complexo, et prius naturaliter in se ut simplicia sunt, secundum quod esse prius mensurant illum conceptum complexum, cui esse priori conceptum complexum conformari est verum esse, difformari est falsum esse; hoc esse est habitudo virtualiter inclusa in extremis ante naturaliter quam extrema comparentur a ratione, sed in simplici nihil est prius naturaliter in extremo, cui conceptus potest conformari et difformari" (*loc. cit.*, n. 9, p. 341).

[41] Unfortunately, Scotus exemplifies the truth of principles (based on the relation of two terms only) and that of conclusions (based on two terms and a middle term) and contingent facts as regards the apprehension of the truth-relation, not as regards the relation as such, but as object of cognition. Cf. *loc. cit.*, n. 10, p. 341bs.

it is a negative proposition; this act of comparison between two simple concepts constitutes as such, and hence necessarily, a mental relation between the one concept and the other. This mental relation is signified or expressed by the copula *est*.[42] The mental relation thus constituted is in conformity with the thing — since we presuppose a true proposition. As is evident from the preceding, this conformity is that of a relation between two simple concepts with the thing. What does this conformity mean? It does not mean that the same relation, which exists as mental relation between the terms, is given in reality or in the thing; for then the statement of identity: *homo est homo* would be false, since, as we understand Scotus, the relation *homo* identical with *homo* is not repeated or anticipated by the thing *homo*.[43] Nor is it necessary to take refuge in the distinction between matter and form, and understand the relation of predication between subject and predicate as reflecting or corresponding to the relation of matter and form. For the proposition as such does not express this relation, and especially the statement: *Deus est Deus*, would then be false.[44] This conformity of the relation expressed by predication can only mean that it reflects or makes explicit what is virtually in the

---

[42] "... sed est actus comparativus unius conceptus simplicis ad alterum, ut eiusdem in affirmativa, vel diversi in negativa; hunc autem necessario sequitur vel concomitatur relatio rationis in utroque extremo ad alterum, quarum habitudinem videtur signare hoc verbum ,est', ut est nota compositionis, scilicet prout est tertium adiacens . . ." (loc. cit., n. 13, p. 344 a).

[43] "Ulterius, ista habitudo rationis conformis est rei, non quod oporteat in re esse relationem aliquam inter extrema, ut in re similem isti rationis, quae est inter extrema ut intellecta, immo ut ab intellectu invicem comparata; nam tunc esset haec falsa, homo est homo" (loc. cit., n. 13, p. 344 a s).

[44] "Nec oportet fugere ad compositionem formae cum materia; tum quia illam non exprimit propositio; tum quia haec esset falsa: Deus est Deus" (loc. cit. n. 13, p. 344 b). St. Thomas, S. Theol., 1, 13, 12: "Sed in propositionibus in quibus idem praedicatur de seipso, hoc aliquo modo invenitur; inquantum intellectus id quod ponit ex parte subiecti, trahit ad partem suppositi, quod vero ponit ex parte praedicati, trahit ad naturam formae in supposito existentis, secundum quod dicitur quod praedicata tenentur formaliter, et subiecta materialiter." Cf. also Metaphys., IX, II, n. 1896—1898.

thing; that means, if the thing were able to produce this relation between the terms of a proposition, it would produce it by its very being. Hence the mental relation conforms with the thing itself and has its objective basis in it, though it does not exist in it. This conformity is that of the sign as proposition with the significatum which is the thing. It is obvious from the preceding that the proposition as sign is not a sign which is similar to the thing, since it belongs to a different order than the thing, and hence it is an equivocal sign; but nevertheless as sign it expresses that which is in the thing. And again, it is not an arbitrary sign of that which is in the thing, but a natural sign.[45]

From all this it follows that, according to Scotus, the truth of a proposition is that of correct signification. The relation between the two extremes of a proposition, signified by the copula *est*, signifies an identity or diversity in regard to the thing about which the proposition is made. And that could be rendered: if both predicate and subject supposit for the same (in an affirmative proposition) or not for the same (in a negative proposition). This is expressed clearly by Scotus in the *Oxoniense*, where he explains the truth-relation of the proposition: *Deus est Pater, Filius, et Spiritus Sanctus*. What the subject-term signifies first, is first posited in this proposition; if now the predicate is the same with it, the affirmative proposition which denotes this identity is true. "God" is the subject in our proposition; "Father, Son and Holy Ghost" is the predicate. What is signified by the subject is the same as that which is signified by the predicate; therefore, the proposition is true.[46]

---

[45] "Sed tunc hic habitudo correspondet rei, quando est talis, qualem res virtualiter continet, sive qualem res de se nata esset facere in intellectu, si faceret habitudinem illam, sive quae est signum non simile sed aequivocum exprimens tamen illud quod est in re, sicut circulus non est similis vino, est tamen verum signum vini, falsum autem lactis, vel huiusmodi; non tamen est omnino simile, quia illud signum est ad placitum huius signati, non sic illa habitudo rei" (*loc. cit.*, n. 13, p. 344b).

[46] "Respondeo, quod propositio est vera, quia terminus subiectus, quod primo significat, hoc primo ponit in oratione; et si illud aliud extremum, quod praedicatur, sit idem, propositio affirmativa denotans talem identitatem, vera est. Deus autem significat naturam divinam ut est nata praedicari de supposito, et illud significatum est idem tribus personis, igitur propositio hoc significans est vera" (*Ox.* I, d. 4, q. 2, n. 2, t. 9, p. 429).

Hence, Scotus too explains his theory of truth with the help of the theory of signification and an equivalent of the theory of supposition.

5. OCKHAM

It is not our intention to explain here in detail the theory of truth according to the Venerabilis Inceptor; for, a full explanation of it presupposes an acquaintance with his theory of signification and supposition, which will be discussed later.[b] Only a general characterization of his theory will be given here briefly.

There seems to be no evidence of the existence of the classical formula of truth: *Adaequatio rei et intellectus*, in the works of Ockham. Not even the term *adaequatio* plays any rôle in his declaration of truth.

Truth and falsity can be predicated only about propositions, mental, oral or written. No *incomplexum* or part of a proposition, but only a proposition and its equivalents in personal supposition can be said to be true or false.[47]

Verum and *falsum* predicated about a proposition mean or express the correspondence between the proposition and the fact, i. e., between the proposition as *signum* and the fact as *significatum*. If, therefore, the proposition signifies the state of thing or the thing as it is, the proposition is true; if it signifies it as it is not, the proposition is false.[48]

This much will suffice for the time being. At any rate, we hope to have made clear that Ockham stands in a line with respectable scholastics who all attribute an important rôle to the theory of signification in the clarification of the notion of truth. The origin of this interpretation is to be found in Aristotle and St. Anselm.

---

[47] "Complexum est verum vel falsum, sed nullum incomplexum est verum vel falsum, sicut patet de istis: homo, album, animal, currit et sic de aliis" (*Expositio aurea, In Praedicam.*, cap. 7, ad: Videtur autem omnis affirmatio . . .).

[48] "Sed veritas et falsitas sunt quaedam praedicabilia de propositione importantia, quod est ita vel non est ita a parte significati, sicut denotatur per propositionem, quae est signum. Unde propositionem esse veram est: ita esse in re, sicut significatur per eam; et propositionem esse falsam est: aliter esse, quam significatur per eam" (*Expositio aurea, In Periherm.*, prooem., ad: Est autem quemadmodum . . .). Cf. *Quodl.*, VII, 4 (ed. Argentina), et alibi.

[b] Cfr. the next two articles in the present volume.

15. OCHHAM'S THEORY OF SIGNIFICATION[a]

Our previous investigation[b] has sufficiently shown that already in the thirteenth century the theory of signification and at least an equivalent of the theory of supposition were linked up with the theory of truth. This historical sketch has proved that Ockham's theory of truth, which is more explicitly based on the theory of supposition than that of any other previous system, remains within the pale of the Scholastic tradition; but it has also prepared the way for making the difference between his own theory and that of his predecessors evident. The Venerabilis Inceptor is in agreement with his predecessors in maintaining that the relation which constitutes the truth of propositions is a relation of correct signification or supposition; but he disagrees with them — in different degrees — regarding the exact specification of this relation.

Ockham follows Aristotle[1] when he refers the predicate "true" or "false" only to propositions, whether spoken, written or mental. Propositions are composed of spoken, written or mental terms. The terms in a proposition have a certain supposition, and supposition in its turn is related to signification. Hence we have to start our analysis with a discussion and explanation of Ockham's theory of signification.

---

[1] Secundo notandum, quod raro invenitur a Philosopho quod ponit aliquam veritatem vel falsitatem nisi in propositione, et ideo, ut communiter, Philosophus non vocat aliquid verum vel falsum nisi propositionem. *Expositio super 1ᵐ librum Perihermenias*, ad: Est autem quemadmodum in anima . . . Cf. P. Wilpert, "Zum Aristotelischen Wahrheitsbegriff", in *Philosophisches Jahrbuch der Görres-Gesellschaft* 53 (1940) 1—16, especially p. 16: "Für eine Entwicklung im Wahrheitsbegriff des Aristoteles können wir feststellen, daß die ontologische Wahrheit Platons mehr und mehr zurücktritt und an ihre Stelle die logische Wahrheit den ersten Platz einnimmt, wenn auch die ontologische Bedeutung des Begriffes nie ganz verschwindet."

---

[a] First published in FrancStud 6 (1946) 143—170.
[b] The preceding article in this volume.

The present article will quote Ockham's texts extensively, partly because these texts are not easily accessible, and mainly because they are almost all revised according to the best manuscripts known to us.

1. THE MEANING OF SIGN NOT CONFINED TO LANGUAGE

A faithful account of Ockham's Semantics must avoid the danger of confusing different types of signs, because he himself has carefully distinguished them. "Sign" can be taken in a very broad sense, but then signs which are terms (spoken, written or mental) are not necessarily a sub-class of sign in general, though they may partly be characterized by the properties of sign in general. Or "sign" can be taken in the specific meaning of language-sign; and so it needs a specific characterization. We shall first deal with the meaning of sign in the broader sense.

According to Ockham, a sign in the broad meaning of the term is everything which, when apprehended, makes something different from itself, which is already habitually known, actually known:

(Signum accipitur) pro omni illo, quod apprehensum aliquid aliud in cognitionem facit venire, quamvis non faciat mentem venire in primam cognitionem eius, sicut alibi est ostensum, sed in actualem post habitualem eiusdem.[2]

This notification of the meaning of sign is undoubtedly inspired by the much quoted definition offered by St. Augustine:

Signum est enim res praeter speciem quam ingerit sensibus aliud aliquid ex se faciens in cogitationem venire.[3]

However, we note immediately that Ockham's wording differs in important details from the definition given by St. Augustine. In fact, Ockham's definition while wider in its scope yet adds a certain limitation.

It is wider in its scope. For Ockham calls "everything which makes something different from itself known" a sign. Hence, by definition, the function of sign is not confined to sensible facts; on the contrary, everything, whether it is a thing or a sign, a material

---

[2] *Summa Logicae*, I, cap. 1 [Edit. Boehner I 9].

[3] *De Doctrina Christiana*, II, cap. 1 (1); PL t. 34, col. 35; cf. the distinction between natural and artificial signs, *loc. cit.* cap. 1 (2) and 2 (3).

or an immaterial reality, can be a sign in this sense if it is the cause of the knowledge of something else. Smoke, for instance, is a sign in this sense, for it can be the cause of the knowledge of fire; or a word, too, is a natural sign in this sense, for it is a natural sign of its cause, *viz.*, the speaker. Furthermore, the barrel hoop in front of an inn is also a sign in this sense, since it can be the cause of knowing that there is wine in the inn.[4] And, let us add, though Ockham does not enumerate an immaterial sign amongst the instances, that a sign in this sense would also be a concept, the cognition of which can call to my mind the cognition of the corresponding word, or the cognition of another concept.

The limitation added by Ockham is very significant. Since it has been usually misunderstood, we are forced to enlarge on it here. Our previous characterization has shown that sign in this sense always means the cognition of something which, in a broad sense, is the cause of the cognition of another thing. Hence, it implies two cognitions, which are distinct, and two objects which are known. By this it is already distinguished from language-sign, for not every language-sign implies two cognitions. This distinction is made even more evident by Ockham when he says that the second cognition, which is caused by the first cognition of a thing (which is the sign), is a secondary cognition or a recordative cognition; that means, the second cognition, which is had through the cognition of the first thing (the sign), has been previously obtained, was stored in the memory (hence habitually known), and is revived or called back or actually known, because of the cognition of the sign. It is the general thesis of Ockham that no sign in this first sense can give us the primary cognition of another thing.

Let us at once take the most shocking case: since an effect is the natural sign of its cause, the effect, too, can lead only to a secondary cognition of its cause, If, therefore, the cause was never experienced before by intuitive cognition, the effect cannot lead to the cognition of the cause. To put this more *in concreto*, if the knowledge

---

[4] Et sic vox naturaliter significat, sicut quilibet effectus significat saltem suam causam; sic etiam circulus significat vinum in taberna. *Summa Logicae*, I, cap. 1 [Edit. Boehner I 9].

of fire is not yet habitually possessed by the knower, the cognition of smoke cannot lead him to the cognition of fire. He must have already had the habitual knowledge of fire and must already know that fire produces smoke before smoke can lead him to the cognition of fire.

We purposely formulated the preceding "illustration" vaguely in order to make understandable (not, however, justifiable) the shock which is usually experienced by those who understand Ockham in such an imprecise manner, and who express his genuine thought in a similar imprecise manner. Anyone who does not follow Ockham himself in his precise terminology will invariably misinterpret Ockham's texts, and the other picture of Ockham as an anticipation of Hume or as a skeptic is then easily constructed.

In order to avoid such confusion we have to bear in mind that Ockham does not say anything about deduction or any kind of inferential operation; he is not even strictly speaking of propositions. He only speaks of cognition. He never has denied the *inference* from an effect to *a* cause. However, he has constantly denied the transition from one simple cognition (which is no proposition) to another simple cognition, if this other simple cognition is not more universal than the former.

What he means by this is best explained as regards one special sign, *viz.*, that of an image or vestige since in dealing with this problem Ockham explains what he means by secondary cognition in opposition to primary cognition, and since he again refers here to his treatment in the prologue of the *Ordinatio* of the transition from one simple cognition to another.[5] Both image and vestige have this in common, that the things which are images or vestiges, are signs making something different from themselves known. For instance, the tracks in the mud bring, or may bring, to one's mind the cognition of an ox. In this case, we have two distinct cognitions: the first is the cause of the second. But, and here is the problem, does the first cognition, *viz.*, that of the tracks, cause a primary cognition of the ox, so that

---

[5] Q. 5 a principalis seu 9 a in ordine. Ockham refers to this question in the *Ordinatio*, d. 3, q. 9, which is used here, and he probably refers to both questions in the above-quoted text in footnote 2.

by itself or with the intellect this first cognition is sufficient to cause for the first time the simple and incomplex cognition of the ox which was never before known?

Before answering this question, Ockham introduces distinctions as regards the transition from one cognition to the cognition of something different from it. Such a transition can be from one cognition either to another primary cognition or to another secondary cognition. The secondary cognition is always understood as recordative knowledge or knowledge which was previously obtained by immediate experience or intuitive cognition and is stored in the memory, and which is therefore, when actually known, the revival of a primary cognition; and for this reason it is called secondary cognition. Now Ockham admits the transition from one cognition to another primary cognition that is a non-recordative knowledge, in two cases: (1) the transition from the cognition of a singular to that of a universal, and (2) the transition from the cognition of the premises in a syllogism to the cognition of the conclusion. Hence, as regards, the cognition of universals and of the conclusions of inferences, the acquisition of primary cognition is explicitly admitted by Ockham, and in these cases no further direct and immediate experience is necessary.[6] But Ockham does not admit such a transition from one cognition to a primary cognition of another thing, if this primary cognition is simple (not composed of more than one notion), if it is proper (not a notion common to several things), if it is *in se* (not in a part of it), if it is incomplex (not a proposition). In such cases inference is ruled out by definition, and simple, proper, *in se*, and incomplex cognition rules out any other cognition which

---

[6] Alia conditio, quod tam vestigium quam imago ducit in notitiam illius, cuius est imago vel vestigium. Sed tamen aliquid ducere in notitiam alicuius potest intelligi dupliciter: vel tamquam causativum notitiae alterius mediante sua notitia, ita quod notitia ipsius sit causa notitiae alterius; vel immediate sine notitia, sicut intellectus ducit tamquam in notitiam cuiuslibet intelligibilis. Primo modo contingit dupliciter: quia vel ducit in primam talem notitiam vel cognitionem, vel tantum facit rememorationem de aliquo habitualiter noto. Primo modo notitia singularis est causa notitiae universalis, et notitia praemissarum est causa notitiae conclusionis. *Ordinatio*, d. 3, q. 9, B.

is not directly based on intuitive knowledge.[7] Hence, Ockham does not contradict himself when he admits that we have knowledge of God by a proper concept composed of common notions, though we do not have a proper and simple knowledge of God.

---

[7] Sed isto modo numquam notitia unius rei incomplexa est causa notitiae primae alterius incomplexae, sicut dictum fuit in prologo; et maxime non est causa sufficiens cum intellectu et aliis quae requiruntur a parte potentiae, sive sit causa partialis cum obiecto sive non. *loc. cit.*

The addition "simple and proper" to incomplex knowledge in our explanation is warranted by Ockham's own back-reference to Prolog. q. 9 (in ordine). Here we read:

Ideo quantum ad istum articulum dico primo, quod universaliter numquam notitia unius rei extra incomplexa est causa sufficiens etiam cum intellectu respectu primae notitiae incomplexae alterius rei... Primum declaratur per experientiam: Quia quilibet experitur in se, quod quantumcumque intuitive et perfecte cognoscat aliquam rem, numquam per hoc cognoscit aliam rem, nisi praehabeat notitiam illius alterius rei. Verbi gratia, si cognoscam ista inferiora et numquam vidissem corpora superiora, nullam notitiam haberem de sole, luna et stellis et huiusmodi corporibus. Et ratio est, quia omnis notitia abstractiva alicuius rei in se *[vel notitia simplex propria alicuius rei]*, naturaliter loquendo, praesupponit notitiam intuitivam eiusdem rei; sed notitia intuitiva alicuius rei numquam potest haberi natuialiter nisi effective vel mediate vel immediate ab illa re, ergo nec notitia abstractiva, et per consequens nulla. Maior patet, et maxime de notitia acquisita, quamvis aliter posset fieri per divinam potentiam; quia, sicut prius argutum est, inter causam et effectum est ordo et dependentia maxime essentialiter et tamen ibi notitia incomplexa unius rei non continet notitiam incomplexam alterius rei. Hoc etiam quilibet in se experitur, quod quantumcumque perfecte cognoscat aliquam rem, quod numquam cogitabit (cogitatione simplici et propria) de alia re, quam numquam prius apprehendit, nec per sensum nec per intellectum. Sicut si aliquis intuitive videret substantiam, numquam per hoc distincte cognosceret aliquod accidens in particulari. *Ordinatio*, Prol. q. 9 (in ordine), F.

The text in the parenthesis (italicized) is in EF1MOOb, but lacking in FTMa (for the meaning of the sigla, cf. our article: "The Text-Tradition of Ockham's *Ordinatio*," in *The New Scholasticism* 16 (1942) 206 ss.) [supra, 113 ff.]. According to our investigations, this addition favorable to our interpretation, is most probably not authentic. On the other hand, the addition in the second parenthesis has to be considered [authentic. It is an addition made by Ockham in his second redaction, since it is lacking in F and is a marginal note in T. Ockham made this addition probably because

Let us apply this to our illustration: the tracks in the mud can lead us to the cognition of some cause in general, of which they are the effect, but that is common knowledge obtained by inference; they can, however, not lead us to the proper and simple knowledge

---

he foresaw a possible misinterpretation, which unfortunately was not even prevented by both the additions which are actually in the edition used by all modern interpreters. We are sorry to be forced again to state that Prof. Gilson's treatment and interpretation of this same passage simply misses the point; cf. *Unity of Philosophical Experience*, New York, Charles Scribner's Sons, 1937, pp. 86 ss. Seen in the light of Ockham's text itself and within its proper setting, the explanations offered by various authors, to say the least, appear to us very confusing. Has not Ockham himself to remind his Scotistic critics (Cf. 1. c. E) that Scotus whom he is criticizing speaks only of incomplex knowledge, and that he is criticizing Scotus only in this regard? On the other hand, Ockham's denial does not concern general common knowledge, that is, abstractive knowledge of the type of universals, nor does it concern inferential knowledge in general, and certainly not the validity of the principle of causality. Cf. the following text:

Concedo, quod notitia unius obiecti continet notitiam alterius obiecti, et hoc contingit per illationem, sicut quando conclusio infertur ex praemissis, vel per compositionem, sicut quando ex notitia termini vel terminorum cognoscitur evidenter aliqua propositio sive contingens sive necessaria; vel per abstractionem, sicut cognito aliquo singulari virtute illius notitiae potest abstrahi aliquod commune et sic cognosci, et tamen sine omni notitia praevia cuiuslibet singularis non potuit cognosci, et ideo notitia illius singularis erit causa notitiae illius communis. Tamen notitia unius singularis numquam est causa sufficiens cum intellectu notitiae alterius singularis, quae non est communis sibi. *loc. cit.* L.

A little before this text the inference from complex knowledge (proposition) of an effect to that of a cause is expressly admitted by Ockham. The following text has bearing on the problem of sign in this connexion, and shows, in an addition, how anxious Ockham was not to be misunderstood:

Ad aliud: quod quando notitia similitudinis causat notitiam illius, cuius est similitudo, illa non est causa sufficiens cum intellectu, sed necessario requiritur notitia habitualis illius, cuius est similitudo. Unde si aliquis videret statuam Herculis et nullam notitiam penitus haberet de Hercule, non plus per hoc cogitaret de Hercule quam de Achille; sed quia prius novit Herculem et remanet in eo notitia habitualis Herculis, ideo, quando postea videt similitudinem suam, virtute illius notitiae habitualis

of the particular ox, if we have never seen that ox before. Consequently, the primary cognition of the ox cannot be caused by the mere intuition of the tracks. Likewise, no one can get the primary knowledge of a person whom he has never seen before, by merely looking at an image of him; for instance, when he is looking at a statue of Hercules, whom he has never seen before, this cognition as such does not lead him to the first cognition of Hercules himself, for as far as the observer is concerned it may resemble any person unknown.

Therefore, what Ockham is driving home here is the fact, confirmed by unbiased experience, that from the incomplex, proper, and simple cognition of one fact, an incomplex, proper and simple cognition of another fact never before experienced cannot be obtained. The transition between such cognitions has been categorically denied by Ockham, but not the transition by inferential operations.[8]

From all this it follows that Ockham takes "sign" in this sense for anything which recalls something else to the knower; only such

---

et istius visionis similitudinis ducitur in actum rememorandi de Hercule et non in notitiam primam ipsius Herculis. (Et ideo dictum est prius, quod notitia unius rei extra non ducit sufficienter cum intellectu in notitiam primam alterius rei in se. Et voco notitiam rei in se, quando illa incomplexa cognitione nec aliqua parte ipsius aliquid aliud ab illa re intelligitur, per quod excluditur instantia, per quam probatur, quod cognosco Papam, quam numquam vidi). l.c. L.

The text in parenthesis is lacking in F and is a marginal note in T, a sure sign that it is an addition of the second redaction.

[8] *Ex superabundanti* let us add one of the earliest texts of Ockham, where the Venerabilis Inceptor expressly admits inferential knowledge of facts which are not experienced and this with the help of common notions:

Item ex notitia incomplexa alicuius rei in se non potest causari notitia incomplexa alicuius rei in se, sicut in prologo dictum est (texts quoted in the preceding footnote). Unde quantumcumque videas essentiam divinam clare, numquam videbis per hoc asinum in se, ita quod una notitia causetur ex alia; igitur si notitia incomplexa creaturae duceret in notitiam incomplexam Dei, hoc erit in conceptu communi creaturae et Deo. Et hoc modo concedo, quod notitia incomplexa alicuius creaturae in se ducit in notitiam alterius rei in conceptu communi. *Report.*, lib. III, q. 9, R.

a sign "re-presents", that is, presents again to the knower what he formerly had known, if we take to "re-present" in its strict meaning.[9]

2. THE MEANING AND FUNCTION OF LANGUAGE-SIGNS

Whilst the term "sign" as explained before has universal applicability, since everything can function as sign in this sense, "sign" in a more restricted sense, which is moreover not necessarily subordinated to the former, applies only to those signs which compose language. Hence, we shall call them "language-signs". Of course, language is by origin related to speech or the utterance of words. However, we do not always take language in this narrow sense, but shall use the term language for written or mental or any other type of language as well, provided it satisfies certain conditions which are to be made explicit. In the course of this investigation, the difference between language-signs and signs in general will become evident.

a. General Characterization of Language-Signs

Ockham defines language-signs in reference to language. Hence the logical course to follow would be, first, to explain what he means by language in general, or mental, spoken and written language. Unfortunately, Ockham has never given us such a general definition of language. He has, however, at least explained what he means by *oratio* as oral expression and locution. From this we are able to gather, in an indirect manner, what he means by language in general. The meaning of mental language, not of written language, will then present certain problems, which will be discussed as we go along.

An oral or spoken language or *oratio* is a composition of verbal expressions or words. Words are sounds which fulfill the following conditions. (1) They must be *voces*, that is, they must be produced by the vocal apparatus of a living being; hence, sounds of instru-

---

[9] Secundo modo una res incomplexa mediante notitia sua potest esse causa partialis rememorationis alterius rei habitualiter notae, ita quod notitia habitualis necessario concurrit in ratione causae partialis. Et tale sic cognitum potest vocari repraesentativum alterius, nec est aliquid aliud proprie repraesentativum. *Ordinat.* d. 3, q. 9, B.

ments, etc., are not considered *voces*. (2) They must signify something or they must have significative function. Hence, they must at least be able to make known something different from themselves. This will be explained more definitely later. (3) Their signification is assigned to them by a voluntary act of man; hence, they are artificial and not natural signs; for natural signs do not signify *ad placitum*, but regardless of any instituted or artificially assigned signification by man.[10]

It is neither our intention nor our task to go into a detailed discussion of the different kinds of words used in the construction of oral language. Ockham, too, leaves most of this to grammarians.

Oratio, which is the placing together of words, that is, of significative sounds as explained, can be understood either in a wide sense or in a narrow and strict sense. In a wide sense, any aggregation of

---

[10] This characterization of "word" is taken from Ockham's explanation of Aristotle's definition of "noun:" Nomen ergo est vox significativa secundum placitum sine tempore, cuius nulla pars est significativa separata. But, as the following text will show, it refers also to words in general:

Secundo notandum, quod per hanc particulam "vox" excluditur sonus qui non est vox, cuiusmodi est sonus instrumentorum musicorum et aliorum inanimatorum. Per hanc particulam "vox significativa" excluduntur voces insignificativae sicut verba et huiusmodi. Per hanc particulam "ad placitum" excluduntur voces significativae naturaliter, sicut risus, ploratus et huiusmodi ... Quinto notandum, quod vox significativa tripliciter accipitur, scilicet strictissime, stricte et large: Strictissime loquendo coniunctiones et praepositiones non sunt significativae dicente Boethio: Coniunctiones et praepositiones nihil omnino nisi tantum aliis coniunctae significant; immo etiam isto modo signa universalia et particularia et universaliter omnia syncategoremata, sive sint nomina large accipiendo nomina sive verba, si quae sunt talia, sive adverbia sive aliae quaecumque partes orationis non sunt significativae; et hoc, quia nullius rei determinatae intellectum faciunt nisi coniunctae cum aliis. Stricte autem vox significativa est illa, quae alicuius rei determinatae intellectum facit, sive per se posita sive cum alio. Et isto modo participia, interiectiones, pronomina et quaedam adverbia sunt significativa, sicut patet de istis: bene, male, legens, disputans et huiusmodi ... Tertio modo accipitur large vox significativa pro omni voce, quae sive per se significat sive quae significat cum alia; et isto modo omnes partes orationis sunt significativae. *Expositio super Periherm.* c. 1, ad: Nomen ergo est vox significativa ... This is a revision of the very corrupt text of the edition.

words is called *oratio*. Thus understood, an *oratio* may have, for instance, a verb, or it may not, since a mere aggregation of nouns and adjectives would already be an *oratio*. Similarly the aggregation of one noun and one adjective would be an *oratio*, and of course the aggregation of a noun and a verb, etc. In a strict sense, however, *oratio* is a suitable arrangement of words, composed of a verb and a noun or the equivalent of it. What is suitable has to be established by grammar; Ockham does not enlarge upon it. Such *orationes* — let us now call them by the common name of sentences, are of various types: they may be imperative sentences which express a command, deprecative sentences which express a prayer or a wish, interrogatory sentences which express a question, etc., and declarative sentences which express a state of affairs.[11] The declarative sentences are also called *propositiones* or *enuntiationes*. They are characterized by their capability of receiving the predicates true or false. Whilst the rhetorician, the poet, and of course all people in ordinary speech make extensive use of all types of sentences, the logician is interested only in those sentences which are true or false.[12] Hence for the rest we shall confine ourselves to propositions or declarative sentences, and to the signs which are found in such sentences.

---

[11] Intelligendum est, quod oratio dupliciter accipitur: Uno modo large; et sic omnis congeries dictionum est oratio; et isto modo definitio quaelibet est oratio sicut tales definitiones: animal rationale, substantia animata sensibilis, informatum albedine; isto modo hoc quod dico: homo albus, et similiter album animal et huiusmodi sunt orationes. Aliter accipitur oratio stricte, et sic oratio est congrua dictionum ordinatio, ubi verbum contingit et nomen vel aliquid loco nominis. Et sic oratio dividitur in indicativam, imperativam, optativam, etc. Et sic definitiones et talia: homo albus, Sortes musicus, non sunt orationes. *Expos. super Perihermenias*, cap. 3, ad: Est autem oratio ...

[12] Dicit (Aristoteles) igitur primo, quod non omnis oratio est enuntiativa, sed illa sola, quae est vera vel falsa. Quod autem non omnis oratio sit enuntiativa patet: quia oratio deprecativa est oratio, et tamen neque est vera neque falsa, et per consequens non est enuntiativa. Et ideo tales orationes, quae nec sunt verae nec falsae, et per consequens non enuntiativae, relinquantur, quia tales magis spectant ad rhetoricam vel poeticam quam ad dialecticam; quia ad dialecticam non pertinet considerare nisi tantum de oratione enuntiativa. *Expos. super Perihermenias*, cap. 4, ad: Enuntiativa vero ...

Since Ockham has explained the parts of spoken propositions to which the parts of mental propositions correspond, we can now from the structure of oral propositions indirectly ascertain what he means by mental language. He uses the following principle as guiding rule: whatever is necessary in oral propositions for a distinct signification, has a corresponding part in mental propositions.[13] This practically comes down to the more definite rule: whatever changes the truth or falsity of a proposition, has its corresponding part in the mental proposition.[14] Then we can say that at least the following parts of oral propositions have an equivalent in mental propositions. (1) Nouns, verbs, conjunctions, prepositions, and adverbs have corresponding or equivalent instances in mental language. (2) The common accidents of nouns, as case and number, too, have corresponding instances in mental language. (3) The common accidents of verbs, as mood, person, tense, and number, again, have corresponding instances in mental language.

As to the other grammatical properties of oral expressions, Ockham partly denies that they have corresponding instances, partly he leaves it in doubt. He is inclined to hold the opinion that participles have no corresponding instances.[15] He leaves it in doubt whether

[13] Sed quod oporteat ponere talia nomina mentalia et verba et adverbia et coniunctiones et praepositiones ex hoc convincitur, quod omni orationi vocali correspondeat alia mentalis in mente; et ideo sicut illae partes propositionis vocalis, quae sunt propter necessitatem significationis impositae, sunt distinctae, sic partes propositionis mentalis correspondenter sunt distinctae. *Summa Logicae* I, cap. 3 [Edit. Boehner I 14].

[14] Quod patet ex hoc, quia omni orationi vocali verae vel falsae correspondet aliqua mentalis composita ex conceptibus; ergo sicut partes propositionis vocalis, quae imponuntur ad significandum res propter necessitatem significationis vel expressionis, — quia impossibile est omnia exprimere per verba et nomina solum quae possunt per omnes partes alias orationis exprimi, — sunt distinctae partes, sic partes propositionis mentalis correspondentes vocibus sunt distinctae ad faciendum distinctas propositiones veras vel falsas, *Quodl.* V, q. 8. Cf. also *Summa Logicae* I, 3, where, however, the text is unfortunately corrupt.

[15] *loc. cit.* As to the participle cf. *Quodl.* V, q. 8: Nulla est necessitas ponendi talem pluritatem in mente, quia verbum et participium verbi sumptum cum hoc verbo "est" in significando aequipollent et sunt synonyma . . .

pronouns have corresponding instances in mental language, and likewise whether abstract and concrete terms must also be distinguished in mental language.[16]

We are not interested here in a detailed discussion of this correspondence. We are interested only in the fact that according to Ockham mental language has a structure similar in a certain degree to that of spoken language, so that every structural element which is in mental language is in spoken language also; but not *vice versa*.[17] For the rest, we shall confine ourselves to signs which have corresponding instances, for they and only they have logical bearing, whilst the others are added merely for the sake of adorning spoken and written language.

Now, we are finally in a condition to understand Ockham's definition of language-signs as distinct from signs in the general meaning of the term. Language signs must fulfill the following conditions: (1) They must be signs, that is, they must make something else known or must be able to make it known. Of course, they share this condition with signs in general; however, Ockham omits here the former characterization that such signs lead only to a secondary cognition on the basis of habitual knowledge derived from a primary cognition. This should not be over-looked, since it shows how careful Ockham is not to burden his logic with epistemological difficulties. Though it is obvious that oral language-signs can function and usually do function like signs in general, this is certainly not generally true for mental language-signs. For according to Ockham these mental language-signs are, as we shall see later, intellections. Since these mental language-signs are intellections or cognitions, which are obtained by intuitive knowledge and not through a species or any other intermediary, they are either the first or direct cognition of an object, and thus make it known or signify or represent it, or they are merely the revival of a former cognition, in which cognition again

[16] Cf. *Summa Logicae*, I, chapters 5 ss., where Ockham treats this question in detail by distinguishing various modes of concrete and abstract terms [Edit. Boehner I 16 ff.].

[17] Est autem inter nomina mentalia et vocalia differentia: quia quamvis omnia accidentia grammaticalia quae conveniunt nominibus mentalibus, etiam nominibus vocalibus sint convenientia, non tamen econverso. *Summa Logicae*, I, cap. 3 [Edit. Boehner I 12].

the object is known without any intermediary. Hence, there is no need for the former double relation between the cognition of a thing which leads to the cognition of another thing. Finally, it is very hard to see how certain language-signs as the *syncategoremata* can have this double relation. (2) They must have a significative function within the realm of language; that is, they must be able to have this function, though it is not always necessary that they actually exercise this function in propositions. Such signs, again, can be of a different type according to their definite or not-definite signification, that is, they can be either categorematic or syncategorematic terms or verbs and other parts of language, or they can be compositions of these different kinds of language-signs or whole propositions.[18] In summarizing we may say that anything which can exercise a significative function in language is a language-sign.

b. The Nature of Mental Language-Signs.

Assuming that the nature of written or spoken language-signs[19] does not present a specific problem within the framework of our

---

[18] Cf. *Summa Logicae*, I, cap. 1: Aliter accipitur signum pro illo, quod aliud facit in cognitionem venire et natum est pro illo supponere vel addi in propositione, cuiusmodi sunt syncategoremata et verba et illae partes orationis, quae finitam significationem non habent, vel quod natum est componi ex talibus, cuiusmodi est oratio vel propositio. *Summa Logicae* I, cap. 1 [Edit. Boehner I 10].

[19] Ockham adopts this distinction from Boethius and partly from St. Augustine. Est autem sciendum, quod sicut secundum Boethium 1⁰ Perihermenias triplex est oratio, scilicet scripta, prolata et concepta tantum habens esse in intellectu, sic triplex est terminus, scilicet scriptus, prolatus et conceptus. Terminus scriptus est pars propositionis descriptae in aliquo corpore, quae oculo corporali videtur vel videri potest. Terminus prolatus est pars propositionis ab ore prolatae et nata audiri aure corporali. Terminus conceptus est intentio seu passio animae aliquid naturaliter significans nata esse pars propositionis mentalis et pro eodem nata supponere. Unde isti termini concepti et propositiones ex eis compositae sunt illa verba mentalia quae beatus Augustinus 15⁰ De Trinitate dicit nullius esse linguae, quae in mente manent et exterius proferri non possunt, quamvis voces tamquam signa eis subordinata pronuntientur exterius. *Summa Logicae* I, 1 [Edit. Boehner I 8—9]. Cf. Boethius in *Perihermenias* editio 2a; PL. t. 64, col. 407 AB; in B Boethius states that this is the common doctrine of the Peripatetics.

present inquiry, we shall deal here only with the thorny question of the nature of mental language-signs. An understanding of Ockham's real thought on this problem will be reached only if we take into account the fact that his teachings on the nature of universals underwent an important development, which we can now trace more exactly than was possible for Hochstetter.[20] We know now that at the beginning of his career Ockham assigned to the universals and to concepts in general only the being of thought-objects *(esse obiectivum)* and not the being of real things as qualities of the mind *(esse subiectivum)*. This first opinion or the Fictum-theory was held by Ockham in his *Reportata* and in the first redaction of the first book of the Commentary on the Sentences. After a short period of hesitation (noticeable in his Exposition of Aristotle's *Perihermenias* and in the second redaction of the *Ordinatio*), he firmly decided in favor of the theory which identifies the universals and concepts in general with acts of cognition, that is, with intellections. We, therefore, have good reason to describe the nature of mental language-signs exclusively according to the so-called intellectio-theory. According to this theory the following can be stated: Mental language-signs are acts of thought, intellections, or cognitions, by which something is thought or conceived.

They are also called concepts, mental terms, *passiones animae*, intentions, at least in so far as they are elements of mental propositions.

They are psychic realities. Hence they are singular things, belonging to the category of quality, inherent in the soul as whiteness is inherent in the wall.[21]

---

[20] E. Hochstetter, *Studien zur Metaphysik und Erkenntnislehre Wilhelms von Ockham*, Berlin 1927, Walter de Gruyter, p. 81 ss. For further references cf. also footnote 4 and our forthcoming article in *Traditio* IV (1946): "The Realistic Conceptualism of William Ockham." [Cf. *supra*, 156 ff.]. Cf. also J. R. Weinberg, "Ockham's Conceptualism" in *Philosophical Review* 50 (1941) 523—525.

[21] This concerns their status as mental or psychic realities. In so far as they have universal meaning, that is, in so far as their significative function is concerned, "quality" could not be predicated about them. Ockham is already very sensitive as regards that paradox of predication which is

These cognitions or intellections conceive either one singular object and represent or signify it in an act of intellection — and then we speak of singular concepts, or they conceive many things indifferently and equally and represent or signify them accordingly in an indiscriminate manner — and then we speak of universal concepts. The latter are also called universals or *intellectiones confusae*, because of their being capable of confused supposition or distribution, as will be explained later in dealing with supposition.[22]

The relation of these mental signs to the things signified by them is that of a natural sign to that which it naturally signifies. This means that their signification does not depend on an act of will: or

---

countered by modern logicians with various devices, one of which is Russell's theory of types.

The two aspects of universals are distinguished in the following text: Dicendum est igitur, quod quodlibet universale est una res singularis, et ideo non est universale nisi per significationem, quia est signum plurium. *Summa Logicae*, I, cap. 14 [Edit. Boehner I 44]. Cf. also the following text which we offer here, since the text of our editions is in a very bad condition: Dicendum, quod qualitas spiritualis non praedicatur de omnibus praedicamentis significative sumptis, sed sumptis pro signis tantum. Et propter hoc non sequitur, quod sit in plus quam quodcumque praedicamentum. Nam superioritas et inferioritas inter aliqua sumitur ex hoc, quod unum significative sumptum praedicatur de pluribus quam aliud significative sumptum. Unde ista est talis difficultas qualis est de hoc nomine "dictio"; nam hoc nomen "dictio" est unum contentum sub nomine; nam hoc nomen "dictio" est nomen, et non omne nomen est hoc nomen "dictio"; et tamen hoc nomen "dictio" est quodammodo superius ad omnia nomina et ad hoc nomen "dictio". Nam omne nomen est dictio, sed non omnis dictio est nomen. Et ita videtur quod idem respectu eiusdem est superius et inferius. Et ita videtur esse de hoc communi "qualitas". Quod potest solvi dicendo, quod argumentum concluderet, si in omnibus propositionibus, in quibus ponuntur tales termini, dicti termini supponerent uniformiter; nunc autem aliter est in proposito. Si tamen hic vocetur inferius, de quo aliquo modo supponente praedicatur aliud et de pluribus, quamvis illud, si aliter supponeret, non praedicaretur de eo universaliter sumpto, potest concedi, quod idem respectu eiusdem est superius et inferius, sed tunc superius et inferius non sunt opposita, sed disparata. *l. c.*

[22] Cf. Quaestio de universali, G, at the beginning of Ockham's Exposition of *Perihermenias*, edited in *Traditio* IV (1946) 324—325: "The Realistic Conceptualism of William Ockham."

in other words, they are not instituted *ad placitum;* positively expressed, their signification depends only on the natural relation between intellection and the object conceived by this intellection. In particular, this relation is that of an effect to its cause, since the object, which becomes known and is conceived in an act of intellection, acts as a partial cause on the intellect, which is the other partial cause. It is well to note here that Ockham has in mind the specific causality between the object of cognition and the intellect and the cognition as the effect of both. Hence the cognition, which is the effect of univocal causes, is similar both to the object and the intellect, to the latter by being immaterial or spiritual, to the former by being a similitude of it; in other words, the act of cognition is a spiritual assimilation of the object known. To specify this similarity further, seems to be impossible, since we are facing here an ultimate fact of cognitive psychology. In order to make clear or rather to suggest what is meant by this assimilation of the intellect with the object in cognition, Ockham uses a circumlocution when he says that the concept or the intellection, be it a singular or universal one, expresses, explains, declares, imports, or signifies the thing.[23]

Summarizing we can say, therefore, that a mental sign of a singular represents or expresses to the mind one thing or one singular object, for instance, the individual Socrates or Plato; a universal mental sign represents or expresses to the mind in an act of intellection the nature, essence, or quiddity of many things indiscriminately, that means, such a universal intellection equally expresses many things without their individual differences.

Further details and a discussion of the process, by which the intellect passes on from singular intellections to universal intellection do not fall within the scope of the present inquiry. It is sufficient for us to have established that according to Ockham there are mental language-signs which are psychic realities and which, because of their natural similitude with their objects, naturally signify their significates. It is their capability of signification which enables them to enter and to form propositions.

---

[23] Cf. *art. cit.* [310—312, and *supra* 171—173]. Second thesis: The content of our thought is in the relation of similitude with reality.

15*

c. The Relation between Mental and Spoken Language-Signs.

We mentioned already that mental and spoken (and written) language-signs are in a certain correspondence, if they have corresponding instances at all. As Ockham stated before, there is correspondence between the elements of mental propositions and the elements of spoken propositions, so that every element of the former has an instance of the latter, but not *vice versa*.[24] In fact synonyms have only one corresponding mental language-sign: equivocal nouns and also analogical nouns which according to Ockham and Aristotle are equivocal nouns *(aequivocum a consilio)*, however, have distinct corresponding mental language-signs.[25] Considering only those mental and spoken language-signs which are corresponding, we must now inquire into which relation of signification these mental and spoken signs fall. Is it such that spoken words immediately signify mental words, and that only mental words immediately signify the significates? For instance: is it so that the spoken word "tree" immediately signifies the concept tree, and that only the concept or mental language-sign "tree" signifies immediately the things which are trees? This question was, as it seems unanimously affirmed, at least by the great Scholastics before Scotus.[26] All these Scholastics quote in their favor Aristotle's remark at the beginning

---

[24] Cf. footnote 17.

[25] Cf. the treatment of such language-signs in the *Summa Logicae*, I, cap. 13 [edit. Boehner I 41—43], and also the problem of the synonymity of certain abstract and concrete terms in the *Summa Logicae*, I, cap. 5 ss. [edit. Boehner I 16 ff.].

[26] In St. Thomas, however, who elsewhere is clearly in favor of an indirect signification of the significate by the word, we read: Et ideo cum in omnibus scientiis voces significent, hoc habet proprium ista scientia, quod ipsae res significatae per voces, etiam significant aliquid. Illa ergo prima significatio, qua voces significant res, pertinet ad primum sensum, qui est sensus historicus vel litteralis. Illa vero significatio, qua res significatae per voces, iterum res alias significant, dicitur sensus spiritualis ... *Summa Theol.* I, 1, a. 10; cf. also: Sicut iam dictum est, sensus isti non multiplicantur propter hoc, quod una vox multa significet, sed quia ipsae res significatae per voces, aliarum rerum possunt esse signa. *loc. cit.* Ad primum.

of *Perihermenias*, where he says that spoken words (φωναί) are symbols — the Scholastics read in their translation *notae* — of the *passiones*, that is, of the concepts which are in the soul.[27] There can be no doubt that Boethius gave ample support for this idea of an indirect signification of spoken words as regards things signified directly by the concepts only.[28]

However, Scotus already broke with this interpretation of Aristotle's text, maintaining that the significate of the word, generally speaking, is not the concept but the thing, and that both word and concept immediately, though in subordination, signify the same significate or thing.[29] In this the Doctor Subtilis was followed by Ockham, although not in every detail, at least in so far as the general idea of direct signification of words is concerned. According to Ockham the word, for instance *homo*, and the corresponding concept of man immediately signify everything which is a man or has been a man or will be a man or is possibly a man. Hence both signs, the natural, which is the concept, and the artificial, which is the noun, are parallel in their signification. Nevertheless, the word or noun *homo* signifies only because it is subordinated under the mental language-sign which expresses man. The spoken sign does not signify primarily and without the mental sign. For only the mental sign signifies the thing primarily and absolutely, that is, without regard

---

27 *Perihermenias*, c. 1.; 16 a 3 s.

28 Cf. *De Interpretatione* ed. 1 a, lib. I; PL. t. 64, col. 297 ss. and editio 2 a *lib*. I; col. 405 ss. Boethius refers to the history of this problem presented by Porphyry (1. c. col. 405 Cs.): Sed Porphyrius hanc ipsam plenius causam originemque sermonis huius ante oculos collocavit, qui omnem apud priscos philosophos de significationis vi contentionem litemque retexuit.

29 *Oxon*. I, d. 27, q. 3, n. 19; ed. Vivès t. 10, p. 378: Ad secundum, licet magna altercatio fiat de voce, utrum sit signum rei vel conceptus, tamen breviter concedendo, quod illud quod significatur per vocem proprie est res, sunt tamen signa multa ordinata eiusdem significati littera, vox et conceptus . . . A thesis (by Fr. John B. Vogel, O. F. M.) is being written under our direction on the problem of the direct signification of the thing according to Scotus; he has discovered a considerable discrepancy between the treatment of this problem in the *Oxoniense* and the *Quaestiones in Perihermenias opus primum* and *secundum*.

to any other sign (the spoken or written one). The spoken language-sign signifies the thing immediately, but in dependence upon the mental language-sign. That is what is meant when Ockham says that the spoken language-sign signifies immediately and directly the significate, which is the thing and not the concept, and in subordination to the mental language-sign or concept.[30] Thus, when somebody uses the noun *homo* appropriately in the proposition *Homo est animal*, the word certainly does not signify the concept *homo*, for this concept *homo* is not an animal, nor is the concept *homo* the concept animal, rather the same thing — any individual man — which is signified by the noun or the mental sign *homo* is also signified by the noun or mental sign "animal."[31]

Here we have an excellent case which will enable us to appreciate the distinction which Ockham makes between the two kinds of signs previously explained. The mental language-sign or the concept is a sign in the restricted meaning of the term "sign", since it makes something known, being the cognition of it, and can take the place of the thing known in a proposition. The same is true for a spoken language-sign. On the other hand, a spoken language-sign is a symbol, since it is an artificial sign. As such it possesses two sign-relations. The first and main relation is that of signifying the significate: thus it is a sign in the restricted meaning. The second is the relation with the mental language-sign. This sign-relation is that of sign in the broader meaning of the term "sign"; since the cognition of the word brings to my mind or revives in my mind a former or an habitual knowledge of the mental language-sign. Wherever a sign, mental or spoken or written language-sign, takes the place or is able to take the place of a thing in a proposition, that is, wherever it has significative function within a proposition, there the language-sign is a sign in the restricted meaning of the term "sign"; where, however, it does not fulfill this condition but revives a cognition associated with the sign, it acts as a sign in the broader meaning of the term "sign".

---

[30] Cf. the text of *Perihermenias* edited in *Traditio* [320] A; (cf. footnote 22).

[31] As to the proof see *loc. cit.* A.

The latter sign-relation, therefore, could aptly be called associative signification.[32]

The following scheme is a visual presentation of the relations between the things signified and the mental and spoken and written language signs. The solid lines indicate the relations of sign in the restricted meaning, the broken line the relation of sign in the broader meaning.

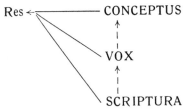

3. GENERAL DIVISIONS AND DISTINCTIONS AS REGARDS LANGUAGE-SIGNS

Of the many distinctions and divisions given by Ockham we shall now select only a few, which will prove to be useful in the forthcoming discussions on supposition. At the same time they will throw more light on Ockham's theory of signification. The word term will be used to designate any incomplex language-sign.[33]

---

[32] Ockham seldom calls this relation signification, obviously not to confound the two kinds of signification. Cf. however, *Ordinatio* d. 27, q. 2, EE: Ad argumentum in oppositum dico, quod non est intentio beati Augustini, quod verbum vocale semper significet verbum mentale, proprie accipiendo significare, sed improprie, secundum quod unum signum significat aliud, quia scilicet imponitur ad significandum illud idem, secundum quod significat aliud signum ... For further details about the relation between *vox* and *conceptus* cf. *Ordinatio*, dist. 22, q. 1, per totum.

[33] Of the three meanings assigned by Ockham to the word "term" we retain, therefore, only the second, which Ockham also usually retains: Uno modo vocatur 'terminus' omne illud, quod potest esse copula vel extremum propositionis categoricae, videlicet subiectum vel praedicatum, vel determinatio extremi vel verbi. Et isto modo etiam una propositio potest esse terminus, sicut potest esse pars propositionis. Haec enim est vera: "Homo est animal," est propositio vera, in qua haec tota propositio: "Homo est animal" est subiectum, et: "Propositio vera," est praedi-

a. Categorematic and Syncategorematic Terms.

At the time of Ockham, this important distinction of language-signs elaborated already by the logicians of the early thirteenth century, was generally accepted.[34] In fact it is very useful for logic and, like many other important discoveries in logic, seems to go back to the Stoics. Approaching this distinction first from the point of view of modern logic, we could vaguely characterize syncategorematic terms (the *syncategoremata*) as the constants of logical discourse which constitute the invariant part of the logical propositions, whilst categorematic terms (the *categoremata*) are terms or instances of the variables in logical frames. Such a frame, for instance, would be:

$$\text{Omnis ( ) est ( ).}$$

Here *omnis* and *est* are constants or *syncategoremata;* everything which can be placed in the blanks or the parentheses is a *categorema*, for instance *homo* and *albus*.

Though this modern approach is not altogether alien to medieval logic, nevertheless, Ockham and all the Scholastics rather explain this distinction from the view of signification. A categorematic term is a sign which has a definite and limited signification, that is, it signifies a certain well-defined class of significates, so that taken alone this sign can represent or take the place of the significates in

---

catum. Aliter accipitur hoc nomen "terminus", secundum quod distinguitur contra orationem. Et sic omne incomplexum vocatur terminus; et sic de termino in praecedenti capitulo sum locutus. Tertio modo accipitur "terminus" praecise pro illo, quod significative sumptum potest esse subiectum vel praedicatum propositionis. Et isto modo nullum verbum nec coniunctio nec adverbium nec praepositio nec interiectio est terminus. Multa etiam nomina non sunt termini, scilicet nomina syncategorematica ... *Summa Logicae*, I, cap. 2 [Edit. Boehner I 10].

[34] One of the early tracts on the *syncategoremata* was edited by J. Reginald O'Donnell, C. S. B., "The Syncategoremata of William of Sherwood," in *Medieval Studies*, III (1941) 46—93. The following syncategorematic terms are treated: *Omnis, Totum, Uterque, Nullus, Nihil, Neutrum, Praeter, Solus, Tantum, Est, Non, Necessario, Contingenter, Incipit, Desinit, Si, Nisi, Quin, Et, Vel, An, Ne, Sive.*

a proposition, either as subject or as predicate. Thus the categorematic term "man" has the definite and limited meaning or signification of being the sign of men only.[35] A syncategorematic term, on the other hand, does not have a definite and limited meaning as regards the significates and does not signify a certain class of objects; it only modifies or determines the signification of categorematic terms. Hence, if taken alone, it has no proper meaning of its own. Consequently it signifies only in connection with categorematic terms. For this reason it is called *syncategorema* or co-predicate. Such syncategorematic terms are the signs of quantification, as *Omnis*, *aliquis*, *nullus*, etc., the copula *est* (and in so far as it is contained in every verb, the verb also), the forms of denial, as *non*, *ne*, *quin*, etc., the conjunctions *si*, *vel*, *et*, *cum*, etc., exclusive, restrictive and reduplicative signs as *tantum*, *solum*, *inquantum*, etc., prepositions and interjections, etc.[36]

We can always determine a given term as a categorematic or syncategorematic sign by testing it when taken alone to find whether it can be meaningfully employed as the subject and predicate of a proposition. According to this rule *omnis* is not a categorematic term. For though *omnis* can be the subject of the proposition *Omnis*

---

[35] Termini categorematici finitam et certam habent significationem, sicut hoc nomen "homo" significat omnes homines, et hoc nomen "animal" omnia animalia, et hoc nomen "albedo" omnes albedines. *Summa Logicae*, I, cap. 4 [edit. Boehner I 15].

[36] Termini autem syncategorematici, cuiusmodi sunt tales: omnis, nullus, aliquis, totus, praeter, tantum, inquantum et huiusmodi, non habent finitam significationem et certam, nec significant aliquas res distinctas a rebus significatis per categoremata; immo sicut in algorismo cifra per se posita nihil significat, sed addita alteri figurae facit eam significare, ita syncategorema proprie loquendo nihil significat, sed magis additum alteri facit ipsum significare aliquid, sive facit ipsum pro aliquo vel aliquibus aliquo modo determinato supponere, vel aliud officium circa categorema exercet. Unde hoc syncategorema 'omnis' non habet aliquod certum significatum, sed additum homini facit ipsum stare seu supponere actualiter sive confuse et distributive pro omnibus hominibus; additum autem lapidi facit ipsum stare pro omnis lapidibus; et additum albedini facit ipsam stare pro omnibus albedinibus. *Summa Logicae*, I, cap. 4 [edit. Boehner I 15]. "Cifra" in the text means "zero".

est terminus, nevertheless, it cannot exercise a significative function as such, and neither can it do so as predicate. The same is true of the copula *est* or the verb.[37]

Of course, there is always the possibility that certain categorematic terms may function at times as syncategorematic terms, or have categorematic terms included in their meaning and *vice versa*. This occasions equivocations often warned against by Ockham.

b. First and Second Intention.

Another distinction which will play an important rôle in Ockham's theory of supposition and consequently in his theory of truth is the distinction between first and second intentions. The matter is, however, a little complicated because this distinction divides not only the mental language-signs, but also the spoken language-signs wherein a new distinction must be introduced, *viz.* that of first and second imposition. We first present the more simple distinction of first and second intention as regards mental language-signs.

Intention is usually taken in the sense of *conceptus animae, passio animae, intellectus, similitudo rei*, that is in the sense of a mental word in opposition to the spoken and written word.[38] Intentions are

---

[37] Sed contra est, quia numquam conceptus syncategorematicus potest supponere pro aliquo, quia tunc posset esse subiectum vel praedicatum, sicut nec dictio syncategorematica. Sed sive dicat conceptum copulae absolutum vel respectivum, solum syncategorematicus est. Igitur non obstante, quod potest significare respectum realem, non tamen potest supponere nec praedicari de aliquo primo modo dicendi per se. Et conceptus categorematicus est qui per se positus aliquid unum significat, sicut homo, animal et talia, quae possunt esse subiecta et praedicata in propositione. Syncategorematica sunt illa, quae per se posita, nihil significant, sicut est 'esse per se', 'inquantum', 'formaliter' . . . *Reportatio* II, q. 1, M.

[38] Illud autem existens in anima, quod est signum rei, ex quo propositio mentalis componitur, ad modum quo propositio vocalis componitur ex vocibus, aliquando vocatur intentio animae, aliquando conceptus animae, aliquando passio animae, aliquando similitudo rei; et Boethius in commento super Perihermenias vocat intellectum . . . Unde quandocumque aliquis profert propositionem vocalem, prius format interius unam propositionem mentalem quae nullius idiomatis est, in tantum quod multi frequenter formant in-

therefore natural language-signs in opposition to artificial language-signs. Since they are natural language-signs, they are able by their very nature to take the place of the things signified by them in mental propositions; in other words, they can supposite for the significates, or they can be parts of mental propositions, as for instance the *syncategoremata*.[39]

An important distinction must be made within intentions of this class. All intentions naturally signify something, either alone or together with another intention. Some intentions, however, naturally signify only such natural signs as are intentions; others naturally signify, alone or together with other intentions, things which are not signs. The intention or the concept of the mind *genus*, for instance, naturally signifies the intentions or natural signs — 'animal,' 'color,' etc. — which in turn signify animals, colors, etc. In other words, they signify the concept of 'animal' or 'color,' etc. For the mental proposition: *Animal is a genus*, is a meaningful proposition. However, 'animal' and 'color' do not signify natural signs, they signify things.

First intention, then, is a natural sign of something which itself is not a sign. If we include within the class of first intentions the *syncategoremata* also, we take 'first intention' in its large meaning; if we exclude them, we take it in its strict meaning. Second intention, on the other hand, is a natural sign which signifies natural signs or first intentions, or is a natural sign which naturally signifies natural signs. Whilst, for instance, the intention or the concept 'man' signifies all men and each individual man, and hence signifies something which is not a sign, the second intention 'species' is a sign of the natural sign 'man' and of other species-intentions, since

---

terius propositiones, quas tamen propter defectum idiomatis exprimere nesciunt. Partes talium propositionum mentalium vocantur conceptus, intentiones, similitudines et intellectus. *Summa Logicae*, I, cap. 12 [edit. Boehner I 39].

[39] Ideo pro nunc sufficiat, quod intentio est quoddam in anima, quod est signum naturaliter significans aliquid, pro quo potest supponere vel quod potest esse pars propositionis mentalis. *Summa Logicae* I, cap. 12 [edit. Boehner I 39—40].

'man' as concept is signified by the intention 'species.'[40] It is obvious that the distinction between first and second intention opens the way for a clear understanding of the *Praedicabilia* and *Praedicamenta*, the former being second intentions, the latter first.

c. Nouns of First and Second Imposition and Intention.

Whilst mental language-signs are either of the first or the second intention, since they are natural signs and therefore independent of a voluntary act of man, the artificial language-signs, which are symbols created by man, admit of another general division. Spoken words or nouns (in a broad sense) are either of the first or of the second imposition, and within this general distinction of nouns, the distinction of first and second intention is only a subclass.

All nouns, that is, all artificial, spoken language-signs (and proportionally all written language-signs), are arbitrarily *(ad placitum)* connected with certain significates, that is, they are imposed by man on certain objects by the relation of signification. Such spoken terms or nouns are of two main types: nouns of the first and nouns of the second imposition. Nouns of the second imposition are nouns of nouns, that is, they are artificial signs or spoken terms which signify artificial signs or spoken terms, as long as and only

---

[40] Tale autem signum duplex est: Unum, quod est signum alicuius rei quae non est tale signum, sive significet tale signum simul cum hoc sive non, et illud vocatur intentio prima, qualis est illa intentio animae quae est praedicabilis de omnibus hominibus, et similiter intentio praedicabilis de omnibus albedinibus, nigredinibus et sic de aliis. Verumtamen sciendum est, quod intentio prima dupliciter accipitur, stricte et large ... Intentio autem secunda est illa, quae est signum talium intentionum primarum, cuiusmodi sunt tales intentiones: genus, species, et huiusmodi. Sicut enim de omnibus hominibus praedicatur una intentio communis omnibus hominibus, sic dicendo: Iste homo est homo, ille homo est homo, et sic de singulis, ita de illis intentionibus, quae significant et supponunt pro rebus praedicatur una intentio communis eis sic dicendo: Haec species est species, illa species est species, et sic de aliis. Similiter sic dicendo: Lapis est genus, animal est genus, color est genus, et sic de aliis, praedicatur una intentio de intentionibus ad modum quo in talibus: Homo est nomen, asinus est nomen, albedo est nomen, praedicatur unum nomen de diversis nominibus. *Summa Logicae* I, cap. 12 [edit. Boehner I 40].

if they are signs. Thus the spoken term 'noun' signifies every noun, for instance 'homo,' 'animal,' 'album,' etc. If we restrict the meaning of the term 'second imposition' to the signification of those nouns which express properties of the spoken language only, that is, of such properties as have no corresponding instances in mental language, then we take the term "second imposition" in its strict meaning; then nouns, which are exclusively used by grammarians and in which the logician is not interested, will be nouns of second imposition. If, however, we include those nouns of nouns which have corresponding instances in mental language, we take the term 'second imposition' in a larger sense. Thus the noun 'conjugation' is a noun of second imposition in the strict sense, since there is no first or second etc. conjugation in mental language; the nouns *nomen* and *verbum* are not nouns of the second imposition in the strict sense, since they have corresponding instances in mental language; nevertheless they are nouns of the second imposition in the larger sense, since they are nouns of nouns.[41]

Nouns of the first imposition, on the other hand, are all nouns which are neither nouns of the second imposition in the strict nor in the large sense.[42]

If we confine the extension of the term 'noun of the first imposition' only to those which are not syncategorematic terms, we take 'noun of the first imposition' in the strict sense; if we include the syncategorematic terms also, we take 'noun of the first imposition' in a larger sense.[43]

---

[41] Verumtamen hoc commune 'nomen secundae impositionis' potest dupliciter accipi, scilicet large, et tunc omne illud est nomen secundae impositionis, quod significat voces ad placitum institutas, sed non nisi quando sunt ad placitum institutae, sive illud nomen sit commune etiam intentionibus animae sive non. Talia autem nomina sunt huiusmodi: Nomen, pronomen, verbum, coniunctio, casus, numerus, modus, tempus et huiusmodi, accipiendo ista vocabula illo modo quo utitur eis grammaticus. Et vocantur ista nomina nominum, quia non imponuntur nisi ad significandum partes orationis . . . Stricte autem dicitur nomen secundae impositionis illud, quod non significat nisi signa ad placitum instituta, ita quod non potest competere intentionibus animae, cuiusmodi sunt talia 'coniugatio', 'figura'. *Summa Logicae*, I, cap. 11 [edit. Boehner I 36—37].
[42] *l. c.*   [43] *l. c.*

Within the class of nouns of the first imposition in the strict sense Ockham introduces the above-mentioned distinction between nouns of the first and second intention, applied here of course to spoken words and not to intentions or mental language signs. The nouns of the second intention are those nouns which are imposed precisely in order to signify intentions of the soul which are natural signs and other signs which are instituted *ad placitum* or signs which follow such signs. Such signs are for instance: 'Genus,' 'species,' 'universal,' predicable.'[44]

It is obvious that the term 'predicable' can be applied to the intention corresponding to the noun of the second imposition *coniugatio* even in the strict sense of the term second imposition. For this reason Ockham introduces a further distinction within the realm of nouns of second intentions. In a large sense a noun of the second intention is any noun which signifies all the mentioned intentions including those intentions which also signify nouns of second imposition. Hence, as regards this large sense of second intention, it is possible that a noun of second intention, for instance, "predicable," and of the first imposition is also a noun of second imposition.[45]

Nouns of the first intention are all those nouns which are nouns of the second intention neither in the broad nor in the strict sense. Such nouns precisely signify things or objects which are not signs

---

[44] Nomina autem primae impositionis stricte accipiendo nomen primae impositionis sunt in duplici differentia: quia quaedam sunt nomina primae intentionis, et quaedam sunt nomina secundae intentionis. Nomina secundae intentionis vocantur illa nomina, quae praecise imposita sunt ad significandum intentiones animae, vel praecise intentiones animae (vel . . . omitted by half of the manuscripts and the edition), quae sunt signa naturalia, et alia signa ad placitum instituta, vel consequentia talia signa. Et talia nomina sunt omnia talia: Genus, species, universale, praedicabile et huiusmodi; quia talia nomina non significant nisi intentiones anomae, quae sunt signa naturalia, vel signa voluntarie insittuta. l. c. [edit. Boehner I 37].

[45] Large illud dicitur nomen secundae intentionis, quod significat intentiones animae, quae sunt naturalia signa, sive etiam significet signa ad placitum instituta, tantum dum sunt signa, sive non. Et sic aliquod nomen secundae intentionis et primae impositionis (et . . . is omitted by two manuscripts out of nine and by the edition) est etiam nomen secundae impositionis. l. c. [edit. Boehner I 38].

and which are not derived from signs,[46] as for instance Plato, whiteness, etc. However, some nouns as *unum, verum, bonum,* viz. the transcendentals, signify things and signs, but nevertheless are considered nouns of the first intention.[47]

Hence Ockham can conclude, somewhat summarizing the preceding: "From all this one may gather: certain nouns precisely signify signs instituted *ad placitum* and only when they are signs; certain nouns, however precisely signify signs, but both those which are instituted *ad placitum* and natural signs; certain signify precisely things which are not such signs as are parts of a proposition; certain indifferently signify such things, which are not parts of a proposition or of language, and also such things; such are the nouns: thing, being, something, one, etc."[48]

The first are nouns of second imposition, the second are nouns of second intention in the broad meaning, the third and fourth are nouns of the first intention. The first concern the grammatical structure of speech, the second the logical structure of thought, the third and fourth the ontological structure of reality. The first belong to Grammar, the second to Logic, the third to the science of reality *(scientia realis)*, the fourth to Metaphysics. This may be stated as being, at least, *"ad mentem* Ockham".

4. THE VARIOUS MEANINGS OF "TO SIGNIFY"

Without going into the further details of Ockham's semantics, and especially leaving out his extensive discussion on the various significative functions of concrete and abstract terms, which are partly the same as connotative and absolute terms,[49] we shall now explain what is meant by the term "to signify." This will afford us

---

[46] i. e. signs of signs.

[47] Nomina autem primae intentionis vocantur omnia alia nomina a praedictis, quae videlicet significant aliquas res, quae non sunt signa nec consequentia talia signa, cuiusmodi sunt omnia talia: Homo, animal, Sortes, Plato, albedo, album, verum, bonum et huiusmodi, quorum aliqua significant praecise res, quae non sunt signa nata supponere pro aliis, aliqua significant talia signa et simul cum hoc alias res. *l. c.*

[48] *l. c.*

[49] For further details cf. E. Moody, *The Logic of William of Ockham.*

an opportunity partly to summarize what has beeen said before, and partly to clarify some points by way of application.

In his *Summa Logicae* and in his *Quodlibeta*,[50] Ockham distinguishes four meanings of the term "to signify". The first two of these types take "sign" only in the restricted sense of language-sign, the other two take "sign" also in the broader sense of "sign."

a) In a first and very restricted sense, "to signify" means that a sign is actually used or can actually be used in a proposition which is categorical and not modal and of the present, so that this sign can be truly predicated about that for which it stands. For instance: *Homo est albus; albus* in this proposition is used as a sign or signifies in this sense, if there is actually a man who is white, for then we are able to point to this individual, saying: This is white. Hence we can say, that if, and only if, at least one white thing exists, that "white" signifies in this restricted sense. It is obvious that a sign does not signify in this sense, if the thing signified by it does not exist, or that a sign loses its signification, if the thing formerly signified by it ceases to exist. Hence signification varies with the actual existence of its significates, and can reach zero-signification, if no significate actually exists.

As a matter of fact this restricted sense of "to signify" is rarely used by Ockham, though it played a major rôle in earlier and later logicians of the Middle Ages. The corresponding use of this signification in a proposition would be *Appellatio*, which Ockham, after having mentioned it once in his *Summa Logicae*, simply dismisses.[51]

---

[50] Cf. *Summa Logicae* I, cap. 33, and Quodl. V, 16 which has almost litterally the same treatment of this division. Our presentation is a paraphrase of both texts.

[51] We presume here that Ockham understands *appellatio* in the sense in which Petrus Hispanus takes it in his *Summulae Logicales:* "Appellatio est acceptio termini pro re existente . . ." Other logicians refer *appellatio* to the indirect signification of connotative terms, that is to connotation, cf. John Buridan's *Summulae*, tract. IV, De Appellatione: Sunt autem terminorum aliqui appellativi et aliqui non appellativi . . . Sed omnis terminus connotans aliud ab eo, pro quo supponit, dicitur appellativus, et appellat illud, quod connotat, per modum adiacentis ei, pro quo supponit, ut album appellat albedinem tamquam adiacentem rei, pro qua iste terminus album est innatus supponere. Ed. Janonus Carcani, Venice, 1499, with commentary of John Dorp.

b) That a sign is actually used or can be used in a proposition of the past, the future, or the present, and in a modal proposition, and in such a way that it takes the place of the significate if a proposition is formulated, constitutes the meaning of "to signify" in a second and broader sense. Since this signification regards not only actually existing significates, but also past or future and even possible significates, it is obvious that a sign still signifies, even if no significate actually exists. For it may signify significates of the past or future; and even if no significate has ever existed or actually exists or will exist (as, for instance "a white thing"), nevertheless, the term "white" can signify or have a significate in a modal proposition (for instance in the proposition: *Album potest currere*) provided only that this proposition is true. Ockham therefore adds with reason: "in a true modal proposition," for the possibility or the non-contradiction of the term has to be assumed.

It is in this sense that Ockham generally takes signification of terms.

c) In a third sense "to signify" prescinds from the possibility or aptitude of taking the place of the significate in a proposition. Ockham has in mind mostly connotative terms, which directly, at least in the second mode of "to signify", signify their subjects, but indirectly signify or connote something else, which they do not signify in the second mode. We may take the instance of *albus* in the proposition: *Homo est albus; albus* here directly signifies the individual man who is white, but *indirectly* signifies, that is, connotes, "whiteness." However, it does not signify whiteness in the second mode; for the proposition: *Albedo est alba* is false. Since, however, the term *albus* calls *albedo* to mind it is said to signify it or to be a sign of it, though it is not a sign of *albedo* in the strict meaning of language-sign.

d) In a fourth sense, "to signify" is taken very generally. Thus any sign that either can be a part of a proposition or a proposition itself may be said to signify when it imports or means something primarily or secondarily, or when it makes something understood or connotes something, or when it signifies something in any mode whether affirmatively or negatively. For instance the term "blind" signifies "sight" negatively, or the term "immaterial" signifies "matter" negatively. In this sense every term signifies.

However, the second, which is only an extension of the first, is the most important meaning of "to signify". This, therefore will be called the proper meaning of the term to "signify". When we use the expression "significative function" we shall always refer to this meaning. In other words, a term has significative function, if and only if it represents something different from itself and so that it can be predicated about it or about the pronoun which stands for it.

Further details of Ockham's semantics are beyond the scope of the present investigation. We intend only to pave the way for a better understanding of Ockham's theory of supposition. Our next task will be to explain this theory of supposition, and to show finally how the predicates "true" and "false" are intimately connected with correct supposition.

16. OCKHAM'S THEORY OF SUPPOSITION AND THE NOTION OF TRUTH[a]

Our discussion of Ockham's theory of signification,[b] though limited to essentials, has prepared the way for an understanding of his theory of supposition and, consequently, of the notion of truth. This ingenious medieval theory of supposition, which unfortunately is much neglected by modern schoolmen and even misunderstood by historians of Medieval Philosophy, will finally answer the question: What is truth or falsity as applied to a proposition? For truth is given when and only when the subject and predicate of the same proposition stand or supposite for the same thing. To be sure, supposition is not *truth*, but supposition enters the definition of truth, at least if we are interested in a semantic definition of *truth* (sometimes called logical truth) and if we are not to indulge in vague circumlocutions about the relation of correspondence between a proposition and a state of affairs, which relation of correspondence in a general

---

[a] First published in FrancStud 6 (1946) 261—292.

[b] Cfr. the preceding art. in the present volume.

way characterizes every scholastic theory of *truth*. As we have shown in our first study on the notion of truth, a semantic elucidation of the notion of truth seems to have been attempted by almost all the scholastics. That Ockham did the same can hardly be called an innovation; that he made a more careful analysis than others before him, is his distinct contribution to scholastic philosophy. In order to show that, we must first acquaint ourselves with Ockham's theory of supposition, and then show its bearing on the notion of truth.

I. OCKHAM'S THEORY OF SUPPOSITION

The *Venerabilis Inceptor* neither invented nor introduced the theory of supposition into Medieval Logic, Philosophy, and Theology. It was already in use among logicians long before the time of Ockham, and had made, as we have shown before, its tentative appearance even in theological writings during the early part of the thirteenth century.[1] Petrus Hispanus, who later became Pope John XXI, merely "codified" or gathered the teaching on supposition in his *Summulae logicales*, a work which later became the classical logical textbook for beginners.[2] However, though Petrus Hispanus professed a Terminism, as all good logicians will do, he still remained along with the other thirteenth century logicians a realist as regards the

---

[1] Cf. also the following studies on medieval semantics: Ernst Schlenker, "Die Lehre von den göttlichen Namen in der Summe Alexanders von Hales. Ihre Prinzipien und ihre Methode", *Freiburger theologische Studien* 46. Heft. (Freiburg Br.) 1938. And Franz Manthey, *Die Sprachphilosophie des hl. Thomas von Aquin und ihre Anwendung auf Probleme der Theologie* (Paderborn) 1937. Valuable notes on the semantics of various scholastics are likewise found in Ernst Borchert, "Der Einfluß des Nominalismus auf die Christologie der Spätscholastik nach dem Traktat De Communicatione Idiomatum des Nicolaus Oresme. Untersuchungen und Textausgabe", in *Beiträge zur Geschichte der Philosophie und Theologie des Mittelalters* (Bäumker), Band XXXV, Heft 4—5, Münster 1940. This study contains an excellent bibliography.

[2] This important work is now partly available in English translation (with Latin text); cf. Joseph P. Mullally, *The Summulae Logicales of Peter of Spain*, "Publications in Mediaeval Studies" VIII; ed. Philip S. Moore, C.S.C. (Notre Dame, 1945).

16*

problem of universals. Ockham on the other hand adapted the same theory to his own conceptualism, simplified it, and gave it a classical form. With Ockham, at least, this theory penetrated the entire field of Philosophy and Theology, and its presence is everywhere felt. He applied it with a rigor and consistency hitherto unknown to the discussion of the relations between faith and reason and to an elucidation of philosophical and theological problems.

a. Supposition in General

In order to explain what supposition is we have to recall what signification means, and especially what *signum* in the sense of language-sign means. As we have seen, *sign* as language-sign must bring something into cognition, and may either stand for something in a proposition or be added to other signs in a proposition or is a composition of various such signs.[3] Now the first part of the disjunction contains the idea of supposition, or, at least, the capability of supposition. Hence it would be awkward to define supposition by referring to *sign*, which was explained by reference to supposition.

Our concern, however, is not a definition of supposition in a strict sense; we only intend to clarify the meaning of the term. For the same reason, Ockham himself seems to have abstained from a definition of supposition. He merely remarks that supposition is a property of terms, but only when they are actually used in propositions, and that supposition is *quasi pro alio positio*.[4] However, he clarifies the meaning of supposition by using circumlocutions and examples.

We first start with examples and then proceed to a characterization of the notion of supposition. In the proposition, *Homo est animal*, both the terms *homo* and *animal* at least stand for the same thing as they signify, which is a man and which is an animal. However,

---

[3] *S. Logicae* I, c. 1 [edit. Boehner I 8 ss.].

[4] Dicto de significatione terminorum, restat dicere de suppositione, quae est proprietas conveniens termino, sed numquam nisi in propositione. ... Dicitur autem suppositio quasi pro alio positio, ita quod quando terminus stat in propositione pro aliquo, utimur illo termino pro aliquo ... (*S. Logicae* I, c. 63 [edit. Boehner I 175]).

we have already said a little too much. What we expressed is correct if the proposition is true, but we have also to take into account false propositions which are false exactly because subject and predicate do not stand for the same thing. For that reason Ockham is careful in his wording, and says that it is denoted that at least one proposition is true, for instance the proposition, *Sortes est animal*. In this proposition the subject is denoted as standing for an individual, so that by pointing at this individual we can form the proposition "This is an animal". And that is meant by the supposition of the subject. Another instance, *"Homo est nomen"*. This proposition denotes that the spoken sign *Homo* is a noun. That which is signified by the spoken word *Homo*, *viz.* the individual man is, of course, not a noun. In this case, again, we can indicate the spoken word *Homo* and say, "This is a noun". But since *Homo* does not stand for its significates, it simply stands or supposits for the spoken word. This is another variety of the supposition of the subject. A third example given by Ockham is the proposition, *"Album est animal."* In this case it is denoted that at least one white thing, let us say this individual to which we can point, is an animal. Therefore, *Album* has supposition. Though up to now we have given only examples of the supposition of the subject, the same can be said about the predicate. For instance, the proposition, *"Sortes est albus,"* denotes that Sortes is this particular thing that has whiteness, and, therefore the term "white" has supposition.[5]

Now we will present Ockham's general characterization of supposition, of which the preceding were only exemplifications. Supposition

---

[5] Sicut per istam: Homo est animal, denotatur, quod Sortes vere est animal, ita quod haec sit vera, si formetur: Hoc est animal, demonstrando Sortem. Per istam autem: Homo est nomen, denotatur, quod haec vox "homo" sit nomen, ideo in ista supponit "homo" pro illa voce. Similiter per istam: Album est animal, denotatur, quod illa res, quae est alba, sit animal, ita quod haec sit vera: Hoc est animal, demonstrando illam rem, quae est alba, et propter hoc pro illa re subiectum supponit. Et sic proportionaliter dicendum est de praedicato; nam per istam: Sortes est albus, denotatur, quod Sortes est illa res, quae habet albedinem, et ideo praedicatum supponit pro ista re, quae habet albedinem (*S. Logicae* I, c. 63 [edit. Boehner I, 176]).

is a property of terms only in propositions. Furthermore, it is a property which one term has in reference to another, *viz.*, of the subject to the predicate and *vice versa*. When we say the subject supposits for something, then it is denoted that the predicate is predicated about the subject as such *(Homo est nomen)* or about the demonstrative pronoun pointing to it or to the individual signified by it. When we say that the predicate supposites for something, it is denoted that the subject functions as subject in regard to it or in regard to the demonstrative pronoun pointing to it.[6] Thus we may say that supposition is the use of a language-sign either as subject or as predicate and in reference to each other within a proposition. However, we cannot say that applied signification is supposition because every signification applied in a proposition is supposition, but not *vice versa*. For supposition also covers cases where signification in the strict sense is not applied, for instance, in the proposition, *Homo est nomen*. This is the reason why supposition can enter the definition of signification, but not *vice versa*.

b. Division of Supposition

Ockham adopts a division of supposition which, as far as we could ascertain, first appears in the works of Raymundus Lullus.[7] This division is different from that offered by Petrus Hispanus and by the other older Logicians, as for instance, William of Shyrswood and Lambert of Auxerre, though it does seem to approach that of William of Shyreswood.[8]

---

[6] Et sic universaliter terminus supponit pro illo, de quo vel de pronomine demonstrante ipsum per propositionem denotatur praedicatum praedicari, si terminus supponens sit subiectum; si autem terminus sit praedicatum, denotatur, quod subiectum subiicitur respectu illius vel respectu nominis demonstrantis ipsum, si propositio formetur [ibid.].

[7] We assert this on the authority of Carl Prantl, *Die Geschichte der Logik im Abendlande.* III (Leipzig) 1867, p. 133, note 596. The text quoted there uses almost exactly the divisions and terms which we encounter in Ockham's writings.

[8] Cf. Martin Grabmann, "Die Introductiones in logicam des, Wilhelm von Shyreswood († nach 1267)," in *Sitzungsberichte der Bayerischen Akademie der Wissenschaften. Philosophisch-historische Abteilung.* Jahrgang 1937, Heft 10, (München) 1937, p. 75.

Three main suppositions are to be distinguished: personal, simple, and material. It is true that a more general distinction could first be made, *viz.* that between a proper and metaphorical supposition. But the Logician is not greatly concerned with this improper supposition of which a few words will be said later.

Personal supposition is had when a term supposits for its significate, whether this significate be a thing outside the mind, or a word, or a concept, or something written, or anything else that could be imagined, as long as it is signified by this term. Hence in each of the following propositions the predicate has personal supposition: "Man is an animal," "Noun is a word," "Man is a concept," "Man is a written word," "Chimaera is an animal." As is evident from the instances, the predicate everywhere exercises its significative function, that is, it signifies something different from itself in the strict meaning of language-sign. In other words it signifies that for which it was originally instituted. For this reason Ockham adds the requirement that in personal supposition the term must be taken in its significative function. Hence we can offer this definition: Personal supposition is had when the subject or predicate of a proposition supposits for its significate and has a significative function.[9] It is obvious that personal supposition can apply only to categorematic terms, which have a definite meaning, while syncategorematic terms, taken alone, can not have personal supposition.[10]

---

[9] Suppositio personalis universaliter est illa, quando terminus supponit pro suo significato, sive illud significatum sit res extra animam, sive sit vox sive intentio animae, sive sit scriptum sive quodcumque imaginabile; ita quod, quandocumque subiectum vel praedicatum propositionis supponit pro suo significato, ita quod significative tenetur, semper est suppositio personalis. (*S. Logicae* I, c. 64 [edit. Boehner I, 177]).

[10] Sciendum, quod solum categorema, quod est extremum propositionis significative sumptum supponit personaliter. Per primum excluduntur omnia syncategoremata, sive sint nomina sive adverbia sive praepositiones, sive quaecumque alia sint. Per secundum excluditur omne verbum ... Per secundam particulam 'extremum propositionis' excluditur pars extremi, quantumcumque sit nomen et categorema, sicut hic: Homo albus est animal, nec 'homo' supponit nec 'albus' supponit, sed totum extremum supponit (*S. Logicae* I, c. 69 [edit. Boehner, I, 188]).

Without going into further details, let us merely state that personal supposition can be subdivided in line with the supposition of the terms of singular, particular, and universal propositions into (1) discrete, (2) determinate (subject and predicate in a particular proposition), (3) common and confused only (the predicate in an affirmative universal proposition), and (4) common, confused and distributive (subject in an affirmative universal proposition).[11] We shall make use of these various suppositions later and at the same time give a few explanations. Let us simply affirm here that they contain the elements of a scholastic quantification-theory.

Simple supposition is had when a term supposits or stands for an intention of the mind, that is, for a concept or mental term when it has no significative function.[12] For instance, in the proposition *Homo est species*, the term *Homo* has simple supposition. For it is evident that the term does not signify in this proposition any one of its significates which are individual men. Since it does not signify any individual or significate, it cannot have, or rather it does not perform, its significative function either. Therefore, the only thing left for which it can stand meaningfully in this connection is the concept *Homo*. This is in complete accordance with Ockham's conceptualism and denial of any universality and any unity less than numerical unity outside the conceptual order. Of course, since according to Ockham the concept or the intention of the mind is a reality, being a quality of the mind, the concept *conceptus* can be truly and correctly predicated about any concept. But as soon as we take any one of the concepts and predicate something about this concept so that pointing to the concept we can say, "This is ...," we mean or intend only this concept, and not what the concept signifies or may stand for. In this case the concept does not stand for anything else but itself. Hence in the proposition *Homo est species*, it is not said that this man or that man, Socrates or Plato *etc.* is a *species*, but only that the concept which is represented by itself or the word *Homo* is a species. Ockham, however, does not forget that

---

[11] Cf. the whole of Chapter 68 of the first part of the *Summa Logicae.*
[12] Suppositio simplex est, quando terminus supponit pro intentione animae, sed non tenetur significative (*S. Logicae* I, c. 64 [edit. Boehner, I, 178]).

there are mental, spoken, and written propositions.[13] The case is simple if we have to deal with a mental proposition for then the subject mentioned stands only for itself. It is more complicated if we have to deal with a spoken or written proposition. For the spoken sign *Homo* is not an intention of the mind, and consequently we cannot say, "This (meaning the spoken word *Homo*) is a species." On the other hand, the spoken word and likewise the written word do not signify the concept with which they are connected. Nevertheless, they are connected, to use a modern expression, through association. As Ockham says, the spoken word is subordinated to the concept but does not signify it in the meaning of a strict language sign, that is to say, it cannot supposit for it in significative function. In spite of this, however, it can supposit for it without a significative function by simply representing it or calling it to mind. Briefly we may say that in a spoken proposition — and the same is true for a written proposition — the term with simple supposition stands for an intention of the mind without signifying it in the strict sense.[14]

Material supposition is had when a term does not supposit in its significative function, but supposits either for a spoken or written sign only. In the proposition *Homo est nomen*, or *Homo scribitur*, *Homo* cetainly does not stand for its significates, nor for its corresponding concept; it stands only for itself, namely the material, written, or spoken sign. It is of course a sign that conveys meaning, but its meaning is disregarded and only the sign as artificial language-sign is considered.[15]

---

[13] Sicut autem talis diversitas suppositionis potest competere termino vocali et scripto, ita etiam potest competere termino mentali, quia intentio potest supponere pro illo, quod significat, et pro seipsa et pro voce et scripto (*S. Logicae*, I, c. 64 [edit. Boehner, I, 179]).

[14] . . . et tamen iste terminus 'homo' non significat proprie loquendo illam intentionem, sed illa vox et illa intentio animae sunt tantum signa subordinata in significando idem, secundum modum alibi expositum (*S. Logicae* I, c. 64 [edit. Boehner, I, 178]). Cf. our preceding article.

[15] Suppositio materialis est, quando terminus non supponit significative, sed supponit pro voce vel pro scripto. Sicut patet hic: Homo est nomen; hic 'homo' supponit pro seipso, et tamen non significat seipsum. Similiter hic: Homo scribitur, potest esse suppositio materialis, quia terminus supponit pro illo, quod scribitur (*S. Logicae*, I, c. 64 [*loc.* cit.]).

After these general descriptions of the three main suppositions Ockham reminds us that every term, be it mental, spoken, or written, can have this threefold supposition. It is important, therefore, to distinguish the various relations of strict and broad signification as regards the terms in mental, spoken, and written propositions. They follow a clear and consistently applied pattern. In order to show this, we shall now present these relations in a visual scheme, using a few simple examples.

Supposition	Thing	Mental term	Spoken term	Written term
Personal Supposition	Sortes	Sortes / est / Homo	Sortes / est / Homo	Sortes / est / Homo
Simple Supposition		Homo / est / Species	Homo / est / Species	Homo / est / Species
Material Supposition for a spoken word		Homo / est / Nomen vocale	Homo / est / Nomen vocale	Homo / est / Nomen vocale
Material Supposition for a written word		Homo / est / Nomen scriptum	Homo / est / Nomen scriptum	Homo / est / Nomen scriptum

A few remarks may explain the meaning of the schematic drawings. We distinguished two kinds of material supposition just as Ockham himself has distinguished them.[16] In every instance the

---

[16] Sed illa (scilicet suppositio materialis) potest subdistingui, eo quod subiectum potest supponere pro voce vel pro scripto. Et si essent nomina imposita, ita posset distingui pro voce et scripto sicut suppositio pro significato et pro intentione animae, quarum unam vocamus personalem et aliam simplicem; sed talia nomina non habemus (*S. Logicae* I, c. 64 [*edit. cit.* 178]).

subject alone has the various suppositions, the predicate retaining always personal supposition. The straight line always indicates that a relation of strict signification is had; the broken line indicates that there is no strict signification but only the relation of subordination, or rather broad signification in the sense of calling to mind or taking the place of the other. For a better understanding let us explain the third drawing: Here *Homo* has material supposition; it simply stands for itself in the spoken proposition and in this spoken proposition it is directly signified in the mental, spoken, and written proposition by the predicate *Nomen vocale* and that in the strict sense of signification. The term *Homo*, exercises no signification in this case; it simply stands for itself. In the mental proposition the mental predicate directly and significatively supposits for the spoken word *Homo*. The mental term *Homo*, however, is merely a substitute for the spoken word *Homo*, it takes its place without signifying it in the strict sense; it calls it to mind, since it is connected with it by voluntary imposition. In the written proposition we have a similar relation.

c. The Primacy of Personal Supposition

The main division into personal, simple, and material supposition means that a term can stand for things or signs of a different order. It makes a great difference whether we use a term or whether we speak of a term. To be alive to this distinction is certainly not a prerogative of modern logicians alone, but of the Scholastics as well. The whole theory of supposition is proof of this.[17] Ockham, therefore tells us that a term must not have a fixed supposition in various propositions, but may supposite *pro alio et alio*.[18] Those

---

[17] The distinction into the *actus exercitus* and the *actus signatus* belongs to the same category, Cf. *S. Logicae* I, c. 65. Ernest A. Moody, *The Logic of William of Ockham*, (London) 1935, p. 43 has assigned much importance to these and similar distinctions. We wholeheartedly subscribe to this and recommend the reading of this book for further details about the theory of supposition.

[18] Circa primum dico, quod suppositio termini variatur dupliciter: vel quia supponit pro alio et alio, vel quia aliter et aliter supponit. Primo modo dividitur suppositio in suppositionem personalem, simplicem et materia-

suppositions *pro alio et alio viz.* personal, simple and material supposition, are, however, not of equal right so to speak. For by natural right a term supposits for that which it signifies in the strict sense. By its original institution every term, and by its original imposition every artificial sign, is meant to signify its significate or at least to signify it in connection with other terms *(cosignificare)*. It is obvious that we use concepts as cognitions of things, but not primarily as concepts in an absolute sense. It is likewise obvious that we use words as signs for their significates, but do not primarily use them as words, that is, as artificial signs without significative function.[19]

From this it follows that personal supposition is the first and most basic supposition and consequently has primacy over simple and material supposition. Ockham does not hesitate from this to draw the conclusion that a term has to be taken in personal supposition as long as no other indication or qualification forces us to take the same term in another supposition. Hence if such an indication is given — Ockham merely says *ratione adiuncti* — the other suppositions may be admitted. Otherwise the term must be taken in personal supposition.[20] Now, such an indication is present if the term, let us for the sake of simplicity say the subject, is compared

---

lem . . . (*Ordinatio* d. 4, q. 1, E). At the beginning of this question Ockham criticizes St. Thomas severely as regards the supposition of the term "Deus". Cf. St. Thomas *S. Th.* I, q. 39, a. 4.

[19] Est etiam sciendum, quod terminus, quantum est ex vi suae institutionis sive impositionis, semper habet, quod supponat pro suis significatis. Cuius ratio est, quia cum utamur vocibus pro rebus, manifestum est, quod utimur vocibus pro suis significatis; igitur semper, quantum est ex vi impositionis vocum, (semper) sumuntur significative, et per consequens personaliter, si sint natae supponere personaliter (*Expos. s. l. Elenchorum*, not yet edited. *MS* Oxford, Bodl. 558, fol. 95 va).

[20] Sed quod vox supponat aliter quam personaliter, hoc est ex ratione adiuncti, quod pertinet ad aliam suppositionem . . . (l. c.). Cf.: Hic tamen est advertendum, quod quandocumque terminus ex se, hoc est natura institutionis, habet supponere pro aliquo, et ratione adiuncti pro alio, ubicumque ponitur ille terminus, semper habet supponere pro primo, sed ratione adiuncti potest supponere pro secundo praecise (*Ordinatio* d. 4, q. 1, F).

to a predicate, which signifies intentions of the mind or spoken or written words.[21]

We will enlarge a little on this primacy of personal supposition since it seems it has been misunderstood. When Ockham says that a term in whatsoever proposition and in whatsoever connection it is used can have personal supposition provided it is not limited by the will of those using it to another supposition,[22] then he does not by any means say that a term always has and *must* always have only personal supposition. He affirms rather that the term *can* also have another supposition. The fact, however, that the term actually has to be taken in another supposition cannot be known from the term alone, but must be ascertained from the other part of the proposition *(ratione adiuncti)* or from the will of those who use the term. For every categorematic term, since only terms of this kind are capable of personal supposition, means something and is instituted, if it is an artificial sign, to signify something. That is its natural right and the reason for its existence. This means that if such a term would not be capable of personal supposition it would not be able to have simple or material supposition for the simple reason that it would not exist at all. Ockham means this when he says that a term can always have personal supposition. For the same reason we have to call personal supposition basic.

However, man has not only the power of obtaining natural signs, that is, concepts of things and of instituting artificial signs of the same things, but he has also the even more amazing power of reflect-

---

[21] Potest igitur ista regula dari, quod quando terminus potens habere praedictam triplicem suppositionem comparatur extremo communi incomplexis sive complexis, sive prolatis sive scriptis, semper terminus potest habere suppositionem materialem, et est talis propositio distinguenda. Quando vero comparatur extremo significanti intentionem animae, est distinguenda, eo quod potest habere suppositionem simplicem vel personalem. Quando autem comparatur extremo communi omnibus praedictis, tunc est distinguenda, eo quod potest habere suppositionem simplicem, materialem et personalem . . . (*S. Logicae* I, c. 65 [*edit. cit.* 180—181]).

[22] Notandum, quod semper terminus, in quacumque propositione ponatur, potest habere suppositionem personalem, nisi ex voluntate utentium arcetur ad aliam (*S. Logicae* I, c. 65 [*ibid.* 179]).

ing upon these first signs, whether natural or artificial, and of obtaining or instituting signs for them. By this fact there is opened to
the human intellect a new world, the world of signs of signs. In this
world, let us call it antonomastically the logical world, the signs of
the former "real" world are individuals, so to speak. But while the
individuals of the real world cannot themselves enter propositions
but only through their names or signs, the "individuals" of the
logical world can enter as such. They do exactly this in simple or
material supposition. But as we can have universal propositions as
regards the real world, so we can have universal propositions as
regards the logical world, as, for instance, "Every concept is predicable," or, "Every proposition is either true or false." In this case
personal supposition reappears for both the subject and predicate.
This personal supposition is, however, not for things but for signs.

   This naturally leads us to a distinction between different levels
of language which were *de facto* clearly held apart by the scholastic
theory of supposition and by Ockham's insisting on the primacy of
supposition. The case where subject and predicate are denoted to
supposit for things which are not signs, is the first level. Here we
have what may be called primary personal supposition. The case
where the subject or predicate, which is a sign of things and not of
signs, does not exercise its significative function and consequently
has simple or material supposition while the other extreme of the
proposition signifies and supposits for it, is the second level. In
such propositions or in such language we are speaking of concepts
or names of things. The third level is the case where both subject
and predicate signify concepts or names. The second and third levels
(and even further levels, if we wish to produce them at will) constitute
the proper realm of logic. But the first level is the proper realm of a
scientia realis of Physics, Mathematics and Metaphysics.[23] This is

---

   [23] Breviter ergo ad intentionem Philosophi est dicendum, quod scientia
realis non per hoc distinguitur a rationali, quia scientia realis est de rebus,
ita quod ipsae res sunt propositiones scitae vel partes illarum propositionum
scitarum, et rationalis non est sic de rebus, sed per hoc, quod partes, scilicet
termini, propositionum scitarum scientia reali stant et supponunt pro
rebus; non sic autem termini propositionum scitarum scientia rationali,

the opinion of Ockham. The second and third levels break down, however, if they are not supported by the first level, or the language which speaks about things.

Since every term can appear and be used in two levels of language, it is necessary to make distinctions if the need arises. But the need never arises when the terms are on the same language-levels. This explains why Ockham demands that certain distinctions be made in certain cases only, but denies the right to make distinctions in other cases. For as long as the two terms of a proposition are used on the same level both have their natural right to personal supposition. But if a term leaves its own level and joins with a term of a higher level, distinctions have to be introduced in order to prevent logical chaos.

Certain rules will serve as guides for the distinction of terms as regards supposition. No proposition need be distinguished as to the supposition of its terms if both terms are first intentions. In other words all propositions which belong to the first level of language are to be accepted without distinctions.[24] We could enlarge this rule, as it seems, to a more general rule by saying that no distinction need be made, if both terms have personal supposition, whether *both* terms be of first intention, second intention, or first or second imposition. Ockham does not say this though he does not deny it either.

When a term capable of the threefold supposition is brought into relation with another term (subject or predicate) of a proposition which is common to spoken or written terms or propositions, then the proposition has to be distinguished; for the first term can have

sed illi termini stant et supponunt pro aliis. *Ordinatio* d. 2, q. 4, O. This text is found in a long digression which Ockham added "propter aliquos inexercitatos in Logica" (M).

[24] Item: Nulla propositio, in qua ponitur nomen primae intentionis est distinguenda primo modo (vel secundo), nisi reliquum extremum sit nomen intentionis secundae vel secundae impositionis (*Expos. s. l. Elenchorum* [cf. note 19]). Cf. *S. Logicae* I, c. 65: Sed terminus non in omni propositione potest habere suppositionem simplicem vel materialem, sed tunc tantum, quando terminus talis comparatur alteri extremo, quod respicit intentionem animae vel vocem vel scriptum [*edit. cit.* 179].

either personal or material supposition. It will be false in one sense and true in the other sense.[25]

When a term that is capable of the threefold supposition is brought into relation with the other extreme of a proposition which signifies an intention of the mind, then a distinction must be made as the term can have simple or personal supposition. It will be true in one sense and false in the other sense.[26]

When a term is brought into relation with another extreme of a proposition so that this other extreme is common to spoken or written words and to intentions of the mind, then the term can have all three suppositions and has to be distinguished accordingly. Such a term common to or predicable of mental, spoken, or written terms is, for instance, "to predicate".[27]

---

[25] Cf. note 21 and *Expos. s. l. Elenchorum* (cf. note 19): "Item, quando nomen primae impositionis, cui non additur signum particulare nec universale, est unum extremum propositionis et aliud extremum est nomen secundae impositionis, illa propositio est distinguenda, eo quod nomen primae impositionis potest supponere personaliter vel materialiter." This rule is narrower and less correct, as it seems, than the formulation given in the *Summa Logicae*. It would exclude the following proposition: 'All men' is two words. The correctness of both formulations of the rule is guaranteed only if we either compare first intentions with second intentions or first impositions with second impositions, but not, necessarily, if both terms are second intentions or second impositions. In the proposition, "All words are spoken terms," we have personal supposition for both terms.

[26] Quando vero comparatur extremo significanti intentionem animae, est distinguenda, eo quod potest habere suppositionem simplicem vel personalem (*S. Logicae* I, c. 65 [*edit. cit.* 180]). Cf. *Expos. s.l. Elenchorum* (cf. note 19): "Item notandum est, quod quandocumque nomen primae intentionis est unum extremum propositionis et aliud extremum est nomen secundae intentionis, potest supponere simpliciter vel personaliter, nisi illi nomini primae intentionis addatur aliquod signum particulare vel universale." This latter rule is narrower than the former. Both formulations do not take into account the case where a second intention is used in simple supposition, for instance, "'Concept' is an intention of the mind."

[27] Quando autem comparatur extremo communi omnibus praedictis, tunc est distinguenda, eo quod potest habere suppositionem simplicem, materialem vel personalem. Et sic est haec distinguenda: Homo praedicatur de pluribus ... (*S. Logicae* I, c. 65 [*edit. cit.* 180—181]). This rule, which seems to be redundant, has no equivalent in the *Expositio super libr. Elenchorum*.

We hope we made it sufficiently clear in the preceding part that at times we went beyond the *littera Ockham*. In order to create no misunderstanding let us state expressly that Ockham *de facto* distinguishes three levels of language: Propositions where subject and predicate are first intentions; propositions where the subject or predicate is a first intention without significative function and the other extreme is a second intention; and propositions where subject and predicate are second intentions each with significative function. We disregard here the case of first and second imposition which could be treated similarly. Ockham is mainly interested in the case where a term of first intention enters into communication with a term of second intention and a term of first imposition with a term of second imposition.

In insisting on the fact that every term primarily has a personal supposition and only secondarily another supposition, and by demanding that an indication must be given if a term has not to be taken in personal supposition, Ockham removes from his logic an element of uncertainty and arbitrariness. According to his rules, we are able to check propositions as to the supposition of their terms. Hence the distinctions that he has introduced are not and cannot be made arbitrarily; they are demanded rather by the matter and by the terms that enter the propositions.[28] However these distinctions

[28] Ockham has made clear how he wants such distinctions to be understood in *Ordinatio* d. 4, q. 1, F: Ex istis patet, quomodo talia quae dixi et quae dicam, scilicet quod hoc potest accipi dupliciter vel tripliciter, vel quod potest accipi sic vel sic, et si accipitur sic, tunc est tale, et si accipitur aliter, tunc est tale, sunt intelligenda: quod non est intelligendum, quod aliquid idem propter acceptionem meam vel considerationem, vel si accipitur sic vel sic, quod sit tale vel tale, sicut alii dicunt, sed est intelligendum, sicut intelligit Aristoteles de ipso termino, quod de eodem secundum quod pro diverso et diverso supponit, aliter et aliter verificatur, immo idem affirmatur et negatur. Sicut si in ista propositione: Homo est nomen, ly homo supponit materialiter, tunc est simpliciter vera, si vero supponit personaliter, est simpliciter falsa et suum oppositum verum: Homo non est nomen. Et ita non est concedendum, quod idem est nomen et non est nomen propter diversam considerationem vel acceptionem, sed quod de eodem termino pro uno vere affirmatur esse nomen et de eodem termino pro alio vere negatur esse nomen. Et ita non est idem, quod est nomen et

do not remove every possibility of equivocation. They and their corresponding rules will indicate whether a proposition can be true or not as far as the formal structure of propositions is concerned and as long as the terms are used in their proper meaning, and this whether they exercise their specific significative function or not. On the other hand they will not suffice if terms are not used in their proper meaning but in their improper meaning. Hence there is need of a more general distinction of supposition which is demanded by the loose manner of speech customary to all authors even in philosophy and theology. Hence, supposition must be divided into *suppositio propria* and *suppositio impropria*. Meanings of words in their improper sense vary according to the various figures of speech.[29] It is obvious that we must know whether we have to take a term in the one or the other sense in order not to end in confusion. It is precisely to avoid such logical chaos that Ockham uses the ancient distinction between the proper and improper sense and the other old distinction between *de virtute sermonis* and *de proprietate sermonis*. It is true that Ockham has made more use of these distinctions than have any other scholastics before him.

DIGRESSION ON THE MEANING OF THE *De Virtute Sermonis*

From the preceding it should be sufficiently evident that Ockham did not consider a proposition simply false if it cannot be true in personal but only in another supposition, or even if it can be true only in an improper supposition. It was the doubtful privilege of certain smaller Ockhamists of Paris to call any proposition simply false which is false in personal suppo-

---

quod non est nomen, sed de eodem termino propter variam suppositionem vere affirmatur et negatur idem.

[29] Oportet autem cognoscere, quod sicut est suppositio propria, quando scilicet terminus supponit pro eo, quod significat proprie, ita est suppositio impropria, quando terminus accipitur improprie. Multiplex autem est suppositio impropria, scilicet antonomatica, quando terminus supponit praecise pro illo, cui maxime convenit, sicut in talibus: Apostolus dicit hoc, Philosophus negat hoc, et similibus. Alia est synecdochica, quando pars supponit pro toto. Alia est metaphorica, quando continens supponit pro contento, vel quando abstractum accidentis supponit pro subiecto, et sic de aliis (*S. Logicae* I, c. 77 [*edit. cit.* 213—214]).

sition; it is regrettable that Michalski has dragged Ockham into their camp by questionable means.

In his (probably) latest publication: "Le problème de la volonté à Oxford et à Paris au XIVme siècle," in *Studia Philosophica* (Lemberg), II (1937), 255 ss (23 ss), this great pioneer in the field of fourteenth-century scholasticism, unfortunately has misrepresented Ockham's position as regards the use of *de virtute sermonis*. After a careful study of the pertinent documents and texts we could not convince ourselves that Michalski has correctly understood the document of condemnation of certain "Ockhamistic errors" issued by the Faculty of Arts in Paris in 1340 (*Charturlarium Universitatis Parisiensis* II, 505—507). Since the publications of the eminent Polish historian are quite often used in an uncritical manner (cf. *Franciscan Studies* 5 (1945) 315, where we promised a more detailed discussion of the point), we are forced once more to the ungrateful task of criticizing a scholar to whom we are very much indebted. However, our following redress of Michalski's misinterpretation is not made with the intention of whitewashing Ockham or even of proving that he was in no way meant by the condemnation of 1340. It is a fact that his name occurs in the document, however not in connection with the problem under consideration. Though we are personally convinced that Ockham's use of the term *de virtute sermonis* was not condemned, nevertheless, we are ready to admit that his frequent use of the term could easily induce a superficial reader to include him in this condemnation. Let us not forget that he had a famous adversary in the Faculty of Arts, Walter Burley, whom he had ridiculed and who had already in 1329 or before that date written a work against him (Cf. *The Tractatus de Successivis...* Franciscan Institute Publications I, [1944], 4). Since the document of condemnation does not state that Ockham's teaching is meant, we are at liberty to presuppose that the authors of it at least did not feel sure about him. We have, therefore, the right to ask whether Michalski's assumptions are correct. We shall do that by first presenting the content of the document of condemnation as regards the use of the expression *de virtute sermonis*, secondly Michalski's interpretation of and comment on it, and finally we shall add the necessary correction.

The decree of the faculty of arts demands the following: No professor is allowed to call a proposition of a "famous" author false in an unqualified sense or false by virtue of expression when he is convinced that the author understood it correctly. In such a case, he must either concede that proposition or separate the true sense from the false sense by making a distinction:

> Nulli magistri, baccalarii, vel scolares in artium facultate legentes Parisius audeant aliquam propositionem famosam illius actoris cujus librum legunt, dicere simpliciter esse falsam, vel esse falsam de virtute

sermonis, si crediderint quod actor ponendo illam habuerit verum intellectum; sed vel concedant eam, vel sensum verum dividant a sensu falso . . . (p. 506).

No one is allowed to call any proposition false in an unqualified sense or by virtue of expression, which would be false, if the terms were taken in personal supposition, since this error leads to the former; for authors often make use of other suppositions. No one is allowed to say that a proposition is to be distinguished, since this leads to the aforementioned errors . . . No one is allowed to say that no proposition is to be conceded if it is not true in its proper sense, since that leads to the aforementioned errors . . .

These are the condemned propositions concerning the expression *de virtute sermonis*. Amann in the *Dictionnaire de Théologie Catholique* (t. 11, I, col. 897) gives a good and cautious summary of them.

Michalski (*l. c.* p. 257) however is convinced that the decree has condemned the doctrine of Ockham concerning the use of *De virtute sermonis*. Since copies of Michalski's article seem to be extremely scarce in this country — we were able to use it only through the courtesy of Prof. Weinberg of Cincinnati — we shall quote him literally:

> La tendance d'Ockham dans la direction de l'actuelle sémantique n'aurait pas sans doute suscité une opposition retentissante dans l'histoire de la philosophie, si elle n'avait pas empiété sur le domaine de la théologie pour attaquer de façon inattendue certaines expressions de l'Ecriture Sainte et des théologiens. Le décret de Paris de l'année 1340 apparut comme une réaction contre cette tendance . . . Je dois immédiatement faire remarquer que le décret ne mentionne pas le nom d'Ockham (this is exact only in the sense that Ockham's name is not mentioned in "condemnations"; however it is mentioned at the end of the decree in another connection); mais, que ce soit bien de lui qu'il s'agissait, nous le savons par Denifle qui rapporte un passage du livre des procureurs de la nation anglaise où la secte des Ockhamistes est désignée expressément.

Michalski is furthermore convinced that the expression *de virtute sermonis* is connected with the old controversy as to whether words have meaning by nature or by institution:

> Comme plus d'une fois elle (viz. the expression "de virtute sermonis") apparaît en opposition avec la formule "ad placitum", il pouvait sembler qu'il s'agit ici de l'ancienne controverse grecque, à savoir si les mots ont leur sens *physei* ou *thései*. Sans aucun doute l'expression elle-même se rattache à cette controverse; pourtant elle a chez Ockham une signification quelque peu différente.

Finally, the "unexpected attacks" made by Ockham against certain expressions of Holy Scripture and theologians, is substantiated by Michalski with a really shocking text of Ockham (note I, p. 257):

Je cite pour exemple la discussion suivante d'Ockham dans son Quodlibet, II, q. 19: Utrum haec propositio "hoc est corpus meum" de virtute sermonis sit vera. Et videtur, quod non est, quia quaero, quid demonstratur per hoc pronomen "hoc". Aut corpus Christi et tunc est falsa, quia quando profertur hoc pronomen "hoc", non est corpus Christi in Eucharistia . . . Aut demonstratur aliquid aliud a corpore Christi et tunc iterum est falsa, qui nihil aliud quam corpus Christi est corpus Christi.

Let us make it expressly clear that no other text and no explanation is added.

Now we are prepared to come to a sound judgment about the meaning of Ockham's *de virtute sermonis* and its alleged connection with the condemnation.

First, we must give credit to Michalski that he succeeded well in exonerating Buridan who added his seal and signature to this decree though he was a determined Nominalist in the medieval sense. Furthermore, Michalski understands *de virtute sermonis* correctly as the sense of a proposition in proper supposition in opposition to improper supposition. Ockham suggests this meaning when dealing with the *suppositio impropia* in chapter seventy-seven of the first part of his *Summa Logicae*. At another place he says that he understands under *de virtute sermonis* the meaning that must be assigned to terms *secundum regulas generales, secundum quas tales iudicari debent* (*S. Logicae* II, c. 19 [edit. Boehner II, 281]).

After these concessions we are forced to part company with Michalski. It is not true, and it is contradicted by every text of Ockham concerning this matter — and they are very numerous — that the expression *de virtute sermonis* has anything to do with the controversy as to whether words have meaning by nature or by institution. Ockham has always maintained with Aristotle and other scholastics that words are instituted *ad placitum*, since they are artificial signs and are not given by nature. However, Michalski says that Ockham *plus d'une fois* opposes *de virtute sermonis* to *ad placitum*. Where? Michalski does not give any text. We do not know any text to that effect. If there should be in the writings of Ockham a passage where *ad placitum* is opposed to *de virtute sermonis* it can have only this meaning: Besides the commonly accepted meaning of terms, one may at will use the terms in improper meaning.

Furthermore it is not proved by Michalski that Ockham's use of the distinction between false in virtue of expression and true according to the intention of the author is condemned. On the contrary it is this very distinction that is demanded by the decree. According to the decree — we again invite the reader carefully to read the text as quoted above — it is not right and allowable to call any famous proposition simply false which is false only in virtue of expression if it has a correct sense according to the intention of the author. If a right sense is intended, then such a proposition must be either conceded as such or it must be distinguished. This implies immediately that it is expressly conceded by this decree that a proposition may be called false in virtue of expression, but true according to the intention of the author. However, it is not allowed to call a famous proposition absolutely false, if and because it is false only in virtue of expression. This point has escaped the attention of Michalski completely. But let Ockham speak for himself:

> One must carefully consider whether a term and a proposition are taken in virtue of expression, and whether they are taken according to the usage of those who are speaking and the authors' intention, because there is hardly any word which is not equivocally taken in some mode of equivocation in the various books of the Philosophers and the Saints and the Authors. Those, therefore, who are decided always to take a word univocally and in one mode, frequently err about the intention of the author and concerning the inquiry of truth, since almost all words are taken equivocally. *Summa Lgicae* I, c. 77 [cfr. edit. Boehner I, 214].

Again:

> And so it is with many authorities from the philosophers which are false in virtue of expression though their intention is true. Therefore, as it is commonly said: Sentences of authorities are to be understood in the sense in which they are made, and not in the sense which they make (*Expositio Aurea, Super 1. Porphyrii*).

Many more passages from Ockham could be accumulated which are all to the same effect. Even Michalski's quotation on p. 256 proves the same. Moreover, the term *de virtute sermonis* and the use of the corresponding distinction was not introduced by Ockham into scholastic theology, but he found it already there, *cf.* for instance St. Bonaventure I S. d. 4, a. u. q. 2; t. I, p. 100 a. We have found it used elsewhere by scholastics of Paris long before Ockham.

However, the "example" of Ockham's radicalism in the use of the expression *de virtute sermonis*, is a little too much. If we allow such a "proof" to be considered seriously, we have to pronounce all the scholastics including St. Thomas the worst heretics. We have only to cut off from their *quaestiones* the *pro* or *contra*, as the case may be, present it without any connection with the rest of the question, and perfect heretics will be created. Let us show this as regards the words of consecration, for the Common Doctor could have really inspired these dangerous lines of Ockham. We read *S. Th.* IV, q. 78, a. 5:

> Utrum praedictae locutiones sint verae. Ad quintum sic proceditur: Videtur quod praedictae locutiones non sint verae. Cum enim dicitur: Hoc est corpus meum, *ly* hoc est demonstrativum substantiae. Sed secundum praedicta, quando profertur hoc adhuc est ibi substantia panis, quia transsubstantiatio fit in ultimo instanti prolationis verborum. Sed haec est falsa: Panis est corpus Christi. Ergo haec est falsa: Hoc est corpus meum.

Michalski simply omitted that in the *corpus quaestionis* where Ockham expresses his own opinion he states that the proposition is true without any distinction.

In summary, therefore, we can say that Ockham, too, could have subscribed to every demand of the decree mentioned above. He uses the expression *de virtute sermonis* only when a term is taken in an improper meaning. If a term is taken in an improper meaning, the Logician must know that he cannot simply apply his established rules, but must proceed carefully and have more regard to the intention of the author and the whole context than to the grammatical and logical structure of the sentences under consideration. What the decree requests from the students in the Faculty of Arts:

> By affirming or denying sentences one must pay more attention to the subject matter than to the proper sense of the sentences; for a disputation which pays attention only to the proper sense of sentences and which does not accept any proposition unless in its proper sense, is only a sophistical disputation (p. 506).

is said by Ockham in other words in the prologue to his *Expositio Aurea:*

> Another use of logic is the ease which it gives in perceiving the virtue of expression and the proper manner of speaking. For by this science one may easily know what is uttered by an author in virtue of expression and what is not uttered by virtue of expression but according to the usual manner of speaking or according to the intention of a teacher — what is said in a proper way and what is said metaphorically. This is highly necessary for all who study the texts of authors. For he who always takes the words of an author in their proper sense and in virtue of expression falls into error and inexplicable difficulties.

II. TRUTH AND FALSITY OF PROPOSITIONS

After these explanations of signification and supposition we are now in a position to understand the concept of truth and falsity in

Ockham. We have simply to apply and to elucidate a little further the previously expounded ideas of signification and supposition. Our aim will be to ascertain the concepts of logical truth and falsity in categorical propositions.

a. Truth and Falsity are Second Intentions

If we restrict the meaning of "true" and "false" or "truth" and "falsity" to the realm of propositions, that is, to logical truth and falsity, the terms are second intentions and not first intentions. For the terms "true" and "false" are predicated about other intentions, *viz.*, propositions. Hence we are not here at all interested in so-called ontological or moral truth and falsity, nor in the so-called truth of simple apprehension or even of concepts. We are interested only in the meaning of the term "true" (or "false") when we say, for instance, "Socrates is white, is true."

The second intentions,[30] "true" and "false", or "truth" and "falsity", signify or stand for propositions. However, when used as predicates, their respective subjects do not necessarily have simple or material supposition. Ockham is well aware of the various ways in which "truth" and "falsity" can be predicated. They can be predicated about the common term "proposition" or *complexum*, *etc.*, by saying for instance: "Every proposition is either true or false," or they can be predicated about the individual propositions as such. There can be no doubt, that in the aforementioned universal proposition "Every proposition" has personal supposition of the

---

[30] Though Ockham does not say expressly that truth or falsity are second intentions, they are nevertheless *de facto* always treated by him as second intentions. We know from *S. Logicae* I, c. 2, that propositions as a whole can be terms. Furthermore, he considers "verum" and "falsum" modalities either qualifying incomplex terms *(sensus divisus)* or propositions *(sensus compositus)*, and as to the latter meaning he introduces our familiar distinctions. Cf. Quamvis ista distinctio communis possit sustineri, nec velim eam improbare, tamen potest aliter distingui et forte magis artificialiter (translate: logically), eo quod dictum propositionis potest sumi materialiter ... et iste sensus est idem cum illo, qui ponitur sensus compositionis, vel potest sumi significative, et tunc est idem sensus cum sensu divisionis (*S. Logicae* III, 1, c. 20 [edit. Boehner II, 375—376]).

type of confused and distributed supposition. In the other case, however, it is quite different as when we say: "Socrates is white, is true." In the first case, it is obvious that the term "proposition" or "every proposition" is not true or false, but only that which is signified by it. In the second case it is likewise obvious that the proposition "Socrates is white" is denoted to be true. In the first case we speak about all the propositions which are signified by the term "proposition"; in the second case, the proposition as such is denoted to be true; and hence it stands for itself. Hence a distinction must be made. The proposition: "Socrates is white, is true" would be false in personal supposition, for the proposition "Socrates is white" denotes a state of affairs, namely the whiteness in Socrates, and this fact or state of affairs is neither true nor false, being no proposition at all. Taken in simple or material supposition, it is only denoted that the proposition "Socrates is white" is true, though of course it is true because it signifies a state of affairs correctly.[31]

We are here not too far from a so-called modern approach to the problem of truth and falsity. Ockham is well aware that we have to distinguish the proposition from the name of the proposition. If we use the name of a proposition, the name has personal supposition — be it a singular or a common name; if we use the proposition as such, we have simple supposition and not personal supposition. In order to show this more definitely, let us briefly discuss an instance where Ockham brings symbolism into the debate. Let "A" stand for the whole proposition *Homo est animal*. In this case "A" is a name of a proposition; it is even a singular name and a sign in

---

[31] Sciendum, quod aliquod incomplexum supponens respectu veri vel falsi potest habere suppositionem simplicem vel personalem; si simplicem vel materialem, sic nullum incomplexum est verum vel falsum, et sic etiam hoc praedicatum verum vel falsum non praedicatur vere de aliquo incomplexo. Si habeat suppositionem personalem, sic de aliquo incomplexo vere praedicatur hoc praedicatum verum vel falsum, sic de hoc termino 'propositio' verificatur, quod aliqua propositio est vera vel falsa. Si tamen subiectum istius propositionis: Propositio est vera vel falsa, supponat pro se, haec esset simpliciter falsa, quia tunc significaretur, quod haec dictio 'propositio' esset vera vel falsa, quod est manifeste falsum. *Expos. s. l. Praedicamentorum* ad: Videtur autem . . .

the strict sense. The term "A" signifies and is able to stand for the proposition *Homo est animal*. Therefore when we say "A" is true, we do not mean to say that this sign "A" is true, but that the proposition which is signified by "A" and for which "A" stands, is true. Hence "A" must have personal supposition; otherwise the proposition would be false.[32]

What we have said here may be illustrated by a drawing in which we distinguish the thing, its state, and three propositions indicating the various suppositions. The thing is the white Socrates; the three propositions are: *"Socrates est albus," "Socrates est albus est verum," "A'* (meaning *Socrates est albus) est verum."*

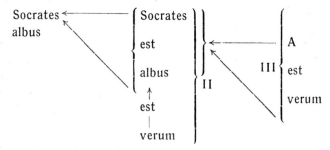

In all of the three the proposition *"Socrates est albus"* plays a role. In the first it is the proposition in its significative function, in the second we predicate *verum* about the same proposition, in the third we predicate *verum* about the name of the proposition. The terms in the first and third proposition have personal supposition; in the second the subject has simple supposition.

This leads us immediately to a before-mentioned distinction between levels of predication. For the first proposition belongs to the language about things in reality, the second speaks immediately

---

[32] Similiter si A instituatur ad significandum hanc propositionem: Homo est animal, tunc haec est vera: A est verum, si A supponat personaliter, et falsa, si supponat pro se. Et isto modo frequenter in respondendo utimur una dictione pro propositione et pro uno complexo, et ita ista dictio neque est vera neque falsa; sed illa propositio, pro qua utimur illa dictione, est vera vel falsa. Sicut si quaeratur a te: Fuisti Romae? et dicas: Ita, tunc hac dictione 'ita' uteris pro tota ista propositione: Ego fui Romae, et ita est de aliis frequenter. *l.c.*

about a proposition of the first level, the third speaks about it mediately through a name of the proposition of the first level. The following drawing is a visual presentation:

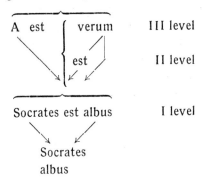

Since the predicates *verum* and *falsum*, being second intentions, are predicated about propositions or names of propositions, it follows that they cannot be predicated about themselves or about any proposition in which they are contained without reference to o t h e r p r o p o s i t i o n s. The famous *Insolubile* is solved by Ockham on the ground of this i m p o s s i b i l i t y. The treatment of the *insolubile* has been ridiculed and labeled as another case of scholastic subtlety and logical absurdity. Modern logicians are reduced to another opinion since in their own logic they must cope with these same difficulties of the scholastic *insolubile*. What they try to remedy by the theory of types or such similar devices is dealt with by Ockham in his theory of supposition and the character of the term true and false which are second intentions predicable about propositions of which they are not a part.[33] The classical example commonly used in the Middle Ages is this: "Socrates says: *Sortes dicit falsum.*" This sentence *Sortes dicit falsum* is his first and last sentence. About this single sentence the sophist now asks: Is it true or false? If it is true then Socrates says something true. But he says only this sentence: *Sortes dicit falsum.* Consequently *Sortes dicit falsum* is true; and consequently: *Sortes dicit verum.* Hence, if Socrates says something

---

[33] Moody, *op. cit.* 43, has first called attention to the relation of the theory of supposition with the "theory of types."

true he says something false. Under the supposition that the sentence is false, similar contradictions will show up. Then it follows that *Sortes dicit falsum* is true; but Socrates utters only this sentence; *Sortes dicit falsum*, consequently it is true, consequently Socrates says something true; hence if Socrates says something true, Socrates says something false. Ockham reminds us that such sophistical argumentation can be made only by using the terms "false" or "not true" or such similar ones.

In his answer Ockham justly remarks that the proposition *Sortes non dicit falsum* under the same condition, namely that no other sentence is uttered, is true, since the term *falsum* does not supposit for any sentence, and that is expressed by the denial. The same can be said about the critical form *Sortes non dicit verum* for if Socrates utters no other proposition, then he does not utter any true proposition for which *verum* could supposit. This is denoted by the negative proposition *Sortes non dicit verum*. However, the sophist will argue: if the proposition *Sortes non dicit verum* is true, and if Socrates does utter this proposition, he utters a true proposition; consequently, we could add, as understood by Ockham: *Sortes dicit verum*. We shall now give Ockham's answer in translation:

> The answer is that this consequence is not valid: "Socrates utters this proposition," and: "This proposition is true," therefore, "Socrates utters a true proposition." The reason for this denial is as follows: In the proposition *Sortes non dicit verum*, the predicate cannot supposit for this entire proposition of which it is a part, yet not precisely because it is a part. Hence the proposition *Sortes non dicit verum* is equivalent to the following: "Socrates does not say something true other than this: *Sortes non dicit verum*." Therefore, as it does not follow: "This (proposition) is true," and: "Socrates utters this (proposition)," therefore "He utters a true proposition other than this," so it does not follow: "Socrates utters this proposition," and: "This is true," therefore "Socrates utters something true." Because as said before these two propositions are equivalent: "Socrates utters something true," and "Socrates utters something true other than the former."

A corresponding answer must be given to the preceding argument. When Socrates starts to say: *Sortes dicit falsum*, and someone asks: Does Socrates say something true or false? We must reply: Socrates says neither something true nor something false. For it must be conceded that he does not say either something true or false other than this. Then it does not follow: "This is false — *Socrates dicit falsum;*" and: "Socrates utters this (proposition);" therefore "Socrates utters something false." As it likewise does not follow: "Socrates utters this, and this is false," therefore, "Socrates says something false other than this." This is so because these two propositions are equivalent: *Sortes dicit falsum* and: "Sortes utters something false other than this," because in the proposition, *Sortes dicit falsum,* the predicate cannot supposit for this proposition. The objection arises: We argue here from the logically lower to the logically higher without denial and without distribution, therefore the consequence is valid. We say in answer: The consequence is not valid if that logically higher in that consequent cannot supposit for that logically lower; hence if in this proposition, "Man is an animal," "animal" cannot supposit for a man, this consequence would not be valid, "Socrates is a man," therefore "Socrates is an animal." In the proposition *Sortes dicit falsum* the predicate cannot supposit for that entire proposition; and for that reason it does not follow "Socrates says this something false," therefore "Socrates says something false."[34]

Hence Ockham's solution of the *Insolubile* comes ultimately down to this: The predicate *verum* and the predicate *falsum* are terms signifying propositions. When used in a proposition in significative function, they require a significate. If no significate is given and the terms *falsum* and *verum* are denied, the propositions are false, since neither *falsum* nor *verum* stand for a significate which by hypothesis is not given. Furthermore, the predicates *falsum*

---

[34] This is a litteral translation from the *Summa Logicae* (revised text). A similar text of the still unedited *Expositio s.l. Elenchorum* (cf. note 19) fol. 135 ra reads: "Sed ex hoc non sequitur, quod simpliciter dicat falsum. Et ita talis consequentia non valet: Sortes dicit hoc falsum, ergo Sortes dicit falsum; sed est fallacia secundum quid et simpliciter. Et hoc, quia in ista: Sortes dicit falsum, ly falsum non potest supponere pro hoc falso, quod est: Sortem dicere falsum. Et per istum modum respondendum est ad omnia insolubilia, negando scilicet consequentiam ab aliquo termino sumpto cum pronomine demonstrativo determinante aliquod contentum ad ipsum terminum sumptum sine tali pronomine. Et non est alia ratio, nisi quia terminus communis non potest supponere in illa propositione pro illo inferiori, quamvis in aliis propositionibus possit pro eo supponere." Prantl's assumption that the chapter on the "Insolubile" in the *Summa Logicae* is non-authentic is without foundation. Cf. Philotheus Boehner, O.F.M., "Zur Echtheit der Summa Logicae Ockhams," in *Franziskanische Studien* 26 (1939) 190—193 [*supra,* 65—70].

and *verum* cannot be predicated about a proposition, of which they are a part, precisely because they require a significate which is a proposition. We know from our treatment of Ockham's theory of signification that sign and significate are different; for sign is something that makes something different from itself known. It is in fact Ockham's ingenious and carefully developed theory of signification and supposition which prevents the *Insolubile* from causing any trouble. For truth and falsity are second intentions predicable only of entire propositions which they signify and for which they can stand in a proposition. But by definition the proposition in which "truth" and "falsity" are predicates will be at least one level higher than the proposition of which or for which they are predicated.

b. Truth and Falsity are Connotative Terms

However, we are not yet at the end of our analysis of the terms "true" and "false". Though we know that "truth" and "falsity", being second intentions, are predicates about or properties of propositions, we wish to know what such properties are. A proposition is either true or false, but whether it is true or whether it is false does not simply depend on the proposition as such — at least if we speak of categorical propositions. Hence true and false are connotative terms. They signify propositions directly and connote something else.

What is it that the terms "true" and "false" connote? When we say about a proposition that it is true, we mean that the proposition signifies a thing or a state as it is; and when we say that a proposition is false, we mean to say that the proposition does not signify a thing or state as it is.[35] By saying this, we have reached

---

[35] Sed verum et falsum sunt quaedam praedicabilia de oratione connotantia aliquid a parte rei. Unde oratio dicitur vera, quia significat sic esse a parte rei, sicut est. Et ideo sine omni mutatione a parte orationis ex hoc ipso, quod primo significat, sicut est a parte rei, et postea propter mutationem rei significat, sicut non est a parte rei, dicitur oratio, primo vera et postea falsa. Sicut quando Sortes sedet, quia illa oratio: Sortes sedet, significat, sicut est a parte rei, ideo est illa oratio vera, et quia quando Sortes surgit, significat, sicut non est in re, sine omni sibi adveniente, est oratio falsa . . . (*Expos. s. l. Praedicamentorum*, cap. 9 ad: Sed si quis . . . Cf. *Quodl.* V, q. 24 [ed. Argentina]).

Aristotle's notification of truth, which though sometimes it may appear trivial,[36] nevertheless remains on safe ground:

This is clear in the first place, if we define what the true and the false are. To say of what is that it is not, or of what is not that it is, is false; while to say of what is that it is, and what is not that it is not, is true.[37]

It appears, however, that this definition is not so trivial after all. It has even found favorable comment in a recent study by one of the leading scholars in modern Logic.[38] Nevertheless, it does not say all that can and should be said in order to make the connotation of "true" and "false" explicit. Ockham leads us a step further when he says that a true proposition signifies a state of affairs as it is, and a false proposition signifies a state of affairs as it is not. When does a proposition signify or not signify a state of affairs as it is or as it is not? The answer constantly given by Ockham is: If subject and predicate supposit for the same or do not supposit for the same. If and only if there is the coincidence of supposition of subject and predicate will a proposition be true. Hence, the *connotatum* of the term "true" is the coincidence of the supposition of subject and predicate, and the *connotatum* of "false" is the lack of the coincidence of the supposition of subject and predicate. In accordance with his teachings, a definition of true would therefore be: "True" is a predicate predicable only of propositions connoting coincidence of supposition of subject and predicate. In similar fashion a definition of "false" would be: "False" is a predicate predicable only about propositions connoting lack of coincidence of subject and predicate. Or, and this comes closer to the wording of Ockham: "True" is a predicate predicable about propositions and connoting that subject and predicate stand for the same. A similar definition could be given for "false".[39]

---

[36] This may be the reason why it is usually overlooked by modern scholastics.

[37] *Met.* VI, 7, 1011b25 (Oxford translation). Cf. *Categor.* c. 5, and *Periherm.* c. 9.

[38] Cf. Alfred Tarski, "The semantic conception of truth and the foundations of Semantics," in *Philosophy and Phenomenological Research* 4 (1944) espec. 342ss.

[39] Ockham has never given an explicit definition of "true" or "false"; however, the definition *(quid nominis)* here presented is in perfect accor-

Since truth is had if and only if subject and predicate supposit for the same, it is sufficient, but not required, that subject and predicate are the same term and have the same meaning, as in cases where we have propositions of identity. Yet, subject and predicate are usually not the same, not only in true negative propositions but also in true affirmative propositions. For they are two different words or two different concepts and hence two different entities. On several occasions Ockham has made it clear that the truth of a proposition does not imply the identity of subject and predicate; the truth of an affirmative proposition only implies that subject and predicate signify or at least stand for the same.[40]

If however, we want to retain the equivocal expression "In a true proposition subject and predicate are the same," we have to distinguish two possible meanings of it. In one sense it could say that in every true proposition subject and predicate are truly identical. It is obvious that, taken in this sense, the expression is false.

---

dance with his explanation. The first part is based on what has been said in footnote 35. The second is amply substantiated by many texts, of which a few will be quoted later. For the time being the following text may suffice: Dicendum, quod per istam propositionem: Sortes est albus, non denotatur, quod Sortes sit vox, quantumcumque vox praedicetur hic. Cuius ratio est, quia per propositionem non denotatur, quod subiectum sit praedicatum, sed denotatur in tali propositione, quod illud, pro quo subiectum supponit, sit illud, pro quo praedicatum supponit. Et propter hoc in tali propositione, ubi praedicatur concretum tale, quale est hoc concretum 'albus', denotatur, quod aliqua talis res, sicut albedo, competit illi, pro quo subiectum supponit. Et ideo quia in illa: Sortes est albus, subiectum et praedicatum supponunt pro eodem, et Sortes est illud, pro quo supponit praedicatum, quamvis non sit ipsum praedicatum, ideo haec et vera. *Expos. s.l. Porphyrii* (De genere) ad: Eorum quae praedicantur . . .

[40] Sed quando subiectum et praedicatum habent suppositionem personalem et supponunt non pro seipsis sed pro suis significatis, tunc non requiritur, quod subiectum et praedicatum sint idem, sed oportet, quod supponunt pro eodem, et hoc in propositione simpliciter de recto et simpliciter de inesse, quamvis non semper hoc sufficit. Unde in illa propositione prolata: Homo est animal, subiectum et praedicatum non sunt idem, quia si essent idem, praedicaretur idem de se, quod nullus concedit; et tamen haec est vera, quia subiectum et praedicatum supponunt pro eodem. *l.c.*

Ockham even takes pains to prove that.[41] In another sense the expression is true. Then it means: Every affirmative, true proposition requires for its truth that subject and predicate signify the same and supposit for the same. This refers, of course, to propositions where both subject and predicate are taken each in personal supposition though it could as easily be enlarged to cover propositions with different suppositions for the terms. Taken in this sense, there is an identity given, not the identity of subject and predicate but only the identity of the thing which is signified with terms which are different. In other words, in such propositions subject and predicate are identified in the thing that they signify.[42]

c. Application of Truth and Falsity to Various Propositions

By way of application let us now exemplify what has been said about the notions of truth and falsity. We cannot take into consideration all possible cases. A few may suffice to show the usefulness of Ockham's theory. We are here following Ockham through the second part of the *Summa Logicae* where he treats of various propositions and also always adds the requirements for their truth or falsity.

Singular propositions in the strict sense are propositions in which the subject is a proper name or a demonstrative pronoun (in the singular case) with or without a common term. For instance: *Sortes*

---

[41] Cf. various proofs in *Quodl.* III, q. 5 ed. Argentina (ed. Paris III, 12). May we recall here that this is also the teaching of St. Thomas. Cf. *S. Theol.* I, 13, 12.

[42] Alius intellectus praedictae propositionis est, scilicet quod omnis propositio affirmativa vera requirit ad veritatem suam, quod subiectum et praedicatum significant idem vel (so Ms. Vat. 3075; the editions *et*) supponant pro eodem. Et iste intellectus est verus, quia omnis propositio affirmativa vera est vera propter identitatem rei significatae per subiectum et praedicatum, et quia per talem propositionem non denotatur, quod subiectum sit praedicatum, sed denotatur, quod res importata per subiectum sit res importata per praedicatum, quia utimur vocibus pro rebus et terminis non pro se sed pro re, quam significant (*Quodl.* III, 5; Ms. Vat. and ed. Paris III, 12).

18 Boehner, Articles on Ockham

currit, Iste currit, Iste homo currit.[43] According to our definition, these are true if subject and predicate stand for the same thing. This needs no further explanation, since we have used similar examples to clarify the meaning of supposition and of truth and falsity.[44] The supposition of the subject in such singular propositions is called "discrete" supposition, since the subject stands precisely for one thing.[45] Falsehood of such a proposition would of course be had if the subject were not to stand for anything for which the predicate stands.

Particular propositions, that is, propositions in which the subject is determined by a particular sign as *aliquis, etc.*, and *indefinite propositions* in which the subject is a common term without a particular or universal sign or a demonstrative pronoun but suppositing personally, demand a more detailed treatment. We first consider the case of such an affirmative true proposition as *Aliquis homo est albus.* Now, this proposition is true, if there is at least one individual for which subject and predicate stand, that is, if there is at least one white man. As regards at least one white man the subject and predicate are identified, not, however, as regards themselves.[46]

Since such a particular proposition requires for its truth at least one instance in which it is true, the supposition of the subject is called determinate supposition. It is a common supposition, since the term that supposits is common, but it is determinate supposition since there must be at least one individual for which it is verified.[47] Though the common term by its very nature is able to stand for all the individuals it can signify, nevertheless, the syncategorematic term *aliquis* causes the subject *aliquis homo* in the proposition *aliquis*

---

[43] *S. Logicae* II, c. 1. Cf. also and for the following, Moody, *op. cit.* p. 192 ss.

[44] Cf. its explicit treatment in *S. Logicae* II, c. 2.

[45] Suppositio autem discreta est, in qua supponit nomen proprium alicuius vel pronomen demonstrativum significative sumptum; et talis suppositio reddit propositionem singularem (*S. Logicae* I, c. 70 [ed. Boehner I, 189]).

[46] *S. Logicae* II, c. 3.

[47] *S. Logicae* I, c. 68.

homo est albus to stand for at least one white man. Or, in other words, it is denoted that subject and predicate meet in at least one individual in which individual they are identified, since each one signifies it and stands for it. Whether subject and predicate meet also in other individuals does not matter.

A negative particular proposition to be true, requires that subject and predicate do not stand for at least one individual. The lack of supposition can be on the part of the subject or of the predicate.[48]

Indefinite propositions are propositions in which the subject is a common term without a particular or universal sign, as for instance: *Homo est animal, Homo est species.* If the subject is taken in personal supposition, Ockham treats them as particular propositions. If, however, the subject is taken in another supposition, then he suggests that they be treated as singular propositions. In the latter case the truth of such propositions is guaranteed if the subject stands for itself and the predicate signifies and stands for the subject.[49]

Universal propositions, that is, propositions in which the subject as such is qualified by a universal sign, as *omnis, etc.* are true if the subject stands for every individual that is signified by it and the predicate stands for every individual that is signified by the subject. Such a universal proposition is, of course, false if subject and predicate are not identified in every individual of the subject, unless such an exception is made explicit. The supposition of the subject

---

[48] Sic igitur patet, quomodo indefinita vel particularis est vera, si subiectum supponat pro aliquo, pro quo non supponit praedicatum. Hoc tamen non semper requiritur, sed quandoque sufficit, quod subiectum indefinitae et particularis negativae pro nullo supponat; sicut si nullus homo sit albus, haec particularis negativa est vera: Aliquis albus homo non est homo, et tamen subiectum pro nullo supponit, quia nec pro substantia nec pro accidente (*S. Logicae* II, c. 3 [ed. Boehner II, 230]).

[49] Sed quid sufficit ad veritatem talis indefinitae, si sit indefinita? Dicendum, quod ad veritatem talis sufficit, quod pro eodem supponat subiectum et praedicatum, si sit affirmativa, vel quod non supponat pro eodem, si sit negativa, sicut hoc sufficit ad veritatem propositionis singularis, quia idem est iudicium de tali propositione et de propositione singulari. Et ideo communiter ponitur, quod talis propositio est singularis, et potest poni satis rationabiliter (*S. Logicae* II, c. 3 [edit. Boehner II, 231]).

18*

of unqualified universal propositions is called *Suppositio confusa et distributiva mobilis;* if at least one of its supposits is excepted or immobilized, as, for instance, in the proposition *Omnis homo praeter Sortem currit,* it is called *Suppositio . . . immobilis.*[50]

We have briefly explained only a few examples of the application of Ockham's theory of supposition to categorical propositions. Ockham makes application to many other types of propositions, to propositions of the past and future (*S. L.* II, c. 7), and to modal propositions (*S. L.* II, 9). It would lead too far afield to present his discussions here, since the nature of such propositions—highly complicated and equivocal—requires lengthy explanations.

There remains, however, one difficulty which we have no intention to pass over in silence. All the scholastic theories of truth and falsity can be more or less easily applied to categorical propositions *de inesse* or *de modo.* All, however, face new problems when they have to deal with hypothetical propositions, that is with conditional, conjunctive or copulative, disjunctive, causal, temporal, and local propositions. It is extremely difficult, not to say impossible, to see how the theory of supposition could immediately be applied to the

---

[50] Est igitur primo sciendum, quod ad veritatem talis propositionis universalis non requiritur, quod subiectum et praedicatum sint idem realiter, sed requiritur, quod praedicatum supponat pro omnibus illis, pro quibus supponit subiectum, ita quod de illis verificetur. Et si ita sit, nisi aliqua causa specialis impediat, propositio universalis est vera. Et hoc est, quod communiter dicitur, quod ad veritatem talis propositionis universalis sufficit, quod quaelibet singularis sit vera (*S. Logicae* II, c. 4 [edit. Boehner II, 234]). As to the various names and distinctions of supposition cf. *S. Logicae* I, c. 70, and Moody, *op. cit.* p. 189—192. Ockham uses *consequentiae* in order to make the various personal suppositions clear. From discrete supposition we can go down to singulars (as to subject or predicate) in a disjunction, for instance: Aliquis homo est albus, ergo vel iste homo est albus, vel iste homo est albus vel . . . From a universal we can go down to all the singulars (of the subject) in a conjunction, for instance: Omnis homo est albus, ergo Iste homo est albus, et iste homo est albus et . . . As to the predicate we can go down only to the disjunct predicate, for instance: Omnis homo est albus, ergo Omnis homo est istud album vel istud album vel . . .

so-called truth and falsity of such composed propositions in so far as they are composed propositions. For even in a certain case where every elementary proposition is false, it can happen that the compound is nevertheless true.[51] As it appears to us, *salvo meliori iudicio*, this problem has been neglected by the scholastics. They seem to have felt this problem since oftentimes for the consequences at least they use the expressions *bona consequentia* or *consequentia valet* or *consequentia tenet*. Hence it seems that they felt at least that the terms "true" and "false" are equivocal. For this reason it would appear that Ockham and the other scholastics do not advocate their theory of signification and supposition in order to ascertain whether such propositions are true or false; rather, they advocate rules of which the compound propositions are instances. These rules are established by the scholastics on purely logical grounds in accordance with the definitions of statement-connectives. They were not considered as "postulates" or "axioms" in the modern sense of these words, but as being evident from an insight into the relations of such propositions. They were, therefore, called *Axiomata*, or propositions of high dignity because of their universal validity. It is, however, beyond the scope of this article to enlarge on this viewpoint. We intended by our remarks only to make clear that we have not dealt with a certain meaning of "truth" and "falsity" which is encountered in scholastic writings.

We hope that one point has, however, been made clear, *viz.*, that the theory of supposition is a considerable help in clarifying the sometimes obscured notions of "truth" and "falsity". As regards non-hypothetical propositions, which are neither explicitly nor implicitly hypothetical, the theory of supposition is of great value.

---

[51] Est etiam sciendum, quod ad veritatem conditionalis nec requiritur veritas antecedentis nec consequentis, immo est aliquando conditionalis necessaria et quaelibet pars eius est impossibilis, sicut hic: Si Sortes est asinus, Sortes est rudibilis (*S. Logicae* II, c. 31 [ed. Boehner II, 315]).

17. THE NOTITIA INTUITIVA OF NON-EXISTENTS ACCORDING TO WILLIAM OCKHAM

With A Critical Study Of The Text Of Ockham's Reportatio[a]

The following study[1] has a threefold aim: 1. to give an historically exact interpretation of the frequently misunderstood teaching of Ockham on the *notitia intuitiva* as regards non-existents; 2. to substantiate this interpretation by a revised edition of one key text[b]; 3. to prepare the ground for this edition by a short critical study of the text of the *Reportatio Ockham*.

I. THE NOTITIA INTUITIVA OF NON-EXISTENTS

Ockham did not discover or propagate the distinction between *notitia intuitiva* and *notitia abstractiva*, which was almost universally adopted by Scholastics of the 14th century. He received this idea from Scotus, who in turn was influenced by Henry of Ghent. By its very origin, the idea of a *notitia intuitiva* is an Augustinian element, and was conceived to replace the mediate cognitive contact with reality (by means of a species) by an immediate contact with reality in intuition. Henry of Ghent, consequently, denied the necessity of a *species intelligibilis*. Scotus, however, who adopted the term "intuitive knowledge" and developed it, did not follow Henry of Ghent to the consequence of a denial of the necessity of a *species intelligibilis*. It was rather his great disciple and critic, Ockham, who turned resolutely back to the "pure position" of Henry of Ghent.

---

[1] I am very grateful for the valuable help given to me in preparing this article by Fr. Sebastian Day, O. F. M., who is working on a comprehensive study on the *notitia intuitiva* under my direction.

The following works will be simply quoted by name and pages: Hochstetter, E., *Studien zur Metaphysik und Erkenntnislehre Wilhelms von Ockham*, Berlin 1927, Walter de Gruyter Co. — Gilson, E., *The Unity of Philosophical Experience*, New York 1937, Charles Scribner's Sons.

[a] First published in Traditio I (1943) 223—275, omitting, however, the text edition with its immediate introduction, 245—275.

[b] Cfr. note a.

Hence we witness in Ockham two tendencies: 1. to base knowledge on the safe ground of reality in intuitive knowledge, and 2. to eliminate any element, as for instance a species, that could becloud the immediate vision of reality and which, preventing the mind from an immediate contact with things, could lead philosophy along the road of skepticism. For, if reality is not grasped immediately, how can we ever ascertain that we grasp reality at all?

If we bear this in mind, it appears both tragical and comical that the very teaching on the *notitia intuitiva* has brought down on Ockham the verdict of skepticism. One may justly suspect, therefore, that something is wrong: either in Ockham's philosophy — which then must be inconsequent — or, perhaps, in the interpretation of his critics who missed the point. That this latter is the case, will be shown in the present study. But before discussing the main problem, a few remarks on Ockham's teaching of *notitia intuitiva* and *abstractiva* in general seems to be necessary.[2]

1. *Perfect and Imperfect Intuitive Knowledge and Abstractive Knowledge*

A proposition or a statement presupposes the apprehension of the terms of this *complexum*, viz. the *incomplexa*. They are united by the *copula* to form a proposition to which the intellect gives its assent or dissent. The cause of the assent or dissent is given in the apprehension of the *incomplexa* or terms. The terms, however, can be apprehended in two essential different ways. We can, for instance, apprehend Socrates and we can apprehend whiteness. In forming the statement or the *complexum:* Socrates is white, we are either able to know evidently that this statement is true, or we are not able to know whether it is true or not, however strong the apprehension of the terms "Socrates" and "whiteness" may be. In the first case our assent is given through the evidence of the fact; in the second case the force of factual evidence is lacking. In other words, in the

---

[2] For further details we refer to Hochstetter, p. 27 ss. and to P. Vignaux, "Nominalisme", in: Vacant, *Diction. de Théol. cath.*, t. 11, pt. 1 (1931), col. 752 s. and 767 ss.

first case the terms of the proposition were given intuitively in sensibly and intellectually seeing the fact; in the second case the terms of the proposition were given without seeing the fact, but simply in imagining and knowing Socrates and whiteness. The first knowledge is intuitive knowledge: *notitia* or *cognitio intuitiva;* the second is abstractive knowledge: *notitia* or *cognitio abstractiva.* The first knowledge gives us evidence of contingent facts; the second does not.[3] The first is the basis of an evident existential proposition; the second, of a non-existential proposition. Since they are the basis of two essentially different propositions, both must be essentially different, as is shown by Ockham at length.

Intuitive and abstractive knowledge can be in the senses and in the intellect, and they can be both of material and immaterial things. The latter is evident, for we know evidently not only material facts but also immaterial facts, as for example, our inner acts which can be known only by the intellect.[4]

Intuitive knowledge, therefore, is that by which our experience starts, which in its turn is the basis of our scientific knowledge of the sensible and spiritual world. For our knowledge starts with contingent facts and proceeds from them to necessary truths.[5]

---

[3] *Ordinatio,* prol. q. 1 X (our edition, Paderborn 1939, Schöningh, p. 19); cfr. below *Rep.* II, q. 15 E. Note that Ockham proves (in X—Y) also that sensitive intuitive knowledge does not suffice for knowing a contingent truth, which, of course, is a proposition, but only *intellective* intuitive knowledge of material or immaterial things: ". . . ad notitiam alicuius veritatis contingentis non sufficit notitia intuitiva sensitiva, sed oportet ponere praeter illam etiam notitiam, intuitivam intellectivam." Y (p. 21).

[4] "Patet etiam, quod intellectus noster pro statu isto non tantum cognoscit ista sensibilia, sed in particulari et intuitive cognoscit aliqua intelligibilia, quae nullo modo cadunt sub sensu . . ., cuiusmodi sunt intellectiones, actus voluntatis, delectatio consequens et tristitia et huiusmodi, quae potest homo experiri inesse sibi . . ." l. c. HH (p. 29); cfr. Y (p. 22).

[5] "Et ista erit intuitiva. Et illa est notitia, a qua incipit notitia experimentalis, quia universaliter ille, qui potest accipere experimentum de aliqua veritate contingente, et mediante illa de veritate necessaria, habet aliquam notitiam incomplexam de aliquo termino vel re, quam non habet

Abstractive knowledge, however, is had of the elements of a non-existential proposition. But we must be on our guard and not misunderstand this abstractive knowledge for conceptual or universal knowledge. It can be that, but it need not be that. For abstractive knowledge, here, only means that such a knowledge abstracts from existence or non-existence, presence or non-presence, inherence or non-inherence of the known object.[6] Hence it does not assure us in any case of the existence etc. of contingent facts.

Besides this distinction between *notitia intuitiva* and *abstractiva*, Ockham adopted from Scotus the distinction between *notitia intuitiva perfecta* and *imperfecta* and developed it especially in the question here edited. In our intellectual life we experience the fact that we make existential statements about the past. Intuitive knowledge, as above described, cannot afford a basis for such a statement, because it regards existence of the present. The basis for statements about the past must therefore be different from the *notitia intuitiva*. Ockham calls it *notitia recordativa* or *notitia intuitiva imperfecta* (*Rep.* II, q. 15 G). Then, the essential difference between notitia intuitiva perfecta and imperfecta is obvious: Whereas the perfect intuitive knowledge cannot be had without the existence of its object, when existence is affirmed, the imperfect one can be had without the actual, but not without any, existence of its object,[7]

---

ille, qui non potest sic experiri. Et ideo sicut secundum Philosophum 1º Metaphysicae et 2º Posteriorum scientia istorum sensibilium, quae accipiuntur per experientiam, de qua ipse loquitur, incipit a sensu, id est, a notitia intuitiva istorum sensibilium, ita universaliter notitia scientifica istorum pure intelligibilium accepta per experientiam incipit a notitia intuitiva intellectiva istorum intelligibilium." l. c. Z (p. 25); cfr. below *Rep.* II, q. 15 G.

⁶ "Notitia abstractiva potest accipi dupliciter: uno modo, quia est respectu alicuius abstracti a multis singularibus, et sic cognitio abstractiva non est aliud quam cognitio alicuius universalis, abstrahibilis a multis . . . Aliter accipitur cognitio abstractiva, secundum quod abstrahit ab existentia et non-existentia et ab aliis conditionibus, quae contingenter accidunt rei vel praedicantur de re . . ." l. c. Z (p. 24).

⁷ Ockham sometimes includes in this imperfect intuitive knowledge the knowledge of future contingent facts also; for instance *Rep.* II, q. 16 JJ; q. 20 E, but he does not give further details.

when existence of the past or future is affirmed (L). The distinction as to the *notitia abstractiva* is not so easily drawn, because this imperfect intuitive knowledge is really a kind of abstractive knowledge (M). Nevertheless it is different from the ordinary *notitia abstractiva* in this, that it is the basis of existential propositions, which abstractive knowledge as such is not.

What is the *psychological* cause of the imperfect intuitive knowledge? In other words: Since imperfect intuitive knowledge refers to experiences of the past which no longer exist, something must be left in the soul, viz. a habit or a disposition which enables us to recall the former experiences and to gain evidence from them for statements about the past. What, then, is the cause of this habit? To answer this question, Ockham has advanced two theories. According to the first, intuitive knowledge as such is the partial cause of a habit of abstractive knowledge, which habit inclines to produce acts of this imperfect intuitive knowledge, which in turn is the basis for an evident existential proposition about the past. In favor of this theory there is, as it seems, experience. Since no other knowledge is experienced in the very act of perfect intuitive knowledge than the *notitia intuitiva perfecta* itself, it is hard to admit that there could be another, viz. an abstractive knowledge, at the same time, which could be the cause of this habit or disposition for imperfect intuitive knowledge (K). Unfortunately, this lack of experience proves only that it is not necessary to posit a cause for the habit different from the *notitia intuitiva*, as long as no other reasons are against it. There are, however, such reasons. For Ockham's first theory meets with a serious objection taken from Aristotelian psychology. According to Aristotle, a habit is produced by similar acts and inclines to similar acts; consequently imperfect intuitive knowledge, which is only a specific abstractive knowledge, would then be caused by perfect intuitive knowledge. According to the Aristotelian axiom, therefore, the perfect intuitive knowledge cannot produce a habit of imperfect intuitive knowledge. Ockham does not dare to challenge this axiom, and therefore he takes refuge in the weak evasion: A habit is produced by acts of the same kind, to which the habit inclines, if the acts are the total cause, not, however, if they are only the partial causes. The

Aristotelian axiom applies to the former, not to the latter case, which is given for the production of the habit of imperfect intuitive knowledge.

Ockham, apparently, was not satisfied with this first theory, and therefore he advanced a second theory. This involves no restriction of the Aristotelian axiom. It admits that concomitant with the *notitia intuitiva* and there is a *notitia abstractiva;* this abstractive knowledge as a partial cause, and the intellect as another partial cause, produce a habit or disposition, or an inclination of the intellect to reproduce the original act, viz. the imperfect intuitive knowledge, which then, is the basis of an evident existential proposition of the past (G—H).

Which theory was finally held by Ockham? An answer to this question was not easy for Hochstetter on account of his limited knowledge of the tradition of the text. The following edition of *Rep.* II, q. 15, together with other indications, clearly points to the second as Ockham's final or, at least, favored theory. The following reasons can be given: First, we see that Ockham mentions the first one only in IV, q. 12 Q. This means that he first advanced this theory, and that he had but this in mind, where he only incidentally touched on the problem. A second indication is found in our edition of q. 15 G, where Ockham strengthens the second theory by a later addition. We have here a case parallel to *Ordinatio* d. 2, q. 8[8], where Ockham, also by an addition, strengthens that solution which finally was held by him. A third indication is that Ockham, in his *Ordinatio,* always speaks of a *notitia abstractiva* as immediately following the *notitia intuitiva* and as immediately caused by the object.[9]

This again proves how useful studies of textual criticism are, tedious though they may be. For Hochstetter, who thinks that the

---

[8] Cfr. our edition in *The New Scholasticism,* 16 (1942), 239 ss.

[9] "Per notitiam abstractivam immediate sequentem notitiam intuitivam nihil fit nec aliquod capit esse praeter ipsam notitiam abstractivam, quia idem totaliter et sub eadem ratione est obiectum notitiae intuitivae et abstractivae immediate sequentis; ergo sicut nihil est medium inter obiectum intuitive cognitum et ipsam notitiam intuitivam, ita nihil est medium inter obiectum et notitiam abstractivam." *Ord.* I, d. 27, q. e J; cfr. prol. q. 1 TT (p. 43 ss).

first theory is Ockham's favored one, was misled — pardonably of course, on account of his meager textual basis (one ms. of Munich = Nr. 11 [M'] of our list). He thinks that the short explanation of the first theory "wie das kurze Aufflackern einer neuen Idee, die er zunächst wieder fallen läßt, erscheint, aber später offenbar eine Modifikation seiner Theorie bewirkt hat" (p. 70 s.). That, however, does not seem to be true, as we found; for it is not the first indication of a new idea, but the fading away of his first idea. What else could be the reason that Ockham strengthened the second theory by a long marginal note? But Hochstetter, who seems to think that the questions of the *Reportatio* were composed in the order in which they are edited, found in his ms. of Munich at the end of II, q. 16 JJ, where our problem is again formulated, not an answer, but a reference to IV, q. 12: *Respondeo in quarto in ultima quaestione quarti.* And he thinks that Ockham will give there his final answer. But the texts do not support his hypothesis. The edition reads: *Responsio huius patet per supradicta.* All manuscripts known to me *(F, Ob, O, M),* however, read: *Responsionem quaere,* and *Ob* adds: *album in li(bro).* In other words, Ockham's original left a space blank, and he did intend to answer, but had, probably, already some doubts as to his final theory.[10]

2. *The Possibility of an Intuitive Knowledge of Non-existents*

Though Ockham develops his doctrine on intuitive and abstractive knowledge following closely Duns Scotus, nevertheless he knows that he is in opposition to the *Doctor Subtilis* as regards at

---

[10] Another point in Hochstetter's interpretation seems to be confused. The excellent interpreter of Ockham finds (p. 75) a difference, if not an opposition, to Ockham's former ideas about the teachings of recordative knowledge (*Quodl.* I, q. 13 and *Rep.* II, q. 15; IV, q. 12). But it is important to note that Ockham deals with different problems. Abstractive and conceptual or universal knowledge are not always the same. In addition, the fact or remembrance is a judgement, and by this surpasses the incomplex or abstractive knowledge or imperfect intuitive knowledge which by definition is no judgement. Of this judgement, *Rep.* IV, q. 12 affords an excellent analysis.

least one main point. Scotus referred the difference between the acts of knowledge to the object, to its causality, and to the relation between knowledge and object.[11] Hence a *notitia intuitiva* is only of an existent and present thing, the *notitia abstractiva* indifferently of an existent and non-existent thing; the *notitia abstractiva* does not reach its object in its proper perfection but only in a similitude or diminutive image; the *notitia intuitiva* reaches its object in its proper perfection; the *notitia intuitiva* is formally caused or motivated by the object in its proper existence; the *notitia abstractiva* by a medium, as for instance, a species; the *notitia intuitiva* necessarily has a real relation to the object; the *notitia abstractiva* has not necessarily a real and actual relation to the object. In the *notitia intuitiva* the object is present in its own existence; in the *notitia abstractiva* the object is present in something which perfectly represents the object.

Ockham, however, holds that none of these differences can be universally applied to the *notitia intuitiva,* as he shows at length in the first question of the Prologue to the *Ordinatio.* From his discussion he draws the conclusion that both acts are essentially different by themselves:

> Ideo dico, quod notitia intuitiva et abstractiva seipsis differunt et non penes obiecta, nec penes causas suas quascumque, quamvis naturaliter notitia intuitiva non possit esse sine existentia rei, quae est vera causa efficiens notitiae intuitivae mediata vel immediata. (*Ord.,* prol. q. 1 GG, p. 29).

Then an immediate consequence is obvious. If existence or presence of an object does not constitute a *notitia intuitiva* in its proper being, and if it is what it is by itself, then the *notitia intuitiva* can exist in itself without the existence and presence of the object which is intuitively known:

> Ex istis sequitur, quod notitia intuitiva, tam sensitiva quam intellectiva, potest esse de re non existente. (HH, p. 29).

Of course, it must be caused. But since every positive effect which can be produced by a natural cause, can be produced by God, intuitive knowledge can be produced in our senses or our intellect by God.

---

[11] See quotations below in *Rep.* II, q. 15E, note 14. Cfr. *Ord.,* prol. q. 1AA (p. 26); the references in the text refer to this question.

It is exactly this doctrine which has earned Ockham the title of a skeptic and of a destroyer of Scholasticism; a doctrine which, however, was completely misunderstood by those critics who so labeled Ockham; and not only by them, for it was misunderstood even by Hochstetter, who is usually very reliable.

In order to obtain a correct understanding, we must not forget (lest right at the beginning we be already in the midst of confusion) that our problem and its solution is a theological one, and not a philosophical one, and that it regards by no means the question how a natural or an everyday proposition of non-existence is known to be true. That our problem belongs to the supernatural order is at least indicated by Ockham always, and sometimes expressly stated. Question II, 15, which is here edited, most probably represents the earliest text on this problem in Ockham's works.[12] Here, in E, we read:

> Ideo oportet, quod cognitio intuitiva, qua cognosco rem non esse, quando non est, sit supernaturalis quantum ad causationem vel conservationem vel quantum ad utrumque.

Hence, the problem concerns only that exceptional and supernatural case where a *notitia intuitiva* of a non-existent would be caused or conserved by God, as Ockham hastens to add *(l. c.)*. A theologian, or at least one who is not unacquainted with theology, should know that no supernatural fact can explain common and ordinary facts of our natural cognition,[13] and neither Ockham, nor St. Bonaventure have made such a theological mistake.

---

[12] Though it is very likely that the *Ordinatio* contains in a revised form the *Reportatio* on the first book, to which II, q. 15 several times refers, nevertheless, we do not know to what extent Ockham revised his original reportation.

[13] That this was imputed to St. Bonaventure's theory of illumination, proves once more that very clear theological notions are imperatively needed. Gilson (p. 55s), finds himself unable to distinguish a more special (but non-supernatural) divine influence on our knowledge from a supernatural influence, if the more special influence is distinct from the general influence of God. And since he would be glad to know what the difference between a more special and natural and a special and supernatural influence could be, I can answer that the one belongs to the natural equip-

This will become more clear, if we now proceed to Ockham's proofs for his main thesis. In the Prologue to the *Ordinatio*, q. 1 HH (p. 29), Ockham reasons: Everything which is absolute, and as to place and subject distinct from another absolute thing, can by the absolute divine power exist without the other thing; for it is not likely that, if God will destroy one absolute thing which exists in the heavens, he is forced to destroy another thing upon earth. But the intuitive vision, sensitive as well as intellective, is something absolute and distinct from the object as to place and subject. For instance, if we intuitively see a star existing in the sky, this intuitive vision, whether it be intellective or sensitive, is distinct as to place and subject from the seen object. Consequently this vision can remain after the star has been destroyed. This means in Ockham's language: It can remain in view of God's absolute power, but it will not remain in view of God's ordained or ordinary power *(potentia ordinata)*.

In this proof, Ockham applies the theological principle of God's omnipotence, which according to him (and Scotus and many other Scholastics) cannot be proved demonstratively by natural reason. Hence the entire reasoning is a theological one and the problem a theological problem. If there should be any doubt left, it is removed definitely by Ockham in one of his latest works, the *Quodlibeta*. There, in VI, q. 6, the *Venerabilis Inceptor* asks: *Utrum cognitio intuitiva possit esse de obiecto non existente*. The formulation of this question is very significant. For he does not ask: How are propositions of non-existents known to be true? He only asks whether a *cognitio intuitiva* of non-existents is possible. To this question he answers in the first conclusion that intuitive knowledge can be had of a non-existent object, and that by divine power; and he proves this by the article of faith: I believe in God the Father Almighty. Accord-

---

ment of *human* nature (like the general influence which is *naturally* added), while the other does not. To the first, nature has a natural right, because it is willed by God in this natural insufficiency; to the other, nature has not a natural right. The first is more special, because it does not concern all creatures, but only intellectual creatures, and nevertheless general, because it concerns all intellectual creatures. Is not some generality even contained in the special supernatural influence? There is a dogma of the generality of redemption.

ing to this article of faith everything is to be attributed to the divine power which does not contain a manifest contradiction. But that intuitive knowledge is possible without the object does not include a contradiction. From this article of faith Ockham takes the famous proposition of the theologians: "God can produce and conserve without the second causes, whatsoever he produces and conserves by means of the second causes," as a principle for another proof, which yields the same conclusion:

> Credo in Deum Patrem omnipotentem, quem sic intelligo: quod quodlibet est divinae potentiae attribuendum, quod non includit manifestam contradictionem; sed illud fieri a Deo non includit contradictionem; ergo etc.[14]

But is there no contradiction really involved? To say that we do not see a contradiction and to say that there is no contradiction are two entirely different statements. The proof that no contradiction is involved is typical of Ockham. For he proves it by the fact that God knows by intuitive knowledge the existence and the non-existence of a thing. Consequently, it cannot be a contradiction to say that there can be intuitive knowledge of a non-existent.[15]

---

[14] "Praeterea: In illo articulo fundatur illa propositio famosa theologorum: quidquid Deus producit mediantibus causis secundis, potest immediate sine illis producere et conservare. Ex ista propositione arguo sic: Omnem effectum, quem potest Deus mediante causa secunda, potest immediate per se; sed in notitiam intuitivam corporalem (om. P) potest mediante obiecto; ergo potest in eam immediate per se. Praeterea: Omnis res absoluta distincta loco et subiecto ab alia re absoluta potest per divinam potentiam existere alia re absoluta destructa; sed visio stellae in caelo tam sensitiva quam intellectiva est huiusmodi: ergo etc." *Quodl.* VI, q. 6. The quotations will be according to the more common Strassburg-edition 1491 (quoted as S), the text is revised according to the Paris-edition 1487 (quoted as P) and the oldest known manuscript Vatic. *lat.* 3075, written in 1333 (quoted as **V**). Because of this revision we will bring almost the entire questions V, 5 and VI, 6 of the *Quodlibeta* into the footnotes, and add variants mostly of V and P.

[15] "Praeterea: Deus per eandem notitiam videt rem esse, quando est, et non esse, quando non est; ergo ita potest esse in proposito sine repugnantia." *Quodl.* V, q. 5. Cfr. *Ord.*, prol. q. 1 HH (p. 29): "Patet etiam ex praedictis, quomodo Deus habet notitiam intuitivam omnium, sive sint, sive non sint, quia ita evidenter cognoscit creaturas non esse, quando non sunt, sicut cognoscit eas esse, quando sunt." — About this knowledge of

This is not the place to discuss and to test the validity of the above mentioned proof of non-contradiction, for it would lead us into the mystery of God's cognition. But it is certainly in Ockham's favor that no theologian can admit that God receives his knowledge from things or that there can be any discursive reasoning in God, and that every theologian admits that God's knowledge is absolutely evident and infallible. Hence God's knowledge must be intuitive, and that of contingent facts also, whether they exist or do not exist. If they do not exist, God must know them by the same intuitive knowledge by which He knows them when they do exist, and vice versa: for no change in God can be admitted. Ockham's "explanation" of God's knowledge of contingent facts stops exactly here, and he refuses to go further and follow either St. Thomas or Duns Scotus in their explanation of God's knowledge, which is a mystery. But the truth remains that God knows intuitively, by His essence, every contingent fact, be it of the past, the present, or the future. Hence, it is obvious that, if intuitive knowledge of non-existents can be in God, then, absolutely speaking, such knowledge must be possible.

But does this imply that we, too, are able to have such intuitive knowledge of a non-existent? Ockham answers: Absolutely speaking: yes. Relatively speaking, however, — i. e. in relation to our natural power — the answer is, no. For such intuitive knowledge cannot be caused or conserved naturally. The reason is obvious: God's intuitive knowledge does not depend on contingent facts; our intuitive knowledge, however, is caused by contingent facts, and therefore depends on them — naturally speaking. A non-existent fact, certainly, can neither produce nor conserve intuitive knowledge; hence, naturally speaking — where knowledge depends on the facts — the fact is required both for the production and the conservation of intuitive knowledge.[16] But this natural impossibility does not exclude a

God, see *Ordin.* I, d. 38, q. un. M, and our edition of the *Tractatus de prae-destinatione* etc., which will be published soon [St. Bonaventure 1945].

[16] "Secunda conclusio est, quod naturaliter cognitio intuitiva non potest causari nec conservari obiecto non existente (*praesente* V). Cuius ratio est: quia effectus realis non potest conservari nec produci de non-esse ad esse ab illo, quod nihil (*non* V) est; et per consequens naturaliter loquendo requirit tam causam producentem quam conservantem." *Quodl.* VI, q. 6.

supernatural possibility, viz. that God can give to us by grace what He Himself has, i. e., the intuitive knowledge of a non-existent or of a non-present.

In order to explain this possibility in a more definite way, Ockham goes a step further. For there still remains the somewhat embarassing situation, that by the same intuitive knowledge sometimes existence is evidently affirmed, and sometimes non-existence evidently affirmed. Is this not an *inconvenientia* and therefore out of the question? Ockham explains: In an evident existential proposition the *notitia intuitiva* is given, and so is the object; both together are partial causes for our evident assent to the proposition: this thing exists (or this thing is here present). In an evident proposition of non-existence (or non-presence) one cause, viz. the object, is lacking. If therefore in this latter case the object does not exist and only the intuition exists, then the intellect must necessarily come to a different assent, viz. to the assent that this object does not exist. Hence one partial cause which acts in conjunction with another partial cause, can and must have, at least for us, a different effect, if it acts alone.[17]

3. *The Infallibility of Intuitive Knowledge*

If we approach our problem in the manner explained above, it becomes clear at once that intuitive knowledge, supernaturally caused or conserved, of a non-existent is the basis of the evident assent to a proposition which states that the thing seen does not exist or is not present. This is always meant by Ockham when he speaks of *notitia intuitiva* as that knowledge by which I evidently know that a thing exists or does not exist (Cfr. *Rep.* II, q. 15 DD). Consequently every assent which is based on perfect intuition knowledge, whether of an existent object or of a non-existent object (in this case supernaturally), is infallibly true. No error is possible, for an error, in this case, would be a clear contradiction.

---

[17] "Probo primum: Quia licet sit inconveniens, quod eadem notitia sit causa totalis unius (om. V) iudicii et iudicii contrarii respectu eiusdem passi, tamen non est inconveniens, quod sit causa partialis unius iudicii, quando res existit, et similiter causa partialis iudicii contrarii, quando res non existit. Et sic est in proposito." *Quodl.* V, q. 5.

This is unmistakably stated by Ockham on several occasions, but especially in *Quodlibeta* V, q. 5, where several objections are brought forward against Ockham, some of which, curious as it may be, do not blame Ockham for admitting that God could deceive us by this supernaturally caused or conserved intuitive knowledge, but blame him precisely because in his teaching there is no room for a deceiving God.

If Ockham's theory is correct, says one objection, then God could not produce in us an act of cognition, by which an object appears to be present, which in reality is absent. This, however, must be false, because it does not include a contradiction that God can do so. And God can do so, because such a cognition is not an intuitive knowledge, for it is not about existence or non-existence but only about presence or non-presence; and it is likewise not an abstractive knowledge, because such a knowledge is not of presence and non-presence.[18]

It is not difficult for Ockham to eliminate this objection. He seldom fails to include in intuitive knowledge the presence and absence of a thing as well. Hence, it is impossible for God to cause in us such a cognition by which a thing evidently appears to be present, while it is absent, precisely because that includes a contradiction. For such an evident cognition implies that a thing is in reality as it is said to be by the proposition to which the evident assent is given. Otherwise, there would be no evident cognition at all. The objection, however, assumed that the thing is absent. From this assumption and the very definition of evident cognition follows the open contradiction: This thing is present and this thing is not present. God, therefore, cannot cause such an evident cognition. He can, however, cause an act of belief; in other words, an act of subjective conviction without factual evidence, so that we are con-

---

[18] "Sed contra: Hoc dato sequitur, quod Deus non posset causare in nobis unum actum cognoscendi, per quem apparet nobis res esse praesens, quae est absens, quod falsum est, cum hoc non includat contradictionem. Assumptum probatur: quia ista cognitio non est intuitiva per te, quia (*et* V) per illam apparet res esse, quando est, et non esse, quando non est; nec abstractiva: quia per illam non apparet res esse praesens." *Quodl.* V, q. 5.

vinced, or believe that an absent thing is present. The cognitive basis for this belief cannot be the *notitia intuitiva*, but only a *notitia abstractiva*.[19]

The second objection aims at the heart of Ockham's theory. Why should it not be possible that the same act which, as to its substance, remains the same whether something else is posited or not, could still produce the same effect? In other words, why should not the *notitia intuitiva*, which is conserved by God's power after the object or the thing is destroyed, be able to produce the same effect, viz., the evident assent to the existential proposition: this thing exists, though the thing does not exist? In other words, why should it be impossible that the supernaturally caused or conserved intuitive knowledge is the cause of an evident assent to a false existential proposition? There is certainly no contradiction, that intuitive knowledge is at least partial cause of this false judgment, and consequently it is possible.[20]

In his answer, Ockham concedes this reasoning in a certain and very definite sense, for he had already admitted that it is possible that God can conserve an intuitive knowledge of a thing after the

---

[19] "Ad primum istorum dico, quod Deus non potest causare in nobis cognitionem talem, per quam evidenter appareat nobis rem esse praesentem, quando est absens, quia hoc includit contradictionem: nam cognitio evidens importat, quod ita sit in re, sicut denotatur per propositionem, cui fit assensus per cognitionem, et per consequens (*per cognitionem* VP, seq. om. V; *ut* P) cum cognitio evidens huius propositionis: res est praesens, importat rem esse praesentem (*et* add. VP), oportet quod res sit praesens. Aliter non erit cognitio evidens. Et tu ponis, quod sit absens. Et ita ex illa positione cum cognitione evidente sequitur manifesta contradictio, scilicet quod res sit praesens et non praesens. Et ideo Deus non potest causare talem cognitionem evidentem. Tamen Deus potest causare actum creditivum, per quem credo rem esse praesentem, quae est absens. Et per talem actum fidei potest apparere res esse praesens, quando est absens, non tamen per actum evidentem." *Quodl.* V, q. 5.

[20] "Praeterea: Quod convenit actui secundum substantiam actus, si substantia eius maneat eadem quocumque alio posito, adhuc tale (om. V) potest sibi convenire; sed substantia visionis manet eadem, re non existente, per potentiam divinam; ergo non repugnat sibi saltem partialiter causare talem assensum, qualem prius causavit, re existente, et per consequens hoc potest sibi competere." *Quodl.* V, q. 5.

destruction of this same thing, and he had likewise admitted that it is not repugnant to such an intuitive knowledge to be partial cause for the evident assent to a proposition of existence or non-existence. Hence such an intuitive knowledge of a destroyed thing is still of itself a partial cause for the assent to the proposition of existence, but only if the other partial causes are also given and work together with the first partial cause which is the conserved intuitive knowledge. What is possible, therefore, to this partial cause, as a partial cause with the other causes, is not only not possible to it, but repugnant to it, as total cause or as partial cause without the other causes. But the existence of the object is such a partial cause for the evident assent to the proposition about its existence; hence naturally speaking (that is to say, if its causality is not supernaturally supplied), such an assent is impossible without the existence of the thing.[21]

The following objection is of a more academic character as regards our problem. In his answer to it Ockham readily admits that it is possible that we can have an intuition produced by God and neither assent nor dissent is given to the corresponding proposition. For the assent and the dissent are acts which, supernaturally speaking, can be suspended by God.[22] Ockham does not say, however, that God can suspend only one act — let us say, the act of dissent —

[21] "Ad aliud concedo, quod si per potentiam divinam visio remaneat, re non existente, non repugnat sibi causare partialiter talem assensum, si omnes aliae causae requisitae concurrant; tamen repugnat sibi causare talem assensum totaliter et partialiter (et p. / om. P) sine aliis causis. Et ita cum existentia rei sit causa partialis illius assensus evidentis, impossibile est, quod causetur naturaliter sine existentia rei." *Quodl.* V, q. 5.

[22] "Praeterea: Hoc dato, sequitur, quod visio posset esse, et tamen quod per illam nec apparet res esse nec non esse. Consequens est contra te. Assumptum probatur per illud principium commune: Ubi (om. V) quodlibet aliquorum convenit alicui contingenter, si non sit contradictio, Deus potest facere ipsum sine omnibus simul. Sic enim probatur potissime materiam posse esse sine omni forma. Sed virtute visionis aliquis potest aliquando scire rem esse et aliquando scire rem non esse. Ergo non est contradictio, quod neutrum sibi conveniat ... Ad aliud concedo illud principium et conclusionem et totam deductionem: quia non est contradictio, quod visio rei sit, et tamen quod per illam visionem nec iudicem rem esse nec non esse, quia Deus potest facere visionem sine omni assensu tali; sed per naturam non (om. V) potest hoc fieri." *Quodl.* V, q. 5.

if the *notitia intuitiva* is conserved by God and the thing does not exist any more, so that only the act of assent would remain and a deception would follow. Nothing of this kind is said by Ockham, who simply states that God can suspend both acts so that neither assent nor dissent is given. In this case we would have a psychological (not logical) *propositio neutra*.[23]

Most instructive, however, is the last objection. For it argues that according to Ockham's theory God cannot cause an evident assent to the contingent proposition, *Albedo est*, if this whiteness does not exist; and a supernatural intuitive knowledge of this whiteness (which does not exist), would, according to Ockham's theory, cause the evident assent to the proposition, *Albedo non est;* and the intellect, as it seems, does not assent at the same time to contradictory statements. In other words, the objection against Ockham here is that God cannot deceive us by intuitive knowledge if his theory were true.[24] The *Venerabilis Inceptor* answers: This is indeed the case. God cannot cause an evident assent to this contingent proposition: *Haec albedo est*, if this whiteness does not exist. For a contradiction would follow. This contradiction was made explicit by Ockham in his answer to the first objection as regards presence and absence of an object. Now he makes this contradiction explicit as regards existence and non-existence. The expression "evident assent" (to the aforesaid proposition) means: It is in reality as it is said to be by the proposition, *Haec albedo est*, to which evident assent is given. Now, this proposition, *Haec albedo est*, says or "imports", that this whiteness really exists. Consequently, if evident

---

[23] On this question, in connection with the problem of a three-valued Logic in Ockham and others, I am preparing a study [published in *Tractatus de praedestinatione . . .* , St. Bonaventure 1945, 58—88]. The treatment of Michalski on this subject needs revision: Cfr. "Le problème de la volonté à Oxford et à Paris au XIV siècle," *Studia philosophica*, 2 (Lemberg 1937), 296 ss.

[24] "Praeterea: Hoc dato non posset Deus causare assensum evidentem respectu huius contingentis: haec albedo est, albedine non existente: quia visio albedinis causat assensum evidentem respectu huius: haec albedo non est, et intellectus non videtur (*potest* P) assentire oppositis simul; ergo etc." *Quodl.* V, q. 5.

assent is given to this proposition, then, by definition this whiteness exists. However, the assumption or hypothesis was made that this whiteness does not exist in reality. Hence it is obvious that it implies a manifest contradiction, viz., this whiteness exists, and this whiteness does not exist.[25]

Evident assent, therefore, never can fail, for it is based on intuitive knowledge, whether it be naturally or supernaturally produced. And since an error in this case necessarily includes a contradiction in terms, it is impossible for God to deceive anybody by intuitive knowledge. Every knowledge, therefore, which is based on intuitive knowledge, is safe from any intrusion of natural or supernatural skepticism.

Not, however, any assent. It is a fact, that we sometimes give our assent to propositions which appear to us as evident, as if they were given to us in intuitive knowledge. The history of human science knows many examples of this kind. Hence Ockham concedes that God can make an assent of that kind which is given to a proposition not based on intuitive knowledge (Ockham most likely thinks of deception of the devil or of cases of *excaecatio*), even if the proposition to which this assent is given does not correspond with the fact. But this assent is not an evident one by definition; it is only an assent of belief or conviction.[26] The epistemological distinction between these two kinds of assent can easily be drawn, for the one is based on intuitive knowledge, which, if natural, implies the existence or

---

[25] "Ad ultimum dico, quod Deus non potest facere assensum evidentem huius contingentis: haec albedo est, quando albedo non est, propter contradictionem, quae sequitur: quia assensus evidens denotat sic esse in re, sicut importatur per propositionem, cui fit assensus; sed per istam propositionem: haec albedo est, importatur, quod albedo sit; et per consequens, si sit assensus evidens huius (om. S): haec albedo est, et positum est, quod haec albedo non sit, et ita hypothesis cum notitia evidente includit manifeste contradictionem, scilicet quod albedo sit et albedo non sit (et ita . . . / om. V). *Quodl.* V, q. 5.

[26] "Concedo tamen, quod Deus potest facere assensum eiusdem (*illius* V) speciei cum illo assensu evidente respectu illius contingentis (*conclusionis* P; seq. . . . . importatur/om. V): haec albedo est, quando illa albedo non existit; sed ille assensus non est evidens, quia non est ita sicut in re, sicut importatur per propositionem, cui fit assensus." *Quodl.* V, q. 5.

presence of the object; and the other is based on abstractive knowledge which does not imply the existence or presence of its object. Hence the assent given to a proposition in intuitive knowledge, if existence is affirmed, cannot be caused by God alone without the existence of the thing as second cause, as it is likewise impossible for God alone to cause a meritorious act, because the former connotes the existence of a thing, the latter connotes the cooperation of the free will.[27]

The psychological distinction of these two acts is not so easily drawn. How do we know practically that our assent is given to intuitive knowledge and not to abstract knowledge, and is therefore an evident assent and not an assent of conviction only? Ockham has not given a direct answer to this question, as far as I know, but it seems in accordance with his teachings to say that in intuitive knowledge the reality is seen (or evidently not seen), and the assent is given to factual evidence, hence cannot fail. Our practical task, therefore, would be to test our conviction as regards contingent facts and to find out by *experience* whether factual evidence is really given or not. In any case, according to Ockham, if factual evidence is given, it is known by the intellect.[28]

---

[27] "Et si dicis: Deus potest facere assensum evidentem huius contingentis mediante existentia rei sicut mediante causa secunda; ergo potest hoc facere se solo. — Respondeo, quod haec est fallacia figurae dictionis, sicut hic (s. h. / om. V): Deus potest facere actum meritorium mediante voluntate creata, ergo potest facere se solo; et hoc est propter diversam connotationem hinc inde." *Quodl.* V, q. 5. As to this favored example see *Summa Log.* III (4) c. 10; ed. Venice 1508, fol. 102 ra.

[28] This would be the answer to Gilson's criticism (p. 81—82). — There are no two answers in Ockham to the same problem, and there is no evidence in Ockham that "the fact remains that human knowledge would be practically indistinguishable from what it is, even though all its objects were destroyed . . ." (p. 82). Consequently it is not correct to say: "In other words, if it is possible for God to make us *perceive as real an object that does not really exist*, have we any proof that this world of ours is not a vast phantasmagoria behind which there is no reality to be found?" (p. 81). In fact, the expression in italics (mine) belongs to an imaginary world, for Ockham had called it a contradiction to perceive *as real* an object that does not exist, not, however, to perceive intuitively an object *as not real.*

The stress laid by Ockham on the infallibility of intuitive knowledge of existence or of non-existence (if supernatural), reveals certainly a considerable optimism as regards human knowledge. It is surprising therefore, to read in Michalski:

> Mais il est une chose qui appartient en propre au novateur d'Oxford, c'est l'idée destructrice qui eut une grosse influence sur les esprits du XIVᵉ siècle . . .: Dieu peut produire en notre esprit une connaissance intuitive sans que l'objet de cette connaissance soit réellement présent à nos sens: dans ce cas l'homme est le jouet d'une illusion . . .[29]

If it is absolutely necessary to find skeptics, why not refer to the leader of the Thomistic School at Paris, Hervaeus Natalis (d. 1323), of whom Michalski quotes the following text:

> Cognitio intuitiva non necessario requirit praesentiam realem obiecti cogniti nec ex parte motionis nec ex parte terminationis . . . Non ex parte motionis, quia omnen effectum causae efficientis potest Deus per ipsum solum facere . . . nec etiam quantum ad terminationem absolute loquendo, quia cognitio falsa non requirit rem talem esse, qualis apparet. (Quodl. IV, q. 11.)[30]

But to call Hervaeus de Nedellec a real skeptic, is not our intention.

We have followed Ockham through his explanation of the *notitia intuitiva* and its infallibility, mostly in his *Quodlibeta*. Since there is no evidence of a contradiction to his ideas in the *Reportatio* and the *Ordinatio*, it may suffice to refer to those comparatively shorter texts (*Ordin.*, prol. q. 1., esp. ZZ, p. 50; *Reportatio* II, q. 15 E and D).[31]

---

[29] Michalski, K., "Les courants philosophiques à Oxford et à Paris pendant le XIVᵉ siècle," *Bulletin international de l'Académie polonaise des sciences et des lettres*, Cracovie 1922, p. 65.

[30] Quoted by Michalski in: "Le criticisme et le scepticisme dans la philosophie du XIVᵉ siècle," *Bulletin* . . . 1926, p. 91.

[31] Let us add that intuitive knowledge can only concern *possibilia:* "Dico, quod contradictio est, quod visio sit et quod (tamen P) illud, quod videtur, non sit in effectu nec esse possit. Ideo contradictio est, quod chimaera videatur intuitive. Sed non est contradictio, quod illud, quod videtur, nihil sit in actu extra causam (*animam* S; seq. om. SP) suam, dummodo possit esse in effectu vel aliquando fuit in rerum natura. Et sic est in proposito. Unde Deus ab aeterno vidit omnes res factibiles, et tamen tunc nihil fuerunt." *Quodl.* VI, q. 6.

4. *Critics of Ockham*

It cannot be the task of this article to write a history of the *notitia intuitiva*, and especially not a history of the fate of Ockham's teachings on the *notitia intuitiva* of non-existents. That will be done, as already mentioned, in a dissertation which Fr. Sebastian Day, O. F. M. is preparing. But it seems to be useful, for the sake of clarity, to hear some of Ockham's critics and to discuss their criticism.

The *Magistri* of Avignon — the Chancellor of Oxford, Luterell, included — seem to be the earliest critics of Ockham's position. In the list of incriminating articles presented to the Pope by Luterell, we read:

> Secundus articulus: Quod notitia intuitiva creaturae secundum se non est necessario plus existentis quam non existentis, nec plus respicit existentiam quam non existentiam.[32]

This doctrine, Luterell maintains (p. 378), has as consequence a dangerous error, viz., that an intellectual creature could be beatified without the divine essence being present to it as object. This article of Luterell, together with literal quotations from Ockham's *Ordinatio*, and his criticism, went into the list of the *Magistri* of Avignon, which was presented to the Pope. The texts which were quoted are already known to us. But the censure which the *Magistri* add is very significant, because they do not take Ockham's statement as a philosophical one, or they do not see in Ockham's position the ruin of our natural certitude; they find in it precisely the theological consequence of which Luterell had been afraid.

It is, however, important to note that the *Magistri* of Avignon were not quite fair to Ockham, because they quote only texts in which Ockham speaks of the *notitia intuitiva* as regards existence and non-existence, and only by means of this selective quotation can they disregard Ockham's statement: *Quod contradictio est Deum non esse, et tamen notitiam intuitivam Dei esse; et ideo non est mirum, si sequatur inconveniens* (*Ord.*, prol. q. 1 ZZ, p. 50). Hence their ob-

---

[32] Koch, J., "Neue Aktenstücke zu dem gegen Wilhelm Ockham in Avignon geführten Prozeß," Recherches de théologie ancienne et médiévale, 7 (1935), 375.

jection that beatific vision could be possible, according to Ockham, without the presence of God. But it is a fact that Ockham, even in his first question of the Prologue, several times refers the *notitia intuitiva* to presence and non-presence also, and treats this knowledge, certainly implicitly, as he treats the knowledge of existence and non-existence.

It is interesting to note that either the objection of the *Magistri* in Avignon, or of Luterell in Oxford, provoked Ockham to a definite and explicit statement. The text of the objection in the list of the *Magistri*, and the text of the same objection in *Quodl.* VI, q. 6 are so much alike that they must be somehow inter-related:

Magistri of Avignon	*Quodl.* VI, q. 6
Dicimus, quod conclusio, quam tenet, est simpliciter falsa, periculosa et erronea, quia secundum raticnem suam sequeretur, quod Deus posset videri intuitive et beatifice, non exhibita praesentia sua actuali in ratione obiecti praesentis actualiter ipsi potentiae. Quod est falsum et erroneum, quia talis cognitio non esset facie ad faciem, qualem describit Apostolus esse visionem beatam [1 Cor. 13]. (Koch, *op. c.*, 8 1936, 93)	Et si dicis, quod secundum istam rationem sequitur, quod Deus posset videri intuitive et beatifice non exhibita sua praesentia actuali in ratione obiecti praesentis actualiter ipsi intellectui, quod falsum est et erroneum.

Ockham answers to his earliest critics that their reasoning is not correct, for they overlook the fact that intuitive knowledge of presence (when the thing is absent) is caused by God, and that by God in his presence: hence if God would cause an intuitive knowledge of his presence though God were absent, it would mean that God causes something where he is not existing. But that really comes down to an elimination of the only possibility under which the supernaturally caused intuitive knowledge of non-presence is possible. For God can supply the causality of second causes but He cannot supply the causality of the *causa prima* which He is Himself.[33]

---

[33] "Respondeo: Hic non est aliqua habitudo (bona similitudo P) arguendo, quod quia Deus potest facere talem visionem sine obiecto creato,

Hochstetter, who is to be recommended for his usually sound interpretation of Ockham's epistemology, became a victim of his lack of theological training. Instead of following Ockham and seeing how a certain problem arose and was formulated by the author under consideration, he gambled with the dangerous historical method of asking his own questions and looking for answers to them. He finds (p. 32) that a difficulty remains in Ockham's teaching as regards the *notitia intuitiva*. It is a fact that there are also negative contingent propositions, viz., the propositions of non-existence, and he asks Ockham: What is the basis for the indubitable evidence of such propositions? To this, his own question, he thinks that Ockham replies with an escape into the supernaturally conserved or caused *notitia intuitiva*, and so he comes to the conclusion:

> Die gesamte Erkenntnis von Nichtexistenz ist überhaupt nur *super-natural* möglich ... Das negative Tatsachenurteil beruht also normaler-weise — wenigstens nach der Fassung des Druckes B — auf einer natür-lichen Verursachung der notitia intuitiva durch ein Object und ihrer über-natürlichen Erhaltung nach dessen Fortfall (p. 22 with reference to *Rep. II, q. 15 E*).

Unfortunately, Hochstetter's problem is not the problem of Ockham, for I do not know of any text where the *Venerabilis Inceptor* formulates this problem. Ockham deals with an entirely different problem, which is given, and only given, when a *notitia intuitiva* is either supernaturally conserved or produced by God, while the object is non-existent or non-present. If and only if, such a super-natural intuitive knowledge is given, then it is the basis for an evident assent to a proposition of non-existence or non-presence. But such a case, by hypothesis, does not belong to our normal and natural life, for it is reserved to the supernatural action of God who can

---

a quo non dependet (illa visio add. *P*) nisi tamquam a causa secunda, ergo Deus potest videri intuitive et beatifice non exhibita sua praesentia ac-tuali in ratione actualiter praesentis ipsi intellectui, a quo obiecto dependet illa visio sicut a causa prima. Quia quamvis secundum doctores Deus potest facere effectus proprios causarum secundarum sine illis causis secundis, non tamen potest aliquem effectum facere sine causa prima. Unde sicut non est possibile, quod color causet effective visionem suam in oculo, nisi sit actualiter praesens, ita non est possibile, quod Deus causet visionem in intellectu nisi exhibita sua actuali praesentia." *Quodl.* VI, q. 6.

grant it, but by no means must grant it. When therefore, Hochstetter calls this solution an appeal to the *Deus ex machina*, or ,,Verlegenheitslösung", it is in reality Hochstetter's *Deus ex machina* and his ,,Verlegenheitslösung".

The distinction of these two problems is aptly confirmed by a Scotist who certainly was no friend of Ockham's. Francis of Mayronis (d. after 1328) asks in the prologue to his *Conflatus* (ed. Basel 1489): *Utrum per potentiam divinam de non existente possit esse notitia intuitiva.* In this question, which refers to a supernatural possibility, two opinions are explained, of which the first concedes the possibility (already in four variations!). The other, which is held by Francis, denies this possibility. In the following question Francis asks: *Utrum potentia sive sensitiva sive intellectiva possit cognoscere naturaliter non existens.* His answer is that neither by intellective nor by sensitive intuitive knowledge is such a knowledge of non-existents possible. The problem of the first question was that of Ockham; the problem of the second question would have been answered by Ockham as it was answered by Francis. It is exactly his second question which constitutes Hochstetter's problem.

Let us add, however, that Hochstetter's problem is a serious one, though it seems that it was not much discussed by Scholastics. Francis of Mayronis is only interested in the negative solution that intuitive knowledge as such is not of non-existence. According to Ockham, i. e., *ad mentem Ockham*, it would be safe to maintain, that he would have based the assent to such propositions indirectly on the *notitia intuitiva* by some kind of inference.

Hochstetter's misinterpretation, unfortunately, was, as it seems, unanimously accepted by those who read and used his book, for instance by Abbagnano,[34] Zuidema[35] and Gilson,[36] but not by Vignaux.[37]

---

[34] *Guglielmo di Ockham*, Lanciano, 1931, p. 68. Abbagnano at least does not see the two different problems, when he writes: "Ritornando sul' argomento, egli finisce per concludere che la concoscenza intuitiva mediante la quale giudico dell' inesistenza di un oggetto è di ordine sopranaturale: è Dio che interviene a conservarla, quando si tratta di un oggetto reale che ha cessato di esistere, o che interveniene a produrla è a conser-

Michalski, however, Gilson, Zuidema and Becher, S. J.,[38] and, somehow, Hochstetter went further, because they are convinced that Ockham's treatment of the *notitia intuitiva* of non-existents opens, and has opened, the road to skepticism. After all that has been said above, there is no reason to answer them. But, I like to add that Michalski's creation of medieval skeptics in his various writings (which are justly appreciated for their many historical details on the little explored Scholasticism of the 14th century) needs a complete revision as to his appreciation of almost every personality, and that Gilson's treatment on Ockham, in his *Unity of Philosophical Experience*, needs overhauling. Ockham was a child of his century, and therefore liable to error, but he did not suffer under the philosophical experience of skepticism.

varla quando si tratta di un oggetto che non è mai esistito. Ma è chiaro che questa conclusione di Ockham non è una soluzione, bensì il riconoscimento esplicito che ogni soluzione logica della difficoltà è da ritenersi impossibile."

[35] *De Philosophie van Occam in zijn Commentaar op de Sententien*, Hilversum, Schipper (s. anno). Zuidema, who knows Hochstetter's study, speaks of a "regelmatige", that is of a regular intervention of God as concerns human cognition.

[36] p. 79s.—G. does not distinguish the two problems either, but proves by his reference to Hochstetter and Abbagnano that he does not think differently, when he writes: "Ockham has several times dealt with the difficulty . . . but his successive answers have merely driven to despair his most conscientious historians" (p. 80).

[37] The most conscientious historian, P. Vignaux, was, as it seems, not driven to despair. He objects against Hochstetter: "Mais il ne faut pas oublier que l'affirmation et la négation d'existence n'ont pas, dans la doctrine, la même place: l'affirmation d'existence, l'évidence du fait sont la donnée première; la négation évidente d'une réalité n'est qu'une possibilité ouverte devant l'esprit." (*l. c.* [cfr. note 2] col. 768.) And as to the deceiving God he remarks (against Hochstetter p. 19 and 57): "Mais Occam ne semble pas s'être posé le problème de discerner l'évidence des déceptions possibles: il ne se demande pas comment aller des idées aux choses, mais tient que selon l'ordre naturel, la connaissance a sa cause dans l'objet; il s'agit seulement de concevoir exactement cet ordre naturel, qui est contingent" (cod. 769).

[38] "Gottesbegriff und Gottesbeweis bei Wilhelm von Ockham," *Scholastik*, 3 (1928), p. 370, note 6. This study is inexact in many respects.

II. A CRITICAL STUDY OF THE TEXT OF OCKHAM'S REPORTATIO

The text of Ockham's *Reportatio*, i. e., his questions to the second, third and fourth books of the Sentences, is in a worse condition than that of any other work of Ockham. Though it has been freely used by almost all historians of Ockham's teachings, none of them, however, has attempted to bring some order into the confusion of the questions. They have noticed, of course, differences between the manuscripts they used and the only edition which exists of this *Reportatio*. But they were prudent enough, as for instance Hochstetter and Baudry, not to generalize their findings. Since we have at our disposal not only their valuable remarks, but also the complete text of four additional manuscripts, it seems justifiable to attempt a first approach to a solution of the problems under consideration. This will, and can, give only certain general, but nonetheless definite outlines of the original state of this work. There should, however, be no illusions as to details, even important ones.

1. List of the Known Manuscripts

In the following list, numbers will be assigned to manuscripts to facilitate future quotations, and some numbers are preceded by letters which will serve as *sigla* in this study. These *sigla* are partly the same as were used in our edition of the first question of the Prologue (Paderborn 1939, Schöningh) and of *Ordinatio* d. 2, q. 8 (*The New Scholasticism*, 16 1942, 206—209). The mss. FMOOb (Ob') and the edition E were already described in our article in The New Scholasticism, hence only a few relevant details are added to them here.

Complete Texts:

1. Bruxelles, Bibl. royale 3512, s. XV (c. 1471?). According to Michalski (*Le criticisme et le scepticisme dans la philosophie du XIVe siècle*, p. 44) this ms. "fait un tout" with the ms. 1284 of the same library. As was shown in our

previous study (p. 113), ms. 1284 was written in 1471 and so badly that it could not be used.

F   2. Firenze, Bibl. Naz. *Conv. soppr.* A. 3. 801, written in a hand different from that of the *Ordinatio*, and of English origin. It is of a smaller size and was later apparently bound together with the *Ordinatio;* but it seems to have the same peculiarities. Though the text is substantially good and valuable on account of certain omissions, it was written by a negligent scribe.

3. Milano, Bibl. Ambros. C. 281 inf. No further details are available.

M   4. München, Universitätsbibl. 52, on vellum, end of s. XIV. It is very much like the text of the *Ordinatio*, with many critical marginal notes; the arrangement of the questions, however, is more disturbed than in the other manuscripts. The text is good.

O   5. Oxford, Merton Coll. 100, on vellum, s. XIV. Like that of the *Ordinatio*, it is not a good text.

Ob(Ob')   6. Oxford, Balliol Coll. 299, written before 1368, vellum. The question here edited is found twice in this manuscript, and the texts differ so considerably from each other that both must go back to different originals. *Ob'* means the second occurrence, and its text is only fair. The text of *Ob*, however, is good.

7. Paris, Bibl. Nat. lat. 16398, s. XV. No further details are available.

Ma   8. Paris, Bibl. Mazar. 893, s. XIV. This ms. was, as it seems, written by the same scribe as 894 and has even the *tabula quaestionum* of the first book. L. Baudry, "Sur trois manuscrits Occamistes", *Archives d'histoire doctrinale et littéraire du moyen-âge*, 10—11 (1936), 157—161 has given a detailed and valuable description of this manuscript.

E   9. Editio Lugdun. 1495. This is the only edition of the *Reportatio Ockham.* The text is worse than that of the *Ordinatio*.

With caution we add Göttingen, Universitätsbibl. *Theol.* 118. No further details are available, and it may even be doubted whether it is not the printed text of G. Biehl's *Collectorium Ockham.*

Fragments:

10. Erfurt, Bibl. Amploniana Q. 109, s. XIV. It is, according to Hochstetter (p. 2), an *Abbreviatio.*

M' 11. München Staatsbibl. 8943, s. XV. It contains parts of the second and fourth books according to Hochstetter (p. 1), who quotes it as A.

12. Padova, Bibl. Anton. 237, on vellum, s. XIV. According to Pelster, in *Gregorianum* 18 (1937), 291—317: "Die Handschrift enthält neben einem Kommentar zum zweiten Buch (dist. 14 bis zum Ende) des Wilhelm von Ockham eine vollständige Erklärung des zweiten Buches." I do not know of any ms. of the *Reportatio Ockham* that has a *distinctio* 14^a. Is this a mistake for *quaestio?* Or is it an indication that it is not Ockham's?

13. Paris, Bibl. Nat. *lat.* 15904 (Nr. 13 of the *Ordinatio*). It starts on f. 183r: *Cum creatio qua Deus . . .* and ends in f. 203v with the question: *Utrum angelus potest loqui alteri* (q. 20 of the edition; this title is in conformity with ms. F). The text of the *Ordinatio* is so bad that it could not be used.

14. Paris, Bibl. Nat. *lat.* 15561, on vellum, s. XIV, in a very bad hand. It contains only *schemata* and a list of questions on ff. 249—270vb.

2. *Elements Which with High Probability Belong to the Reportatio*

For a determination of the elements of the *Reportatio* which most probably belonged to the original inventory we have at our disposal not only the mss. FOb(Ob')OM and the edition, and the descriptions of Baudry and Hochstetter, but also the very important testimony of the *Magistri* of Avignon who literally quoted passages from

Ockham's *Ordinatio* and *Reportatio*. According to Koch's identification, it can be said that the following questions certainly belonged to the original inventory of the *Reportatio:*

II, 17—18, and 26.
III, 1, 3, and 8—9.
IV, 4—6 and 8—10.

None of these questions is missing in the respective parts of the manuscripts. Hence we are safe in stating that at least these questions belonged with certainty to Ockham's *Reportatio*.

Going a step further and taking as criterion the agreement of all the studied mss., we can state that the following questions belonged to the original inventory of the *Reportatio:*

II, 1—2; 4—7; 9—24; 26.
III, 1—3; 5—11.
IV, 4—14 (most probably 1—14)

Most of the mss. (or all?) transpose II, 17—18 to the third book. Ms. M transposes the first questions of II to the end and has other transpositions of the questions.

3. Foreign Elements in the Edition of the Reportatio

The occurrence of the rest of the questions in the mss. may be seen in the following table:

Q. II, 3	found in mss.	O	Ma
II, 8		F O	Ma
II, 20 U ss.			Ma
II, 25		F	Ma
III, 5			Ma
III, 12		O	Ma M
III, 13—15			Ma
Addit. add.		O(1)	Ma

Besides these elements which are found in the edition, there are others which are found in the mss. only and not in the edition. Instead of II, q. 13—15, we find in mss. FOb: *Utrum de anima tam-*

quam de subiecto sit tantum unus habitus. Ms. Ma adds to II, q. 9: *Quid sit nugatio orationis.* — After III, q. 7K. mss. Ma and O add the long fragment: *Ad dubium de positione Johannis, (in secundo* add. Ma) *quomodo beata Virgo potuit stare in originali peccato . . .* — Since IV, q. 1—3 are only missing in ms. F, we do not consider them as foreign elements.

Though many smaller, and even longer, passages and even questions are to be considered as foreign elements in the *Reportatio*, we shall confine our discussion to one question only and to one group of questions.

The question II, 8: *Utrum mundus potuit fuisse ab aeterno per potentiam divinam,* did most probably not figure in the original inventory of the *Reportatio*. First, because it is lacking in many mss. Second, because Ockham is quoted. In the edition we read (J): *Sicut patet in reportatione nostra, ubi tractatur de esse cognito . . .* Mss. F and O, however, read: *sicut patet in reportatione Ockham . . .* Another quotation (also in J) is missing in the edition: *Ut patet in secundo Ockham . . .* Again, according to the two mss. we read (N): *sicut patet diffuse in ordinatione et reportatione Ockham, quere ibi,* whilst instead of *Ockham* the edition has *nostris.* Are these quotations of Ockham a proof against the authenticity of this question? Without further evidence, they are certainly not a definitive proof, because similar quotations of Ockham are found in two mss. of the *Tractatus de praedestinatione* where the explanation is obvious, viz., that they were originally marginal notes and inserted in the text by the scribes. But such quotations are never found in the original stock of the *Reportatio*, and they prove at least that they do not belong to the *Reportatio.* That the second book of Ockham should be quoted in a question that belongs to the second book, is at least surprising. The quotation of the *Ordinatio Ockham* proves the same, because there is much evidence for the assumption that Ockham transformed the first book into the *Ordinatio* after the *Reportatio* on the other books. There are many quotations of the first books in the three others, but they refer to it only as *in primo libro.*

The questions II, 3; III, 12, and the *Additiones additae* form a group or a unit, and it seems that to this unit belongs III, q. 14—15,

20*

too. That they are foreign elements may be proved also by another fact concerning III, q. 12, which is printed in the Strassburg edition of the *Quodlibeta*. Its unproportionately large size, and the fact that it is not in the Paris-edition nor in the oldest ms. of the *Quodlibeta*, prove that it does not belong to the *Quodlibeta* either. That these questions form a unit is proved especially by their cross-references: *Addit. add.* E(2) refers to III, q. 12; so does III, q. 13 J; and II, q. 3 not only treats of a similar subject, but refers in AA to the *Additiones (quaere in fine dubitationis sequentis).* There does not seem to be a valid reason against their authenticity, although III, q. 12 mentions Ockham by name and several times quotes the *Reportatio.* On the contrary, they seem to be the *nucleus* of another work of Ockham, which probably could be called: *Quaestiones disputatae Ockham.* II, q. 3B and III, q. 12 mention an *Opponens,* and the *Additiones* speak several times of an *Adversarius* (L, O, Q: twice). If this theory should be verified, we would have to list another work of Ockham and maybe some light could be shed on his academical career.

4. The critical value of mss. FOb(Ob')OM(E)

Though I am acquainted with only four manuscripts, and with the Lyons Edition, nevertheless it does not seem to be too hazardous to form a fairly sound conclusion as to the value of the mss. which were used for the following edition. Since ms. Ob has our question twice (likewise qq. 13, 17 and 21) and since the edition has at least the value of a late ms., our evaluation is based on six witnesses.

In a first approach, the evaluation of the texts can proceed indirectly. All of them are bound together with the text on the *Ordinatio* and at least mss. ObOb'OM(E) are written by the same scribe who copied the corresponding version of the *Ordinatio.* In our study of the *Ordinatio Ockham* we have shown that ms. Ob ranks amongst the best and so does ms. F; ms. O has only a fair text, likewise E; ms. M has a better text than ms. O and E. If we now test this vague evaluation by a study of the text itself and by the agreement of the variants, we find that ms. Ob ranks first, then comes ms. F, then ms. M, and finally ms. Ob', E and ms. O. Since the results of the indirect and the direct method are in fair agreement, it seems justified to give ms. Ob the preference, if it is not in disagreement with all the other texts, and to give mss. FOb preference over all the others, if no strong reasons militate against them. This rule is followed in the edition. Mss. Ob' and M are often related, but to draw a stemma is beyond our power.

This evaluation may be substantiated by a few details. As for the *Ordinatio*, so likewise for the *Reportatio*, mss. F and M are of special interest. The text of the *Ordinatio* in ms. F certainly represents an earlier redaction. Though it may seem hazardous to speak of different redactions in the *Reportatio*, nevertheless, our question contains a clear indication of a kind of redaction. Hochstetter (p. 69, note 1) vaguely noticed it, though he did not think of an addition. But there is evidence that in II, q. 15 G, Ockham made an addition which starts: Ponendo . . . It was not in the original text: for ms. F omitted it; and it was later added on the margin, for it was transposed by E to the wrong place; and because it is so long, it was inserted by mss. Ob'M partly at the right and partly at a wrong place (similar cases are known in the *Ordinatio*). The absence of this addition, therefore, can be an indication that ms. F has, especially at the beginning of the questions, often a text considerably divergent from that of the edition and the other manuscripts, so that a future edition will have to print these in parallel columns. The parallel texts of ms. F suggest oral delivery more than the others, for they often connect the preceding with the following question and indicate the scheme of a question. It is, however, not always easy to decide whether these parts are remainders of the lectures as such or the first traces of an *Ordinatio*.

Ms. M certainly retains its character as a "critical" text, as in the case of the *Ordinatio*. A very striking example of this is found in II, q. 9, where (in H) the text is omitted from: *Quia omnis respectus subiecti potest manere . . .* to: *. . . quia sicut tu arguis de affirmationibus . . .* Instead of this a marginal note reads:

Sequentia argumenta, ad quae respondet, non sunt scripta, quia non erant scripta in libro Wilhelmi, et ibi (?) in respondendo potest homo videre argumenta; sed unum argumentum est hic et incipit: sicut tu arguis de affirmationibus etc.

Ms. M, then, gives before the answers of Ockham, a brief summary of the arguments to which Ockham answers, usually with the remarks: *Ratio, quae hic solvitur . . .* There are many other similar instances in ms. M. Since, however, these texts are in ms. F, our original hypothesis that ms. F is the earlier redaction would seem to be doomed. That, however, does not necessarily follow. For these omissions are arguments of Scotus, which Ockham apparently did not bother to copy (see also II, q. 15 D and MM). He left this task probably to his secretary. This is a possibility, but it is not meant as a final explanation.

What has been said of ms. M has some bearing on the question edited here. At the beginning of q. 14 we read in ms. M (marginal note): *Istud non fuit positum.* Does this mean that the *pro* and *contra* of question 14 were not in the copy of Ockham? Maybe Ockham dictated it simply from memory. In any case, he answers the *principale* of the first question. Further research may perhaps furnish new details which may help to decide problems, which, although of minor importance, will certainly reveal Ockham at work.

18. IN PROPRIA CAUSA[a]

A Reply to Professor Pegis'
"Concerning William of Ockham"
(Traditio, II [1944], 465—480)

Professor Anton Pegis in a recent article has leveled serious objections against my interpretation of Ockham as laid down in several publications. His criticism mainly concerns my article, "The Notitia Intuitiva of Non-existents according to William Ockham," which appeared in *Traditio*, I (1943), 223—275 [*supra* 268 ff.]. Since my answer to these objections could have appeared in the same periodical only

---

[a] First published in FrancStud 5 (1945) 37—54.

after the lapse of an entire year,[1] I gratefully accept the offer of the editors of *Franciscan Studies* to present my comment here. This will concern, first, the main issues; and, secondly, minor details.

I. MAIN ISSUES

Professor Pegis states that I have raised "three distinct issues in the interpretation of Ockham, all related in different ways to the problem of his skepticism." To these he adds a fourth.

I. Is Ockham's use of the doctrine of the divine omnipotence open to the charge of skepticism?

II. Does not Ockham's inability to prove the liberty and the omnipotence of God, against Greek and Arabian philosophers, suppose the natural impotence of the human reason to disprove the errors of the philosophers and therefore the *substitutional* use of faith against them?

III. There is also the particular issue, raised by Father Boehner's defense of the Ockhamistic doctrine of intuitive knowledge against Gilson's interpretation of it as in principle skeptical.

IV. I should like to add, finally, that the problem of interpreting Ockham, as Father Boehner has shaped it, is not so much *whether* Ockham is a skeptic but *when* a philosopher may be so called (p. 465).

Of these four distinct issues, Professor Pegis has devoted about four pages (465—469) to the first two, about ten pages (469—479) to the third, and only one page to the last. Accordingly, I shall answer only the third in extenso.

AD I

Doctor Pegis' discussion of this issue moves only in generalities, reiterating what he has said before. But the repetition of statements does not contribute in any way to their truth. He imputes to me that I accept Baudry's interpretation of the meaning of Ockham's philosophy. Now I am the one most competent to judge of that and, as far as I know my own mind, I can only state that I do not accept

---

[1] The editors of *Traditio* regret in their note to Professor Pegis' article that it has not been possible because of technical difficulties beyond their control to include my reply in the same number. My correspondence with the editors has convinced me of their sincerity.

the views of this excellent Ockhamistic scholar *in toto;*[2] certainly not as to the particular interpretation of Ockham's philosophy "as a philosophy of divine omnipotence." Hence I am happy to agree with Professor Pegis:

> But it is not at all clear that this doctrine of omnipotence was, in fact, the starting point of Ockham's philosophical activity (p. 466).

If Ockham used his *theological* principle of omnipotence in order to prove philosophical propositions, then I would consider it a serious confusion; and then at least the charge of theologism or fideism would be true, and probably the charge of skepticism also. However, my firm conviction, based on an intensive study of Ockham's texts themselves, is that Ockham *in praxi* very often (in fact, always where the opportunity is given) makes the distinction between a philosophical truth and a theological truth (including a theological conclusion) more apparent than St. Thomas. In theory, I believe, all Scholastics are equally clear as to the distinction between philosophy and theology.

AD II

Unfortunately the discussion concerning the second issue also moves in generalities, and hence it is useless to discuss it, except to present a few clarifications.

1. I emphatically deny the truth of this statement made by Professor Pegis:

> In principle, Father Boehner is contesting the Thomistic ideal of an autonomous philosophy which could refute the errors of the philosophers on it own ground and with the light of reason (p. 468).

I do not remember having ever contested this Thomistic ideal, nor have I ever intended to do so even in principle. In addition, I have never contested the following statement of Professor Pegis, though I do contend that it is specifically Thomistic, and not Scotistic or Ockhamistic:

> It cannot be stressed too much that Thomism in the thirteenth century meant an attitude which insisted that truth, philosophy and demonstration

---

[2] My own copy of Baudry's work shows at least eight question marks in the margin, made as early as four years ago.

were on the same side of the dispute between Hellenism and Christianity, and not at all opponent (p. 468).

I agree, provided, of course, that we take "philosophy" as the ideal of a system of true statements only, and that Professor Pegis, as a good Aristotelian, takes "demonstration" in the technical Aristotelian sense as a necessary inference from necessary propositions to a necessary conclusion. I would really be grateful to be informed where I have denied that.

Several times I have pointed out how important is the difference between "demonstration" in the strict sense and the more general term "proof" and "persuasio" — at least when reading Scotus and Ockham. "Persuasio" is a natural reason, and in this sense, a proof which convinces a man of good will; but it is not invulnerable against the logical subtleties of the "protervus", who so often makes his appearance in Ockham's writings. Hence, in my opinion, "persuasio" comes pretty close to what neo-Scholastics call "moral certitude". This disposes of the following remark of Professor Pegis:

But Ockham, whom Father Boehner defends, accepts the divine omnipotence as a doctrine which he is powerless to prove against the necessitarianism of the philosophers (p. 468).

If "to prove" means "to demonstrate", Ockham agrees; if it means "persuasiones", Ockham denies it.

2. Professor Pegis writes:

His [that is my own] view of the Thomistic ideal, and particularly his willingness to follow Ockham in conceding that the errors of the philosophers were not philosophically refutable, is as old as St. Bonaventure's observation that the philosopher *must* fall into some error unless he is aided by the light of faith: "necesse est enim philosophantem in aliquem errorem labi nisi adiuvetur per radium fidei" (p. 468).

This is a relief. For from now on I am in the company of the Seraphic Doctor and, as I shall show, in the company of another illustrious champion of Christian philosophy. The first part of this quotation is, of course, not true, either for me or for St. Bonaventure. Let us mention only the question of the eternity of the world. St. Bonaventure believes, against all the philosophers, that he has demonstrations to disprove it. St. Thomas denies that we have any valid demonstration to disprove the eternity of the world, or even to prove this an impossibility. The second part of the quotation is certainly not the proof of the first, nor equivalent to a proof. It is interesting, however, that Doctor Pegis has italicized "must". Is it not obvious that St. Bonaventure here speaks, not of logical necessity, but only of a psychological or moral necessity? Is it not Catholic teaching that the power of human reason is very limited and exposed to many errors, as Pope Leo says in his encyclical *Aeterni Patris:*

> Etenim cum humana mens certis finibus, iisque angustis, conclusa teneatur, pluribus erroribus et multarum rerum ignorationi est obnoxia.

And is it not a fact that all ancient philosophers without exception fell into many errors, because they lacked the light of faith? Hence without faith it was psychologically necessary for them to fall into at least some errors. I do not think that Professor Pegis thinks differently. I believe we both subscribe to the words of Pope Leo:

> Quod si, Venerabiles Fratres, ad historiam philosophiae respiciatur, cuncta, quae paulo ante diximus, re ipsa comprobari intelligetis. Et sane philosophorum veterum, qui fidei beneficio caruerunt, etiam qui habebantur sapientissimi, in plurimis deterrime errarunt. Nostis enim, inter nonulla vera, quam saepe falsa et absona, quam multa incerta et dubia tradiderint de vera divinitatis ratione . . . (*Opera S. Thomae*, ed. Leonina, t. I, VIII).

3. Professor Pegis says:

> Now it is a fact that the whole Thomistic view of the nature of God is implicit in the proof of the divine omnipotence as St. Thomas understands it (p. 468).

As far as I know, this is not the commonly accepted interpretation of St. Thomas, and hence Professor Pegis' private affair with other Thomists. The same is true also of the conclusion from his view on St. Thomas:

> To think in this way, however, is nothing less than to ruin philosophy, for such an attitude consists in accepting by faith that which St. Thomas thought was philosophically demonstrable (p. 468).

I have no comment to offer on this unhappy thought.

4. Professor Pegis finds it puzzling that I have given Ockham the title "defender of the faith".[3] The title really does not matter. By it I meant this: Ockham confessed in all honesty that he was unable to *demonstrate certain* truths, which others believed they had demonstrated, because he feared that the good of the faith is endangered if we base ourselves on insufficient reasons. In this sentiment, though not in its wider application, he had St. Thomas as a good companion, for the Angelic Doctor confessed that he was unable to refute demonstratively the infinite duration of the world, and justified the necessity of acknowledging this failure as follows:

Has autem rationes [for a finite duration of the world], quia usquequaque non de necessitate concludunt, licet probabilitatem habeant, sufficit tangere solum, ne videatur fides catholica in vanis rationibus constituta et non potius in solidissima Dei doctrina (*Contra Gentiles*, II, 38).

And again:

Unde mundum incoepisse est credibile, non autem demonstrabile vel scibile. Et hoc utile est ut consideretur, ne forte aliquis, quod fidei est demonstrare praesumens, rationes non necessarias inducat, quae praebeant materiam irridendi infidelibus, existimantibus nos propter huiusmodi rationes credere quae fidei sunt (*Summa Theologica*, I, q. 46, a. 2 c.).

Does not Scotus repeat that? He says:

Adducere tamen sophismata pro demonstrationibus, periculosum esset contra infideles, quia ex hoc exponeretur fides derisioni (*Oxoniense*, II, d. 1, q. 3, n. 8, ed. Vivès, t. 16, 136).

And is this not exactly the position of Ockham also?

AD III

We now come to the most decisive part of Professor Pegis' "not-polemical" reflections, the part which concerns the very problem which I have discussed in my article in *Traditio*. Here he takes up a determined defense of Gilson's accusation of Ockham.

Gilson's accusation comes down to this, that for Ockham "human knowledge would be practically indistinguishable from what it is, even though

---

[3] Incidentally, there is a no less startling "paradox" in Ockham's *Dialogus*, 1 a pars, lib. 2, c. 19 *et seq.* This could merit Ockham the title "Defender of St. Thomas" — against the *Articuli Parisienses*.

all its objects were destroyed; nothing is necessarily required to make knowledge possible but the mind and God." That is to say, "if God can converse in us the intuition of something that is not actually existing, how shall we ever be sure that what we are perceiving as real is an actually existing thing? In other words, if it is possible for God to make us perceive as real an object that does not really exist, have we any proof that this world of ours is not a vast phantasmagoria behind which there is no reality to be found?"

To this I say: For Ockham, human knowledge, even though its objects were destroyed, would be both practically and theoretically distinguishable from what it is. It is true that, to make knowledge *possible*, nothing is necessarily required except the mind and God — if, and only if, nothing exists besides God and the mind. If, however, something exists outside God and the mind, this reality is necessarily required as partial cause for the *evident judgment* that it exists. Hence the possibility of distinguishing in theory and in practice. Neither Gilson nor Pegis has ever offered to the contrary a text in which Ockham denies either this possibility or this necessity.

On the last part I have commented in my article in *Traditio* as follows:

Ockham had called it a contradiction to perceive *as real* an object that does not exist, not, however, to perceive intuitively an object *as not real* (p. 235, n. 28), [*supra,* 286].

Professor Pegis finds in Ockham's *Commentary to the Sentences*, Report. II, q. 15 E, two distinct discussions, which have to be carefully distinguished:

In the first part of this text Ockham is discussing intuitive knowledge and judgments of existence. In the second part, the discussion turns on the relations between intuitive knowledge and judgments of non-existence. Now the difficulties posed by these two discussions are entirely different. The first discussion produces these two difficulties:

I. Whether by intuitive knowledge we can apprehend a reality, given that that reality does not exist?

II. Whether we can assent to a thing as existing, given that it does not exist?

On the other hand, the second discussion is concerned with the intuition and the judgment of non-existence, given that a thing does not exist. Gilson's charge of skepticism, which Father Boehner thinks he has answered, lies primarily in the Ockhamistic context of judgments of existence, a context whose virtualities Father Boehner's own discussion has tended to obscure (p. 470).

Let us, for the time being, note here only that Doctor Pegis emphasizes that the *context* proves the charge against Ockham, and that I have tended to obscure the *virtualities* of this context. This has to be kept well in mind.

After a long interpretation of the text of Ockham taken from my edition in *Traditio* (an interpretation which I cannot accept in every detail,[4] but which for the present can be the basis for further discussion), Professor Pegis finds himself confronted with this aporia:

> After this exposition Ockham concludes that it is clear how intuitive knowledge is that knowledge by which I know a thing to be when it is, and not to be when it is not (p. 475).

This is correct and would, in my opinion, make Professor Pegis' further comment and his desperate attempt to save Gilson superfluous. However, he continues — and this now comes as a surprise:

---

[4] I cannot even agree with his interpretation of St. Thomas. For on page 471, footnote 26, he writes: "For St. Thomas Aquinas, the proper object of the judgment is *ipsum esse rei* (*In B. De Trinitate*, q. V, a. 3, Resp.*). In this sense, a judgment cannot but be an assent — an assent to the being of a thing." And a little further: "For, in St. Thomas Aquinas, the distinction does not lie between judgment and assent, as it does in Ockham; the distinction rather lies between a direct and reflexive judgment, both of which are assents. The direct judgment is an assent to being while the reflexive judgment is an assent to one's own act of assenting to being (cf. St. Thomas, *Sum. Theol.* I—II, q. 17, a. 6, Resp.)." Cf., however, P. Wilpert, "Das Urteil als Träger der Wahrheit nach Thomas von Aquin," *Philosophisches Jahrbuch*, 46 (1933), 56—75. This author maintains that judgment (an expression which is true or false) and assent to a judgment have to be distinguished according to St. Thomas. Cf. p. 74: "Gewiß kennt Thomas eine zweifache Bedeutung des Begriffes judicium. Erst im Urteil ist der assensus möglich, notwendig dafür aber, daß ein Gedankeninhalt das Prädikat der Wahrheit erhalte, ist er indes nicht." The identification of judgment and assent which Professor Pegis maintains is, according to Wilpert, a false interpretation of St. Thomas, adopted by Joannes a St. Thoma and Suarez, while he himself gives valuable evidence for the interpretation of Cajetanus and Mercier, who both deny this identity. Ockham, then, would go with the latter. As to myself, I would prefer to say with Spinoza: "Non sum actor huius scenae, sum solum speculator."

It is sufficient for our purpose if we propose three questions for consideration on the basis of Ockham's text *In II Sent.*, q. 15 E.

I. Does not Ockham hold that it is possible, given a supernaturally caused intuitive knowledge, to judge that a thing exists when it does not exist?

II. How is it possible for Ockham to derive opposite conclusions from a supernaturally caused knowledge of a non-existent thing? For does he not hold that by a supernaturally caused intuitive knowledge I can judge both that a thing exists and that a thing does not exist (assuming in both cases the non-existence of the thing)?

III. If these two points are true, does not Ockham's omnipotentism lead him to violate the principle of contradiction in at least two distinct ways (p. 475)?

Here are my answers:

To I: No! Ockham does not hold that it is possible, given a supernaturally caused intuitive knowledge, to judge that a thing exists when it does not exist. Ockham has denied this on several occasions, and has never affirmed it.

To II: No! It is not possible, according to Ockham, to derive opposite conclusions from a supernaturally caused knowledge of a non-existing thing. It is assumed, of course, that there is no change outside this cognition. For if there is an intuitive cognition of a non-existing being, and this non-existing being comes to existence, the opposite assent on the basis of this cognition plus the existence of the thing is forced on the mind, and consequently the opposite assent to the judgment is then warranted: "The thing exists." Hence the answer to the second part of the question: Ockham does not hold that by a supernaturally caused intuitive knowledge I can judge both that a thing exists and that a thing does not exist (assuming in both cases the non-existence of the thing). It is assumed, of course, as before, that no change occurs in the thing of which intuitive cognition is given.

To III: Since Professor Pegis is mistaken as regards points I and II, he is wrong in concluding that Ockham's "omnipotentism" leads him to violate the principle of contradiction.

I am certainly grateful to Professor Pegis for having formulated his questions (or theses) in so clear a manner. That makes an equally clear answer possible.

Where are the proofs for Professor Pegis' theses? For the first and the most basic one, Professor Pegis offers the following text as proof (I prefer to quote it in Latin, though his translation seems to be correct):

Ex istis sequitur, quod notitia intuitiva, tam sensitiva quam intellectiva, potest esse de re non existente. Et hanc conclusionem probo aliter quam prius sic: Omnis res absoluta distincta loco et subiecto ab alia re absoluta, potest per potentiam divinam absolutam existere sine illa, quia non videtur verisimile, quod si Deus vult destruere unam rem absolutam exitentem in coelo, quod necessitetur destruere unam aliam rem existentem in terra. Sed visio intuitiva, tam sensitiva quam intellectiva, est res absoluta distincta loco et subiecto ab obiecto. Sicut si videam intuitive stellam existentem in coelo, illa visio intuitiva, sive sit intellectiva sive sensitiva, distinguitur loco et subiecto ab obiecto viso; ergo ista visio potest manere, stella destructa (*In I Sent.*, Prol. q. 1 HH, ed. Boehner, p. 29).

To this text Professor Pegis adds:

Certainly Ockham thinks here that he sees the star when the star no longer exists. Is Gilson wrong in attributing such a view to Ockham? If texts such as this mean anything, there is surely no way of avoiding Gilson's conclusion (p. 476).

Now, there is no doubt that this text does mean something, but not what Professor Pegis or Gilson (according to Pegis) *imply* or read into Ockham's words. For Pegis *infers* from this text that Ockham holds that it is possible, given a supernaturally caused intuitive knowledge, to *judge* that a thing exists when it does not exist, or to judge of the *existence* of a *non-existing* thing, given that God caused in us an intuitive knowledge. He only infers that Ockham here admitted this contradiction. However, Professor Pegis' speculation is neither good interpretation nor good logic, and for the following reasons.

First: Where, in this text, does the term "to judge", or its equivalent, occur? It is not to be found. There is here poor interpretation and a *petitio principii*. Ockham only infers: "Ergo ista visio *potest* manere, stella destructa." According to good Aristotelian, Thomistic, and Ockhamistic logic, the mood of possibility is equivalent to the mood of non-impossibility; for "impossibility" in the logical sense we can substitute "contradiction" or its equivalent; hence the "potest" in Ockham's text comes exactly down to "non-contradiction". In other words, it is no contradiction that intuitive cognition is given and that the object of this cognition outside the mind does not exist. The object in the sky is a real thing; the cognition is a psychic reality; both are distinct by distance and subject. If I have an intuitive cognition of this object, my cognition is a psychic reality corresponding to the thing; and if now this psychic reality is supernaturally conserved by God while the object in the sky is destroyed, then it only follows that I have an intuitive cognition of an object which does not exist. Does it follow from this that I then *judge* and *give my evident assent* to the statement: "This object exists?" By no means! For the simple apprehension must be distinguished from the complex or statement: "This thing exists," and also from the judgment or assent to this statement. The assent to the statement always, without any exception, depends on the existence or non-existence of the thing. If the thing exists, its existence is partial and necessary cause for the evident assent to the statement: "The thing exists." If the thing does not exist, its non-existence or the lack of any causality from the side of the thing is the basis for the evident assent to the statement that the thing does not exist.

Again let us ask: Where does Ockham say, either in this text or in any other, "that it is possible, given a supernaturally caused intuitive knowledge, to *judge* that a thing exists when it does not exist?" Professor Pegis cannot, and in fact does not, maintain that Ockham *says* it. He maintains, however, that it is *implied* by this text. Unfortunately he does not make this implication explicit; hence it is *his personal assumption.*

Of course, on the basis of such an assumption, not proved by any text of Ockham, it is easy to construct the logical monstrosity:

How can Ockham possibly assert that we can judge of the *existence* of a *non-existing* thing, given that God caused in us an intuitive knowledge of it (p. 476).

When he continues, saying: "That is certainly a problem, not to say a contradiction," let us say with Ockham: "That is a contradiction." Ockham has always conceded it as such. Professor Pegis himself admits this to some extent, with, however, a distinction:

True enough, Ockham has tried in the *Quodlibeta* to prove that it would be contradictory to assert the existence of a non-existing thing. If we take this decision seriously, then we are led to wonder whether Ockham did not finally give up the position he adopted in the *Commentary on the Sentences*. For this amounts to saying that it is impossible to have an intuition of a thing, as well as an evident judgment of the existence of a thing, without being given that existence (p. 477).

Instead of asking now, as Professor Pegis does:

What happens, then, to the view which we have already seen, namely, that there can be an intuitive knowledge when the object is a *purum nihil?* (p. 477),

we might rather ask the Professor himself: What happens now to your own conclusion, drawn from your own inference from a statement of Ockham, an inference which Ockham had never drawn, and for which you are unable to give the evidence of any text? If the object is a *purum nihil*, it is no contradiction that there be an intuitive cognition of the object; but it is a contradiction in this case to judge that it exists.

Some readers may have wondered how Ockham can maintain this, namely, that there can be the possibility of intuitive cognition without the existence of the object. Ockham's answer is that such a cognition is in God; consequently it is possible. For God knows everything, including the *possibilia*, which are a *purum nihil* as to their existence. How does God know that certain things do not exist? Not through a discursive process; hence by incomplex knowledge. The incomplex knowledge which is the basis for judgments of existence and non-existence is called by Ockham *notitia intuitiva* (which comprises the Thomistic *scientia visionis* and *simplicis intelligentiae*). Since God has intuitive knowledge of non-existents, intuitive cognition of non-existents is possible. Hence Ockham can write already in the *Ordinatio*, right after the text which is the basis for Professor Pegis' imputation:

Patet etiam ex praedictis, quomodo Deus habet notitiam intuitivam omnium, sive sint, sive non sint, quia ita evidenter cognoscit creaturas non esse, quando non sunt, sicut cognoscit eas esse, quando sunt *(loc. cit.)*.

Consequently Ockham would answer Professor Pegis' charge by asking: How can God have the *scientia simplicis intelligentiae* of something that does not exist, if discursive reasoning and any kind of inference is excluded?

But let us return to Professor Pegis. He is not quite satisfied with the assumption of a revision made by Ockham. For he finds the same contradiction admitted by Ockham in the very next *Quodlibetum* after the *Quodlibetum* in which Ockham had called Professor Pegis' assumption a contradiction. There, in *Quodl.* VI, q. 6, we read:

> Dico quod contradictio est, quod visio sit et quod illud quod videtur, non sit in effectu nec esse possit. Ideo contradictio est, quod chymaera videatur intuitive. Sed non est contradictio, quod id quod videtur nihil sit in actu extra animam, dummodo possit esse in effectu vel aliquando fuerit in rerum natura.

I am at a loss to find in this text any contradiction to the former statement of Ockham. For Ockham says here that it is a contradiction to have an intuitive cognition of something which is not possible and hence cannot be in reality. He excludes from the objects of intuitive cognition only the *impossibilia*, i. e., contradictory objects, not however non-existents. On the contrary, he states here again *expressis verbis* that there is no contradiction in the notion of intuitive knowledge of a *non-existent*, but *possible*, thing, and I am especially at a loss to understand Professor Pegis' discovery of a contradiction, since he italicizes the important words: "nor be capable of being" and "but it is not a contradiction that that which is seen should be actually nothing outside the soul, provided that it can actually be or has been in reality" (cf. p. 477). But it seems that Professor Pegis is haunted by the expression of Ockham that something which is possible, but does not exist, is a *purum nihil*. Here he finds it again in the expression: "quod id, quod videtur, *nihil* sit." Ockham, of course, means by this that a thing which is possible, but does not exist, is a *purum nihil* as regards its existence and existential reality. The cognitive content of such intuitive knowledge of a possible but non-existing thing, of course, is a psychic reality, according to Ockham.

We have already anticipated some of Professor Pegis' discussions concerning the second problem. How does he prove his second thesis? I shall not criticize the formulation of it, and I take it for granted that Professor Pegis too understands the problem, expressed in Ock-hamistic terminology, exactly thus: How can the *same* intuitive cognition be the basis of an evident judgment that the object exists, if the object exists, and that it does not exist, if the object does not exist? We have already made the answer clear. In the first case, the evident judgment that the thing exists is made because the object, which is partial cause for the evident assent, is given; in the second case, the evident judgment that the thing does not exist is made because the object, which is partial cause, is lacking, and this lack of the partial cause, together with the same intuitive cognition as before, is now the cause for this assent. That a partial cause *together* with another partial cause and *without* the other partial cause can have contradictory effects, can hardly be denied by Professor Pegis.

But Doctor Pegis does not consider this exactly as an answer, and makes the surprising statement:

This is not exactly an answer, for it assumes that the existence of a thing makes a difference in our judgment of its existence. To hold this, however, Ockham would have to ruin the very point of his examples about the star and the object in far-away Rome. Hence, Ockham cannot possibly hold that the existence of a thing can make a difference between the judg-ment of its existence and the judgment of its non-existence, if he has already granted that (supernaturally speaking) its existence is not necessary for our intuition of it. In short, if the existence of a thing is not necessary to the (supernaturally caused) intuitive knowledge of it; if, in other words, the existence of a thing need not, absolutely speaking, act as a partial cause of our intuitive knowledge of it, why should the non-existence of a thing affect intuitive knowledge in any way? No doubt, Ockham must say that the thing is a partial cause of the judgment that it exists, and he must explain in this way the judgment of its non-existence. But there is absolutely no reason why he should say this, since he has already said that intuitive knowledge can be caused without the existence of things (p. 477).

This statement speaks for itself. And a prudent reader is asked only to read it again, having in mind that the position by which Ockham is said to ruin himself is a construction of Professor Pegis, and furthermore that Ockham carefully distinguishes between *intui-tive cognition* (which can be produced without an object outside the mind, but then not without God's supernatural interference) and

21*

the *assent* to the statement: "This thing does not exist; this thing does exist." For if the thing does not exist, and supernaturally produced intuitive knowledge is given, the lack of one partial cause for the assent, plus the intuitive cognition, is the basis of the statement: "The thing does not exist." If the thing exists, the existence of the thing acts together with intuitive cognition of it as partial cause for the statement: "The thing exists." If Professor Pegis does not see a reason why Ockham should say this, Ockham himself certainly saw a reason: namely, that evidence should always be based ultimately on existence or non-existence.

From now on Professor Pegis moves more or less in pure constructions. When he says (p. 478):

> After all, it remains true to say that for Ockham there can be an intuitive knowledge of a thing which is in itself a *nihil*, provided this *nihil* is a *possible* being,

Ockham would say: "Concedo" (in the sense previously explained).

Then Professor Pegis goes on to say:

> That is the main point on which I should like to insist. If non-contradiction in the objects of intuitive knowledge is sufficient for Ockham, then he evidently does not need actual things outside the soul.

To this Ockham could answer in his own defense: Say it rather thus (the antecedent of your conditional being granted, of course): Then I evidently do not need actual things outside the soul (except God) for the evident assent that this thing does not exist; for if, and only if, the thing does not exist, the (supernaturally possible) intuitive cognition alone would be sufficient cause for the evident assent to the judgment: "This thing does not exist." However (and please take my words as they stand, for I have repeated it time and again), I evidently need the existence of the thing as partial cause for the evident assent to the statement: "This thing exists."

Thus the whole chain of further inferences which Professor Pegis has so neatly arranged breaks down. It seems utterly useless to refute them or repeat them individually, for the simple reason that they are essentially constructions based on the former assumptions.

AD IV

I have virtually no comment to make on this point, because it moves entirely in generalities and, as far as I am able to see, does not even answer the questions posited by Professor Pegis himself. For I have not found there a definition of a skeptic, nor a statement which tells *"when* a philosopher may be so called." Perhaps Doctor Pegis tacitly invites the reader to think that any philosophy of a kind of vague Platonism is skeptical. For the sake of curiosity I would like to quote one passage:

> With Platonism, Ockhamism has in common the gulf which it places between thought and the world of things. But Ockhamism is fundamentally Platonism minus the Ideas (p. 479).

I wonder what other historians of philosophy would think of a Platonism from which the Ideas have vanished!

II. MINOR DETAILS

1. Concerning my edition: On page 470, Professor Pegis criticizes my paragraphing of the text of E. What he says seems to me to be well founded, and I regret that I did not make the more desirable arrangement. On page 473, footnote 28, Professor Pegis criticizes the adoption of "determinata" in preference to "debita". Here he has justly made use of the advice which I expressed as follows: "To read the variants, too, is sometimes very important, for a prudent reader may justly prefer it to the adopted text" (p. 245). Instead of "it" I should have said "some of them".

This gives me an occasion to answer a friendly criticism offered by Father R. Arbesmann in his review of my article (cf. *Theological Studies*, V [1944], 388). My doubt regarding the authenticity of the Padova Manuscript could hardly convince anybody not in constant contact with Ockham's manuscripts. Though I was personally convinced of the non-authenticity of this work, and though the reason I offered was for me sufficient, I must still have had in my memory a vague recollection of that decisive proof in my files which I did not explicitly adduce. For Dom H. Bascour, O. S. B., to whom I owe valuable notes on the manuscript-tradition of Ockham's works, has written in a private letter concerning this manuscript as follows:

Padova Anton. 237: l. II, d. 14 jusqu'à la fin, d'après F. Pelster, *Gregorianum* 1937, p. 310; mais ce doit être une erreur. J'ai vérifié sur des photographies du ms. et n'ai rien trouvé de semblable. Il doit avoir confondu avec Scot, qui commence en effet l. II, d. 14 (f. 92 vb).

2. On several occasions Professor Pegis makes reference to Professor Gilson, and to my criticism of his position. Some of his remarks might create the impression that I was too radical in my criticism.

First, I believe that my criticism, which lacks any personal note, can at most contribute to Gilson's generally accepted eminence in matters of medieval research. His excellent and scholarly work is unanimously appreciated. But he is the last to claim that he is infallible.

Secondly, I believe that I am personally as much indebted to Professor Gilson as Doctor Pegis is — and probably even more. For I am indebted to him not only spiritually but materially also. I shall never cease considering him "amicum et patrem nostrum", as I have said in the preface to the edition of the first question of Ockham's *Commentary on the Sentences*. He has awakened in me a great love of the Seraphic Doctor, and of the Scholastics in general, and even of Ockham by exhorting me, in personal conversations, to undertake much-needed editions of Ockham. The translating of three of his books into German has recompensed me considerably more than the tedious work of translation could be expected to, by shaping my own intellectual development. I am indebted to him especially for that very attitude of mind which has forced me to criticize his interpretation of Ockham. For I have learned from him, what I later found expressed in Scotus: "Ex dictis eorum volo rationabiliorem intellectum accipere quem possum" (*Oxoniense*, I, d. 8, q. 5, n. 8, ed. Vivès, t. 9, 745). We are at one in that attitude; we are at variance only in a concrete interpretation, that is in the application of this attitude. Taught by many years of personal acquaintance with him, I am sure that his magnanimity well stands a difference of opinion on the part of his friends, even if such a difference seems very fundamental. A man's greatness is measured by that which he can bear. To destroy the work of his life, however, or even that of the last fifteen years, is entirely alien to my intentions.

But if I should have hurt the feelings of my friend, that would cause me more sorrow than it does Professor Pegis. In this case, I infinitely regret having criticized his position in public, even though my criticism was limited to the mild enough expression: "Gilson's treatment of Ockham, in his *Unity of Philosophical Experience*, needs overhauling" (p. 240). Hardly a "sweeping criticism" or a "grave and radical charge"!

But I know well that Professor Gilson is capable of a benevolent smile at the "rigor Minorum qui nemini parcunt". And he may rest assured that his *Philosophie de saint Bonaventure* is one of those rare and precious gifts for which the "turba Fratrum Minorum" will always be grateful.

3. Professor Pegis quotes a passage from my article: "The Text-tradition of Ockham's *Ordinatio*" (*The New Scholasticism*, XVI [1942], 222 [and *supra* 127] in which he finds the following "defiant words":

If one is not able to grasp the meaning of Ockham's conceptualism and his criticism (not skepticism[5] — this disease certainly is in Holkot) and his serious endeavour to find a new solution for Christian philosophy in a new situation, a solution which satisfied him and others, and even Saints, he may take our advice and leave the Venerabilis Inceptor alone (p. 467).

Unfortunately Professor Pegis did not quote enough. For before I gave this advice, I said that a new edition of the *Ordinatio* will not yield new discoveries in Ockham, but will necessarily lead to a revision of certain prejudices:

New discoveries concerning the doctrine of Ockham can hardly be expected from a future critical edition of this first book. Such an edition, however, will have another effect, viz., a revision of the exposition of Ockham's doctrine in our textbooks and of many articles written by incompetent students.

Then follow the "defiant words".

When I wrote these words, I did not realize that they could possibly hurt any of the competent students. If they do, I regret

---

[5] I have here corrected Professor Pegis' misquotation of my original. I wrote "skepticism", not "nominalism".

them. But I am happy to make explicit now at least, that I did not consider Professors Pegis or Gilson incompetent students. I had in mind certain articles — but "nomina sunt odiosa". The remark on Holkot, the Dominican Scholastic of Oxford, does not seem wholly happy now to me either.

In this connection, I would request Professor Pegis not to call Ockham's theory as regards universals "Nominalism". We both agree that "nomina sunt ad placitum". But even neo-Scholastics usually distinguish clearly between Conceptualism and Nominalism. Ockham has never identified universals with "flatus vocis". I insist on the distinction in order to keep Professor Pegis safe from these "defiant words".

4. On page 468 of Professor Pegis' article we read:

The doctrine of the divine omnipotence is an excellent example of the issue between St. Thomas and Father Boehner.

Here I am embarrassed, and also a little flattered. But I refuse to be pushed into the ring with the great St. Thomas. I cannot enter this Gigantomachia; I am only a spectator at this great battle between the giants St. Thomas and Scotus and Ockham. I am only a historian who unfortunately sides, as spectator, with Scotus or Ockham.

This dispenses likewise with the insinuation expressed in this form:

For does not such a defense free Ockham of the charge of skepticism on the condition of involving St. Thomas in it? (p. 469).

The context of the text quoted by Professor Pegis shows that I am speaking there about Ockham and his fear, which he indeed expresses, without mentioning St. Thomas.

This may suffice. There are, of course, more points on which I might comment. But I hope that I have answered at least the main ones. As far as I am concerned, the discussion is closed. As soon as Professor Pegis, or anyone else, should offer evidence on the basis of *texts*, and not on the basis of speculation or of a scheme of the history of philosophy into which facts are pressed, however ingeniously, I shall abandon my position. Doctor Pegis himself will realize, I hope, that my position is sound. No human being is free from prejudice. But instead of interpreting Ockham from the standpoint of my own philosophical position, I have tried to be guided only by *his* views in interpreting *his* texts. I have the impression that Doctor Pegis has interpreted Ockham too much according to his own philosophical position. As he knows, I do not share all his views. However, we both are one in affirming the essential basis on which various Scholastic systems can be constructed, which systems are not always necessarily contradictory. Thus let us both enjoy the generous liberty which the Church in her wisdom and her Catholicity, that is in her universality, has granted us.

I conclude by quoting what was, once at least, a "traditional" view on William Ockham. The great Irish historian of the Franciscan order, Luke Wadding, wrote:

> Neque vero depravatorem theologiae ... aut philosophiae fuisse Occhamum, probant ipsa eius scripta philosophica et theologica, quae passim in scholis leguntur, approbantur, commendantur: confirmantque destinata sibi subsellia in quibusdam orthodoxis academiis, ex quibus solae Occhami sententiae tum philosophicae, tum theologicae, designatis stipendiis edocentur ... Non eam ego sumo provinciam, ut velim omnes libros Occhami defendere, et quidquid scripserat, commendare; immo aperte condemno, et ex corde detestor omnia quae in Joannem Pontificem insolenter evomuit. Theologicis censuris dignum existimo Opus Nonaginta Dierum .. Illud solum velim, quae communi scholasticorum methodo vel scripsit in Aristotelem vel in libros Sententiarum, aut elaboravit absque bile ante indignationem conceptam contra Joannem Pontificem, catholica esse in scholis recepta absque acri censura, et proinde immerito atque iniuste depravatorem dici philosophiae seu theologiae (*Annales Minorum*, ad annum 1347, t. VIII [nova editio, Quaracchi, 1932], n. xxx—xxxi, 17—18).

19. DOES OCKHAM KNOW OF MATERIAL IMPLICATION[a]

The present study has two main purposes. First, it will try to determine whether Ockham had any idea of material implication as understood by modern logicians; secondly, through the pertinent discussions, it will serve as a test for ascertaining whether certain recently discovered tracts on logic can be attributed to Ockham.

---

[a] First published in FrancStud 11, Commemorative Volume (1951) 203—230.

In a previous article[1] we showed that at least three systematical works on logic, or *Summae* of logic, are attributed in certain manuscripts to Ockham. Let us briefly summarize the *status quaestionis*. There is no doubt that the famous *Summa Logicae* is a work of Ockham; its authenticity *in toto* and in its parts is well documented. In the following discussions, this *Summa* will be called S1. A manuscript of Munich (*Staatsbibliothek* 1060) written in 1348 attributes another *Summa* (S2) to Ockham. It is called by the author *Elementarium*, and by the scribe *Tractatus medius logicae Ockham*. Another manuscript, *Assisi* 690, written probably in the 14th century, also attributes a logic to Ockham. The scribe calls it *Tractatus minor logicae Ockham* (S3). All three *Summae* are distinct works. S1 is the longest, S3 the shortest. There is no question, however, of any one of the *Summae* being an abbreviation of another, but all three are independent, though related, treatments of the same subject. S2 seems to be closer to S3. All of these logics show characteristic features of Ockham's teaching and arrangement of subject matter. Up to now, our study of these *Summae* has not showed any serious discrepancy between them, except perhaps one, which will be dealt with in this article, and, as we hope, explained in the course of our discussion. Thus we hope to shed new light on the problem of their authenticity; at the same time, we intend to determine whether an equivalent of the material implication of modern logicians is to be found in Ockham's logic.

In all three *Summae* there are two distinct places where information on our problem is to be found, *viz.*, in the treatment of conditional propositions and of the *consequentiae*.

I. ON CONDITIONAL PROPOSITIONS

According to medieval logic, hypothetical propositions in contradistinction to categorical propositions are understood as compound propositions, that is, as propositions which are composed of at least two categorical propositions. Usually five main subclasses

---

[1] "Three Sums of Logic attributed to William Ockham," in *Franciscan Studies* XI (1951), 173—193; [*supra*, 70—96].

of hypothetical propositions are enumerated, though as Ockham does not fail to emphasize, more can be adduced. There are the conditional, the copulative, the disjunctive, the temporal, and the causal propositions. In order to reach an exact understanding of the conditional proposition and the relation prevailing between *its* component parts, we shall deal first with the relations existing between the parts of conjunctive, disjunctive, and causal propositions. This will be done by comparing the texts, especially of S1 and S2, since S3 has very little to say about the present matter.

In order to make a more exact presentation of the following discussions, we shall resort to the following symbols:

p, q, r, s   are symbols of propositions

.   is the symbol of "and"

—   in front of, or above, another symbol is the symbol of negation

v   is the symbol of "or"

∫   is the symbol of not specified implication (sequitur)

∫'   is the symbol of material implication

∫*   is the symbol of strict implication

≡   is the symbol of equivalence

Imp   is the symbol for "impossible that"

Poss   is the symbol for "possible that"

Parentheses and brackets etc. are used to distinguish parts of complex expressions.

A conjunctive or copulative proposition is composed of at least two categorical propositions linked up by the statement-connective "and" (.). Necessary condition for such a proposition is the truth of all its parts. Hence, if (p . q) is true, then p is true and q is true.

Therefore, inference from the whole copulative proposition to each part is valid, but not vice versa. Hence:

$$(p \cdot q) \int p \quad \text{or} \quad (p \cdot q) \int q$$

The inverse inference from the part to the whole is incorrect. If one part of a copulative proposition is false the entire proposition is false. In other words (though it is not expressly stated in any of the pertinent texts of Ockham, but clearly hinted at) the falsity of one part is sufficient condition for the falsity of the whole proposition. Hence a copulative proposition is false, if either

$$- p \int - (p. q)$$
or: $\quad - q \int - (p . q)$

From this, the famous so-called De Morgan Law is immediately deduced by Ockham: *The contradictory opposite of a copulative proposition is an affirmative disjunctive proposition in which both parts of the former are denied.* Hence we have the equivalence:

$$- (p . q) \equiv (- p \text{ v} - q)$$

S2 has nothing that is not in S1, but since S2 is not edited, the text of S2 (fol. 142 vb) we shall here present as proof of this:

> Copulativa est, quae componitur ex duabus categoricis mediante coniunctione copulativa, ut: 'Sortes currit et Plato disputat.' Et ad veritatem ipsius requiritur, quod quaelibet pars eius categorica sit vera. Sic ad veritatem ipsius: 'Sortes currit et Plato disputat,' requiritur, quod haec sit vera: 'Sortes currit,' et similiter ista: 'Plato disputat.' Unde, si aliqua pars est vera et alia sit falsa, tota copulativa est falsa. Et ideo contradictoria copulativae est disiunctiva composita ex contradictoriis partium copulativae seu aequipollens tali disiunctivae. Unde ista: 'Non: Sortes disputat et Plato currit,' aequipollet isti: 'Sortes non disputat vel Plato non currit.' A copulativa ad utramque partem divisim est bona consequentia, sed non econverso. Sequitur enim: 'Sortes est albus et musicus, ergo Sortes est albus,' et similiter: 'ergo Sortes est musicus.' Sed a parte copulativae ad totam copulativam non valet consequentia, quia non sequitur: 'Sortes non currit, ergo Sortes non currit et Plato non disputat.'

A disjunctive proposition is composed of at least two categorical propositions linked up by the statement-connective "or" (v). Sufficient condition for its truth is the truth of at least one part. Hence, either part infers the whole proposition. Therefore, it follows:

$$p \int (p \text{ v } q) \text{ and } q \int (p \text{ v } q)$$

The opposite inference, *viz.*, from the whole to its parts, is not valid.

It is to be noted that S2 has here a definitely better wording than S1. While S2 says that the truth of at least one part is a sufficient condition (and this made our symbolization easier), S1 says that it is a necessary condition (requiritur) which is at least not as elegant an expression as that in S2. We would then have to say: If (p v q) is true, then at least one of the two parts is true. It is to be noted, furthermore, that in all these texts only the inclusive disjunction, or "alternation", is considered; the exclusive meaning is not even mentioned. For that reason the so-called De Morgan Law can be formulated: The contradiction of a disjunctive proposition is a copulative proposition in which both parts are denied:

$$- (p \lor q) \equiv (- p . - q)$$

The text of S2 reads (fol. 243 ra)

Disiunctiva est, quae componitur ex pluribus categoricis mediante coniunctione disiunctiva, ut: 'Sortes est homo vel Plato currit.' Ad veritatem disiunctivae sufficit, quod altera pars sit vera. Et ideo ab altera parte disiunctivae ad totam disiunctivam est consequentia bona, sed non econverso. Sequitur enim: 'Sortes currit, ergo Sortes currit vel disputat,' sed non econverso. Et propter hoc contradictoria disiunctivae est copulativa composita ex contradictoriis partium disiunctivae, seu aequipollens ei. Unde ista: 'Non: Sortes currit vel disputat,' aequivalet isti: 'Sortes non currit et Sortes non disputat.'

Still more important as an introduction to our problem can be a discussion of the causal proposition. A causal proposition is composed of at least two categorical propositions linked up by the statement-connective "because" or its equivalents. The necessary condition for the truth of a causal proposition is that both parts are true, and, furthermore, that it is true that the one contains the reason for the truth of the other. Hence, not only consistency is required, but in addition, it is required that the cause of the truth of the first is the cause of the truth of the second proposition. Hence in a causal proposition the inference from the two parts in conjunction to the whole causal proposition is not valid. Therefore if we symbolize the causal relation or statement-connective with "Ca" (p . q) $\int$ (p Ca q) is not valid.

However the inverse inference is valid:

(p Ca q) $\int$ p (and also (p $\int$ q) and also q)

For this reason the denial of a causal proposition is equivalent to a disjunctive proposition in which each part is denied, hence, we have the equivalence:

$$ - (p \ Ca \ q) \equiv [- p \ v - q \ v - (p \int q)] $$

This is what is expressed by both texts of S1 and S2; we present here the wording of the latter (fol. 143 rb).

> Causalis est, quae componitur ex pluribus categoricis mediante hac coniunctione 'quia' vel aequivalenti seu consimili, ut: 'Sortes irascitur, quia Plato iniuriatus est ei.' Et ad veritatem causalis requiritur veritas cuiuslibet partis et quod una importet causam vel occasionem alicuius importati per reliquam. Et ideo causalis infert utramque partem, sed ambae partes non inferunt eam; non enim sequitur: 'Sortes currit, Plato disputat, ergo Sortes currit, quia Plato disputat,' sed econverso bene sequitur. Contradictoria causalis est disiuntiva composita ex contradictoriis partium causalis et una tertia, qua denotatur, quod non est vera; ut contradictio istius: 'Petrus dormit, quia Plato currit,' aequivalet isti: Petrus non dormit vel (*ms.* et) Plato non currit' vel haec non est vera: 'Petrus dormit, propter hoc quod Plato currit.'

Since we believe that a certain significance should be attached to this relation of "causality", because it seems to include the idea of strict implication, we now will make additional clarification after S1, which goes into more detail. First we have to ask, what is meant by "cause"? S1 explains: Cause is taken here not in a strict, but in a large sense, that means, it is not required that by positing one proposition another proposition is also posited or brought to existence, but it is sufficient that one proposition expresses the reason for the truth of the other proposition, or it is required that one proposition is logically prior to the other, and hence the one is deducible from the other.[2]

In our opinion a causal proposition is the combination of a copulative proposition with a *natural* consequence composed of the prop-

---

[2] Et est sciendum, quod hic accipitur causa large et non stricte; non enim requiritur ad veritatem causalis, quod una propositio sit causa, quare alia ponitur in esse, sed sufficit, quod exprimat causam requisitam ad hoc quod alia propositio sit vera..., vel requiritur, quod propositio illa sit prior alia, ita quod praedicatum antecedentis prius praedicetur... S. L. II, c. 33 [ed. Boehner c. 34, II 318].

ositions of the copulative proposition, as we have explained and symbolized before. By natural consequence, we mean a consequence in which the truth of one proposition depends on the truth of another proposition either because of physical or logical causality. If there is logical causality, the consequent is deducible from the antecedent because of a class-inclusion. The scholastics simply say, a natural consequence holds in virtue of an intrinsic means. This will be explained later.

After these clarifications we now can approach a careful study of the conditional proposition. Here we have at our disposal reasonably long texts of all three *Summae*. Before discussing them we shall present them in parallel columns.

S1	S2	S3
II. Pars, c. 30	f. 242 vb	f. 231 v
. . . Sed quia conditionalis aequivalet uni consequentiae, ita quod tunc conditionalis est vera, quando antecedens infert consequens, et non aliter, ideo differatur usque ad tractatum de consequentiis. Hoc tamen sciendum, quod illa hypothetica dicitur conditionalis, quae componitur ex duabus categoricis coniunctis mediante hac coniunctione "si" vel aequivalenti ei. Propter istud ultimum est dicendum, quod ista est conditionalis: 'Sortes non legit, nisi sit magister', quia aequivalet isti: 'Si Sortes non est magister, Sortes non legit'. Et universaliter,	Conditionalis est, quando ponitur haec **coniunctio "si", et sem**per aequivalet consequentiae. Et ideo, sicut consequentia potest esse bona, quamvis neutra propositionum sit vera, et quamvis antecedens sit falsum et consequens verum, sed numquam est bona, si antecedens sit verum et consequens falsum, sic propositio hypothetica conditionalis potest esse vera, licet neutra categoricarum, ex quibus componitur, sit vera, et licet prima sit falsa et secunda vera (*ms.:* prima sit vera et secunda falsa!), sed non, si prima sit vera et secunda falsa; haec enim est vera:	Conditionalis componitur ex pluribus categoricis per hanc **coniunctionem "si"**. Sicut ista: 'Si homo est animal, homo est corpus.' Ad cuius veritatem veritas neutrius partis (*ms.:* neutra pars veritatis) requiritur. Haec enim est vera: 'Si homo est asinus, homo est rudibilis' (*ms:* rationalis), et tamen neutra pars est vera. Et sic conditionalis verae quandoque neutra pars est vera, quandoque altera tantum; sed si altera tantummodo est vera, oportet, quod illa sit consequens; quia quandocumque antecedens est vera, oportet quod consequens sit vera, quia in

quando duae proposi-
tiones coniunguntur
mediante coniunctione
aliqua, et totum aequi-
valet uni conditionali,
illa propositio dicetur
hypothetica et condi-
tionalis.

Est etiam sciendum,
quod ad veritatem con-
ditionalis nec requiri-
tur veritas anteceden-
tis nec veritas conse-
quentis, immo est ali-
quando conditionalis
necessaria et quaelibet
pars eius est impossi-
bilis, sicut hic: 'Si
Sortes   est   asinus,
Sortes est rudibilis.'

'Si asinus est homo,
asinus est risibilis,' et
tamen neutra pars est
vera. Haec similiter est
vera: 'Si omne animal
est risibile, omnis ho-
mo est risibilis' et ta-
men prima est falsa et
secunda vera. Sed ista
est falsa: 'Si omnis ho-
mo est risibilis, omne
animal est risibile;' prima est vera et secunda
falsa.

nulla conditionali vera
est possibile, quod an-
tecedens sit verum et
consequens sit falsum.
Omnis enim conditio-
nalis est vera, in qua
antecedens non potest
esse verum sine conse-
quente.

According to S1 "conditional proposition" and *"consequentia"* are equivalent terms, hence they can be interchanged. Let us immediately add that S2 also expressly states the interchangeability of these terms, whilst S3, which in general has a much shorter text, omits it. Hence, we can follow the rule that whatever holds of a conditional proposition holds also for a *consequentia* and vice versa. We shall make use of this equivalence.

S1 states that a conditional proposition or a *consequentia* is true *when* the antecedent infers the consequent. This expression "infert" is found only in the text of S1. It is to be noted that the inference of the consequent from the antecedent is not introduced as a condition but only in a temporal proposition. More important is to find out, what is meant by *"infert"*. Since it is not explicitly stated, we must determine its meaning by the remarks which are added later, at the end of this passage. For there again it is stated, now in a more exact logical form, though negatively, that the necessary condition for the truth of a conditional proposition is neither the truth of the antecedent, nor the truth of the consequent. Hence the following inferences are false:

$$(p \int q) \int p \text{ and}: (p \int q) \int q$$

On the contrary sometimes when the antecedent is false and the consequent is false, or even impossible, the *consequentia* is necessary. An instance for that is given: "If Socrates is a donkey, then Socrates is not capable of education". Since we are not interested right here in the modalities, and since they do not expressly enter the instance, we have the true conditional proposition:

$p \int q$, where both components are false, or
$$(- p \cdot q) \int (p \int q)$$

Let us gather our results in the form of a matrix which will serve as a definition of the conditional proposition. Four combinations as to the truth and falsity of the two propositions are possible, *viz.*, that the antecedent and consequent are both true or false, or that the antecedent is true and the consequent is false or vice versa. If T indicates the truth, F the falsity we have the following results so far obtained:

	p	q	$p \int q$
1.	T	T	T
2.	F	T	
3.	T	F	
4.	F	F	T

If someone should object that we have immediately treated the truth or falsity of conditional propositions as a truth-function, that is, regardless of any other relation between the propositions, — of the kind, for instance, that we introduced into the causal propositions, — we have to answer that Ockham himself does not give, or treat of, any other relation than a truth-function.

Thus far, we have expressly stated by Ockham case (1) and (4) where a conditional proposition is true. What about the other cases? We have to substitute here one of the consequential rules, to which, however, Ockham expressly refers, in order to determine whether the other cases are true or false. According to Ockham the first rule of the *consequentiae* reads:

Ex vero numquam sequitur falsum; et ideo quandocumque antecedens est verum et consequens est falsum, consequentia non valet.

S1 III, III. c. 27.

Thus, we are able to determine case (3) as being a false conditional
proposition. This we can express in the following form as a thesis:

$$(p \cdot - q) \int - (p \int q)$$

Since it was stated in our text on conditional propositions that
neither the truth of the antecedent nor the truth of the consequent
is required for the truth of a conditional proposition, and, furthermore, the case of the antecedent being true and the consequent being
false is qualified as false, it remains that the other case (the antecedent
being false and the consequent being true) is admitted as true.
However, for that we can also rely on the consequential rule: *Ex
falso potest sequi verum (loc. cit.).* Hence, case (2) is expressly admitted as yielding a true condition. Thus we arrive at a complete
matrix for the truth or falsity of a conditional proposition:

	p	q	p $\int$ q
1.	T	T	T
2.	F	T	T
3.	T	F	F
4.	F	F	T

Now this is the definition of material implication as well. For
only material implication is defined as a truth-function in this manner.
And, as we have seen, Ockham uses only truth-function in order to
ascertain the value of a conditional proposition. He does not make
use of any inner connection between the propositions as he explicitly
did in the case of the causal proposition. For this reason strict implication, which requires by definition more than a truth-function
for the determination of its value, cannot be defined by a truth table
on the basis of only truth-function. The point we are making here is
not that the matrix offered above does not apply to strict implication
at all, for even in strict implication from an impossibility anything
follows; but, that neither modern logicians for material implication,

nor Ockham for the truth-value of a conditional, make use of any other relation but truth-functions. This is, in our opinion, a sufficient proof for the statement that he not only knows, but makes use of material implication. The fact that most of the conditional rules or *consequentiae* are also strict implication, results simply from the fact that every strict implication is also a material implication, but not vice versa.

When we now go on to S3 — which according to our investigations has been written after S1 and before S2 — we find that it is in perfect agreement with S1; it even seems to lead definitely further. Only truth-functions are mentioned. It clearly admits the following cases:

1. If p is false and q is false, then (p ʃ q) is true
2. If p is false and q is true, then (p ʃ q) is true
3. If p is true and q is true, then (p ʃ q) is true
4. If p is true and q is false, then (p ʃ q) is false

No modalities are introduced either. The impossibility of the truth of the consequent, when the antecedent is true, is only the impossibility which results from the definition of a conditional proposition; it is not an impossibility which is based on the relation between the propositions, as the context clearly proves. For it is said: "... in no true conditional proposition is it possible that the antecedent be true and the consequent be false. For every conditional is true in which the antecedent cannot be true without the consequent (being true)." In other words, if there is a true conditional (p ʃ q), and p is true, then it is impossible, because it is a contradiction that q be false. This is in perfect harmony with material implication; though of course, it holds in strict implication as well.

However, we believe that we can still go a step further. We read the quite elegant formulation: "But if one part only is true, it must be the consequent." This in our opinion expresses very nicely the basic definition of material implication as offered by modern logicians. For if we assume that one proposition is true and only one, then it must be the consequent. Hence, if we assume that q is true, it follows:

$$p \, \int \, (\leftarrow p \, \int \, q)$$

22*

This according to our author is true in any case, even if q were false also. And furthermore, if we assume that p only is true, then it follows.

$$p \int (q \int p)$$

But again according to our author this is true, even if q were true also. Now these two formulas are exactly the definition of material implication according to modern logicians. For they state that a true proposition is inferred by any proposition, be it true or false. Since our author omits modal relation we do not see any objection against this interpretation.

S2 in our opinion gives, perhaps, the clearest presentation of material implication which we can expect. The text is rather remarkable and deserves to be literally translated:

And therefore, as a *consequentia* can be valid, though neither one of the propositions be true, and although the antecedent is false and the consequent is true, but is never valid, if the antecedent is true and the consequent is false; so likewise a hypothetical conditional proposition can be true, though neither one of the categorical propositions of which it is composed is true, and though the first is false and the second is true, but not, if the first is true and the second is false.

There is hardly any need to go into a discussion of this text. All possible cases of a matrix are enumerated and evaluated. No modalities enter the explanation. The implication is clearly conceived as a truth-function. However, what is really striking is that we find here, instead of antecedent and consequent, the expression "the first" and "the second", which definitely reminds us of the Stoics. The examples which are given, however, hold in strict implication as well. We do not, however, consider this an instance against our interpretation. The reason for that will be given later when we deal with consequential rules in S2. Here we only want to add a few historical notes which will illustrate or even justify this interpretation.

Boethius[3] makes a distinction between a natural *(secundum naturam)*, and an accidental *(secundum accidens)* conditional proposition. The interesting text reads as follows:

---

[3] *De Syllogismis hypotheticis*, PL 64, 825 B.

Sed quoniam dictum est idem significari 'si' conjunctione et 'cum', quando in hypotheticis propositionibus ponitur, duobus modis conditionales fieri possunt: uno secundum accidens, altero, ut habeant aliquam naturae consequentiam. Secundum accidens hoc modo, ut cum dicimus: Cum ignis calidus sit, caelum rotundum est. Non enim quia ignis calidus est, coelum rotundum est, sed id haec propositio designat, quia quo tempore ignis calidus est, eodem tempore coelum quoque rotundum est. Sunt autem aliae quae habent ad se consequentiam naturae. . . .

From this we gather that he expressly admits the truth of a conditional proposition in which there is no inner connection between the propositions.[4]

There can be no doubt that most of the logicians we have consulted, except William Shyrswood,[5] expressly demanded an inner connection between the antecedent and the consequent. Petrus Hispanus, for instance, writes:

Ad veritatem conditionalis exigitur, quod antecedens non possit esse verum sine consequente, ut: Si homo est, animal est; unde omnis conditionalis vera est necessaria, et omnis conditionalis falsa est impossibilis. Ad falsitatem eius sufficit, quod antecedens possit esse vera sine consequente, ut: Si homo est, album est.[6]

In the *Ars brevis* of Raymundus Lullus, written in 1308, the truth of a conditional proposition is defined as follows:

Ad veritatem conditionalis requiritur quod antecedens nequeat stare sine consequente, ut: Tu es homo, ergo tu es ens. Ad cuius cognitionem habendam considerctur, si oppositum consequentis repugnat antecedenti. Ad falsitatem vero requiritur, quod antecedens possit stare sine conse-

---

[4] It seems that this distinction is, though not exactly in the sense Boethius understood it, still found in the distinction between a *consequentia naturalis* and *accidentalis*. We read in Burleigh's still unedited *De puritate artis logicae* (tr. 2, in the beginning): Consequentia simplex est duplex, quaedam naturalis, et est quando antecedens includit consequens, et talis consequentia tenet per locum intrinsecum. Consequentia accidentalis est, quae tenet per locum extrinsecum, et est quando antecedens non includit consequens, sed tenet per quandam regulam extrinsecam [Ed. Boehner 61].

[5] Cf. *Introductiones in Logicam* (München, 1937), p. 37.

[6] *Summulae logicales*, ed Bochenski, 1. 23; p. 8. This is even more strongly expressed in the *Summa Logicae* falsely ascribed to St. Thomas, tr. 7, c. 14.

quente, quod etiam poterit videri, considerando quod oppositum consequentis non repugnat antecedenti, etc.[7]

Hence, the mode of impossibi!ity, or necessity, is introduced into
the determination of the truth or falsity of a conditional proposition
as is done by Petrus Hispanus. The relation between the antecedent
and the consequent, that is their compossibility, is expressed in a
slightly different way in the texts of Peter of Spain and Raymundus
Lullus. For the truth of a conditional proposition, both give the same
necessary reason, *viz.* the impossibility that the antecedent be true
and the consequent false. Hence we have the symbolization

$$(p \int q) \int Imp (p . - q)$$

This is definitely strict implication.

For the falsity of a conditional, it is sufficient reason, according
to Peter of Spain, and necessary reason according to Raymund, that
the antecedent can be true without the consequent. Hence, Peter
would symbolize:

$$Poss (p . - q) \int - (p F q)$$

Raymund would symbolize:

$$- (p \int q) \int Poss (p . - q)$$

In our opinion either one expresses strict implication. It is interesting to note that Buridan in his *Tractatus Summularum*, which is a
revision of Peter's text, follows Peter exactly in the qualification of
the truth of a conditional proposition, but follows Raymundus in
the qualification of the falsity of such propositions.[8]

---

[7] Ed. Argentinae, 1599, p. 159.

[8] "Ad veritatem conditionalis requiritur quod antecedens non possit
esse verum sine consequente. Unde omnis conditionalis vera est necessaria;
est enim necessaria consequentia. Et falsa est impossibilis. Ad falsitatem
conditionalis requiritur quod antecedens possit esse verum sine consequente, ut: Si Sortes est, Sortes est albus . . ." Dorp in his commentary,
however, restores a "sufficit" into the qualification and makes a false
conditional proposition *equivalent* with a modal proposition expressing
that it is *possible* that the antecedent be true and the consequent be false.
(ed. Janonus Carcanus, 1499.)

Now we are in position to make a clear distinction between strict and material implication. It is obvious according to the aforesaid that in any implication, material or strict, the following thesis is valid:

$$(p \int q) \int - (p . - q)$$

Hence, we can write this also as strict implication and as material implication:

$$(p \int^* q) \int - (p . - q)$$
$$(p \int' q) \int - (p . - q)$$

Furthermore, according to the aforementioned equivalence, it also follows in both kinds of implications:

$$(p \int q) \int (- p \vee q)$$

However the inverse relation is not valid in strict implication, but only in material implication. Hence the following expressions are false in strict implication:

$$- (p . - q) \int (p \int^* q)$$
$$(- p \vee q) \int (p \int^* q)$$

On the contrary, these implications are valid in material implication. Hence, if we succeed in finding either:

$$- (p . - q) \int (p \int q)$$

as being asserted, or:

$$(- p \vee q) \int (p \int q)$$

we can immediately also maintain that he who asserts these inferences (which are then equivalences) knows of material implication. With this in mind we will now proceed to a discussion of the *consequentiae*.

II. DIVISION OF *Consequentiae*

Let us now turn to a discussion of the division of *consequentiae*. The divisions offered by Ockham are commonly accepted by the medieval logicians, at least of the 14th century, though not always

exactly in the same meaning. It is well to keep in mind that, as
Ockham does not fail to say, the various distinctions are not mutually
exclusive. They may, and in fact, do overlap.

Since we want to compare also the treatment of these distinctions in the three *Summae*, we shall first communicate their texts
in parallel columns and then discuss them.

1. *Absolute and factual consequentia (simplex et ut nunc)*

S1 III, III, cap. I	S2 f. 157rb	S3 f. 236v
Consequentia quaedam est ut nunc, quaedam simplex. Consequentia ut nunc est, quando antecedens pro aliquo tempore potest esse verum sine consequente, sed non pro isto tempore. Sicut ista consequentia est ut nunc solum: Omne animal currit, igitur Sortes currit, quia pro illo tempore, pro quo Sortes est animal, non potest antecedens esse verum sine consequente. Et tamen pro aliquo tempore poterit antecedens esse verum sine consequente, quia quando Sortes erit mortuus, poterit antecedens esse verum consequente existente falso. Consequentia simplex est, quando pro nullo tempore poterit antecedens esse verum sine consequente. Sicut	Est enim consequentia quaedam ut nunc et quaedam simplex. Consequentia simplex vocatur, quae omni tempore et in omni casu tenet, si formetur, dummodo termini non cessent significare nec mutent significationes suas. Sic syllogismi, conversiones, inductiones et plura alia argumenta sunt consequentiae simplices, si vocantur consequentiae. Consequentia ut nunc vocatur, quae tenet pro aliquo determinato tempore, ita quod pro isto tempore antecedens non potest esse verum sine consequente. Dicentes enim consequentiam aliquam esse bonam ut nunc, non intendunt aliud dicere, nisi quod antecedens non potest esse verum sine consequente, quamdiu	Consequentiarum quaedam est ut nunc, quaedam simplex. Consequentia ut nunc est illa, quae non tenet omni tempore [sed tantum] determinato. Sicut ista: Omnis homo est animal, ergo Jacobus est animal. Ista non tenet omni tempore, sed solummodo, quamdiu Jacobus vivit et est homo. Et talis consequentia communiter per medium intrinsecum tenet formatum de eisdem terminis, quod est contingens; sicut praedicta consequentia tenet per hoc medium: Jacobus est homo. Consequentia simplex vocatur, quae omni tempore tenet, sicut (*ms.* et) talis est simplex: Omnis homo est coloratus, ergo aliquod animal est coloratum;

ista consequentia est simplex: Nullum animal currit, igitur nullus homo currit; quia numquam poterit haec esse vera: Nullum animal currit, nisi ista sit vera: Nullus homo currit, si formetur.

aliqua res aliquo determinato modo est vel se habet. Sicut quando dicunt istam consequentiam: Omnis homo currit, ergo Sortes currit, esse bonam ut nunc, non intendunt dicere, nisi quod, quamdiu Sortes est in rerum natura, sicut nunc [est], est impossibile hanc esse veram: Omnis homo currit, nisi haec sit vera: Sortes currit. Voces autem sunt ad placitum; ergo . . .

et tenet communiter talis consequentia per medium necessarium extrinsecum (*ms.* intrinsecum) non formatum cum eisdem terminis; sicut praedicta consequentia tenet per hanc regulam: Ab inferiori ad suum superius non distributum sed particulariter sumptum est bona consequentia.

As far as we see all three texts are in substantial agreement. They state that an absolute *(simplex) consequentia* and a factual *(ut nunc) consequentia* are distinguished by this that the former is always true regardless of the time when it is formulated—in the past, the present or the future—but that a factual *consequentia* is valid only at a certain time. According to Ockham "always true" is the mode of necessity, "always false" is the mode of impossibility. Hence, we can symbolize such an absolute *consequentia* thus:

$$(p \int q) \int Imp \, (p \, . - q)$$

In other words, if $(p \int q)$ is an absolute *consequentia* then $(p \, . - q)$ is always false. A factual consequence, however, does not require that the antecedent and the denial of the consequent are always false. On the contrary, it is expressly stated that they are, or that they can be, true together. Only at a certain time are they false. Hence, we cannot qualify, in a factual *consequentia*, the *consequentia* as such as necessary, or its denial as impossible. An impossibility is given only if and under the condition that the antecedent be true. Now in virtue of the definition of the truth of a conditional proposition, when the antecedent is true, then the consequent must be true also; it is impossible that, if the antecedent is true, the consequent can be false. This we would like to express in the following definition of the factual *consequentia:*

$$\text{Imp } [(p \int q) \int (p \cdot - q)]$$

However, this is true of material implication as well. For according to material implication, it is this case that according to definition is always false, hence impossible.

We conclude, therefore, that the modality invested into the formulation of factual *consequentia* does not argue for strict implication. This as also confirmed by the example given: "Every animal is running, therefore Socrates is running." For by no logical method is it possible to deduce the consequent: "Socrates is running," from the antecedent: "Every animal is running." Furthermore, the denial of the consequent is quite consistent with the affirmation of the antecedent except at the time *when* Socrates exists. However, we agree that there is a certain connection between the consequent and the antecedent in our example. This could be misleading. Whilst S1 in its formulation is non-committal, S3 states that "commonly" such a factual *consequentia* holds in virtue of an intrinsic means, in other words, that a factual *consequentia* is "commonly" an *enthymema*. This would almost efface the distinction between an absolute and factual consequence. S2, however, purposely, as it seems, avoids the reduction of a factual consequence to an *enthymema*, and thereby to a syllogism, for in the example given it does not add, as could have easily been done, the missing premiss. On the contrary, it only adds a new proposition which is a necessary reason for the truth of the consequent. But even if all these propositions are given: "Every man is running," and: "Socrates exists," logically it does not follow: "If every man is running, then Socrates is running." We still need the premiss: "Socrates is a man." However, we hope to give further corroboration to our interpretation when we come to formal and material *consequentia*.

2. *Consequentia that holds by an intrinsic or an extrinsic means*

Since S3 has no special distinction of this kind, though it mentioned it in the previous text, we shall present here only the texts of S1 and S2.

S1

III, III, cap. I

Alia distinctio est, quod aliquando tenet per medium extrinsecum, aliquando per medium intrinsecum. Illa consequentia tenet per medium intrinsecum, quando tenet per aliquam propositionem formatam ex eisdem terminis. Sicut ista: Sortes non currit, igitur homo non currit, tenet virtute illius medii: Sortes est homo. Unde nisi haec esset vera; Sortes est homo, non valeret consequentia.

Consequentia autem, quae tenet per medium extrinsecum est, quando tenet per aliquam regulam generalem, quae non plus respicit illos terminos quam alios. Sicut ista consequentia: Tantum homo est asinus, igitur omnis asinus est homo, non tenet per aliquam propositionem formatam ex istis terminis "homo" et "asinus", sed per istam regulam: Exclusiva et universalis de terminis transpositis idem significant et convertuntur. Et per talia media tenent omnes syllogismi.

Et si dicatur contra istam distinctionem, quod ista consequentia: Sortes non currit, igitur homo non currit, tenet per istud medium extrinsecum: A singu-

S3

(Vide supra)

S2

f. 157va

Rursus, quaedam consequentiae tenent per medium intrinsecum, scilicet per unam propositionem formatam ex terminis ipsius consequentiae. Sicut ista consequentia: [Sortes currit, ergo] homo currit, tenet virtute istius propositionis: Sortes est homo, et illud (*ms.* aliud) non vocatur regula.

Quaedam autem tenent per medium extrinsecum, scilicet per regulam, quae non componitur ex terminis ipsius consequentiae. Sicut ista: Tantum homo currit, ergo omne currens est homo, tenet per istam regulam: Ab exclusiva ad universalem de terminis transpositis est consequentia bona. Primae consequentiae possunt [esse] ut nunc, eo quod medium potest esse verum ut nunc et non semper est necessarium; secundae consequentiae sunt simplices, quia regulae, per quas tenet, sunt necessariae.

lari ad indefinitam post-
posita negatione est bona
consequentia, quod est medium extrinsecum. — Di-
cendum est, quod tenet per
illud medium mediate et
quasi remote et insuffici-
enter, quia praeter istam
regulam generalem requi-
ritur plus, scilicet quod
Sortes sit homo. Et ideo
magis immediate et magis
sufficienter tenet per illud
medium: Sortes est homo.

The distinction between these two kinds of *consequentiae* is made sufficiently clear by the texts. We may summarize it briefly. A *consequentia* holding in virtue of an extrinsic means is that which holds in virtue of a logical rule. Without going into the thorny question, how far the scholastics were aware of the distinction between logical rule and logical thesis, let us but make explicit here that what they call rules of *consequentiae* seem to be logical rules in the modern sense as well. For a logical rule does not contain the terms of the thesis and cannot be converted into a thesis by substituting appropriate terms; a logical rule governs a logical thesis or a *consequentia;* it tells us that, if certain conditions are fulfilled, the thesis can be asserted. Both texts give practically the same instance of such an extrinsic means or rule. There is a good *consequentia* (or even an equivalence according to S1) from an exclusive universal proposition to a universal proposition in which the terms of the former are interchanged. Hence the *consequentia:* "Only man is running, therefore everything that is running is a man," is valid. It is obvious that such *consequentiae* holding in virtue of an extrinsic means are absolute *consequentiae*, and hence necessary, since they are always true. For it follows, if $(p \int q)$ is a *consequentia* holding in virtue of an extrinsic means, then it is necessary that $(p \int q)$.

A *consequentia* holding in virtue of an intrinsic means is always an *enthymema*, for intrinsic means is the same as a proposition which is composed of a term of the antecedent and the consequent. Hence, if we would add such a proposition, we would obtain a true syllogism. The instances in both S1 and S2 are obvious. However, as soon as such *consequentiae* are converted into syllogisms, they definitely cease to be factual *consequentiae*, for they become absolute *consequentiae*. Now, S2 expressly states (this is not in S1 which is non-committal) that such *consequentiae* holding by an intrinsic means can be factual *consequentiae*. If we will not risk to incur a contradiction, we have to say that the "intrinsic means," or the additional proposition, is not considered to be a premiss in the *consequentia*. Hence, we cannot and must not understand such a *consequentia* so that the intrinsic means enters the *consequentia*. For then they would become absolute consequences.

3. *Formal and material consequentiae*

We first shall present the texts of the three *Summae:*

S1 III, III, cap. I	S2 f. 157 rb	S3 f. 236 v
Alia distinctio est ista, quod consequentiarum quaedam est materialis et quaedam formalis. Consequentia formalis est duplex, quia quaedam tenet per medium extrinsecum, quod respicit formam propositionum, sicut sunt tales regulae: Ab exclusiva ad universalem de terminis transpositis est bona consequentia. Ex maiori de necessario et minori de inesse sequitur conclusio de necessario, et huiusmodi. Quaedam tenet per	Item consequentiarum quaedam vocatur formalis, quae tenet ratione formae propositionum, ita quod tenet, quandocumque talis modus arguendi servatur. Sicut: Ab inferiori ad superius sine distributione est consequentia bona; sequitur enim: Sortes currit, ergo homo currit. Et potest esse consequentia ut nunc. Et ita non omnis consequentia formalis est consequentia simplex.	Consequentia autem dividitur, quia quaedam vocatur formalis, et est illa, quae tenet ratione formae propositionum in materia omni, ubi est syllogisticus modus arguendi; sic syllogismus et inductio, conversio et multi alii modi arguendi (*ms.* ordinandi?) sunt consequentiae formales.

medium intrinsecum immediate et mediate per medium extrinsecum respiciens generales conditiones propositionum, non veritatem vel falsitatem, nec necessitatem vel impossibilitatem, cuiusmodi est ista: Sortes non currit, igitur homo non currit.

Consequentia materialis dicitur, quando tenet praecise ratione terminorum et non ratione alicuius medii extrinseci respicientis praecise generales conditiones pro positionum, cuiusmodi sunt tales: Si homo currit, Deus est; Homo est asinus, igitur Deus non est, et huiusmodi.

Consequentia materialis est, quae non tenet virtute modi arguendi, sed gratia terminorum, ex quibus componitur. Sicut sequitur: Animal disputat, ergo homo disputat, non quia a superiori ad inferius sit consequentia bona, sed quia istud praedicatum "disputare" non potest competere alicui animali nisi homini; et potest talis consequentia esse simplex, sicut in proposito.

Consequentia materialis vocatur illa, quae tenet solummodo gratia terminorum ibidem positorum, et in aliis terminis non tenet talis modus arguendi.

This distinction should give us definite information about the problem, whether Ockham knew of material implication, or not. Yet, we have to be cautious. Let us not make the mistake of hastily identifying material *consequentia* with material implication. This will become clear through our discussion of the text. We may start with S1.

A formal *consequentia* is said to be that which holds in virtue of an extrinsic means, either immediately or mediately. Therefore, in any case, it is governed by a logical rule which only concerns the form of the propositions, not their content. By "form" of propositions the scholastics, both the realists and the so-called nominalists, mean the same, namely the structure (or form) of propositions which is given by the syncategorematic terms of propositions and the position of the terms, *viz.* the syncategorematic and categorematic terms as well. Syncategorematic terms are the logical terms in the proper sense, as "every", "some", "not", "if-then", "or", "only" etc. The categorematic terms, as for instance, "man", "stone", "white" etc., belong to the matter of propositions. This distinction between form and matter of propositions corresponds pretty much to the distinction introduced by modern logicians between constants (syncategorematic terms) and variables (categorematic terms). In the following proposition, the italicized parts belong to the form (including also the position of the terms), the others to the matter: "*Tantum* homo *est* animal, *ergo omne* animal *est* homo."

It is obvious that a formal *consequentia* which is governed *only* by an extrinsic means is in any case an absolute *consequentia*. And hence, we can always add the mode of necessity. It is likewise obvious that in the case that also an intrinsic means governs such a *consequentia*, it can still be an absolute *consequentia*. The instance given is quite to the point: Socrates is running, therefore a man is running. For we can formulate it as follows:

$$(p \int q) \int \text{Imp} \ (p \ . \ - \ q)$$

The intrinsic means "Socrates is a man" makes the impossibility based on class inclusion and on the expository syllogism *only* explicit. But it is not said by S1 that it must always be an absolute *consequentia*. The question whether it must be an absolute *consequentia* has to be left open.

There is, however, an interesting addition of great importance which further explains what is meant in our case by an extrinsic means. Let us present this text first in translation:

> Some *consequentia* holds in virtue of an intrinsic means immediately, and mediately in virtue of an extrinsic means which concerns the general conditions of propositions, not their truth or falsity, nor their necessity or impossibility.[9]

---

[9] Many manuscripts, approximately half of the 30 examined by us, read here *propositionis* instead of *propositionum;* however, their number

According to this text a formal consequence holding in virtue of an extrinsic means does not hold because of the truth or falsity, or the necessitiy or impossibility, of the parts of the *consequentia*, that is of the propositions. Hence truth functions are expressly excluded, and also the stronger truth function of necessity or its opposite. Here, it is sufficient for us to know that a formal *consequentia* is not based only on the truth function.

In the light of this exclusion we have to read now the qualification of material *consequentia*. We translate:

> A *consequentia* is called material when it holds precisely because of the terms and not because of an extrinsic means concerning precisely the general conditions of propositions; such *(consequentiae)* are the following: If a man is running, God exists; A man is a donkey, therefore God does not exist, and such similar ones.

This text evidently proves that a material *consequentia* is precisely based on truth-functions; however, it is not only based on simple truth-functions, but also on the stronger truth-function of necessity and impossibility. However, it is not said that it must be the stronger truth-function. On the other hand, are we allowed to say that simple truth-functions are sufficient? Unfortunately the two examples given are open to various interpretations. For the first *consequentia* is always true, because the consequent "God exists" is *de facto* always true, though not on purely logical grounds. The second is always true, because the antecedent "Man is a donkey" is *de facto* always false, but again, not on purely logical grounds. From this we may immediately gather that a *consequentia* can, at the same time, be qualified as material and as absolute; hence, these

---

decreases at the following two occurrences in favor of the reading of the better manuscripts, *viz., propositionum.* The following "not" is very crucial for our interpretation. Salamucha, *Die Aussagenlogik bei Wilhelm Ockham*—translated from the Polish by J. Bendiek, O. F. M., in *Franziskanische Studien,* 32 (1950) 108—109, found that of the 9 manuscripts he has examined only three make sense. Of the manuscripts examined by us 9 (and the better ones) have "non", 6 "nec", 12 have "ut" (easily mistaken for "nec"); the edition has "scilicet" and one ms. over an erasure has "vel". The following "nec" is omitted by 21 mss., but is found in at least three mss. which are to be considered the better ones.

two qualifications are compatible. It is obvious that the aforementioned *consequentiae* are not formal. Not only because they are material *consequentiae*, but also, because they do not hold in virtue of an extrinsic means concerning the general conditions of propositions.

However, it could be objected that they are instances of strict implications, and therefore are also formal *consequentiae*, because they hold in virtue of the rule: "From something impossible anything follows," and: "Something necessary follows from anything." Could Ockham have overlooked this? We hardly believe so, or rather, he definitely did not overlook this. For later, in the chapter on the general rules of *consequentiae* (S1, III, III, cap. 37), he expressly states that *consequentiae* governed by these rules are material *consequentiae*, and at that place similar instances are given *(see toward the end)*. However, we admit that this does not yet completely take care of the objection. For a material *consequentia* is not governed by an exterior means, and here we have a "rule" which as such is an exterior means, and governs a material *consequentia*. The obvious answer must be this, that in this case we do not have an exterior means or rule which concerns the *general conditions of the propositions*, but exactly such conditions as truth and falsity, necessity and impossibility, which were excluded from the exterior means. In other words the "rule" under consideration is not a logical rule strictly speaking, since it concerns only factual truth or falsity and factual necessity or impossibility. But factual impossibility is different from logical impossibility.

In order to make this peculiar situation as clear as possible, let us distinguish the following cases:

1. If p is a factually impossible proposition, for instance, "Man is a donkey," then the following will be an absolute material consequence:

$$(p \int q)$$

2. From a contradiction follows, in formal consequence, anything:

$$(p \cdot - p) \int q$$

3. From a proposition, which is qualified as impossible, follows, in formal consequence, anything:

$$\text{Imp } p \int q$$

for a logically expressed impossible proposition is always equivalent to a contradiction.

4. Hence the following will be also a formal *consequentia:*

$$\text{Imp } p \int (p \int q)$$

It is obvious that 2.—4. represent formal *consequentiae* and strict implications. For 2. we have the express statement of other scholastics who not only qualify it as a formal *consequentia* (the classical instance is: Socrates is sitting and Socrates is not sitting, therefore, a stick is in the corner), but even prove it.[10] 3. and 4. also can be shown to be always true simply on the basis of the form of the proposition. This is by no means possible for 1. Only terms themselves, *viz.,* the matter, can decide the truth of it, and nothing else. We have here a material *consequentia* which is absolute.

We are convinced, therefore, that the two instances have to be interpreted as material implications, and hence that we can symbolize the first (A man is running, therefore, God exists) as follows:

$$q \int' (p \int' q)$$

The second (If man is a donkey, then God does not exist) is unfortunately not so clearly to the point, since both propositions are impossible. However, as is indicated by the rule, that from an impossible proposition anything follows, we can symbolize it thus:

$$p \int' (- p \int' q)$$

It is to be emphasized again, that no modalities enter these *consequentiae.*

When we now turn to S3, we do not obtain further information, because of its brevity. S2, however, presents certain difficulties which deserve closer attention.

---

[10] Cf. for instance Albertus de Saxonia, *Perutilis Logica,* tr. IV, cap. 2 (ed. Venetiis, 1518), fol. 24 vb.

S2 defines a formal *consequentia* in a manner similar to S1. It explicitly states that this can be a factual *consequentia* also, yet, without explaining it. This, of course, would be the case, when a formal *consequentia* immediately holds in virtue of an intrinsic means and mediately in virtue of an extrinsic means, or by a logical rule. Besides other things, this text also leaves out the express denial of truth-functions. However, this cannot be construed as an opposition to S1. On the other hand, the qualification of material *consequentia* could appear at first sight different from, or even in opposition to, S1. Nevertheless, we believe that this difference is only apparent, and not a real one. We may even go a step further and maintain that material implication is affirmed. The text in translation reads as follows:

Material *consequentia* is that which does not hold in virtue of the mode of argumentation, but because of the terms of which it is composed. For instance, it follows: "An animal is debating, therefore, a man is debating", not because there is a valid *consequentia* from the logical higher to the logical inferior, but because the predicate "debating", can belong to no other animal but a man. And this *consequentia* can be an absolute one, as it is in our case.

We are not so much interested now in the case which is presented here, for that would lead us only into similar discussions as before. The point to which we would like to call attention is this, that a material *consequentia* can be a factual *consequentia*, since it is stated that it may be an absolute *consequentia* also. Now, a factual material *consequentia* excludes by definition that it is valid by a logical rule and that it *must* always be true. It also does not hold by an intrinsic means, for then it would be a kind of formal *consequentia*. Hence, it can hold only because of the truth or falsity of the consequent and the antecedent.

We believe, therefore, that material implication and material *consequentia* have much in common, and that in any case a material factual *consequentia* is always a material implication. As to material absolute *consequentia*, we leave the question open as to whether it is *always* a material implication.

23*

Thus, we also reach the conclusion that there seems to be no serious difference between the treatment on the *consequentiae* in the three *Summae*. We can safely state, therefore, that in this regard S1, S2 and S3 can have been written by the same author.

III. THE *Consequentiae* RULES

For a final test, let us now at least enumerate the general rules of *consequentiae* as presented by the three tracts and discuss a few of them which may shed further light on our problem. First, we will present the texts in parallel columns. S1 has these rules at the end of the tract on topical rules, S2 and S3 have them at the beginning of this tract.

S1 III, III, cap. 36	S2 fol. 158ra	S3 fol. 237v
Regulae generales sunt multae. [1] Una est, quod ex vero numquam sequitur falsum. Et ideo, quando antecedens est verum et consequens falsum, consequentia non valet. Et haec ratio est sufficiens ad probandum consequentiam non valere. . . . [2] Alia regula est, quod ex falsis potest sequi verum. Et ideo ista consequentia non valet: Antecedens est falsum, igitur consequens est falsum. Sed ista consequentia est bona: Consequens est falsum, igitur et antecedens. . . .	Post hoc ponendae sunt aliquae regulae paucae de multis, quibus consequentiae tenentur, cognoscuntur et probantur, praecipue contra protervos. Et primo magis generales. [I] Est ergo regula talis: Quando aliqua consequentia est bona, quidquid sequitur ad consequens, sequitur ad antecedens. . . . [II] Ex ista regula sequitur alia regula, quod scilicet quidquid antecedit ad antecedens antecedit ad consequens, non tamen eodem modo.	Sunt autem regulae tales, per quas tamquam per media extrinseca quae possunt vocari loci [tenent consequentiae], quarum aliquae sunt magis generales. [a] Quarum una est: Si aliqua consequentia est bona, quidquid sequitur ad consequens, sequitur ad antecedens. Unde, consequentia si est bona: Omnis substantia est ens, ergo omne animal est ens, quidquid sequitur ad ista omne animal est ens. . . . [b] Ex ista regula sequitur alia regula generalis, quae est:

[3] Alia regula est: Si aliqua consequentia sit bona, ex opposito consequentis sequitur oppositum antecedentis. . . .

[4] Alia regula est: Quidquid sequitur ad consequens, sequitur ad antecedens. . . .

[5] Et ex ista regula sequitur alia, scilicet, quidquid antecedit ad antecedens, antecedit ad consequens, quia aliter aliquid sequeretur ad consequens, quod non sequeretur ad antecedens. . . .

[6] Ex istis sequuntur aliae regulae. Una est, quod quidquid stat cum antecedente, stat cum consequente . . .; sed non, quidquid stat cum consequente, stat cum antecedente. . . .

[7] Alia regula est: Quidquid repugnat consequenti, repugnat antecedenti. . . .

[7a] Et ideo tales consequentiae sunt bonae: Oppositum consequentis stat cum antecedente, igitur consequentia non valet Oppositum consequentis non stat cum antecedente, igitur consequentia est bona. Sed sciendum, quod conse-

[III] Sequitur etiam, quod quidquid sequitur ex antecedente et consequente, sequitur ex antecedente per se, sed non eodem modo. . . .

[IV] Sequitur etiam, quod quidquid sequitur ad consequens cum aliqua propositione addita, sequitur ad antecedens cum eadem propositione addita.

[V] Alia regula est: Si ex opposito consequentis sequitur oppositum antecedentis, prima consequentia erat bona. . . .

[Va] *(for syllogism)* Si ex opposito contradictorio consequentis et una parte antecedentis sequitur contradictorium alterius partis, primum argumentum erat bonum.

[VI] Alia regula est, quod quidquid repugnat antecedenti, repugnat consequenti.

[VII] Alia regula est, quod quidquid stat cum antecedente, stat cum consequente.

[VIII] Alia est: Si oppositum consequentis non stat cum antecedente, consequentia erat bona. Et in omni consequentia bona op-

Quando aliqua consequentia est bona, quidquid antecedit ad antecedens, antecedit ad consequens.

[c] Alia est: Si ex opposito consequentis sequitur oppositum antecedentis, prima erit bona.

[c*] Si autem in antecedente sunt plures propositiones categoricae, tunc istae regulae sic sunt intelligendae: Si aliqua consequentia est bona, ex opposito consequentis et una parte antecedentis, sequitur oppositum alterius partis — prima consequentia erat bona. Et istae regulae numquam fallunt. Accipiatur hic oppositum pro contradictorie opposito.

[d] Alia regula est: Quidquid repugnat consequenti, repugnat antecedenti, et non econverso.

[e] Alia est: Quidquid stat cum antecedente stat cum consequente, et non econverso.

[f] Alia est: Si oppositum consequentis non stat cum antecedente, prima consequentia erat bona.

quentia poterit esse bona ut nunc, quamvis ut nunc oppositum consequentis posset stare cum antecedente; sed si oppositum consequentis stet vel possit stare cum antecedente, non poterit esse consequentia simplex.

[8] Alia regula est, quod ex necessario non sequitur contingens.

[9] Alia regula est, quod ex possibili non sequitur impossibile. Istae duae regulae sunt intelligendae de consequentia simplici. Nam ex necessario consequentia simplici numquam sequitur contingens, nec ex possibili impossibile. Tamen consequentia ut nunc bene poterit sequi; sicut sequitur: Omne ens est, igitur omnis homo est, et tamen antecedens est necessarium et consequens contingens. Similiter bene sequitur: Omne coloratum est homo, igitur omnis asinus est homo, et tamen antecedens est possibile et consequens impossibile: et consequentia est bona solum ut nunc. . . .

positum consequentis repugnat antecedenti.

[IX] Alia est, quod quidquid sequitur ex opposito antecedentis sequitur ex opposito consequentis.

[X] Alia est, quod quidquid antecedit ad oppositum consequentis, antecedit ad oppositum antecedentis. ...
Regulae autem falsae sunt tales: Quidquid sequitur ad antecedens, sequitur ad consequens.
Quidquid antecedit ad consequens, antecedit ad antecedens.
Quidquid repugnat consequenti, repugnat antecedenti.
Si aliqua consequentia est bona, ex opposito antecedentis, sequitur oppositum consequentis.
Quidquid stat cum consequente (*ms.* antecedente), stat cum antecedente (*ms.* consequente). Et multae regulae tales.

[g] Alia est: Quando oppositum consequentis non stat cum antecedente, sed ei repugnat, est bona.

[10] Aliae regulae
dantur, quod ex im-
possibili sequitur quod-
libet, et quod neces-
sarium sequitur ad
quodlibet. Et ideo se-
quitur: Tu es asinus,
igitur tu es Deus. Et
sequitur: tu es albus,
igitur Deus est trinus
et unus. Sed tales
consequentiae non sunt
formales nec sunt mul-
tum usitandae.

The first two rules of S1 have no equivalent in S2 or S3. The first
rule states, at least in the tenor of material implication, that sufficient condition for the falsity of a *consequentia* is that the antecedent
be true and the consequent be false. Hence, we can formulate the
following thesis:

$$(p \ . - q) \int - (p \int q)$$

If we combine this rule with the second where it is stated that
from falsity truth may follow, and that, if the consequent is false,
the antecedent must be false also, then we obtain the following thesis:

$$(- p \ . - q) \int (p \int q)$$

where both antecedent and consequent are false. But, we also obtain
the thesis:

$$- p \int (p \int q)$$

in which it is assumed that the antecedent is false, and where it is
irrelevant whether the consequent may be true or false. Furthermore, since a true consequent may follow from an antecedent which
is either true or false, we also obtain the thesis:

$$q \int (p \int q)$$

Now, the last two theses are characteristic of material implication.
However, we have still another clear indication for Ockham's knowledge and use of material implication.

Rule 7a which has its equivalent in VIII (S2) and f (S3) reads in translation:

> Therefore, the following *consequentiae* are valid: The opposite of the consequent is true together with the antecedent, therefore, the *consequentia* does not hold; the opposite of the consequent is not true together with the antecedent, therefore, the *consequentia* may be valid as a factual one, although factually the opposite of the consequent might be true together with the antecedent. But, if the opposite of the consequent should be true, or could be true, together with the antecedent, it cannot be an absolute *consequentia*.

The first part of these rules does not yield anything new. We already formulated the thesis:

$$(p \cdot - q) \int - (p \int q)$$

The second part is of greatest interest. For here, we finally meet with the crucial *consequentia* for which we were looking. For, when the contradictory opposite of the consequent does not stand together, or is not true, together with the antecedent, that is, if the copulative proposition formed by the antecedent and the denial of the consequent is false, then the *consequentia* is valid. Hence, we have the thesis:

$$- (p \cdot - q) \int (p \int q)$$

In fact, if we go a little further and apply Ockham's equivalence between the denial of a copulative proposition and a disjunctive proposition, we obtain the much-used thesis of modern logic:

$$(- p \vee q) \int (p \int q)$$

which is an equivalence, as could easily be proved.

The texts of S2 (VIII) and S3 (f and g) are substantially the same. They are, however, of special interest, since a distinction is made between "*stare cum*" and "*repugnare*". S2 presents first the rule in the milder form of "not being true together" *(stare cum)*, but then, we could say, spoils this clear presentation by adding, that "in every valid *consequentia* the opposite of the consequent is *repugnant* with the antecedent". "*Repugnare*" is stronger than "*stare cum*". S3, however, keeps both terms clearly apart, and has put the stronger expression into a special rule, *viz.* g.

The rest of the *consequentiae*—10 of S1 has been discussed already— is of no particular concern here. The interested reader is referred to Salamucha's article where they are presented in modern symbolization.[11]

Again, we come to the conclusion that it can hardly be denied that Ockham knew of material implication in the modern sense. Furthermore, there is no real contradiction on this point between the three *Summae* of logic which are attributed to Ockham.[12]

20. THE MEDIEVAL CRISIS OF LOGIC AND THE AUTHOR OF THE CENTILOQUIUM ATTRIBUTED TO OCKHAM[a]

The purpose of the following study is twofold: to show that there was a crisis of Logic in Scholasticism, especially of the fourtheenth century; and to show that while Ockham is not, the author of the *Centiloquium* is a representative of logical scepticism. The basis of our study will be the text of the *Centiloquium* edited in the previous numbers of FRANCISCAN STUDIES [1941—1942].

---

[11] Cf. footnote 9.

[12] Our opinion that the recently discovered *Sums* of Logic (S2 and S3) are authentic works of Ockham has found an unexpected corroboration in the discovery of another manuscript of S3 by Ludger Meier, O.F.M. ("Aufzeichnungen aus vernichteten Handschriften des Würzburger Minoritenklosters," in *Archivum Franciscanum Historicum*, XLIV (1951), 194. Though the codex *I 63* has been destroyed in 1945, we are grateful to Ludger Meier for having taken the following notes (probably in a hurry, since they are evidently partly incorrect): *Bl.* 1r—12r. *Inc.:* Logica cum dicat.—*Expl.:* Vel negativa formata ex eisdem sit vera vel . . .[?] universaliter tenenda. — Explicit Compendium Logicae Oquam [?] collectum ab eodem et scriptum . . . [?] per manus Fratris Hugonis Kuenemani A.D. 1345 circa . . . Simonis et Iudae. This indeed is the *Tractatus minor logicae Ockham of Assisi 690*, which has the better reading for the *Incipit:* Logica cum dicatur . . . and for the *Explicit:* . . . vel negativa formata ex eisdem sit vera vel concedenda. Explicit minor tractatus novae logicae fratris Gwilelmi ocham. Especially precious is the indication of the date 1345 (Ockham died in 1349).

---

[a] First published in FrancStud 4 (1944) 151—170.

Since Ockham was especially interested in the field of Logic, and since the author of the *Centiloquium* always attacks his problems from a logical point of view, an essential doctrinal difference between both will certainly be a most conclusive criterion for eliminating Ockham as a possible author of the *Centiloquium*. Such an essential difference is found as regards at least two logical problems which are basic, namely, the problem whether or not Logic is formal, and the problem whether or not the principle of the excluded middle is universally valid. Both problems are of interest at the present time, when research in Logic is making considerable progress. The present study will be confined to the medieval problem: Is Logic formal?

I. THE MEANING OF

Discursus Formalis

There is considerable confusion among Neo-Scholastics as to the meaning of the expression "Formal Logic". Some of them reject this term;[1] others, apparently more faithful to Scholastic tradition, defend the usage of the expression and of its counterpart "Material Logic".[2] Neither side, however, would seem to be aware that it has no part in the spirit of Scholastic Logic, which in this case is the spirit of Aristotelian Logic. For neither Aristotle nor the Scholastics knew anything of a Formal Logic as opposed to Material Logic (Epistemology!). They knew only a science which was called — not by Aristotle, but by the Scholastics — Logic, and was essentially formal. More precisely and more correctly, they knew one Logic which contains logical forms, namely, formal syllogisms or, more generally, formal discourses.

What is a formal discourse? Partially following H. Scholz,[3] we may state that, according to Aristotle (that is to say, while it is not

---

[1] For instance, G. H. Joyce, S. J., *Principles of Logic (Stonyhurst Philosophical Series)*, 3rd edn., pp. 12 *et seq.*

[2] For instance, J. Maritain, *An Introduction to Logic* (Sheed and Ward, New York, 1937), pp. 8 *et seq.*

[3] *Geschichte der Logik (Geschichte der Philosophie in Längsschnitten)* (herausgegeben von W. Moog, Berlin, 1931), pp. 3—4.

expressly taught by Aristotle it is easily abstracted from his treatment of logical problems), Logic deals with perfect logical forms. A mere logical form is an expression which contains at least one constant and one variable. Constants are expressions like "est", "omne", etc.; variables are indicated by letters. Therefore the expression "Omne A est album" would be a logical form. If we interpret A simply as an empty place into which any meaningful term can be put, this logical form is neither true nor false, but can become true or false, provided the variable be replaced by a suitable term.[4] A perfect logical form, then, is an expression which contains only constants and variables, for instance: "A est B," or: "Omne A est B." Aristotelian Logic, however, does not deal with such simple perfect logical forms. It deals with a combination of them, namely, with a combination of at least three forms which we shall call F_1, F_2, F_3, so that these three perfect forms constitute one expression in which, if the truth of F_1 and F_2 (or the premises) be affirmed, the truth of F_3 (or the conclusion) is affirmed also. This is performed by the logical operation which is called *syllogismus*, or inference. The inference, in its turn, has to be made under the guidance of certain rules, namely, the syllogistic rules of the different figures and modes which were formulated by Aristotle for the first time in history. The syllogistic rules guarantee that a syllogistic form always yields a true conclusion if the variables are replaced by suitable terms. The formality of Aristotelian Logic, therefore, is equivalent to the expression: Universal validity, regardless of the terms or the matter of the propositions.[5]

Aristotelian, and consequently Scholastic, Logic is therefore essentially formal. And this character of formality is best expressed and emphasized by symbols which, indeed, were applied by Aristotle and the Scholastics, though still in a primitive way.

---

[4] This is not exactly Aristotelian or Scholastic, for according to them the expression: *Omne odium est album*, is false; according to modern logicians, it is meaningless.

[5] This can be applied to modern Logic also, though formality assumes another and more abstract meaning in mathematical Logic. Cf. the chapter on "Formality" in W. Van Orman Quine, *Mathematical Logic* (Norton, New York, 1940), pp. 283 *et seq.*

This idea of formality was to some extent in the mind of the author of the *Centiloquium* when he wrote: "Nullus discursus est formalis, cui poterunt inveniri termini, in quibus ratio, id est, in quibus praemissae similis discursus sunt verae et conclusio falsa" (Concl. 56). He evidently intends to say that a syllogism or any discourse cannot be called formal if its terms are replaced by others so that the premises are true and the conclusion becomes false; or, to express this in our terms: A syllogism is not formal if the variables in F_1, F_2, and F_3 are replaced by corresponding terms so that F_1 and F_2 are true, and F_3 is false. The author of the *Centiloquium* states correctly that this ideal of the formality of Logic was developed by Aristotle in the *Prior Analytics*, and that Aristotle does not regard any syllogism as formal as soon as an instance can be found in which true premises yield a false conclusion. And indeed, as Ockham remarks,[6] this in the ultimate means by which Aristotle proves the validity of a syllogism.

As far as the present writer is aware, there can be no doubt that this is the commonly accepted doctrine of all Scholastics, though the exact formulation given by some may show defects. The most striking expression, however, is found in Adam Wodham: "Diceres, Aristoteles sic exemplificat: Omne B est A, omne C est B, igitur omne C est A, quasi diceret: applices ubi volueris, et similis syllogismus erit bonus . . ."[7]

---

[6] *Summa Logicae*, III (1) c. 4: "Ista narrata non possunt probari nisi per modum, quo probat Aristoteles, quod quatuor modi [sc. primae figurae] sunt utiles, per hoc quod non contingit inferre instantiam" [edit. Boehner II 333].

[7] Adam Goddam (Wodham) *Super quatuor libros Sent.* (this is the abbreviation made by Henry of Oyta) (Paris, 1512), fol. 81 va. Cf. for a similar expression Scotus, *Super 1. Elench.* q. 4, n. 3; ed. Vivès t. 2, pp. 5 *et seq.* For the Thomistic tradition, cf. the pseudo-thomistic *Summa Logicae*, Tract. VIII, c. 5: "In hoc opere tractetur de syllogismo simpliciter, scilicet de forma ipsius syllogismi inquantum syllogismus est, non applicando ad aliquam materiam; et ideo illa erit vera forma syllogismi, quae applicata cuicumque materiae semper si praemissae erunt verae, sequetur ex eis conclusio vera . . ." (ed. Mich. Maria, 1886, pp. 108 *et seq.*).

II. THE NON-FORMALITY OF ARISTOTELIAN LOGIC ACCORDING TO THE AUTHOR OF THE *Centiloquium*

The author of the *Centiloquium* unequivocally states: "Nullus discursus, quem Aristoteles vel aliquis antiquorum posuit, est formalis" (Concl. 56). The meaning of this negative conclusion admits of no doubt. Since *discursus* has to be taken in the sense of any inferential operation, it includes the *consequentiae* as well as the syllogisms. And since, for a medieval logician, a *discursus* stated by Aristotle or one of the old philosophers is equivalent to a *discursus* of the traditional Logic known in the Middle Ages, the negative conclusion just cited amounts to the statement: No *consequentia* and no syllogism of the traditional Logic is universally valid.

This is proved for different discourses:

1. The *syllogismus expositorius* is not formal or universally valid. Aristotle used the *syllogismus expositorius* in order to prove valid modes of the third figure.[8] Hence it must be most formal. But this syllogism meets with many difficulties when expressed in terms of the Blessed Trinity; e. g.,

> "Haec essentia est Pater;
> Haec essentia est Filius;
> Ergo Filius est Pater."

The premises are true and are arranged correctly as to figure and mode; but the conclusion is false according to the teaching of the Church. Consequently, the syllogism is not valid, and not formal or universally true. The author of the *Centiloquium* does not expressly deny that the expository syllogism is valid in terms of creatures, though he simply states that this is the opinion of many; but he does deny that it holds in terms of the Blessed Trinity: "Quia quamvis multis appareat in materia naturali et in materia creata, non tamen

---

[8] It seems that the author of the *Centiloquium* confines the *syllogismus expositorius* to the third figure, as Ockham did, against the author of the *Summa Logicae* attributed to St. Thomas, and the author of the *Quaestiones in 1. Priorum* attributed to Duns Scotus.

tenet in materia increata et praecipue in propositionibus sive terminis divinae Trinitatis" (Concl. 55 C, ad primum). Of course, Aristotle did not see this deficiency, for he had no knowledge of the mystery of the Blessed Trinity. Hence he believed that this discourse was universally valid. But after the time of Aristotle, and after this mystery was revealed, the "summi doctores theologici" found that this syllogism meets a particular case contrary to the general rule; that is to say, it is not formal *(loc. cit.)*.

2. Syllogisms of the first figure are not formal or universally valid. This again is proved by the author of the *Centiloquium* in giving true premises, arranged according to figure and mode, which yield a false conclusion. From among other instances, the following two may serve as illustrations:

> "Omnis essentia divina est Pater;
> Omnis Filius in divinis est essentia divina;
> Ergo omnis Filius in divinis est Pater" (Concl. 56).

> "Nullus Filius in divinis est Pater in divinis,
> Haec essentia est Filius in divinis,
> Ergo haec essentia non est Pater in divinis" (Concl. 55).

The same is true for a *syllogismus enthymematicus*, as shown in Concl. 61 C.

3. A formal consequence is not valid. Formal consequences can hold between propositions or between terms. Of this latter type is the following: *Ab inferiori ad superius affirmative sine distributione, consequentia valet* ("Socrates is white," consequently "A man is white"). This formal consequence runs into a difficulty in the following cases: "Pater in divinis generat; ergo Deus generat;" or "Filius in divinis generatur; ergo essentia divina generatur" (Concl. 58). In all these instances, our author asserts, the consequence proceeds from the logical inferior to the logical superior, affirmatively and without (universal) distribution.

From all three statements it becomes evident that the author of the *Centiloquium* denies the character of formality or universal validity in Aristotelian Logic.

III. THE IDEA OF A SUPERNATURAL LOGIC ACCORDING TO THE AUTHOR OF THE *Centiloquium*

Not satisfied, however, with the denial of any formal discourse in Aristotelian Logic, the author proceeds to the idea of another Logic namely, a supernatural Logic which is formal.[9] According to him, formality of Logic can be obtained by a supernatural rule. We read in Concl. 59: "In omni materia valet aliquis discursus formaliter qui ab aliquo philosophorum ponebatur, utpote discursus expositorius et discursus in modo et figura regulatus, quorum conclusiones vel consequentiae masculine vel neutraliter resolvuntur." This means: Aristotelian Logic can be made really formal and universally valid, if we formulate an additional rule which affects the grammatical subject of the conclusions, and this additional rule is formulated on the basis of revelation. This becomes clear in taking an example.

"Iste Pater in divinis generat;
Iste Pater in divinis est essentia divina."

Instead of concluding: "Essentia divina generat," we must conclude: "Aliqua Persona, quae est essentia divina, generat;" or "Aliquis, qui est essentia divina, generat."

The author of the *Centiloquium* gives more details of this supernatural Logic which, being irrelevant, we shall not consider here.

The universal validity of certain syllogisms with his additional rule is simply guaranteed by the declaration *(Extra) De Summa Trinitate:* "Pater est alius a Filio et Filius est alius a Patre, non tamen aliud" (Concl. 55 H, ad 6^m). In all the cases where he comes in conflict with this declaration, he applies his additional rule. Hence the decision of naturally valid or supernaturally valid has to be made entirely on theological grounds.

By way of summary, therefore, the author states: "Ex quibus omnibus plane sequitur, quod nullus discursus naturalis, id est naturaliter inventus, est formalis, sed aliquis discursus supernaturalite inventus est formalis" (Concl. 59 B).

---

[9] This has nothing to do with St. Bonaventure's idea of a Christian Logic in *Collationes in Hexaemeron*, I, 30; t. 5, p. 334.

Let us add that the author of the *Centiloquium* does not deny the principle of contradiction. In Concl. 55 B (6) he formulates it as follows: "Contradictoria sibi invicem contradicentia respectu eiusdem significati non sunt simul vera." According to him, this law of contradiction is not violated in terms of the Blessed Trinity, because the term *essentia* which can be predicated about one Person in one statement of identity and of another in another statement of identity — for instance, "Essentia divina est eadem Filio; Essentia divina est eadem Patri" — is not convertibly identical with each Person *(non est convertibiliter eadem)*. The meaning of this "nonconvertibility", however, is not explained by advocating any distinction in God. It is simply stated that though the one essence is identical with the one Person, nevertheless it is not true that it is identical with another Person *(non tamen est alicui alteri per se a Filio non eadem)*. In any case, the author does not believe that his statements violate the principle of contradiction.

IV. OCKHAM AND THE UNIVERSAL VALIDITY OF ARISTOTELIAN LOGIC

The problem discussed by the author of the *Centiloquium*, and solved by him in a negative sense, was not of merely academic interest in the Middle Ages. It is, in fact, one case of the many clashes between reason and revelation which proved to be stimulating factors in the progress of Scholasticism. And progress there is, even in the fourtheenth century, and even as regards the problem of the relation between reason and faith.[10] It is a fact that the scientific

---

[10] Cf. A. Lang, *Die Wege der Glaubensbegründung bei den Scholastikern des 14. Jahrhunderts (Beiträge zur Geschichte der Philosophie des Mittelalters*, Bd. 30, H. 1—2) (Münster, 1930) p. 253: "So hat auch das 14. Jahrhundert das Problem der Glaubensbegründung um ein gutes Stück der Lösung nähergebracht . . ." On page 241 the author remarks that looking back at his research on the fourteenth century, "die erste Beobachtung, die sich aufdrängt [ist], daß die Scholastik des 14. Jahrhunderts zum großen Teil besser ist als ihr Ruf." Lang, like Card. Fr. Ehrle, S. J., was, however, not able to appreciate the excellent Logic of the fourteenth century.

culture of the fourteenth century was far ahead of that of the thirteenth. And this fact accounts, to a great extent, for a deeper and more penetrating treatment of the relation between reason and faith. If Scholasticism is always characterized as a *Fides quaerens intellectum*, then the first and most general problem will be to ascertain whether the statements of revelation are susceptible of a rational process, and to what extent; in other words, to ascertain whether the statements which cannot be known by natural reason, and which are given to us by unerring Truth, can be treated logically and can be instances of logical forms. Only if this question be answered affirmatively is speculative theology safe and scientifically justified. If the answer is negative, the road to the *Credo quia absurdum* is open.

The great Scholastics of the thirteenth century took the universal validity of Logic for granted. After a rapid development of Logic under the powerful influence of the *Summulae Logicales* of Petrus Hispanus (Pope John XXI),[11] the problem became more acute. While certain Scholastics gave up hope for a universally valid Logic, Ockham, with the majority of the Scholastics, defended the formal character of Logic as regards the statements of revelation.

1. The *syllogismus expositorius* is valid, regardless of its matter. In *Summa Logicae*, III (1), c. 16, Ockham deals with the *syllogismus expositorius* as an appendix to the discussion of modes of the third figure. Here he gives the following characterization of it.[12] The

---

[11] The error of Prantl, still maintained by Bartholomaeus Roth (see below), according to whom Petrus Hispanus translated his work from a Greek original, is definitely eliminated by M. Grabmann, *Handschriftliche Forschungen und Funde zu den philosophischen Schriften des Petrus Hispanus, des späteren Papstes Johannes XXI († 1272) (Sitzungsberichte der Bayerischen Akademie der Wissenschaften, Philosophische-historische Abteilung*, 1936, Heft 9) (München, 1937).

[12] "Est igitur sciendum, quod syllogismus expositorius est, quando arguitur ex duabus singularibus in tertia figura, quarum singularium subiectum supponit pro aliquo uno numero, quod non est plures res nec est idem realiter cum aliquo, quod est plures res. Et quia in creaturis nulla una res numero est plures res realiter quaecumque, ideo generaliter quando arguitur ex propositionibus singularibus praedicto modo, fit syllogismus expositorius, hoc addito, quod minor sit affirmativa..." [edit. Boehner II368].

premises of a *syllogismus expositorius* must be two singular propositions; these two propositions must be arranged according to the third figure (therefore, the minor must be affirmative); the conclusion can be either singular or particular or indefinite, but never universal. In order to safeguard himself and Logic from the disaster which threatened as the result of the teaching of certain theologians, Ockham adds: the subject of the singular propositions must be a term which really stands for, or "supposits", one thing which is not several things, and which is not really the same as something which is several absolute or relative things, and which only and precisely stands for one such thing.

The last precision is necessary. For if the subject term — be it a demonstrative pronoun, or a proper noun, or a demonstrative pronoun with some other term — stands for something which, though in itself unique and simple and numerically one and most singular, nevertheless is several things, then the consequence cannot be valid by reason of the *syllogismus expositorius*. Ockham proves this by taking an analogical case. Such a term which stands for one thing that is several things is similar to a common term, e. g., "homo". If we predicate about this term two proper names, for instance: "Homo est Sortes", "Homo est Plato", the conclusion "Plato est Sortes" would not be true and the consequence would not be valid. For in this case one premise is verified for one man, and the other can be verified for another man. Another analogical case which is developed on the basis of Platonic realism may show the same defect. Let us presuppose that the term "Haec humanitas" stands precisely for one thing, and that nevertheless Plato and Sortes are several men. If then we should reason: "Haec humanitas est Sortes; Haec humanitas est Plato; Igitur Plato est Sortes," the conclusion would be false and the consequence would not be valid. Since we presupposed that Plato and Sortes are distinct, and since each premise is verified, either by the fact that Sortes is Sortes or that Plato is Plato, it can only follow: "Ergo haec essentia est tam Plato quam Sortes."

This latter case is to some extent given in syllogisms in terms of the Blessed Trinity. For there we have terms which signify really different Persons, and we have one term which signifies a reality which is not really distinct from each Person. Hence the following syllogism cannot be a *syllogismus expositorius:*

> "Haec essentia est Pater;
> Haec essentia est Filius;
> Igitur Filius est Pater."

For the term "essentia" stands for one thing which is three Persons; and though the term "Pater" stands for the divine essence, the term "Pater" does not stand for the Son, etc. Therefore these terms as such cannot enter a valid *syllogismus expositorius;* and they cannot enter because they are of a special and unique nature. This idea could be expressed in other words by saying that terms of the Blessed Trinity are not always suitable replacements of variables in a *syllogismus expositorius.* Consequently, the validity of the syllogism cannot be disputed, but the correctness of the replacement of the variables must be disputed.

The universal validity of the *syllogismus expositorius* is expressly stated by Ockham on another occasion. In *Summa Logicae,* II (c. 27), the *Venerabilis Inceptor* proves a conversion of modal propositions with the help of the *syllogismus expositorius.* This reminds him that the validity of this syllogism has been disputed by contemporary theologians. Against them he emphatically states:

> Est autem probatio sufficiens, quia syllogismus expositorius est per se evidens nec indiget ulteriori probatione. Et ideo multum errant, qui negant talem syllogismum in quacumque materia . . . Et quia syllogismi expositorii, qui sunt ex se evidentes, frequenter negantur a modernis theologis, et ideo contra tales non est disputandum cum negent per se nota, ideo aliqualiter disgrediendo a proposito, ponam exempla, in quibus non est syllogismus expositorius, quamvis videatur [ed. Boehner II. 304—305].

Then Ockham enumerates a long list of syllogisms which have the appearance of a *syllogismus expositorius,* and he unmasks them as fallacies. From among these, he discusses at length a so-called *syllogismus expositorius* in terms of the Blessed Trinity, which he reduces to a *fallacia consequentis* or *accidentis.*

2. Every syllogism which is governed by the rule of *Dictum de omni vel de nullo* is formally valid. Since the syllogisms of the first

figure are directly governed by this rule, they are most formal. This is shown by Ockham in *Summa Logicae*, III (1), cc. 4—5. In this section, too, Ockham discusses terms of the Blessed Trinity which sometimes prevent such a syllogism from being governed by the universal rule. Such a syllogism would be:

> "Omnis essentia divina est Pater;
> Filius est essentia divina;
> Ergo Filius est Pater."

Ockham acknowledges readily that Aristotle would have admitted this syllogism as valid and as governed by the *Dictum de omni*. The reason for this, however, is that Aristotle did not admit, or at least did not know of, such terms: "Quia non posuit unicam rem simplicem esse plures res distinctae realiter." Theologians, on the other hand, do admit such terms, and therefore they must deny that the above-mentioned syllogism is regulated by the *Dictum de omni:*

> Sed Theologi, qui ponunt secundum veritatem unam rem numero esse plures res, quia dicunt quod essentia divina simplex et indivisibilis est plures personae distinctae realiter, habent dicere, quod praedicti discursus non valent nec regulantur per dici de omni vel de nullo [ed. Boehner II 337].

On the basis of theology it is easy to show that this syllogism is not ruled by the *Dictum de omni,* because in saying "Omnis essentia divina est Pater", it is not meant that we can predicate the term "Pater" about everything which can be predicated about the subject "essentia divina". For we also predicate about the essence the term "Filius", but we do not say: "Filius est Pater."[13]

---

[13] "Et ratio est quia per istam: omnis essentia divina est Pater, non denotatur, quod de quocumque dicitur hoc subiectum essentia divina, de eodem dicatur hoc praedicatum Pater. Tunc enim necessario iste syllogismus regularetur per dici de omni: omnis essentia divina est Pater, Filius est essentia divina, igitur Filius est Pater. Sed ista esset tunc falsa: omnis essentia divina est Pater, sicut ista est falsa: de quocumque dicitur hoc subiectum essentia divina, de eodem dicitur hoc praedicatum Pater. Sed per istam: omnis essentia divina est Pater, denotatur, quod omne illud, quod est omnis res absoluta et relativa quae est essentia, est Pater, et hoc est verum. Sed tunc si uniformiter acciperetur minor, ipsa esset falsa; tunc enim per istam: Filius est essentia divina, denotaretur, quod Filius

From this we again gather that Ockham does not deny the character of formality in any valid Aristotelian syllogism, but he denies that certain terms are suitable replacements in valid perfect forms. The fact that certain terms are not suitable replacements, however, can be known only by revelation, and this for the obvious reason that the terms themselves are known only by revelation.

3. The *fallacia accidentis* (or *consequentis*) is easily committed in terms of the Blessed Trinity. If certain syllogisms in terms of the Blessed Trinity yield a false conclusion, and their formality is admitted, then there must be a fallacy. This fallacy, according to Ockham, is the *fallacia accidentis* or *consequentis*.

A *fallacia accidentis* is a fallacy which concerns terms. Ockham explains in his treatment of this fallacy that *accidens* has to be taken in the sense of *term*, either of the subject or of the predicate term. Every term which can be the subject or predicate as regards another term, is its *accidens*. The reason of deception or of the *apparentia fallaciae* is found in the identity of predication which is assumed between the two terms because they are predicated about each other. Because we find that one term is predicated affirmatively or negatively about another term, we believe that whatever is affirmed or denied of the one is affirmed or denied of the other also. This, however, is not necessary; hence the fallacy. Therefore the fallacy consists in the connection of two terms of the premises in the conclusion, though this connection is not warranted by the premises.[14] For instance, it is not necessary to unite the terms "asinus" and "homo" in the

---

esset quaelibet res respectiva quae est essentia divina, quod falsum est, quia non est Pater, et tamen essentia divina est Pater . . ." (*loc. cit.*, c. 4 [edit. Boehner II 337]). This is condensed to the rule: "Quando per maiorem non denotatur praedicatum vere affirmari vel vere negari de pronomine demonstrante quodcumque quod est realiter idem cum significato per subiectum, tunc accipiendo 'sub' aliquid tale, non erit syllogismus regulatus per dici de omni vel de nullo" (*loc. cit.*, c. 5 [edit. Boehner II 345]).

[14] "Et responsio generalis ad omnes paralogismos accidentis est dicere, quod non est necesse conclusionem sequi ex praemissis, hoc est, non est necesse praedicatum conclusionis dici de subiecto conclusionis propter unionem illorum in praemissis cum aliquo uno" (*Summa Logicae*, III [4], c. 11).

conclusion because they were united in the premises: "Homo est animal" and "Asinus est animal". This general rule, however, needs a specification as to why, in certain cases, the connection of terms is not warranted.

Ockham distinguishes two forms of the *fallacia accidentis,* of which the first is of special interest to us. This fallacy is committed if the premises are arranged as to figure, but not as to mode, according to the general rules. In order to exclude such fallacies, the rules of Aristotle are sufficient, except in one case, and that is the case of certain syllogisms in term of the Blessed Trinity. These theological terms, of course, need a theological characterization which prevents a logical disaster.

> Et debet specialis regula assignari talis: Quia una essentia est plures Personae, quae Personae sunt distinctae inter se, non oportet quod omne nomen Personae, de quo praedicatur nomen essentia, praedicetur de nomine alterius Personae.

Because the one essence is several Persons who are really distinct, it does not follow that the predicates which are predicated about the same subject — namely, this essence in three Persons — are predicated about each other also.

This theological rule has to be applied only in cases where theology tells us that it must be applied. It must be applied, according to a device given by St. Anselm, where an opposition of the relations is involved. In all other cases it must not be applied.

> Propter quod ubi non obviat relationis oppositio, quod conceditur de una Persona, concedendum est de alia. Ubi autem obviat relationis oppositio, non est concedendum de qualibet Persona, quod de una conceditur. Et ad hoc semper est aspiciendum in repondendo ad discursus ex terminis importantibus divinas Personas *(loc. cit.).*

It is obvious, and expressly stated by Ockham on several occasions, that we know of this peculiarity of these terms only by revelation. And nobody, certainly no theologian, can deny that — if we set aside the doubtful rationalism of Richard of St. Victor. But — and this is also clear from Ockham's teachings and his explanations given on many occasions — this peculiarity of these terms does not affect Aristotelian Logic in its formal character; it simply prevents us from putting these terms into certain valid forms of syllogisms. The structure of these syllogisms is not affected. Logic, therefore, is formal. That is to say, it is universally valid whether the terms applied be terms of created or uncreated things. This was Ockham's position from the beginning to the end of his philosophical career.[15]

4. The *distinctio formalis* is the safeguard of the formality of Logic. Ockham does not sacrifice Logic for a theological irrationalism. Instead, he escapes into the only possible refuge, namely, the mystery of the Blessed Trinity itself. His guide is Duns Scotus, and his hiding-place is the *distinctio formalis* or the *non-identitas formalis*. Though Scotus did not actually introduce the idea of a *distinctio formalis* into Theology and Philosophy,[16] he certainly is the most powerful and unrestricted defender of this greatly disputed distinction. Ockham is much less enthusiastic about this distinction, which is so difficult to understand; and if he had seen a way of avoiding it he would undoubtedly have abandoned it. But, rather than endanger Logic and the highest principle of reason, the principle of contradiction, he preferred to follow Scotus. If the statements: "Paternitas non est Filiatio," and "Paternitas est essentia", and "Filiatio est essentia", have any meaning as to the reality they concern, they must mean that "Paternitas" and "Filiatio" point to really distinct relations; and, consequently, that the predication of "Paternitas" or "Filiatio" about "essentia" cannot be a predication of formal identity; and, further, that there must be between the "Paternitas"

---

[15] This is clear on the evidence of texts taken from the *Summa Logicae,* which was one of Ockham's latest non-polemical work. The same teaching is found even in his first work, the *Ordinatio.* The following text should suffice: "Et quando dicitur, quod omne argumentum [falsum] peccat in materia vel in forma — Concedo, quamvis hoc non possit sciri evidenter." This is explained in the addition of the second redaction: "Unde illud argumentum: essentia divina est Pater, essentia divina est Filius . . . peccat in forma; et tamen nullus potest de communi lege evidenter sciri, quod illud argumentum peccat in forma, sicut nullus potest evidenter cognoscere de communi lege, quod una res absoluta est plures Personae relativae distinctae realiter . . . (*I Sent.,* prol., q. 3 princ., sive 7 in ord. Q.).

[16] Cf. B. Jansen, S. J., "Beiträge zur geschichtlichen Entwicklung der Distinctio formalis," *Zeitschrift für katholische Theologie* (Innsbruck), vol. 53 (1929), pp. 371 *et seq.,* and 517 *et seq.*

or the "Filiatio" and the "essentia" a distinction of formal non-identity.[17] This formal non-identity between the essence and the three Persons which are one and the same essence, prevents us from an unrestricted predication of identity and enables us to reduce certain false syllogisms in terms of the Blessed Trinity to a *fallacia accidentis*.

5. Ockham did not deny the principle of contradiction. The *distinctio formalis* saves Ockham's Logic as to its character of universal validity, but does it save the principle of contradiction as well? From what has been said, it should be clear that Ockham intended to save the basic principle of contradiction by the formal distinction. It is very surprising, therefore, and it adds a new example to the collection of careless judgments passed upon Ockham, that an otherwise excellent work on the *distinctio formalis* in Francis of Mayronis[18] should picture Ockham as a representative of those

---

[17] While Scotus speaks of a *distinctio formalis* and of *non-identitas formalis*, Ockham admits the *distinctio formalis* only in the negative sense: "Non est aliud dicere, quod essentia et Personae distinguuntur formaliter secundum unum intellectum, nisi quod essentia est tres Personae et Persona non est tres Personae. Similiter nihil aliud intelligo per istam: essentia et paternitas distinguuntur formaliter nisi istam propositionem: essentia est filiatio, et paternitas non est filiatio, et tamen paternitas est essentia. Similiter: paternitatem et spirationem activam distingui formaliter non est aliud quam dicere, quod paternitas non est filiatio, et quod spiratio activa est filiatio, et tamen quod paternitas est spiratio activa. Et ita universaliter: de aliquibus verificari distingui formaliter non est aliud quam de uno istorum aliquid vere affirmari et de alio vere negari, et tamen unum illorum vere affirmari de alio contingit sine omni variatione et aequivocatione alicuius vel verificatione pro diversis, sicut contingit in particularibus et indefinitis..." (*Summa Logicae*, II, c. 2 [edit. Boehner II 228]).

[18] Bartholomaeus Roth, O.F.M., *Franz von Mayronis, Sein Leben, seine Werke, seine Lehre vom Formalunterschied in Gott* (*Franziskanische Forschungen*, Heft 3) (Werl, 1936), p. 330: "Als Vertreter der Ansicht, daß zwar für die Philosophie nichts zugleich Eines und Vieles sein könne, wohl aber in der Theologie, die ja lehre, daß 1—3 sei, läßt sich Ockham feststellen." The author may to some extent be excused for this error, as he used as his main source Prantl who believed the *Centiloquium* to be an authentic work of Ockham's.

who denied the validity of the principle of contradiction in God. The author is able to quote some marginal notes of an old manuscript of Mayronis which refer this opinion to Ockham; and there is a strong possibility that this remark can be found in manuscripts of other Scholastics as well. For there was in the fourteenth century among some Scholastics a persistent conviction that Ockham denied this principle. The reason for this view, however, is not that Ockham anywhere expressly denied the principle of contradiction, but rather (and this should surprise a Scotist!) that he taught the *distinctio formalis*. Holkot and Gregory a Rimini[19] cannot see anything but a flat contradiction in the *distinctio formalis*. And for this reason they allege against Ockham, as well as Scotus, a violation of the principle of contradiction. This fact at least should caution Scotists against condemning Ockham for a doctrine which he has in common with Scotus.

Yet we will admit that Ockham's expressions could suggest to a careless reader that he excluded the principle of contradiction from God; or that he admitted that contradictory statements can be made about God, in the sense that the same in exactly the same sense is affirmed and denied in God. We read, for instance, in *I Sent.*, d. 1, q. 5 E:

Difficillimum est intelligere contradictoria verficari de eadem re, nec est hoc ponendum nisi propter solam fidem; ergo hoc non est ponendum, nisi ubi fides compellit; sed fides non compellit ad aliquid ponendum nisi quod habetur ex Scriptura Sacra vel ex determinatione Ecclesiae vel evidenter et formaliter infertur ex talibus. . . .

Does the expression *contradictoria verficari de eadem re* mean that the same in exactly the same sense is denied and affirmed in God? Ockham certainly never taught such arrant nonsense. And when the *Venerabilis Inceptor* uses the expression "One thing is three things", he does not mean that one essence is three essences; he means that one essence is in three Persons, of which each one is really distinct from the others, and each one really the same as the essence. Therefore, to simplify his formula to the impossibility "1=3" is an elementary fallacy and should be left to Averroes

---

[19] Cf. *infra* in the historical discourse.

and some modern objectors. The problem which Ockham views is not how "1=3" can be possible, but how one thing can be three things — i. e., three Persons — and how, nevertheless, each Person can be the same essence. Ockham sees very well the gravity and intricacy of the problem. If contradiction is the most powerful way to prove a real distinction, in case we have a simple denial of an affirmation as regards real things and provided no linguistic qualification admits the verification of this affirmation and denial at the same time, then we have to conclude to a real distinction wherever we verify contradictory statements. This rule is sufficient as regards all creatures and many facts in God. But as to some statements about the Blessed Trinity the case is different. There we have the choice either to deny the validity of the principle of contradiction, or to admit a distinction which is not a mental distinction and not a real distinction — namely, the *distinctio non-identitatis formalis*. Ockham chooses the latter alternative. Hence his proof of the *distinctio formalis* is the Blessed Trinity itself; and his reason is to safeguard the principle of contradiction.[20]

Ockham, however, is well aware that he does not give a solution of the difficulty, if solution means the elimination of the problem by reducing it to better-known statements. For the *distinctio formalis* is a mystery of the same degree as the mystery of the Blessed Trinity itself.

[20] "Contradictio est via potissima ad probandum distinctionem realem, quando ita est, quod est negatio simpliciter, ita quod per nullam circumlocutionem potest alterum contradictoriorum verificari de illo a quo negatur. Sed quando per talem circumlocutionem contingit alterum contradictoriorum verificari de illo a quo negatur, tunc tantum erit via et est via ad probandum distinctionem formalem. Et sic est in proposito; quia quamvis haec sit vera: paternitas non est communicabilis, haec tamen est vera: paternitas est illa res quae est communicabilis. Similiter, quamvis haec non sit vera: Pater est Filius, tamen haec est vera: Pater est illa res quae est Filius, quia Pater est illa essentia quae est Filius. Et universaliter, quando ita est, tunc est illa distinctio possibilis: sed numquam ita est, nisi in Deo, et ideo est in solo Deo ponenda. Unde dico, quod non potest esse distinctio formalis nec talis contradictio verficari, nisi ubi sunt distinctae res realiter, quae tamen sunt una res realiter, quod solum est possibile de Personis divinis, quia sunt tres Personae realiter distinctae, et tamen sunt una res, quia sunt una essentia numero" (*I Sent.*, d. 2, q. 11, O).

Quia tamen est difficillima [sc., the distinctio formalis] ad ponendum ubique, non credo eam esse faciliorem ad tenendum quam Trinitatem Personarum cum unitate essentiae, ideo non debet poni, nisi ubi evidenter sequitur ex traditis in Scriptura Sacra vel determinatione Ecclesiae, propter cuius auctoritatem debet omnis ratio captivari... (*I Sent.*, d. 2, q. 1 F).

But from this, as we have seen, Ockham does not conclude to an irrationality in God or to the *Credo quia absurdum.* He concludes to a mode of non-identity in God which, though it cannot be grasped by any human understanding, nevertheless excludes a violation of the principle of contradition. We may object to Ockham — but, in that event, to Scotus as well — that he implicitly violated the principle of contradiction; but to allege against him that he intentionally denied that principle is an historical error. My personal opinion is that he neither intended to deny the principle of contradiction, nor denied it even implicitly.

V. THE DIFFERENCES BETWEEN THE AUTHOR OF THE *Centiloquium* AND OCKHAM

The differences between the author of the *Centiloquium* and Ockham are much more far-reaching than at first glance would appear. The main ones are as follows:

1. The author of the *Centiloquium* states: Logic as developed by Aristotle is not formal and universally valid. Ockham, however, states that Aristotelian Logic is essentially formal and universally valid.

2. The author of the *Centiloquium* states: The *syllogismus expositorius*, when applied to terms and propositions about the Blessed Trinity, has no defect, and nevertheless is not valid. Ockham states that in these cases there is a defect which can be unmasked as a *fallacia accidentis.*

3. The author of the *Centiloquium* states: A formally valid syllogism can be obtained by an additional supernatural rule which concerns changes in the nature of the conclusion. Ockham, however, knows nothing of such an additional rule. He simply sounds a warning as to the terms of the Blessed Trinity. Because these terms are of a unique nature, not known (of course) to Aristotle but known

only to theologians, they are therefore not suitable replacements of variables in formally valid syllogisms.

4. The uniqueness of terms of the Blessed Trinity is expressed by Ockham when he advocates the *distinctio non-identitatis formalis*. The author of the *Centiloquium*, on the other hand, does not mention any distinction; he states only that certain terms are not convertible.

These differences between the author of the *Centiloquium* and Ockham are of such a nature that, historically speaking, an identification of Ockham with the author of the *Centiloquium* is impossible. A change of mind on the part of Ockham is excluded, because he has substantially the same teaching in his first work, the *Ordinatio*, and in one of his last philosophical writings, the *Summa Logicae*.

VI. THE HISTORICAL POSITION OF THE AUTHOR OF THE *Centiloquium* AND OF OCKHAM

In this final section we shall try to indicate the group of Scholastics to which Ockham belongs, and that to which the author of the *Centiloquium* belongs. Only a short and necessarily incomplete outline will be given.

The thirteenth century Scholastics, at least implicitly, believed in the formality of Logic as regards the mystery of the Blessed Trinity. However, the first one to realize the gravity of the problem involved was, as it seems, Scotus "qui alios in subtilitate iudicii excellebat" (Ockham, *I Sent.*, d. 2, q. 6 B). He deals with our problem *in extenso* in *Ox.*, I, d. 2, q. 7, nn. 47 *et seq.* (Viv. ed., t. 8, pp. 630 *et seq.*). His solution is slightly different from that of Ockham, since he unmasks certain syllogisms in terms of the Blessed Trinity as *fallaciae figurae dictionis*, though he admits that they can be *fallaciae accidentis* as well.

The unknown author of the *Quaestiones in libros Priorum* (which have been attributed to Scotus) maintains the formality of Logic and shows in particular that it holds for the *syllogismus expositorius* (Cf. *op. cit.*, 9. 11: "Utrum syllogismus ex-positorius teneat gratia formae" — Viv. ed., t. 2, pp. 108 *et seq.*). According to him, the *syllogismus expositorius* is not confined to the third figure. This, however, is a matter of mere terminology.

Within the Scotistic school, the most vigorous defender of the formality of Logic is Francis of Mayronis. His first question of the *Conflatus* (ed. Basel, 1489) is a masterpiece of formal treatment of the principle of contradiction. Other texts relevant to our problem have been published by Fr. Bartholomaeus Roth, O. F. M.,[21] whose work contains many historical details relative to our topic.

To this Scotistic group of defenders of the formal character of Logic Ockham belongs also, because he too acknowledges the necessity of a *distinctio formalis*, though, like many other Scotists, in the negative form.

Closely related to Ockham is Adam Wodham, O. F. M., who is usually called an Ockhamist, though strictly he should be considered as belonging to no particular school. His discussion of the problem of the formality of Logic is found in *I Sent.*, d. 33, q. 3 (ed. cit., foll. 81 *et seq.*): "Utrum sit aliqua regula vel ars, per quam consequenter solvi possunt paralogismi facti circa materiam Trinitatis et talibus similes." The formal distinction is stated by him in the first question of distinction 33, where he says: "Octava conclusio: Deitas non est formaliter vel per se primo modo aliqua Persona divina." Wodham's criticism of Scotus and Ockham regards more the formulation of the solution than the solution itself.

Gregory of Rimini, likewise an Ockhamist, criticizes Ockham severely, and thinks that Ockham's solution implies a denial of the universal validity of Logic. He defends the formal character of Logic but denies, however, the *distinctio formalis*.[22] Gregory of Rimini is sometimes enumerated among the defenders of the *distinctio formalis*. But this seems to be an error, because he denies any distinction *a parte rei*. Let the texts speak for themselves:

Secunda [conclusio]: quod deitas nullo modo distinguitur ex natura rei a proprietate personali, sic quod extra animam deitas et personalis proprietas sint aliquae duae quaevis entitates qualitercumque illae nominentur.

Gregory admits only that the *predication* of the essence and the personal property is not formal: "Quarta: quod neutrius praedicatio de altero est formalis."

---

[21] *Op. cit.*, esp. pp. 336—347 (*Quodl.*, I).

[22] *I Sent.*, d. 33 et 34, q. 1: "Respondeo ergo . . ." (ed. Gugl. Militis, Paris, 1482).

Holkot represents the furthest point of development from the Scotistic and Ockhamistic solution. For this so-called Ockhamist, who is fond of quoting St. Thomas often, denies the *distinctio formalis* in any sense, and also denies the formal character of Logic. But he does not deny the principle of contradiction. In *Quodl.*, q. 2 (Ms. Royal 10 C VI), he ridicules the *distinctio formalis*.

> Frustra fingitur iste modus loquendi in materia ista, quia non dilucidat nec contradictionem vitat nec plus invitat quam quicumque modus alius. Nam omnis catholicus concedit quod aliquid praedicatur de essentia, quod non praedicatur de Patre, et haec est difficultas, quomodo hoc potest esse... Cf. also *Determinationum* q. 10, sextum dubium Q (ed. Lyons, 1497).

In *Quodl.*, q. 3, Holkot states:

> Tertio dico quod [catholicus] non debet concedere contradictoria, potest tamen concedere propositiones, quae videntur esse contradictoriae vel implicantes contradictionem, sicut illae duae propositiones videntur includere contradictionem: Deus est res simplicissima, et Deus est tres res...

The formality of Aristotelian Logic is denied, and a supernatural Logic affirmed, in the following text *(loc. cit.)*:

> 10^0 dico, quod catholicus nulla logica debet uti in concedendo vel negando propositiones sive consequentias nisi determinatione ecclesiae, nec aliquibus regulis humanitas adinventis sic quod illae regulae sint mensura suae concessionis vel negationis in materia de credibilibus. Patet hoc, quia in materia tali deficit logica naturalis; nam aliquando in syllogismo expositorio oportet concedere utramque praemissarum et tamen negare conclusionem. Et tamen secundum logicam naturalem discursus non habet instantiam, sed est syllogismus optimus. Verbi gratia, si arguitur sic: Haec res est Pater, haec res est Filius, ergo Filius est Pater, videtur optima consequentia. Similis instantia (non) potest inveniri in universo mundo. Unde Aristoteles arbitratus est, quod talis forma arguendi est notior et evidentior quam syllogismus quicumque factus ex universalibus vel ex universali et particulari.

From this short exposition it follows that the historical position of the author of the *Centiloquium* is not in the neighborhood of Ockham, but rather in the neighborhood of Holkot.*

---

* I wish to express my thanks to Fr. Sebastian Day, O. F. M., for his kind help in preparing this article. The texts of Ockham quoted in this paper are corrected on the basis of many manuscripts. *P. B.*

21. THE METAPHYSICS OF WILLIAM OCKHAM[a]

It may seem rather daring to speak and write about the Metaphysics of William Ockham. The judgment of historians of Medieval Philosophy should perhaps restrain anyone from such a venture. Time and again it has been stated that Ockham has no Metaphysics at all, or at least, that he has no right to have a Metaphysics. After all, according to these historians, Ockham's "accomplishment" for Scholasticism has been to destroy the very foundation of Metaphysics. Ockham, we are told, does not admit universal essences, which would guarantee unity and order amongst the confusing multitude of individuals. Furthermore, his conceptualism has forced him to sever the bond between the order of thought and the order of reality so that each order is left in hopeless isolation. If he does have anything that somehow resembles a metaphysical doctrine, it is nothing more than a badly disguised theologism, that is, a theology which uses a metaphysical language and thus gives the impression of being a philosophy.

It is unnecessary to make a direct refutation of these and similar statements and insinuations which occur frequently in the fast growing literature on medieval thought. The fact is, Ockham does have a Metaphysics. It could even be called a well-developed Metaphysics. To show that this is the case, is already to refute completely the denials that Ockham has a Metaphysics.

Basically, it is not simply a question of deciding whether or not there is a Metaphysics in the philosophical system of Ockham; it is a question of how Metaphysics will have changed after its submission to the catalytic operation of Ockham's Conceptualism.

This problem was formulated clearly by Ritter:

Im einzelnen bedürfte es noch der genaueren Untersuchung, wie sich Ockham auf Grund seines "Nominalismus" prinzipiell zu dem Problem der Metaphysik gestellt hat . . .[1]

---

[1] Gerhard Ritter. ,,Studien zur Spätscholastik" 1. Marsilius von Inghen und die ockhamistische Schule in Deutschland, In *Sitzungsberichte der Heidelberger Akademie der Wissenschaften*, Philosophisch-historische Klasse, Heidelberg 1921, 4. Abhandlung, p. 112.

[a] First published in *The Review of Metaphysics* 1 (1947—1948) n.4 59—86.

This problem has been practically neglected by almost all those who have passed judgment on the Metaphysics of Ockham. Without taking into consideration the sequence of Ockham's thought they have usually judged his Metaphysics according to the standards of the very principles which Ockham had rejected. The result, of course was bound to be essentially negative. If, however, we stand with Ockham on his own ground, and evaluate his metaphysics in its own terms and in terms of its consequence for his own system and on its own value, quite a different picture will result. The value of Ockham's Metaphysics must not be ascertained by comparing it with other systems, but only by confronting it with reality, of which it claims to be the highest science.

Ockham never denies the possibility of Metaphysics. He always speaks as if Metaphysics were something acknowledged by everybody to be there and about which everybody made intelligent statements. Hence he did not feel the need of proving that Mataphysics is possible. After all whatever is there, is possible. A perusal of all his works, existing either in old prints or in manuscripts, has not yielded one passage in which Ockham has made it clear to his readers that he felt obliged to prove the right of speaking about things which transcend our experience. If he had any doubt at all in this regard it certainly did not concern his own position. He entertained serious doubts only with regard to the position of those who denied the univocity of the term "being". For he doubted whether they could come to any knowledge of God; and thus an important part of Metaphysics would be closed to them, namely natural theology. Hence our study cannot and will not offer any direct justification of Metaphysics, nor does it have the intention of burdening itself with the thankless task of explaining how it could happen that Ockham was termed or labeled an adversary or destroyer of Metaphysics. If, however, there is any justification needed, this justification in its most convincing form will be the presentation of Ockham's metaphysics itself. And that we shall outline.

When we study Ockham's scattered remarks on physics or rather on metaphysical problems, we should always keep in mind, that the Venerable Inceptor never wrote a textbook of Metaphysics. In this he does not differ from the other great scholastics. However, St. Thomas and Duns Scotus have commented on the *Metaphysics* of Aristotle. Ockham did not do this. Yet, we know that he intended to write an exposition of the *Metaphysics of Aristotle*.[2] Circumstances already well known, prevented him from fulfilling his promises. For this reason we are confined chiefly to his theological writings for information about his Metaphysics. We have to collect his teachings on Metaphysics partly from occasional remarks, partly from entire questions found in his *Commentary on the Sentences*, his *Quodlibeta*, and to a lesser extent, in his writings on Logic and Physics. Our task will be to gather and reconstruct from these texts a synthesis which, it must be acknowledged, will necessarily suffer from a certain arbitrariness. Nonetheless it is intended not merely as a subjective reflexion on the texts of Ockham, but as a Metaphysics according to the mind of Ockham.

Our presentation of Ockham's ideas on Metaphysics or metaphysical problems will depart somewhat from the usual treatment of historical questions. We shall offer our own interpretation, but we also shall try to have Ockham speak for himself, wherever the occasion may be given. Thus, the reader will be in a position to check our interpretation on the sources themselves. Since the texts of Ockham are not easily accessible and the available texts are not always in a trustworthy state, we shall publish them here in a revised edition based on the oldest manuscripts; for practical reasons we shall add an English translation.

[2] Ockham expressed this intention in his *Expositio sup. lib. Porphyrii, sup. lib. Elenchorum* and in his *Summa Logicae.*

For a list of non-political works on Philosophy and Theology, cf. Philotheus Boehner, O. F. M., *The Tractatus de Successivis attributed to William Ockham.* Edited with a Study on the Life and Work of Ockham, Franciscan Institute Publications, Philosophy series No. 1, The Franciscan Institute, St. Bonaventure, N. Y., 1944, pp. 16.

We wish to emphasize that the Centiloquium attributed to Ockham by the Lyon's edition of the Commentary on the Sentences (1495) will not be used for our present study. In our opinion this work has not been proved to be authentic. Cf. our study on this work in Franciscan Studies (1941 to 1942). Any serious study on Ockham's Philosophy or Theology should avoid the use of this work for documental evidence.

1. THE MEANING OF "BEING" AND ITS DERIVATIVES

Before delving into strictly metaphysical problems it seems to be necessary to clarify Ockham's terminology. There are certain terms which are commonly counted amongst those absolutely necessary for a methaphysical language. The term "being", and its derivatives, belongs to them without any doubt, since Metaphysics is supposed to deal with being *qua* being. By first clarifying the notion of being we are adhering to the spirit of Ockham who seldom omits to determine the meaning of the terms of a problem before discussing the problem itself.

Our task in this particular case proves to be quite difficult, since we are dealing with basic notions, the meanings of which escape clear cut definition.

The difficulty is increased by the fact that during the classical period of Scholasticism the Scholastics did not commonly use an unequivocal and clear terminology. New terms were being introduced[3] and their meanings often remained fluctuating. And even if Scholastics seem to be settled on a definite terminology, yet critical differences will appear as soon as we try to confront the teaching of one of them with the teaching of another. Many a famous debate, we are convinced, goes back more to a difference in the use of certain terms — *a difficultas verbalis* as Ockham would say — than to differences in the solution of the problem.[4]

---

[3] Cf. the very illuminating philosophical and philological study of E. Gilson, "Notes sur les Vocabulaires de l'Etre", in *Medieval Studies*, Vol. VIII, pp. 150—158, Toronto 1946. Pontifical Institute of Mediaeval Studies.

[4] For instance the term "existence" seems to be used in a different meaning by St. Thomas and certainly by Thomists on the one hand and by Scotus and Ockham on the other. When St. Thomas is said to admit a real distinction between essence and existence in the thing and Duns Scotus and Ockham consider this distinction to be a fiction, they are not using the same language. In our opinion, the Scotistic term *"haecceitas"* comes closer to the Thomistic term *"existentia"*, at least in the sense that the two terms mean the ultimate reality *(actus ultimus)* of a thing. However, Scotus identifies this ultimate reality with individuality, which according to St. Thomas and Ockham is not a distinct entity (or 'reality', in the terminology of Scotus). It is evident from this that the historian has to face a rather involved terminology!

For Ockham, as for every Scholastic philosopher, there are things given, that are independent of our thinking. We are aware of these things, we find them, we do not create nor produce them by our thoughts. He is a realist, since he admits the existence of things *(res)*, even if no one thinks of them. Hence he is utterly ignorant of that idealism, according to which the objects of our intellect are thoughts or ideas and nothing more. As we have shown elsewhere,[5] even the critical *Aprioria* of Kant is foreign to Ockham's thought. Ockham is a naïve realist who firmly believes that he is in immediate contact with objective reality, with the things outside the mind, be they material or spiritual, and that our sense experiences are faithful representations of their objects. Consequently, he is convinced that the universe of his experience is composed of many things which evidently show a definite order. Of these things — which are individuals, substances or accidents — we can predicate some very general notions if we also use either names or demonstrative pronouns as subjects.

Some of these general notions are now to be explained. They are properly speaking metaphysical notions, though they may have bearing on Logic as well.

"Being" — "Ens".

The term "being" signifies any thing and every thing that is given in this universe, be it outside or inside the mind. We could also say that "being" signifies any and every individual, if we equate "things" (res) with "individual".[6] Since we are at the systematic

---

[5] Cf. *The realistic conceptualism of William Ockham*, in *Traditio*, Vol. IV (1946) p. 307, espec. p. 312 s. [and *supra*, 163 ff.].

[6] Nunc logice loquendo tripliciter accipitur singulare et individuum. Uno modo dicitur singulare quod est una res numero et non plures res. Alio modo dicitur singulare res extra animam quae est una et non plures nec est signum alicuius. Tertio modo dicitur singulare signum proprium uni quod vocatur terminus discretus. *Quodlib.* V, 12 (edit. Argent.). The third meaning is purely logical. However, strictly speaking we cannot equate "thing" with "individual" in meaning, though they have the same extension, because "individual" is considered to be a necessary attribute of a being. As such it belongs to the *passiones entis* and is related to the attribute "one". Cfr. *Ordinatio* d. 36, q. 1 G—J.

25*

beginning of Metaphysics, which has to presuppose the knowledge
of the term "being" and its signification, we are able only to point
at what is meant or signified by this term, as referring to any and
every thing of our experience. We could likewise hint at the meaning
of this term by saying that in a progressive process of generalizing abstraction we can reach a concept which is so general that it can be
predicated about any and every thing that is in the universe.

Whilst the first approach to a clarification of the notions of being
is not explicitly developed by Ockham, — though he uses it, —
the second approach is explicitly stated in the *Summa Logicae*,
where it is linked up with the teaching on the univocation of being.
We will not now refer to this text in order to deal with the doctrine
of the univocity of being, but only to make evident that according
to Ockham it is always possible for us to transcend two distinct concepts of distinct things and to form a concept which is higher than at
least one of them and which can be predicated of both of them. If all
distinct concepts are surpassed, the most common notion predicable
about things will be reached, to give us the notion of "being".

Let us now listen to Ockham himself:

Summa Logicae, 1. 38[b]

"Concerning "being", let it be first known that "being" can be taken
in a twofold sense: In one sense, the noun "being" is taken, insofar as there
corresponds to it one concept which is common to all things and which can
be predicated about all in such a way that it answers the question "What
is it?" and this in that manner, in which a transcendental can be predicated
in answer to the question "What is it?" The statement, that for all things
there is one concept common to and predicable about all things, can be
'persuaded' by the following reason: If there is not such a common concept,
then diverse concepts which are A and B are common to diverse things.
However, I show, that there is a concept which is more common than both
A and B and which is predicable about any of them, viz., C, for example:
As the three spoken propositions: C is B, C is A, C is something, can be
formulated, so likewise such three mental propositions can be formulated;
of these two are doubtful and the third is known; for it is possible that
someone doubts both: C is B, C is A, and that he nevertheless knows: C is

[b] Fr. Boehner originally had here first the Latin text; we prefer to
refer to his edit. of the *Summa Logicae* I 98—100 lines 6—68. Better
translation in *Ockham-Philosophical Writings* (Edinburgh 1957) 90—92.

something. With this assumption I argue in the following manner: Two of these propositions are doubtful and one is known, and all three propositions have the same subject, consequently they have distinct predicates. For if they did not have distinct predicates, then the same proposition would be known and dubious, since two are here supposed to be doubtful. If they have distinct predicates, then there is another predicate in this proposition: C is something, which is not predicate in one of these: C is B, C is A; therefore, this predicate is distinct from the other predicates. Yet, it is manifest that this predicate is not less common nor coextensive with at least one of them; consequently it is more than at least one of them: That was to be proved, viz., that some concept of the mind other than these less extensive concepts is commom to every being, which must be conceded. For about every being or about the pronoun pointing to any being, a concept of the mind can be truly predicated as the same word can be truly predicated about everything.

Notwithstanding the fact that there is a concept thus common to every being, the noun "being" is equivocal. For it is not predicated as one concept about all its possible subjects taken in their significative function; rather to the noun "being" there correspond diverse concepts, as I have explained in the Exposition of Porphyry.

Furthermore it is known, that according to the Philosopher in the fifth book of *Metaphysics* [*1. c.* c. 7; 1017a7] "being is spoken of in an accidental manner; and, in itself." This distinction does not mean that some being is in itself and another in an accidental manner. Aristotle rather shows a diverse mode of predication of one about the other by means of the verb "to be". That is sufficiently clear from the examples of the Philosopher. He says: "We say: The musical in an accidental manner is just, and also: The musician is in an accidental manner a man, and: We say that the musical in an accidental manner is building". From this it is apparent, that he is speaking only about a diverse mode of predication of the one about the other. For something is said about something by itself, and something is said about something by accident. For, it is manifest, that there is not one such thing which is by itself and another that is by accident, since there is no thing unless it is a substance or an accident; but both, substance and accident is a being by itself; therefore . . . However, notwithstanding this, something is predicated about another by itself and something by accident.

Likewise, there is the distinction of being in potency and being in act. This does not mean that something which is not in the universe, but can be in the universe, is truly a being, or that something else which is in the universe, is also a being. Rather Aristotle in dividing "being" in potency and act (in the fifth book of *Metaphysics* — *1. c.* 1017b 1.) has in mind that this noun "being" is predicated about some thing by means of the verb "is" in a proposition merely about an actual state of thing and in such a way that this proposition is not equivalent to a proposition about possibility for instance: Socrates is a being; Whiteness is a being. About something, however, "being" is not predicated unless in a proposition about the possible or in a proposition equivalent to one about the possible; for instance saying: The Antichrist can be a being, or: The Antichrist is a being in potency. In like manner it is with others. Hence he declares in the same place, 'that being is divisible by potency and act as that which knows and that which rests'; but nothing is knowing or resting unless it be actually knowing or resting."

Explanatory Remarks

For an explanation of the difficult expression: *Praedicari in quid* and *praedicari in quale*, we refer to Ockham's explanation in his *Expositio Aurea* (Sup. Porphyr. cap. de gener, ad: A differentia vero). Something is predicated *"in quale"*, "in how", as qualifying a subject or in the manner of a quality or attribute which answers the question: How is something? For instance when we ask: How *(qualis)* is a man, we can answer: He is rational, or: How is a raven? we can answer: It is black. We are thus answering by something which is either a difference, or an accident or a property of a thing. All these predications are, generally speaking, "in quale". However, as it is obvious from the examples, they do not predicate a predicamental accident. In fact, the distinction does not concern the predicamental line at all, that is the line of predicates about things, but it concerns the manner in which predicates are predicated. Where on the other hand we predicate in the manner of a genus or species, we call the corresponding predication a predication *in quid*, since it answers the question: What is it? For if we ask: What is a man? we can conveniently answer: An animal. Thus we ask about the whole, when we ask "What", and do not ask about a qualification. However, we can also ask about a part: What is it? For instance if we see the quality whiteness, we can ask: What is it? and answer: It is color. Color is also predicated "in quid", though it is an accidental form (according to the scholastics).

Connotative predicates are predicated *in quale*, absolute predicates *in quid*. Since "being", too, is predicated about the whole, though it is neither a genus nor a species, but precisely the subject, concerning real predication, "being" too, is said to be predicated "in quid". And hence, Ockham says, "being" like any generic or specific or individual concept is predicated "in quid", yet in that manner in which a transcendental can be predicated because it is not a generic concept.

Some mss. read: *Primo modo praedicandi per se*. The form "*prae*dicandi per se" is not the usual one. We usually read: *dicendi per se*. The first mode of saying something by itself about something is given, when the predicate defines the subject. For instance: Man is an animal. It is true, that "being" is predicated in the first mode, but not the other transcendentals, as one, true, good etc. For, though "being" is not a definitorial part (genus or specific difference) of any term or quiddity, nevertheless it is a kind of highest genus. Hence in saying: *Unum est ens*, Or: Man is a being "ens" or "being" in these cases would be predicated in the first mode of predication.

Either reading, therefore, makes sense, but we preferred the first, because it makes better sense.

Ockham also mentions in this text, that in spite of the fact that there is one univocal term predicable about every thing, being is equivocal. The problem does not concern us now, since Ockham here refers to his theory about the meaning of the categories of Aristotle. According to Ockham, there are only two categories, which signify really distinct entities or absolute things, viz., substance and quality. Therefore, "being" cannot be predicated about the other categories as about distinct entities. About this problem more will be said in our later discussion of the problem concerning the univocity of being. Ockham refers to: *Expositio Aurea sup. Porphyr.* cap. De specie, ad: Sed in familiis.

Finally Ockham uses in the text the term *"persuasio"* in the form, "can be persuaded". It means that his proof is not a demonstration in the strict sense, but yields "probability" or in modern terminology moral certitude. The proof is no demonstration since it lacks necessarily true premises.

The net result of this text is that the highest notion common to all things and predicable about every thing in its totality and absolutely is the notion of "being". It can, therefore, be equated and is equated by Ockham with "thing", "something", and even with "nothing". Ockham does not hesitate to equate it also with "reality", since the abstract term, certainly in this particular case, is synonymous with its corresponding concrete term.

Furthermore, we can gather from this text that "being" primarily signifies any thing that is in the universe. Hence in a proposition like this: Man is a being, the term "being" is used to signify and to stand for a thing which is a man. The proposition is true, therefore, if there is at least one individual which is a man. In this case the term "being" is used for an actually existing thing, here and now. However, the term "being" can also be used in propositions which are not of the present and do not express an actual or present state of thing, but which are of the future or the past or express a possible state of affairs.

In such cases, too, the term "being" can be applied, and that in its original meaning, but as qualified by the form of a proposition, viz., by the form of being of the past or future tense or by containing the modality of possibility. For, the following propositions can be true: This pen is a being, This pen was a being, This pen will be a being, This pen can be a being. In all these cases, we do not change the meaning of "being", we are only changing or enlarging the range of signification of "being" or its supposition.

This consideration of the logical function of the term "being" in propositions about the present, the past, the future and the possible, discussed by the scholastics in their tracts on "*Appellatio, Ampliatio,* or *Suppositio* in general, leads Ockham to a new circumlocution of the notion of "being". Since it is sufficient to take into account only the term "being" as it functions in propositions about the possible, (what was, was possible; what will be, will be possible; what is, is possible), we can now determine "being" as saying: Something to which it is not repugnant to be in the actual order of things (aliquid cui non repugnat esse in rerum natura). If taken in this sense, we shall call it "being" in an unrestricted signification or supposition, or simply "being" in its unrestricted form; if it is restricted to something that here and now is in the universe, we shall call it "being" in restricted signification or supposition, or simply "being" in its restricted form.

This distinction between the unrestricted and restricted signification or supposition of "being" is brought out by Ockham in discussing a term which is the opposite of "being", viz., "nothing", which in turn leads us to the other circumlocution of "being", namely "not-nothing".

In order to avoid any equivocations, we must eliminate from our metaphysical terminology the syncategorematic term "nothing". "Nothing", as syncategorematic term, can be considered to be a logical constant of discourse. When we say, for instance: Nothing is running, we mean to say, that every instance of the propositions: This is running, or That is running etc. is false. In other words, "nothing" in this sense, contains the universal quantifier "every" plus the negation, which excludes every subject.

On the other hand "nothing" can be understood in its categore-matical meaning, and as such it is the opposite of "being" and an important term of our metaphysical language. It is the negation of "being" either in its restricted or in its unrestricted form. In its unrestricted form "being" is predicated about everything to which it is not repugnant to be in the actual order of things. The negation of this, or the corresponding "nothing", is the absolute nothing or that to which it is repugnant to be in the actual order of things. In its restricted form "being" is predicated only about things which are here and now in the actual order of things. The negation of this, or the corresponding "nothing", is the relative "nothing": namely, that which actually is not in the actual order of things, or, which comes down to the same, that which does not have actual or real being. An instance of the absolute nothing would be signified in the proposition: Chimaera is nothing. An instance of the relative nothing would be signified in the proposition, famous in the Middle ages: The Antichrist is nothing. The latter proposition is consistent with: The Antichrist is a being in potency or can be a being. The former proposition is not consistent with: Chimaera can be.[7]

Further clarifications will be given in the following sections, where the interchangeability of "being" and "to be", that is of "ens" and "esse", will also be mentioned. For the rest we shall keep in mind that "being" which signifies every *thing* or reality in the universe comprehends in its widest extension that to which it is not repugnant to be in the actual order of things.

---

[7] Ideo dico quod nihil multipliciter accipitur. Uno modo syncategore-matice, et sic est unum signum universale negativum includens suum distri-buibile secundum modum loquendi logicorum, sicut dicimus: Nihil currit, Nihil est intelligens. Alio modo accipitur categorematice pro aliquo quod dicitur unum nihil. Et hoc potest accipi dupliciter: quia uno modo nihil accipitur et dicitur illud quod non est realiter nec habet aliquid esse reale. Et isto modo dicendum est quod angelus ab aeterno fuit nihil, quia nullum esse ab aeterno fuit nisi solus Deus. Aliter accipitur nihil pro illo quod non tantum non habet esse reale, sed etiam sibi repugnat esse reale, et isto modo dicimus quod chimaera est nihil; et sic non fuit homo nihil ab aeterno, quia numquam sibi repugnabat esse in rerum natura. *Ordinatio* d. 36, q. 1, P.

2. "To Be", ESSE

The discussion of this extremely elusive term "to be" or "esse" which was freely being used by Scholastic philosophers, constitutes a link between the preceding explanation and later discussions. We encounter this term "esse" in various contexts which have to be carefully analyzed in order to keep in line with a consistent terminology and to avoid expressions which may be misleading. An opportunity to clarify this term is presented to Ockham, when he meets such a proposition as: The *Esse intelligibile*[8] or the *Esse repraesentatum* of a creature is not really distinct from the divine essence. Ockham's logical mind is very suspicious of such expressions. In fact, he considers them "irrational", though he readily admits that it is rather a matter of terminology than a real problem.[9] For the sake of a clear and precise terminology, he proposes certain distinctions. Three meanings of "to be" or "esse" are distinguished by Ockham, to which he adds a discussion of grammatical expressions in which "to be" appears.

a) "To be" can mean "to exist". In this sense the verbal variations of the term used to be called the "secundum adiacens" by the scholastics, which means, that "is" (est) constitutes the whole predicate, as for instance in the proposition: Socrates is; for which we usually say, Socrates exists.

b) "To be" can also mean the same as "being", in the sense that we have explained above, viz., that to which it is not repugnant to be in the actual order of things. However, "to be" in this sense is not much in use.

c) "To be" can also be used merely as the copula in a proposition. As such it is the "tertium adiacens" and unites the predicate with the subject and indicates or signifies that the predicate is predicated about the subject.

---

[8] This should be translated as "The intelligible to be" or, however, not so correctly: "The to be intelligible." The expression is discussed later.

[9] Sed ista opinio videtur mihi irrationalis; quia tamen plus constat in verbis quam in re et verba sunt ad placitum et unusquisque potest vocare esse intelligibile creaturae sicut placet, ideo arguere contra istam opinionem est arguere ad nomen et non ad rem ... *Ordinatio,* d. 36, q. 1, D.

After these more general distinctions of the term "to be", Ockham goes on to discuss the meaning of this term in various grammatical connections, some of which are peculiar to Latin and will resist an appropriate translation into idiomatic English. In our explanation, therefore, we have to have recourse to the Latin expressions quite frequently.

It may happen, that the infinitive "to be" (esse) is followed by the genitive case, as for instance in the expression: "The to be of a creature" *(esse creaturae);* The to be of God *(esse Dei).* In such cases, and if no other term interferes, "to be" is taken in its significative function and stands for or 'supposits' for an existing being *(esse existere),* that is, it has the meaning of being in its restricted form; or at least it 'supposits' for something to which it is not repugnant to be in the natural order of things, it has therefore the meaning of "being" in its unrestricted form.[10] Hence we could aptly translate such expressions as "The to be of a creature", with: "The actual being of a creature," or simply: "The being of a creature." It only depends on whether we choose the restricted or unrestricted form "of being".

The infinitive "to be" in Latin can be followed by the accusative case of a noun. This noun, in turn, may be either a substantive or an adjective. In order to simplify the rather involved analysis made by Ockham, let us distinguish here two main instances, viz., first "to be" is followed by a noun in the accusative case which is either a substantive or an adjective, but so that the adjective is not a qualification of "to be". Secondly the adjective is a true adjectival determination of the expression "to be".

In the first case, expressions like: "To be an animal", "To be white" etc. are incomplete expressions, since they require something to be added. The first example for instance, would be completed by saying: Man to be an animal (hominem esse animal); the second: Man to be white (hominem esse album). Such expressions are called "dictum" and play a major role in modal propositions. As dicta,

---

[10] Si primo modo accipitur, semper tale esse, nisi forte ratione adiuncti, accipitur significative et supponit pro esse existere, vel saltem pro aliquo cui non repugnat esse in rerum natura. *Ordinatio,* d. 36, q. 1, G.

they require, of course, still a further addition, a modality for instance, so that the whole sentence would be: Man to be an animal is possible. They do not concern us here. May it suffice to state that "to be" exercises here the function of the copula "is" and that the dictum can be understood to have simple supposition.

In the second case, "to be" is taken in significative meaning and is qualified or determined by an adjective, in the same manner as the term "man" is qualified or determined by the term "white" in the expression: "White man." Sentences which contain the term "to be" qualified by an adjective are apt to be false; for they must fulfill certain necessary conditions for their truth. For instance, the expression: A white man is an animal, requires for its truth the truth of the following propositions: Man is an animal, Something white is an animal, and: Man is white. If we apply to the following true proposition (Ockham gives only a false instance): "Divine to be is eternal" (esse divinum est aeternum), the analysis will yield these three propositions: A to be is eternal, Something divine is eternal, and A to be is divine. It appears immediately that "to be" is understood either in the sense of actual being, or in the sense of being in its unrestricted form, that is, as "existence" or as "that to which it is not repugnant to be in the actual order of things".

We shall now present in translation a text where such an analysis is given concerning a false expression containing "to be" qualified by an adjective, viz., the expression: "The represented to be", (esse repraesentatum).

Ordinatio, d. 36, q. 1. O.

Et quod dicitur postea, quod esse repraesentatum creaturae est idem realiter cum forma repraesentante, et quod esse cognitum est idem realiter cum cognitione, verum non est. Et huius ratio est: nam hic esse cognitum creaturae ly esse ibi non potest stare illo modo quo stat in dicto propositionis quia non potest assignari propositio cuius potest esse dictum; et ideo oportet quod stet pro esse existere vel pro esse cui non repugnat esse in rerum natura. Sed sive sic sive sic, omnes tales sunt falsae. Nam si in ista: Esse repraesentatum creaturae est idem cum Deo, ly esse stet pro esse existere, oportet quod ad veritatem istius propositionis omnes istae sint verae: quod esse creaturae sit repraesentatum, quod esse creaturae sit idem realiter cum Deo, et quod repraesentatum sit idem realiter cum Deo. Sicut ad veritatem huius: Anima intellectiva Sortis est forma, requiruntur omnes istae, scilicet: quod anima sit forma, quod anima sit intellectiva, et quod aliquid intellectivum sit forma. Et hoc propter implicationem importatam per talem propositionem, cuius extremum componitur ex tali determinabili et determinatione vel determinationibus. Et est manifeste notum exercitatis in Logica.

Sed in proposito ista est falsa: Esse existere creaturae est idem realiter cum Deo ab aeterno. Tum quia non fuit ab aeterno, et per consequens non fuit Deus ab aeterno. Tum quia esse existere creaturae vel est realiter ipsa creatura vel est aliquid in creatura, quorum neutrum est idem realiter cum Deo. Similiter haec est falsa: Aliquod repraesentatum est Deus realiter, quia Deus secundum eos non est repraesentatus sed repraesentans. Eodem modo est haec falsa: Esse existere cognitum creaturae est idem realiter cum Deo, quia implicatur quod esse existere creaturae sit idem realiter cum Deo. Propter idem, si esse ibi stet pro omni illo cui non repugnat esse in rerum natura, adhuc est falsa, qui haec est falsa: Esse creaturae est idem realiter cum Deo. Nam esse creaturae non potest esse aliud realiter a creatura.

What is said (later on) that *the represented* to be of a creature is really the same with the representing form, and that *the known* to be is really the same with cognition, is not true. The reason for this is the following: In the expression: "*The known* to be" of a creature, the "to be" can not have the same supposition as it has in the dictum of a proposition, since there cannot be assigned a proposition of which it is the dictum; therefore it must have the meaning of "to be actually" or of "being to which it is not repugnant to be in the actual order of things". But in either case all such sentences are false. For, if in the proposition: *The represented to be* of a creature is the same with God, the "to be" has the meaning of "to be actually", then the truth of this proposition requires, that all these propositions be true: The to be of a creature is represented; the to be of a creature is really the same with God; and Something represented is the same with God. In the same manner the truth of the proposition: The intellective soul of Socrates is a form, requires all these propositions: The soul is a form; the soul is intellective; and Something intellective is a form, because of the implication which such a proposition has, of which the subject is composed of something determinable, and of a determination or determinations. This is a manifest truth for those who are trained in Logic. However, in our case this proposition is false: *The to be actually* of a creature is really the same as God since eternity. First, because it was not from eternity, and consequently it was not God from eternity. Secondly, because *the to be actually* of a creature is really the creature itself, or it is something in the creature, neither of which is really the same as God. Likewise this proposition is false: Something represented is really God; for according to the opponents, God is not represented but representing. In like manner this proposition is false: *The known to be actually* of a creature is really the same with God, since it is implied that the *to be actually* of a creature is really the same with God. And for the same reason, if "to be" has the meaning of "everything to which it is not repugnant to be in the actual order of things", then, too, it is still false, because the proposition is false: The to be of a creature is really the same with God. For the to be of a creature cannot really be anything else but the creature.

3. EXISTENCE AND ESSENCE

We know that Ockham was not much in favor of abstract terms. According to him they lead easily to confusion, since most of them signify the same as their corresponding concrete terms, unless they include certain syncategorematic terms or signify an absolute form or a reality, as for instance "whiteness" or "heat" etc. Ockham believes that many abstract terms are introduced for convenience sake, partly as abbreviations, partly only as an ornament of language. This applies also to the terms "essence" and "existence". Hence it seems that we could dispense of them. For "being" (ens) could be substituted for the abstract term "essence", and" to be" (esse) or "to exist" (existere) could be substituted for the abstract term "existence". Moreover, even the terms "to be" and "being" are interchangeable, as we have seen, unless we understand the one term in the restricted form of "being" and the other in the unrestricted form of "being".

According to Ockham's metaphysical language, therefore, we could say: This (pointing at Socrates, for instance) is a being, and likewise: This is, or: This exists, and again: This is an essence, or: This is an existence. All of these propositions are equivalent or can be made equivalent. Only their grammatical structures are different. In any case, the meaning of the terms under consideration is the same, though their extensions may vary. In fact we could dispense with all of them in favor of the verb "to be", more exactly in favor of the verbal form of "to be", i. e., "is", which not only signifies the binding of the predicate with the subject, but also that there is or can be a state of affairs which satisfies, or as Ockham prefers to say, which verifies the proposition. Hence, if there is a proposition, in which both subject and predicate are terms or signs of things — Ockham would say, signs of first intentions — and if both terms have significative function or have personal supposition, then the verbal form "is" (or its derivatives) signifies that there is something that verifies the proposition. Hence "is", used with predicative function on this level of language, has always for Ockham — and as far as we know for all scholastics — an existential import, or the import of being, signifying reality. And in this he is in line with Aristotle himself, when he gives his famous definition of falsity and truth:

> To say of what is that it is not, or of what is not, that it is, is false, while to say of what is that it is, and of what is not that it is not, is true; so that he who says of anything that it is, or that it is not, will say either what is true or what is false. (*Metaph.* IV, 7; 101 b 26.)

We could say, therefore, if we exclude subjectivistic or idealistic interpretations, that being and all its derivatives are obtained from the verbal form "is", we could even say that they are obtained from the copula "is", provided that we do not understand the copula only as copula. Consequently it would not make any difference, as to the meaning, if we substituted nouns for the verbal variations of "is". Only the customs of language are barriers here.

These and other points, or at least the equivalences hinted at, are brought out by Ockham in a text, where he asks whether essence and existence in an individual are the same, or whether they are really distinct. By really distinct he means, whether there are two things (res) in an individual, one of which is its essence, the other its existence. Two texts can be referred to in this connection, one treating the matter in a more general way, the other applying it to a concrete case viz., to an angel.

Summa Logicae, P. III, 2, cap. 27.

Et quia tactum est de esse existere, aliquantulum digrediendo considerandum est, qualiter esse existere se habet ad rem, utrum scilicet esse rei et essentia rei sint duo extra animam distincta inter se. Et mihi videtur quod non sunt talia duo, nec esse existere significat aliquid distinctum a re.

Quia si sic, aut esset substantia aut accidens. Non accidens, quia tunc esse existere hominis esset quantitas vel qualitas, quod est manifeste falsum, sicut inductive patet. Nec potest dici quod sit substantia, quia omnis substantia vel est materia vel forma vel compositum, vel substantia absoluta; sed nullum istorum potest dici esse, si esse sit alia res ab entitate rei.

Item si essent duae res, aut facerent per se unum, aut non. Si sic, oporteret, quod unum esset actus et reliquum potentia, et per consequens unum esset materia et aliud forma, quod est absurdum. Si non facerent per se unum, igitur essent unum aggregatione tantum vel facerent tantum unum per accidens, ex quo sequitur, quod unum esset accidens alterius.

Item, si essent duae res, non esset contradictio, quin Deus conservaret entitatem rei in rerum natura sine existentia, vel econverso existentiam sine entitate, quorum utrumque est impossibile.

Ideo dicendum est, quod entitas et existentia non sunt duae res, sed ista duo vocabula res et esse idem et eadem significant, sed unum nominaliter et aliud verbaliter. Propter quod unum non potest convenienter poni loco alterius, quia non habent eadem officia. Unde esse potest poni inter duos terminos sic dicendo: Homo est animal. Non sic est de hoc nomine res vel entitas. Unde esse significat ipsam rem. Sed significat causam primam simplicem, quando dicitur de ea non significando ipsam ab alio dependere. Quando autem praedicatur de aliis, significat ipsas res dependentes et ordinatas ad causam primam, et hoc quia istae res non sunt res, nisi sint sic dependentes et ordinatae ad causam primam, sicut non sunt aliter. Unde quando homo non dependet ad Deum, sicut tunc non est, ita tunc non est homo. Et ideo non est plus imaginandum, quod essentia est indifferens ad esse et non esse, quam quod est indifferens ad essentiam et non essentiam. Quia sicut essentia potest esse et non esse, ita essentia potest esse essentia et non esse essentia. Et ideo talia argumenta: Essentia potest esse et non esse, igitur esse distinguitur ab essentia: Essentia potest esse sub opposito essentiae, igitur essentia differt ab essentia. Et ideo non plus sunt essentia et esse duae res quam essentia et essentia sunt duae res; et ita esse non est alia res ab entitate rei ...

Causa autem quare Sancti et alii dicunt Deum esse ipsum esse, est quia Deus sic est esse quod non potest non esse; immo necessario est esse, nec ab alio est. Creatura autem sic est esse, quod non est necessario esse, sicut nec necessario est res, et ab alio est, sicut ab alio est res effective. Et ideo non differunt in Deo quod est et quo est, quia non est aliquid aliud a Deo quo Deus est; sed in creatura differunt, quia illud quod est creatura et quo est creatura sunt distincta simplicter, sicut Deus et creatura differunt.

Since we touched upon the "to be to exist", we have to make a digression for a while in order to consider, how the "to be to exist" is related to the thing, viz., whether the to be of a thing and the essence of a thing are two (entities) outside the thing distinct from each other. It appears to me that there are not two such (entities); nor does the "to be to exist" signify something distinct in the thing. For, if that were the case, it would be either substance or accident. It is not an accident, because then the "to be to exist" of a man would be a quantity or a quality; that is manifestly false, as becomes clear by way of induction. Nor can it be said that it is a substance, because every substance is either matter or form or the compositum (of both), or it is an absolute substance. But if the "to be" is another thing different from the entity of the thing, it cannot be said that it is anything of these.

Furthermore: If essence and existence were two things, either they would make something that is one by itself, or not. If so, it would be necessary, that the one be act and the other potency, and consequently, the one would be matter, the other form, which is absurd. If they do not make something that is one by itself, then they would be only something one by aggregation, or they would make something that is ore in an accidental manner, and from that it follows, that the one would be an accident of the other.

Furthermore: If they were two things, then it would be no contradiction, that God could preserve the entity of a thing in the actual order without existence, or vice versa, the existence (of a thing), without entity; both of which are impossible.

Therefore, it must be said that entity and existence are not two things; rather these two words "thing" and "to be" signify the same and the same things, but the one does it in the manner of a noun, the other in the manner of a verb. For that reason, the one cannot conveniently put in the place of another, since they do not have the same task to fulfill. Hence, "to be" can be put between two terms, saying thus: Man is an animal. However, it cannot be done thus with the noun "thing" or "entity". Hence "to be" signifies the thing itself. But it signifies the first simple cause, when it is predicated about it, without signifying that it is depending on something else. When, however, it is predicated about others, it signifies that these things are depending on and ordered to the first cause. And this is so because these things are things only if they are thus depending on and ordered to the first cause; for, otherwise they do not exist. Hence, when a man is not depending on God, as he then is not, so he is then not a man. Therefore, there is no more reason to imagine that essence is indifferent to to be and to not to be, than that it is indifferent to essence and existence. For, as essence can be and cannot be, so essence can be essence and cannot be essence. For this reason such arguments as: Essence can be and cannot be, therefore the to be is distinguished from essence; Essence can be under the opposite of to be, therefore, essence is distinguished from to be, are not valid, as likewise such ones are not valid: Essence can not be essence, and it can be essence, therefore, essence differs from essence. Hence, there is no more reason that essence and to be are two things, than that essence and essence are two things. Thus to be is not another thing from the entity of a thing...

Yet, the reason, why the Saints and others say that God the very to be, is this: God is in such a manner to be that he cannot not be; rather, He is to be in a necessary manner, and He is not from something else. A creature on the other hand, is to be in such a manner, that it is not necessary to be, as it is not necessarily a thing, and that means, it is from something else, like a thing is from something else as from its effective cause. For this reason, in God, there is no distinction between "what is", and "by which He is", since there is not something different from God, by which God is; but in a creature they do differ, since that which is a creature and by which it is a creature, are simply distinct, as God and creature are distinct.

We add to this text an entire question from the Quodlibeta of Ockham. Though it contains some repetitions, nevertheless it adds certain viewpoints in its concrete applications.

Quodlibet II, q. 7.

Utrum existentia angeli distinguatur ab essentia eius.

Quod sic: Quia existentia angeli est separabilis ab essentia, ergo distinguitur. Assumptum patet, quia essentia aliquando existit, aliquando non.

Contra: Tunc existentia esset accidens essentiae, quod falsum est.

Ad istam quaestionem dico quod existentia angeli non est alia res ab essentia. Quod probatur: Quia non est accidens essentiae — patet inductive — nec est alia substantia, quia nec est materia nec forma nec compositum ex his.

Si dicis, quod est respectus dependentiae creaturae ad Deum.

Contra hoc: Quia tales respectus sunt superflui.

Praeterea: Si sic, posset angelus esse sine tali respectu dependentiae. Consequens est falsum. Consequentia patet; quia minus dependet angelus a tali respectu quam effectus a sua causa et accidens a suo subiecto et forma a materia: sed omnia ista potest Deus facere sine aliis; ergo etc.

Item: Tunc existentia angeli esset accidens angeli, et per consequens prius natura esset essentia quam eius existentia.

Similiter: Substantia est prius natura quam accidens, ergo potest esse sine eo.

Item: Omnem rem priorem naturaliter potest Deus facere sine posteriori, ergo posset essentiam facere sine existentia.

Item: Si sic, aut facerent unum per se aut unum per accidens. Si unum per se, igitur unum esset materia et aliud forma. Si per accidens, ergo angelus esset unum per accidens.

Ideo dico, quod nullo modo distinguuntur.

Sed contra: Quod simul distinguitur ab aliquo, semper distinguitur ab eodem; sed existentia angeli aliquando distinguebatur ab angelo, puta quando angelus non fuit: ergo.

Praeterea: Quod est indifferens ad esse et non esse distinguitur ab utroque; sed essentia est indifferens ad esse et non esse; ergo etc.

Praeterea: Quando angelus non fuit, haec fuit vera: Essentia est essentia, sive: Angelus est angelus, et non ista: Angelus est existentia, nec illa: Angelus est; ergo distinguuntur.

Praeterea: Sequitur: existentia angeli non est essentia angeli, ergo existentia distinguitur ab essentia angeli. Antecedens est verum, ergo consequens.

Praeterea: Quando angelus non fuit, aut existentia angeli fuit idem cum essentia angeli aut distinctum; non idem, quia tunc non existebat; ergo distinctum ab illo.

Ad primum istorum dico, quod existentia angeli numquam distinguebatur a sua essentia, et tamen aliquando existentia non fuit essentia; sicut essentia angeli numquam distinguebatur ab essentia, et tamen aliquando essentia angeli non fuit essentia, quia aliquando fuit nihil.

Ad aliud dico, quod non magis est essentia indifferens ad esse et non esse quam existentia, quia sicut essentia potest esse existentia et potest non esse existentia, ita existentia potest esse essentia et potest non esse essentia. Unde idem omnino significatur et consignificatur per unum et per reliquum. Tamen esse aliquando est nomen, et tunc significat omni modo grammaticali et logicali idem cum essentia. Aliquando vero est verbum, et tunc significat illud verbaliter quod essentia significat nominaliter. Et ideo unum non ponitur convenienter loco alterius, qul non habent eadem officia, sicut nec nomen est verbum. Et ideo aliquando esse ponitur inter duos terminos dicendo: Homo est animal, vel: Homo potest esse animal, inter quos non convenienter ponitur essentia, quia nihil est dictu dicere: Homo essentia animal. Ita est de cursu et currere et multis talibus. Sic est ergo indifferens ad esse et non esse, quia utraque pars contradictionis potest esse vera successive.

Ad aliud dico, quod quando angelus non fuit haec fuit falsa: Angelus est angelus, sive: Essentia angeli est essentia, sive: Angelus est substantia sive ens, sicut ista: Angelus est existentia. Quia per omnes tales implicatur quod angelus sit aliquid. Ideo quandocumque haec est vera: Angelus est essentia vel ens, haec est vera: Angelus est existentia vel: Angelus existit, quia existentia et essentia idem omnino significant.

Ad aliud nego istam consequentiam: Existentia angeli non est essentia angeli, ergo existentia angeli distinguitur. Quia per antecedens non importatur angelum esse, scilicet per illam negativam, sed per consequens importatur angelum esse; ergo etc.

26*

Ad aliud dico, quod nec sunt idem nec distinctum, quia idem et distinctum sunt differentiae entis.

Contra: Quando non fuit angelus, plus distinguebatur asinus ab angelo quam angelus ab angelo, sive idem a se; ergo illae differentiae conveniunt non enti.

Respondeo, quod non plus distinguebatur tunc de facto; sed plus potuerit distingui, quando utrumque ponitur in effectu.

Ad principale dico sicut patet ex praedictis quod nec essentia est separabilis ab existentia nec econverso, licet utraque pars illius contradictionis: esse non esse, possit successive praedicari tam de essentia quam de existentia.

Whether the existence of an angel is distinguished from his essence.

This is affirmed: For, the existence of an angel is separable from the essence; therefore, it is distinguished. The antecedent is clear, since at one time the essence existed, at one time it did not exist.

On the contrary: If so, then existence would be an accident of the essence, which is false.

To this question I answer, that the existence of an angel is not a thing different from the essence.

This is proved: Because existence is not an accident of the essence — as is clear by induction —, nor is it another substance, since it is neither matter nor form nor a composition of both.

If you say, it is the relation of dependency of a creature upon God, then it is to be objected:

Such relations are superfluous.

Furthermore: If that were the case, then an angel could be without such a relation of dependency. The consequent is false. The consequence is clear: For, an angel is less dependent on such a relation than an effect on its cause and an accident on its subject and a form on matter. But God can make all these without the others; therefore etc.

Again: In this case, the existence of an angel would be an accident of the angel and consequently in the order of nature his essence would be prior to his existence.

Likewise: A substance is in the order of nature prior to an accident, therefore, it can be without it.

Furthermore: God can make every thing which in the order of nature is prior, without its posterior; therefore He could make an essence without an existence.

Furthermore: If it were the case that existence and essence are distinct they would make something that is one by itself or one by an accident. If one by itself, than one would be matter, the other form. If one by accident, then an angel would be something one by accident.

Therefore, I say, that they are in no way distinct.

But, to the contrary: That which is distinguished from something at one time is distinguished from the same at all time; but the existence of an angel was at some time distinguished from the angel, viz., when the angel did not exist, therefore . . .

Furthermore: That which is indifferent to *to be* and to *not to be* is distinguished from both; buth the essence is indifferent to *to be* and to *not to be:* therefore.

Again: When an angel did not exist, this proposition was true: An essence is an essence, or: An angel is an angel, but not this proposition: An angel is an existence, nor this: An angel is. Therefore essence and existence are distinguished.

Again: It follows: The existence of an angel is not the essence of an angel, therefore, the existence is distinguished from the essence of an angel. The antecedent is true, also, therefore, the consequent.

Again; When an angel did not exist, either the existence of the angel was the same with essence of the angel or it was distinct; it was not the same, since he did not exist at that time, therefore, it was distinct from him.

To the first of their arguments I reply: The existence of an angel was never distinguished from his essence; nevertheless at some time the existence was not the essence; as likewise the essence of an angel never was distinguished from his essence, and nevertheless at some time the essence of an angel was not an essence, because at some time he was nothing.

To the other argument I reply: The essence is not more indifferent to *to be* and to *not to be* than existence; for just as essence can be existence and can not be existence, so existence can be essence and can not be essence. Hence absolutely the same is signified and cosignified by the one and by the other. Yet, some times "to be" is a noun, and then it signifies the same as "essence" in any manner, grammatical or logical. Sometimes it is a verb, and then it signifies in the manner of a verb that which "essence" signifies in the manner of a noun. For this reason the one is not suitably put in the place of the other, since they do not have the same task to fulfill. Therefore, sometimes "to be" is put between two terms by saying: Man is an animal, or: Man can be an animal, between which "essence" is not suitably put, since it is no sentence at all to say: Man essence animal. The same applies to "the run" and to "to run" and to many others. Therefore, it is thus indifferent to *to be* and to *not to be,* because either part of the contradiction can be true in succession.

To the other argument I reply: When an angel did not exist, then this proposition was false: An angel is an angel, or: The essence of angel is an essence, or: An angel is a substance or a being, just as this was false: An angel is an existence. For all such propositions imply that the angel is something. Therefore, whenever this proposition is true: An angel is an essence or a being, this also is true: An angel is an existence, or: An angel exists, because "existence" and "essence" signify absolutely the same.

Concerning the other argument, I deny the consequence: The existence of an angel is not the essence of an angel, therefore the existence of an angel is distinguished. For by the antecedent, that is, by the negative proposition, there is not given to be understood that an angel exists, but by the consequent it is given to be understood that an angel exists; therefore etc.

To the other I reply: They are neither the same nor distinct, since "same" and "distinct" are differences of being.

To the contrary: When an angel existed, a donkey was more distinguished from an angel than an angel from an angel, or than the same from itself; these differences, therefore, apply also to non-being.

I answer: At the time that donkey was not distinguished more *de facto:* but it could have been more distinguished, when both the donkey and angel are posited to be in reality.

To the main objection I reply: It is clear from the aforesaid, that neither essence is separable from existence, nor vice versa; though either part of the contradiction, to be, not to be, can be predicated successively about both essence and the existence.

From these texts it follows clearly that the problem of a distinction between essence and existence does not exist in the Metaphysics of Ockham, since such a distinction is meaningless as regards reality. It follows likewise that such a distinction cannot be used in order to distinguish certain beings. For instance, the difference between God and creature cannot be expressed by saying: God is His essence, God is His existence, and In God essence and existence are the same. For, it can likewise be said of every creature: This creature is its essence, This creature is its existence, and In this creature essence and existence are the same. This rejection of one distinction does not of course imply that Ockham knows no other distinction between the being that is God and the being that is a creature. He only rejects the aforementioned distinction, because he cannot admit it on terminological and semantical grounds, and partly, also, because of the underlying theory of universals which Ockham considers to be very questionable — not to say even false.

Nevertheless, the distinction between the being that is God and the being that is a creature remains clear and definite in Ockham's system of Metaphysics, as it is in any other theory of the great

Scholastics. He only refuses to project semantical differences or even grammatical differences into reality. For that reason he emphasizes true metaphysical distinctions or differences which are more in line with transcendental notions and modalities. Thus he determines the being that is God as that being which is being necessarily or which necessarily is, or exists. A creature is a being that is not being necessarily, or which is or exists necessarily. God is a being for which there is no cause of its being or its essence or existence; a creature is a being which in its being, that is in its essence or existence, is dependent or is caused. God is from Himself, a creature is from God.

In this sense, Ockham even admits the famous distinction introduced by Boethius, viz., the distinction between "quo est" (by which a thing is) and "quod est" (what a thing is), a distinction which sometimes and wrongly is interpreted as the distinction between essence and existence. There is, of course no distinction in God, viz., between "by which God is" and "what God is", since "what God is" is God himself, and God is by Himself. In creatures, however, there is a distinction between "what the creature is" and "by which the creature is"; and even a real distinction, that is a distinction, just as between thing and thing, since the creature is that which it is, viz., it is itself, but it is by something else, viz., it is by God.

4. QUIDDITY, WHATNESS

We add a short discussion of this term also, because of its close relation to the term "essence". The term "quiddity" is formed from the interrogative particle "Quid". According to Ockham it is used in various meanings.[11]

In a first sense, "quiddity" is applied to any entity or to any thing which is one by itself. This particular man, for instance is a quiddity, since this individual is one by itself and represents a distinct entity. Hence in general, every thing that is a being is a quiddity, be it a substance or an accident, as long as it represents a distinct being. It is also called a "real quiddity" or a "quidditative entity".

---

[11] Cfr. *Reportatio* IV, q. 11, E and also *Ordinatio* d. 2, q. 6, Q.

This term would, therefore, also apply to the Scotistic "Haecceitas" (the thisness or the individual difference), which according to Scotus is not identical with the real nature of a thing, and likewise the term "quiddity" would apply to the Thomistic "existence" which is supposed to be really distinct from the real essence. If Ockham had admitted them, he would call "Haecceity" and "Existence" quidditative entity or quiddity. In this sense therefore, "being", "essence", "existence" and "quiddity" are interchangeable, as we have explained them before.

In a second sense, the term "quiddity" is applied only to the ultimate form of a compound thing by which it is distinguished from other things. For instance, the quiddity of man in this sense would be, the intellective soul. This "quiddity" of course cannot be equated with the whole thing, but only with a part of it. Yet this difference will disappear when we consider separate forms, like the angels or God.

In a third sense "quiddity" is applied to the definition which is composed of the genus and the specific difference. Since the definition is in the conceptual order, "quiddity", which is predicated about the definition cannot be applied to things. In other words, the definition of a thing and the thing itself are not really the same.

Quiddity or essence as that which precedes the individual being in any manner, logical or natural, has disappeared completely from Ockham's Metaphysics.

Thus we have shown what certain basic notions connected with the notion of being have become after having passed through Ockham's realistic conceptualism. All of them go back ultimately to the one notion of being, which signifies either the actually existing individuals or things in this world, or that to which it is not repugnant to be in the actual order of things. All Platonic ideas have disappeared from this Metaphysics, and likewise the mitigated Platonism of Aristotle in which the essence or quiddity is still something that precedes at least logically and naturally, though not in time, the individual. For Ockham the individual is equated with its essence, as it is also equated with its existence, and both are different names for the thing itself, which is either a being in the actual order of things or something to which it is not repugnant to be in the actual order of things.

Does this Metaphysics lose by this simplification? According to Ockham it loses only verbal difficulties and endless discussions about problems which originate from Grammar. And this according to the Venerable Inceptor can be only a gain.

22. ZU OCKHAMS BEWEIS DER EXISTENZ GOTTES

Texte und Erklärungen[a]

Obwohl seit einiger Zeit eine Revision der Deutung und Beurteilung der Philosophie Ockhams auf der ganzen Linie eingesetzt hat, wie die Arbeiten Vignauxs, Hochstetters, unsere eigenen und anderer Forscher beweisen, so ist es leider immer noch der Fall, daß wir auch in jüngster Zeit Darstellungen begegnen, die diese Forschungen ganz oder doch zum wesentlichen Teil unberücksichtigt lassen. Es ist natürlich leicht, etwas zusammenzuschreiben, von dem man glaubt, es sei wahr, und was gewissermaßen Traditionsgut einer oberflächlichen Geschichtsschreibung geworden ist; es ist aber unter Umständen recht schwer und auf jeden Fall recht mühsam herauszufinden, wie es denn nun wirklich gewesen ist. Die erste Aufgabe einer ernsten Geschichtsschreibung muß sein, die Dokumente zu befragen und gestützt auf sie die Geschehnisse und die Gedanken exakt zu beschreiben und dann zu deuten. Leider wird der umgekehrte Weg zu häufig von philosophierenden Historikern betreten, und das Ergebnis sind gewöhnlich Zerrbilder. Einem solchen Zerrbild der Philosophie Ockhams begegnen wir in De Wulfs Histoire de la Philosophie Médiévale.[1] Es ist durchaus nicht diesem Geschichtswerk eigen. Es ist aber typisch für viele Darstellungen der Ockhamistischen Philosophie. Nur weil es typisch ist, haben wir dieses Zerrbild einer kritischen Prüfung an anderer Stelle[2] unterzogen. Und aus dem-

[1] T. 3, éd. 6, Louvain 1947.
[2] A recent presentation of Ockham's philosophy, in: FrancStud 9 (1949) 443—456; [vgl. oben 137—156].

[a] Erst herausgegeben in: FranzStud 32 (1950) 50—69.

selben Grunde möchten wir an dieser Stelle wenigstens einen Teil, nämlich die Darstellung der Theodizee Ockhams, dem Zeugnis der Dokumente gegenüberstellen. Das Ergebnis wird vernichtend sein. Wir werden zunächst De Wulfs Darstellungen in Thesen aufteilen; wir werden sodann zwei einschlägige Texte Ockhams edieren und endlich von diesen Dokumenten aus Stellung nehmen.

I. EINE TYPISCHE DARSTELLUNG DER THEODIZEE OCKHAMS

Nach De Wulf[3] lassen sich über die natürliche Gotteslehre Ockhams folgende Behauptungen aufstellen:

1. Soweit die Hauptprobleme dieser Theodizee in Frage kommen, schwimmen wir geradezu in einem vollen Agnostizismus.

2. Ockham erklärt die Theodizee des Duns Scotus für falsch. (Ob diese These und die vorhergehende in einem inneren Zusammenhang stehen, ist eine offene Frage. De Wulf scheint sie zu bejahen.)

3. Ockham bestreitet die Gültigkeit des Scotischen Beweises der Existenz Gottes.

4. Das Dasein Gottes ist nicht Gegenstand des schauenden Erkennens, sondern ist unserm Verstande nur durch abstrakte Begriffe zugänglich.

5. Wie alle abstrakten Begriffe, so hat auch der Begriff der Ursache keine Tragweite oder Bedeutung für die Wirklichkeit, da sie nur Fiktionen des Verstandes sind (figmentum de l'esprit).

6. Das Kausalgesetz kann das Dasein Gottes nicht im strengen Sinne beweisen; denn: Es ist schwierig, wenn nicht unmöglich zu beweisen, daß Ursachen sich nicht ins Unendliche ohne einen Halt (sans arrêt!) aneinanderreihen können. Hier wird der Satz zitiert: Quia difficile est vel impossibile probare contra philosophos, quod non est processus in infinitum in causis eiusdem rationis (I Sent. d. II, q. 5; es muß aber heißen: q. 10 Q).

---

[3] A. a. O. 41.

7. Sollte man aber, um einen Regreß ins Unendliche zu vermeiden, doch eine erste Wirkursache annehmen, dann ist diese zweifellos ein Wesen, das an der Spitze von allen anderen Wesen steht. Es bleibt aber die Frage offen, ob es das möglichst vollkommene Wesen ist.

8. Ergebnis (conclusion): Die Existenz Gottes ist Gegenstand des Glaubens und nicht des Beweises (démonstration): Non potest sciri evidenter quod Deus est (Quodl. I, 1).

9. Auch die Eigenschaften Gottes sind unbeweisbar. Keiner der Beweise des Duns Scotus findet Gnade in den Augen Ockhams.

Es ist unmittelbar klar, daß die erste These zu Recht besteht, wenn all das, was unter 2—8 gesagt worden ist, wahr ist. Sind diese Behauptungen, vor allem die unter 5, 6 und 8, wirklich die Lehre Ockhams, dann haben wir einen vollen Agnostizismus vor uns, und dann werden wir vergebens noch irgendwelchen positiven Beiträgen Ockhams zur natürlichen Gotteslehre suchen. Dann wird aber auch die Behauptung an Gewicht gewinnen, daß Ockham für den Niedergang der Scholastik verantwortlich zu machen ist, und nur aus diesem Grunde könnte sein Werk noch das Interesse des Historikers erwecken.

Es könnte aber auch der Fall sein, daß wir in den oben angeführten Thesen Ockham überhaupt noch nicht gehört haben, oder doch nur in einer solchen Form, die Ockham selbst befremden müßte. Tatsächlich sind wir der Überzeugung, daß es Ockham schwerfallen, ja unmöglich sein würde, sich in den neun Thesen zu entdecken. Damit wollen wir nicht sagen, daß er alle neun Thesen schlechthin ablehnen müßte. Er würde sicher zugeben, daß Gott für uns im Pilgerstande und rein natürlicherweise kein Gegenstand des schauenden Erkennens, sondern nur des abstraktiven Erkennens ist und sein kann. Aber er würde uns doch wenigstens fragen dürfen, wer denn der Scholastiker sei, der das Gegenteil dieser Lehre vorgetragen habe. Nicht einmal der hl. Bonaventura habe einen Ontologismus gelehrt, geschweige denn ein direktes Schauen Gottes als eine natürliche Gabe des Menschen.

Auch die neunte These könnte Ockham mit Einschränkungen zugeben. Wenn die Eigenschaften angeführt werden, die De Wulf aufzählt, nämlich die Einzigkeit Gottes, die Allmacht, die Freiheit und

das Monopol der Schöpfermacht, so würde Ockham allerdings ein-
gestehen, daß er ihre Beweisbarkeit bestritten hat. Aber es dürfte
ihm doch wenigstens erlaubt sein zu bemerken, daß er die Beweisbarkeit (demonstrabilitas) und nur diese geleugnet habe, daß er aber
unter Beweisbarkeit als guter Aristoteliker etwas verstanden habe,
was kaum noch in einem neuscholastischen Handbuch der Philosophie
zu finden sei. Vor allem würde er auch noch sagen, daß er nicht
daran zweifle, daß die Güte Gottes, seine Geistigkeit usw. im strengen
Sinne bewiesen werden könne.

Aber damit würden Ockhams Zugeständnisse ziemlich zu Ende
sein; denn was die übrigen Thesen behaupten, könnte er schwerlich
zugeben, ohne sich selbst zu widersprechen, oder wenigstens ohne
wichtige Unterscheidungen zu machen.

Er würde sicher die These 5 radikal ablehnen. Die Begriffe sind
für ihn niemals Fiktionen gewesen, wohl aber, und zwar zu Anfang
seiner wissenschaftlichen Laufbahn, Gedankengebilde, d. h. Gegen-
stände eines Denkaktes, denen nur Gedacht-Sein und kein reales
Sein zukommt. Solche Gedankengebilde hat er wohl „ficta", aber
nicht „figmenta" genannt. Denn einem „figmentum" entspricht
nichts in der Wirklichkeit, einem „Fictum" oder einem Gedankengebilde oder einem Denkinhalt entspricht etwas in der Wirklichkeit.
Schon bald hat Ockham diese „Fictum"-Theorie aufgegeben zu-
gunsten einer anderen Theorie, nach der die Begriffe ein reales Sein
(esse subiectivum) und nicht bloß ein gedankliches Sein (esse obiectivum) haben, und zwar aus dem sehr überraschenden Grunde, weil
die Realität des Begriffes seine Ähnlichkeit mit den realen Gegen-
ständen besser gewährleistet. Wer über Ockhams Theorie der Begriffe schreibt, sollte niemals leugnen, daß Ockham die reale Tragweite und die Ähnlichkeit der Begriffe mit der Wirklichkeit bestritten
hat, oder aber er müßte die eigenartige Tatsache erklären, daß Ockham diese Ähnlichkeit immer eigens hervorhebt. Über diese Fragen
haben wir eine besondere Studie veröffentlicht, die unsere Behauptungen mit einschlägigen Texten belegt.[4] Wir konnten darin sogar
nachweisen, daß Ockham überzeugt ist, daß Kants „Verlegenheit",

---

[4] The Realistic Conceptualism of William Ockham, in: Traditio IV
(1946) 307—335; [vgl. oben 156—174].

wie wir a priori wissen, für seine Theorie der Erkenntnis gar nicht in Frage kommt, sondern nur für jene Theorie, die annimmt, daß es keinen unmittelbaren Kontakt des erkennenden Subjektes mit der Wirklichkeit gibt, sondern nur einen mittelbaren, nämlich über die Spezies, die ja wenigstens als „medium quo" angenommen wird und darum wenigstens ein Mittel ist. Es liegt eine gewisse Ironie des Schicksals darin, daß von Historikern das Gegenteil von dem, was er gesagt hat, Ockham so oft in den Mund gelegt wird. Ockham würde sich heute als Realisten bezeichnen müssen. Und wenn er plötzlich in unsere Zeit versetzt würde, ohne inzwischen etwas dazugelernt zu haben, würde er sich sogar als naiven Realisten bezeichnen müssen. Was er natürlich immer geleugnet hat, ist dies: es gibt keine Art von wirklicher Allgemeinheit in irgendeiner Form außerhalb der begrifflichen Welt.

Doch wir haben bereits zuviel für Ockham geredet. Die beste Kritik der typischen Darstellung seiner Theodizee wird Ockham selbst geben können. Wir wollen zunächst ihm das Wort geben und aus diesem Grunde einen Text veröffentlichen, auf den De Wulf ausdrücklich verweist, und wollen ihm einen anderen hinzufügen, der bislang der Forschung kaum zugänglich war, da er einem Werke entnommen ist, das noch nicht ediert ist.

II. TEXTE ZUR NATÜRLICHEN GOTTESLEHRE OCKHAMS

Als ersten Text wählen wir den Anfang der ersten Quaestio des ersten Quodlibet. Gerade dieser Text hat vielfach zu falschen Deutungen Anlaß gegeben.[5] Um ihn in möglichst gesicherter Form vorzulegen, wurde er mit zwei Inkunabel-Ausgaben der Quodlibeta verglichen und mit einer Reihe von Handschriften. Da aber Hochstetter noch kürzlich darauf hingewiesen hat, haß die Echtheit der Quodlibeta, vor allem Quodl. V—VII, noch einer kritischen Nachprüfung bedarf,[6] so wollen wir wenigstens einige Bemerkungen zu diesem Problem voranschicken.

[5] Z. B. H. Becher S. J., Gottesbegriff und Gottesbeweis bei Wilhelm von Ockham, in: Scholastik 3 (1928) 369—393.

[6] Vgl. Ockham-Forschung in Italien, in: Zeitschr. f. philosoph. Forsch. 1 (1947) 559 ff.

Von den Quodlibeta Ockhams sind mehrere Ausgaben bekannt, die durchaus nicht, wie es gewöhnlich bei den älteren Drucken der Fall ist, genau denselben Text bringen. Wir haben folgende zwei benützt, die sowohl im Quästionenbestand als in der Anordnung der Quästionen und im Text verschieden sind.

E¹ wahrscheinlich Paris 1487
E² Straßburg 1491

Von Handschriften der Quodlibeta sind die folgenden bekannt:

B   Basel, Stadtbibliothek, F. II. 24; 14. Jahrhundert. Unvollständig (bis Quodl. II, 15 der Straßburg-Edition).
C   Vaticana, Chigi, B. VII. 93; 14. Jahrhundert.
G   Göttingen, Universitätsbibliothek 118; 15. Jahrhundert.
L   Vaticana 956; 14. Jahrhundert.
M   Paris, Bibl. Mazarine 894; 14. Jahrh. Unvollständig wie B.
N   Paris, Bibl. Nationale 17841; 15. Jahrh. Unvollständig.
P   Paris, Bibl. Nationale 16398; 15. Jahrhundert.
S   München, Staatsbibliothek 8943; 15. Jahrhundert. Nur einige Quästionen.
V   Vaticana 3075; 14. Jahrhundert (1333?).
W   Wien, Dominikanerbibliothek 153; 15. Jahrhundert. Unvollständig. Brüssel, Bibl. Royale 4771; 15. Jahrhundert.

Alle mit Siglen versehenen Handschriften standen uns zur Verfügung, zum großen Teil durch Vermittlung unseres Freundes Dom Hildebrand Bascour O. S. B. Ferner hatten wir Zugang zu ausführlichen Beschreibungen des Quästionenbestandes der Handschriften L und V (Pelzer) und S und G (Hochstetter und James Sullivan).

Von unserer kurzen Untersuchung können wir die Handschriften B, M und S ausscheiden, da die beiden ersten nur bis Quodl. II, q. 15 reichen, die Münchener Handschrift S aber nur je eine Quaestio aus dem II. und III. Quodlibet und fünf aus dem IV. Quodlibet bringt.

Von den übrigen 8 Handschriften enthalten C, G, L, P und V alle sieben Quodlibeta. Wahrscheinlich dürfen wir zu diesen vollständigen Handschriften auch die von Brüssel rechnen, da sie nach der kurzen Angabe des Katalogs 230 Blätter enthält. Die restlichen zwei Handschriften haben nicht die drei letzten Quodlibeta. Die Handschrift W hat aber die ersten vier vollständig, während N mit der 18. Quästio des IV. Quodlibet abbricht. Es sei hervorgehoben, daß die beiden letztgenannten Handschriften dem 15. Jahrhundert angehören und voneinander abhängig zu sein scheinen.

Die Anordnung der Quästionen folgt im allgemeinen nicht der Straßburger Ausgabe, sondern kommt der Pariser Ausgabe näher. Quodlibet IV, q. 6 der Straßburger Ausgabe fehlt in allen Handschriften mit Ausnahme von C. Auch die Pariser Ausgabe hat sie nicht. Wie bekannt, ist sie auch als 12. Quaestio des 3. Buches der Reportatio Ockhams in der Lyoner Ausgabe gedruckt, wohin sie aber auch nicht gehört, wie wir anderswo nachgewiesen haben,[7] zumal sie eine Quaestio disputata zu sein scheint. Quaestio 14 des Quodl. VII findet sich nur in der Straßburger Ausgabe und in C und G. Es fehlen jedoch in C Quodl. IV, qq. 10—39; in G Quodl. III, qq. 10 und 18 und Quodl. IV, qq. 12, 13 und 20—29. In L fehlen Quodl. IV, qq. 19 und 39. Wie wir bereits erwähnt haben, folgen wir der Numerierung der Quästionen in der Straßburger Ausgabe, die wohl am häufigsten benützt wird. Leider scheint aber ihre Anordnung nicht die ursprüngliche und auch der Text am unzuverlässigsten zu sein.

Der Stil der Quodlibeta ist, wenigstens was die knappe Ausdrucksweise anbelangt, von Ockhams Stil in anderen edierten Werken verschieden, aber sehr nahe mit der Form der Quaestiones super libros Physicorum verwandt, die sonderbarerweise nur die Quodlibeta, und zwar recht häufig, zitieren. Die Quodlibeta zitieren aber den Sentenzenkommentar Ockhams (vgl. Quodl. I, q. 1). Wir glauben nicht fehlzugehen, wenn wir in den Quodlibeta im wesentlichen Entwürfe sehen, die Ockham nicht weiter ausgeführt hat, weil er die Zeit dazu nicht fand. Es ist möglich, daß er die Quodlibeta im Hausstudium gehalten hat. Wir sehen keinen vernünftigen Grund, an der Echtheit der Quodlibeta zu zweifeln.

Die folgende Edition eines Teiles der ersten Quaestio des ersten Quodlibets[b] gibt den Handschriften des 14. Jahrhunderts den Vorzug.

---

[7] Vgl. The notitia intuitiva of non-existents according to William Ockahm... In: Traditio I (1943) 243; [oben 249 ff.].

[b] Auch (Latein-Englisch) *Ockham-Philisophical Writings* 125—126.

Wir betrachten sie nur als eine vorläufige. Von den Varianten sollen nur die wichtigeren angemerkt werden.

Quodlibet I[m]

Quaestio 1[a1]

Utrum possit probari per naturalem rationem[2], *quod tantum est unus Deus.*

Quod sic: Quia unius mundi est tantum unus princeps, 12⁰ Metaphysicae; sed probari potest naturali ratione, quod tantum est unus mundus, secundum Philosophum 1⁰ De Caelo; ergo potest probari naturali ratione,[3] quod tantum est unus princeps; sed ille est Deus; ergo etc.

Ad oppositum: Articulus fidei non potest evidenter probari; sed quod tantum sit[4] unus Deus est articulus fidei; ergo etc.

In ista quaestione primo exponam, quid intelligendum est[5] per hoc nomen Deus; secundo respondebo ad quaestionem.

Circa primum dico, quod hoc nomen Deus potest habere diversas descriptiones. Una est, quod Deus est aliquid nobilius et melius omni alio a se. Alia descriptio est, quod Deus est illud quo nihil est melius et[6] perfectius.

Circa secundum dico,[7] quod accipiendo Deum secundum primam descriptionem non potest demonstrative[8] probari,[9] quod tantum est unus Deus. Cuius ratio est, quia non potest[10] evidenter sciri, quod Deus est, sic[11] accipiendo Deum;[12] ergo[13] non potest evidenter sciri,[14] quod tantum est unus Deus, sic[15] accipiendo Deum. Consequentia plana est. Antecedens probatur: Quia haec[16] propositio: Deus est, non est per se nota, quia multi[17] dubitant de ea; nec potest probari ex per se notis, quia in omni ratione accipietur[18] aliquod dubium vel creditum; nec est nota per experientiam — manifestum est; ergo etc.

Secundo dico, quod si posset evidenter probari, quod Deus est, sic accipiendo Deum, quod unitas Dei tunc[19] posset evidenter probari. Cuius[20] ratio est, quia si[21] essent duo dii A et B, tunc[22] per illam descriptionem

---

¹ Quaestio prima est E¹ LVW.   ² p. n. r.] naturali ratione BMV.
³ n. r.] naturaliter E² E¹ GNW; *om.* L.   ⁴ sit E² E¹ CGLPV.
⁵ i. e.] intelligitur BM; intelligo E².   ⁶ vel E² G; nec BCMP.
⁷ primo *add.* BCM.   ⁸ demonstratione P.   ⁹ d. p.]demonstrari V.
¹⁰ ... non potest *om.* MP.   ¹¹ ... Deum *om.* E² NC.
¹² *om.* LV.   ¹³ Similiter C.   ¹⁴ probari CM
¹⁵ ... Deum *om.* E¹ LM.   ¹⁶ ... quia *om.* L.
¹⁷ infiniti P (*marg.* M?).   ¹⁸ acciperetur BGW.
¹⁹ *om.* E² VW.   ²⁰ ... est *om.* BM.   ²¹ *om.* P.
²² *om.* E² E¹ GL (*quod add. post praec.* B, *et ibi*, W: sic).

A esset perfectior omni alio a se, et ita[23] esset[24] perfect.or B, et B esset imperfectior[25] A. Similiter,[26] B esset perfectior A, quia Deus est, per positum; et per consequens B[27] esset perfectior et imperfectior quam A, et A quam B, quod est manifesta contradictio. Ergo si posset probari evidenter, quod Deus est, sic accipiendo Deum, posset evidenter probari unitas Dei.

Tertic dico, quod unitas Dei[28] non potest[29] evidenter probari accipiendo secundo modo. Et tamen haec negativa:[30] Unitas Dei[31] non potest evidenter[32] probari, non[33] potest demonstrative probari, quia non potest demonstrari,[34] quod unitas Dei non possit[35] evidenter probari nisi solvendo rationes in contrarium. Sicut[36] non potest[35] demonstrative probari,[37] quod astra sint paria, nec potest demonstrari[38] Trinitas personarum. Et tamen illae negativae non possunt evidenter[39] probari: Quod[40] non potest demonstrari quod astra sint paria, non potest demonstrari Trinitas personarum.

Sciendum[41] tamen, quod potest demonstrari Deum esse secundo[42] modo prius dicto, quia aliter esset processus in infinitum, nisi esset aliquid in entibus, quo non est aliquid prius nec perfectius. Sed ex hoc non sequitur, quod potest[43] demonstrari, quod tantum est[44] unum tale; sed[45] hoc fide tantum tenetur.[46]

Unde ad rationes Scoti in contrarium respondeo . . .

Es folgt hier eine längere Diskussion der Argumente des Doctor Subtilis für die Einzigkeit Gottes, die Ockham als nicht streng beweisend ablehnt.

Die folgende Edition einer Quaestio[c] der Quaestiones super libros Physicorum gründet sich auf zwei Handschriften, und zwar die einzigen, die, soweit wir bis jetzt wissen, dafür überhaupt in Frage kommen. Sie sind: Vaticana 956 (14. Jahrh.) und Paris, Bibl. Nat. 14841 (15. Jahrh.). Die beiden Handschriften stimmen so sehr über-

---

[23] A *add.* E[2] GP.   [24] est M.   [25] . . . esset *om.* E[1] CLW.

[26] . . . quia *om.* V.   [27] *om.* E[2] W; Deus P; *pro seq.* est P.

[28] hic *add.* V.   [29] sic *add.* M   [30] est necessaria M.

[31] *om.* L; sic accepti *add.* CP; sic accepta *add.* E[2] BM.   [32] *om.* L.

[33] non E[2] VW *om.* L.   [34] demonstrative probari C.

[35] posset E[2] LVW.   [36] ergo C; sed E[1].   [37] d. p.] demonstrari L.

[38] . . . trinitas personarum *om.* CMP.   [39] demonstrative L.

[40] *om.* BV; scilicet L; *pro seq.* enim V.

[41] . . . fide tantum tenemus *om.* LW (*marg.* V).   [42] primo B.

[43] possit E[2] C.   [44] sit C.   [45] . . . tenetur *om.* BM.

[46] tenemus E[2] GM.

---

[c] Auch (Latein-Englisch) *Ockham-Philosophical Writings* 122—125.

ein, daß wir glaubten, von einer Angabe der wenigen unwesentlichen Varianten Abstand nehmen zu dürfen.

Quaestiones super libros Physicorum

[Quaestio 136ª]

Utrum possit sufficienter probari primum efficiens esse per conservationem.

Quod non: Quia conservare est efficere; sed per efficientiam non potest probari primum efficiens; igitur nec per conservationem.

Contra: Omnes causae conservantes effectum concurrunt simul ad conservationem; si igitur in causis conservantibus sit processus in infinitum, infinita essent simul in actu; hoc est impossibile; igitur etc.

In ista quaestione dico breviter, quod sic. Quod probatur: Quia quidquid realiter producitur ab aliquo, realiter vel ab aliquo conservatur, quamdiu manet in esse reali — manifestum est; sed ille effectus producitur — certum est; igitur ab aliquo conservatur, quamdiu manet. De illo conservante quaero: aut potest produci ab aliquo, aut non. Si non, est efficiens primum sicut est conservans primum, quia omne conservans est efficiens. Si autem istud conservans producitur ab aliquo, de illo alio quaero sicut prius; et ita vel oportet procedere in infinitum, vel oportet stare ad aliquid quod est conservans et nullo modo conservatum; et tale efficiens est primum efficiens. Sed non est processus in infinitum in conservantibus, quia tunc aliqua infinita essent in actu, quod est impossibile; nam omne conservans aliud, sive mediate sive immediate, est simul cum conservato; et ideo omne conservatum requirit actualiter omne conservans. Non autem omne productum requirit omne producens actualiter, mediate vel immediate. Et ideo quamvis posset poni processus in infinitum in produccionibus sine infinitate actuali, non potest tamen poni processus in infinitum in conservantibus sine infinitate actuali.

Sed contra: Videtur quod ratio ista sit evidens de prima productione sicut de conservatione. Arguitur sic: Aliquid est productum. Quaero de suo producente: aut est producens non productum, et habetur propositum, aut est productum ab alio; et non tamen in infinitum, igitur est status ad aliquod producens nec productum. Assumptum probatur in essentialiter ordinatis:

Tum, quia in essentialiter ordinatis omnes causae simul requiruntur ad productionem effectus; si igitur essent infinitae, infinita essent actu.

Tum, quia tota multitudo causatorum essentialiter est causata, et non ab aliquo illius multitudinis, quia tunc idem causaret se, igitur causatur ab aliquo non causato quod est extra multitudinem causatorum.

Similiter: In accidentaliter ordinatis patet quod tota multitudo causatorum actualiter est causata, et non ab aliquo illius multitudiris, quia sic causaret seipsam causando totam multitudinem, igitur causatur ab aliquo extra illam multitudinem; et tunc aut est idem non causatum, et sic habetur propositum, aut causatur a causis essentialiter ordinatis, et tunc stat prima pars istius argumenti.

Respondeo: Quod per solam primam productionem non potest sufficienter probari, quod non it processus in infinitum, saltem in causis accidentaliter ordinatis, nec formaliter in essentialiter ordinatis.

Et ad primam probationem pro essentialiter ordinatis dico, sicut prius patet, quod non omnes causae essentialiter ordinatae concurrunt ad primam productionem effectus.

Ad utrumque sequens dico, quod tota multitudo tam essentialiter ordinata quam accidentaliter est causata, sed non ab aliquo uno quod est pars illius multitudinis, vel quod est extra illam multitudinem; sed una causatur ab uno quod est pars multitudinis et aliud ab alio et sic in infinitum; nec per primam productionem potest sufficienter oppositum probari; et tunc nec sequitur, quod idem causat totam multitudinem nec quod idem causat se, quia nihil unum est causa omnium.

Ad argumentum principale dico quod per efficientiam, secundum quod dicit rem immediate accipere esse post non esse, non potest probari primum efficiens esse; sed per efficientiam, secundum quod dicit rem continuari in esse, bene potest probari, hoc est per conservationem. Et sic patet ad illam quaestionem.

III. DER LEHRGEHALT DER TEXTE

Der erste der von uns veröffentlichten Texte hat nicht die Existenz Gottes zum Gegenstand, sondern die Beweisbarkeit der Einzigkeit Gottes. Es ist aber ohne weiteres klar, daß die Frage nach der Beweisbarkeit der Einzigkeit Gottes mit der Frage nach der Beweisbarkeit der Existenz Gottes verknüpft ist. Die Beweisbarkeit der Existenz Gottes ist notwendige Bedingung für die Beweisbarkeit der Einzigkeit Gottes. Ist sie aber auch hinreichende Bedingung? Diese Frage hat im Mittelalter zur Diskusssion gestanden und ist von den Scholastikern durchaus nicht einmütig bejaht worden. Die Einzigkeit Gottes ist ja ein absolutes Attribut Gottes, zu dem es von den Geschöpfen aus keinen unmittelbaren Zugang gibt. Wenn wir darum die Einzigkeit Gottes zu beweisen versuchen, kann es nur mit Hilfe des Begriffes geschehen, zu dem wir von den Geschöpfen gelangen, indem wir die Existenz Gottes beweisen. Ockham behauptet nun in dieser 1. Quaestio des 1. Quodlibet, daß kein Beweis Gottes uns zu einem Begriff Gottes führt, der hinreichende Bedingung für die Behauptung der Einzigkeit Gottes ist. Wir können also natürlicherweise und im strengen Sinne die Einzigkeit Gottes nicht beweisen. Wie das Contra zeigt, sind für Ockham zunächst theologische Gründe maßgebend: Die Einzigkeit Gottes ist ein Glaubensartikel; Glaubensartikel können aber, nach allgemeiner Lehre der Scholastiker, nicht im strengen Sinne bewiesen werden.[1] Ockham mag aber auch, wie andere Scholastiker (etwa Wilhelm von Ware) unter dem Einfluß des Moses Maimonides gestanden haben, der gegen einen philosophischen Rationalismus die Notwendigkeit einer Offenbarung dartun wollte und aus diesem Grunde die Beweisbarkeit der Einzigkeit Gottes bestritt. Sicher aber haben Ockham rein logische Erwägungen zu seiner Stellungnahme bewogen. Diese logischen Schwierigkeiten werden in unserer Quaestio angedeutet, und es wird in längeren Ausführungen, die wir ausgelassen haben, den Beweisen, die Scotus für die Einzigkeit Gottes beigebracht hat, die strenge Gültigkeit abgesprochen. Übrigens unterläßt es Ockham nicht hervorzuheben, daß auch der negative Satz: Gottes Einzigkeit läßt sich nicht im strengen Sinne beweisen, nicht Gegenstand einer Demonstration sein kann.

Aber um diese Frage dreht es sich hier nicht. Was für uns wichtig ist, liegt in dem, was Ockham gewissermaßen nebenbei über den Beweis der Existenz Gottes sagt. Was erfahren wir darüber in diesem Text, der verschiedentlich und auch von De Wulf angerufen worden ist, um zu zeigen, daß Gottes Dasein sich nicht streng beweisen lasse?

Ockham schickt zunächst, wie es seine Gewohnheit ist, Unterscheidungen voraus. Der Sinn des Wortes „Gott" läßt verschiedene Umschreibungen oder Begriffserklärungen zu. Er gibt zwei an, die auf den ersten Blick eng zusammenzuliegen scheinen und doch tief verschieden sind. Nach der ersten Umschreibung ist Gott etwas, das erhabener und besser ist als alles andere; nach der zweiten ist Gott etwas, im Vergleich zu dem es nichts Besseres und Vollkommeneres

[1] Vgl. Quodl. II, q. 3: Utrum articuli fidei possint demonstrari.

gibt.[2] Wenn wir nun diese beiden Begriffsumschreibungen an die Stelle des Subjektes in dem Satze: Gott ist (oder existiert) setzen, so erhalten wir die folgenden zwei Sätze, die für Ockhams Stellungnahme von größter Bedeutung sind:

1. Das, was erhabener und besser ist als alles andere, existiert.
2. Das, im Vergleich zu dem es nichts Besseres und Vollkommeneres gibt, existiert.

Ockham verneint nun, daß der erste Satz durch sich einleuchtend ist und mit unserer natürlichen Vernunft im strengen Sinne der aristotelischen Demonstratio bewiesen werden könne; denn er ist weder aus der Erfahrung evident, noch kann er aus Sätzen, die durch sich einleuchtend sind, gefolgert werden. Hervorgehoben sei, daß die Möglichkeit oder Unmöglichkeit eines Regressus in infinitum in diesem Falle mit keiner Silbe erwähnt wird. Ockham bemerkt jedoch, daß der erste Satz den Satz inferiert: Es gibt nur einen Gott. Da der erste Satz nicht streng bewiesen werden kann, kann auch der zweite, von ihm abhängende, nicht streng bewiesen werden.

Anders aber steht es mit dem Satz 2. Dieser Satz läßt sich nach Ockham streng beweisen. Aber aus diesem Satze läßt sich nicht der andere ableiten: Es gibt nur ei n e n Gott.

Damit ist eine Tatsache historisch sichergestellt, die von De Wulf bestritten wird. Ockham behauptet, daß die Existenz eines Wesens, das an Vollkommenheit von keinem anderen Wesen übertroffen wird, streng bewiesen werden kann. Ein solches Wesen nennt er Gott; und er kann ein solches Wesen Gott nennen, weil tatsächlich die Bestimmung, von keinem anderen Wesen an Vollkommenheit übertroffen zu werden, keiner anderen Natur als nur Gott zukommt. Es bleibt aber die Frage offen, die auch Scotus sehr scharf gesehen hat, ob die Vervielfältigung einer solchen Natur in verschiedenen

---

[2] Vgl. unter anderem Augustins Umschreibung: Nam cum ille unus cogitatur deorum Deus, ab his etiam qui alios et suspicantur et vocant et colunt deos sive in caelo sive in terra, ita cogitatur, ut aliquid quo nihil melius sit atque sublimius, illa cogitatio conetur attingere. De Doctr. christ. I, 7, 7 (PL 34, col. 22). Auch nach *Augustin* ist offenbar die Einzigkeit Gottes in diesem Begriffe von Gott nicht eingeschlossen.

Individuen möglich ist. Was Ockham verneint, ist, daß diese Möglichkeit durch den Satz 2 ausgeschlossen ist oder ausgeschlossen werden kann. Was Ockham beweist, ist die Existenz des christlichen Gottes, weil der vor-christliche Begriff Gottes im Sinne von 2 nur für den christlichen Gott supponiert; nicht bewiesen ist aber der Begriff des christlichen Gottes, der die Einzigkeit Gottes einschließt. Diese scharfe logische Distinktion ist Ockham sehr geläufig, leider aber nicht manchen seiner Kritiker. Obwohl also Gott im Sinne von 1 nicht bewiesen werden kann, so supponiert nichtsdestoweniger der Begriff Gottes im Sinne von 2 für denselben christlichen Gott. Ja, derselbe Begriff supponiert sogar für die Wesenheit, die eine in drei Personen ist, also für die Trinität selbst. Wollte man ganz exakt sein, so müßte man sagen, daß der Satz: Gott existiert, falls an die Stelle des Subjektes der echte christliche Gottesbegriff, der die Dreipersönlichkeit der einen Natur einschließt, eingesetzt wird, nicht bewiesen werden kann, da alle unsere Gottesbeweise nur die Persönlichkeit Gottes dartun können. Es wird aber keinem christlichen Philosophen einfallen, daraus zu schließen, daß er die Existenz des christlichen Gottes nicht bewiesen habe. Wenigstens Ockham kann zugeben, daß der christliche Gott, der eine Natur in drei Personen ist, bewiesen worden ist, da der vorchristliche Begriff „das höchste Gut" präzise für diesen Gott supponiert.[3]

---

[3] Es sei uns erlaubt, hier einen Text wiederzugeben, der zeigt, daß Ockham sich dieser Verhältnisse sehr klar bewußt ist: ... concedo quod ex puris naturalibus possumus cognoscere istam propositionem: Deus est summum bonum, et tamen ipsa essentia divina non plus cognoscitur secundum tales conceptus quam trinitas personarum, quia illud quod cognoscimus ita vere competit trinitati personarum sicut divinae essentiae; ita enim realiter et ita vere trinitas personarum est summum bonum, sicut divina essentia est summum bonum, quamvis ista propositio sit nobis nota: Essentia divina est summum bonum, et haec non: Trinitas personarum est summum bonum, et hoc quia isti termini pro eisdem supponunt, quamvis hoc nesciatur a nobis ... Ita est in proposito: quia nescitur pro quo supponit iste terminus "summum bonum", quando dicitur: Deus est summum bonum, utrum scilicet pro uno supposito absoluto vel pro tribus suppositis respectivis, quamvis aliqui credant se scire quod supponit pro supposito absoluto et non pro tribus suppositis relativis ... Ordinatio d. 1, q. 5, M.

Es ist also sicher, daß Ockham glaubt, die Existenz Gottes nachweisen zu können, und zwar des Gottes, dessen Einzigkeit nach ihm nicht streng bewiesen werden kann. Diesen Satz hat er nie zurückgenommen. Wenigstens ist uns nach jahrelanger und fast täglicher Beschäftigung mit den gedruckten und ungedruckten Werken Ockhams keine Stelle begegnet, wo er die Möglichkeit eines strengen Beweises für die Existenz Gottes geleugnet hätte. Eine solche Stelle müßte uns erst noch gezeigt werden. Wohl aber hat er häufig das gerade Gegenteil behauptet.

Wir können uns nicht enthalten, hier auf das Zeugnis eines Scholastikers des späteren 14. Jahrhunderts hinzuweisen, der unsere Behauptung bestätigt. Petrus von Candia wirft in der dritten Quaestio des ersten Buches seines Sentenzenkommentars die Frage auf: Utrum sit naturaliter demonstrabile quamlibet conditionem primitatis simpliciter alicui enti per rationem propriam convenire. Darauf antwortet er wie folgt:

> Pro declaratione primi articuli est advertendum quod inter doctores multiplex diversitas reperitur. Prima est contradictionis, secunda probationis. Diversitas contradictionis est, quia quidam tenent quod aliquid esse primum sit per se notum, quia Deum esse, et per consequens cum propositio per se nota nullo modo sit demonstrabilis, tenent quod Deum esse et aliquid esse primum, quod pro eodem habent, non est demonstrabile, eo quod per se notum. Et istius opinionis videtur fuisse magister Aegidius, ut apparet in opere suo primo distinctione III, quaestione II. Alii doctores, quos videre potui, tenent quod talis propositio non est per se nota, sed est bene demonstrabilis. Et huius opinionis fuerunt beatus Thomas, Doctor Subtilis, Ockham, Adam (Wodham), Johannes de Ripa; sed eorum diversitas est in modo probandi ... (nach ms. Vat. lat. 1081, fol. 42vb s).

Ockham darf sich also noch am Ende des 14. Jahrhunderts unter den Vertretern der Beweisbarkeit der Existenz Gottes im strengen Sinne in der Gesellschaft des hl. Thomas und Duns Scotus wohlfühlen.

Aber, hat De Wulf nicht das Recht oder sogar die Pflicht, Ockham aus dieser ehrenwerten Gemeinschaft zu verweisen? Er zitiert doch einen Text, der klar und deutlich zeigt, daß Ockham die Beweisbarkeit Gottes geleugnet hat. Er lautet: Non potest sciri evidenter, quod Deus est. Da De Wulf für diese Stelle auf den hier veröffentlichten Text des Quodlibet I, q. 1 verweist, hat der Leser die direkte Möglichkeit, sich selbst zu überzeugen, wie oberflächlich, ja wie leichtfertig es war, diese Stelle anzuführen. Es ist oberstes Gesetz treuer Geschichtsforschung, einen Satz nie zu verstümmeln und dadurch seinen Sinn zu ändern oder einen Satz nie losgelöst aus seinem Zusammenhang zu interpretieren. Beide Verstöße gegen die Regeln echter Geschichtsforschung sind in Bezug auf diese Stelle vorgekommen. Daß der Satz verstümmelt wiedergegeben worden ist, läßt sich einigermaßen entschuldigen. Der aufmerksame Leser wird das Zitat im zweiten Abschnitt des Corpus Quaestionis, der mit Circa secundum ... beginnt, wiederfinden. In unserem hier edierten Text ist aber der bedeutsame Zusatz „sic accepto Deo" zu lesen, der leider in der Straßburger Edition ausgefallen ist, den aber die andere Edition und auch alle Handschriften mit Ausnahme von C haben. Dieser Zusatz qualifiziert aber den Satz: Es kann nicht bewiesen werden, daß Gott existiert, so daß das Subjekt des Nebensatzes, nämlich „Gott", im Sinne unserer ersten Umschreibung genommen werden muß. Ockham behauptet darum nur, daß Satz 1 nicht bewiesen werden kann.

Es zeigt sich aber dann, daß De Wulf gegen die andere Regel, nie einen Satz losgelöst aus seinem Zusammenhang zu interpretieren, ganz sicher verstoßen hat. Denn zu Anfang des Abschnittes sagt Ockham ausdrücklich, daß er „Gott" im ersten Sinne seiner Begriffsbestimmungen verstanden wissen will. Aus diesem Grunde wäre auch der Zusatz, der sich nicht in der Straßburger Edition findet, eigentlich überflüssig. Liest man also den ganzen Text, wie er von Ockham gegeben wird, so ist er im Grunde harmlos, und dann fügt er sich ungezwungen in die Linie des folgenden Abschnittes ein. Denn hier wird nun ausdrücklich behauptet, daß der Satz 2 streng beweisbar ist: Potest demonstrari Deum esse secundo modo prius dicto. Und warum ist er beweisbar? Wieder müssen wir eine Überraschung erleben, denn Ockham antwortet, daß man einen Regressus in infinitum annehmen müßte, wenn es unter den Seienden nicht ein Wesen gäbe, im Vergleich zu dem kein früheres oder vollkommeneres existierte. Es ist also gerade die Unmöglichkeit des Regressus in infinitum, die uns nach Ockham zwingt, ein Wesen, das wir Gott nennen, anzunehmen.

Damit stehen wir wieder mit einer Behauptung De Wulfs in Widerspruch. Es gibt nicht nur einen strengen Beweis für die Existenz Gottes, dieser strenge Beweis stützt sich sogar auf die Unmöglichkeit des Regressus in infinitum. Trotzdem glauben wir, daß sich dieser Widerspruch eines Textes Ockhams mit der Behauptung De Wulfs mildern läßt, aber dann nur dadurch, daß wir De Wulf eine andere grobe Nachlässigkeit nachweisen müssen. Denn wir müssen wieder feststellen, daß ein Satz aus dem Zusammenhang gerissen wurde und damit zur Unverständlichkeit verurteilt ist.

Fragen wir uns zunächst, ob Ockham einen Regreß ins Unendliche zugegeben hat. Diese Frage muß bejaht werden. Sie muß aber auch bejaht werden für den hl. Thomas, für Duns Scotus und viele andere Scholastiker, nicht aber für den hl. Bonaventura, der hier eine rühmliche Ausnahme bildet. Ein Regreß ins Unendliche für Wirkursachen derselben Art wird von all denen angenommen, die die Möglichkeit der Ewigkeit der Welt zugeben. Nach ihnen gibt es, oder genauer gesagt, kann es Ursachenreihen geben, die kein erstes Glied haben, die also anfanglos sind. Diese Annahme hat natürlich mit der Leugnung des Kausalgesetzes nichts zu tun, setzt es vielmehr voraus. So sagt z. B. der hl. Thomas (Summa contra Gentiles II, c. 38):

> Quod etiam quinto obiicitur non cogit, quia causas agentes in infinitum procedere est impossibile, secundum philosophos, in causis simul agentibus; quia oporteret effectum dependere ex actionibus infinitis simul existentibus; et huiusmodi sunt causae per se infinitae, quia earum infinitas ad causatum requiritur. In causis autem non simul agentibus hoc non est impossibile, secundum eos qui ponunt generationem perpetuam...

In der Stelle, die von De Wulf aus dem Zusammenhang gerissen zitiert wird, finden wir den gleichen Gedanken von Ockham ausgesprochen. Sie steht in der 10. Quaestio (oder der 7. Quaestio der 4. Hauptquaestio) der 2. Distinktion des ersten Buches oder der Ordinatio. Ockham diskutiert hier die Frage: Gibt es nur einen Gott? Nachdem es Skotus' Beweise für die Existenz eines ersten Wesens in der Ordnung der Wirkursächlichkeit, der Zielursächlichkeit und der Vollkommenheit kurz wiedergegeben hat und ebenfalls die Beweise für die Einzigkeit Gottes, schließt er daran eine Kritik bestimmter von Scotus verwandter Begriffe an, die uns hier nicht

interessiert. Darauf nimmt Ockham selbst Stellung, zunächst zum
Beweis der Existenz eines ersten Wesens in der Ordnung der Wirkursächlichkeit oder der causa efficiens im engeren Sinne. Er führt aus:

> Ich sage zum ersten Artikel, daß der Beweis, der die Erstheit eines
> ersten Bewirkers dartut, ausreichend ist. Er ist ja der Beweis aller Philo-
> sophen. Es scheint aber, daß die Erstheit des ersten Bewirkers mit größerer
> Evidenz geführt werden kann, wenn die Erhaltung eines Dinges durch
> seine Ursache, als wenn seine Hervorbringung zugrundegelegt wird, in-
> sofern Hervorbringung eines Dinges besagt, daß es Sein unmittelbar nach
> dem Nichtsein erhält. Der Grund dafür ist dieser: es ist schwierig oder un-
> möglich, gegen die Philosophen zu beweisen, daß es in Ursachen derselben
> Art, von denen die eine ohne die andere sein kann, keinen Processus in
> infinitum gibt.

Wir stehen hier wiederum vor einem der vielen Rätsel, die uns
in der Literatur über Ockham begegnen; denn unsere Übersetzung
zeigt deutlich, daß das von De Wulf herangezogene Zitat nicht mehr
bedeutet als das, was auch der hl. Thomas behauptet hat. Das wäre
in De Wulfs Zitat sofort deutlich zutage getreten, hätte er nicht
einen verstümmelten Text angeführt. Ockham sagt nämlich: quia
difficile vel impossibile est probare contra philosophos, quod non sit
processus in infinitum in causis eiusdem rationis, quarum una
potest esse sine alia. Der von uns hervorgehobene Teil des Textes
findet sich in der Edition und auch in allen Handschriften, nur nicht
in De Wulfs Werk. Ockhams Zweifel an einer effektiven Ausschaltung
des Regressus in infinitum bezieht sich also nur auf Ursachreihen, in
denen die eine Ursache ohne die andere existieren kann, oder für die
die Simultaneität aller Ursachen derselben Reihe nicht feststeht.
Wo die Simultaneität feststeht, lehnt er, wie St. Thomas und Scotus,
den unendlichen Regreß ab.

Um dies noch deutlicher hervortreten zu lassen, haben wir einen
Text aus den Quästionen zur Aristotelischen Physik dem Quodlibet-
Text hinzugefügt. Wir werden uns auf seinen wesentlichen Inhalt
beschränken, müssen aber den Zusammenhang dieser Quaestio mit
den anderen kurz darlegen. Die Quaestio 132 (oder nach anderer
Zählung 133) lautet: Utrum in causis essentialiter ordinatis secunda
dependeat a prima. Die Frage wird verneint, und zwar in einem gewissen Sinne, den wir hier nicht weiter angeben wollen, da unser

Kollege, P. Allan Wolter O. F. M., demnächst darüber eine ausführliche Untersuchung anstellen wird. Es folgt dann die Frage: Utrum in causis essentialiter ordinatis causa superior sit perfectior. Auch sie wird verneint. Quaestio 134 (oder 135) lautet: Utrum causae essentialiter ordinatae necessario simul requirantur ad producendum effectum respectu cuius sunt causae essentialiter ordinatae. Wiederum antwortet Ockham verneinend. Darauf folgt eine Quaestio, die bereits auf Ockhams Gottesbeweis im Gegensatz zu Scotus' Gottesbeweis abzielt: Utrum possit sufficienter probari primum efficiens per productionem distinctam a conservatione. Nochmals lautet die Antwort verneinend; denn, so heißt es am Schluß: „Gestützt auf die erste Erzeugung (productio) läßt sich nicht hinreichend beweisen, daß es in Wirkursachen, von denen die eine zeitlich nacheinander (successive) von der anderen verursacht wird, keinen Regreß ins Unendliche gibt; denn daraus folgt keine aktuelle Unendlichkeit." Jetzt folgt schließlich die von uns hier mitgeteilte Quaestio. Wir haben ihr nichts weiter hinzuzufügen als nur dies, daß Ockham im wesentlichen seinen Beweis aus der Ordinatio wiederholt und unzweideutig den Regreß ins Unendliche ablehnt, falls es sich um eine Ursachenreihe handelt, in der jedes Glied ohne zeitliche Sukzession also simultan mit jedem anderen gesetzt wird.

Um es anders auszudrücken: Ockham lehnt eine Form der Unmöglichkeit des Regressus in infinitum ab, nämlich diejenige, die von einer horizontalen oder zeitlichen Reihe von Ursachen ausgesagt wird. Die Möglichkeit eines solchen Regressus läßt er offen. Ockham lehnt aber nicht die andere Form der Unmöglichkeit eines Regresses ins Unendliche ab, nämlich genau jene, die von einer vertikalen oder simultanen Reihe von Ursachen ausgesagt wird. Alle Texte, die uns von Ockham zu Gesicht gekommen sind, drücken sich unzweideutig im gleichen Sinne aus.

Nun wird aber auch klar, warum Ockham soviel Gewicht auf den Beweis aus dem Erhaltensein der Dinge legen muß. Was im Sein erhält und das, was im Sein erhalten wird, müssen simultan existieren. Der Aristotelische Deismus, nach dem Gott die Welt weder erzeugt oder schafft noch im Sein erhält, ist für den Beweis der Existenz Gottes auf seine unhaltbare teleologische Bewegungsmechanik ge-

drängt worden. Da ein solcher Deismus der christlichen Weltanschau-
ung direkt widerspricht, kann der Aristotelische Beweis nur mit
tiefgreifenden Änderungen übernommen werden. Am weitesten und
tiefsten scheint uns hier Ockham vorgedrungen zu sein. Denn in
Ockhams natürlicher Gotteslehre erscheint der Deus conservans der
christlichen Theologie. Produzierende Ursachen verlangen ihrem
Wesen nach keine Simultaneität; werden die Ursachen, von denen
sie selbst produziert worden sind, erhaltende Ursachen, so verlangen
sie Simultaneität. Und in diesem Gedanken sehen wir einen äußerst
wertvollen Beitrag der Theodizee Ockhams zur christlichen Philosophie. Obwohl er nie — trotz der gegenteiligen Behauptungen De
Wulfs, die vielleicht noch auf Manser zurückzudatieren und bereits
von Hochstetter im Jahre 1927 zurückgewiesen worden sind — die
Gültigkeit des Kausalitätsgesetzes geleugnet hat, hat er mit scharfem
Blick Schwächen in der Tragfähigkeit der Wirkursächlichkeit, oder,
um es ganz scharf auszudrücken, der Erzeugungs-Ursächlichkeit
gesehen, die von der Erhaltungs-Ursächlichkeit, die übrigens auch
eine Wirkursächlichkeit ist, vermieden werden.

Wir wollen jetzt unsere Ergebnisse in der Paraphrase der Thesen
De Wulfs zusammenfassen:

1. Soweit die Hauptprobleme dieser Theodizee in Frage kommen,
setzt Ockham die Tradition der scholastischen Philosophie fort und
hält sich von Agnostizismus fern.

2. Ockham erklärt die Theodizee des Duns Scotus nicht einfach
für falsch, sondern nur in bestimmten Punkten, und in anderen ver-
besserungsbedürftig. Ockham hat die Scotische Theodizee weitergeführt.

3. Ockham bestreitet nicht die Gültigkeit des Scotischen Beweises
der Existenz Gottes schlechthin; er sagt vielmehr ausdrücklich, daß
dieser Beweis hinreichend ist. Er weist aber darauf hin, daß seine
Stringenz gegen die Philosophen bedeutend gewinnt, wenn er nicht
auf eine beliebige Wirkursächlichkeit, sondern auf die Wirkursächlichkeit des Erhaltens gestützt wird.

4. Das Dasein Gottes ist nicht Gegenstand des schauenden Erkennens, sondern ist unserm Verstande nur durch abstrakte Begriffe

zugänglich, und nur mit Hilfe eines Beweisverfahrens, wenigstens natürlicherweise und solange wir hier im Pilgerstande sind.

5. Wie alle abstrakten Begriffe, die von der Wirklichkeit gewonnen sind, so hat auch der Begriff der Ursächlichkeit Tragweite für die Wirklichkeit; denn sie sind weder figmenta noch ficta, sondern natürliche, vom Objekt bestimmte, gedankliche Ähnlichkeiten des Wirklichen.

6. Das Kausalgesetz kann das Dasein Gottes im strengen Sinne beweisen. Denn obwohl es schwierig, wenn nicht unmöglich ist zu beweisen, daß Ursachen sich nicht bis ins Unendliche ohne einen Halt oder ein Ende aneinanderreihen können, so ist es doch unmöglich, daß Ursachen, die simultan existieren müssen, wie im Falle des Erhaltens und Erhaltenseins, sich ins Unendliche aneinanderreihen können.

7. Da man, um einen Regreß ins Unendliche zu vermeiden, einen ersten Erhalter annehmen muß, gibt es zweifellos ein Wesen, das an der Spitze einer solchen Reihe steht; es bleibt aber die Frage offen, ob es nur ein solches Wesen gibt, d. h. ob es vollkommener als jedes andere Wesen ist. Es läßt sich stringent beweisen, daß Gott ein Wesen ist, im Vergleich zu dem kein besseres und vollkommeneres Wesen existieren kann; es läßt sich aber nicht stringent beweisen, daß Gott ein Wesen ist, das alle anderen überragt. Wäre dies Letztgenannte beweisbar, so wäre auch die Einzigkeit Gottes beweisbar. Für die Einzigkeit Gottes stehen uns somit nur Gründe zur Verfügung, die uns überzeugen können (persuasiones), die uns aber nicht zu einer evidenten Zustimmung zwingen.

8. Ergebnis: Die Existenz Gottes ist beweisbar: Potest demonstrari Deum esse secundo modo prius dicto, quia aliter esset processus in infinitum, nisi esset aliquid in entibus, quo non est aliquid prius nec perfectius (Quodl. I, 1).

9. Viele Eigenschaften Gottes sind unbeweisbar, aber nicht alle, wie z. B. die Geistigkeit, die Güte, die Weisheit Gottes usw.

Mit unseren voraufgehenden Ausführungen glauben wir die Darstellung der Theodizee Ockhams in De Wulfs Histoire de la Philosophie Médiévale auf jenes Maß zurückgeführt zu haben, das die

Dokumente zulassen. Wir wollen zum Schluß noch besonders hervorheben, daß De Wulf von einer Benützung des Centiloquiums abgesehen hat. Das war sehr klug gehandelt; denn weder die Echtheit dieser eigenartigen Schrift ist bisher bewiesen, noch der Sinn dieses Werkes genügend erhellt worden. Was den Sinn dieser Schrift angeht, so möchten wir es als eine Anwendung der Disputationskunst interpretieren, wie sie in den mittelalterlichen Traktaten De Obligationibus festgelegt worden ist. Der neuerliche Versuch Iserlohs,[4] die Echtheit des Centiloquiums zu retten, scheint uns mit recht unzulänglichen Mitteln unternommen zu werden. Ohne Handschriftenforschung läßt sich diese Frage nicht endgültig entscheiden. Inzwischen ist es unserm Freund Dom Bascour O. S. B. gelungen, eine dritte Handschrift dieses Werkes aus dem 15. Jahrhundert in Spanien zu entdecken. Was aber noch wichtiger ist: Wir glauben endlich dem zweiten Teil des Centiloquiums, auf das in unserer Ausgabe nur hingewiesen wird, auf die Spur gekommen zu sein. Mit diesem neuen Material hoffen wir zu gegebener Zeit Iserlohs Versuch kritisch würdigen zu können.[d]

23. OCKHAM'S TRACTATUS DE PRAEDESTINATIONE ET DE PRAESCIENTIA DEI ET DE FUTURIS CONTINGENTIBUS AND ITS MAIN PROBLEMS[a]

Ockham, as well as all the great Scholastics, gives evidence of great interest in the problem of the prescience of God as regards free and contingent facts. He not only deals with it in his Commentary on the Sentences and, to a certain extent, in his *Summa Logicae* and in his *Quodlibeta*, but he also devotes a whole treatise to this problem: the *Tractatus de praedestinatione et de praescientia Dei et de futuris*

---

[4] Um die Echtheit des "Centiloquium". Ein Beitrag zur Wertung Ockhams und zur Chronologie seiner Werke, in: Gregorianum 30 (1949) 78—103; 309—346.

[d] Vgl. oben 33 ff.

---

[a] First published in: Proceedings of the American Catholic Philosophical Association, vol. XVI (Washington, D. C. [1941]) 177—192.

contingentibus. This tract, though of great value for an interpretation of the true doctrine of Ockham, was nevertheless often overlooked, and that even by Schwamm.[1] I do not mean to blame this scholar to whom we are obligated for his research-work on our problem in the 14th century. On the contrary, Schwamm may easily be excused by the inaccessibility of this tract of Ockham's, for it is hidden in the edition of the *Expositio aurea super artem veterem*[2] of Ockham, edited by Marco di Benevento. The rarity of this work is known to everyone who has had occasion to look for it. It may appear strange, that a treatise on predestination should have been added to a logical work, but soon it will become clear that Marco di Benevento had good reasons for placing it so. Our problem is not only a theological and metaphysical, but also a logical one. Ockham views it chiefly from the logical standpoint.

In my following exposition of the teachings of the Venerabilis Inceptor I used the above mentioned treatise, and only took into account other works in order to explain further details. I did so chiefly because this treatise is less known, and secondarily it seemed to afford a good basis-test for a panel.[b] However, I did not use the above mentioned Incunabula-edition of Marco di Benevento, but I preferred my own text prepared during the last two years on the basis of eight Manuscripts.[3]

---

[1] Cfr. Hermann Schwamm, Das göttliche Vorherwissen bei Duns Scotus und seinen ersten Anhängern. (Philosophie und Grenzwissenschaften, V. Band, 1.—4. Heft.) Innsbruck 1934, Felizian Rauch, p. 126—130.

[2] Expositio aurea et admodum utilis super artem veterem edita . . . cum quaestionibus Alberti parvi de Saxonia, Bononiae 1496.

[3] I wish to express my thanks to Mr. Etienne Gilson who made the five manuscripts of Paris available to me. [The tract has been edited: The tractatus de praedestinatione et de praescientia Dei et de futuris contingentibus of William Ockham, edit. Ph. Boehner, O. F. M. (Franciscan Institute Publications, Philosophy Series n. 2) St. Bonaventure 1945; in this edition eight manuscripts were used; more manuscripts are in existence].

---

[b] Members of the panel were: Anton Pegis, Hunter Guthrie, Wm. O'Meara; leader: Philotheus Boehner.

A. SCHEME OF THE TRACTATUS DE PRAEDESTINATIONE
ETC.

Before I start dealing with Ockham's teachings on this difficult problem, it may be worth while to present a brief scheme of the entire tract:

In the introduction Ockham states that everyone who is of the opinion that predestination or reprobation is a distinct entity either in God or in the human person, has to admit contradictory propositions. After it he discusses five dubia.

1. Dubium: Even he who is opposed to real distinct relations has to admit contradictory propositions. Ockham's final answer is found in 9 suppositions which we will discuss later.

2. Dubium:[4] Has God determined certain, infallible and necessary knowledge? Here Ockham closely follows the same arrangement as Scotus in his Commentaries, taking each attribute separately.

3. Dubium: How can we save the contingency of the created and uncreated will in causing something outside themselves?

4. Dubium: Is there any cause of predestination in the predestinated person, and any cause of reprobation in the reprobated person?

5. Dubium: since propositions like these: Peter is predestinated, Peter is condemned, are opposed, why cannot the one succeed the other in truth?

B. THE SUPPOSITIONS OF OCKHAM

William Ockham always likes to state a problem as precisely as possible. Therefore he defines the terms he uses and indicates what he presupposes. He certainly was not the first Scholastic who considerably enlarged the frame of a simple *Quaestio*, so that a simple *Quaestio* almost became a treatise, but his personal contribution to the old scholastic method seems to be the logical strictness which he applied to the enlarged form of the *Quaestio*. Hence we see that

---

[4] The following dubia are wanting in three manuscripts [of those known to the author at the time of the redaction of the present article], but their authenticity cannot be doubted.

Ockham as elsewhere, in dwelling with our problem, after a comparatively short scholastic skirmish first states suppositions which prepare the solution of the problem to be discussed. All the critical problems are already touched on in the suppositions, which are a model of logical clarity.

1. supposition: Active predestination and active reprobation are not distinct, in whatsoever sense distinction may be taken, from God or the Divine Persons; and passive predestination and passive reprobation do not imply anything distinct from the predestinated person. Predestination in the active sense signifies God Himself insofar as he will give eternal life to a person; passive predestination signifies a person to whom eternal life will be given. Consequently active predestination signifies three things: God, eternal life, and the receiving person. The same holds for passive and active reprobation.

2. supposition: The second supposition is a logical one and, like the two others, very important. Ockham states: All propositions in this matter, whether of the present, the past or the future time, are contingent propositions. No proposition is a necessary one. According to Aristotelian Logic a statement about a contingent present fact turns at once into the necessary statement that it is impossible that it should not be a fact. If the fact: *Sortes sedet* is true then no power upon earth or in heaven, can falsify the statement: *Sortes sedet*, and it will be necessarily true forever. Our present supposition, however, excludes from this law all propositions about predestination and the prescience of God. Consequently the statement: *Petrus fuit praedestinatus* is as contingent and not necessary as the other statement: *Petrus praedestinabitur*. That is, of course, provided that Peter is still alive.

3. The third supposition further explains, why such a statement is not necessary. Ockham says: It is universally true that certain propositions of the present time which are of the present time as they sound *(secundum vocem)* and as they really are *(secundum rem)*, have a corresponding necessary proposition of the past, for instance: *Sortes sedit*. After this moment, *Sortes sedit* is necessarily true for ever. But there are still other propositions of the present time which are of the present time only as they sound not as

they really are, and they are in reality equivalent to propositions of the future time, because their truth depends upon the truth of future time. Here the law, that a proposition of the present time has a corresponding proposition of the past time, is not valid. Ockham reminds us, that this fact is not so exceptional as it at first may seem to be. Because there are certain propositions of the past and future times which have no corresponding true proposition of the present time, for instance the statement: *album fuit nigrum, album erit nigrum:* the corresponding proposition of the present time, *album est nigrum*, would be false.

4. The fourth supposition gives the ultimate reason why all the propositions in this matter are contingent, because all propositions in this matter, whether of the past or the present time, are really of the future time. Consequently they have no corresponding necessary proposition of the past time, therefore they are absolutely contingent.

5. The fifth proposition makes a very important statement about Aristotle's Logic and Metaphysics. Ockham says: According to Aristotle — or, Ockham is very careful, according to the intention of Aristotle, — God does not know which part of a contradiction is true or false in propositions of future contingent facts or in propositions equivalent to them. Therefore these propositions are neutral to God, that is to say, neither true nor false to God. That means: though one part must be true, nevertheless God does not know which part will be true.

6. The sixth supposition opposes the Christian dogma to this Aristotelian opinion: According to faith God knows all future contingent facts, so that he knows which part of a contradiction of these statements will be true, and he knows it with certitude. But Ockham reminds us at once, that God does not know future contingent facts in a necessary way, but only in a contingent way. Here Ockham adds his criticism on Scotus and explains his own opinion.

7. The seventh supposition states that *"scire"* is taken broadly, and so it means a cognition of every possible and impossible, contingent and necessary thing or fact. If *"scire"* is taken in a strict sense, then it means cognition of something true.

8. The eighth supposition declares, that some propositions of this matter are to be distinguished acccording to the *sensus compositionis et divisionis*. For instance: *Possibile est Petrum praedestinatum damnari;* this statement is true *in sensu divisionis,* false *in sensu compositionis.*

9. The ninth and last supposition defines the term cause. It can be taken either in the sense of a thing which has something as effect; that means: something whose existence is followed by the existence of another thing, because if the cause is posited, the effect is posited too. Or cause can be taken in a more logical sense, if it implies the priority of a proposition as regards consequence. So we call the antecedent cause of the consequence and not viceversa, if there is a natural consequence from one proposition to another.

These are the suppositions. And Ockham affirms that they contain the solution of all questions concerning the prescience of God and future contingent facts.

C. DISCUSSION OF SOME PROBLEMS

Now we will proceed to the discussion of some problems.

1. The problem of contingency.

Our problem presupposes the possibility of future contingent facts. Is there contingency at all? And how can we prove it?

Contingency, here, means, as Peter d'Ailly declares, *possibile non necessarium.* It is the *contingens ad utrumlibet.* According to the great Cardinal, the Dominus Cameracensis, who deeply admired Ockham without following him slavishly, *contingens ad utrumlibet* does not mean: something which will be and will not be, nor something which will neither be nor not be, but only: illud quod erit et potest non fore, vel quod non erit et potest fore.[6]

The fact that after the creation of the world there are actions which are possible without being necessary, or more exactly: which will be and could not be, is something which cannot be demonstrated

---

[6] [Note 5 is missing in the first edition.] Cfr. Quaestiones magistri Petri de Aylliaco super libros Sententiarum, Argentinae 1490, q. 12, B.

a priori. But according to Scotus who quotes Avicenna, there is a good *argumentum ad hominem* to prove, that contingency is in the world: *Et ita etiam isti, qui negant aliquod esse contingens, exponendi sunt tormentis, quousque concedant quod possibile est eos non torqueri.*[7]

This contingency necessarily presupposes liberty. Therefore liberty is defined by Ockham in his Quodlibeta as: the power, by which I am able indifferently and contingently to posit an effect, so that I am able to cause the effect and not to cause the effect without any change being made in this power.[8] This *contingenter causare et non causare* means as Ockham explains in his Commentary on the Sentences: the will is in absolute possession of itself, so that the will is able, not to act even if all the necessary requirements to an act are given.[9] Therefore according to Ockham liberty is not only the power of free choice which would presuppose the choice between two objects, but ultimately the power of self determination or the dominion of the will over its own act.

The quaestio iuris being solved, there remains the quaestio facti: is there such a free cause or liberty? Philosophy is absolutely sure about one free cause, about our own free will. Though this statement, that I am able to act freely, cannot be demonstrated (in the Aristotelian sense), nevertheless we are absolutely certain, that we are able to act freely; because we know it by our own experience with intuitive knowledge, or in modern terms by introspection. So we know that we are able not to do what reason tells us to do.[10]

---

[7] Oxon. I, d. 39, q. u. n. 13; ed. Vives t. 10, p. 625.

[8] Voco libertatem potestatem, qua possum indifferenter et contingenter effectum ponere, ita quod possum eundem effectum causare et non causare, nulla diversitate circa illam potentiam facta. Quodl. ed. Argentinae 1491, quodl. 1, q. 16.

[9] Praeter istos modos adhuc est unus modus, quo potest voluntas creata cessare ab actu causandi, scilicet se sola, quantumcumque nullum praedictorum desit, sed omnia sint posita, et hoc est et non aliud voluntatem contingenter causare. I Sent. d. 38, q. 1, G.

[10] Non potest probari per aliquam rationem, quia omnis ratio probans accipit aeque dubia et aeque ignotum conclusioni vel ignotius. Potest tamen evidenter cognosci per experientiam, per hoc, quod homo experitur, quod quantumcumque ratio dictet aliquid, potest tamen voluntas hoc velle vel nolle. Quodl. 1, q. 16, ed. cit.

Therefore a philosopher is sure by assertoric evidence, that the human will is free. But, is he equally sure about a free will and consequently a free cause in God? Against such certitude is the old opinion of Philosophers who think God a necessary being in every respect, and the world, if produced, an effect of God's necessary causality.[11] The presence of the Arabian philosophy forced every Scholastic to respect it. St. Thomas is convinced that he is able to refute their necessitarian view by reason, Duns Scotus knows the position of these Philosophers, and for him it proves the necessity of revelation: *Proprietas etiam istius naturae (sc. Dei) est causare contingenter, et ad oppositum huius magis deducunt effectus in errorem, sicut patet per opinionem philosophorum ponentium primum necessario causare.*[12] In order to prove liberty in God, Scotus thinks it necessary first to remove an obstacle still existing in the teachings of St. Thomas, viz. the statement that it is possible for the first cause to be necessary, whilst the second cause causes contingently. But this proof does not please Ockham, as we shall see later. The Venerabilis Inceptor too is convinced that according to the philosophers (Aristotle included), God only produces and preserves immediately and entirely the separate substances and the celestial bodies, but He does not produce immediately generable and corruptibile things upon earth. The reason is, because the Philosophers could not imagine any contingency in God; but if they referred the production of contingent things to God, contingency would be proved in God: *Causa autem quare Philosophus dicit, quod non est causa immediata generabilium et corruptibilium est, quia tunc posset probari naturali ratione, quod esset causa de novo omnium inferiorum, et sic posset probari in eo contingentia.*[13]

After having rejected St. Thomas' proofs[14] and likewise the proofs of Duns Scotus, Ockham concludes: God's liberty cannot be proved

---

[11] Cfr. A. C. Pegis, Necessity and liberty: an historical note on St. Thomas Aquinas, in: The New Scholasticism, Vol. XV (1941) p. 19 ss.

[12] Oxon. prol. q. 1, n. 14: ed. Vives t. 8, p. 34.

[13] Sent. II, q. 6, in fine.

[14] Cfr. A. C. Pegis, 1. c. p. 25 ss. Pegis gives a correct exposition of Ockham's criticism, therefore we can pass it over here. However, we do not

by any natural reason to which an unbeliever[15] would not be able to find an objection. Therefore liberty in God is to be held by faith, and we are able to develop this anti-philosophical idea because we are instructed by revelation, and so we are absolutely sure, that there is liberty in God. Nevertheless, he agrees that there is a good persuasion *(persuasio)* in favor of the liberty in God which runs as follows: Every cause which cannot be hindered and which equally regards many or infinite things, if it acts one of these and not another, as a contingent and a free cause. Because of its equally regarding all things and in the same way, and because of its not being able to be hindered, there seems to be no reason but its liberty, why it could produce the one thing and not the other. God is such a cause.[16]

Therefore we conclude: According to Ockham and the so-called nominalistic school contingency is a fact; this fact presupposes a free cause; this free cause certainly is the free will of man, but also, according to Faith, the free will of God, who caused everything freely.

This position of Ockham remains in the frame of Christian tradition and certainly in the frame of Christian dogma; the Venerabilis Inceptor acknowledges liberty in God because he acknowledges revelation as an indisputable fact. He knows the well established tradition developed by the Fathers of the Church from clear scriptural sources; but he also knows, like the Fathers and all the great Scholastics, the necessitarian view of almost all the Greek Philosophers who either thought the world as necessary and eternal as God — for instance Aristotle and he agrees with St. Thomas that there is no evident natural reason against the possibility of an eternal world —; or who thought the world a necessary product of the divine essence — for instance Plotinus and Avicenna, and Ockham respects their reasons as he respected the reasons of Aristotle. In both cases the problem of liberty and contingency does not exist.

---

agree with Pegis' interpretation of Ockham's attitude. Ockham's denial of natural proofs for any Christian truth begins exactly where the Credo starts: Credo in *unum* Deum . . . Ockham could be called "Defensor fidei" in a very literal sense.

[15] The answers of Ockham's unbeliever, see I. Sent. d. 43, q. 1, O.

[16] Sent. II, q. 5, E.

Therefore no Pagan Philosopher reached the true problem of contingency. It was brought to our mind by revelation. In stating this Ockham does not make a simple concession to Neoplatonism just as St. Thomas did not make a simple concession to Aristotelianism in admitting the possibility of an eternal world. In my opinion it is a question of intellectual honesty. Behind the criticism of Ockham is the sound Thomistic principle that we should be very severe with our own proofs: *ne fides derideatur*.

Therefore here, we face a true problem of Christian Philosophy. It is interesting to see how the Christian philosophers struggle with the necessitarian idea of Hellenism and of the Arabian Philosophers. The first step was to safeguard liberty in God as regards the universe which is a free creation of God's will and unbounded goodness — St. Thomas gave the classical formula of the solution; the second step was to liberate the essences of created things from their fetters of necessity and to submit them, too, to the productive will of the *ars aeterna*, as Ockham did; a third step was to safeguard the contingency of God's will and knowledge as regards all contingent facts, as did St. Bonaventure, Scotus and Ockham in opposition to St. Thomas. About this we shall hear in the third problem.

II. Aristotle and the problem of God's prescience of future contingent facts.

From this fact that there are contingent or free actions arise most difficult problems in Philosophy as well as in Theology.

The first problem concerns both the History of Philosophy and Logic.

1. The historical problem. According to Ockham, Aristotle denied the prescience of God as regards future contingent facts, if not with expressed words, certainly in the consequence of his teachings. At the end of the first book of Perihermenias Aristotle discusses the problem, whether in propositions about future contingent facts is truth or falsity. His answer is, that there is no determinated truth in such propositions, though of course they must be either true or false. We cite here one important passage in the Oxford English translation (19a—b): "Since propositions correspond with facts, it

is evident that when in future events there is a real alternative, and a potentially in contrary directions, the corresponding affirmation and denial have the same character. This is the case with regard to that which is not always existent or not always non-existent. One of the two propositions in such instances must be true and the other false, but we cannot say determinatedly that this or that is false, but must leave the alternative undecided. One may indeed be more likely to be true than the other, but it cannot be either actually true or actually false. It is therefore plain that it is not necessary that of an affirmation and a denial one should be true and the other false (determinatedly adds the translation in a footnote). For in the case that which exists potentially, but not actually, the rule which applies to that which exists actually does not hold good."[17]

As Ockham stated in the fifth supposition, according to this text it is the intention of the Philosopher, that even God does not know, which part of a contradiction in propositions about future contingent facts is true, because there is no determinated truth at all.[18]

It is true, historically speaking, that, according to Aristotle, God does not know future contingent facts, knowing of course taken in the Aristotelian sense: knowing truth? Ockham answers, the consequence is clear. If neither part of such a contradiction is true or false, that is to say, if either part is neutral in itself, it is neutral for any

---

[17] It may be of some interest to compare this translation with the Latin version which most probably is not far from the text Ockham had before him: Quare quoniam orationes similiter verae sunt quemadmodum et res, manifestum est quoniam quaecumque sic se habent, ut ad utrumlibet sunt et contraria ipsorum contingere queant, necesse est similiter se habere contradictionem, quia vel quod contingit in hiis, quae non semper sunt et non semper non sunt, horum enim necesse est quidem alteram partem contradictionis veram esse et falsam, non tamen hoc aut illud sed utrumlibet, et magis quidem alteram veram, non tamen iam veram vel falsam. Quare manifestum est, quoniam non est necesse omnes affirmationes vel negationes oppositarum hanc quidem veram, illam autem falsam esse. Neque enim quemadmodum in hiis, quae sunt, sic se habent etiam in hiis, quae non sunt, possibilibus tamen esse aut non esse; sed quemadmodum dictum est. — Expositio aurea, ed. cit. in fine libri primi Periherm.

[18] Cfr. also Ockham, I Sent., d. 38, q. 1, M, and the important text of the Expositio aurea.

knowing subject, God included. Peter d'Ailly[19] is of the same opinion and adds that Aristotle never speaks about the prescience of God. Gregory a Rimini thinks it foolish to deny this as historical fact. This interpretation of Ockham's is adopted by all the so-called Nominalists, and Aureoli. St. Bonaventure seems to be of the opinion when he says: *Dicendum quod istam rationem facit Philosophus ad ostendendum, quod in futuris non est veritas; et est sophistica.*[20] More plainly he accuses Aristotle in the Hexaemeron: "Hence he says (viz. Aristotle), that God knows only Himself and needs no knowledge of any other thing and moves things only as the object desired and loved . . . From this error follows another, namely, that God has neither prescience nor providence, since He has no reasons of things in Himself, through which He may know. They also say, that there is no truth concerning the future, except the truth of necessary things; and the truth of contingent things is no truth."[21]

The position of St. Thomas does not seem to be clear. In his Commentary on the text of Aristotle the Doctor Communis declares: "*. . . dicit (Aristoteles) manifestum esse ex praedictis quod non est necesse in omni genere affirmationum et negationum oppositarum, alteram determinate esse veram et alteram falsam: quia non eodem modo se habet veritas et falsitas in his quae sunt iam de praesenti et in his quae non sunt, sed possunt esse vel non esse. Sed hoc modo se habet in utrisque, sicut dictum est, quia scilicet in his quae sunt, necesse est determinate alterum esse verum et alterum falsum: quod non contingit in futuris quae possunt esse et non esse.*"[22] That there is no determinated truth in future contingent facts was explained by St. Thomas, according to the text of Aristotle, in Lectura XIII. In Lectura XIV St. Thomas discusses different theories and explains his own theory, that God knows which part of such a contradiction is true, determinatedly true, as I believe, because these facts are present to God's eternity. But, as far as I see, the Doctor communis does not try to bring into

---

[19] Qual. Magistri de Aylliaco super libros Sent., Argentinae 1490 q. 12 a.

[20] Sent. I, d. 38, a. 2, q. i, ad 3; t. I, p. 675.

[21] Coll. in Hexaem. VI, 2—4; t. V, p. 360.

[22] In libros Perihermenias expositio, l. I, c. 9, lect. XV; ed. Leon. t. I, p. 74.

agreement Aristotle's Logic and his own Christian theory, or perhaps we had better say, he presupposes that Aristotle presupposes the prescience of God. But, unfortunately, he does not say it. The editors explain that *"determinate"* means *"necessario"*.[23] A last explanation could be, that he charitably passes over this sore spot.

Scotus[24] seems to be not far from Saint Thomas.

My own opinion is that Aristotle was opposed to the prescience of God in the Christian sense. And we may conclude this part with the almost too careful remark of Silvester Maurus, S. J.: *Quaeritur an haec Aristotelis doctrina sit vera, vel erronea et contra fidem? Respondeo, quod si ita intelligatur, ut neget solum propositiones de futuro contingenti habere de praesenti veritatem determinatam naturaliter in rebus creatis, est vera; si autem ita intelligatur, ut neget tales propositiones habere veritatem determinatam etiam in scientia divina atque in supernaturalibus revelationibus, est falsa, contra fidem et impia."*[25]

We must at least give credit to Ockham for having seen a possible non-Christian interpretation in explaining Aristotle.

2. The logical problem. There is no doubt, that in a Christian Logic the above-mentioned neutral propositions are not admitted. Almost all the Christian thinkers agree on this point. The only exceptions I know are Aureoli,[26] the author of the Centiloquium[27] attributed to Ockham and Albertus de Saxonia.[28]

---

[23] l. c.

[24] That is to say only in his work: In duos libros Perihermenias, operis secundi, quod appellant, quaestiones octo, q. 7; ed. Vives, t. I, p. 597.

[25] Aristotelis opera omnia, t. I, Paris 1885, p. 73.

[26] Cfr. Peter d'Ailly, ed. cit. q. 12, M: Ex his patet manifeste, quod periculosa est et fidei contraria opinio Aureoli, quae dicit, quod haec est falsa: Deus scit quod Antichristus erit, et similes omnes, quibus significatur Deum determinate scire aliqua futura. Cuius rationem assignat, quia talis propositio de futuro contingenti non est determinate vera, et per consequens nec determinate scita. Et iterum dicit, quod ista est impropria: Deus scit, quid est futurum, quia nihil est determinate futurum, sed tantum sub distinctione hoc vel illud; et sic etiam Deus scit hoc vel illud sive quod affirmatio vel negatio erit futura, sed determinate nescit, quod affirmatio sit futura, quia non est determinate futura. Deus autem non potest scire, quod non est etc.

Ockham, however, does not admit neutral propositions in a Christian Logic. He expressly states it, because God knows determinatedly, which part of such a contradiction will be true. But he sees, too, that there is a cause, where natural Logic following its own course, easily may develop into a non-Christian Logic, or into a Logic of more values thant wo, namely of three values: either true or false or neutral. Ockham, the great logician clearly sees this possibility, though he does not admit it, and he also sees, that in this case the validity of certain universal principles would be shaken.[29] For instance, in such a polyvalued Logic the rule: *Ab universali ad singularem est bona consequentia* does not hold good. It is universally true that in propositions about future contingent facts one part of the contradiction is true or false, but a *propositio singularis* is neutral: neither true nor false. An other rule does not hold good in this matter, namely: *Universale sufficienter inducitur ex suis singularibus.* Because the following consequence would not be valid: this future contingent fact will not be, this will not be, and so for every contingent fact, therefore no future contingent fact will be. Because in this case the consequent is determinatedly false, but the antecedent is not determinatedly false.

It is of great interest to see, how closely Ockham approaches modern logic here, the so-called polyvalued Logic. In order to give an idea of it I quote K. Menger.[30] "In geometry besides Euclidean

Cfr. also Schwamm, op. cit. p. 118 and 121 s., who refers to Aureoli's printed Commentary on the Sentences, Romae, 1596, p. 901[a].

[27] Cfr. for instance Conclusio 84, ed. Lugduni 1495 (together with Ockham's Commentary on the Sentences); [ed. Boehner in: Franciscan Studies 2 (1942) 293]. The most probable non-authenticity of this work will be proved in an article to be published in the first issue[s 1941—1942; cfr. Introduction, *supra*] of "Franciscan Studies".

[28] "Tertia conclusio: sive sit vera sive falsa, tamen nec est determinate vera nec determinate falsa, quia licet sic erit, quod Sortes leget, tamen antequam sic erit, possibile est, quod non leget; propter hoc sic erit falsa: Sortes legit: et per consequens antequam Sortes leget, nondum praedicta propositio est determinata in veritate. Et consimiliter arguitur de falsitate." In the edition of the Expositio aurea of Ockham (ed. cit.).

[29] For the following cfr. the Text of the Expositio aurea.

[30] The new Logic, Philosophy of Science, 4, July (1937) p. 325 s.

geometry there have been deduced from other axioms other geometries which are quite different from one another and of which each is a system closed within itself. Similarly there have been constructed numerous logics which differ from one another; and each of these is a system closed within itself. Some examples are the so-called polyvalued logics which originated with Lukasiewicz and Post. In the ordinary logic, all propositions are divided into two classes, the class of so-called true and the class of so-called false propositions, so that every proposition belongs to one and only one of the two classes, as expressed by the principle of the excluded middle or third. Likewise there has now been developed a logic in which propositions are divided into three classes, and a principle of excluded fourth holds. The assumption that through one point there are many parallels to a given line leads to a system which is not only abstract but can even be illustrated by models; similarly, it is possible to get an illustration of the three-valued false ones . . . However, the mere existence of different logics and of different mathematics belonging to them is of interest, for until recently any such state of affairs was regarded as out of the question." The last statement of Menger apparently is not correct, because at least Ockham saw this possibility as a consequence of Aristotelian logic and metaphysics, long before the great Polish scholar Lukasiewicz discovered this possibility in Aristotle again.[31]

---

[31] Cfr. C. A. Baylis: Are Some Propositions Neither True Nor False? in: Philosophy of Science 3 (1936) p. 156—166. In this article are found references to Lukasiewicz and others. K. Michalski expressly directed the attention to Ockham. I was not able to use his article which I read years ago: Le problème de la volonté à Oxford et à Paris au XIVe siècle, in: Studia philosophica, Lemberg, II, 1937, p. 233—265. See also H. Scholz: Die mathematische Logik und die Metaphysik, in Philosophisches Jahrbuch 51 (1938) p. 257—291. If Scholz is correct, the statement of Michalski is incorrect, namely: ". . . daß kein geringerer als Wilhelm von Ockham sich als Logiker und als Philosoph für eine dreiwertige Logik mit den ihr eigentümlichen propositiones neutrae eingesetzt hat." p. 265. Ockham saw the possibility of a three-valued Logic, but was opposed to it. In his latest [?] philosophical work, in the Summa Logicae, Ockham states: Ad veritatem autem disiunctivae requiritur, quod altera pars sit vera. Et hoc est intelligendum, quando propositiones sunt de praesenti, non de futuro nec aequivalentes propositionibus de futuro, et hoc diceret Philosophus. Tamen

3. Problem: The necessity of God's prescience.

Ockham stated in the second supposition, that all propositions in this matter are contingent propositions. This is directed immediately against some artists[32] (in the old sense) and mediately against St. Thomas:

According to St. Thomas, God's knowledge, which is the first cause, is necessary, though the *scita* are contingent: *Scita a Deo sunt contingentia propter causas proximas, licet scientia Dei, quae est causa prima, sit necessaria* (ad 1^m). In his answer to the second objection the Doctor communis remarks: *Quidam dicunt, Deus scivit hoc contingens futurum, non est necessarium, sed contingens: quia licet sit praeteritum, tamen importat respectum ad futurum. — Sed hoc non tollit ei necessitatem: quia id quod habuit respectum ad futurum, necesse est habuisse, licet etiam futurum non sequatur quandoque* ... And a little later: *Unde dicendum est, quod hoc antecedens est necessarium absolute. Nec tamen sequitur, ut quidam dicunt, quod consequens sit necessarium absolute* ...[33]

---

secundum veritatem ad veritatem disiunctivae requiritur, quod altera pars sit vera, quia secundum veritatem propositio de futuro est vera vel falsa, quamvis evitabiliter. (Instead of the *evitabiliter* of the manuscripts, the edition has: *non evidenter.*) Summa Logicae, p. II, c. 33, ed. Venet. 1508, fol. 43 rb—va; [ed. Boehner II, p. 317].

[32] Verumtamen pro aliquibus artistis est sciendum, quod quantumcumque Deus sciat de omnibus futuris contingentibus, quae pars erit vera et quae falsa, tamen haec non est necessaria: Deus scit quae pars erit vera, immo est contingens intantum, quod quantumcumque haec sit vera: Deus scit, quod haec pars contradictionis erit vera, tamen possibile est, quod haec numquam fuit vera, et in isto casu potentia est ad oppositum illius sine omni successione, quia possibile est, quod numquam fuit vera. Sent. I, d. 38, q. 1, N.

[33] Summa theol. I, q. 14, a. 13. It is worthwhile to read the long explanation of this article by Cajetanus. He says, it caused much trouble to Thomists and thinks that with the help of God and an inspiration of St. Thomas, he had found a good solution, namely: For God in His eternal "Nunc" there are no real past or future facts, because all facts are present to Him; consequently as such they are necessary according to the principle: Omne quod est, quando est, necesse est esse (See Ockham's criticism of this principle in Sent. II, q. 8), and he admits: Appellatur tamen Deus, vel

Scotus[34] does not agree with this statement of St. Thomas, because from it there would follow, that if the first cause is necessary, the second cause would be necessary too. Ockham does not agree with St. Thomas either, but he thinks it possible, for the first cause to be a necessary one and the second cause contingent.[35] Therefore he admits the conclusion of Scotus: *Et illam conclusionem dicit Sco-*

---

eius scientia, causa necessaria, propter necessitatem non simpliciter, sed immutabilitatis, quae in eo, etiam in quantum causa, formaliter salvetur. Ed. Leonina, p. 191, XXIV.

The Scoliastes of St. Bonaventure declare (t. I, p. 680): Ad quaestionem duplex est responsio. S. Thom. (S. I, q. 14, ar. 13, ad 2, et I Sent. hic q. 1, a. 5, ad 4.) docet, propositionem: Deus scivit hoc contingens esse futurum, esse „necessariam absolute" (quod intelligendum esse videtur non de necessario absoluto in *rigore*, sed de necessario *immutabilitatis*). — S. Bonav. vero cum Scoto (I. S. d. 39, q. 4), Richard. (d. 39, a. 1, q. 2.) et plurimis aliis, etiam nonnullis ex scola S. Thomae, vult, propositionem esse *simpliciter* contingentem, et necessariam *tantum secundum quid.*

[34] Scotus does it in a very objective manner in Ox. I, d. 39, q. u. n. 11. Adam Wodham, here a disciple of Scotus, seems to go too far, when he connects the opinion of St. Thomas with the necessitarian view of Hellenism. Cfr.: Sed haec opinio secundum illud, quod sonat, stare non potest, quia tunc omnia illa, quae solum a Deo fuerant producenda, necessario fuissent futura, antequam essent, et tunc Deus necessario produxisset caelum et omnes angelos, quod esset erroneum et contra fidem. Probatur: Quidquid undecumque est necessarium omnibus pensatis, est necessarium, licet illam necessitatem non habeat a qualibet eius causa; igitur si omnia futura ut relata ad divinam praescientiam vel ad primam causam necessario evenirent, sequitur, quod absolute loquendo omnia simpliciter futura necessario evenirent, quod est erroneum et contra Augustinum 5° De Civitate, cap. praenotatis. Hoc enim tolleret arbitrii libertatem, et per consequens meritum et demeritum, et necessitaret ad inconvenientia immutabilia (sic!). Item: Contra hoc est articulus Parisiensis sic dicens: Quod nihil contingenter eveniat considerando omnes eius causas — error. Item: Alius articulus dicit sic: Falsum est omnia esse praeordinata a causa prima, quia sic omnia evenirent de necessitate, quod est error . . . Sent. II, d. 14, q. 3; Paris 1512, fol. 120vb. The printed text is the "Abbreviatio" of Henry of Oyta.

[35] Sent. II, q. 4 et 5, E: Sed potest dici, quod ex contingentia causae secundae non potest argui contingentia in prima . . .

tus,[36] not his proof of the statement that God does not know a contingent future fact in a necessary way.

Ockham's first criticism on this opinion of some artists and of St. Thomas is found in the second supposition, and he makes it asking: Is it possible that Peter who is predestinated, be condemned? If not, it follows that he will be necessarily saved; if so, and we take this case, then the following proposition is true: *Petrus est damnatus*, and after this moment, it will be true for ever: *Petrus fuit damnatus*. According to the opponents it would be also true to say: *Petrus fuit praedestinatus*, true forever, consequently both propositions would be true: *Petrus fuit reprobatus, Petrus fuit praedestinatus*. That is impossible.

But according to Ockham's third supposition this reasoning is simply false, because no proposition in this matter is a proposition of the present or the past time, consequently, in a purely logical sense, there is no necessity at all. This statement however, would be denied by St. Thomas. And Cajetanus explains it, as it seems, saying that for God any proposition in this matter is a proposition of the present.

In order to explain his position which, as far as I see, is close to the teachings of Duns Scotus, Ockham clearly distinguishes between the necessity of God's knowledge as it regards God's substance, and the necessity of God's knowledge as it regards contingent facts. The former necessity is to be held, because it is identical with God's essence, the latter necessity is to be denied, lest we should introduce necessity into contingent facts. Though God has this knowledge of every contingent fact, nevertheless he has not this knowledge as a necessary one, because a contingent fact is not necessarily a fact, and if it did not exist, God would not have this knowledge, as God is not necessarily Lord over the world, but only when the contingent fact of the existence of the world is posited. By this fact the proposition: God is Lord over the world becomes true, in the same way the statement:

---

[36] In the second supposition [ed. Boehner, p. 12]. Cfr. Scotus: Rep. Par. I, d. 40, q. u. n. 11; ed. Vivès, t. 22, p. 477; Oxon. I, d. 39, q. u. n. 22 and 26, t. 10, p. 637 and 650.

God knows a contingent fact, is in God per praedicationem: *Dico, quod illud, quod est in Deo vel potest esse in eo formaliter, necessario est Deus; sed scire A non est sic in Deo, sed tantum per praedicationem, quia est quidam conceptus vel nomen, quod praedicatur de Deo, et aliquando non; et non oportet sic, quod sit Deus, quia hoc nomen dominus praedicatur de Deo contingenter et ex tempore, et tamen non est Deus.*[37]

In other words no knowledge of any kind which regards non-divine things *is* a reality in God. God only *has* it, and He *has* it as *esse obiectivum*. God *is* His knowledge, He *has* knowledge of all other things. The same is to be said of His will: He *is* His will as regards Divine things, He has a will as regards other things *"per praedicationem"* not *per essentiam*. Consequently no knowledge and no activity which concerns created things can change Him. Further, this knowledge and this will can change as created things change, because their mutation does not affect by any means God's own immutability. For instance, if it is true now: *Sortes sedet*, and after a few moments, *Sortes non sedet:* God first knew that the statement: *Sortes sedet* was true, and now he knows, that this statement is false. And only in this sense we can say: God's knowledge can change. And the ultimate reason is, because God's knowledge does not impose any necessity upon contingent facts, and it does not impose any necessity, because they are outside of His own necessity.[38]

4. *Problem: How does God know a future contingent fact?* We know by experience that there are contingent facts, we know by faith that a proposition about a future contingent fact is determinatedly true or false, because God knows it, we know by reason that this knowledge is contingent. By then there remains the difficult problem, how to explain this knowledge of God's, His prescience? Ockham is opposed

---

[37] Tractatus de praedestinatione etc. Cfr.: Dico, quod quamvis Deus sit primo non sciens hoc et postea sit sciens hoc, tamen non sequitur Deum mutari, quia ad verificandum talia contradictoria de Deo sufficit sola mutatio in creatura, sicut ad hoc, quod sit primo non creans et postea creans sufficit sola mutatio creaturae. Sent. I, d. 39, q. u. D.

[38] Cfr. Sent. I, d. 39, q. u.: Utrum Deus possit scire plura quam scit? and the Tractatus de praedestinatione...

to any solution which denies or implies that these facts are not really future for God — here he admits Dun Scotus' criticism on St. Thomas, as is evident from his discussion of the whole problem;[39] and Ockham is equally opposed to any solution which could endanger the liberty of the created will. Just as nothing was nearer Scotus' heart than to safeguard contingency *(salvare contingentiam)*, so Ockham was preoccupied with safeguarding liberty. Therefore he directs his criticism especially against the theory of Duns Scotus. We find his criticism as well in the Commentary on the Sentences, used by Schwamm, as here in our treatise *De Praedestinatione etc.* in the sixth supposition. In our tract he first briefly explains the theory of Duns Scotus: Scotus states, the intellect of God knows both sides of the possibility regarding future contingent facts, first without any determination; then the will of God determines one part has to be true, and now the intellect knows through the determination of the Divine will, which part will be true.

Ockham objects: From this theory follow untenable consequences:

a) What about the free will of man? Does the free will necessarily follow the determination of God's will or not? If necessarily, then there would be no free will, if not necessarily, it follows that the human will is able not to do as the Divine will determined; therefore God is not able to know by the determination of His will, which part will be true. Consequently any determination of the will of God taken as a means of knowledge cannot lead us out of the dilemma: if necessary, then no free will, if not necessary, then no Divine Prescience.

Schwamm mentions this objection of Ockham's and finds it a little superficial, because Scotus had already said, that this determination of the will of God is a contingent one. But this contingent determination is excluded by this reasoning of Ockham too, and he explains it further in his second objection.

b) The second objection of Ockham takes the second possibility: no necessary determination, in other words: God determines contin-

---

[39] Cfr. for instance: Sent. I, d. 38, q. u. M: et hoc non esset, quia futura contingentia essent sibi praesentia.

gently, which part of a contradiction concerning future contingent facts will be true. But even granted, that it would be contingent, answers Ockham, such a contingent determination does not guarantee certitude and infallibility to the Divine Knowledge, because of its being a contingent determination, the fact could be different.[40]

Then we have to ask: What remains for a solution? How can we explain God's prescience, its certitude, its infallibility etc.? Is there any solution of this problem? Ockham confesses in the Commentary on the Sentences: *Sed modum exprimere nescio.*[41] The solution of this problem escapes the limits of a human understanding. And in our tract he says: It is impossible to express clearly the way God knows future contingent facts, but it is to be held, that He knows them, and He knows them in a contingent manner. The basis of this statement is revelation; human reason has to acknowledge it, even if no clear solution can be given.

Nevertheless we are able to point in some direction where a possible solution could be found: Our intellect is able to know evidently, which part of a contradictory statement is true, for instance of the proposition: A exists, A does not exist, and our intellect is able to do so by the *notitia intuitiva.* In the same way it can be conceded, that the divine essence, which is so perfect and so clear, that it is evident and intuitive knowledge of all past and future things, that it knows, which part of a contradiction will be true, and which part will be false.

Ockham refuses to give any further details. But somebody may object: How can God know such a future fact, because it is contingent and neither true nor false? Ockham answers: One part is true, now, so that it is not false, and this means: it is contingently true.

But why is it true? would the opponent ask again. Ockham answers: one part is determinatedly true, so that it is not false, because the will of God wills that this part be true and the other part be

---

[40] For further details see Schwamm, l. c.

[41] Sent. I, d. 38, q. u. M; and in N he says: Sed hoc evidenter declarare et modum quo scit omnia futura contingentia exprimere est impossibile omni intellectui pro statu isto.

false. But he wills it contingently, and He is able not to will this part, and He can choose the other part, and the other part would be true.

Here, the will of God suddenly interferes. Does this mean, Ockham falls back on the Scotistic solution? I do not think so. Because it only would be the Scotistic solution, if God knew the truth of a future contingent fact by the determination of His will. This, however, is excluded. But the fact that one part will be true or a fact, of course, is due to the will of God which causes everything. Therefore the will of God is the cause of the truth not the knowledge of this truth. The knowledge has to be explained neither by the determination of the will of God, nor through God's presence, nor through the ideas in God, but only through the immensity of God's knowledge which is His essence.

Conclusion: I only chose some problems which could be of some interest even to Philosophers. Perhaps I created the impression that the different problems are without connection. Nevertheless they all point in the same direction, and this is: The absolute contingency of every created being and the sovereignty of God over every created being. In other words in the direction of a Christian God and a Christian world entirely depending upon God. But this dependance does not mean the suppression of gifts freely given by God: Therefore no necessity in God as regards creatures, neither in His will nor in His knowledge; but also no necessity in the created will. This contingency excludes any means of knowledge or prescience of God: it cannot come from the things nor from the determination of God's will nor from his ideas, nor from the presence of creatures before the eternal *Nunc* of God, because that would destroy their temporality. Therefore there only remains the immensity of God's essence which embraces every creature: and because every creature is known by God's essence, hence it is, that there is determined truth in the present, the past and the future facts and no room for neutral statements, and hence it is that the eternal eye of God infallibly, without necessity, knows every fact, may it be present, past or future.[42]

---

[42] I am indebted to Prof. [Thomas] Merton for assistance in preparing the manuscript for publication.

OCKHAM'S POLITICAL IDEAS*

WILLIAM OCKHAM, the *Venerabilis Inceptor* and the *Doctor plus quam subtilis*, started his academic career simply as a theologian and philosopher who did not have, or at least did not evince, the slightest interest in political questions. By 1324 or at least by 1327, he had composed all his purely theological or philosophical works of which we have any knowledge.[1] In all these writings there is no trace of any political idea worth mentioning. Even the struggle about the Franciscan ideal of poverty had left no impression on the lines written by Ockham prior to 1327. While he was in England he was either too remote from the theatre of war of (and this seems to be more likely) he was too much engrossed in the construction of his conceptualistic system of philosophy and theology. In any case, we know from his own words that he did not take part in the struggle about poverty — not even to the extent of reading the pertinent documents — before or during his enforced stay at Avignon until the beginning of 1328.

After 1328, however, Ockham did enter into the field of polemical and political writing, and so radical was this change that henceforth he was solely a polemical and political theologian. So completely were his energies absorbed in this new task that he no longer found time to complete some of his more philosophical and theological works.

---

* The author wishes to express his indebtedness to Fr. Sebastian Day, O.F.M. for his assistance in preparing the manuscript for publication. [First published in: *The Review of Politics* 3 (1943) 462—487].

[1] These are: *Reportatio* (quaestiones in 2m 3m 4m librum Sententiarum), *Ordinatio* (quaestiones in 1m 1. Sententiarum), the Commentaries on Porphyry's Isagoge, Aristotle's Categories, Perihermenias, De Sophisticis Elenchis and on the Physics, Summulae in libros Physicorum and Summa Logicae; Ockham had composed most probably at this time *Quodlibeta* VII, *Quaestiones in libros Physicorum*, his two treatises on the Holy Eucharist and some Quaestiones disputatae. Of these works *Expositio in libros Physicorum*, *Summulae in libros Physicorum* and *Reportatio* are unfinished. Ockham did not fulfill his promise to write on Aristotle's Metaphysics and other works.

This sudden change in his life occurred when, at the request of his superior, Fr. Michael de Cesena, the General of the Franciscan Order, he studied the bitterly debated problem of the Franciscan ideal of poverty. Because of this question Michael was held under arrest at the papal court in Avignon from December, 1327 and Ockham who had been held at the same court since 1324 because of an impending trial concerning suspicious doctrines in theology, read and studied then for the first time the decretals of Pope John XXII. He soon became convinced that there were contradictions between these decretals and those of former Popes, especially those of Popes Nicholas III; and he found in these contradictions an excuse to renounce obedience to a Pope whom he considered heretical.[2] With his superior and two other friars, Ockham escaped from Avignon on May 26, 1328. He took refuge with the Pope's enemy, Louis the Bavarian. This event marks the beginning of Ockham's bitter and relentless fight against Pope John XXII and his successors and, at the same time, marks the beginning of his career as a polemical and political writer.

At first, however, the purely political questions concerning the relation between the secular and ecclesiastical power did not occupy Ockham's interest. During the years 1328—1335 his pen was, as it seems, mainly devoted to the interests of his Order in matters of Franciscan poverty. In this, of course, he gave at least indirect

---

[2] Noveritis itaque et cuncti nover nt Christiani, quod fere quatuor annis integris in Avinione mansi, antequam cognoscerem praesidentem ibidem pravitatem haereticam incurrisse, quia nolens leviter credere, quod persona in tanto officio constituta haereses definiret esse tenendas, const - tutiones haereticales ipsius nec legere nec habere curavi. Post modum vero, ex occasione data, superiore mandante, tres constitutiones seu potius destitutiones haereticales ... legi et studui diligenter ... L. Baudry, *La Lettre de Guillaume d'Occam au Chapitre d'Assise*, in *Revue d'Histoire Franciscaine* III (1926) p. 207. Cf. also pp. 207 and 213 where Ockham states that this was the reason for his escape from Avignon. It does not seem likely that Ockham escaped for fear of an imminent condemnation in his trial; for this assumption meets with the objection that Ockham was never condemned by the Pope because of "suspicious doctrines" which were examined by the Pope's commission, though it would have been an effective weapon in the hands of the Pope.

support to the German Emperor, Louis the Bavarian, who, for his own cause and because of his own purely political struggle against the Pope, exploited the opposition of the friars against the Supreme Pontiff. However, it was only natural that Ockham, fighting for the cause of Franciscan poverty, should favour the side of the German Emperor against the common enemy. Nevertheless, there seems to be a deeper reason why Ockham finally gave direct support to the Emperor's cause. Louis the Bavarian fought for the independence of secular power (and of the Roman Empire in particular) against any interference by the Pope.[3] He had been elected by a majority of German princes; a minority, however, disputed the election. In such a case, the Pope (John XXII) claimed the right to decide who was to be the lawful Roman Emperor. The struggle, therefore, of the Franciscan Order and the struggle of the Emperor against the Pope was one struggle for inviolable rights, as Ockham saw them. The Franciscans fought for a right guaranteed by Holy Scripture and by declarations of previous Popes,[4] and the Emperor fought for a right guaranteed by divine and natural law. Hence, to Ockham's way of thinking, both cases were but one as to their fundamental issue; for both were one in their opposition to an unjust claim of the supreme ecclesiastical power, which was prejudicial to lawful rights. Thus, the essential problem of the entire struggle became the question of the limits of papal authority, and from about 1335 Ockham focused his main interest on this problem. This is evident from even a very cursory reading of his political writings. These begin, roughly speaking, with his monumental and unfinished work, the *Dialogus*, on which Ockham probably worked from 1334.

---

[3] It should be noted that wherever Ockham refers to the "Roman Empire", he understands by this term the Ancient Roman empire *and* its continuation, the so-called "Holy Roman Empire."

[4] Ockham with the friars — and not only with the so-called Spirituals — was convinced that the ideal of Franciscan poverty, expressed in the Franciscan rule, confirmed by the Bull of Honorius III and the decretal of Nicholas III, was revealed by the life of Christ. There can be no doubt that Pope Nicholas III believed it, too, although in a strict theological sense, he had not defined it *ex cathedra*. Since Pope John XXII denied it, there ex sted for Ockham a contradicton between two definitions of Popes.

A correct interpretation, therefore, of these so-called political writings, where the problem of evangelical and Franciscan poverty plays only a subordinate role, must never lose sight of this central idea. The crucial problem was not simply that of the relation between Church and State or between the Pope and the Emperor; it was rather this same problem but with a definite qualification. Ockham's problem was the actual extent of the Pope's power; still more correctly and precisely, it was the actual limits of the papal power. This was the problem which inspired Ockham to write all his political works, and even the problem of the right and extent of secular power and jurisdiction was subordinated to it. For, contrary to some scholars, Ockham did not write for the benefit of the Emperor, or, at least, that was not his main concern. The scholars to whom we refer have attached too much significance to the much quoted words which were never spoken by Ockham at all: "O Emperor, defend me with the sword and I shall defend you by the word." Ockham was not a courtier who had sold himself to a secular prince and who now earned his life and protection by such servility. In denying the absolute fullness of the papal power he denied the absolute fullness of the Emperor's power as well; and he always maintained the autonomy and higher dignity of the Pope. For Ockham was a theologian who, for the benefit of the Church and for the love of peace between Church and State, tried to define the proper authority of the Church and its jurisdiction side by side with those of the State. Though excommunicated by the Pope and expelled from the Order, he did not renounce the Church or his Order. Neither did he deny the supremacy of the Pope or any defined dogma of the Church — except those defined by Pope John XXII and his successor, because he thought them heretical. (Cf. note 19 for Ockham's attitude towards the infallibility of the Pope.)

It is apparent, therefore, that the only logical and psychological starting-point, even of a short outline of Ockham's political ideas, are Ockham's notions concerning the limits of the papal power. Consequently, to base Ockham's political ideas on, or to develop them from, his so-called Metaphysics, as has been done by Al. Dempf,[5]

---

[5] Cf. Al. Dempf, *Sacrum Imperium.* (München and Berlin 1929), esp. pp. 504—510.

appears to us more as an adventure and certainly as a construction of the writer. We do not deny that there are inner connections. These connections, however, can be seen only if the philosophical and theological system of Ockham is correctly interpreted. Seldom has this been done hitherto, and certainly not by Al. Dempf, who presents a rather vague and partly very incorrect interpretation of Ockham's Metaphysics. One should be on his guard against all such conctructions of Hegelian coinage because even Bartholomaeus de Lucca, the confessor of St. Thomas and probable continuator of his *De regimine principum*, and likewise Aegidius Romanus, another disciple of St. Thomas and leading Thomist of the 13th century, arrived at a very unsound political theory of an unrestricted absolutism of the Pope, in spite of their Thomistic metaphysical principles. Ockham's political ideas in their great outlines could have been developed, so far as we can see, from any of the classical metaphysics of the 13th century; for, as will be shown, they coincide with a sound Catholic political theory.

Our starting-point, therefore, will be Ockham's starting-point: his very personal problem of the limits of the Pope's power. His disobedience to the Pope cannot be justified; it is, however, understandable if we take into account the confusion which prevailed at his time concerning the actual power of the Pope. Ockham suffered from this confusion to which the friends of the Pope contributed at least as much as the enemies of the Pope. Ockham, therefore, saw his task, first and above all, as the definition and determination of the right and authority of the successors of Peter. In natural consequence of and in dependence on this first task, he had to deal with secular power and also its rights and limits.[6]

---

[6] That the limits of the papal power were Ockham's chief concern finds a remarkable expression in *Breviloquium de potestate Papae:* Porro, si secundum istos tenendum est, quod papa non habet praedictam plentitudinem potestatis a Christo, dicatur ergo quam potestatem habet a Christo et quam non habet, quod tamen a nullo ampliantium potestatem papae adhuc est dictum. Et utinam aliquis eorum hoc expressis verbis dicere non formidet! Ex hoc enim excogitata (or exagitata? Cf. *Consultatio de causa matrimoniali*, ed. *infra cit.* p. 282, I n. 18) veritas clarius elucescet. Lib. 1, c. 13; ed. *infra cit.* p. 42 f. We gladly acknowledge that N. Abbagnano,

In order to find out Ockham's personal views, one must start with works in which the *Venerabilis Inceptor* expresses his own opinions because his main work, the *Dialogus* (composed between 1334 and 1339) and also the *Octo quaestiones de potestate Papae* (probably written between 1340 and 1342) were both written in the style of mere discussions of the problem without revealing the personal opinion of the author. His own opinions are expressed in less-known works of which we shall use the *Breviloquium de Potestate Papae* (composed about 1340), *An Princeps* (composed between 1338—1339), and the *Consultatio de causa matrimoniali* (composed about 1341). After Ockham's opinion has been sufficiently ascertained on the basis of these three works, one may be permitted to identify his opinions as expressed in the other writings. As to the *Octo quaestiones*, a generally valid rule would seem to be this: That opinion which, in comparison with the others, is disproportionately more developed and proved represents Ockham's own opinion.[7]

I. THE NATURE AND ACTUAL EXTENT OF PAPAL POWER

In order to give a faithful historical account of Ockham's political ideas, we must not only see the problem to be solved as Ockham saw it, but we must also see with Ockham's eyes the historical facts which stimulated his inquiry into the limits of papal power. In Pope John XXII's claim of the right to interfere in matters pertaining to the empire, the *Venerabilis Inceptor* certainly saw a usurpation of

---

Guglielmo di Ockham, (Lanziano n. d.), p. 309 ff and S. Tornay, *Ockham, Studies and Selections*, (La Salle, III, 1938) p. 79 f substantially come to the same conclusion. As to the latter, however, his introduction to Ockham's political philosophy," p. 77, contains many errors concerning biographical data.

[7] We used the following editions: *Dialogus* (Lyons 1494); *Breviloquium de potestate Papae*, ed L. Baudry (Etudes de Philosophie Médiévale, dir. Et. Gilson. t. 24). (Paris, Vrin, 1937); *Octo quaestiones de potestate Papae* (ed. J. G. Sikes), *An Princeps pro suo succursu, scilicet guerrae, possit recipere bona ecclesiarum, etiam invito Papa* (ed. H. S. Offler and R. H. Snape). *Consultatio de causa matrimoniali* (ed. H. S. Offler) in *Guillelmi de Ockham Opera Politica accuravit* J. G. Sikes etc. Vol. 1 (Manchester 1940).

unlawful rights. The very title of one of Ockham's main works, which expresses his own personal opinions, is really significant and speaks for itself: *Breviloquium on the tyrannical power over things divine and human, especially, however, over the empire and over the subjects of the empire, usurped by certain people called highest Pontiffs.*[8] Ockham was convinced of the historical fact of a tyrannical power usurped by certain Popes.

We, however, shall dismiss here the *quaestio facti* as irrelevant to our purpose, and shall simply take Ockham's contention as our starting-point. Then, we must ask: What is meant by usurped and tyrannical power of the Pope? Ockham defined this in each one of his political writings, and never tired of coming back to it and refuting it vehemently. What he called usurped and tyrannical power was in reality an absolutistic and universal supremacy of the Pope which, in its fantastic exaggerations, had been developed by the so-called Curialists, such as Bartholomaeus (or Tolomaeus) de Lucca, Aegidius Romanus, Augustinus Triumphus, and others.[9] This development, moreover, had not come about without at least the effective influence of Popes Innocent IV and Boniface VIII. Ockham is well aware that there were differences and nuances in their positions. In any case, the opinion existed that the Pope had full (that is, absolute) power over all things, spiritual and temporal, or over the Church and the State. That this power was absolute meant that it was not limited by any human law or institution or treaty, or by a human promise, vow or oath. The only restriction of the power of the Pope was imposed by the divine law and the immutable and indispensable natural law. In other words, things which were directly forbidden by God and the natural law to all human beings without exception, because they are illicit in themselves, could not be commanded by the Pope, but outside of this single restriction, all human beings were subjects of the Pope and he may command them to do whatever he wills. If he commanded within the limits of the aforesaid restriction, his

---

[8] Baudry has changed this challenging title into the very innocent one: *Breviloquium de potestate Papae*, for typographical reasons.

[9] For introductory information in this regard cf. Al. Dempf, op. cit. p. 441—468.

orders were binding in conscience, even though the Pope in so commanding should commit a sin.[10]

Ockham considered such an idea of the Pope's absolute power regarding temporal and even spiritual things as false, dangerous for society, and heretical. In the name of the liberty of the Holy Gospel he protested against such a usurpation of absolute power. For him the new law of the Holy Gospel is a law of free men in Christ, and by its very nature it does not admit of any servitude which even equals, let alone surpasses, the yoke imposed upon the Jews by the Old Law. It is a flagrant contradiction of the Holy Gospel to make all men slaves *(servi)* of the Popes and thus create a most horrid state of bondage. Besides this theological reasoning, it is easy to imagine all the dangerous consequences which would follow if such a power were placed in the hands of one human being. For such a man could turn the whole of society upside down; he could take away justly-owned property from everyone and could give it to his favorites; he could depose kings and prelates at will and could appoint criminals as rulers, without violating any right.[11]

But in advocating the divine right of the liberty of the Holy Gospel, Ockham by no means makes a plea for libertinism. He cautions his readers that "liberty of the Holy Gospel" can be understood in a correct and in a false sense. It is correctly understood if it is taken as the denial of an absolute power of the Pope; but it is falsely understood if it is taken as the denial of any power of the Pope whatsoever. Consequently, it must be rather negatively understood, in the sense that the evangelical law does not admit a grave yoke or that anybody is made by it the slave of another.[12] This presupposes

---

[10] *An princeps, c.* 1.; p. 232. Cf. *Breviloquium, lib.* 2, *c.* 1; p. 17 and *c.* 13; p. 42; *Octo quaestiones,* q. 1, *c.* 2; p. 15; *Dialogus,* pars III, *lib.* 1, *c.* 1 ffs; fol 81va; *Consultatio,* p. 284 f.

[11] *Breviloquium, lib.* 2, *c.* 3; ff. To the references to the other works on p. 20, note 2, add also *Consultatio,* p. 234 ff.

[12] Iterum, quia legem evangelicam esse legem perfectae libertatis ex quo patet papam non habere talem plenitudinem potestatis, potest bene et male intelligi, est advertendum quod legem evangelicam esse legem perfectae libertatis non debet intelligi, ut omnem servitudinem tollat et nullam patiatur etiam christianis . . . sed debet magis intelligi negative, quia scilicet

that the Pope has a supreme power, although Ockham is usually not too much concerned with the actual content of the supreme ecclesiastical power. Yet, since to limit something implies that there is something which can be limited, the actual content of the Pope's power is more or less clearly seen in Ockham's criticism of the exaggerated claims.

At least once he expressed his own opinion of the actual extent of papal authority, in his treatise *An princeps*. However, since the essential elements of his explanations are more systematically arranged in the *Dialogus*, we shall follow his determinations in the latter work, with references to the former. Ockham's discussions of the powers of the Pope in the *Dialogus*, are likewise governed by the idea of a limitation of the supreme ecclesiastical power to its just limits. After having stated that the Pope's power is not absolute *(plenissima potestas)*, he nevertheless admits that it is grand, singular and very great. He then explains the actual extension of it in the following steps:

1. Christ has constituted Peter as the head, the prince, and the prelate of the other Apostles and of all the faithful. Hence Peter was not elected by the Apostles or by others and instituted by this election in his right. Every successor of Peter possesses the same right and privilege as Peter.[13]

2. The Pope, as successor of Peter, has the regular supreme power in all spiritual matters, that is, in matters which pertain to the evangelical law and which are proper to it, and which do not belong to another law, at least not to another human law. The Pope has, therefore, the regular supreme power as regards the dispensation of

---

per legem evangelicam nullatenus iugum grave inducitur et nullus per ipsam fit servus alterius, nec tantum onus quoad exteriorem cultum divinum per ipsam imponitur christianis quanto Judaei passi sunt. *Breviloquium,* lib. 2, c. 4; p. 21.

[13] *Dialogus,* pars III, tract 1. lib. 1, c. 17; fol. 88vb. In *An princeps* this truth is more presupposed as basis than formally expressed; for instance: Tertium notabile, quod ex praedictis habetur est, quod a Deo non solum instituta est potestas papalis ... c. 4; p. 243; Amplius, Christus constituens beatum Petrum caput et praelatum cunctorum fidelium ... l. c., c. 2; p. 236 and elsewhere.

the Sacraments, the ordination of priests, and the institution of clerics or the promotion of those who have to govern and teach the Christian peoples. In brief, the Pope has the regular supreme power as regards faith (including morals) and the divine cult and as regards all those things without which the Church cannot conveniently be ruled.[14]

3. Within the frame of this regular supreme power, the Pope has, however, no absolute power; his power is limited to those things which are necessary to be done or omitted. Hence his power does not regard works of supererogation. For instance, the Pope has no right to oblige anybody to the observation of the evangelical counsels or to works without which neither faith nor good morals would be endangered. He can, however, in case of necessity or of great utility, prescribe such works.[15]

4. Moreover, the Pope has regular coercive power; that is, he has not only a jurisdiction as regards the confessional or the *forum internum* concerning the remission of sins, but he has also the right to enforce his order by punishment. This coercive power, however, must be (regularly, at least) restricted to ecclesiastical crimes which are directly committed against the Christian law as such and which, therefore, are not considered as crimes by any other law. As regards purely secular crimes, he has no regular power over them, and has to leave their punishment to the secular law. However, in the case of sinners and criminals who are already judged by a civil court, he

---

[14] *Dialogus*, l. c. Cf. *An princeps*, c. 4; p. 244. Cf. also p. 253 about the Pope as delegate of Christ and especially p. 255: Licet potestas papae, quae spiritualia respicit, sit nobilior et dignior potestate saeculari, quemadmodum spiritualia sunt temporalibus digniora, et papa quoad quaedam spiritualia habeat etiam potestatem super illos qui sunt in sublimitate saeculari constituti, tamen non habet super ipsos talem plenitudinem potestatis, licet sub bono intellectu posset concedi, quod, quemadmodum asserunt sancti patres, papa habet plenitudinem potestatis, quia quoad omnia spiritualia quae sunt de necessitate facienda et super quae expedit caput fidelium potestatem habere, ipse regulariter plenitudinem obtinet potestatis.

[15] *Dialogus*, l. c. This restriction is contained in the liberty of the Holy Gospel. Cf. also *An princeps*, c. 4; p. 244, and *Breviloquium*, lib. 2, c. 17; p. 52 f.

may inflict on them additional punishments in order to bring them to true repentance. In any case, his vindictive power must not extend to a violation of the lawful rights of others, nor must it be exceedingly severe and in contradiction of the spirit of the Holy Gospel.[16]

5. Every Pope who is lawfully elected in *ipso facto* free and not subject to any secular power or to any secular jurisdiction. If, therefore, a Pope before his election had been a slave or subject to any secular ruler, by the fact that he is instituted the Supreme Pontiff he is free and not subject to a secular jurisdiction. This admits, however, of an exception. Though the Pope is regularly not subject to a secular power, he may lose his liberty and sovereignty through his own fault, because of heresy or a crime that endangers public security.[17]

6. The Pope, like the Church, has the right to ask the faithful for all necessary temporal goods without which a fruitful government of the Church cannot be established and realized. This, of course, does not mean that the Pope can expropriate any Christian, but it means that he has the right to get the necessary support as to temporal things for his divine work.[18]

This is, according to Ockham, the regular power of the Pope, as it can be established by the teaching of the Holy Gospel, of the

---

[16] *Dialogus*, l. c. It is surprising that Al. Dempf, *op. cit.*, p. 518 denies that, according to Ockham, the Pope has coactive power. He probably failed to make necessary distinctions. Ockham denies the coactive power of the Pope as regards purely secular crimes and "*in foro contentioso*" which apparently, here refers only to temporal contests or disputes. Cf. *An princeps*, c. 4; p. 244 and *Octo quaestiones*, q. 3, c. 3; p. 104 f.

[17] *Dialogus*, l. c. This privilege of the Pope is not stated in *An princeps*. It is, however, expressed in *Octo quaestiones*, q. 3, c. 3, p. 105, where in the following chapters which certainly represent Ockham's opinion, it is proved that such an exemption is not repugnant to the best form of government.

[18] *Dialogus*, l. c. Cf. *An princeps*, c. 4; p. 243. Though the Franciscan formulation of this privilege is striking, nevertheless Ockham certainly admits that the Pope and the Church own those temporal goods which were donated by the Christian people; the Pope and the Church own them, however, not by divine, but by human law. Cf. *An princeps*, c. 8; p. 258 ff.

Fathers of the Church, and of saintly theologians — especially St. Bernard, whom Ockham, it seems, follows closely. Though this demarcation of the Pope's power is definite in its general outlines, Ockham is, nevertheless, aware that not every situation is covered by it. Should any doubt arise whether certain things belong to the Pope's power or not, the problem has to be decided first by going back to two infallible guides, namely, Holy Scripture and right reason. Everyone who understands Holy Scripture in a sound way (not merely in its mystical sense, which cannot be used as a strict proof), and who bases himself on an infallible reason, has the right and the duty to explain and to declare by a true and faithful statement whether a certain case falls under the Pope's power or not. For it is obvious that nothing which is against Holy Scripture or right reason can belong to the papal jurisdiction. Furthermore, it is the task of a General Council and also of the Pope (if he is able to understand the truth correctly) to make authentic decisions and determinations as regard the Pope's power. Such determinations bind all Christians in conscience and do not allow them to teach, explain or determine an opinion contrary to the definition of the General Council or the Pope. If, however, the Pope's definition is against truth, then nobody has to believe him under any circumstance. In such a case, anyone who by Holy Scripture or by a necessary reason knows that the Pope is in error has the duty not to believe the Pope, and he has even the duty to refute his errors in order that he may not appear to assent to them; but such a one must observe the appropriateness and propriety of place, time, and all other circumstances.[19]

---

[19] *An princeps*, c. 5; p. 254. This, of course, is Ockham's *Apologia pro vita sua*, also. In any case, Ockham does not believe in the infallibility of the Pope, which, at this time, was not yet a defined dogma; nor does he seem to believe in the infallibility of a general Council, but only of the Church, though his discussions on this topic in the *Dialogus* should be more cautiously used than is commonly done. In any case, Ockham did not make the necessary distinction between a definition *ex cathedra* and other statements of the Popes. Hence the unfortunate instances of erroneous statements of Pope John XXII about beatific vision prevented him from believing in the infallibility of the Pope.

By these determinations Ockham constituted the papal power in its own (i. e., in its spiritual) realm, where it is supreme and a full power, though by no means an absolute power. Every Christian is subject to the Pope as to his lawful spiritual superior, according to divine institution — and the Emperor is no exception. But according to the same divine institution, the Pope is not a lord or ruler in the secular sense, nor is he a tyrant. He may be truly called "Lord", but only because of his dignity. For, in truth the Pope is the servant of all Christians. This idea of the *ministerium* of the Pope, and not of a *dominium*, equally emphasized by Dante, probably has its source in St. Bernard's *De Consideratione ad Eugenium Papam.* Impressed by this idea, Ockham reminds the Pope: "Let him know that, by the general legation, it is not conceded to him by any means to command *(imperare)* by austerity and force; let him know, therefore, that not the Lordship *(dominium)* but the ministry *(ministerium)* is given; let him know that he is a prelate over all not for himself but for the benefit of others, because it was not provided principally for him but for the others; let him know that he received the power in the Lord for edification, not for destruction and perturbation, and to diminish the rights of others."[20]

The papal power, therefore, is not without limits which are imposed upon it by God. These limits are defined by the actual and positive content of the ecclesiastical authority, and also by the God-given rights possessed by others (which is only the reverse of it). The next task of Ockham, therefore, was to prove the existence of such divine rights outside the ecclesiastical realm, and consequently not dependent on the Pope. In fulfilling this task, Ockham had to develop what could be called a political philosophy.

II. MAN'S NATURAL RIGHT OF PROPERTY AND DOMINION

Ockham begins with the premise that man has the natural right, granted to him by natural and divine law, to acquire property and to set up a ruler or a government endowed with jurisdiction. This right is independent of man's belief or unbelief, since God does not cease

---

[20] *An princeps,* c. 6; p. 254.

to give life and health, material and spiritual goods to all men, regardless of their creed. Hence, they are capable of possessing them and of ruling over them; or in other words, they have the right of acquiring property and of setting up a government, Nobody, therefore, has the right to deprive anyone of these natural perogatives without a just reason.[21]

While this right to acquire property was given by God to man as regards temporal things, this property is either common to all men. or is private property. The common property of temporal things was granted to Adam and his wife, not only for themselves but also for all their descendants. This ownership *(dominium)* gave man the right to dispose of temporal things and to use them for his personal benefit. It did not, Ockham continues, include the right of private property in any form because it was the will of God that all men should own all temporal things in common, as befitted man in his original innocence. Sin, however, made it necessary to grant to man the right of private property, and for this reason the right of private property was introduced by God into the right of common property.

The Franciscan influence on this idea is worth noting.[22] Ockham here follows closely and almost literally Duns Scotus. The right to acquire private property, he argues, is not a sign of perfection. For in perfect man, such as Adam and Eve were in their original innocence, there is no avarice nor any greediness to acquire or to use any temporal thing against the dictates of right reason. Consequently, there was no necessity nor even utility in possessing any temporal thing so long as man remained in his original innocence. Sin, however, changed this happy state. After man's sin there arose and grew in him avarice and greediness to possess and to use temporal things in an improper manner. In order to restrain this immoderate desire to

---

[21] *Breviloquium*, lib. 3, c. 6; p. 84.

[22] Cf. the same (traditional) idea of only the right of common property before sin in St. Bonaventure, *Sentent.*, II, d. 44, a 2, q. 2, ad 4; ed. Quaracchi t. 2, p. 1009. The connection with Franciscan poverty is seen in *De perfectione evangelica*, II, a. 1; t. V; p. 129. Cf. Alexander Halensis (to be exact William of Melitona), *Summa Theologica.* 1ª IIae, n. 521 f.; (ed. Quaracchi) t. 3; p. 777 ff. Scotus, Oxoniense, IV, d. 15, q. 2, n. 3—4; ed. Vives t. 18, p. 256 f.

possess temporal things, and, at the same time, to prevent man from neglecting the due management and procurement of temporal things (for common things which belong to all men are usually neglected by bad men), it was necessary that all temporal things should not be common property but that some of them should be acquired as private property. This is the reason why, after the sin of Adam and Eve, the right *(potestas)* to acquire private property was introduced by divine law. The right of private property, therefore, is a restriction of the common possession of all temporal things, a restriction in those things which are necessary and useful for a good and honest life not only for man as an individual but also for man as a citizen in a perfect society. Hence actual society cannot be like the Republic of Plato, where all things are in common, and Aristotle was right when he rejected Plato's conception. Aristotle considered the actual state of man and knew that the average man is inclined to evil.[23]

But just as the right to acquire private property was given to man as an adjustment of his actual state, so for the same reason God has given man the right to set up rulers endowed with temporal jurisdiction. This implies that temporal jurisdiction reserved to a ruling person or persons was foreign to the original state of man, but became necessary for man's actual state in which it is necessary and useful to set up rulers for a good social life. Furthermore, he says, the right to institute a jurisdiction was immediately given by God, and not by any human intermediary or cooperation.[24]

These assertions of Ockham do not imply that temporal jurisdiction or the state is bad in itself. Though the need of forming a state and of instituting a ruling body is one of the effects of the first sin, the institution of a government is not an effect of sin, but is only occasioned by sin, that is, as a natural remedy for the effects

---

[23] Cf. *Breviloquium*, lib. 3, c. 7; p. 85 ff. Cf. Scotus l.c. Ockham develops these ideas in extenso in his *Opus nonaginta dierum* which was not used here.

[24] Potestas ergo appropriandi res temporales personae et personis aut collegio data est a Deo humano generi. Et propter rationem consimilem data est a Deo, absque ministerio et cooperatione humana, potestas instituendi rectores habentes jurisdictionem temporalem, quia jurisdictio temporalis est de numero illorum quae sunt necessaria et utilia ad bene et dolitice vivere ... *Breviloquium*, lib. 3, c. 7; p. 87.

of sin. From this it follows that temporal jurisdiction outside the Church and outside any religious authorization (by the Pope, for instance) is valid and good.[25]

This twofold right to acquire private property and to institute a government is immediately granted by God to all men, believers and unbelievers alike. It contains an affirmative precept, and, as such belongs to man's moral and natural duties. As every man, believer and unbeliever, is obliged by a precept of God to honor his parents and to assist his neighbor, so every man is obliged, as soon as a corresponding situation is given, to acquire private property and to set up a ruler in secular matters.[26] He is obliged to do so, however, only if a corresponding situation exists because, since this is an affirmative precept, it obliges always but not for every moment *(semper sed non pro semper)*. The corresponding situation where the precept obliges is the case of necessity. In other words, man is not obliged to appropriate property or to institute a government so long as his well-being and a sound social life are not in danger. If this well-being and a sound social life are not in danger, he can use his right, but he is not obliged to use it. Consequently he can renounce this right, as he does, for instance, by the vow of poverty or obedience.[27]

From this right to acquire private property and to institute a ruler endowed with jurisdiction, we must distinguish the actual appropriations of temporal things and the actual setting up of a government. The right comes immediately from God by natural law; the actual appropriation and setting up of a government is usually the act of man and of human law. Man, therefore, using his divine right, owns certain temporal things as private property by the act of appropriation in a lawful way. That means that according to human ordination certain things belong to one and others to another.

---

[25] The other view found its significant expression in the formula: Extra ecclesiam omnia aedificant ad gehennam, et ideo extra ecclesiam nulla est ordinata potestas sed ibi est solummodo potestas permissa et non concessa, *Breviloquium*, lib. 3, c. l. p. 68. Ockham's purpose is to refute this opinion (based on Rom. 14, 23), which implies that at least the Roman Empire, if it does not "build up towards hell," is from the Pope.

[26] *Breviloquium*, lib. 3, c. 8; p. 87 f.

[27] *Breviloquium*, l. c. p. 88.

30*

God has left the division of temporal things ordinarily to man, though in exceptional cases He has given certain things to certain persons or nations. In this latter case, of course, the person or persons own temporal things by divine right and not by human right.[28]

The actual setting up of a lawful jurisdiction or of a ruler endowed with jurisdiction according to this explanation, is at least partly by human ordination and human law. There is, however, one exception to be mentioned. The jurisdiction of the husband over his wife, and likewise the jurisdiction of the father over his children, is not by human institution but by divine institution and right, or by natural law. The jurisdiction of rulers, that is to say, of judges in cities or of kings in their kingdoms, etc., is not actually set up by natural or divine law, at least not ordinarily; it is ordinarily set up by human action and by human laws — for instance, by election or heredity or the like.[29]

III. THE DIVINE RIGHT OF SECULAR POWER

It is clear that according to Ockham true dominion over temporal things and true jurisdiction over persons was instituted not only by an act of God, but also and mainly by acts of human beings. If we leave aside the exceptional cases where God has instituted Judges or Kings, we have to ask: By what right does a secular power possess what is given to it by an act of the people? In this case does a secular power possess its jurisdiction and its dominion over lands and other properties by human right or by divine right? Ockham answers that such a secular power possesses its power by divine and not by human right, although it is instituted by an act or acts of human beings. In

---

[28] As to human ordination or human right, cf.: Ius proprietatis et dominii primo introductum fuit iure humano et civili, appellando ius civile omne ius quod non est ius divinum nec naturale. Postea autem quaedam dominia introducta fuerunt iure divino, quia ex speciali consecratione divina; quaedam autem introducta fuerunt iure humano quod non erat ius regum sed populi vel aliorum minoris dignitatis quam sint reges; quaedam introducta fuerunt iure regum. *Breviloquium*, lib. 3, c. 15; p. 98.

[29] l. c.

other words, such a secular power has its dominion and its jurisdiction but not its institution immediately from God.

What does "to have power immediately from God" mean? It can be understood in three different senses. That a power be immediately from God can mean, in a first sense, that this power is immediately given by God and without the help and co-jurisdiction of any creature. In this way, Moses had his authority as leader of the Israelites immediately from God and in no way from the people.[30] In a second sense, a power can be immediately from God, because it is given only by God, not, however, without the help of creatures. In this way for instance, every Pope after Peter has his power and his pontificate immediately from God, not, however, without human cooperation; for the Pope has to be elected. But the electors of the Pope do not give him any power, just as the performer of the baptismal rite does not confer grace; the power, like the grace in Baptism, is immediately conferred by God alone.[31]

In a third sense (and this is the most important one for our purpose) a power can be understood to be immediately from God or from God alone, if somebody had the power and the dominion first (i. e., when he was instituted) because of a concession or a donation or the resignation of another and is nevertheless after these acts dependent only on God for his power and dominion, so that only God is his superior in these matters.[32]

There cannot be the slightest doubt that Ockham was convinced that only in this third sense did every secular power come immediately from God alone, unless in a particular case it could be proved by a special divine revelation that it was from God in the first or second sense. In any case, the Roman Empire, like almost all the other kingdoms and empires, received its power and dominion in the third sense immediately from God alone.

---

[30] Cf. *Octo quaestiones*, q. 2; c. 3; p. 74. The same distinction is found in *Breviloquium*, lib. 4, c. 5; p. 109, though here is specification as to jurisdiction.

[31] *Octo quaestiones*, l. c. Cf. *Breviloquium*, l. c. The instance of the Pope is here introduced with: Isto modo videtur aliquibus ...

[32] *Octo quaestiones*, l. c. Cf. *Breviloquium*, l. c.; p. 110.

It is important now to explain what is meant by saying that a secular power has the supreme power by divine right, yet is instituted by the people. It means, first, that a supreme secular and sovereign power has its power by the ordination of the people, so that the people at the beginning have transferred or given the supreme power to the ruler. In other words, the people did not simply consent or acknowledge that the ruler had and actually exercised the supreme power, but the people really and truly conferred this power. The electors or those who perform the coronation ceremony may simply indicate or confirm the fact that somebody has the supreme power, without giving him power; the people's election, however, conferred the power on a ruler and transferred it to him from themselves. This power includes that over temporal goods and jurisdiction.

To say that a secular power has the supreme power, yet is instituted by the people means, secondly, that the people did not transfer this power to a private person and for the personal benefit of an individual, but to a person or persons for the common benefit. Or, as Ockham says, they conferred it not on a person but on a dignity. Hence a ruler cannot use his power for personal purposes, but only for the common good. If he uses, for instance, temporal things which belong to his dignity, not to his person, for his personal benefit, he is obliged to restitution.

This statement means, thirdly, that a ruler to whom the people transferred the supreme power possesses this power not as the people's power but as a divine power, or not by the right of the people but by divine right. In one word, after the transfer has been accomplished the ruler has no other superior but God, and is regularly dependent on no one but God. In certain cases, however, when the ruler proves to be unfit, he is subject to the people or to another person — for instance, to the Pope — and he can be deposed.[33]

From this it follows that since the lawful ruler possesses his power in dependence on God alone, although it was given to him by the people, the power cannot be taken away from him without a just cause. Some might think that the cause of the constitution of a

---

[33] *Octo quaestiones,* q. 2, c. 6; p. 78 ff. *Breviloquium,* l. c.; p. 111. As to the deposition of an emperor cf. *Breviloquium,* lib. 5, c. 2; p. 157 f.

lawful government is also the legitimate cause of its dissolution. According to this since the will of the governed has constituted the government, so the will of the governed can lawfully, without any just cause *(sola voluntate et dissensu)*, dissolve the government. Ockham, however, objects violently against this reasoning: *Sed hoc habet minime veritatem.* For when someone submits himself freely to the dominion of another, he cannot, without the other's consent, retract this submission without guilt.[34]

IV. THE JUST CONSTITUTION OF A COMMONWEALTH

Ockham's interest as a political theoretician was focused on the relation between the Roman Empire and the Papacy. After having established the fact that true secular power in its dominion and jurisdiction exists without being authorized by the Pope and that the supreme power, after having been constituted, possesses its right in immediate dependence on God alone, he goes on to show how a lawful empire can be constituted without ecclesiastical interference. He bases his discussions on the special case of the Roman Empire. He enumerates three ways in which a lawful empire can be constituted. The third, however, may be disregarded here, since it envisages a direct divine intervention. Of the remaining two ways, the first is by consent, the second by force.

The first way is simply by consent. All who are born free have the right from God to submit themselves to a higher authority, so long as they are not subject to another authority,[35] as was already explained. Hence a nation can submit itself *in toto* to another authority and thus become an integral part of a larger commonwealth. In this way, all the people who belonged to the Roman Empire could, at the same time or at different times, have become parts of the Roman Empire.

---

[34] *Breviloquium*, lib. 4, c. 12—13; p. 124 f. This is said in connection with the submission of the people and nations to the Roman Empire, but it holds generally too. Cf. also p. 125.

[35] *Breviloquium*, lib. 4, c. 10; p. 121.

The other lawful way is by force — that is to say, by a just war. A war could be just either because other nations declared war and were then subjected in a defensive war; or a war is just because the nation against which war is waged has refused to do that to which it could be justly compelled — for example, if they refuse to return things which they have stolen, or have committed injuries or other crimes. But these must be of such a nature that it is just to punish them for these crimes by subjugation and captivity.

What is said here about a just war which gives the right to subjugate other nations is somehow vague. And in the special case of the Roman Empire, it seems very likely that it was constituted, not only by free consent and by just wars, but also by unjust war and by oppression of other nations. Ockham, therefore, is forced to show how, in spite of an initial injustice, a lawful and just dominion over other nations can be obtained. This would not be true, of course, in every case. If the Romans oppressed other nations and forced them into their Empire for an unjust reason, and if those nations never have consented to this incorporation, then they do not belong rightfully and lawfully to the Roman Empire. Consequently, Ockham implied that they can break away from it at any convenient time. But there are possibilities of healing the initial injustice and of converting an unjust and unlawful dominion into a true and lawful one, just as an invalid marriage and unjustly possessed property can be validated and legalized. An unjust subjugation of other nations can be converted into a just and lawful dominion of these nations either by a subsequent free submission and assent of these people, or by a later just war, or because the population of a certain territory is exterminated and the land is thus opened to the right of occupation.[36]

But these are only deliberations of possibilities. Ockham himself admits that he does not know when the Roman Empire began to be a just and lawful one. In any case, he knows by a theological reason that it was lawful at least in the time of Christ, because Christ and

---

[36] *Breviloquium*, lib. 4, c. 10; p. 122; cf. c. 11; p. 123 f; *Dialogus,* pars III, tract. 2, lib. I, c. 27; fol. 2rr vb.

the Apostles, by their own acts and words, acknowledged it as a true and lawful empire.[37]

Behind all these considerations of Ockham was a twofold pre-occupation. First, he desired to prove that the Roman Empire, now ruled by Louis the Bavarian, was a true and lawful commonwealth, constituted by the people and ruled by divine right; hence it was not dependent on the Pope, nor did it admit of any interference, at least not regularly, from the side of the Pope. The second preoccupation of Ockham was his ideal of one commonwealth of nations. The Roman Empire once realized this ideal. Everyone who is concerned with the common good of all nations should contribute, as much as he can, to bring the world nearer to this ideal. Or, as Ockham himself puts it: "Therefore he is not truly zealous for the common good, who does not desire and work, as much as he can in his station, that the whole world be subject to one monarch."[38]

V. STATE AND CHURCH

There can be no doubt that Ockham was a champion of a strong and autonomous monarchical form of government, which has been instituted by the people or the representatives of the people, has its right and power in dependence only on God, is not subordinated to any human authority, and has its only reason for existence in the common good of all its subjects. To enlarge, however, on this description, is a temptation which will be resisted here. For, besides a few scattered remarks in his minor works, where Ockham really expresses his own opinions, the main source of information would be the *Dialogus*. Yet, the *Dialogus* conceals Ockham's own opinions

---

[37] Sed quando et qualiter coepit esse verum imperium fateor me nescire. Dubium enim est mihi an, quando Romani dominari coeperunt de facto, tyrannice solummodo sibi dominium supra alios usurpaverunt, et ideo non constat modo utrum ab initio vel postea verum imperium habuerunt. Quamvis enim a Christo et apostolis habeamus quod eorum temporibus erat verum imperium, tamen ipsi minime expresserunt quando coepit esse verum imperium. Quod autem illi non definierunt, nec ergo definire prae-sumo. *Breviloquium*, lib. 4, c. 10; p. 120 f.

[38] *Breviloquium*, lib. 4, c. 13; p. 126.

more than any other work, and to disentangle his own viewpoint from the discussions with any degree of probability needs more textual substantiation than can be afforded here. In any case, Ockham has proved this much: temporal power and jurisdiction exist alongside the papal power and jurisdiction. Hence it is not included in the dominion of the Pope or the Church.

But then we have to ask a final question of Ockham: How did he understand the relation between the two highest powers here upon earth? Unfortunately Ockham has never directly answered this question, for he was, as we have repeatedly said, interested above all in the limits of the Pope's power. Hence an elaborated and complete theory as regards the relation between the two powers cannot be expected from him. But by gathering some scattered remarks, and presupposing what has just been said, we can try at least to reconstruct a theory about the relation between Church and State, between Pope and Emperor, according to Ockham.

Ockham certainly arrived at a clear distinction between secular and ecclesiastical power. On the other hand, a divorce or separation of these supreme powers did not even enter his mind. Divorce does not admit of order; distinction, however, does admit of order, for it admits coordination and colloboration. Such a coordination and colloboration is guaranteed first by the unity of both powers as regards their common source — for both are immediately from God: "By God not only is papal power instituted, but also many others — i. e., the secular powers are instituted by Him."[39] This needs no further corroboration. The coordination and collaboration between both powers is furthermore guaranteed by their unity as regards their same end, for both exist not for any private good, but only for the common good: "The apostolic or papal principality is not less instituted because of the common benefit of believers than is the secular, moderate, and just principality for the benefit of its subjects."[40] This likewise does not need further corroboration. The coordination and collaboration between both powers is finally guaranteed because of their necessity for this world. This necessity is

---

[39] *An princeps*, c. 4; p. 243.
[40] *Breviloquium*, lib. 2, c. 5; p. 22.

caused by the same fact, namely, original sin. This condition is obvious as regards the Church and the Pope; for the Church is the institution of salvation, and the keys of the kingdom of Heaven are entrusted to Peter and his successors as regards all sins without exception.

Thus the Pope's delegation, which he received from Christ, "is useful for the community of all believers, necessary and wholesome.[41] And the secular power is mainly and above all other ends instituted so that order may be maintained, crimes prevented and criminals punished; otherwise preachers and professors would suffice for the common good.[42] Hence both powers exist under the shadow of the lost Paradise. This, however, does not mean that Church and State have only a negative function caused by sin. But it remains true that the only power is a spiritual, and the other a temporal, remedy for sin. Nevertheless, Ockham does not overlook the positive and constructive task of both powers. There is no need to show this for the papal and ecclesiastical institution. But since this positive task was denied to the State, it may be good to hear from Ockham that, besides the main task of the State to prevent crimes, there are others as well: "Namely to give to each one his rights and to save them, to make the necessary and just laws, to institute the subordinate judges and officials, (to decide) which handicrafts *(artes)* are to be exercised and by whom, to prescribe acts of all virtues, and many other things."[43]

We have, however, to admit that these proofs for a coordination and collaboration between Church and State are not systematically developed by Ockham. They are not, however, mere constructions by juxtaposition of texts. This becomes clear when we now study with Ockham in some detail the mutual relations of both powers. These relations concern the interference of each power with the other. In order to understand his ideas correctly, it will be necessary to

---

[41] *An princeps,* c. 6; p. 253; cf. c. 4; p. 244.

[42] *Octo quaestiones,* q. 3, c. 8; p. 113.

[43] *Octo quaestiones,* q. 3, c. 8; p. 112. Al. Dempf, *op. cit.,* p. 522, thinks that according to Ockham, "die optimistische Sozialphilosophie, die den Staat aus der natürlichen und politischen Haltung des Menschen ableitet, ist ersetzt durch eine pessimistische Gewaltauffassung des Staates wie bei

introduce a distinction favoured by Ockham, that is, between regular and casual power. A servant, for instance, has no regular power over his master, but he has a casual power over him in a case of necessity; because a servant is obliged in a case of necessity, even by using force, to prevent his master from a grave crime or an imminent danger.[44]

The following matters do not fall under the regular power of the Pope: 1. The lawful rights of the emperors, kings, and of all Christians and non-Christians, which in no way are against good morals, the honor of God and the observance of the law of the Gospel. The Pope cannot interfere *(turbare vel minuere)* with these rights, at least not regularly, without being guilty of sin. So long as secular princes exercise their legitimate power carefully and justly, the Pope, according to Christ's ordination, must not meddle with their rights, at least it they do not invite him to intervene.[45]

2. Neither can the Pope regularly interfere with the liberties conceded by God and by nature to all men. Hence the Pope cannot impose upon Christians more than is contained in the Holy Gospel, or more than is necessary or so useful that it equals necessity. In any case, the liberty of the Holy Gospel must be respected.[46]

3. The Pope must guard against too harsh and too onerous a procedure within the limits of his power, and he has no regular power whatsoever as regards capital punishment *(indicium sanguinis)*.[47] Hence the Pope cannot regularly interfere in temporal matters.

Casually, however, the Pope may justly interfere in temporal matters. This is explained by Ockham in two instances: 1. The Pope

---

Marsilius . . ." We admit that Ockham's theory is not optimistic in a naturalistic sense, because it takes into account the supernatural truths of original sin, Christ's atonement and doomsday, which do not admit optimism as regards man's nature, though no absolute pessimism either. St. Bonaventure, Duns Scotus and Ockham have to remind those who take Aristotle's theory as the "natural" one, that it is based on the requirements of fallen nature, which Aristotle mistook for nature as such. We do not believe that St. Thomas thinks essentially otherwise.

[44] *Breviloquium*, lib. 4, c. 4; p. 108.
[45] *Breviloquium*, lib. 2, c. 16; p. 48 ff.
[46] L. c. c. 17; p. 51 ff.   [47] L. c. c. 18; p. 54 ff.

may, in certain circumstances, help in the deposition of a king or Emperor. Ockham is not very definite about this, but he certainly holds as more probable that the Pope cannot directly depose any secular ruler. In any case, two possibilities have to be distinguished. First, the emperor or king has to be deposed because of a secular crime or insufficiency *(defectus)*. In this case the decision and subsequent deposition of the ruler is up to those who have elected him — ultimately, of course, to the people. Since the Pope is a member of the Roman Empire, he may as such help in the deposition of the Emperor, not however as the spiritual head of Christendom. Secondly, if the Emperor or king has to be deposed because of heresy or another crime that is condemnable only by the Christian law, the examination and trial as to the fact belongs to the Pope as the head of Christianity, but the condemnation and execution of the sentence belongs to those who have elected the ruler, or to the people, as before.[48] 2. The Pope may casually interfere even as regards war. Ockham discusses this case in explaining the famous contention that "the two swords" are given to the Pope. This can be understood (Ockham is careful in saying "it is answered") either in the sense that the Pope may inform or exhort or even command a secular power to unsheath the sword and to do justice, if the secular power is ignorant or neglects its duty. Or, in a second and much stronger sense, it may mean that, if the secular power fails to do its duty and the highest utility and necessity is in question, the Pope himself may unsheath the sword justly, manfully, and powerfully.[49]

This is about all that can be said about an interference of the Pope in secular matters. If we now ask Ockham whether the State or the Emperor may interfere in spiritual matters as well, he gives us even less information. In any case, to say that the Pope is subject to the Emperor or that the Church is subordinated to the State, is not warranted by any text which expresses Ockham's own opinion.[50]

---

[48] *Breviloquium*, lib. 6, c. 2; p. 156 ff.

[49] *An princeps*, c. 6; p. 250.

[50] Tanquerey, *Synopsis Theologiae Dogmaticae* t. 1 (Benziger Bros., New York, 1920) p. 591 (n. 910) who imputes this to Ockham and Marsilius, is incorrect as to Ockham.

If that were true, why then should Ockham try to prove that the exemption of the Pope even in temporal things from the jurisdiction of the secular power is possible and does not detract from the best form of government? In any case, Ockham stated that the State has the highest jurisdiction only in temporal matters.[51] It is certain that, according to Ockham, the Emperor or any secular power had no right to interfere in spiritual matters, so long as the security of society was not endangered. That means, however, that the secular ruler can only casually interfere. As regards this casual interference, it seems that Ockham admitted certainly that the Emperor can punish a Pope who has committed grave crimes against public security, for that is required by the common good. It seems probable that Ockham admitted a casual interference of the Emperor in the case of the crime of heresy committed by a Pope, if the Emperor was a Catholic. For the responsibility of removing a heretical Pope belongs to all Christians.[52] If we add to this that the State has, in a case of grave necessity, the right to use the temporal goods of the Church (in case of a just war, for instance),[53] or that the Emperor has the right to settle matrimonial cases, insofar as their civil side is concerned, even the right to declare a marriage invalid or to admit a marriage in certain cases where the law of the Church (not the divine law and the sacrament) is against it,[54] we have said about all that can be said with any historical certitude about Ockham's position.

From all that has been said about Ockham's political ideas, it becomes evident that the *Venerabilis Inceptor*, who was driven into political discussions by personal necessity and in defense of his disobedience to a Pope, remained moderate in his theory. As has been justly stated, his place, it seems, is to be sought in the company of Dante and not of Marsilius. Indeed, one wonders whether Dante's *De Monarchia* was not known to him.

---

[51] Cf. *Octo quaestiones*, q. 3, c. 3; p. 104.

[52] This may be gathered from the *Dialogus*.

[53] This is the topic of *An princeps*.

[54] This is the topic of *Consultatio de causa matrimoniali*. Ockham admits matrimonial cases *as causae mixtae*, and distinguishes clearly between the sacramental and civil aspect of marriage.

INDEX AUCTORUM

William of Nottingham, 128
William of Shyreswood, 83, 222, 236, 331
William of Ware, 410

Wilpert, P., 182, 190, 193, 201, 307
Wolter, A. B., 22, 417

Zuidema, S. U., 291, 292

INDEX RERUM

Missiology Series

1. *Imperial Government and Catholic Missions in China During the Years 1784—1785*, by Bernward H. Willeke, 1948. $ 2.25.

2. *The Negotiations Between Ch'i-Ying and Lagrené 1844—1846*, by Angelus Grosse-Aschoff, 1950. $ 2.00.

Theology Series

1. *The Eucharistic Teaching of William Ockham*, by Gabriel Buescher, 1950. Exhausted.

2. *De Corredemptione Beatae Virginis Mariae*, by Juniper Carol, 1950. $ 4.00.

3. *The First-Gospel. Genesis 3:15*, by Dominic J. Unger, 1954. $ 4.50.

4. *Transiency and Permanence. The Nature of Theology According to Saint Bonaventure*, by George H. Tavard, 1954. $ 3.75.

5. *The Sacrament of Confirmation in the Early-Middle Scholastic Period*, by Kilian F. Lynch, vol. I: Texts, 1957. $ 9.00. vol. II: Doctrine, in preparation.

Text Series

1. *Walter Burleigh, De puritate artis logicae [tractatus brevior]*, edit. Ph. Boehner. Exhausted, but see below, under No. 9.

2. William Ockham, *Summa Logicae*, vol. I: Pars Prima, edit. Ph. Boehner, Photomechanic reprint of the 1951 edition, 1957. $ 2.50. Vol. II: Pars Secunda et Tertiae prima, edit. Ph. Boehner, 1954. $ 2.25. Vol. III, edit. Innocent Daam, in preparation.

3. Peter Aureoli, *Scriptum super Primum Sententiarum*, edit. E. M. Buytaert, vol. I: Prologue and Distinction I, 1953. $ 5.00. Vol. II: Distinctions II—VIII, 1956. $ 8.50. Vol. III—VIII in preparation.

4. *Guidonis de Orchellis Tractatus de Sacramentis ex eius Summa de Sacramentis et Officiis Ecclesiae*, edit. Damian and Odulph Van den Eynde, 1953. $ 5.00.

5. Henry of Ghent, *Summa quaestionum ordinariarum*. Photomechanic reprint of the 1520 edition. 2 volumes, 1953. $ 6.00 each.

6. Saint John Damascene, *Dialectica*. Version of Robert Grosseteste, edit. Owen A. Colligan, 1953. $ 1.00.

7. *Gregorii Ariminensis Super Primum et Secundum Sententiarum*. Photomechanic reprint of the 1522 edition, 1955. $ 7.50.

8. Saint John Damascene, *De fide orthodoxa*, Versions of Burgundio and Cerbanus, edit. E. M. Buytaert, 1955. $ 9.00.

9. Walter Burleigh, *De puritate artis logicae tractatus longior*. With a Revised Edition of the *Tractatus brevior*, edit. Ph. Boehner, 1955. $ 4.50.

10. Henrici de Werla *Opera omnia*, edit. Sophronius Clasen, vol. I: *Tractatus de immaculata conceptione B. V. Mariae*, 1955. $ 2.25. Vol. II—IV in preparation.

11. Petrus Thomae, O.F.M., *Quodlibet*, edit. M. Rachel Hooper and E. M. Buytaert, 1957. $ 6.00.

12. William Ockham, *Tractatus logicae minor et medius*, edit. Ph. Boehner and E. M. Buytaert. In preparation.

II. WORKS OF SAINT BONAVENTURE

Latin Text, with English Translation and Commentary.

1. *De reductione artium ad theologiam*, by Emma Thérèse Healy, 1955. $ 2.25.

2. *Itinerarium mentis in Deum*, by Ph. Boehner, 1956. $ 2.00.

Several others in preparation.

III. GUILLELMI OCKHAM,
OPERA OMNIA PHILOSOPHICA ET THEOLOGICA

edit. E. M. Buytaert. (Some 25 volumes projected; subscribers to the entire collection will receive a discount of 10%).

1. *Expositionis in libros artis logicae prooemium* et *Expositio in librum Porphyrii de praedicabilibus*, edit. Ernest A. Moody. At press.

PRINTED BY FERDINAND SCHÖNINGH AT PADERBORN, GERMANY